C000225703

STREET ATLAS
Bristol
and Bath

First published in 1995 as 'Bristol and Avon' by

Philip's, a division of
Octopus Publishing Group Ltd
2–4 Heron Quays, London E14 4JP

Second colour edition 2003
First impression 2003

ISBN 0-540-08524-3 (spiral)

© Philip's 2003

oʀˢ Ordnance Survey®

This product includes mapping data licensed
from Ordnance Survey® with the permission of
the Controller of Her Majesty's Stationery Office.
© Crown copyright 2003. All rights reserved.
Licence number 100011710.

Printed and bound in Spain
by Cayfosa-Quebecor

Contents

III	**Key to map symbols**
IV	**Key to map pages**
VI	**Route planning**
VIII	**Administrative and Postcode boundaries**
1	**Street maps** at 3½ inches to 1 mile
141	**Street maps of Bath and Bristol city centres** at 7 inches to 1 mile
144	**Town maps with indexes** of Chippenham and Trowbridge
146	**Index** of towns and villages
147	**Index** of streets, hospitals, industrial estates, railway stations, schools, shopping centres, universities and places of interest

Digital Data

The exceptionally high-quality mapping found in this atlas is available as digital data in TIFF format, which is easily convertible to other bitmapped (raster) image formats.

The index is also available in digital form as a standard database table. It contains all the details found in the printed index together with the National Grid reference for the map square in which each entry is named.

For further information and to discuss your requirements, please contact Philip's on 020 7644 6932 or james.mann@philips-maps.co.uk

Key to map symbols

III

	Motorway with junction number (22a)
	Primary route – dual/single carriageway
	A road – dual/single carriageway
	B road – dual/single carriageway
	Minor road – dual/single carriageway
	Other minor road – dual/single carriageway
	Road under construction
	Tunnel, covered road
	Rural track, private road or narrow road in urban area
	Gate or obstruction to traffic (restrictions may not apply at all times or to all vehicles)
	Path, bridleway, byway open to all traffic, road used as a public path
	Pedestrianised area
DY7	Postcode boundaries
	County and unitary authority boundaries
	Railway, tunnel, railway under construction
	Tramway, tramway under construction
	Miniature railway
Walsall	Railway station
	Private railway station
South Shields	Metro station
	Tram stop, tram stop under construction
	Bus, coach station

	Ambulance station
	Coastguard station
	Fire station
	Police station
	Accident and Emergency entrance to hospital
H	Hospital
+	Place of worship
i	Information Centre (open all year)
P	Parking
P&R	Park and Ride
PO	Post Office
	Camping site
	Caravan site
	Golf course
	Picnic site
Prim Sch	Important buildings, schools, colleges, universities and hospitals
River Medway	Water name
	River, weir, stream
	Canal, lock, tunnel
	Water
	Tidal water
	Woods
	Built up area
Church	Non-Roman antiquity
ROMAN FORT	Roman antiquity
87 / 228	Adjoining page indicators and overlap bands. The colour of the arrow and the band indicates the scale of the adjoining or overlapping page (see scales below)

Acad	Academy	Inst	Institute	Recn Gd	Recreation Ground
Allot Gdns	Allotments	Ct	Law Court		
Cemy	Cemetery	L Ctr	Leisure Centre	Resr	Reservoir
C Ctr	Civic Centre	LC	Level Crossing	Ret Pk	Retail Park
CH	Club House	Liby	Library	Sch	School
Coll	College	Mkt	Market	Sh Ctr	Shopping Centre
Crem	Crematorium	Meml	Memorial	TH	Town Hall/House
Ent	Enterprise	Mon	Monument	Trad Est	Trading Estate
Ex H	Exhibition Hall	Mus	Museum	Univ	University
Ind Est	Industrial Estate	Obsy	Observatory	W Twr	Water Tower
IRB Sta	Inshore Rescue Boat Station	Pal	Royal Palace	Wks	Works
		PH	Public House	YH	Youth Hostel

■ The small numbers around the edges of the maps identify the 1 kilometre National Grid lines

■ The dark grey border on the inside edge of some pages indicates that the mapping does not continue onto the adjacent page

The scale of the maps on the pages numbered in blue is 5.52 cm to 1 km • 3½ inches to 1 mile • 1: 18103

0   ¼   ½   ¾   1 mile
0   250 m   500 m   750 m   1 kilometre

The scale of the maps on pages numbered in red is 11.04 cm to 1 km • 7 inches to 1 mile • 1: 9051

0   220 yards   440 yards   660 yards   ½ mile
0   125 m   250 m   375 m   ½ kilometre

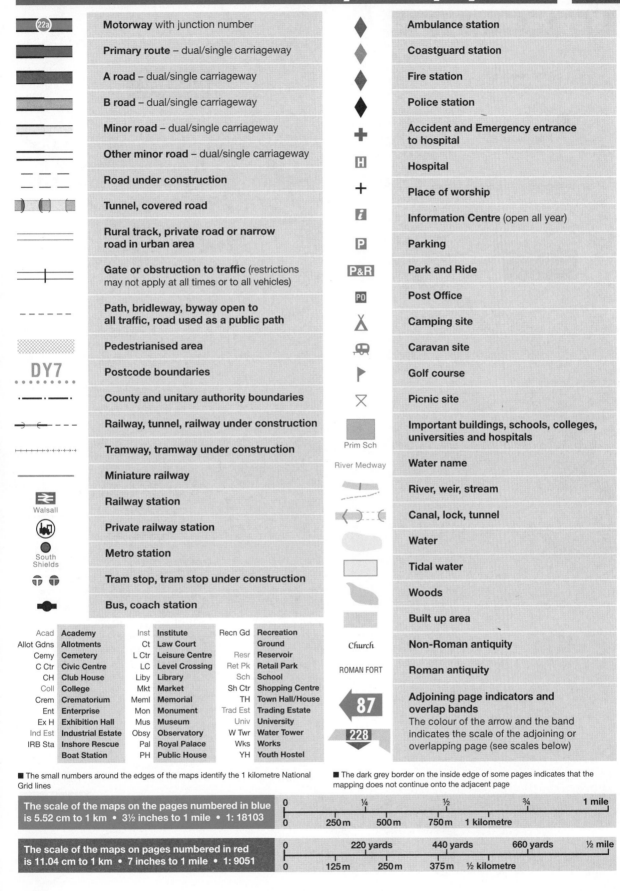

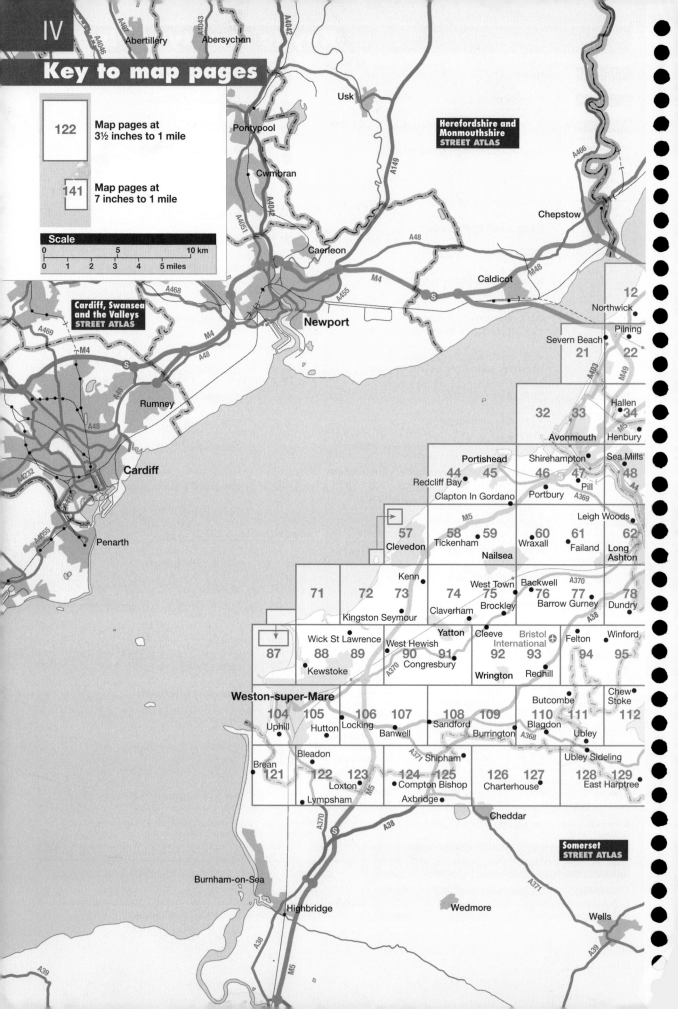

Key to map pages

122	Map pages at 3½ inches to 1 mile
141	Map pages at 7 inches to 1 mile

Scale

0   5   10 km

0   1   2   3   4   5 miles

Abertillery Abersychan

Usk

Herefordshire and Monmouthshire STREET ATLAS

Pontypool

Cwmbran

Chepstow

A48

Caerleon

Caldicot

M4

Newport

Cardiff, Swansea and the Valleys STREET ATLAS

Northwick **12**

Rumney

Severn Beach **21** Pilning **22**

Cardiff

Hallen **34**

32 **33**

Avonmouth Henbury

Penarth

Portishead Shirehampton Sea Mills

44 **45** **46** **47** **48**

Redcliff Bay Pill

Clapton In Gordano Portbury

Leigh Woods

57 **58** **59** **60** **61** **62**

Clevedon Tickenham Wraxall Failand Long Ashton

Nailsea

Kenn

West Town Backwell

71 **72** **73** **74** **75** **76** **77** **78**

Claverham Brockley Barrow Gurney Dundry

Kingston Seymour

Yatton Cleeve **Bristol International** Felton Winford

Wick St Lawrence West Hewish

87 **88** **89** **90** **91** **92** **93** **94** **95**

Congresbury Wrington Redhill

Kewstoke

Weston-super-Mare

Butcombe Chew Stoke

104 **105** **106** **107** **108** **109** **110** **111** **112**

Uphill Hutton Locking Sandford Blagdon Ubley

Banwell Burrington

Bleadon Shipham Ubley Sideling

Brean **121** **122** **123** **124** **125** **126** **127** **128** **129**

Loxton Compton Bishop Charterhouse East Harptree

Lympsham Axbridge

Cheddar

Somerset STREET ATLAS

Burnham-on-Sea

Highbridge Wedmore Wells

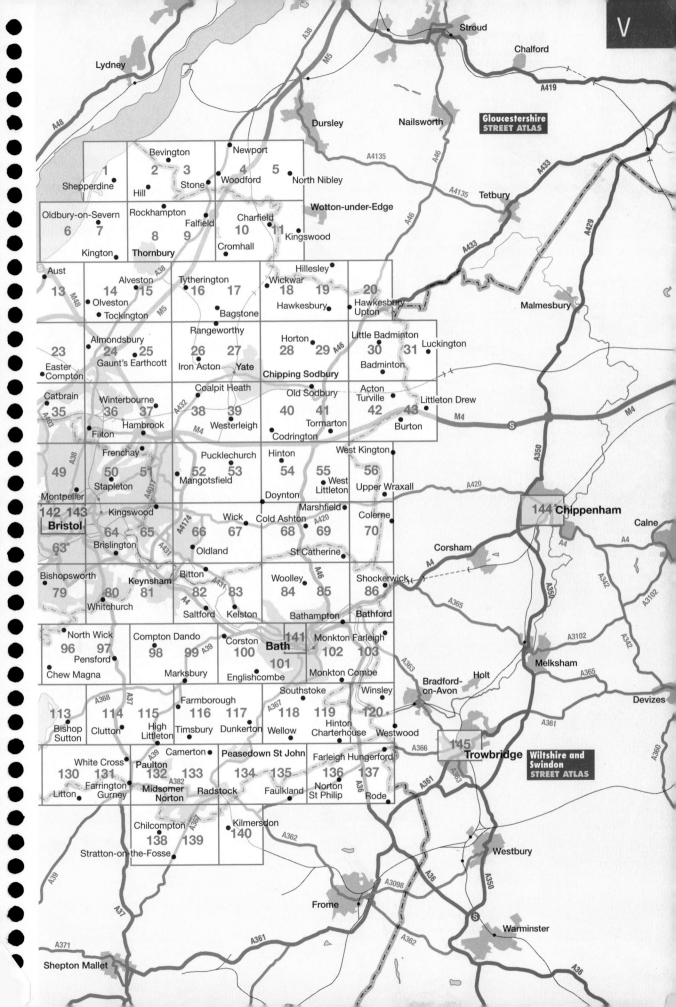

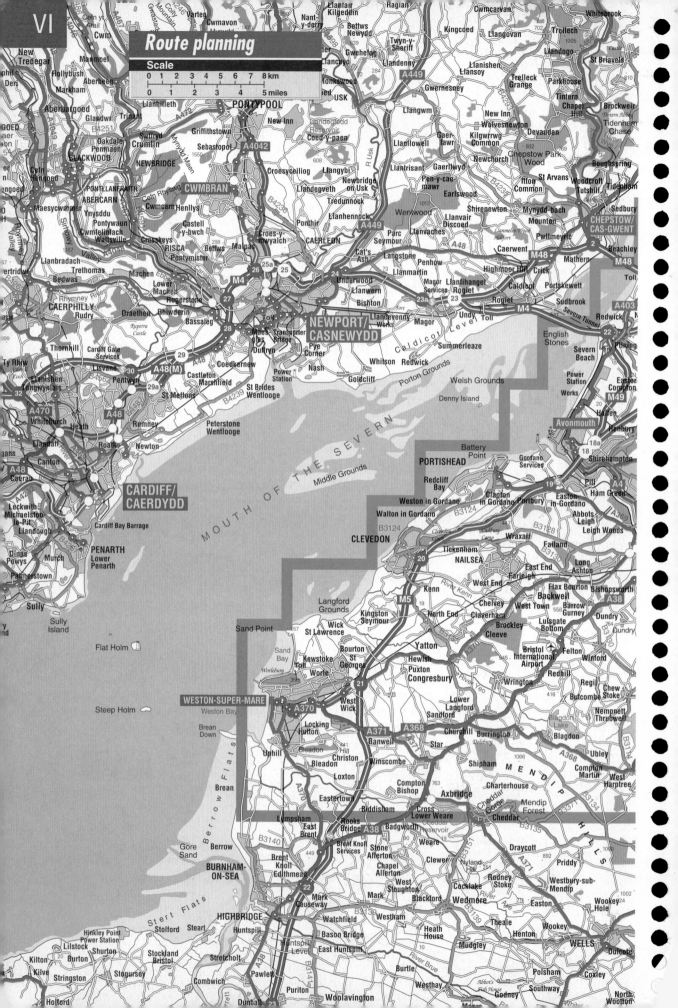

Route planning

Scale

0 1 2 3 4 5 6 7 8 km

0 1 2 3 4 5 miles

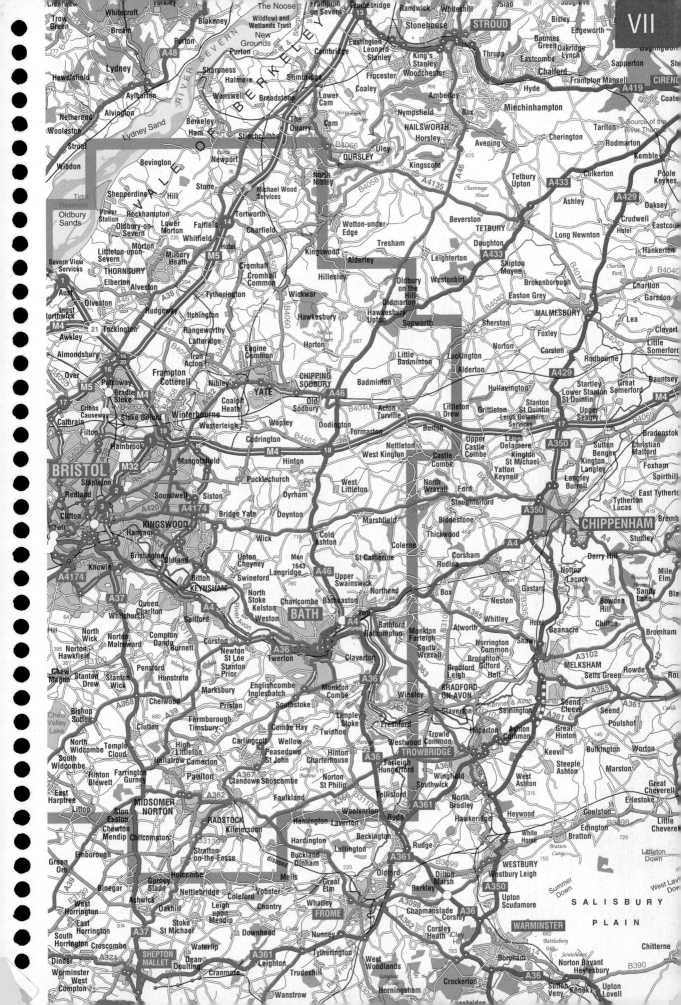

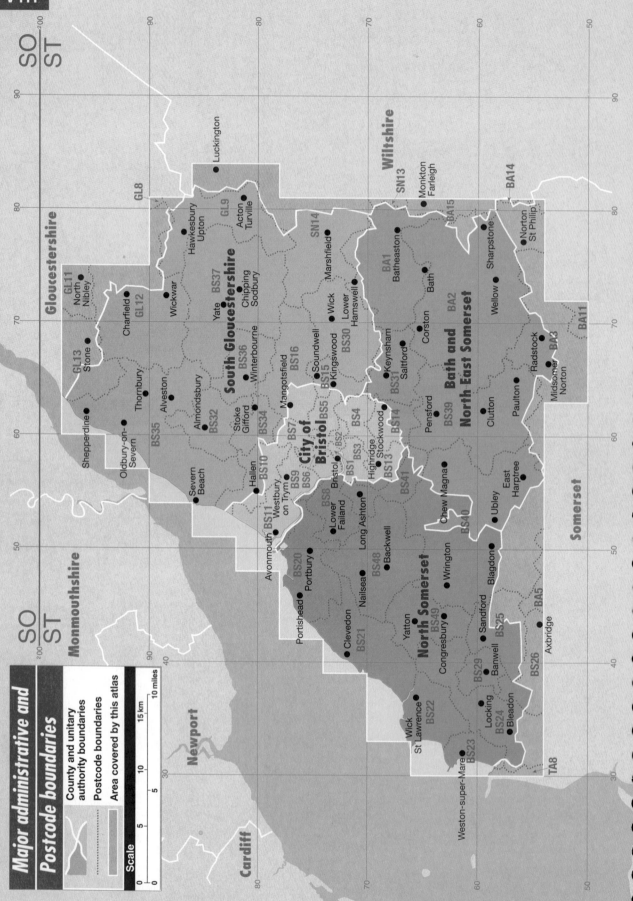

Major administrative and
Postcode boundaries

County and unitary
authority boundaries
Postcode boundaries
Area covered by this atlas

Scale
0   5   10 miles
0   5   10   15 km

SO
ST
200

SO
ST
200

Monmouthshire

Cardiff

Newport

Gloucestershire

GL8

GL11
North
Nibley

GL12
Charfield

GL13
Stone

Thornbury

Alveston

GL9
Acton
Turville

Hawkesbury
Upton

Luckington

Wickwar

Yate BS37

Chipping
Sodbury

South Gloucestershire

BS36
Winterbourne

Almondsbury

Stoke
Gifford

BS32

BS34

BS35

Shepperdine

Oldbury-
on-
Severn

Severn
Beach

Hallen

BS10

BS7

Mangotsfield

BS16

BS15

Soundwell

BS5

Kingswood

Wick

Lower
Hamswell

BS30

Marshfield

SN14

Wiltshire

SN13

Monkton
Farleigh

BA15

BA1
Batheaston

Corston

Bath

BA2

Norton
St Philip

Sharpstone

Wellow

BA14

BA11

BA3
Radstock

Midsomer
Norton

Keynsham

BS31

Saltford

Pensford

BS39

Bath and
North-East Somerset

Clutton

Paulton

BA5

Somerset

City of
Bristol

BS9

BS6

BS11

Westbury
on Trym

Avonmouth

BS20

Portbury

Portishead

Clevedon

BS21

BS8

Lower
Failand

Long Ashton

Bristol

BS1

BS2

BS3

BS4

BS13

Highridge

Stockwood

BS14

BS41

Chew Magna

BS40

Ubley

East
Harptree

Blagdon

Backwell

BS48

Nailsea

North Somerset

Yatton

BS49

Wrington

Congresbury

Sandford

BS29

Banwell

BS25

BS26

Axbridge

Weston-super-Mare

BS23

BS24

Locking

Bleadon

BS22

Wick
St Lawrence

TA8

River Severn

White House

Chapel House

Severn Way

Manor Farm

NUPDOWN RD

The Laurels

PH

Shepperdine Farm

North Ham Corner

Shepperdine Farm

Shepperdine

Brickhouse Farm

Shepperdine Withybed

BS35

GL13

SHEPPERDINE RD

Harecrest La

Jobsgreen Farm

Lowgoods Farm

Power Station

Knight's Farm

Visitor Ctr

Mast

HILL LA

GL13

River Severn

Severn Way

Willis Elm

SEVERN LA

WORLDSEND LA

Worldsend
Farm

Blisbury
Farm

Stample La

Pennyhay La

BEVINGTON LA

Bevington

Longpool La

Stuckmoor La

Dayhouse
Farm

Brick House
Farm

Manor Farm

Upper Hill

Cat Grove

Nupdown

TRANTON LA

Nupdown
Farm

NUPDOWN RD

BS35

GL13

Upper Hill
Farm

Yew Tree Farm

Hill
Court

Scotlands
Farm

Hill

Roundhouse
Wood

Maniards
Green

Court
Farm

HILL LA

Church-hill
Wood

BS35

Beggarsbush La

Rockhampton Rhine

WOODEND LA

63   64   65

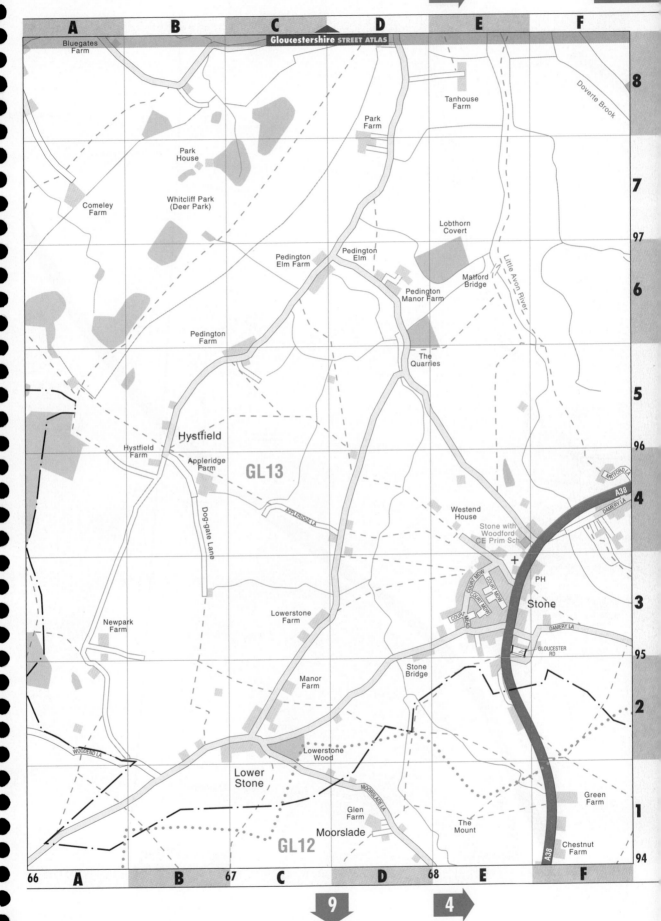

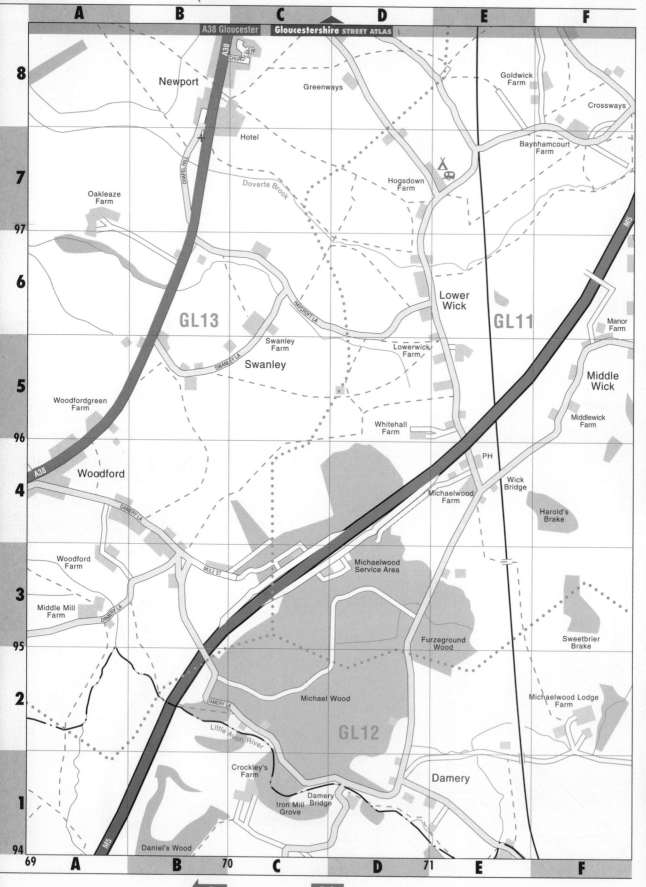

A38 Gloucester

Gloucestershire STREET ATLAS

A B C D E F

8

Newport

Greenways

Goldwick Farm

Crossways

7

Hotel

Baynhamcourt Farm

97

Oakleaze Farm

Doverte Brook

Hogsdown Farm

6

CHAPEL HILL

Lower Wick

GL11

Manor Farm

GL13

HAYCROFT LA

Middle Wick

5

Swanley Farm

Swanley

Lowerwick Farm

Middlewick Farm

SWANLEY LA

96

Woodfordgreen Farm

Whitehall Farm

PH

A38

Woodford

DAMERY LA

Michaelwood Farm

Wick Bridge

Harold's Brake

4

Woodford Farm

MULE ST

Michaelwood Service Area

3

Middle Mill Farm

DAMERY LA

Sweetbrier Brake

Furzeground Wood

95

Michaelwood Lodge Farm

2

DAMERY LA

Michael Wood

GL12

Little Avon River

Crockley's Farm

Damery

1

Iron Mill Grove

Damery Bridge

94

M5

Daniel's Wood

69 A B 70 C D 71 E F

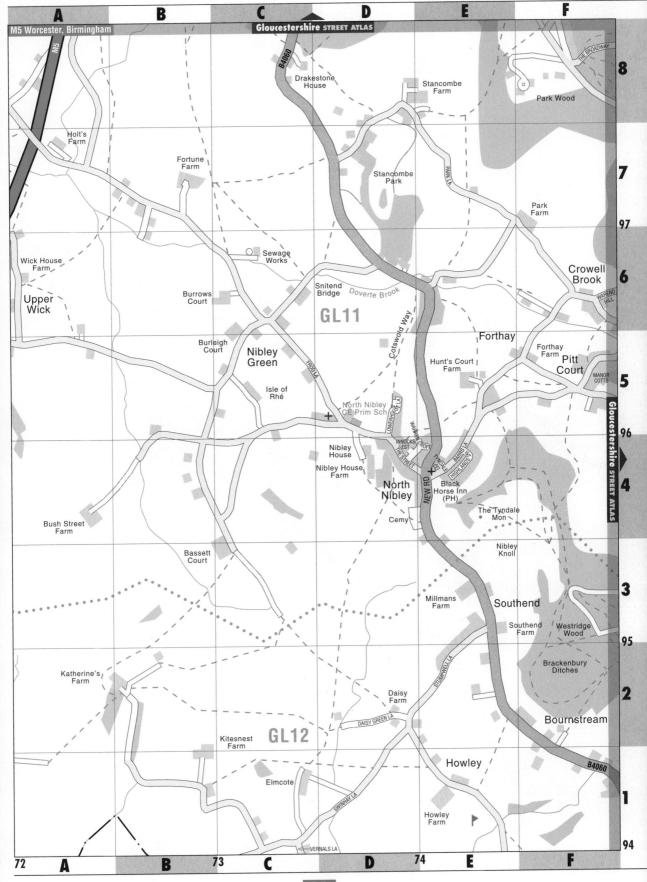

M5 Worcester, Birmingham

M5

B4060

Drakestone House

Stancombe Farm

Park Wood

THE BROADWAY

Holt's Farm

Fortune Farm

Stancombe Park

Park LA

Park Farm

Wick House Farm

Sewage Works

Snitend Bridge

Doverte Brook

GL11

Crowell Brook

WAREND HILL

Upper Wick

Burrows Court

Cotswold Way

Forthay

Forthay Farm

Pitt Court

Burleigh Court

Nibley Green

Hunt's Court Farm

MANOR COTTS

FROG LA

Isle of Rhé

North Nibley CE Prim Sch

LOWERHOUSE LA

Bush Street Farm

WARREN CROFT

INNOCKS CL EST

BARRS LA

Nibley House

THE STREET

TYNDALE CT

HIGHLANDS CL

Black Horse Inn (PH)

Bassett Court

Nibley House Farm

NEW RD

North Nibley

The Tyndale Mon

Cemy

Nibley Knoll

Millmans Farm

Southend

Westridge Wood

Katherine's Farm

Southend Farm

Brackenbury Ditches

Daisy Farm

STUMPWELL LA

Bournstream

GL12

DAISY GREEN LA

B4060

Kitesnest Farm

Howley

Elmcote

SWINHAY LA

Howley Farm

VERNALS LA

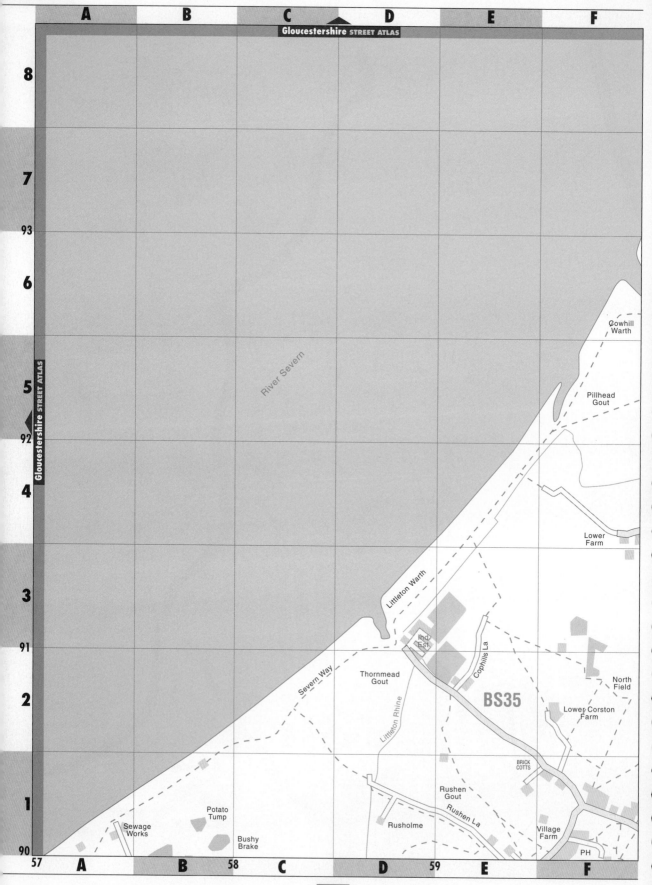

6

A B C D E F

Gloucestershire STREET ATLAS

8

7

93

6

Cowhill Warth

Pillhead Gout

River Severn

5

92

4

Lower Farm

Littleton Warth

3

91

Ind Est

CopHills La

North Field

Severn Way

Thornmead Gout

BS35

Lower Corston Farm

2

Littleton Rhine

BRICK COTTS

Rushen Gout

Rushen La

1

Potato Tump

Rusholme

Village Farm

Sewage Works

Bushy Brake

PH

90

57 A 58 B C 59 D E F

Gloucestershire STREET ATLAS

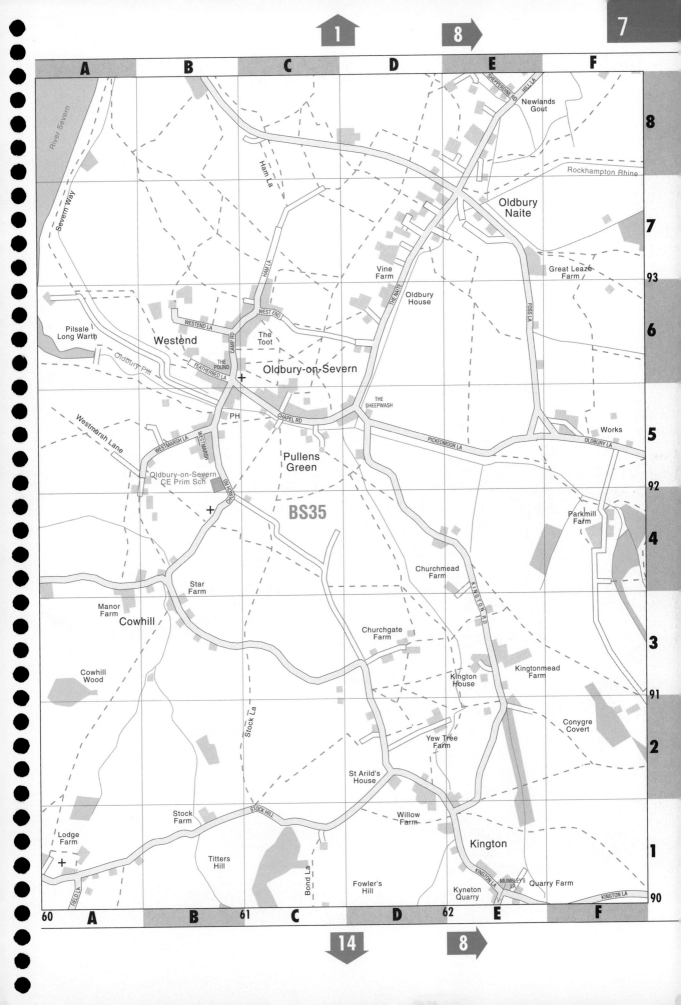

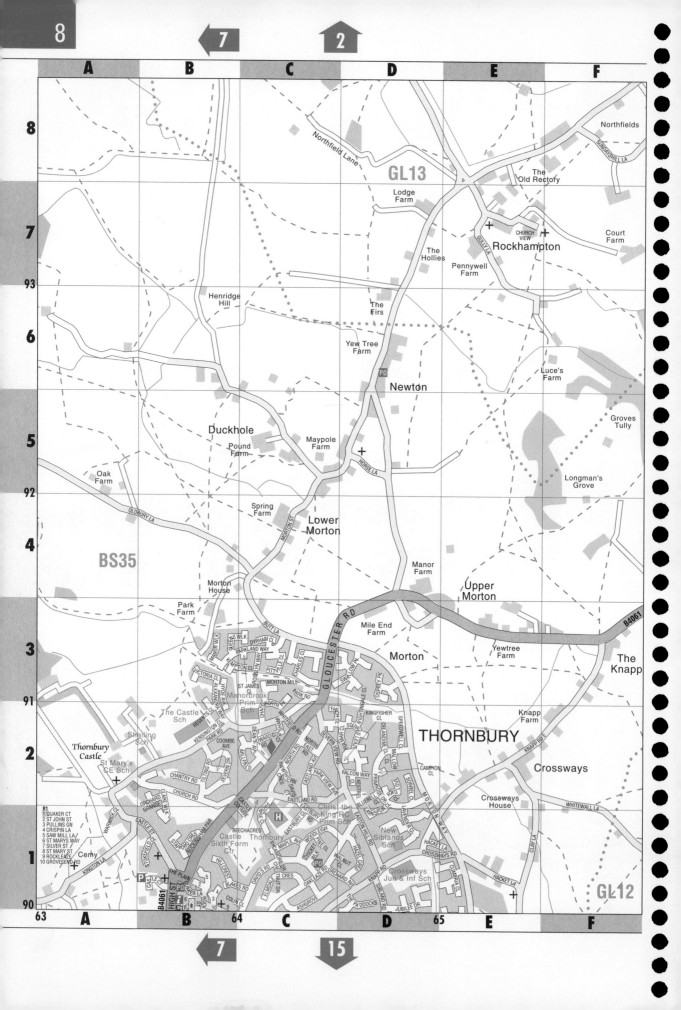

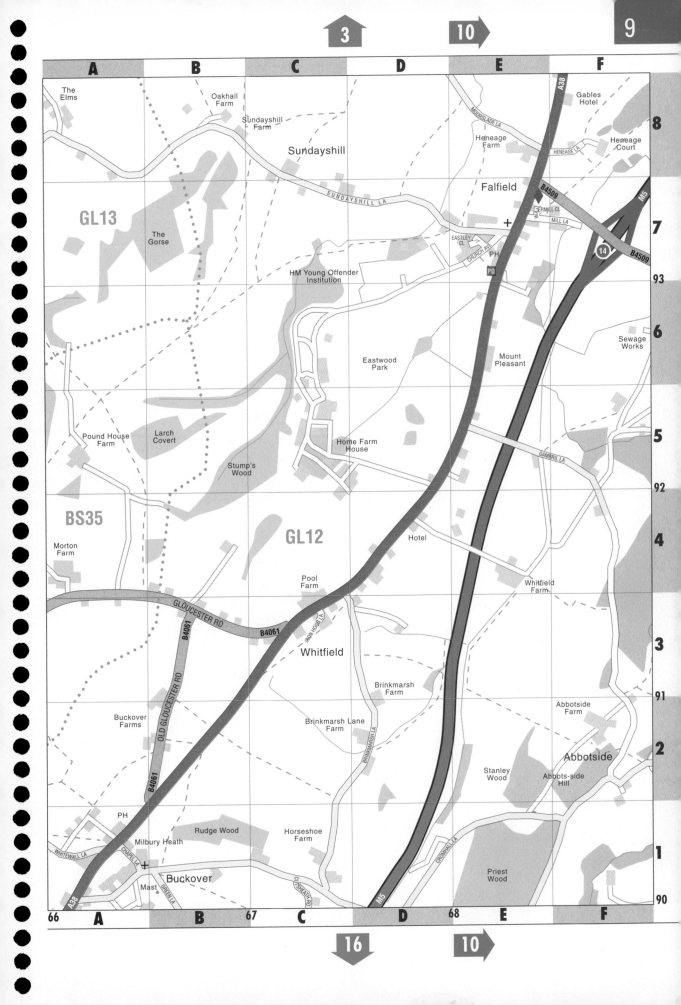

A B C D E F

8

Daniel's Wood

Avening Green

Huntingford

Huntingford Farm

Old Court Farm

M5

Old Court

Little Tortworth Copse

Little Avon River

Hotel

7

Brook Farm

Howcroft Cottages

Tortworth

+ Chestnut

B4509

93

Tortworth Prim Sch

Old Lodge Farm

Kennel Plantation

Tortworth Copse

Underwood Farm

6

Gall Pond

Arboretum

Lodge

Tortworth Green

Elmtree Farm

Poolfield Farm

Charfield Prim Sch

Tortworth Court Hotel

HM Prison

5

Charfield Hill

WOTTON RD B4058

PO

MINOR LA

92

The Lake

Tortworth Park

Tafarn-bach

B4509

The Old Rectory

GL12

4

Harris's Wood

PARK RD

WOODLAND RD

MEADOW RD

Woodend Farm

Hammerley Down

B4509

Poundhouse Farm

Bloody Acre

Leyhill

CHURCHEND LA

3

Parkend

Royal Oak (PH)

Manor Farm

+

KNAPP LA

Wicks' Hill

Brand Wood

Churchend

91

Sodam Mill

Bibstone

FARLEIGH LA

Church Farm

PERRY LA

2

PO

THE BURLTONS

TOWNWELL

Talbotsend Farm

CHURCH LA

LONGCROSS

BRISTOL RD

+

St Andrew's CE Prim Sch

Cromhall

Talbot's End

1

Court Farm

RECTORY LA

B4058

B4509

90

69 A B 70 C D 71 E F

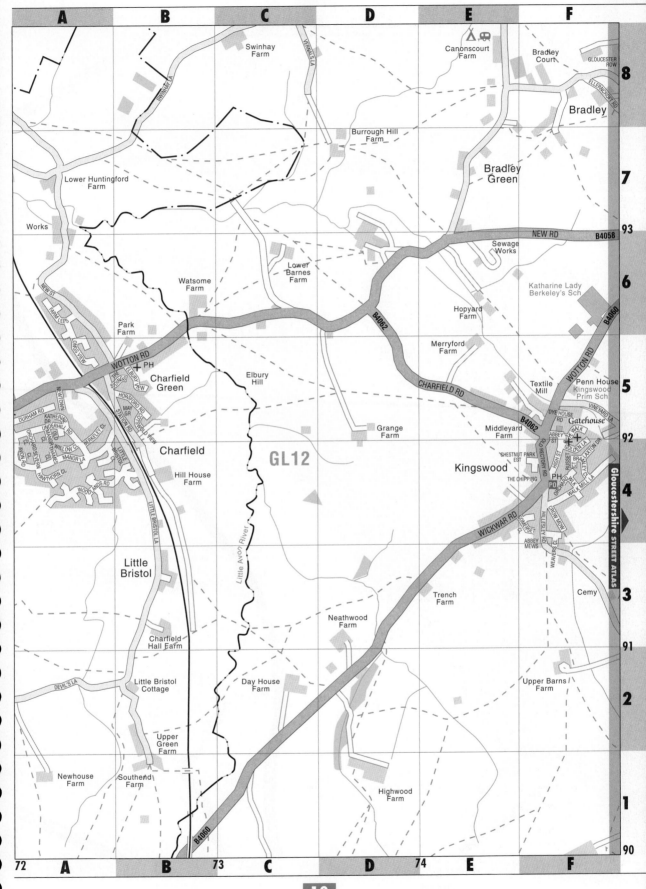

A B C D E F

8

7

93

6

5

92

4

3

91

2

1

90

Swinhay Farm

Canonscourt Farm

Bradley Court

GLOUCESTER ROW

ELLERNCROFT RD

Bradley

VERNAL'S LA

SWINHAY LA

Burrough Hill Farm

Bradley Green

Lower Huntingford Farm

NEW RD

B4058

Works

Sewage Works

Katharine Lady Berkeley's Sch

NEW ST

Watsome Farm

Lower Barnes Farm

B4062

Hopyard Farm

B4060

FARM LEES

LONGS VIEW

Park Farm

Merryford Farm

WOTTON RD

WOTTON RD

Penn House

Kingswood Prim Sch

NEWTOWN

THE SIDINGS

ELBURY VIEW

PH

Charfield Green

Elbury Hill

CHARFIELD RD

Textile Mill

VINEYARD LA

DYE HOUSE RD

Gatehouse

DURHAM RD

KATHERINE DR

HORSFORD RD

ROSSMORE VIEW

MAY GR

B4062

Middleyard Farm

ABBEY WALK

HIGH ST

RUSSET CL

GOLDEN LA

BRADLEY CL

LAXTON DR

92

UNDERHILL RD

ORCHARD CL

BERKELEY CL

WILLOW CL

Charfield

Grange Farm

Kingswood

CHESTNUT PARK EST

ORCHARD WAY

RECTORY RD

PH

PO

WALK MILL LA

ORCHARD SEVERN

AVON RD

MANOR LA

WOODLANDS RD

HAWTHORN CL

Hill House Farm

THE CHIPPING

CROWN CL

WICKWAR RD

SOMERSET

HILLESLEY RD

WEAVERS CL

ABBEY MEWS

Cemy

LITTLE BRISTOL LA

Little Bristol

Little Avon River

Trench Farm

DEVIL'S LA

Charfield Hall Farm

Neathwood Farm

91

Little Bristol Cottage

Day House Farm

Upper Barns Farm

Upper Green Farm

Newhouse Farm

Southend Farm

Highwood Farm

B4060

GL12

Gloucestershire STREET ATLAS

A B C D E F

8

7

89

6

5

88

4

3

87

2

1

86

54 A B 55 C D 56 E F

Herefordshire & Monmouthshire STREET ATLAS

M48

Footpath/Cycle Way

Severn Road
Bridge

Mast •

Toll

Severn Way

Aust
Cliff

PASSAGE RD

New House
Farm

Old
Passage

Old Passage
House

Aust Warth

Foss Ditch

A403

River Severn

Cake Pill

Cake Pill
Gout

Asnum
Copse

Lords Rhine

Severn Way

Bilsham Rhine

Bilsham
Farm

Northwick Pig
Farm

BS35

WARTH LA

AUST RD

Laural
Farm

Church
Farm

Northwick

Redwick & Northwick
CE Prim Sch

Mill
Farm

BILSHAM LA

DANGER
AREA

B4055

Manor
Farm

Red
Lodge

Rifle Range

North Worthy
Farm

Holm Rhine

REDWICK RD

Severn
Lodge
Farm

REDWICK RD

BLANDS
ROW

New
Passage

B4064

A403

SEVERN RD

NORTHWICK RD

B4055

M4

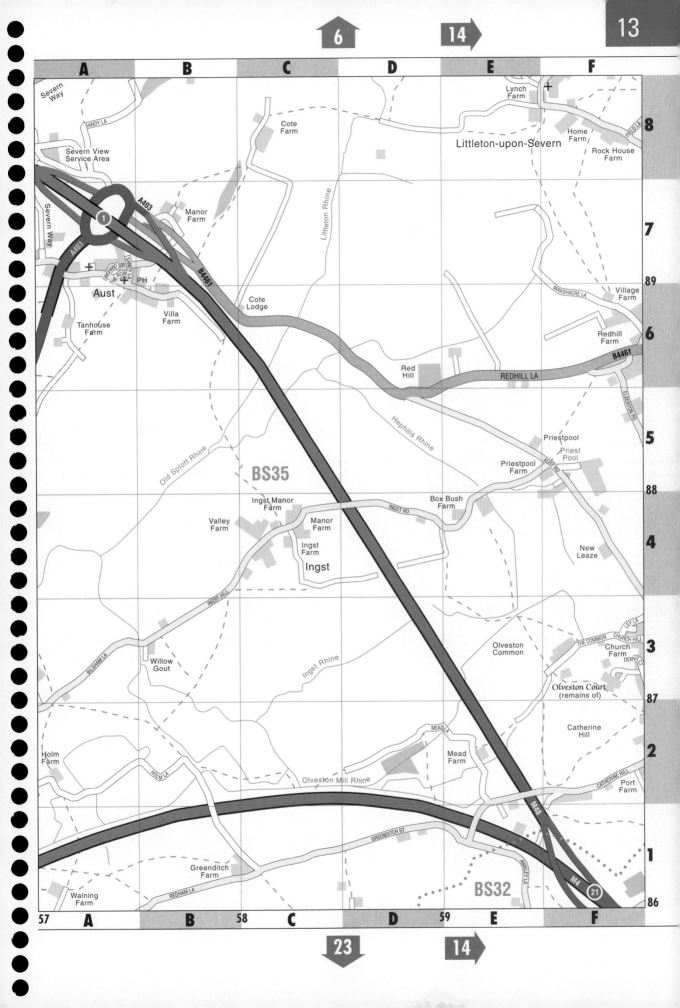

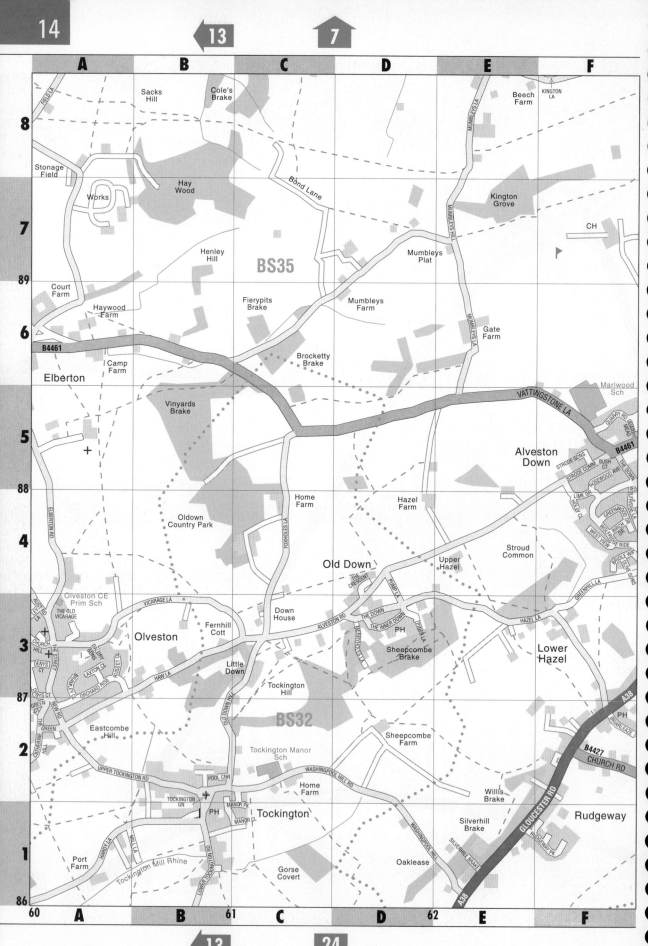

Stonage Field

Works

Sacks Hill

Cole's Brake

Hay Wood

Bond Lane

Beech Farm

KINGTON LA

CH

Kington Grove

Mumbleys Plat

BS35

Henley Hill

Court Farm

Haywood Farm

Fierypits Brake

Mumbleys Farm

Gate Farm

Elberton

B4461

Camp Farm

Brocketty Brake

Vinyards Brake

VATTWGSTONE LA

Marlwood Sch

QUARRY RD QUARRY MEAD

B4461

STRODE GDNS

Alveston Down

STRODE COMM
BUSH CT
THE DOWN

ROSEWOOD AVE

LIME DR

HOLLY CL

GREENWOOD DR

BIRCH DR

WOLFRIDGE DR

WOLFRIDGE RIDE

WEST VIEW

BRIDLE WAY

CLIVE GDNS

Elberton Rd

Oldown Country Park

Home Farm

FOXHOLES LA

Hazel Farm

Stroud Common

Upper Hazel

GREENHILL LA

Olveston CE Prim Sch

THE OLD VICARAGE

VICARAGE LA

Olveston

AUSTLEY LA

DALORY GDNS

Fernhill Cott

Down House

THE CRESCENT

PUMP LA

ALVESTON RD

Old Down

THE DOWN
THE INNER DOWN

PH

PINES LA

HAZEL LA

Lower Hazel

CHURCH HILL

DENYS CT

LAXTON CL

RUSSEL CL

HAW LA

Little Down

NERRYHOLES LA

Sheepcombe Brake

DENYS CT

GREEN CT

ORCHARD RISE

Tockington Hill

BS32

THE GREEN

NEW RD

CATHERINE HILL

Eastcombe Hill

UPPER TOCKINGTON RD

POOL CNR

OLD DOWN INN

Tockington Manor Sch

WASHINGPOOL HILL RD

Home Farm

Sheepcombe Farm

Willis Brake

A38

PH

BRIARLEAZE

B4427

CHURCH RD

TOCKINGTON GN

PH

MANOR PK

MANOR CL

Tockington

Silverhill Brake

GLOUCESTER RD

RUDGEWAY PK

Rudgeway

Port Farm

HARDY LA

MILL LA

OLD TOCKINGTON RD

Tockington Mill Rhine

Gorse Covert

WASHINGPOOL HILL

SILVERHILL BRAKE

Oaklease

A38

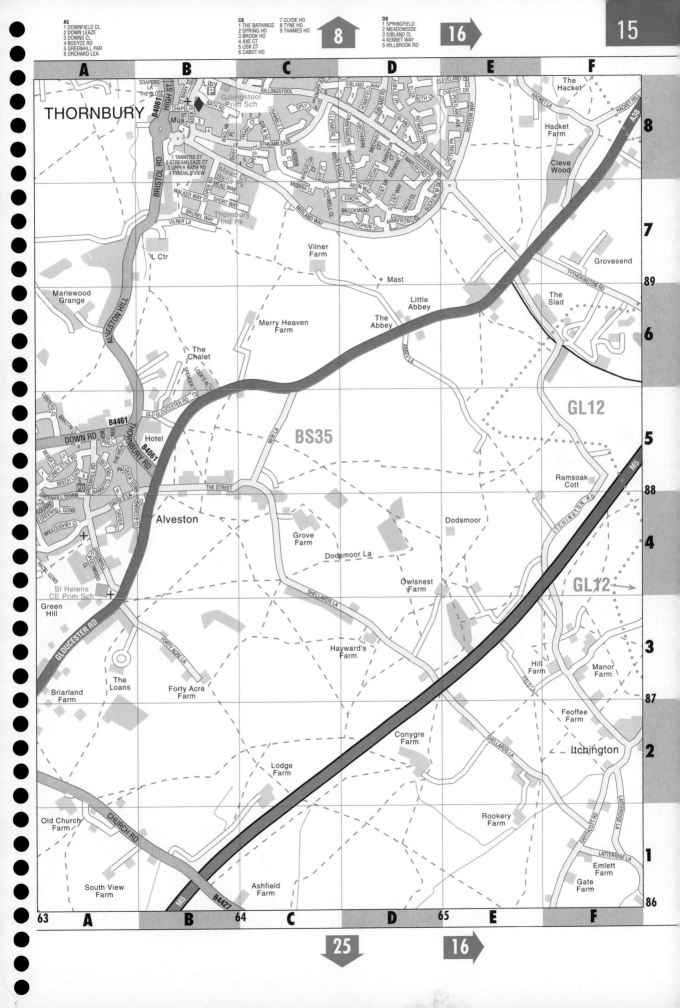

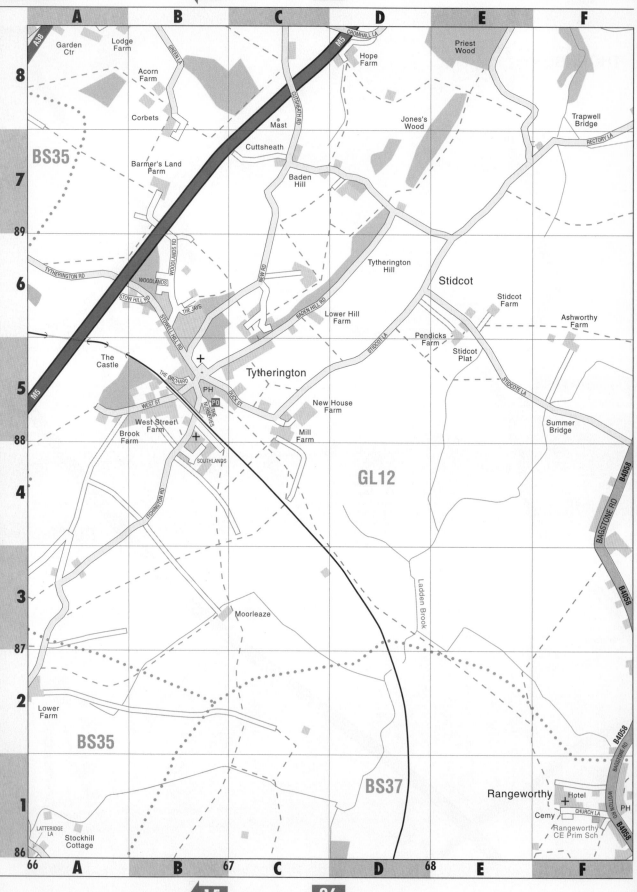

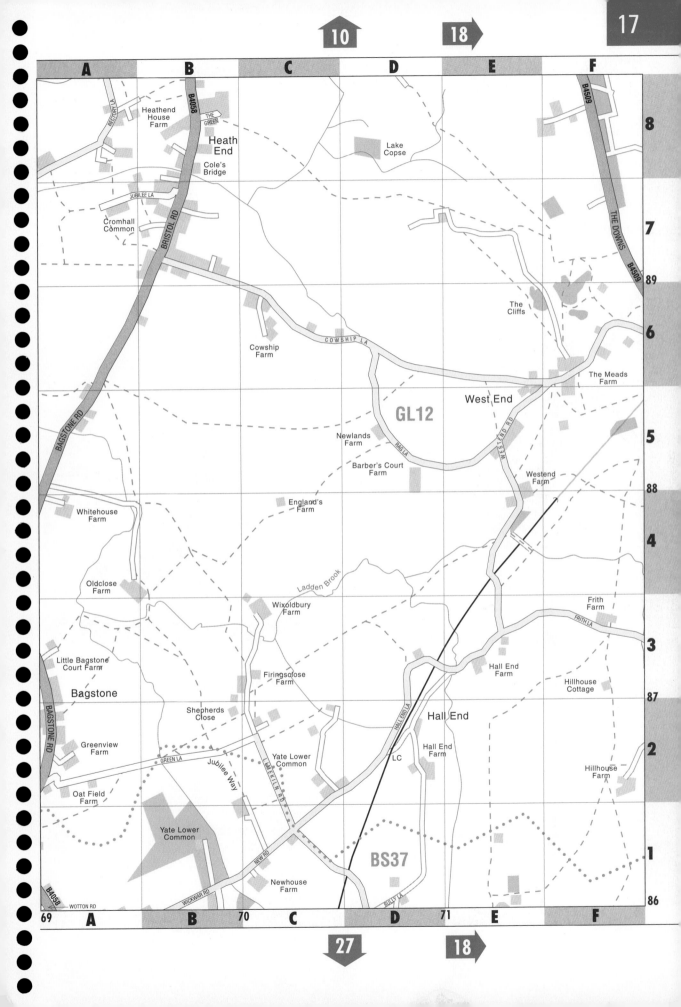

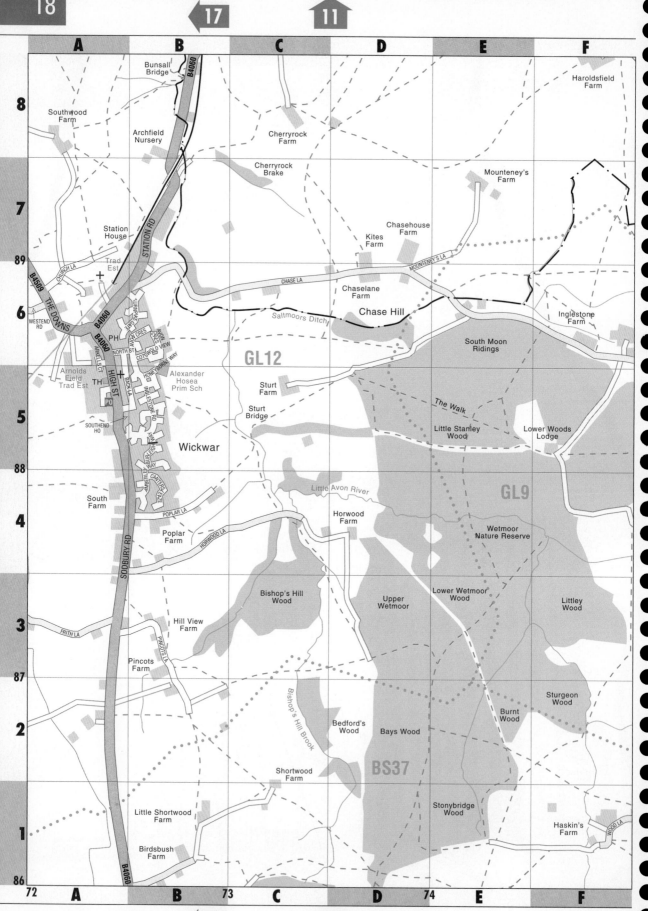

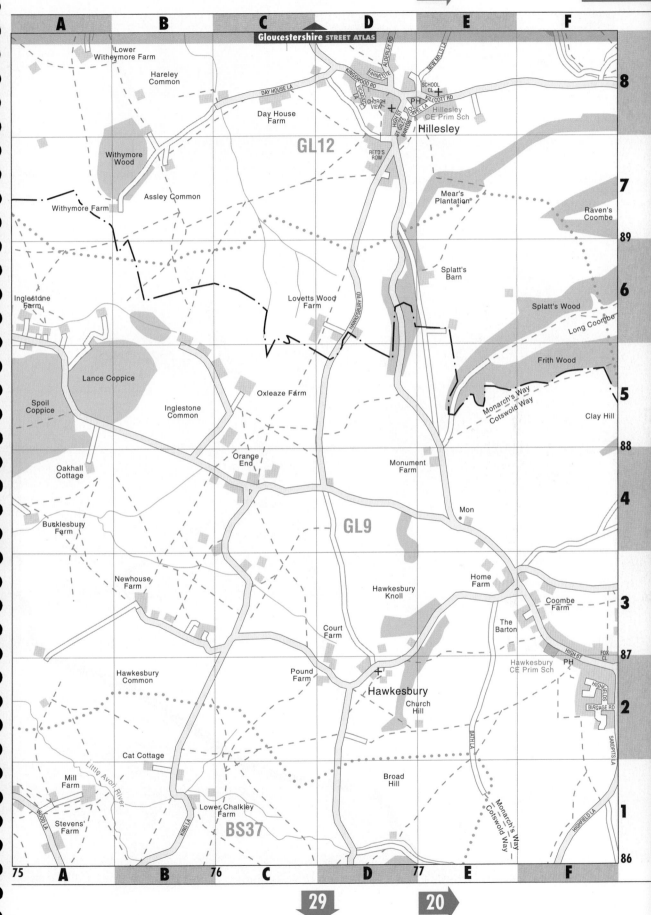

Lower
Witheymore Farm
8
Hareley
Common

DAY HOUSE LA

ALDERLEY RD

FARMCOTE

NEW MILLS LA

SCHOOL
CL

KILLCOTT RD

KINGSWOOD RD

VICARAGE

Day House
Farm

CHURCH
VIEW

PH

Hillesley
CE Prim Sch

HIGH ST

ST GILES

BARTON

CHAPEL LA

Hillesley

GL12

REED'S
ROW

Withymore
Wood

7

Mear's
Plantation

Raven's
Coombe

Assley Common

89

Withymore Farm

6

Splatt's
Barn

HAWKESBURY RD

Lovetts Wood
Farm

Splatt's Wood

Inglestone
Farm

Long Coombe

Frith Wood

Lance Coppice

Monarch's Way

Clay Hill

Oxleaze Farm

Cotswold Way

Spoil
Coppice

Inglestone
Common

5

88

Orange
End

Monument
Farm

Oakhall
Cottage

4

Mon

Bucklesbury
Farm

GL9

Newhouse
Farm

Home
Farm

Coombe
Farm

3

Hawkesbury
Knoll

The
Barton

HIGH ST

FOX
CL

87

Court
Farm

Hawkesbury
CE Prim Sch

PH

Hawkesbury
Common

HIGHFIELDS

BIRGAGE RD

Pound
Farm

Hawkesbury

2

SANDPITS LA

Church
Hill

BATH LA

Cat Cottage

Broad
Hill

Little Avon River

Monarch's Way

Mill
Farm

Cotswold Way

HIGHFIELD LA

WOOD LA

Lower Chalkley
Farm

1

Stevens'
Farm

KING LA

BS37

86

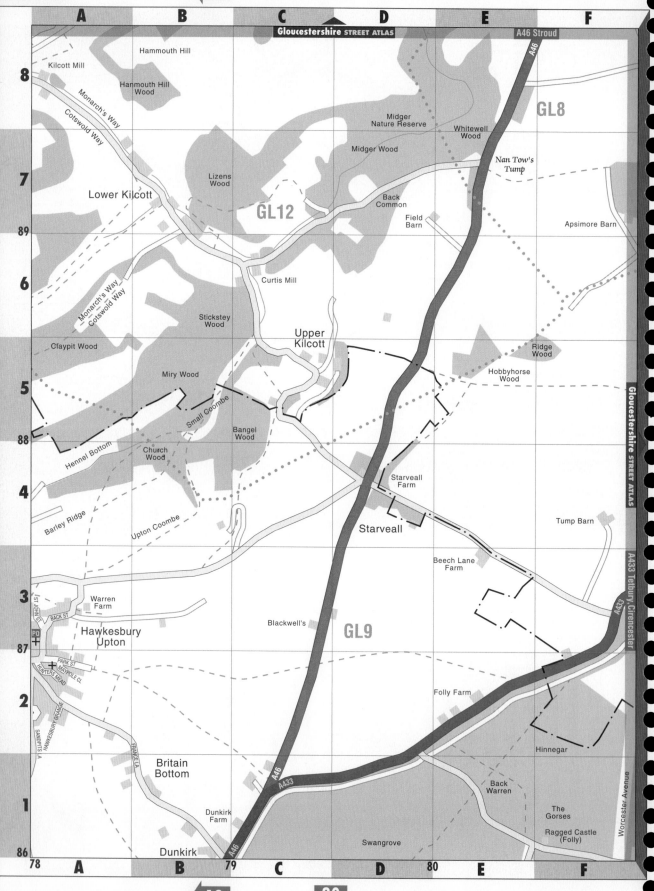

A46 Stroud

GL8

A B C D E F

8

Kilcott Mill

Hammouth Hill

Hanmouth Hill Wood

Monarch's Way

Cotswold Way

Midger Nature Reserve

Whitewell Wood

Nan Tow's Tump

7

Lower Kilcott

Lizens Wood

Midger Wood

Back Common

GL12

Field Barn

Apsimore Barn

89

6

Monarch's Way

Cotswold Way

Curtis Mill

Upper Kilcott

Ridge Wood

Hobbyhorse Wood

Stickstey Wood

Claypit Wood

Miry Wood

5

Small Coombe

Bangel Wood

Hennel Bottom

Church Wood

Starveall Farm

88

4

Barley Ridge

Upton Coombe

Starveall

Beech Lane Farm

Tump Barn

A433 Tetbury, Cirencester

3

Warren Farm

1ST JOHN'S ST

BACK ST

Hawkesbury Upton

Blackwell's

GL9

87

PO

PARK ST

MAYPOLE CL

HUNTERS MEAD

HAWKESBURY GRANGE

Folly Farm

2

SANDPITS LA

FRANCE LA

Britain Bottom

Hinnegar

Back Warren

Worcester Avenue

1

Dunkirk Farm

A46

A433

Swangrove

The Gorses

Ragged Castle (Folly)

86

Dunkirk

A46

78 A B 79 C D 80 E F

Gloucestershire STREET ATLAS

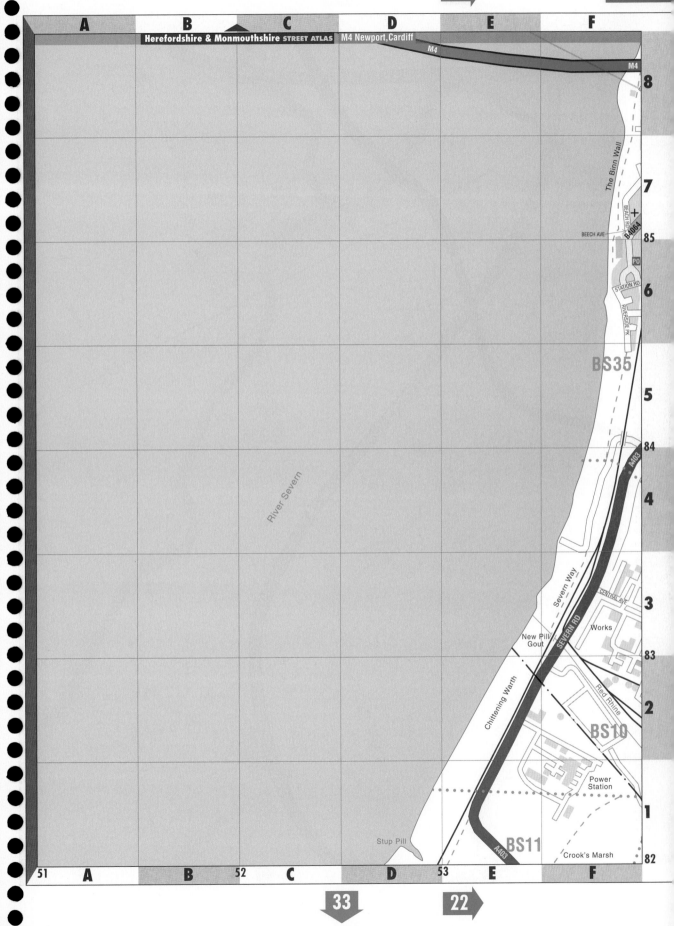

22

Herefordshire & Monmouthshire STREET ATLAS

M4 Newport, Cardiff

M4

M4

The Binn Wall

8

7

BEECH AVE

85

B4064

BEACH RD

PO

STATION RD

6

RIVERSIDE PK

BS35

5

84

A403

4

Severn Way

CENTRAL AVE

3

Works

New Pill Gout

SEVERN RD

83

Chittening Warth

Red Rhine

2

BS10

Power Station

1

Stup Pill

BS11

A403

Crook's Marsh

82

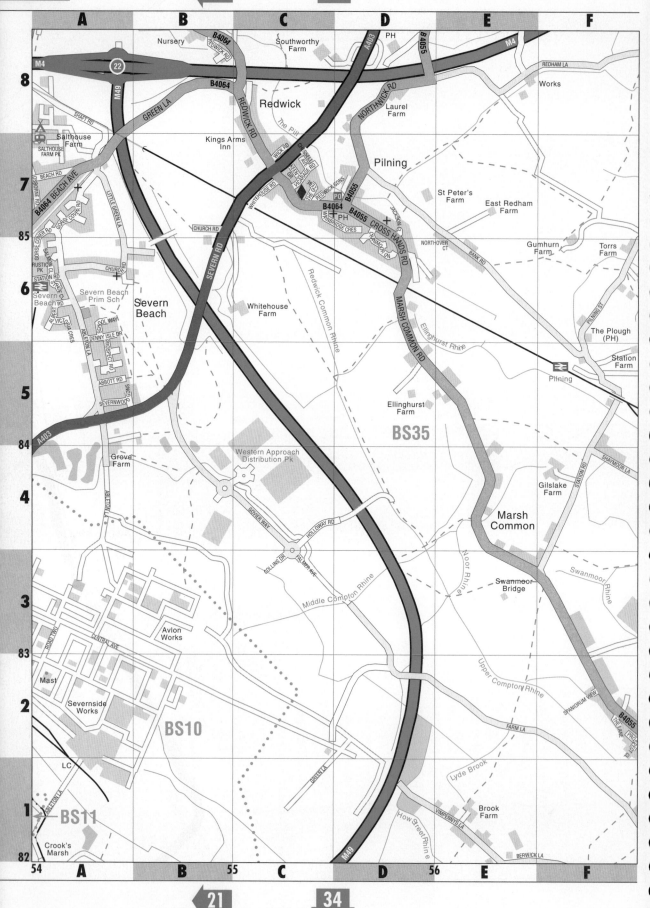

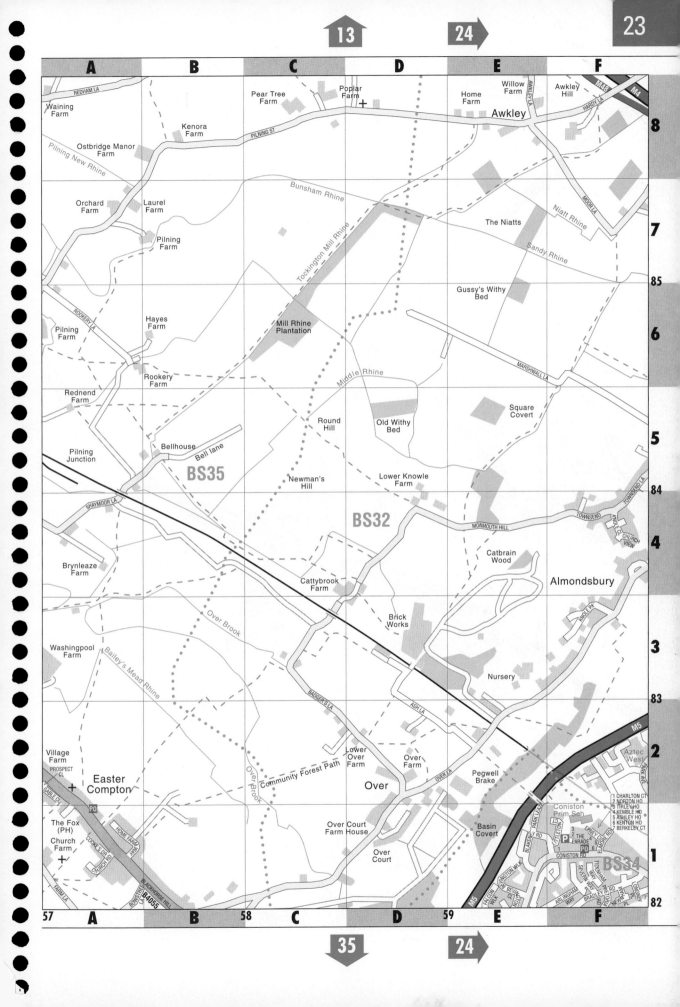

C2
1 WOODLANDS CT
2 BRADLEY PAVS
3 BROAD CROFT

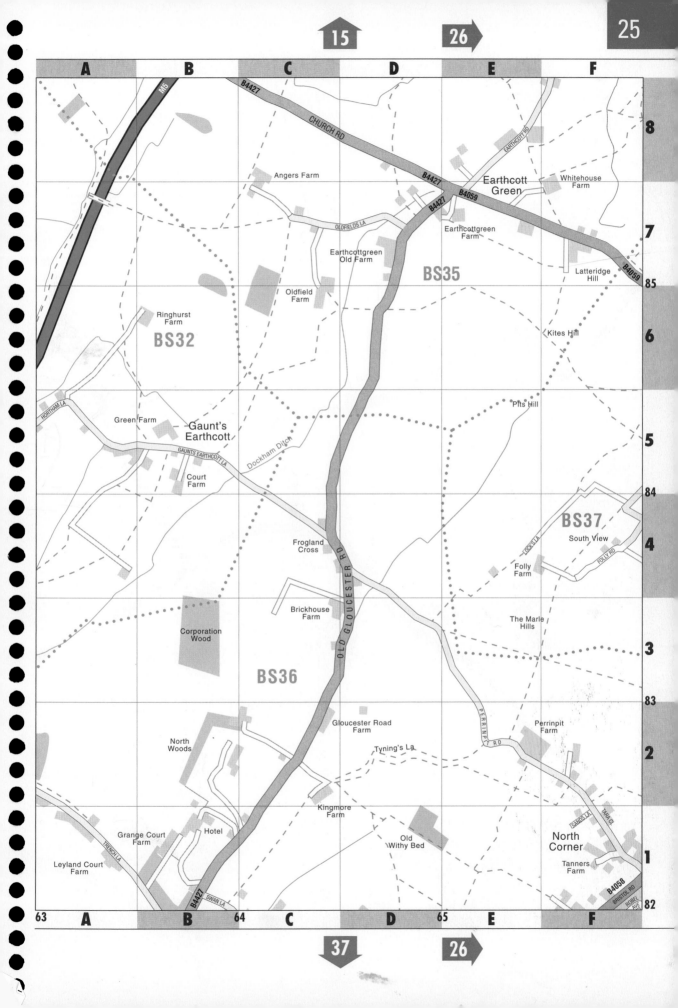

25   16

A   B   C   D   E   F

8

BS35

Lower Lark's Farm

LATTERIDGE LA

LARK'S LA

Dowell's Farm

Patch Elm Farm

7

PATCH ELM LA

B4058

85

B4059

Mudgedown Farm

NORTHBREAD LA

6

Ladden Bows Bridge

Northend Farm

Chaingate House

CHAINGATE LA

WOTTON RD

Latteridge

Two Pools Farm

Beckfield Farm

LC

5

Sheephouse Farm

Ladden Brook

BS37

Acton Court

Acton Lodge

84

Hill House

FOLLY RD

4

Laddenside Farm

LC

Elm Farm

B4059

LATTERIDGE RD

PARK ST

PH

HIGH ST

WOTTON RD

B4058

B4059

Isle of Rhee

PH

PH

Iron Acton

HOLLY HILL

Iron Acton CE Prim Sch

VATE RD

B4059

Cogmill La

STATION RD

LC

CHILLWOOD CL

ALGARS DR

Robins Wood

NIBLEY LA

Lavenham Farm

3

BRISTOL RD

River Frome

Brake Farm

Algars Manor

83

Cog Mill Farm

Frome Valley Walkway

FRAMPTON END RD

2

Hover's La

Tubb's Bottom

BS36

Chestnut Farm

1

PH

B4058

WESTERN AVE

CONIFER CL

CHURCH RD

SCHOOL RD

MILL LA

Mayshill

BADMINTON RD

A432

Cemy

82

66   A   B   67   C   D   68   E   F

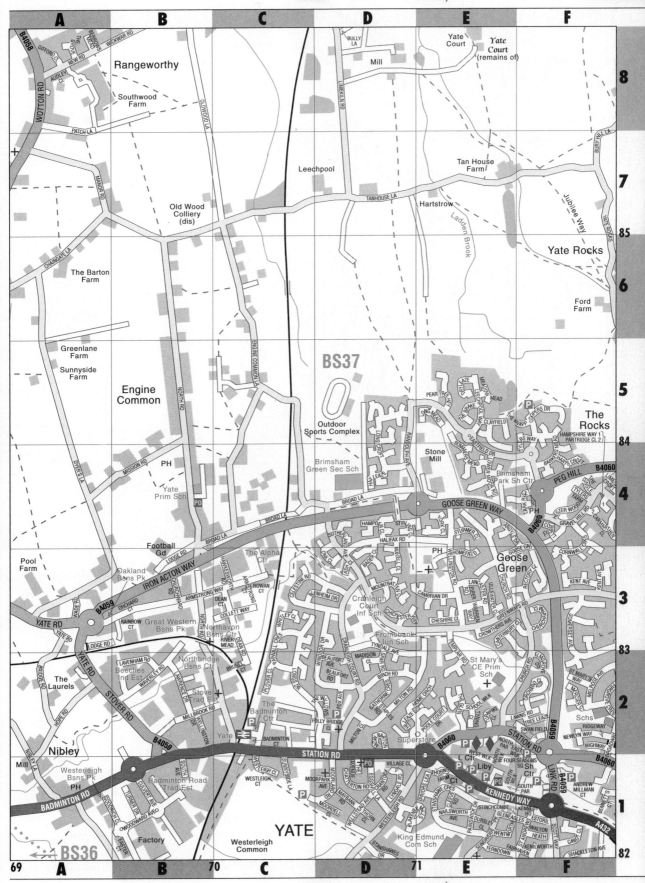

27
18

A B C D E F

8

Oxwick Farm

B4060

Lady's Wood

Horwood Riding Farm

BURY HILL LA

The Chase

Springfield Farm

VINNEY LA

Bury Hill

Lattimore Farm

Little Wood

7

Brinsham Wood

MAPLERIDGE LA

85

Hares Farm

Brinsham Farm

Brinsham Bridge

Ashlea Farm

6

BRINSHAM LA

WICKWAR RD

Horton Bushes

Quarry

5

BS37

Totteroak

Home Farm

Quarry

Sodbury Common

GRAVEL HILL RD W

Rockwood

84

Totteroak Farm

ROCKWOOD HO

Star Vale Farm

B4060 PEG HILL SOUTHFIELD WAY

LOVE LA

Winchcombe Farm

4

LIME CROFT

BARNHILL CL

Little Sodbury End

HORTON RD

CARMARTHEN CL

Jubilee Way

Greystone Ct

WILTSHIRE AVE

SHAWMANS LA

GREEN LA

Great House Farm

3

YATE

Stub Riding

Mead Riding

CH The Windmill

Monarch's Way

DORSET WAY

WALNUT LA

MELROSE AVE

Lodge

83

J.M.HIRST GDNS

JUBILEE GDNS

Portway La

2

BROADWAY

AIRSPORT WAY

MELROSE CL

Hardwoodgate Farm

River Frome

Park's Farm

RIDGEWAY

CAROLINE CL

DOWDING CL

COUZENS CL

HOPTON RD

BROOKFIELD CT

ST JOHNS WAY

NAPIER WAY

COMMONMEAD LA

HIGHWAY

Cemy

BARNHILL RD

ROSS CL

Chipping Edge Est

TT Trading Est

VAYRE CL

GRACE CL

B4060 STATION RD

Bowling Hill Bsns Pk

Works

Mill

P

BRIDGE ST

Stone House Mews

BEAUFORT MEWS

HYTERS CL

BATTEN CT

FROME RD

CORLANDS RD

BRANDASH RD

WALSHE AVE

RIDINGS

1

BENNETT

BOWLING HILL

QUARRY RD

THE PARADE

ROUNCEVAL ST

HIGH ST

TH

BROAD ST

PO

LANE DR

WHITEFIELDS

HARTLEY CL

CHIPPING SODBURY

A4320

CHERRY

STEGA

RIVERSIDE

WISTARIA

RIVER MEAD

CHESTNUT

CULVERWELL RD

TEAM LA

Liby

COTSWOLD CL

ARNOLD CT

MELBOURNE DR

CESSON CL

82

VIRGINIA

HIGHFIELD RD

GRASSINGTON DR

HORSESHOE LA

Prim Sch

HOUNDS CL

B4060 HORSE ST

MEAD RD

A B C D E F

72 73 74

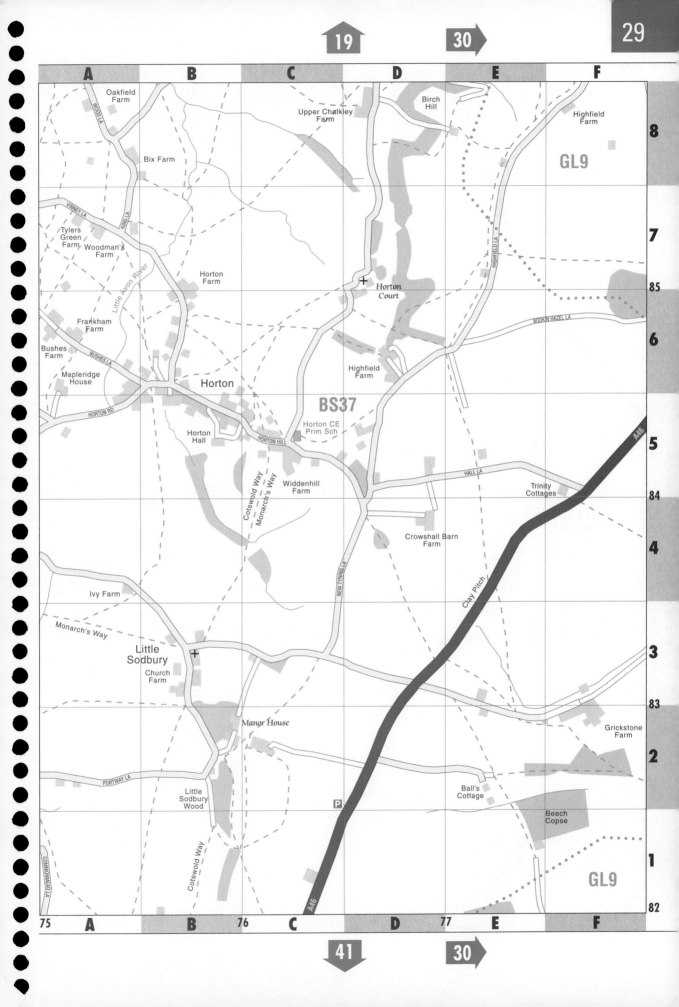

A   B   C   D   E   F

8

Swangrove House

Marshfield Path

Petty France Farm

Hotel

Petty France

Bodkin Wood

7

Worcester Avenue

85

Bodkin Hazel Wood

BODKIN HAZEL LA

6

Worcester Clump

Shepherd's Lodge

SN14

A46

Withy Bed

Little Badminton Farm

Seven Mile Plantation

American Barn

CHURCH LA

Little Badminton

5

GL9

WELL LA

84

BS37

Peaked Down Clump

4

Badminton Park

Mount Pond

Deer Park

The Mount

Landing Strip

Park Pond

3

83

Slait Lodge

Badminton House

SHOP LA

KENNEL DR

2

Castle Barn

The Tyning

HIGH ST

Badminton

Bath Lodge

Bath Verge

ROACH'S LA

THE LIMES

HAYE'S LA

SCHOOL LA

Vicarage Plantation

LIME AVE

STIRTON RD

1

OLD DOWN RD

Badminton Farm

Cape Farm

82

78   A   B   79   C   D   80   E   F

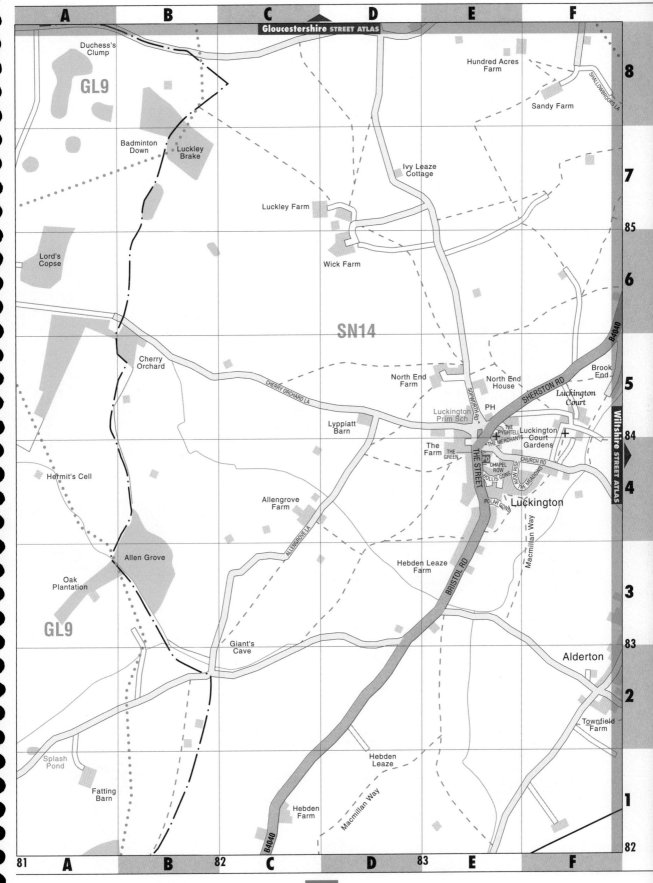

GL9

Duchess's Clump

Badminton Down

Luckley Brake

Lord's Copse

Cherry Orchard

SN14

Hermit's Cell

Allengrove Farm

Allen Grove

Oak Plantation

GL9

Giant's Cave

Splash Pond

Fatting Barn

Hundred Acres Farm

Sandy Farm

Ivy Leaze Cottage

Luckley Farm

Wick Farm

CHERRY ORCHARD LA

Lyppiatt Barn

ALLENGROVE LA

North End Farm

North End House

SOPWORTH RD

Luckington Prim Sch

PH

SHERSTON RD

Luckington Court

Brook End

B4040

The Farm

THE GREEN

THE PYGHTELL

THE MERCHANTS

Luckington Court Gardens

CHURCH RD

THE STREET

PO

CHAPEL ROW

TOLLIS GDNS

NOVA RISE

THE MEADOWS

POLAR GDNS

Luckington

BRISTOL RD

Hebden Leaze Farm

Macmillan Way

Alderton

Townfield Farm

Hebden Leaze

B4040

Hebden Farm

Macmillan Way

81   82   83

River Severn

Jetty
(dis)

Piers

King Road

BS11 Docks

East Pier

River Avon
Swash Channel

BS20

West Pier

SEA BANK RD

RIVER RD

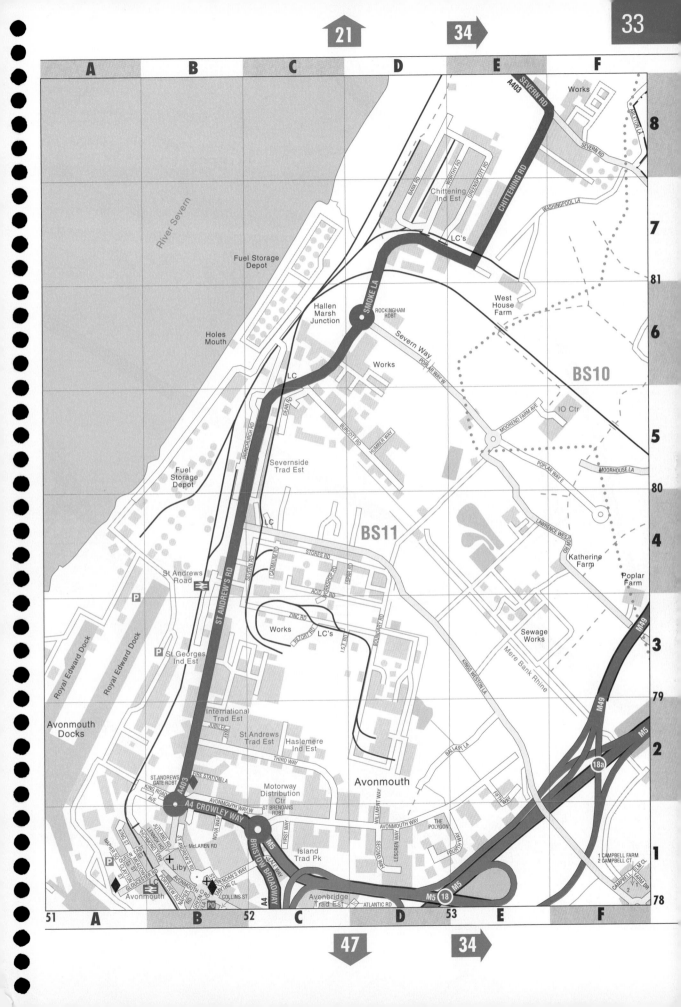

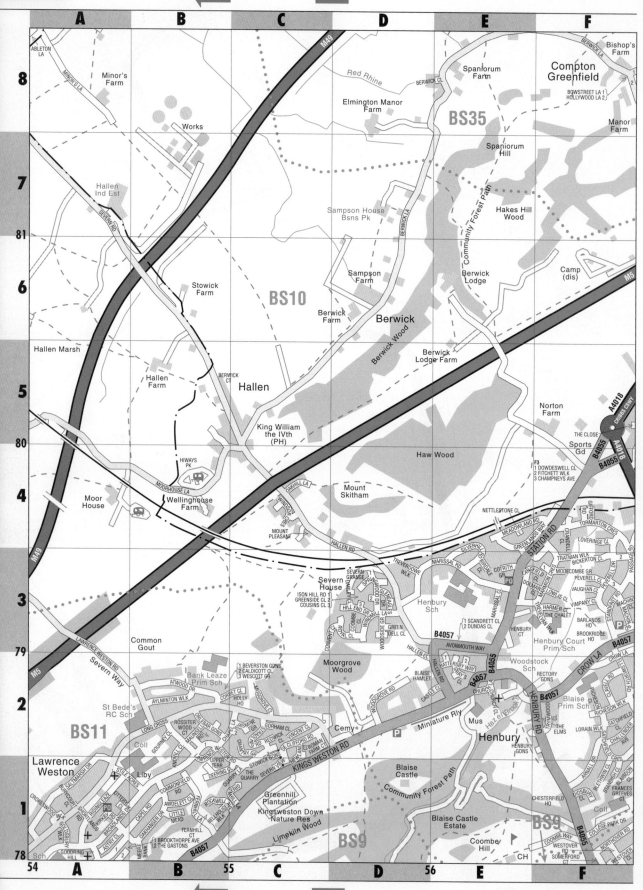

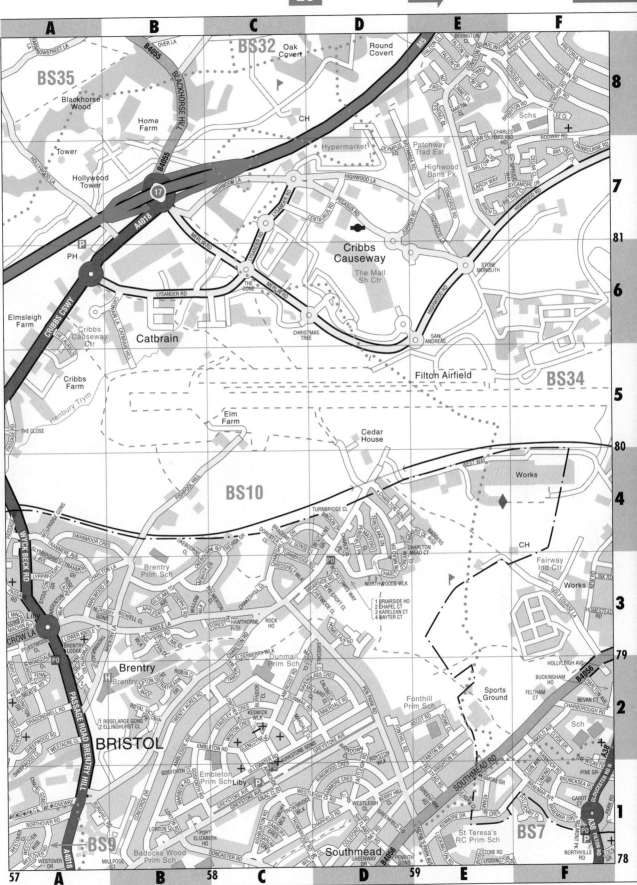

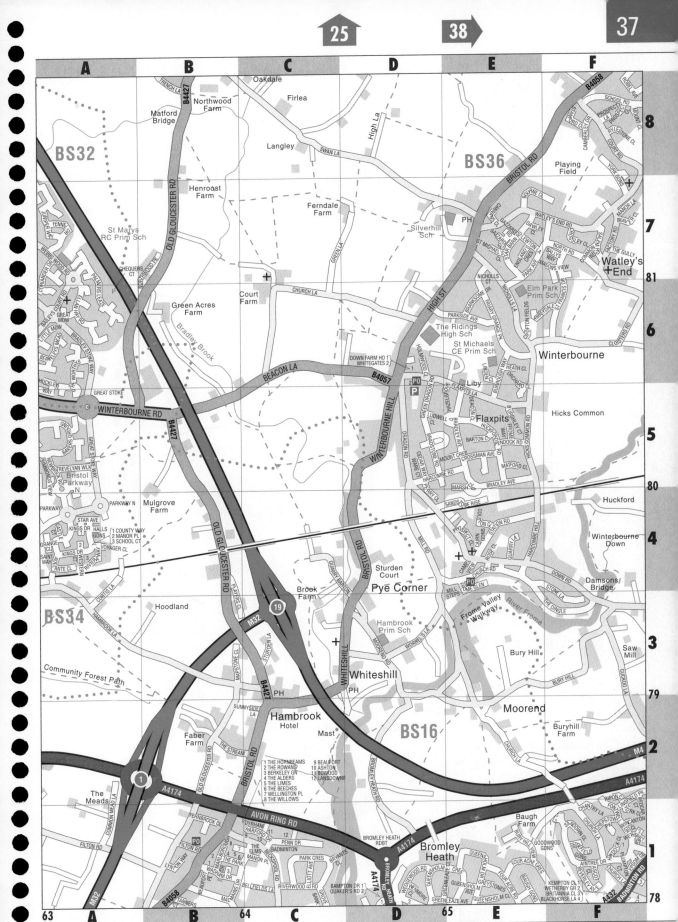

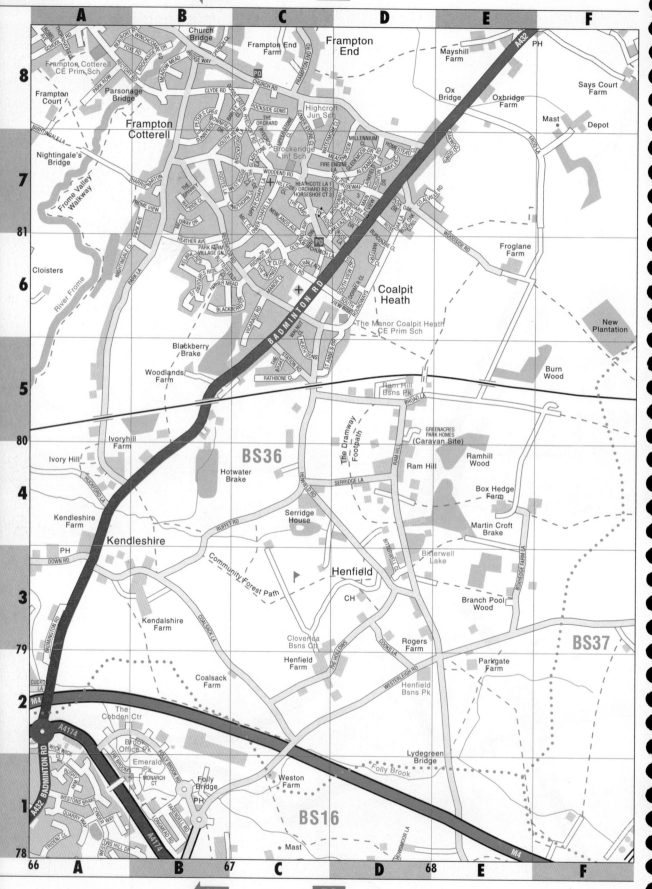

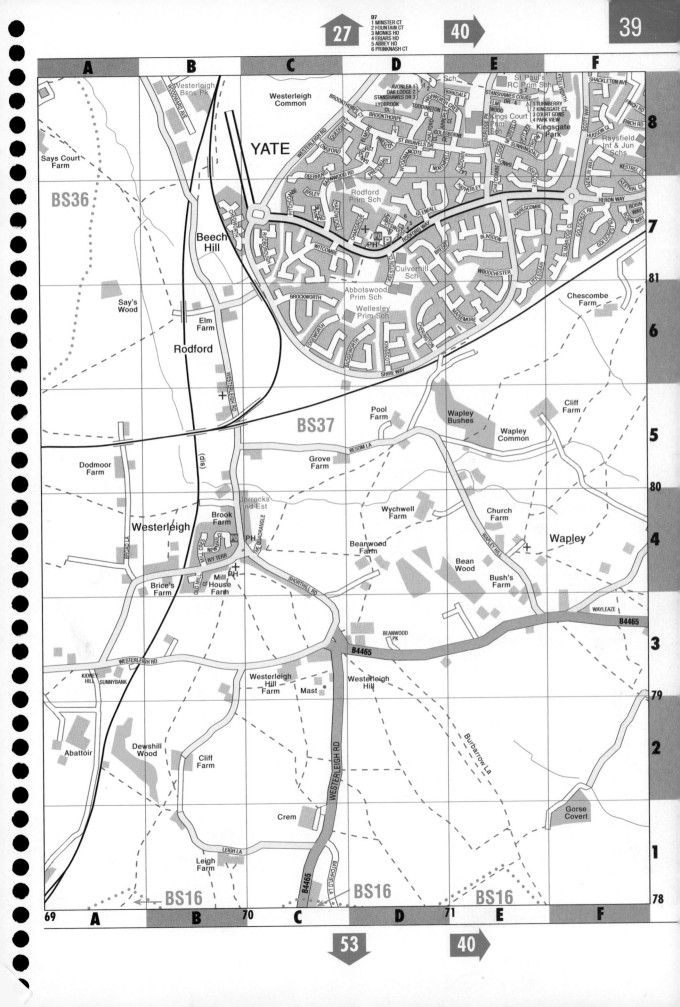

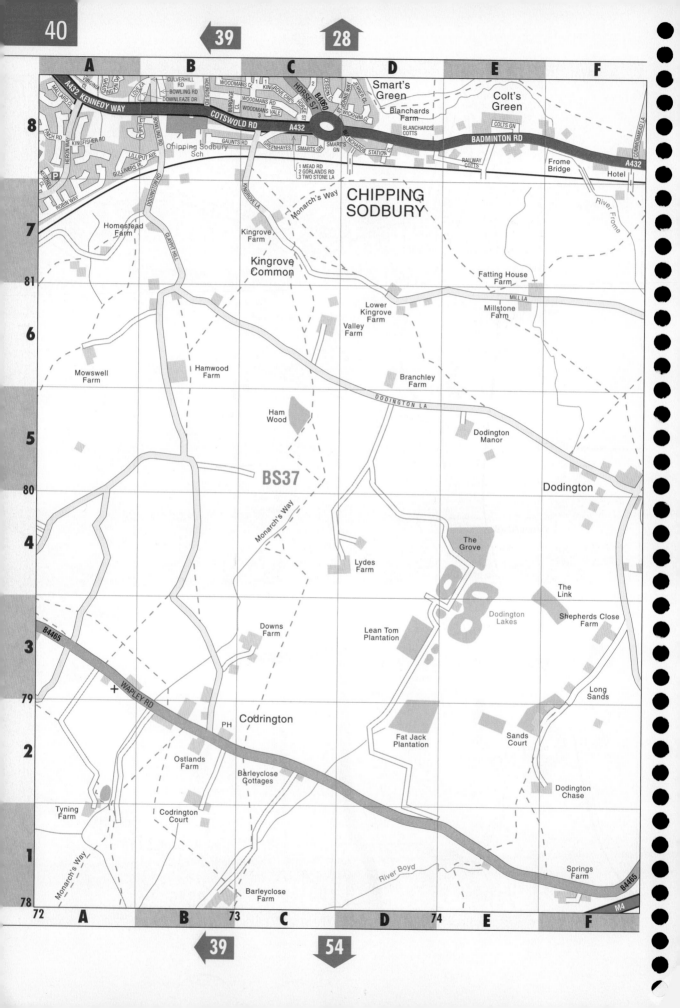

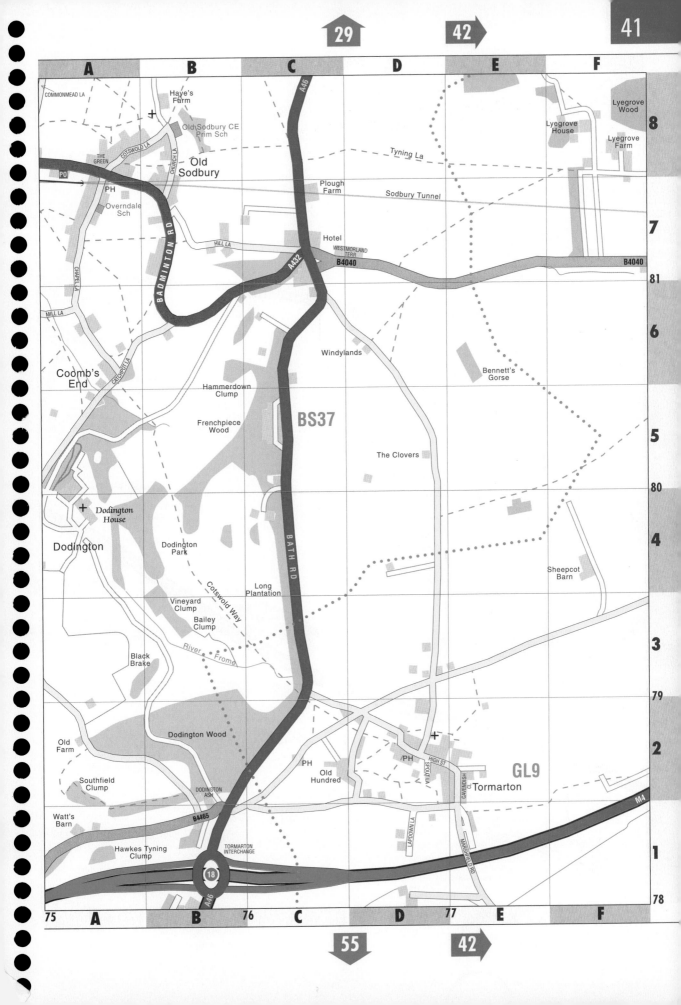

41
30

A **B** **C** **D** **E** **F**

Lyegrove Wood

8

Egg Clump

LIME AVE

OLD DOWN RD

Withy Moor

STATION RD

Sodbury Tunnel

7

B4040

Limes Farm

81

Newhouse Farm

Acton Turville

B4039

B4040

THE STREET

6

GL9

PH

BURTON RD

TORMARTON RD

B4039

Vicarage Cottage

OAKES LA

5

80

Warren Barn

Fagot Pile

M4

Pike Cottage

4

Old Warren

Wall Leaze Wood

Parks Farm

Brotton Hill Wood

3

Warren Gorse

79

2

Westfield Farm

M4

Phyldornick

Little Westfield

SN14

1

Fox Covert

78

78 **A** **B** 79 **C** **D** 80 **E** **F**

A B C D E F

Centre Walk
Brake

B4040

8

Cranhill
Wood

Alderton Grove
Farm

7

Alderton
Grove

81

GL9

6

HOLLYBUSH LA
CHAPEL LA
CHESTNUT LA
LITTLETON DREW LA

ALDERTON RD

Trinity CE
Prim Sch

Goulter's
Gorse

Hollybush
Farm

VINER'S LA

Manor Farm

Littleton Drew

5

Ivy Leaze

+

Townsend
Farm

+

80

Withy
Beds

MARSHLA

Mast

4

HILLSIDE

New House
Farm

PH

New Town

M4 Swindon, Reading

Wiltshire STREET ATLAS

M4

GL DOWN
FREDERICKS WAY
CHURCH HILL
THE STREET
THE MEADS
BURTON FARM CL

Horsedown

The
Gibb

3

SN14

SUMMER LA

PH

Burton

+

Step Hill
Plantation

79

B4039

The
Piggeries

Littleworth
Plantation

Goulter's Hill
Farm

NETTLETON RD
EDGE CORNER LA

Nettleton & Burton
CE Prim Sch

Fosse Bridge

2

Green
Farm

Priory
Farm

Macmillan Way

Lugbury
Long Barrow

Mill

Gatcombe
Plantation

PO

Gatcombe
Hill

Nettleton
Green

Gatcombe
Wood

1

Hanger
Wood

Elm Tree
Farm

Manor Farm

Square
Plantation

Garrick
Wood

Long Leaze

78

81 A B 82 C D 83 E F

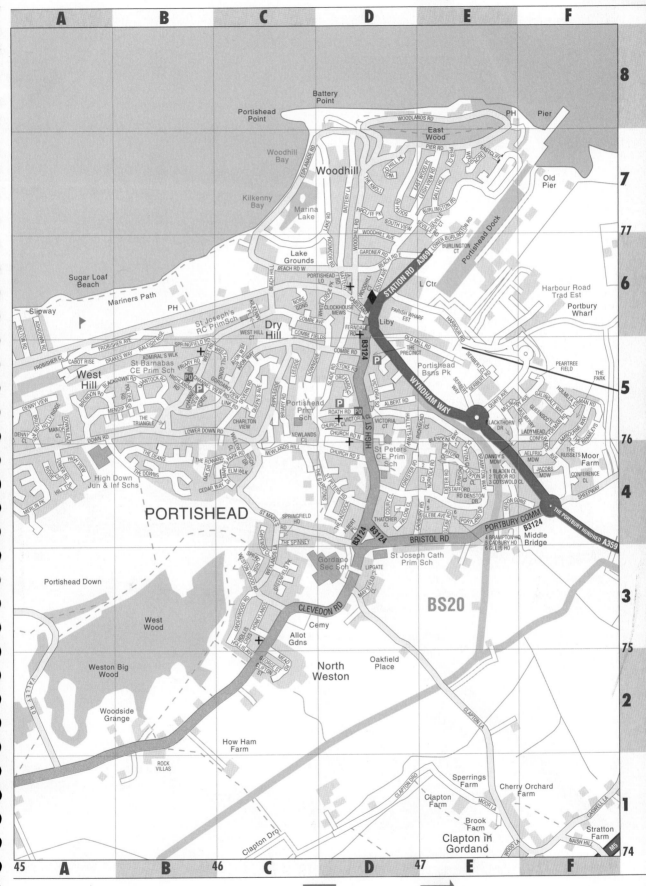

A B C D E F

8

King Road

7

Drove Rhyne

Sewage Works

77

6

Portbury Wharf

5

Atherton House

WHARF LA

SHEEPWAY LA

Sheepway

SHEEPWAY

Sheepway Gate Farm

76

Elm Tree Farm

ELM TREE PK

BS20

4

Cole Acre

STATION RD

THE PORTBURY HUNDRED

A369

Priory Farm Trad Est

The Priory (remains of)

PH

PRIORY RD

PRIORY WLK

Portbury

3

St Mary's CE Prim Sch

CHURCH LA

HIGH ST

75

CASWELL LA

Caswell Cross

Conygar Hill

HILLSIDE

FORGE END

BRITON PL

MILL LA

MILL CL

Bulling's Wood

Longlands Wood

2

Upper Caswell Farm

Lower Caswell House

CASWELL HILL

The Mount

FAILAND LA

Honor Farm

1

M5

Rifle Range

Prior's Wood

CHARLTON DR

Birch Wood

PORTBURY LA

Oakham Farm

COOMBE LA

74

BS48

Budding's Wood

BS8

48 A B 49 C D 50 E F

River Avon

Nelson Point

River Quay

The Royal Portbury Docks

Gordano Quay

SEA BANK RD

GORDANO RD

THE DROVE

St George's Quay

ST GEORGE'S RD

SHEEPHOUSE CARAVAN PK

NORMANS WAY

Marsh Lane Ind Est

MARSH LA

REDLAND RD

RIVER RD

BS 11

Wr Twr

ROYAL PORTBURY DOCK RD

FIRST AVE

GARONOR WAY

Gordano Way

Portbury Way

BANTANG RD

Bradley Rd

Drove Rhyne

ROYAL PORTBURY DOCK RD

M5

19

Gordano Service area

MARTCOMBE RD

A369

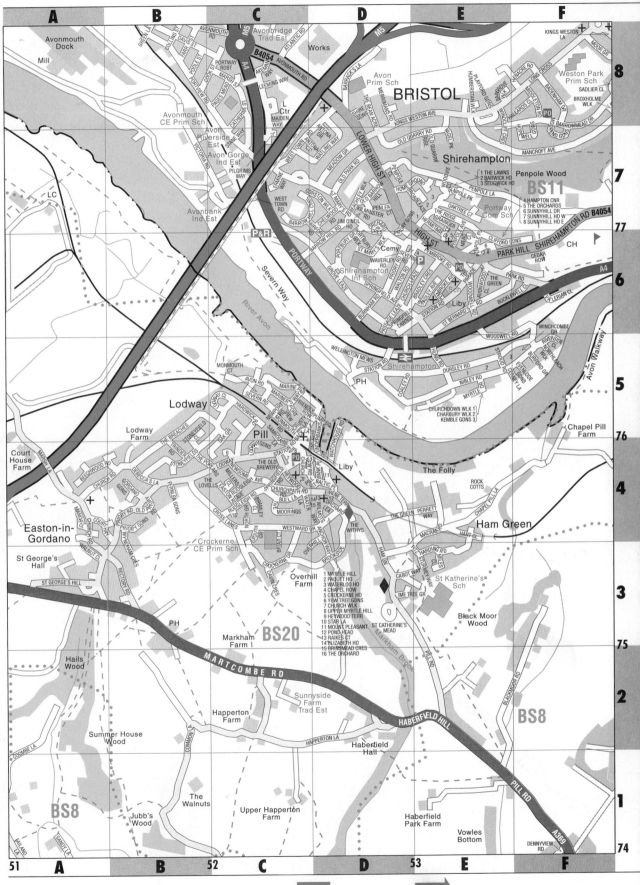

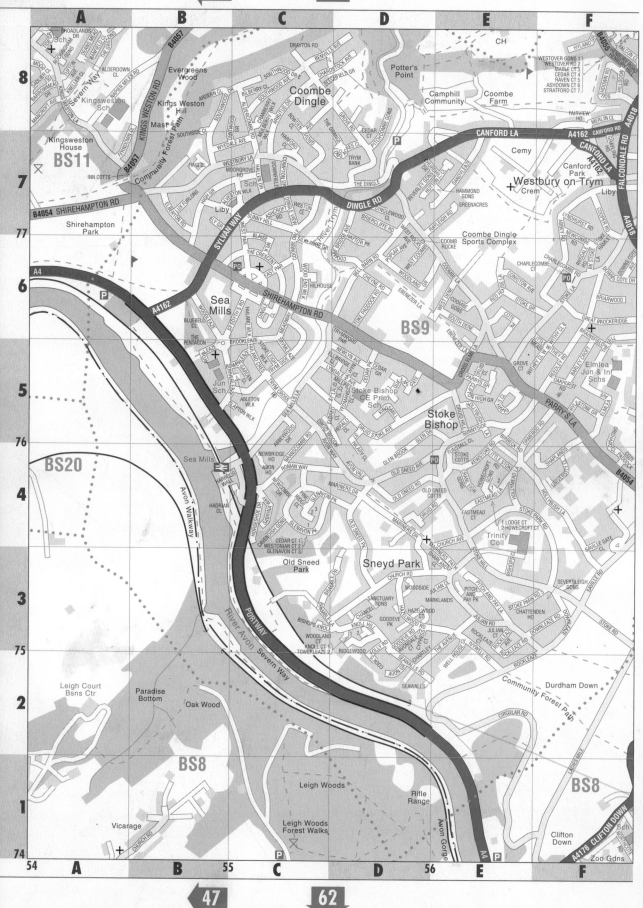

A B C D E F

8

7

77

6

5

76

4

3

75

2

1

74

BROADLANDS DR
Sch
BEANS HEAD
BANFIELD CL
THE GASKINS
B4057
DRAYTON RD
BENVILLE AVE
CHARDSTOCK AVE
BEECHFIELD GR
CH
WESTOVER GDNS 1
WESTOVER RD 2
MAPLE CT 3
CEDAR CT 4
RAVEN CT 5
ASHDOWN CT 6
STRATFORD CT 7
B4055 HENBURY RD
FALCON CL
HYLAND GR

Evergreens
Wood
SOUTHWOOD DR E
SOUTHWOOD AVE
Potter's
Point
Camphill
Community
Coombe
Farm
Coombe
Dingle

Kingsweston
Sch
ALDERDOWN CL
Kings Weston
Hill
Mast
Community Forest Path
BILBERRY CL
SOUTHWOOD CL
ARDERN CL
CRANBERRY
MULBERRY CT
ARBUTUS DR
BOWDEN
THE GRANGE
GROVE RD
PITCHCOMBE GDNS
CEDAR CT
FAIRVIEW HO
MERLIN CL

Kingsweston
House
BS11
INN COTTS
KINGS WESTON RD
FERNDOWN CL
SOUTHSIDE CL
WYEDALE AVE
RAILB DL
DOWNFIELD
COMPTON CL
HALLEN DR
HARFORD CL
GROVE
THE DINGLE
TRYM
BANK
BEVERLEY RD
HUTTON CL
SANDYLEAZE
HAMMOND
GDNS
GREENACRES
CANFORD LA
A4162
CANFORD RD
Cemy
Westbury on Trym
Crem
Canford
Park
Canford
LA
A4162
Liby
FALCONDALE RD
A4018

B4054 SHIREHAMPTON RD
LIBERTON RD
HIGH LA
WESTBURY LA
MOORGROVE
HO
Sch
MOORGROVE
KINGS WESTON RD
Liby
DINGLE RD
WESTON CL
SUNNY HILL
ASHCROFT RD
DINGLE VIEW
BRIERCLIFFE RD
RAYLEIGH RD
WEST ROCKS
COOMB
ROCKE
COOMBE DINGLE GDNS
Coombe Dingle
Sports Complex
LYNDHURST RD
ABBEY RD
NEWCOMBE
RD
COOPER RD
DOWNS COTE DR

Shirehampton
Park
SYLVAN WAY
WEST PAR
ELY GR
BLAISE
THE CRESCENT
EAST PAR
WOOD END WLK
HILHOUSE
SILKLANDS GR
COOMBE LA
WEST COOMBE
WOODLAND
WEST DENE
COOMBE
DR
COTE LA
CHARLECOMBE
RD
CHARLECOMBE LA
BK SEDALE
DOWNS COTE DR

A4
A4162
SHIREHAMPTON RD
BLUEBELL CL
SEDDITUS CL
River Trym
THE PENTAGON
BROOKLEAZE
FARLAND WLK
MEADWAY
CHEYNE RD
BELL BARN RD
POPLAR AVE
EBENEZER LA
CONISTON AVE
STOKE LA
RED RD
COTE
BS9
GROVE
EBENEZER LA
BRIARWOOD
GREAT BROCKERIDGE
BRAINSFIELD

Sea
Mills
WOOD LEAZE
STOKE CELLS
FARLAND CRES
TRYM CROSS
TRYM SIDE
MILLFIELD
NEWLYN AVE
CEDAR
GR
LYNDALE AVE
HERALD
KINGS
Stoke Bishop
CE Prim
Sch
PARRYS GR
HOLLYBUSH LA
DRUID HILL
SUNNYSIDE
GROVE
CT
WITHEY CL W
REEDLEY RD
BARLEY CROFT
OAKHURST
PARRY'S LA
BEECHEN CLI
ELMLEA
Elmlea
Jun & Inf
Schs

Jun
Sch
BOWSE GREEN
ABLETON
WLK
CLAPTON WLK
ABBEYWOOD
DR
Newbridge
HO
ABON HO
ROMAN WAY
DRUID WOODS
DRUID STOKE AVE
AVON WAY
GLEN BROOK
OLD SNEED RD
AVON VALE
STOKE COTTS
CRANLEIGH
GDNS
TUNSTALL CL
KEWSTOKE RD
LITTLE STOKE
SHAPLANDS
LINDORS
RICHARDS CL
STOKE GR
ELM LA
GROVE RD
STONE CL
B4054

BS20
Sea Mills
HARBOUR
WALL
HADRIAN
CL
Avon Walkway
NEWBRIDGE
HO
PINE RIDGE
GLENAVON PK
HORSESHOE DR
SABRINA
CAVENDISH GDNS
CEDAR CT 1
WESTONIAN CT 2
GLENAVON CT 3
MARINERS DR
OLD SNEED PK
OLD SNEED
COTTS
DRUID RD
EASTMEAD LA
EASTMEAD
HOMECROFT
GDNS
Trinity
Coll
1 LODGE CT
2 HOWECROFT CT
SAVILLE GATE
STOKE PARK RD
HOLLYBUSH LA
SEVERNLEIGH
GDNS
SAVILLE RD
STOKE RD

Old Sneed
Park
BROMLEY
BRAMBLE
KNOLL HILL
CHURCH AVE
MARINERS PATH
CHURCH RD
PITCH
AND
PAY LA
STOKE HILL
MARINERS
CHATTENDEN
HO
DOWNLEAZE RD
STOKE RD

Leigh Court
Bsns Ctr
Paradise
Bottom
Oak Wood
River Avon Severn Way
PORTWAY
BISHOPS KNOLL
WOODLAND
KNOLL
KNOLL CT 1
TOWERLEAZE 2
RIDGEWOOD
SANCTUARY
GDNS
CHANCEL
CL
GOODEVE
PK
HAZELWOOD
CT
Sneyd Park
Woodside
JULIAN CL
MARKLANDS
GOODEVE RD
AVONLEAZE
CYPRESS
S CLOS
THE AVENUE
WELL HOUSE CL
JULIAN RD
IVYWELL RD
ROCKLEAZE
AVE
SEAWALLS RD
SEAWALLS
AVON GR
SEAWALLS
ROCKLEAZE
Community Forest Path
Durdham Down
CIRCULAR RD

BS8
Vicarage
CHURCH RD
Leigh Woods
Leigh Woods
Forest Walks
Rifle
Range
Avon Gorge
Clifton
Down
A4
Sch
NORTHOTE
LABURNUM
A4176 CLIFTON DOWN
Zoo Gdns
BS8

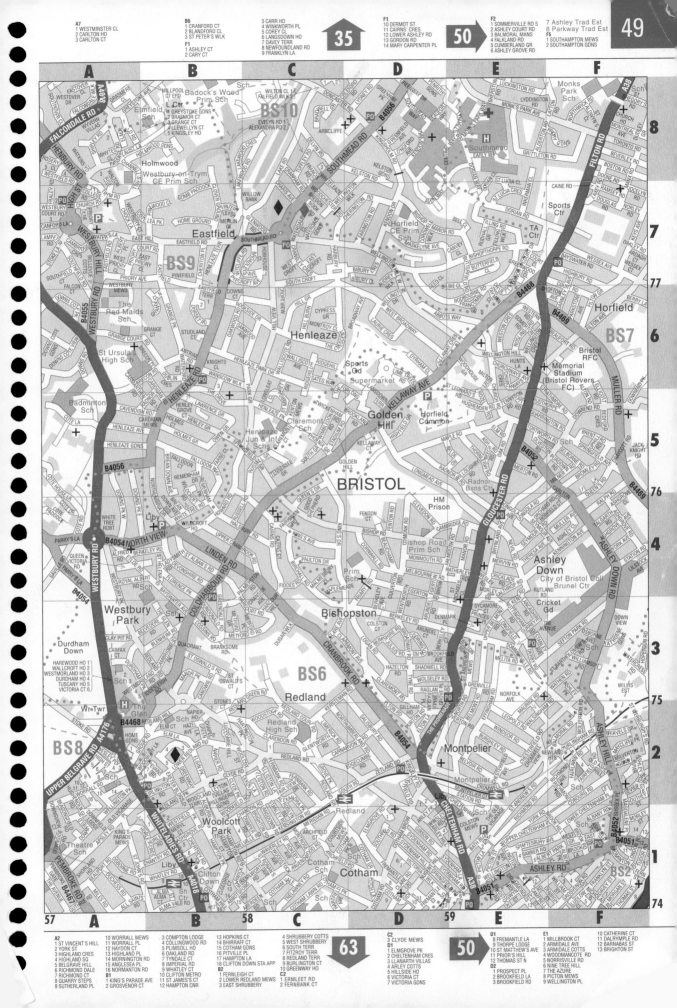

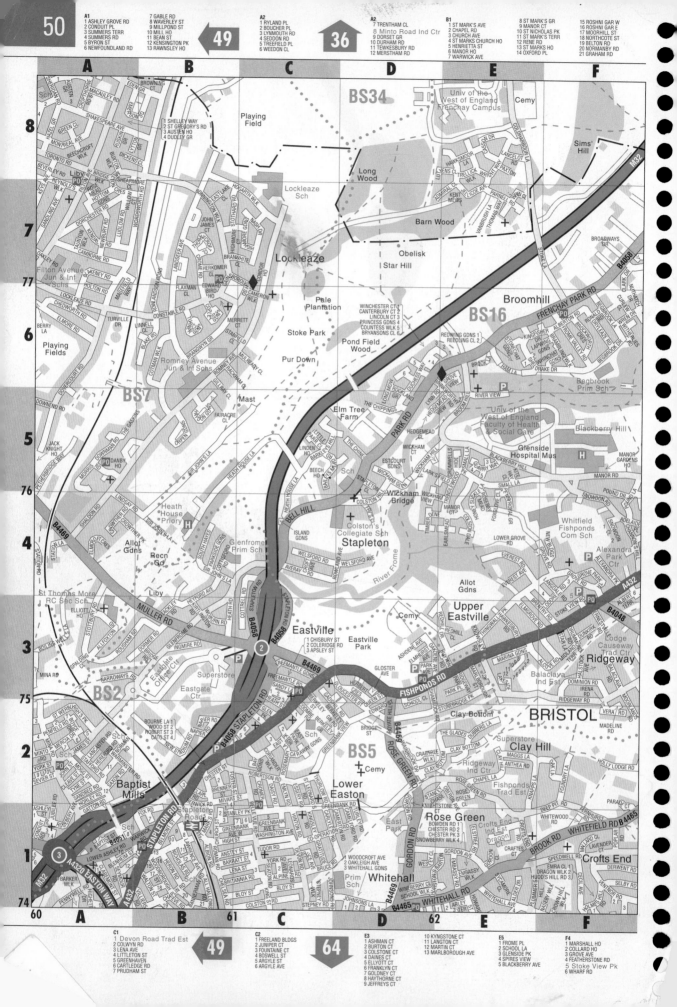

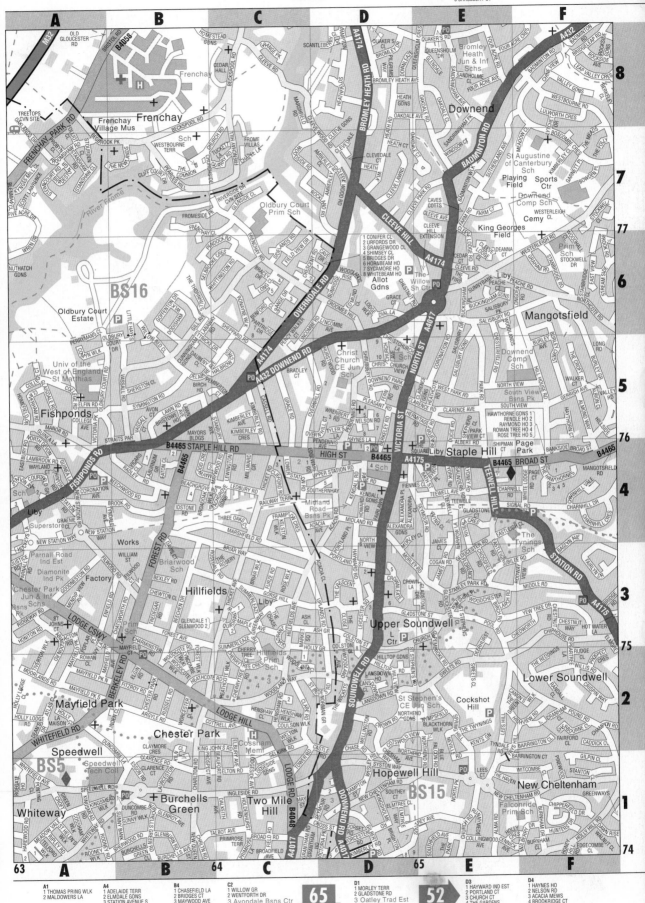

37

52

D5
1 BRITANNIA CT
2 OVERNHURST CT
3 GARTON HO
4 PLEASANT HO
5 PENDENNIS HO
6 SHRUBBERY CT

7 BERKELEY HO
8 NELSON HO
9 VICARAGE COTTS
10 ORCHARD COTTS

A1
1 THOMAS PRING WLK
2 MALDOWERS LA

A4
1 ADELAIDE TERR
2 ELMDALE GDNS
3 STATION AVENUE S
4 LOWER STATION RD

B4
1 CHASEFIELD LA
2 BRIDGES CT
3 MAYWOOD AVE
4 PARKHURST AVE

C2
1 WILLOW GR
2 WENTFORTH DR
3 Avondale Bsns Ctr
4 Lonsdale Bsns Ctr

D1
1 MORLEY TERR
2 GLADSTONE RD
3 Oatley Trad Est
4 KENNINGTON AVE
5 ALSOP RD
6 MAPLE CT
7 Kingswood Trad Est
8 PARK RD
9 HICKING CT

D3
1 HAYWARD IND EST
2 PORTLAND CT
3 CHURCH CT
4 THE GARDENS
5 BEAZER CL
6 ST CLEMENTS CT
7 WESLEY CL
8 WHITFIELD CL

D4
1 HAYNES HO
2 NELSON RD
3 ACACIA MEWS
4 BROOKRIDGE CT
5 KENSINGTON RD
6 EXHIBITION HO

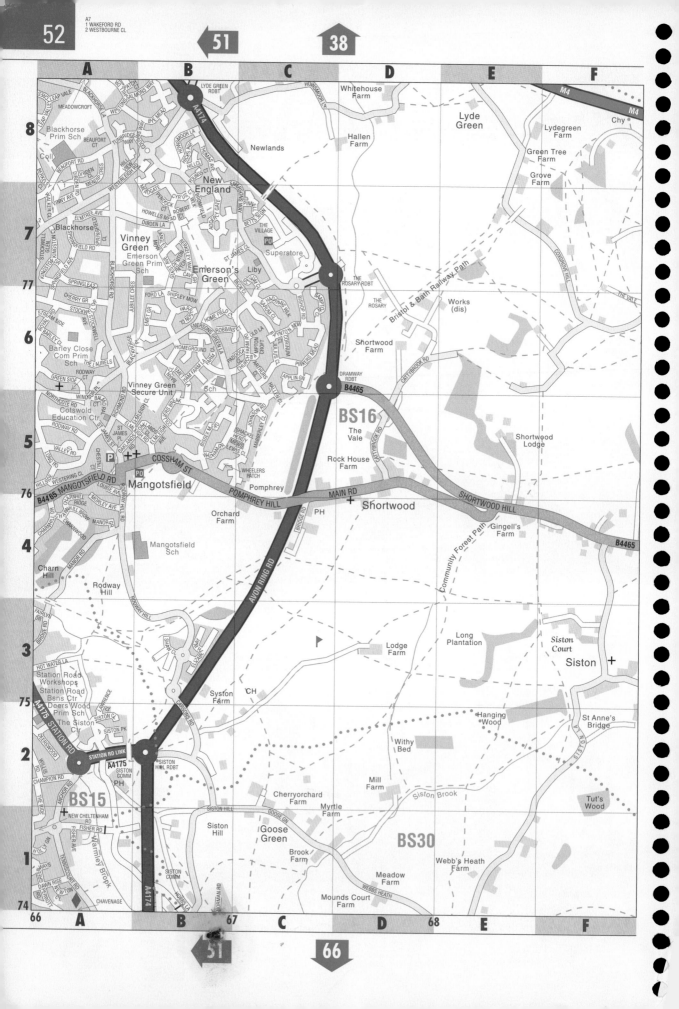

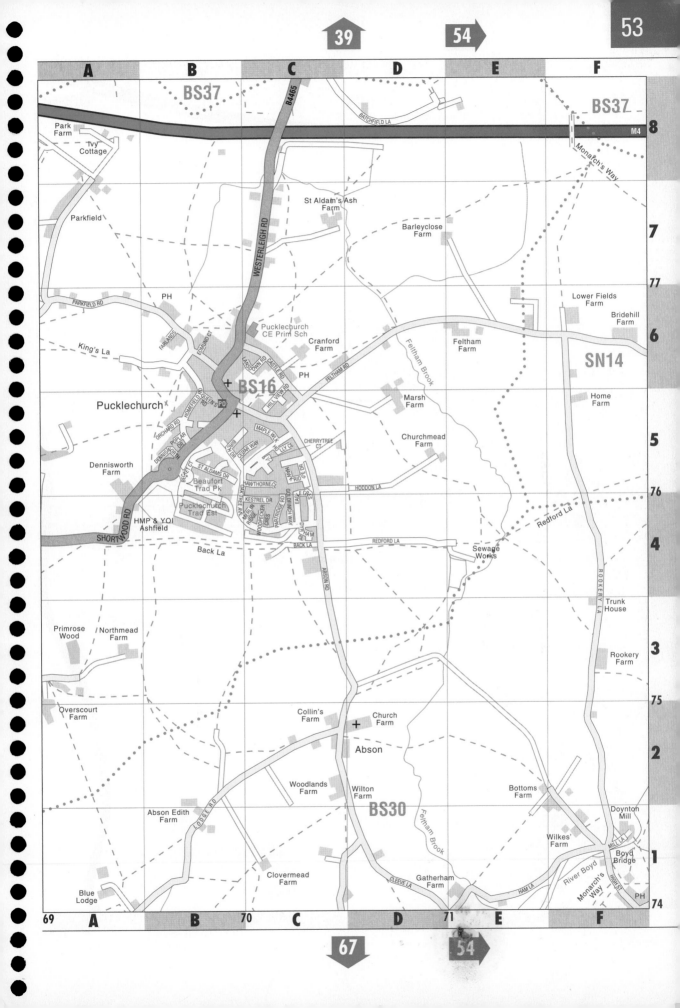

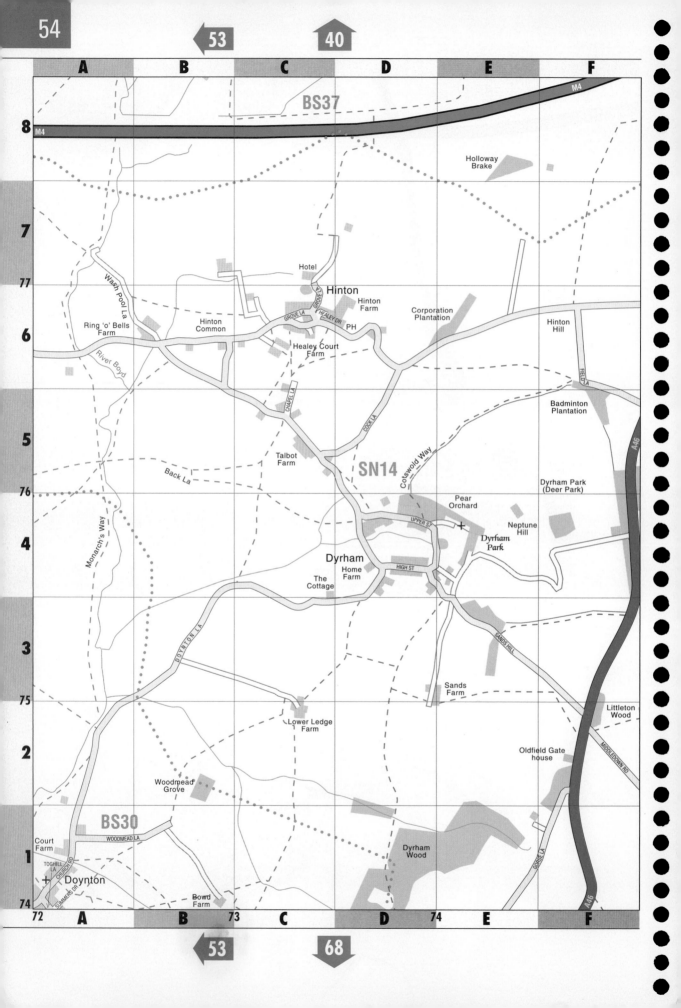

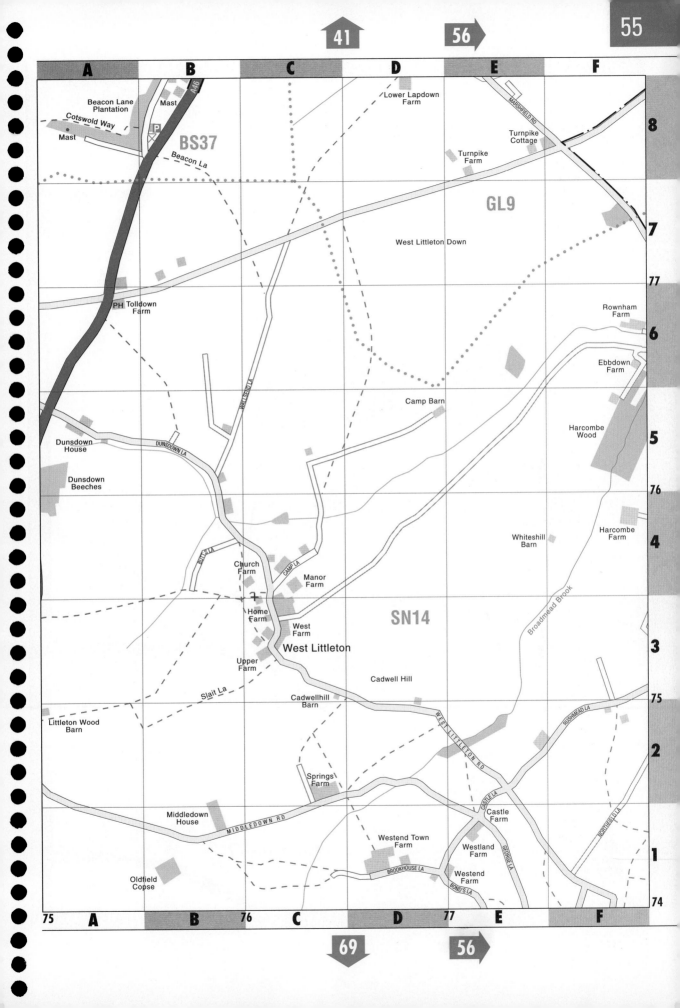

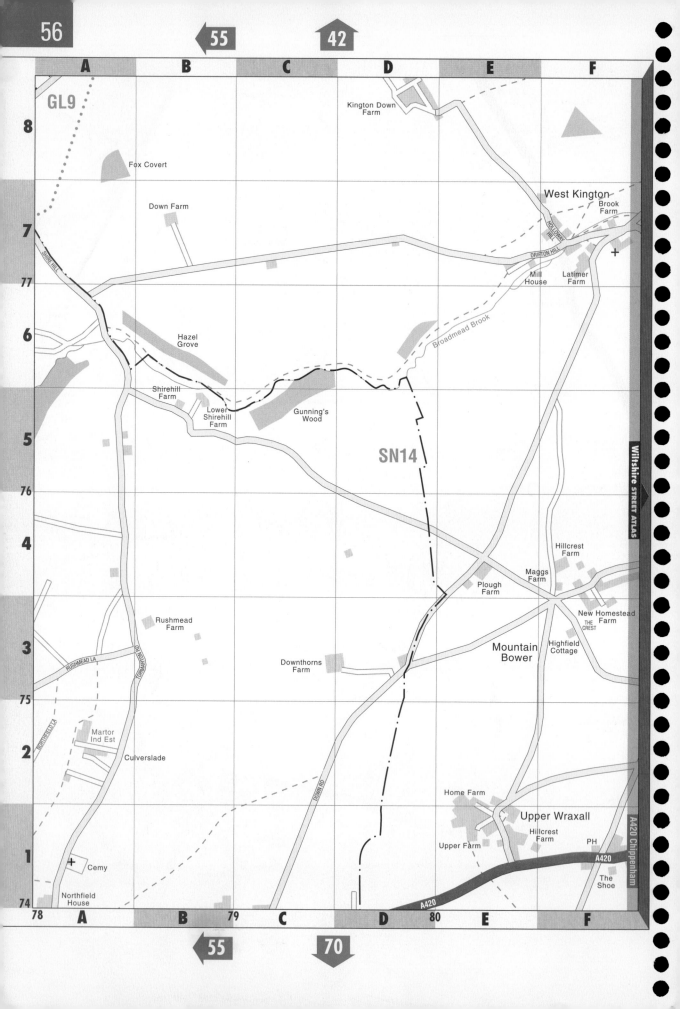

55
42

A B C D E F

8

GL9

Fox Covert

Down Farm

Kington Down
Farm

West Kington

Brook
Farm

7

SHIRE HILL

HOLLOWAY HILL

DRIFTON HILL

Mill
House

Latimer
Farm

77

Hazel
Grove

Broadmead Brook

6

Shirehill
Farm

Lower
Shirehill
Farm

Gunning's
Wood

SN14

5

76

4

Hillcrest
Farm

Maggs
Farm

Plough
Farm

New Homestead
Farm

THE
CREST

Rushmead
Farm

Downthorns
Farm

Mountain
Bower

Highfield
Cottage

3

RUSHMEAD LA

TORMARTON RD

DOWN RD

75

NORTHFIELD LA

Martor
Ind Est

Culverslade

2

Home Farm

Upper Wraxall

Hillcrest
Farm

PH

A420 Chippenham

Upper Farm

A420

Cemy

1

A420

The
Shoe

Northfield
House

74

78 A 79 B C 79 D 80 E F

55
70

Wiltshire STREET ATLAS

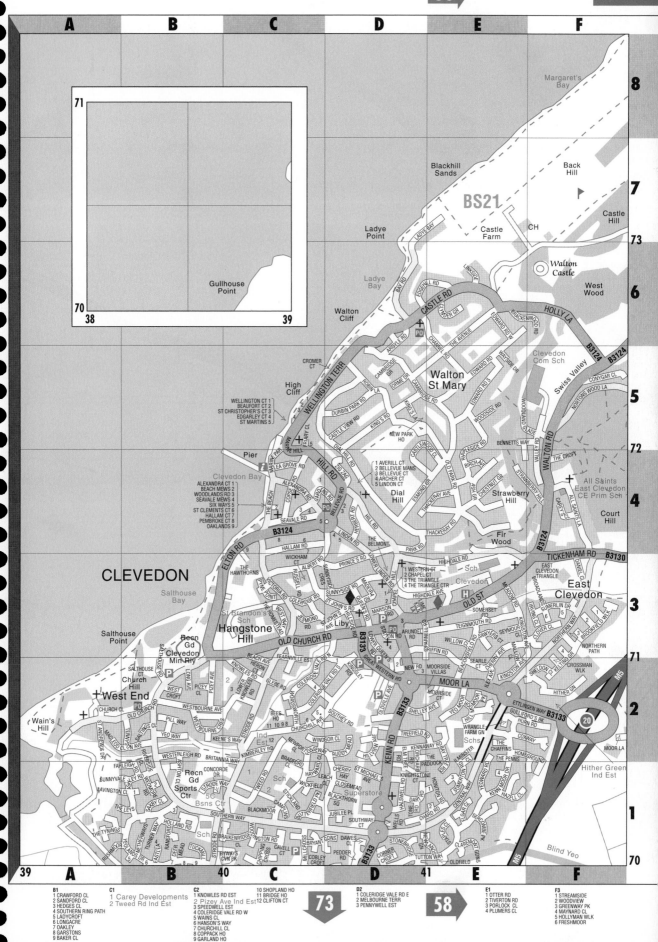

A   B   C   D   E   F

8

Margaret's
Bay

Blackhill
Sands

Back
Hill

BS21

7

CH   Castle
Hill

Ladye
Point

Castle
Farm

73

Walton
Castle

West
Wood

6

Ladye
Bay

CASTLE RD   HOLLY LA

Walton
Cliff

Clevedon
Com Sch

B3124   B3124

5

CROMER
CT

Swiss Valley

NORTONS WOOD LA

WELLINGTON TERR

High
Cliff

Walton
St Mary

72

WALTON RD

Pier

i   Clevedon Bay

New Park
Ho

Bennetts Way

The Croft

All Saints
East Clevedon
CE Prim Sch

4

HILL RD

ALEXANDRA CT 1
BEACH MEWS 2
WOODLANDS RD 3
SEAVALE MEWS 4
SIX WAYS 5
ST CLEMENTS CT 6
HALLAM CT 7
PEMBROKE CT 8
OAKLANDS 9

1 AVERILL CT
2 BELLEVUE MANS
3 BELLEVUE CT
4 ARCHER CT
5 LINDON CT

Dial
Hill

Strawberry
Hill

B3124

Court
Hill

B3124

TICKENHAM RD   B3130

ELTON RD

CLEVEDON

The
Belmont

Fir
Wood

EAST
CLEVEDON
TRIANGLE

East
Clevedon

3

Salthouse
Bay

St Brandon's
Sch

Hangstone
Hill

OLD CHURCH RD

1 WESTERN CT
2 CHAPEL CT
3 THE TRIANGLE
4 THE TRIANGLE CTR

Sch

Clevedon

OLD ST

H

Somerset
Rd

71

Salthouse
Point

Recn
Gd
Clevedon
Min Rly

B3133

GREAT WESTERN RD

MOOR LA

NORTHERN
PATH

M5

2

Church
Hill

West End

PO

Moorside
Villas

B3133

Moorside
Rd

ETTLINGEN WAY   B3133

20

MOOR LA

Wain's
Hill

Ind
Est

Superstore

WRANGLE
FARM GN

Schs

THE
CHAFFINS

THE PENNS

HOMEGROUND

Hither Green
Ind Est

1

Recn
Gd
Sports
Ctr

Bsns Ctr

Blackmoor

KEN RD

Blackthorn
Sq

Blind Yeo

70

39   A   40   B   C   40   D   41   E   F

B1
1 CRAWFORD CL
2 SANDFORD CL
3 HEDGES CL
4 SOUTHERN RING PATH
5 LADYCROFT
6 LONGACRE
7 OAKLEY
8 GARSTONS
9 BAKER CL

C1
1 Carey Developments
2 Tweed Rd Ind Est

C2
1 KNOWLES RD EST
2 Pizey Ave Ind Est
3 SPEEDWELL EST
4 COLERIDGE VALE RD W
5 WAINS CL
6 HANSON'S WAY
7 CHURCHILL CL
8 COPPACK HO
9 GARLAND HO
10 SHOPLAND HO
11 BRIDGE HO
12 CLIFTON CT

D2
1 COLERIDGE VALE RD E
2 MELBOURNE TERR
3 PENNYWELL EST

E1
1 OTTER RD
2 TIVERTON RD
3 PORLOCK CL
4 PLUMERS CL

F3
1 STREAMSIDE
2 WOODVIEW
3 GREENWAY PK
4 MAYNARD CL
5 HOLLYMAN WLK
6 FRESHMOOR

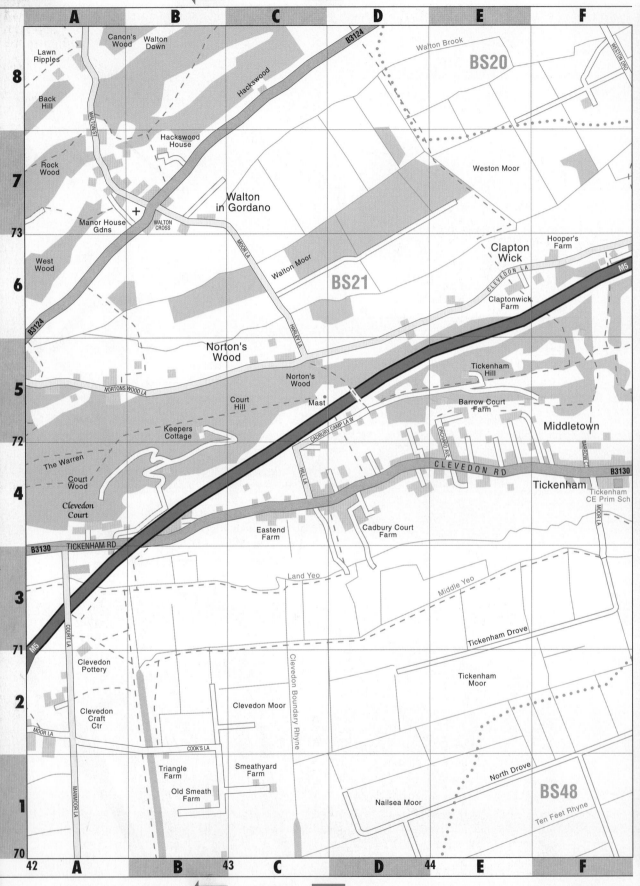

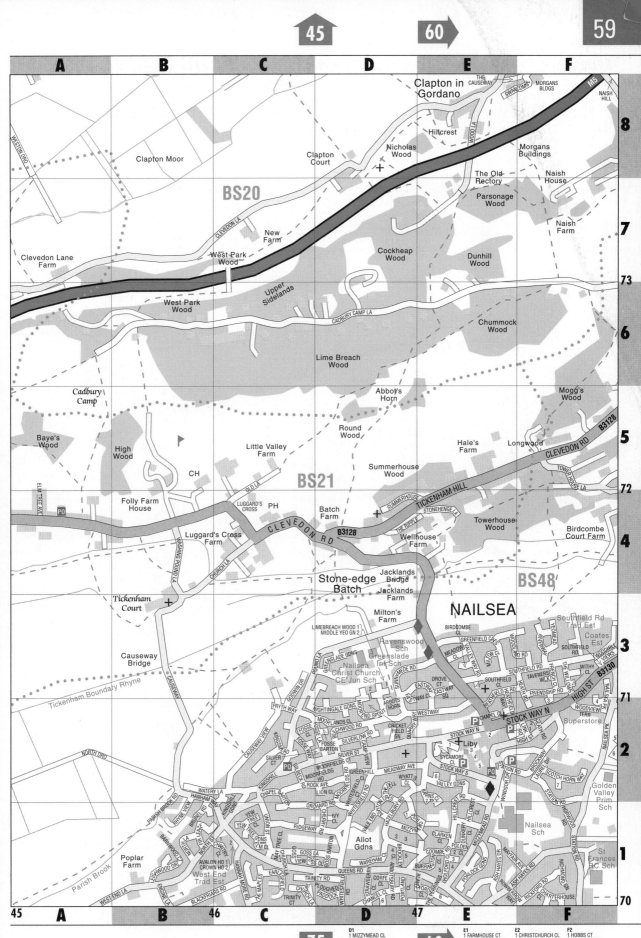

59
46

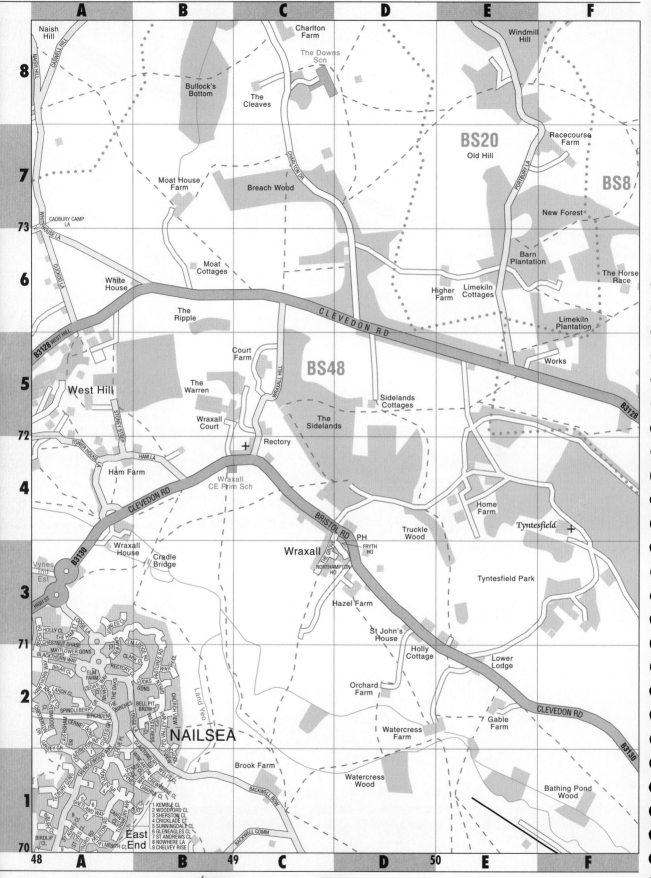

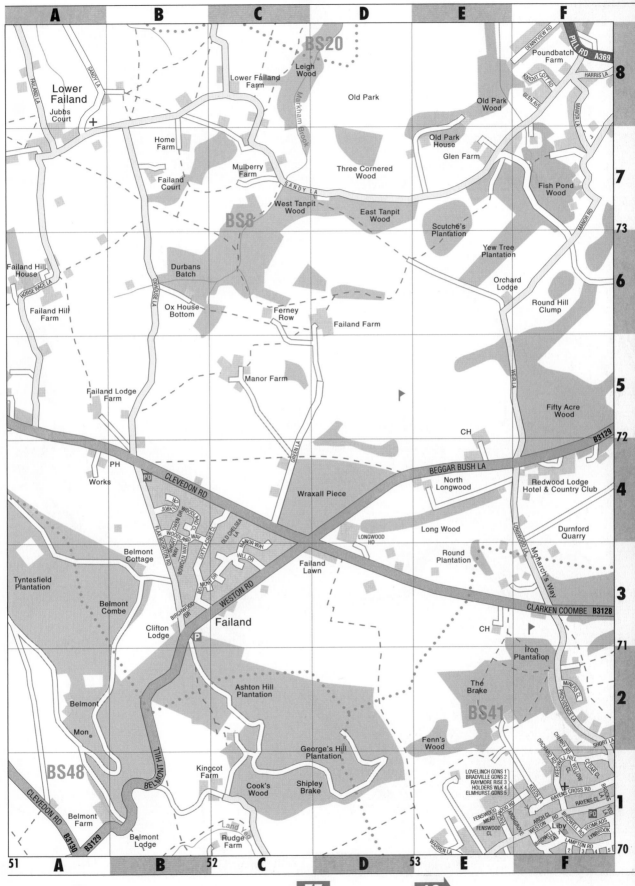

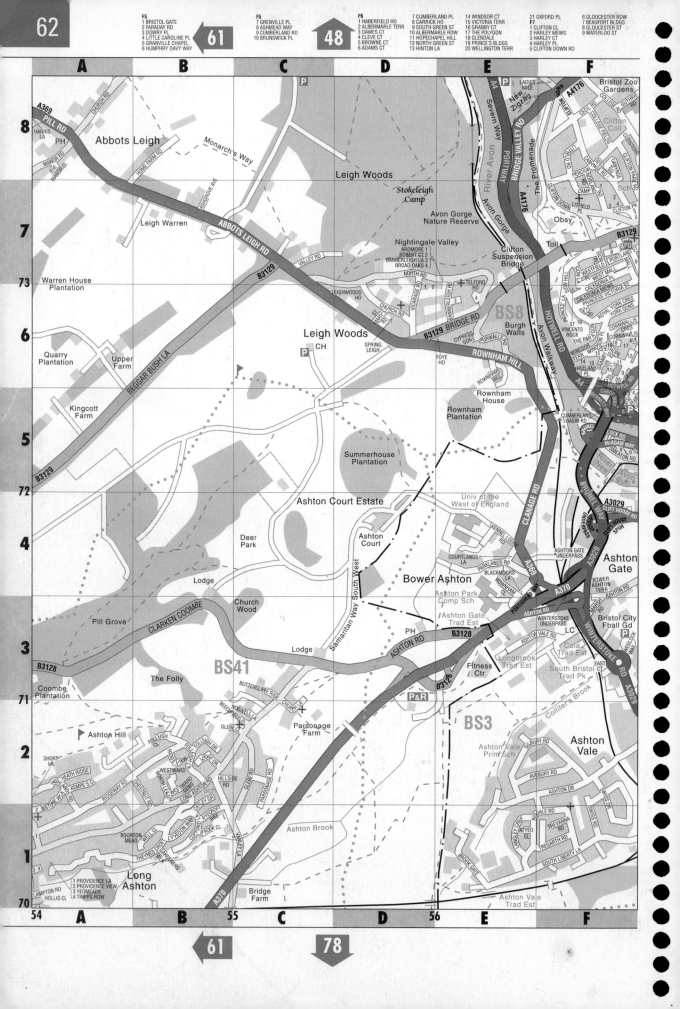

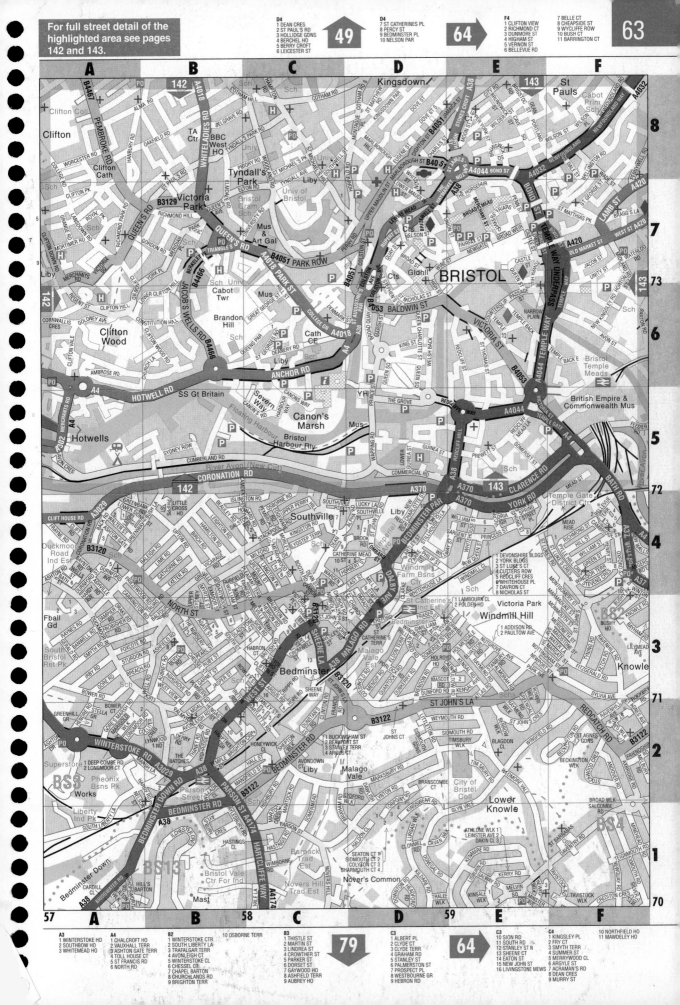

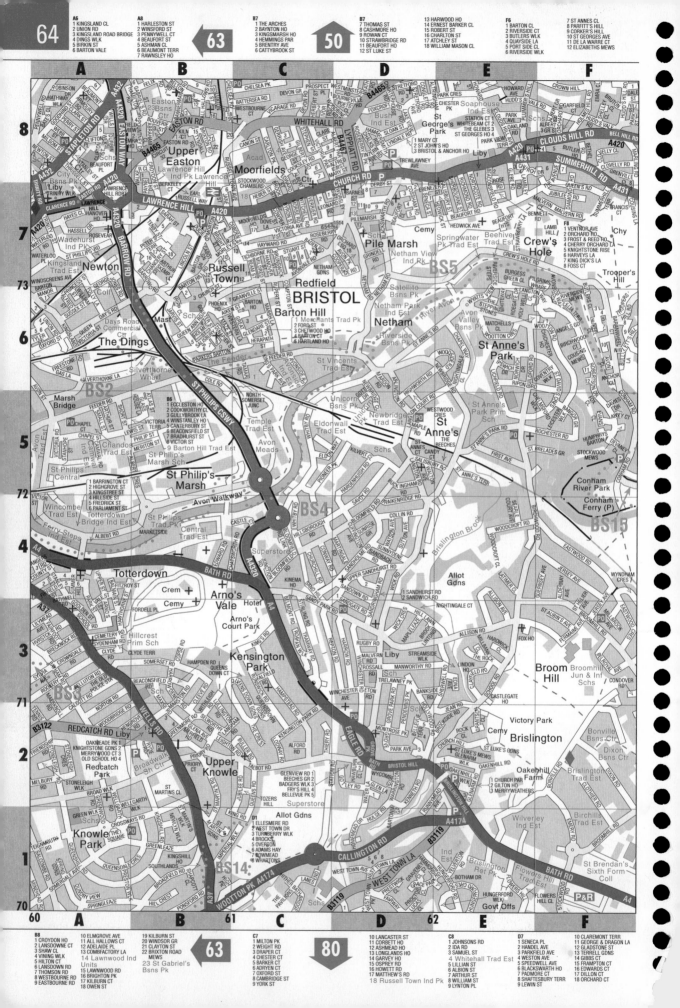

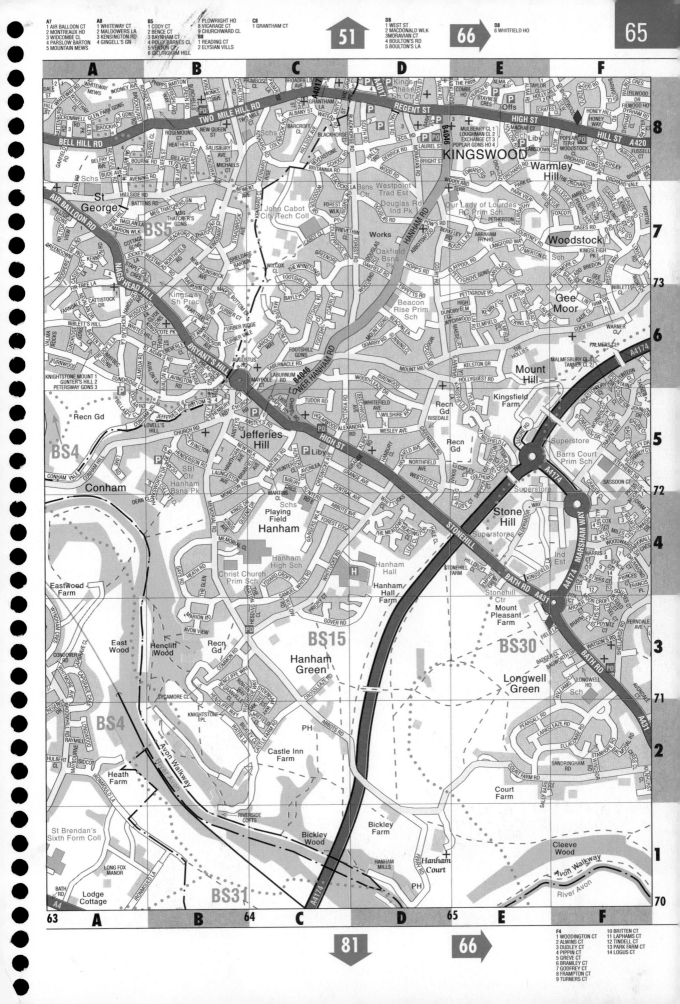

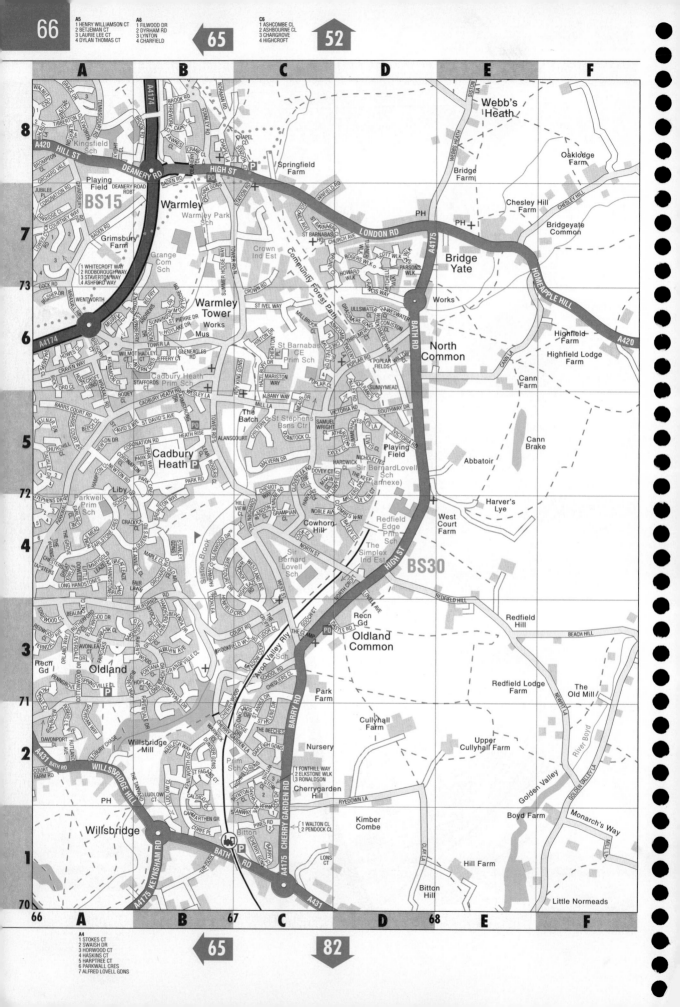

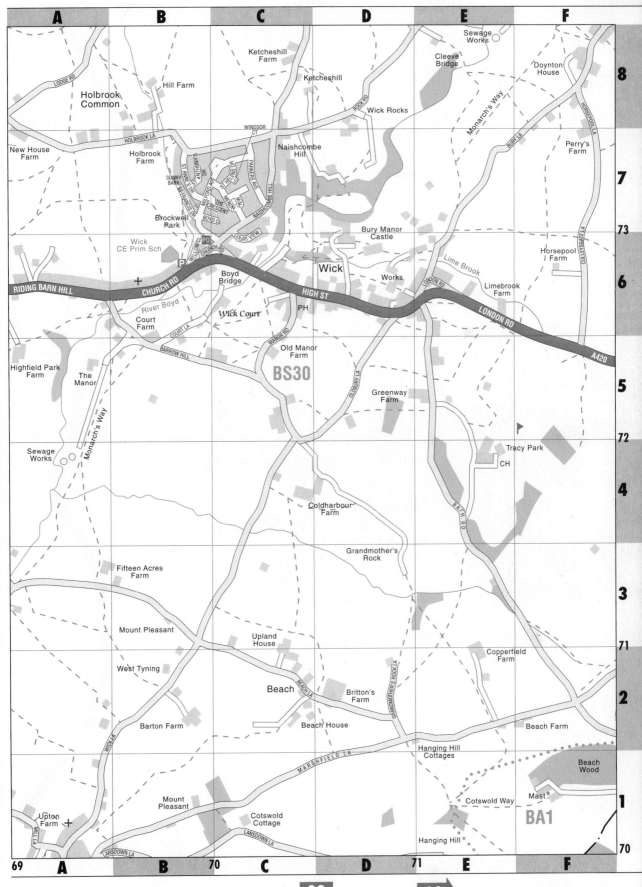

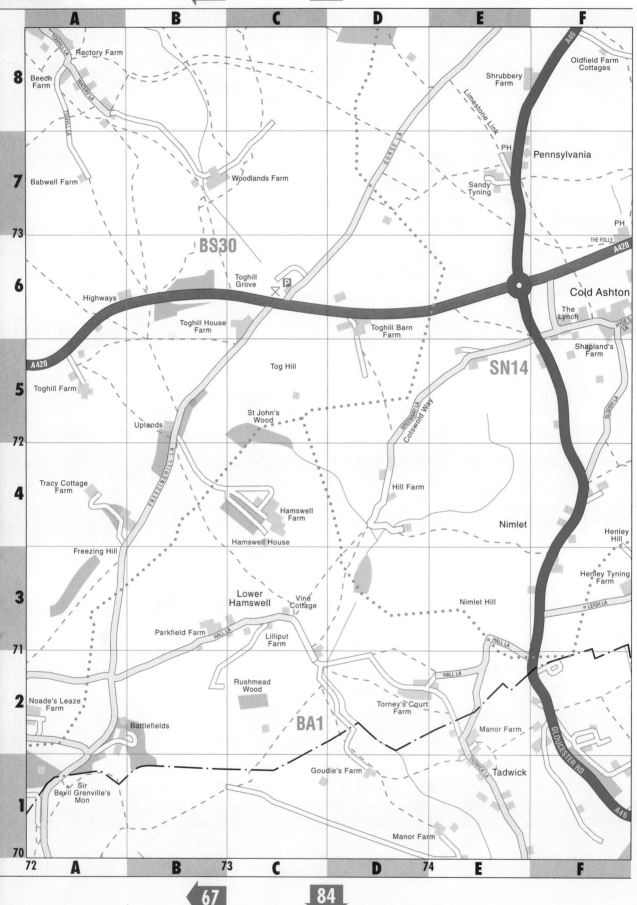

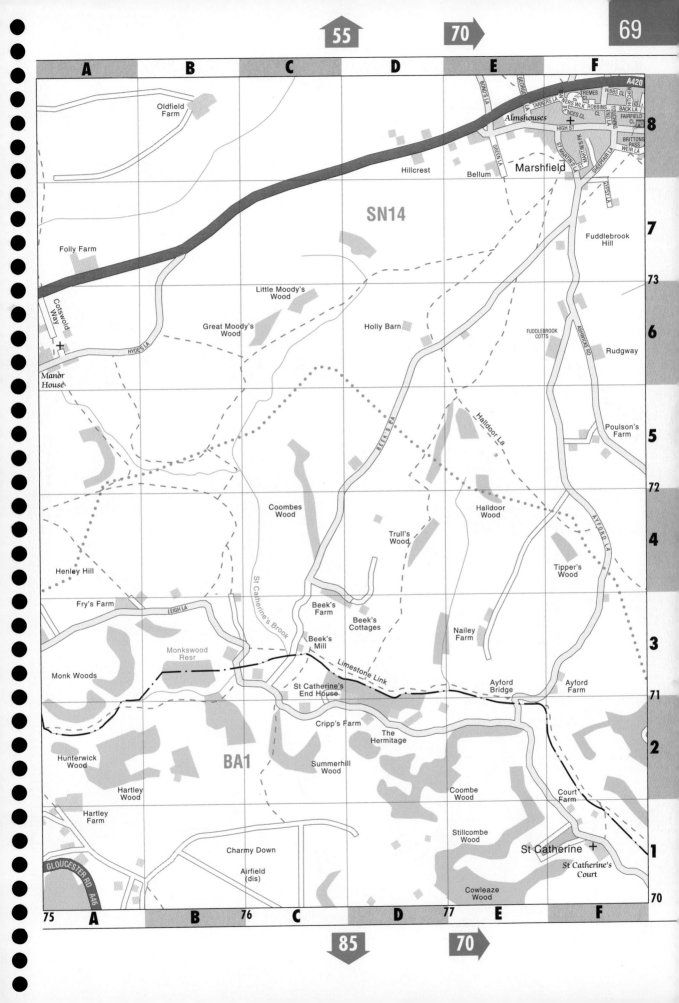

A B C D E F

8
7
73
6
5
72
4
3
71
2
1
70

Oldfield Farm

A420

TREMES
HIBBS CL
TANNERS LA
BOND'S LA
GEORGE

BENCE'S CL
ROBBINS CL
END LA
BACK LA
FAIRFIELD CL
PO

Almshouses
HIGH ST

BRITTONS PASS
WEIR LA
GREEN LA
ST MARTIN'S LA
SHEPPARD LA
Marshfield

Hillcrest
Bellum

GIPSY LA

SN14

Fuddlebrook Hill

Folly Farm

Cotswold Way

Little Moody's Wood

FUDDLEBROOK COTTS
ASHWICKE RD
Rudgway

Great Moody's Wood

Holly Barn

HYDE'S LA

Manor House

Halldoor La

Poulson's Farm

BEEK'S LA

Coombes Wood

Halldoor Wood

AYFORD LA

Trull's Wood

Henley Hill

Tipper's Wood

Fry's Farm

LEIGH LA

St Catherine's Brook

Beek's Farm

Beek's Cottages

Nailey Farm

Monkswood Resr

Beek's Mill

Limestone Link

Monk Woods

St Catherine's End House

Ayford Bridge

Ayford Farm

Cripp's Farm

The Hermitage

Hunterwick Wood

BA1

Summerhill Wood

Coombe Wood

Court Farm

Hartley Wood

Hartley Farm

Stillcombe Wood

St Catherine

St Catherine's Court

GLOUCESTER RD
A46

Charmy Down

Airfield (dis)

Cowleaze Wood

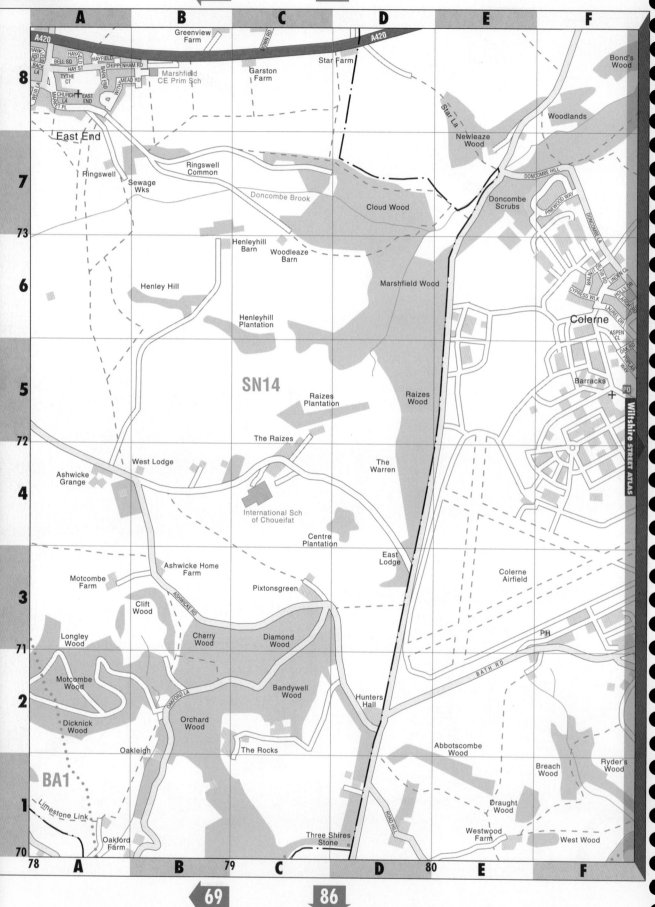

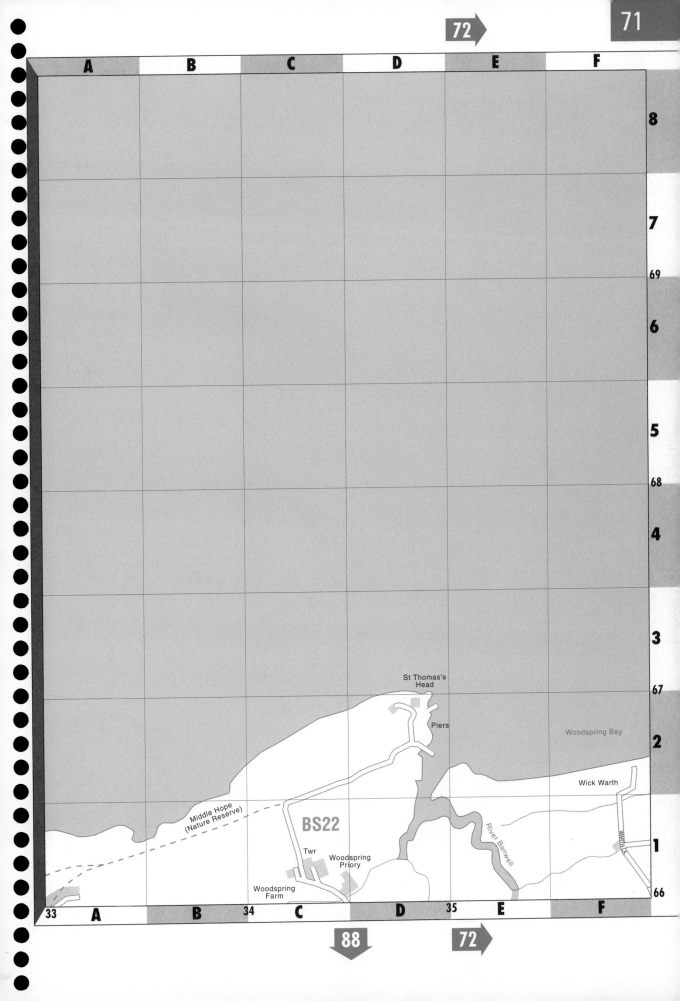

A B C D E F

8

7

69

6

5

68

4

3

67

St Thomas's
Head

Piers

2

Woodspring Bay

Wick Warth

Middle Hope
(Nature Reserve)

BS22

River Banwell

WARTH

1

Twr

Woodspring
Priory

Woodspring
Farm

66

33 A B 34 C D 35 E F

71

A | B | C | D | E | F

8

7

69

6

Dowlais Ditch

Kingston Pill

Hook's Ear

Seawall Farm

Treble House Farm

5

68

Sewage Works

4

Channel View Farm

BS21

MIDDLE LA

MIDDLE LA

Broadstone Rhyne

3

Broadstone Farm

BROADSTONE LA

67

Wharf Farm

New House Farm

2

HAM LA

Ham Farm

Pool Farm

Ham Rhyne

Sewage Works

1

Mendip View Farm

Yeo Bank Farm

YEO BANK LA

BS22

MOOR DA

Mill Leaze Rhyne

66

36 | A | B | 37 | C | D | 38 | E | F

71
89

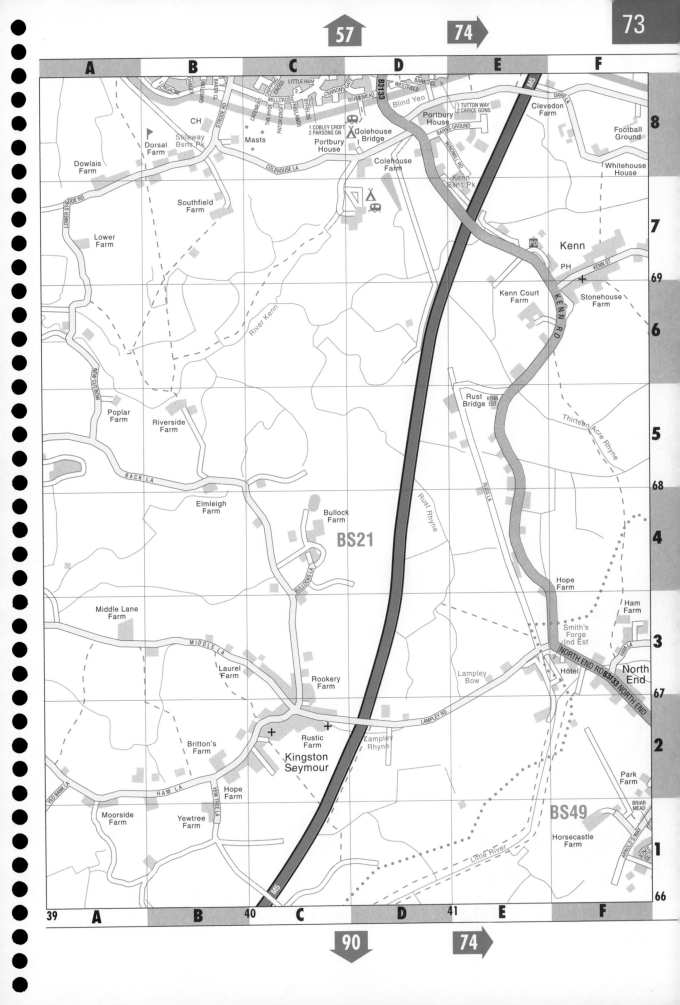

73
58

A B C D E F

8

Mannmoor La
Blind Yeo
Davis La
Davis La
Nailsea Wall
Ten Feet Rhyne
BS48

Kenn Pier Farm
River Kenn
Moorside Farm

7

Parish Brook
West End
Nailsea Wall La
Nailsea Moor La
Breach La
West End La

Yew Tree Farm
Kenn St
Duck La
West End Farm
Elm Tree Farm
McPherton Wood La
PH
Myrtle Farm

69

6

Kenmoor Rd
Western Drainage Rhyne
Kenn Moor
Lilypool Dro
Blackditch Rhyne
Decoypool Rhyne
Eastern Dro
BS21

Meadmoor Rhyne
Manor Farm
Mawkin's Bridge

5

Decoypool Dro
Says Rhyne
River Kenn

68

Barberry Farm
Claverham Dro

4

Little River
Kenn Moor Gate

3

Ham La
Laurel Bank

Moorstreet Bow
Claverham Court
Lower Claverham

67

Chestnut Farm
Mud La
LC
BS49
Chestnut Farm

2

B3133
North End
Stowey Rhyne
Moor Rd
Horsecastle
The Grange
Hillsea
Laurel Farm
Manor Farm
Claverham
Jasmine La
Brockley Way
Broadcroft Ave

1

Arnolds Way
Hawthorn Cres
Gregory Mead
Macquarie Platn
Briar Mead
Horsecastle Farm La
The Lawns
Avalon Cl
Wemberham Cres
Grange Farm Cl
Kenn Moor Rd
The Park
Prime Cl
Elmcroft
Market Ind Est
South View Terr
Park Rd
Park Ave
Stowey Rd
Laurel Gdns
B3133
Station Rd
1 Laurel Terr
2 Atlay Ct
3 Durban Way
Ramcross
St
High St
Chestnut Dro
Broadcroft Cl
Dunsters Rd
Anvil Rd
Orchard Ct
Chapel La
Bishops Rd
Franklin's Way
Court-de-Wyck CE Prim Sch
PO

66
Yatton
Claverham Farm

42 A B 43 C D 44 E F

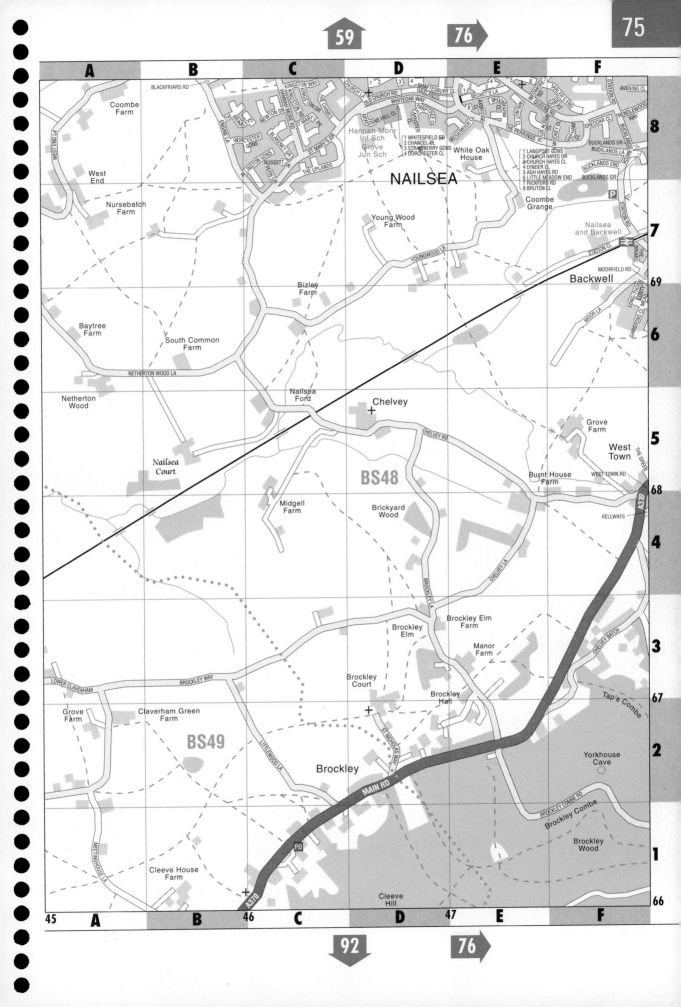

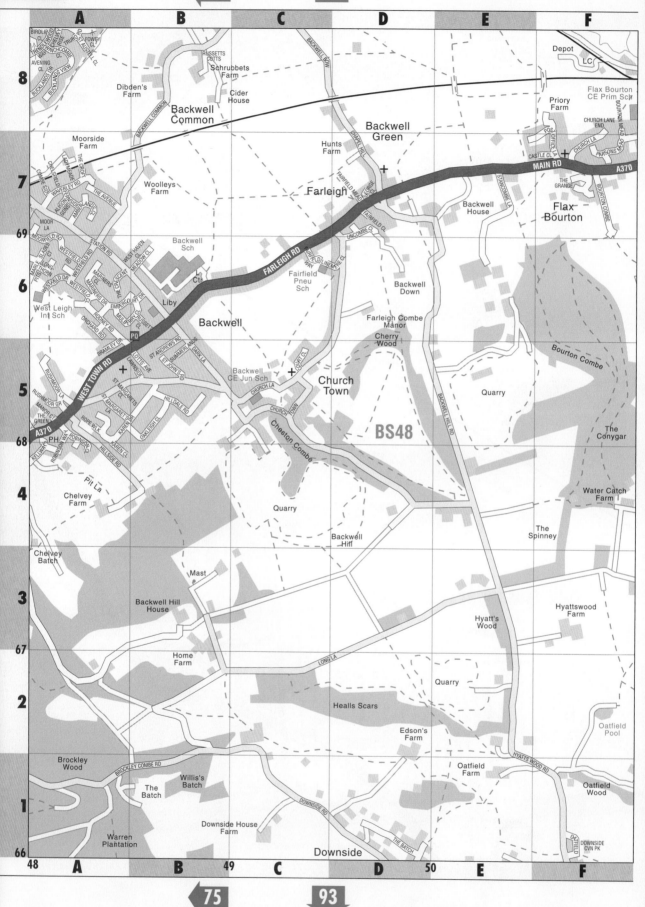

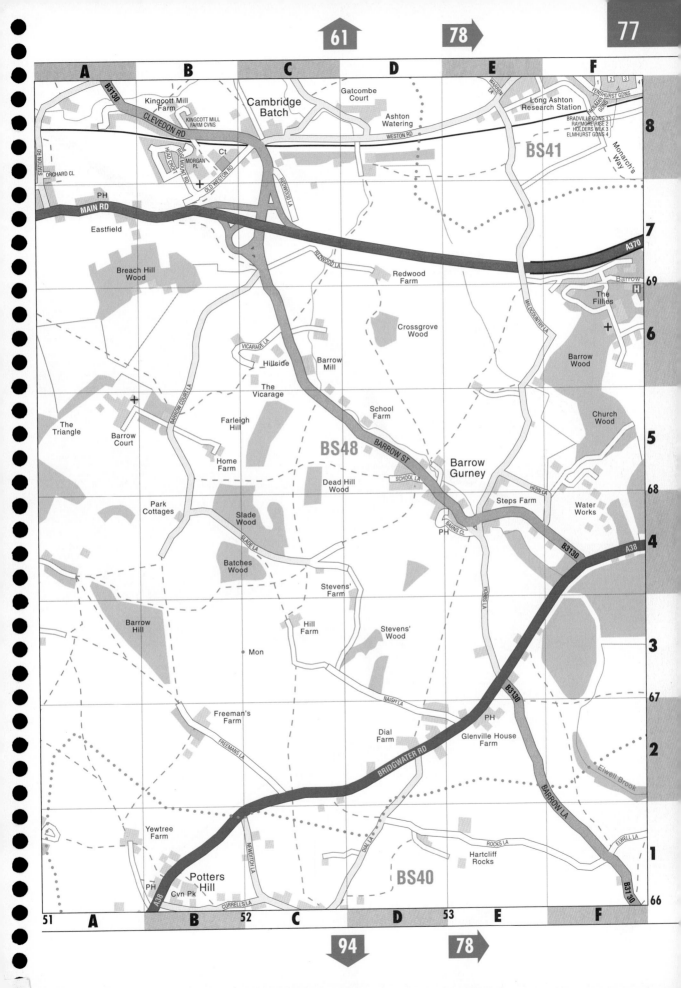

B3130

Kingcott Mill Farm

CLEVEDON RD

Kingcott Mill Farm CVNS

Cambridge Batch

Gatcombe Court

Ashton Watering

WESTON RD

Long Ashton Research Station

FENSHURST GDNS

1 2 3 4

BRADVILLE GDNS 1
RAYMORE RISE 2
HOLDERS WLK 3
ELMHURST GDNS 4

BS41

8

WARREN LA

Monarch's Way

HEAD CROFT

ROSEMONT PL

MORGAN PL

Ct

OLD WESTON RD

REDWOOD LA

STATION RD

ORCHARD CL

PH

MAIN RD

Eastfield

7

A370

Redwood Farm

REDWOOD LA

Barrow

69

H

The Fillies

Breach Hill Wood

Crossgrove Wood

WILDCOUNTRY LA

6

Barrow Wood

VICARAGE LA

Hillside

Barrow Mill

BARROW COURT LA

The Vicarage

Farleigh Hill

School Farm

Church Wood

The Triangle

Barrow Court

BS48

BARROW ST

Barrow Gurney

5

Home Farm

Dead Hill Wood

SCHOOL LA

HERM LA

68

Park Cottages

Slade Wood

SLADE LA

PH

BARNS CL

Steps Farm

Water Works

B3130

A38

4

Batches Wood

Stevens' Farm

HOBBS LA

Barrow Hill

Hill Farm

Stevens' Wood

3

Mon

B3130

67

NAISH LA

Freeman's Farm

PH

Dial Farm

Glenville House Farm

2

FREEMANS LA

Elwell Brook

BRIDGWATER RD

BARROW LA

Yewtree Farm

DIAL LA

ROCKS LA

ELWELL LA

1

NEWDITCH LA

Hartcliff Rocks

PH

Potters Hill

Cvn Pk

BS40

A38

B3130

66

CURRELLS LA

51   A   B   52   C   D   53   E   F

← 77   62

A B C D E F

8

Yanley

Yanley Farm

HOLLIS CL
FENSHURST GDNS
Birdwell Prim Sch

A370

Hanging Hill Wood

BS3

Crem

Mast   Cemy

Elm Farm

A38

Colliters Brook

Yewtree Fram

Rose Meare Gdns

BRUNEL
BLACKWELL
LANGFORD RD
YATTON CL
Bedminster Down Sch
DINGLE CT
PO

7

A370

A370

Castle Farm

BS13

Highridge

PUPP AR RD
MARGUERITE RD
DONALD RD
RISDALE RD
KINGS HEAD LA
ALEXANDRA RD

KINGS WLK
HIGHRIDGE WLK
GREYLANDS RD
WESTWARD RD

OLDMEAD
WLK
LOCK GDNS

MARLFIELD

69

Barrow
Wood

BARROW
H

Ridings Wood

CH

Colliter's Brook Farm

Motel

BRIDGWATER RD

Highridge Farm

DANCEY MEAD

SPARTLEY WLK
SPARTLEY DR
MARLEPITY
GR

Highridge Inf Sch

Bishopsworth CE Jun Sch

ANNINGTON CL
WATCHILL CL
VICARAGE RD

HAYES CL
SANDBURROWS
RD
SANDBURROWS
WLK
GEOFFREY CL

6

The Wild Country

BS48

Monarch's Way

YANLEY LA

YANLEGH CL

Barrow Big Wood

Winford Arms (PH)

WINFORD
TERR

Community Forest Path

BS41

OAKTR-E GDNS

COLDPARK GDNS
COLDPARK RD

GILLON
SHUTER
KERLE LA

Highridge Common

SOLON
CT

KING GEORGE'S RD
BROADWAY
RD

SPINNEY
CROFT

BISHOPS
COVE

TEMPLELAND
RD

WELLS RD
THREE

5

68

The Peart

HIGHRIDGE RD
GREENBRIDGE CL
MYRTLEGATE WLK
PEART DR
FOUR ACRES
STILLMAN CL
THE COPPICE

HUNTINGHAM RD

ELMTREE DR

WILGROUND RD

ROUNDMOOR

WITHYWOOD GDNS

CLEYLAND WLK

WITHYWOOD

COWLEER
WLK

WITHYWOOD RD

LAKEMEAD
GDNS

4

A38

Barrow Common

Valley View Farm

Highridge Farm

Four Acres Prim Sch

PO

HIGHMEAD GDNS
MALAGO WLK
CHALCROFT WLK

HERSEY GDNS

BUBBLEYON
RD

FARMER RD

HORSEPOOL RD

RUSHAM

QUEEN'S RD

LONGMEAD
CROFT

BROAD OAK
RD

BEAR CL

MARGARET RD
TAYLOR GDNS
CORBOLE DR
CENTREPIECE
RD

3

67

Greenditch Farm

DUNDRY LA

Lower Grove Farm

Highridge

SHERRIN WAY

BILLAND CL

REDFORD CRES

STRAWBERRY LA

OXLEAZE LA

BROADWAY HILL

2

Castle Farm

Masts

Grove Farm

Dundry CE Prim Sch

Dundry Down

Masts

Dundry Inn

Dundry

HILL RD
ABEECH

HAM LA

DOWNS RD

THE MEAD
CHURCH RD

AMBRUSS DRO

WEST DUNDRY LA

EAST DUNDRY LA

PH

Maiden Head

CASTLE FARM LA

CRABTREE LA

1

BS40

ELWELL LA

WINFORD LA

Elwell Farm

LITTLETON LA

CRABTREE CL

WELLS RD

UPTON LA

Mast

Upton Farm

Watercress Farm

66

54   A   55   B   C   56   D   E   F

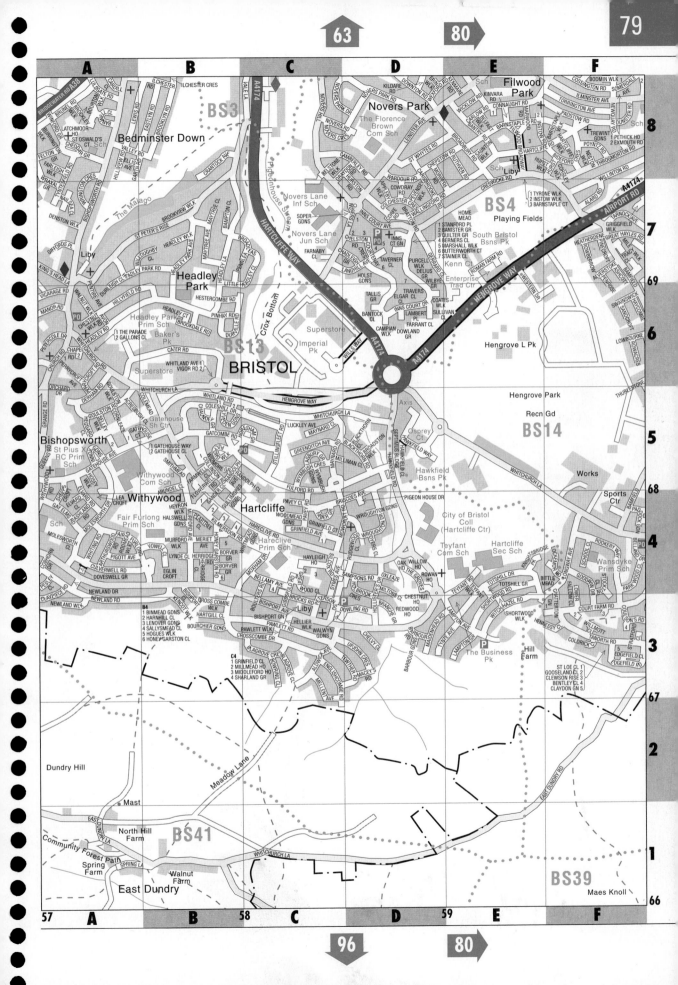

79 64

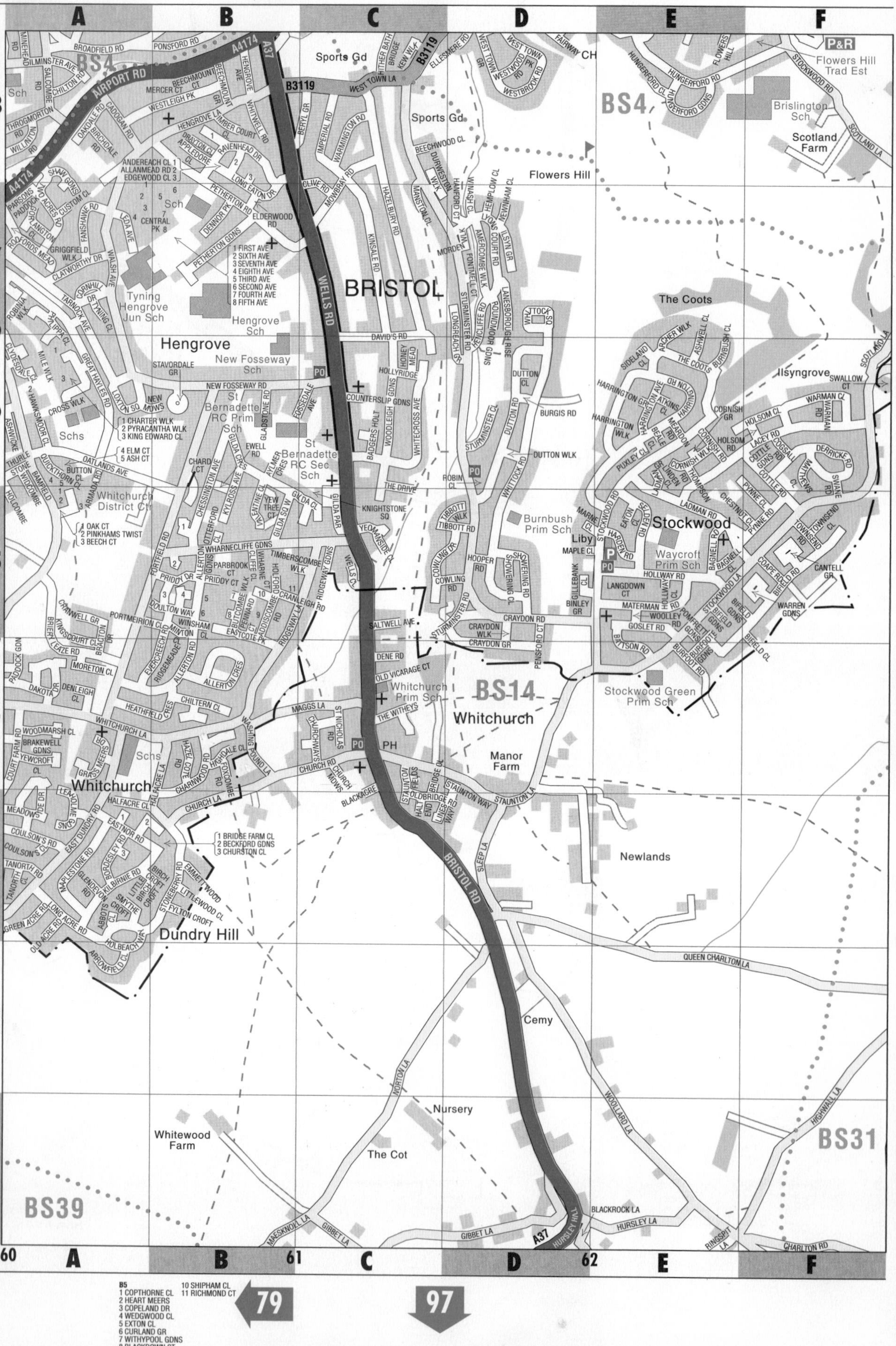

A B C D E F

8
7
69
6
5
68
4
67
2
1
66

BS4
BS14
Bristol
Hengrove
Whitchurch
Stockwood
Dundry Hill
BS39
BS31

B5
1 COPTHORNE CL
2 HEART MEERS
3 COPELAND DR
4 WEDGWOOD CL
5 EXTON CL
6 CURLAND GR
7 WITHYPOOL GDNS
8 BLACKDOWN CT
9 WANSDYKE CT
10 SHIPHAM CL
11 RICHMOND CT

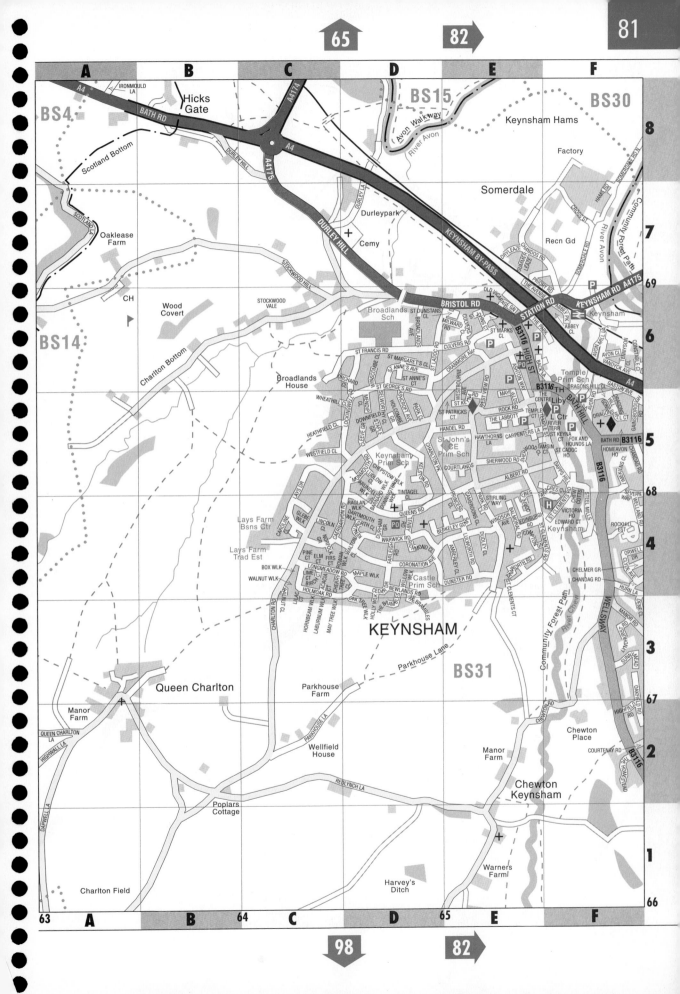

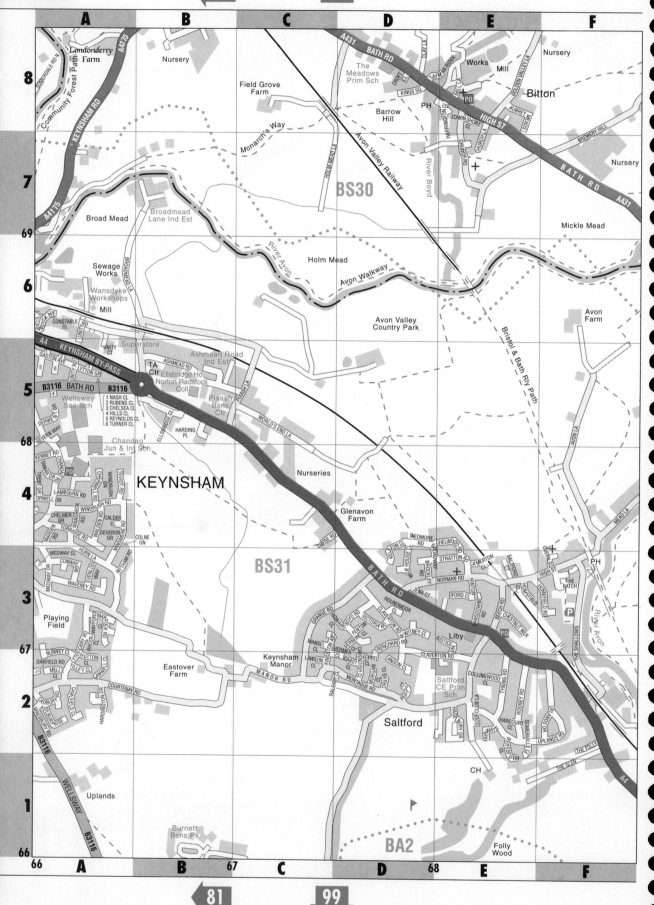

A B C D E F

8

Londonderry Farm
Community Forest Path
KEYNSHAM RD
A4175
Nursery
Field Grove Farm
Monarch's Way
A431 BATH RD
The Meadows Prim Sch
CROFT
CLAYTA
LAYMAN RIDGE
KINGS SQ
Barrow Hill
Works
Mill
Nursery
Bitton
HARBROUGH
GOLDEN VALLEY LA
AUBREY MEADS
CHURCH LA
HIGH ST

7

A4175
Avon Valley Railway
River Boyd
PH
EDWIN SHORT CL
CHURCH RD
BATH RD A431
Nursery
BS30

69

Broad Mead
Broadmead Lane Ind Est
BROADMEAD LA
Mickle Mead

6

Sewage Works
Wansdyke Workshops
Mill
River Avon
Holm Mead
Avon Walkway
Avon Valley Country Park
Avon Farm
Bristol & Bath Rly Path

5

WICK AVE
CONSTABLE CL
UNITY RD
A4 KEYNSHAM BY-PASS
GASTON AVE
UNITY CT
LYTTON GR
Superstore
TA Ctr
ASHMEAD RD
Ashmead Road Ind Est
Ellsbridge Ho
Norton Radstock Coll
ELLSBRIDGE CL
PIXASH LA
Pixash Bsns Ctr
WORLD'S END LA
AVON LA

B3116 BATH RD B3116

68

Wellsway Sec Sch
DERWENT GR
SEVERN WAY
1 NASH CL
2 RUBENS CL
3 CHELSEA CL
4 HILLS CL
5 REYNOLDS CL
6 TURNER CL
HARDING PL
Chandag Jun & Inf Sch
Nurseries

4

KENNET RD
TAMAR DR
TRENT DR
ORWELL DR
PO
CHANDAG RD
CHISNALL RD
WINDRUSH
Lambourn RD
WINDRUSH RD
WANSBECK
WALDER AV
CALDER CL
DEVERON GR
KINGSMERE
COLNE GN
KEYNSHAM
Glenavon Farm
CHELMER GR
MARROW
TORRIDGE RD
HURN LA
CORSE RD
WEDMORE RD
KESTON CL
CHELWOOD RD
WHICH HOUSE LA
BROADWAY
STRATTON
BROCKLEY
CAMERTON CL
SALTFORD CL
OVERN ST

3

Playing Field
MEDWAY CL
CONWAY RD
EVENLODE WAY
WAVENEY RD
BS31
GRANGE RD
ROUNDMOOR
BATH RD
JENA CT
NORMAN RD
IFORD CL
HILTON CL
HONEYWOOD
BEECH RD
CHESTNUT WLK
THE BATCH
PH
P
River Avon

67

OAKFIELD RD
NUNNEY CL
MELLS CL
TILLEY'S CL
BANNELL CL
RHODE CL
WAYFORD CL
Eastover Farm
Keynsham Manor
MANOR RD
LAWSON CL
KINGSTON CL
CLAVERTON RD
VICTORIA CL
FENTON
WITNEY CL
TRENCHARD RD
LANSON CL
CLAVERTON RD
Liby
PO
COLLINGWOOD CL
TYNING RD
ROONEY RD
THE SHALLOWS

2

CADBURY
MAESBURY RD
CAYFORD CL
SALBURY RISE
HARDINGTON CL
COURTENAY RD
MANSEL CL
HERMES CL
CABOT CL
KEPPEL CL
MONTAGUE CL
RALEIGH CL
MORGAN CL
DRAKE CL
HASELBURY GR
Saltford
Saltford CE Prim Sch
GOLF CLUB LA
FAIRWAYS
HARCOURT CL
SOMERVILLE CL
BEECH RD
UPLANDS RD
SOMERVILLE DR
THE FOLLY
A4

1

WELLSWAY
B3116
Uplands
Burnett Bsns Pk
CH
THE GLEN
Folly Wood

66

B3116
BA2

66 A B 67 C D E 68 F

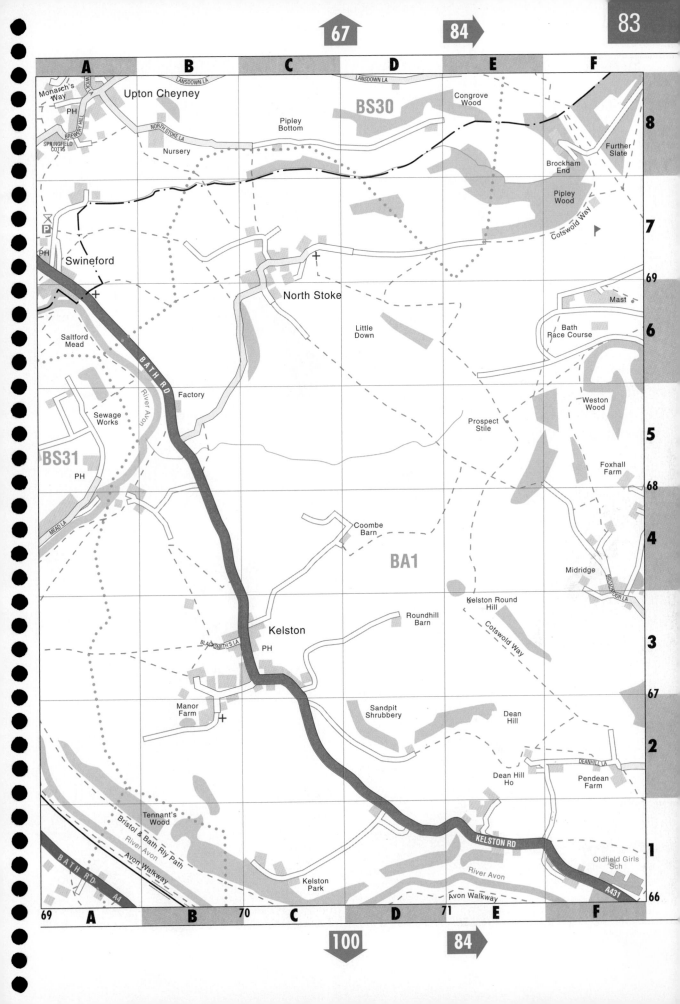

83
68

A B C D E F

8

Midfields

The Grove

Court Farm

Langridge House

LANGRIDGE LA

Langridge

Ashcombe Farm

Ashcombe House

Upper Langridge

7

Upper Farm

Aldermoor Wood

TADWICK LA

Lam Brook

Hall

69

Lansdown Hill

Upper Langridge Farm

Mill Farm

6

CH

Lansdown

PH

Bath Race Course

HIGH ST

CHURCH

Woolley

WOOLLEY LA

Heather Cottage

Charlcombe Grove Farm

5

Ravenswell House

P&R

Soper's Wood

68

Aldermead

BA1

Govt Offices

View Point Farm

4

Heather Farm

COLLIERS LA

LANSDOWN LA

Beckford's Twr

GRANVILLE RD

Charlcombe

Cemy

Upper Weston Farm

HAMILTON HO
STONELEIGH CT

LANSDOWN PK

CHARLCOMBE LA

3

Upper Weston

NAPIER RD
FALCONER RD
LEIGHTON RD
DUNCAN GDNS
BERESFORD GDNS
PURLEWENT DR
BROADMOOR LA
HAVILAND GR
GREENACRES
THE MACIES

67

Weston All Saints CE Prim Sch

SIX STREAMS

Rohannon Farm

Dean Hill Nursery

MICHAELS MEAD

HOLCOMBE GN

BLIND LA

FONTHILL RD

Kingswood Sch

LANSDOWN RD

VAN DIEMEN'S LA

CHARLCOMBE WAY

Royal High Sch

FAIRFIELD PARK RD

CHARLCOMBE RISE

SOLSBURY WAY

2

WESTMEAD GDNS

HOLCOMBE GN

BROOKFIELD PK

WELLINGTON BLDGS

WEALTERR

THE WELLS

1 BROOKSIDE HO
2 KNIGHTSTONE PL
3 SHEPPARDS GDNS
4 THE OLD BREWHOUSE
5 GAINSBOROUGH CT
6 CHELSCOMBE
7 EDGECOMBE MEWS
8 PROSPECT PL

BATH

HAMILTON RD

COLLEGE RD

Lansdown

NEWLAND RD

NORTHFIELDS

Prim Sch

Richmond HILL

BELTON CT

BIBURY HO

HARCOURT GDNS

SOUTHLANDS

Primrose Hill

Summerhill Park

LAGGAN GDNS

WALDEGRAVE RD

RICHMOND HO

NORTHFIELDS

RICHMOND HILL

1

Penn Hill

Cotswold Way

St Mary's RC Prim Sch

ANCHOR RD

GRENFELL

CHURCH RD

LANSDOWN RD

LUCKLANDS RD

HOCKLEY CT

ST CLEMENTS

WESTON PARK E

PRIMROSE HILL

MOUNTAIN ASH

Kingswood Day Prep Sch

SION RD

HERMITAGE RD

1 LANSDOWN PL W
2 LANSDOWN CRES

NORTHFIELDS CL

Weston

Liby

66

Sch

PENN HILL RD

NEWBRIDGE GDNS

FRANKLAND CL

CHANDLER CL

BERNARD IRELAND HO

Royal United H

THE GROVE

MANOR VILLAS

MONTROSE COTTS

Weston Park

WESTON PK

Summerfield Sch

WOODLAND

SUMMERHILL RD

Summerfield Sch

Sion Hill

SION HILL PL

Coll

WINIFRED LA

SOMERSET LA

SOMERSET PL

UPPER LANSDOWN MEWS

Mount Beacon Pl

Beacon Hill

ST STEPHEN'S

72 A B 73 C D 74 E F

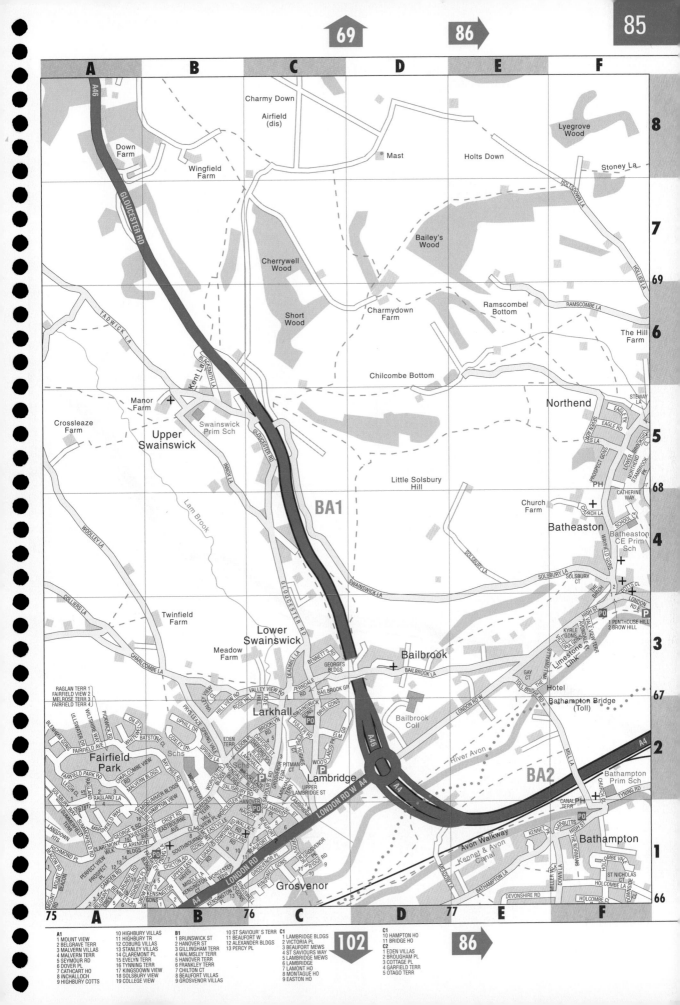

A B C D E F

8 7 69 6 68 5 4 3 67 2 66

Charmy Down
Airfield
(dis)

Mast

Holts Down

Lyegrove
Wood

Stoney La

Bailey's
Wood

Down Farm

Wingfield
Farm

Cherrywell
Wood

Ramscombe
Bottom

RAMSCOMBE LA

The Hill
Farm

Short
Wood

Charmydown
Farm

Chilcombe Bottom

Northend

EAGLE PK
EAGLE RD

STEWAY LA

Manor
Farm

Swainswick
Prim Sch

Little Solsbury
Hill

PROSPECT GDNS

PH

CATHERINE
WAY

Crossleaze
Farm

Upper
Swainswick

BA1

Church
Farm

CHURCH LA

SCHOOL LA

Batheaston

Batheaston
CE Prim
Sch

WAYFIELD GDNS

Lam Brook

SOLSBURY LA

SOLSBURY
CT

THE BATCH

SCOTTS CL

LONDON
RD

P

Twinfield
Farm

SWAINSWICK LA

HIGH ST

PO

1 PENTHOUSE HILL
2 BROW HILL

KYRLE
GDNS

VALE VIEW TERR

AVONDALE PL

VICTOR TER

Lower
Swainswick

Meadow
Farm

DEADMILL LA

Bennett's Rd

GEORGES
BLDGS

BAILBROOK LA

Bailbrook

Hotel

Limestone
Link

Bathampton Bridge
(Toll)

CHARLCOMBE LA

VALLEY VIEW RD

FERNDALE
RD

BAILBROOK GR

Larkhall

SWAINSWICK
GDNS

ORIEL GDNS

PO

Bailbrook
Coll

LONDON ROW

River Avon

BA2

Bathampton
Prim Sch

RAGLAN TERR 1
FAIRFIELD VIEW 2
MELROSE TERR 3
FAIRFIELD TERR 4

Fairfield
Park

Schs

ROSE HILL

FULLER RD

TYSSE R RD

P

Lambridge

UPPER LAMBRIDGE ST

LONDON RD W

A4

A46

Avon Walkway
Kennet & Avon
Canal

Bathampton

ST NICHOLAS
CT

CANAL
TERR

PH

PO

HIGH ST

TYNING RD

CHURCH LA

London Rd

Grosvenor

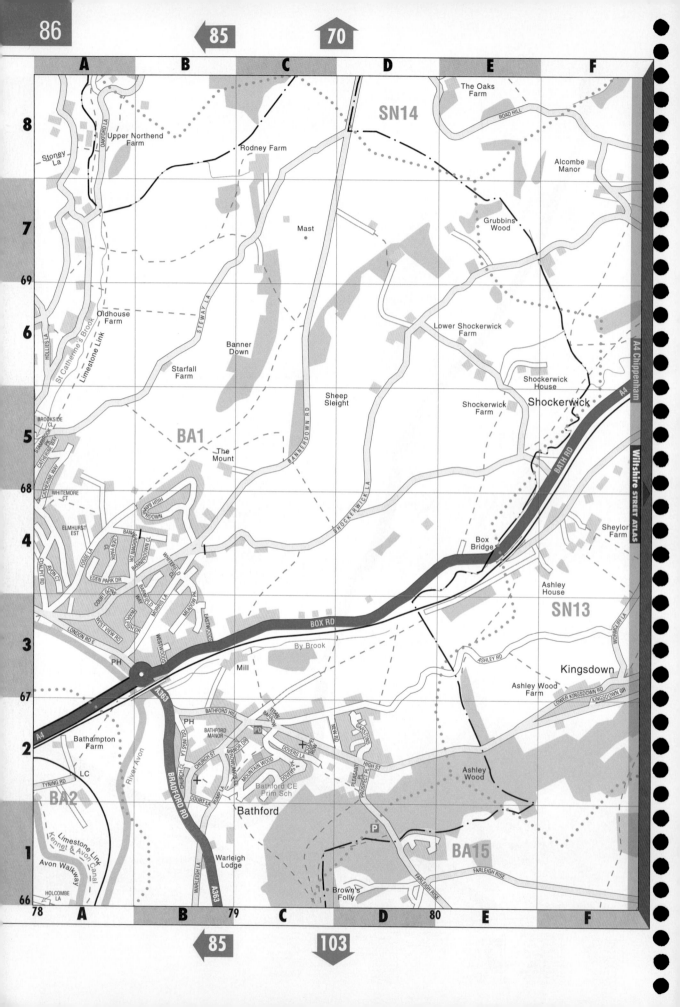

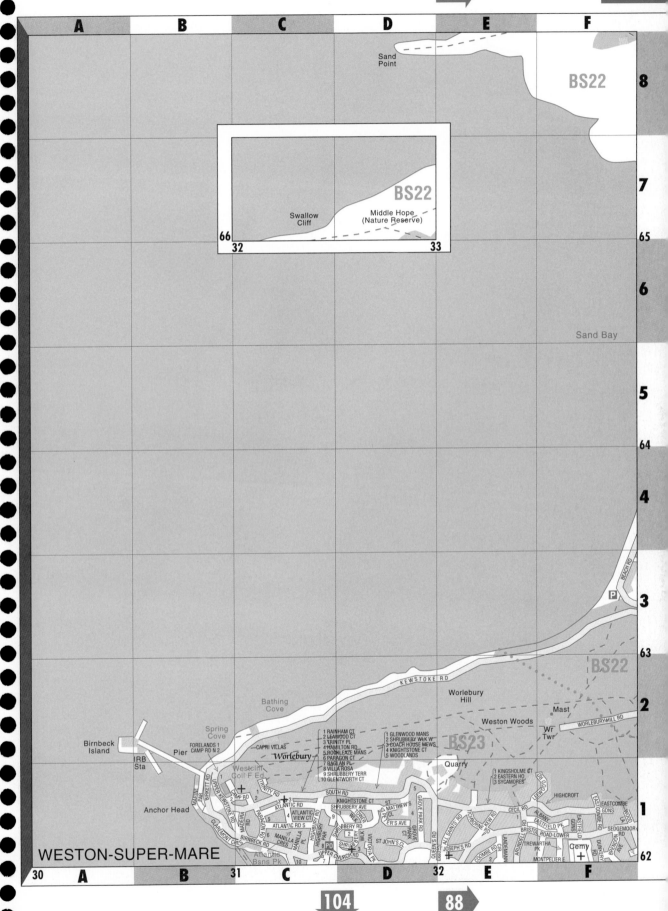

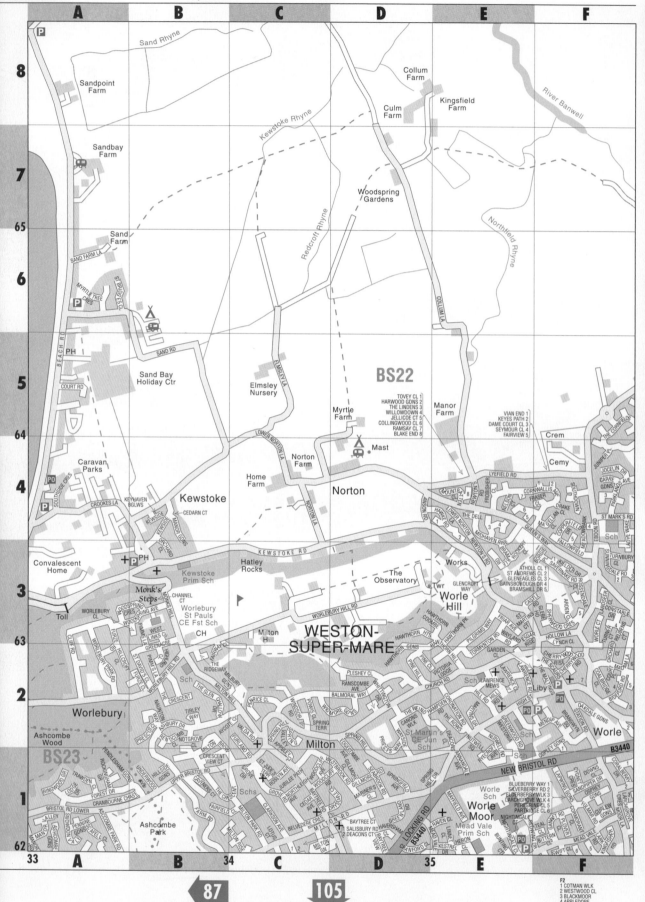

F2
1 COTMAN WLK
2 WESTWOOD CL
3 BLACKMOOR
4 APPLEDORE
5 BAMPTON
6 KENNFORD
7 KNIGHTSTONE PL

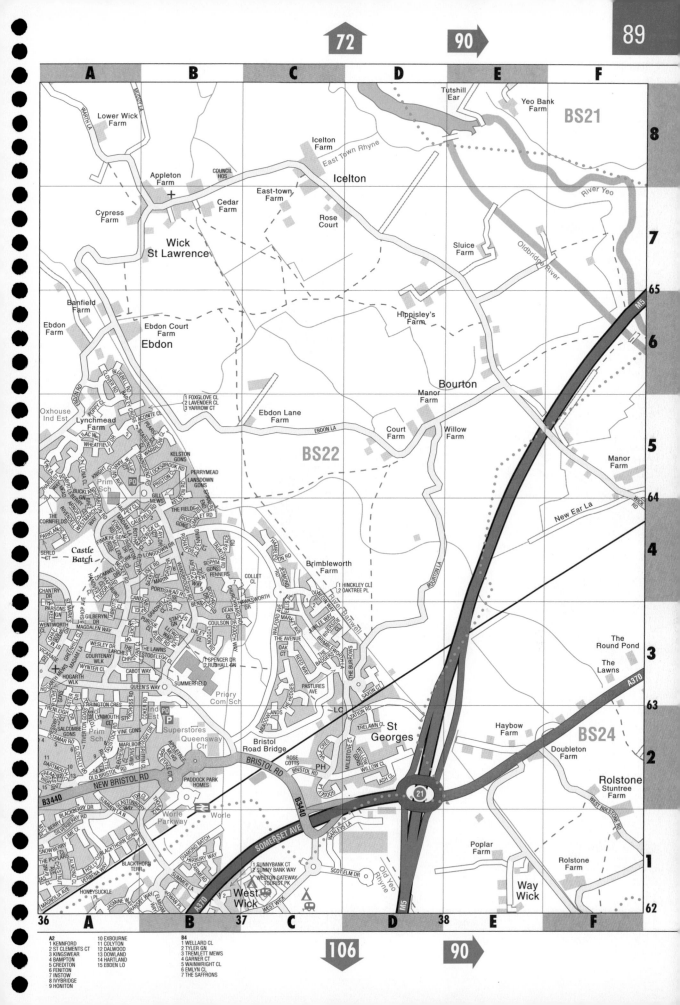

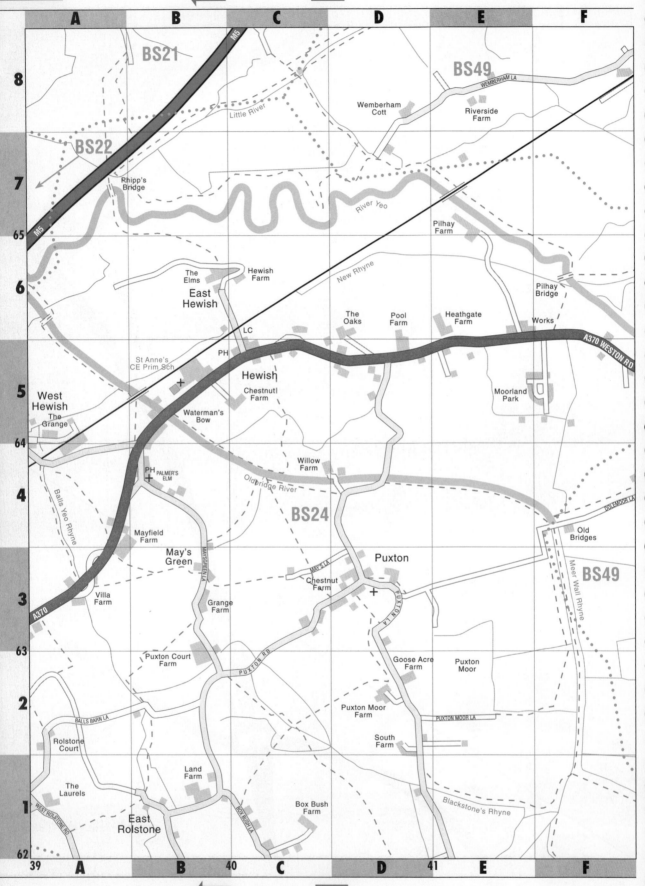

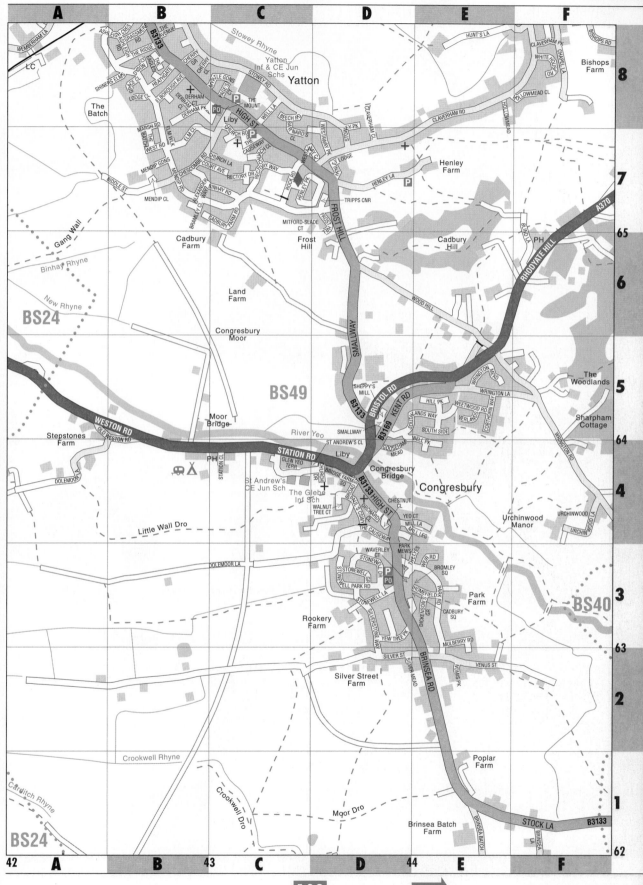

A B C D E F

8

Cleeve
Cleeve Combe
MEETINGHOUSE LA
A370
BISHOPS RD
GRAITNEY CL
CLEEVE DR
WOODVIEW DR
MILLIER RD
WARNER CL
Cleeve Court
Walnut Tree Farm
Cleeve Toot
PH
PENDER ST
P
Saw Mill
Wrington Warren
BS48

7

RHODYATE LA
RHODYATE HILL
CHAPEL LA
BS49
CLEEVE HILL RD
Goblin Combe
Warren House
Brockley Mini Farm

65

Bickley
King's Wood

6

Woolmers
Corporation Woods
Wrington Hill
Wrington Hill Farm

5

Urchin Wood
Ball Wood
Oatlands
Bracken Hill

64

The Island
Montreux Farm
The Grove
BS40
Bullhouse Lane

4

Udley
Uplands
Simshill Wood
WRINGTON RD
Yeowood
Littler Plantation
Prestow Wood
Barley Farm
WRINGTON HILL

3

Iwood
WEST HAY RD
West Hay
Piercehay
Maines Batch
CHAPEL HILL
YEOMANS ORCH
ROPER'S LA
HOME ORCHARD CL
BRANCHES CROSS
OLD HILL
Barley Wood

63

IWOOD LA
Iwood Farm
Iwood Manor
ALLEYS
HIGH ST
BELL WLK
SCHOOL RD
SOUTH
LONG LA
Barley Wood Walled Garden
Wrington CE Prim Sch

2

LADYWELL
PO
BROAD ST
Court Farm
CHURCH WLK
LAWRENCE CL
HANNAH MORE RD
MEMORIAL
SILVER ST
RICKYARD RD
Congresbury Yeo
WILTONS
BAKER'S BLDGS
WESTWARD CL
THE COTTAGES
BROOM HILL
OLD STATION CL
GARSTONS
GARSTONS ORCH

1

Butt's Batch
BUTT'S BATCH
KINGS RD
Wrington
Stoney Croft House
Beam Bridge
Cox's Green
HALF YD
HAVYAT RD
COX'S GN
Burnett Ind Est
Oakdene Farm
NATES LA
MILL LA
STOCK LA
B3133
Havyat Road Trad Est

62

45 A 46 B C 47 D E F

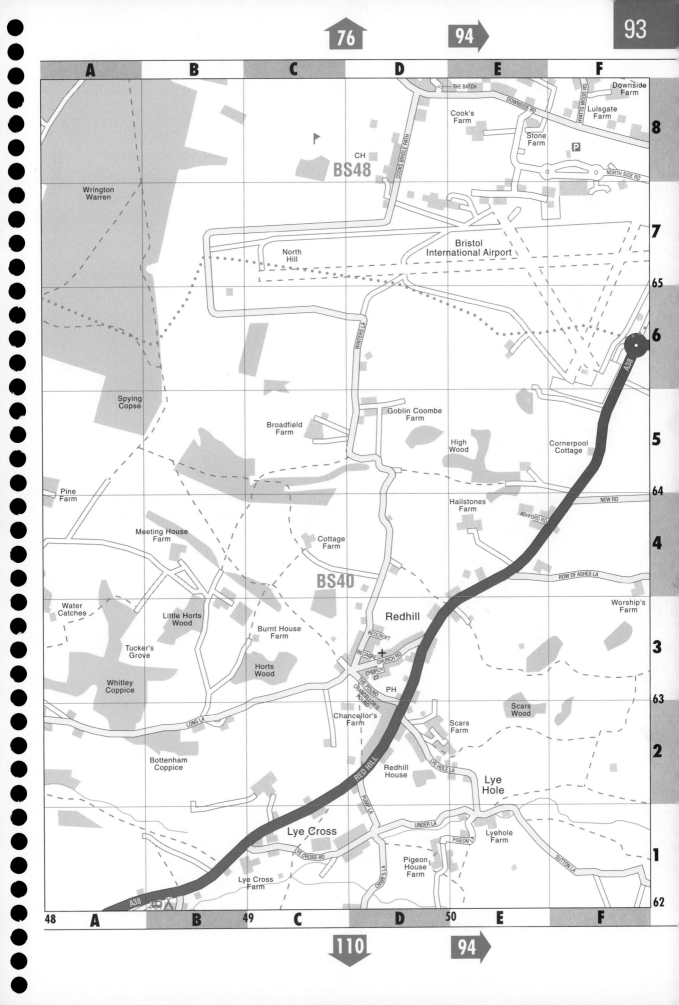

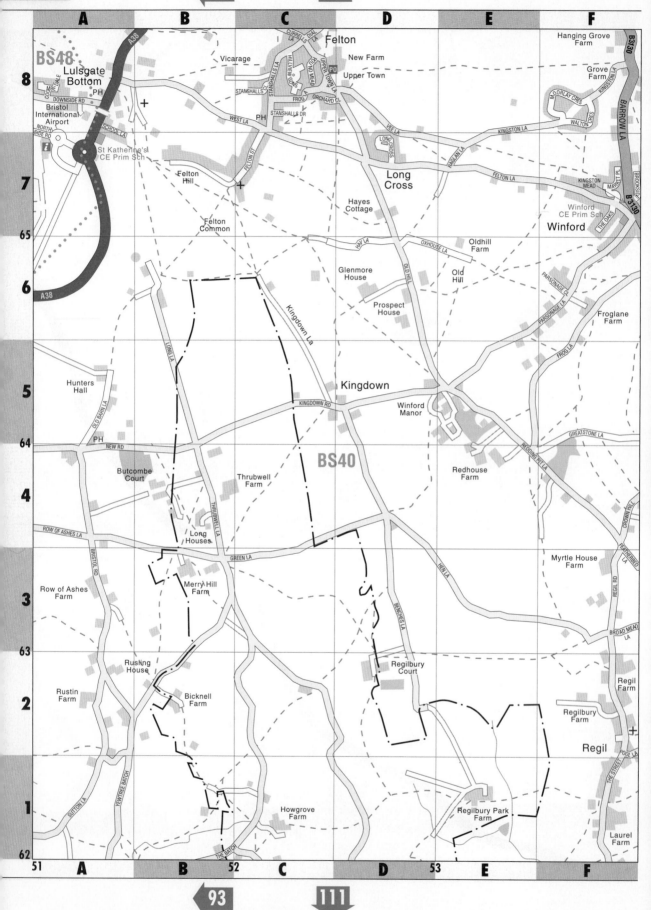

93
77

A   B   C   D   E   F

BS48

Lulsgate
Bottom

8

Vicarage

Felton

New Farm

Upper Town

COTSWOLD
MBE
DOWNSIDE RD
PH

A38
STANSHALLS LA
CURRELLS LA
DIAL LA
HILLVIEW GDNS
DIAL NO MEAD
UPPER TOWN LA
PO
ORCHARD CL
FROG LA

Bristol
International
Airport

NORTH
SIDE RD
SCHOOL LA

WEST LA
PH
STANSHALLS DR

St Katherine's
CE Prim Sch

FELTON ST

Felton
Hill

7

Long
Cross

LONG CROSS

VEE LA

RAGLAN LA

FELTON LA

KINGSTON LA

KINGSTON MEAD
MARKET PL

Hanging Grove
Farm

Grove
Farm

MOORLAY CRES
WALTON CRES

KINGSTON LA

B3130

BARROW LA

BROOKSIDE
B 3130
THE OAKS

Winford
CE Prim Sch

Winford

Felton
Common

65

Hayes
Cottage

HAY LA
OXHOUSE LA

Oldhill
Farm

6

A38

Kingdown La

Glenmore
House

Prospect
House

OLD HILL

Old
Hill

PARSONAGE CL

PARSONAGE LA

FROG LA

Froglane
Farm

Hunters
Hall

5

LONG LA

OLD BACH LA

Kingdown

KINGDOWN RD

Winford
Manor

REDDINGTON LA

GREATSTONE LA

64

PH

NEW RD

Butcombe
Court

Thrubwell
Farm

BS40

Redhouse
Farm

CROWN HILL

4

ROW OF ASHES LA

THRUBWELL LA

Long
Houses

GREEN LA

HEN LA

Myrtle House
Farm

FEATHERBED LA

REGIL RD

BRISTOL RD

Row of Ashes
Farm

3

Merry Hill
Farm

BROAD MEAD
LA

63

Rusling
House

Regilbury
Court

BENCHES LA

Regil
Farm

Rustin
Farm

2

Bicknell
Farm

Regilbury
Farm

Regil

THE STREET

POOL LA

SUTTON LA

YEWTREE BATCH

1

Howgrove
Farm

Regilbury Park
Farm

Laurel
Farm

62

THE BATCH

51   A   B   52   C   D   53   E   F

93
111

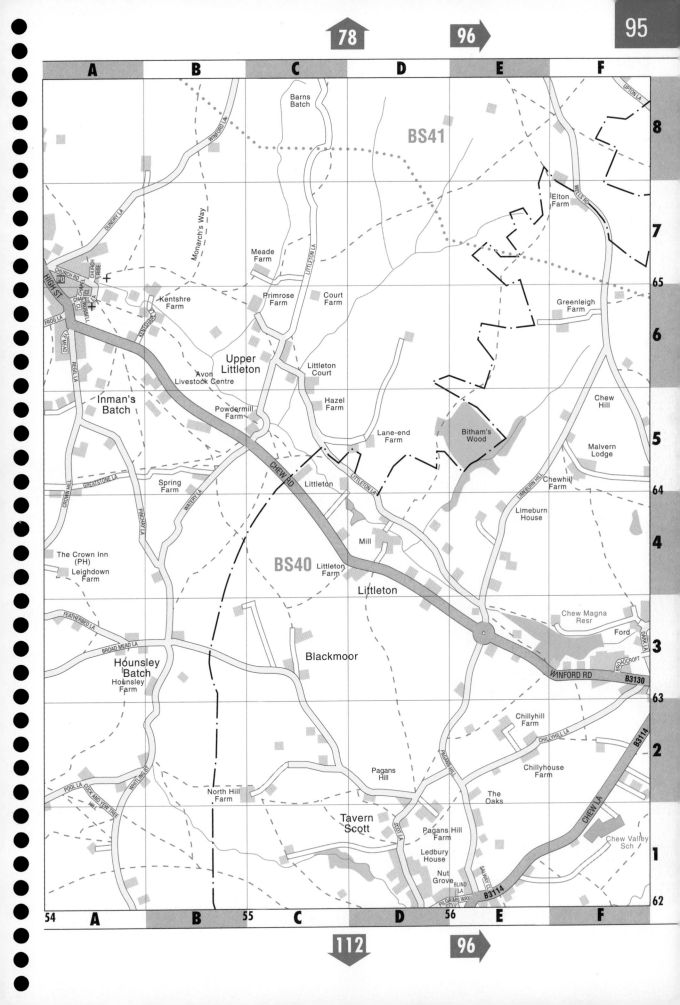

95
79

A B C D E F

8

Rattledown Farm

Waterloo Farm

North Wick

BS41

Yewtree Farm

Maes Knoll Farm

Manor Farm

7

Model Farm

NORTHWICK RD

NORTON LA

Norton Malreward Court

65

Community Forest Path

Norton Hawkfield

6

Whistley Wood

5

Wr Twr

Blacklands

NORTON LA

64

BS40

BS39

4

BUTHAM LA

North Chew Farm

Halfway Farm

B3130

CHEW HILL

Fairfield House

Chew Magna

NUTGROVE LA

Chew Magna Prim Sch

STONELEIGH

River Chew

Stanton Court

The Rookery

NORTON CL

Mill Place

SPRATTS BRIDGE

SILVER ST

THE BATCH

NORTH CHEW TERR

Rosedale

Church Farm

3

Sacred Heart Prep Sch

LOWER BATCH

Bridge Farm

SANDY LA

BATTLE LA

HARFORD

PO

Chew Court Farm

PH

B3130

HIGH ST

CHEW ST

SOUTH PAR

STANTON RD

PH

WINFORD RD

MADAM'S PADDOCK

P

THE CHALKS

63

CHEW LA

PINE CT

Mill

B3114

CRICKBACK LA

DUMPERS LA

Tun Bridge

Paradise

TYNING LA

UPPER STANTON

TUNBRIDGE CL

TUNBRIDGE RD

Tunbridge Farm

2

Chota Castle

Stanton Drew

MOORLEDGE RD

BROOKLEY RD

HIGHFIELDS

THE DRIVE

DENNY LA

Pitt's La

THE CRESCENT

1

Roundhill Farm

MOORLEDGE LA

Moorledge

Moorledge Farm

62

57 A B 58 C D 59 E F

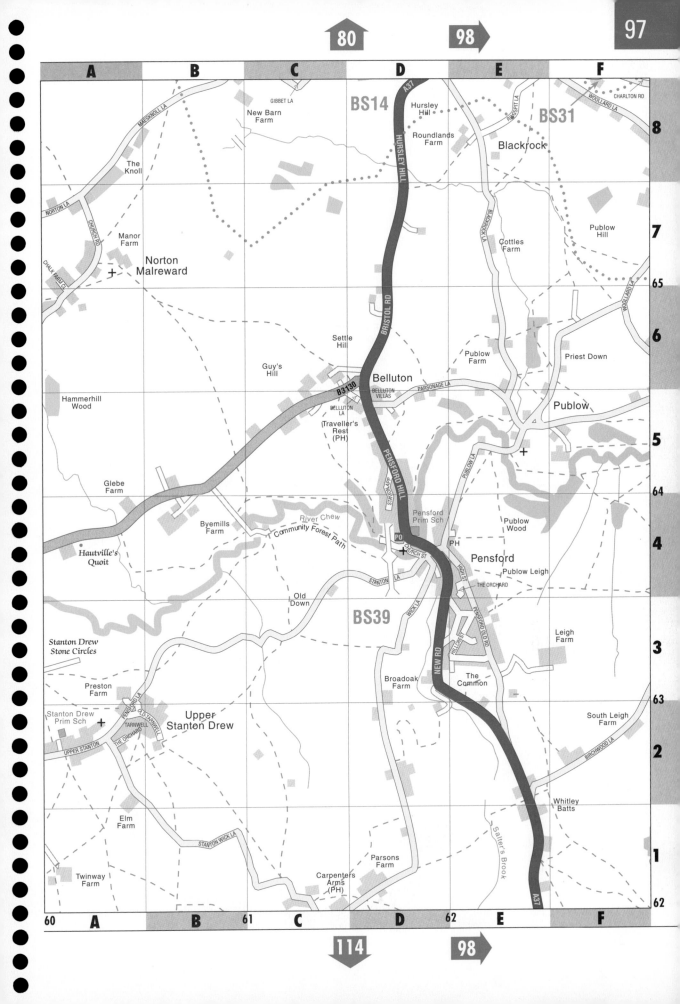

A   B   C   D   E   F

8

CHARLTON RD
DAPWELL LA

Great
Wood

Elm Park
Farm

BS31

WOOLLARD LA

Wooscombe Bottom

SLATE LA

7

BS14

Knowle
Farm

Fairy Hill

65

Pepper
Shells

PEPPERSHELLS LA

FAIRY
HILL

Lye Hill

SMALLBROOK LA

Community Forest Path

6

Langford's
Farm

Park
Copse

River Chew

Fairy
Hill

Compton Dando

Bathford Brook

Lye Hill
Farm

WOOLLARD LA

PARADISE ROW

Woollard

Catsley
Wood

VICARAGE LA

CHURCH LA

COURT HILL

CULVERHAY

The
Compton Inn
(PH)

THE GREEN

Compton
Green

BATHFORD HILL

5

Woodboro Mill
Farm

COCKERS HILL

RANNESS LA

Glebe
Wood

TUCKINGMILL LA

64

Compton
Common

BS39

Tuckingmill
Farm

4

Birchwood
House

Nutgrove
Farm

Allens Brake

Atgrove Wood

3

BIRCHWOOD LA

Lord's Wood

63

Wick
Farm

Roundhill
Wood

2

Hunstrete

Common
Wood

BA2

Hunstrete
Plantation

The
Hawhaw

1

Lady
Farm

School
Label

Fir
Copse

62

63   A   B   64   C   D   65   E   F

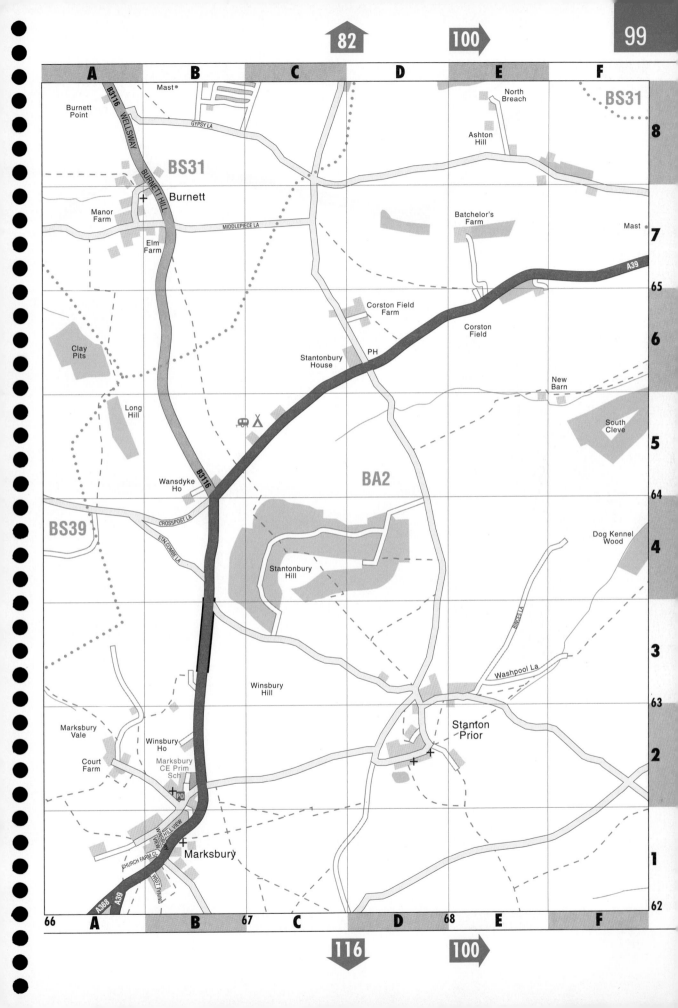

A B C D E F

BA31

BA1

8

BATH RD

BRISTOL RD

River Avon

Bristol & Bath Rly Path

Avon Walkway

New Bridge

NEWBRIDGE RD

P&R PH

KELSTON RD

A431

A4

Avon Walkway

HOMEMEAD

GOOLD CL

CORSTON LA

THE BARTON

Newton Bridge

LOWER FARM LA

THE PADDOCK

MEADLANDS

COTTON MEAD

Corston

PO

A4

A39

A4

Bristol Rd

A36

LOWER BRISTOL RD

A36

7

Church Farm Bsns Pk

WELLS RD

A39

BROOK COTTS

Long Shrub

PH

Seven Acre Wood

Camp Site

65

Corston Brook

CORSTON DR

PENNYQUICK

WALTINING LA

Mill

DAY CRES

REDLAND PK

REDLAND

Woodenhouse Covert

PO

Home Farm

Newton St Loe

Clays End

HINTON CL

Sch

CLEEVE GN

NEWTON RD

CAMELEY GN

CAMELEY GN

6

Newton Park

Claysend Farm

SHANS WAY

Sch

BOYCE CL

TANNERS LONG WK

WICK LN

CL RD

SHERIDAN RD

GARRICK RD

Bath Spa University Coll (Newton Park Campus)

ALEC RICKETTS CL 1
KELSTON VIEW 2
POOLE HO 3
GARRE HO 4

WHITEWAY RD

WEDGWOOD RD

POOLEMEAD RD

PO

5

Park Wood

St Loe's Castle

BA2

Newton Brook

Whiteway

Haycombe Farm

Crem

Cemy

WRIGHTSON CL

4

64

Whistling Copse

Ashery Gully

HAYCOMBE LA

Nursery

3

Park Farm

Pennsylvania Farm

63

WASHPOOL LA

2

Wilmington Farm

Manor Farm

Tithe Barn

Englishcombe

LENNOX GR

1

Wilmington

Wilmington La

62

69 A B 70 C D 71 E F

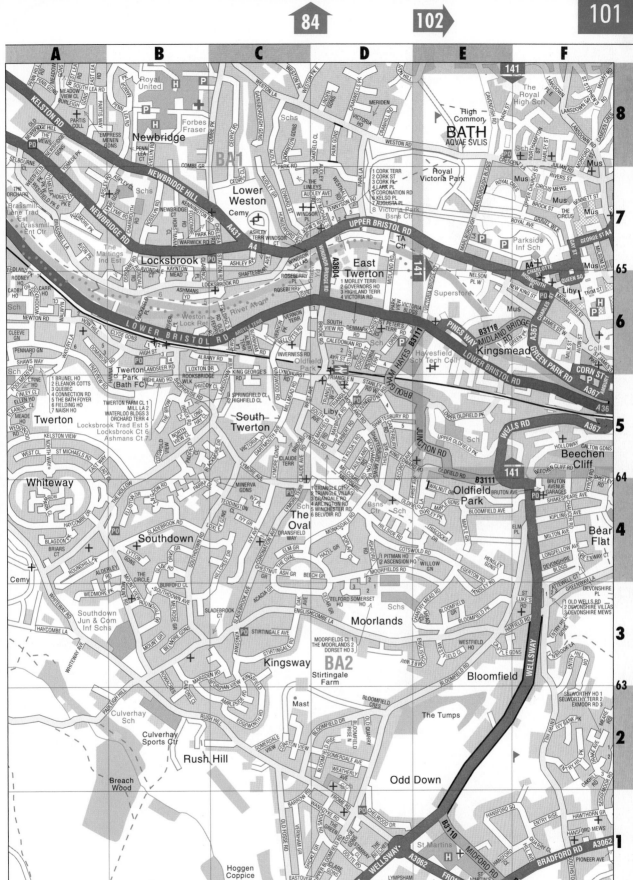

For full street detail of the highlighted area see page 141.

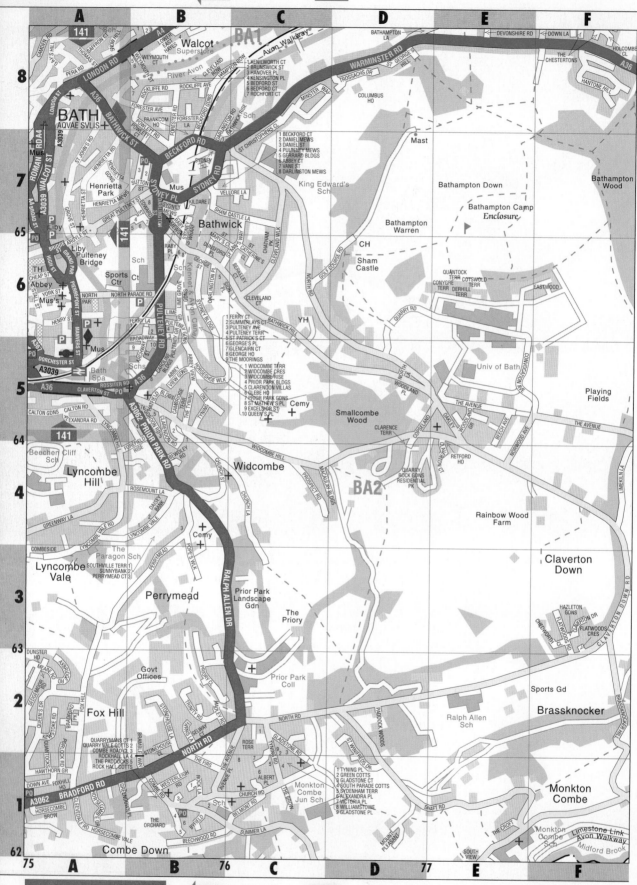

101 85

For full street detail of the highlighted area see page 141

101 119

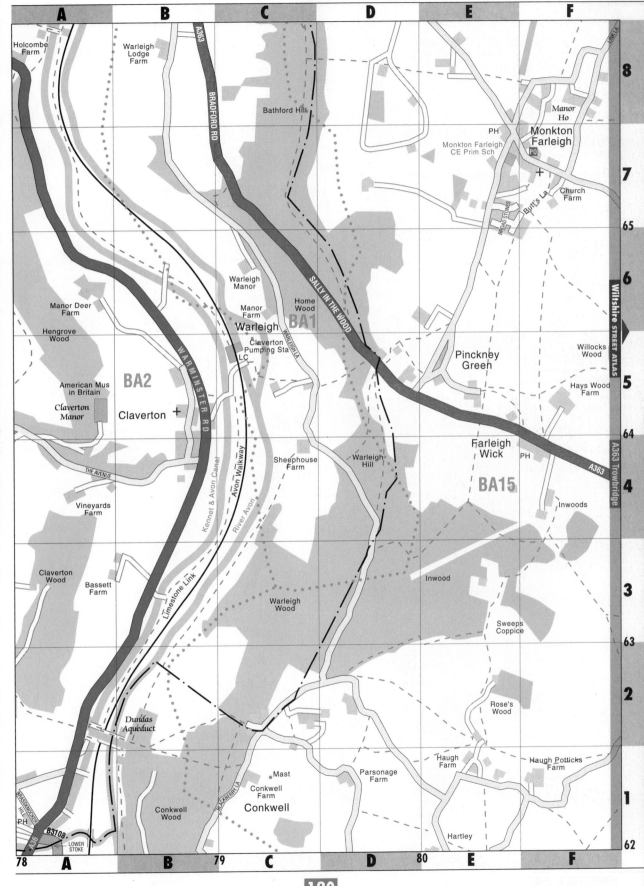

86

A   B   C   D   E   F

8
7
65
6
5
64
4
3
63
2
1
62

Holcombe Farm

Warleigh Lodge Farm

BRADFORD RD

A363

Bathford Hill

SALLY IN THE WOOD

Monkton Farleigh

Manor Ho

PH
Monkton Farleigh CE Prim Sch
PO

Broad Stones
Butt's La
Church Farm

LINK LA

Wiltshire STREET ATLAS

A363 Trowbridge

Manor Deer Farm

Hengrove Wood

Warleigh Manor

Manor Farm

Warleigh
BA1

Home Wood

Pinckney Green

Willocks Wood

Hays Wood Farm

BA2

American Mus in Britain

Claverton Manor

Claverton   +

WARMINSTER RD

Claverton Pumping Sta
LC

WARLEIGH LA

THE AVENUE

Kennet & Avon Canal

Avon Walkway

River Avon

Sheephouse Farm

Warleigh Hill

Farleigh Wick
PH

BA15

Inwoods

Vineyards Farm

Claverton Wood

Bassett Farm

Limestone Link

Inwood

Warleigh Wood

Sweeps Coppice

Rose's Wood

Dundas Aqueduct

Haugh Farm

Haugh Potticks Farm

Mast

BLACKBERRY LA

Conkwell Wood

Conkwell Farm

Conkwell

Parsonage Farm

PH
B3108
A36
LOWER STOKE
BRASSKNOCKER HILL

Hartley

78   A   79   B   C   80   D   E   F

120

87

WESTON-SUPER-MARE

Marine Lake

Knightstone

Steep Holm

Rudder Rock

Gull Research Station

Tower Rock

Calf Rock

Split Rock

Weston Bay

Somerset STREET ATLAS

Grand Pier

Sea Life Ctr

Tropicana Leisure Pool

Model Yacht Pond

Clarence Park

Miniature Rly

BS23

Broadoak Com Sch

OXFORD ST

Superstore

Weston-super-Mare

LOCKING RD

B3440

WINTERSTOKE RD

Recn Gd

Drove Road

Wyvern Sch

Bournville Jun Sch

Westhaven Sch

Uphill

West Links Sch

Weston Sixth Form Coll

General

BS24

TA8

Brean Down Farm

Black Rock

Slimeridge Farm

Marina

West Mendip Way

Windmill

River Axe

DEVONSHIRE RD

BEACH RD

MARINE PAR

UPHILL RD N

A370

BRIDGWATER RD

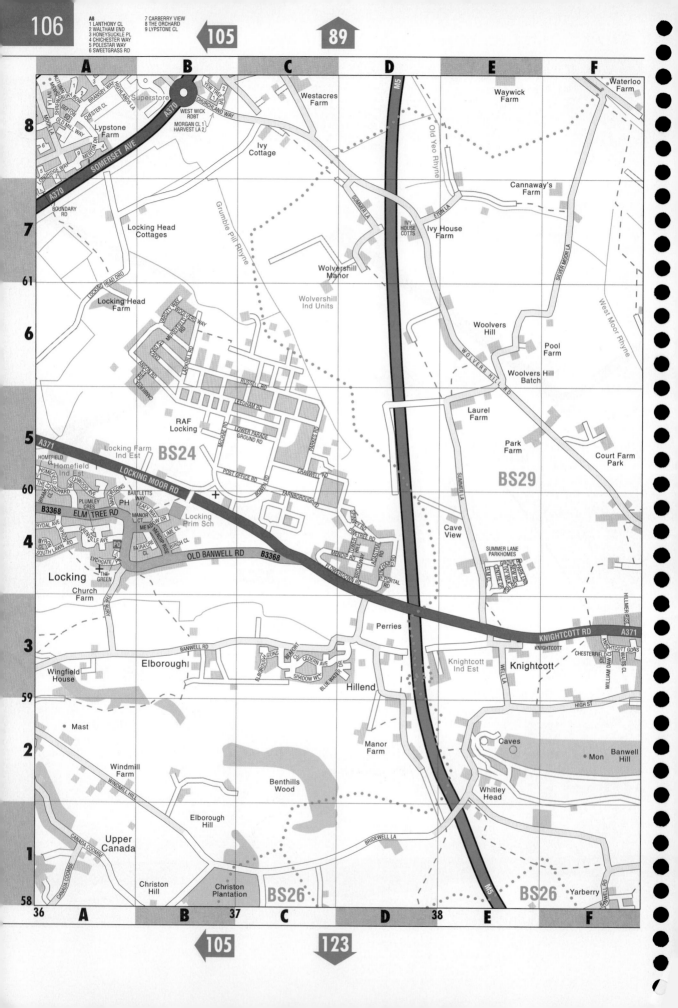

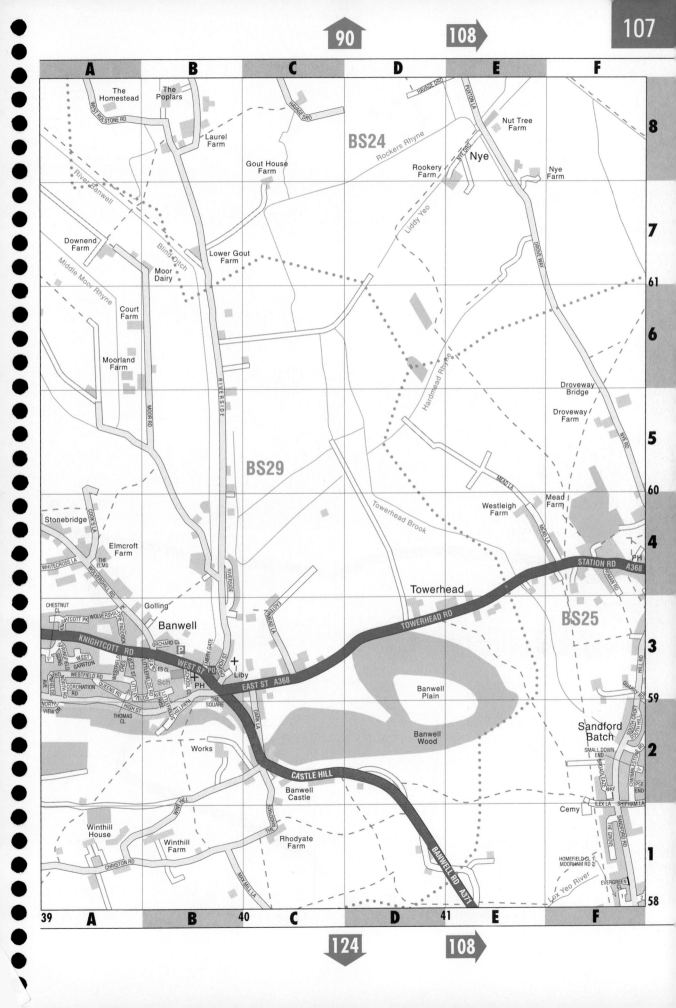

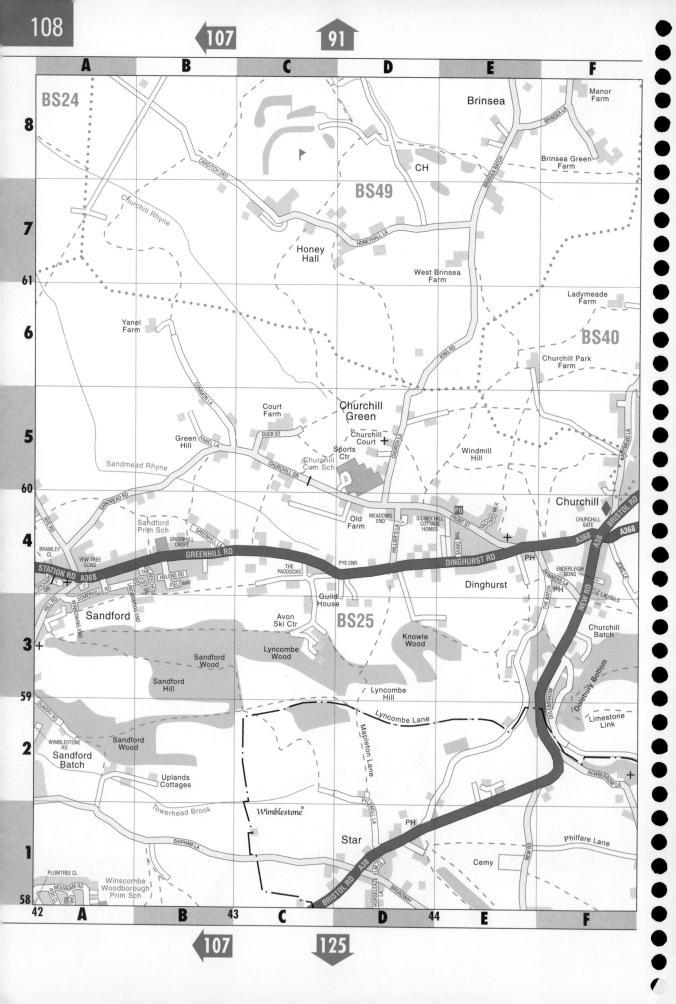

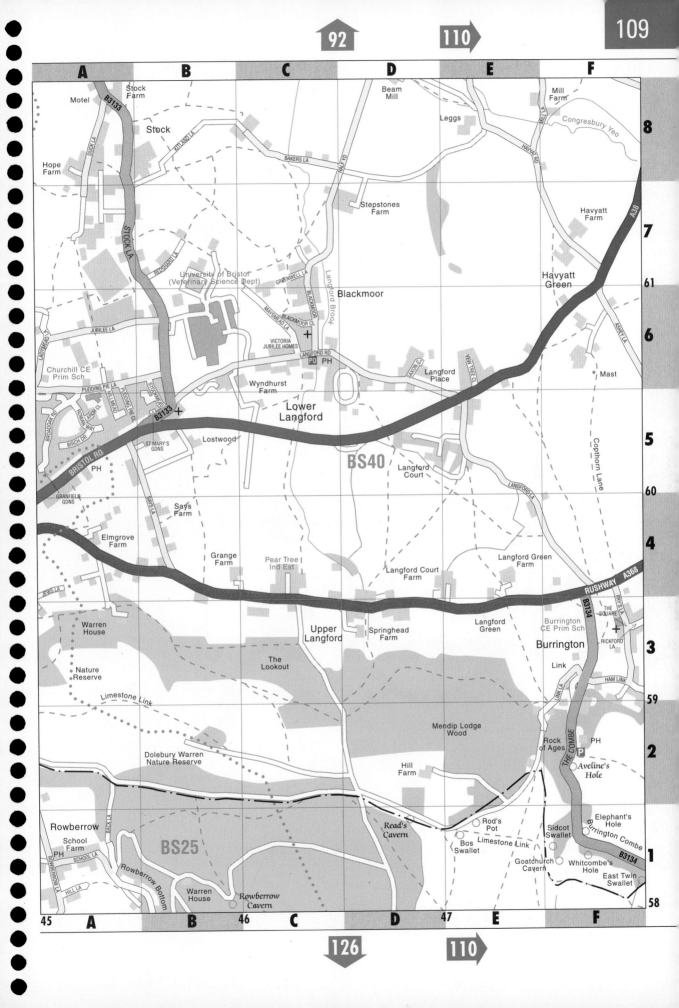

A B C D E F

8
7
61
6
5
60
4
59
3
2
1
58

Motel
Stock Farm
B3133
Stock
Hope Farm
DUCK LA
KITLAND LA
STOCK LA
REDSHARD LA
LADYMEAD LA
JUBILEE LA
University of Bristol (Veterinary Science Dept)
GREENWELL LA
MAYSMEAD LA
BLACKMOOR CL
BLACKMOOR
Langford Brook
Blackmoor
Churchill CE Prim Sch
PUDDING PIE LA
HILLMEAD
ROWAN WAY
LARCH CL
STOCKMEAD
PUDDING PIE LA
BROADOAK RD
BIRCH DR
VICTORIA JUBILEE HOMES
LANGFORD RD
PO PH
SAXON ST
Langford Place
YEW TREE CL
Mast
B3133
Wyndhurst Farm
Lower Langford
Lostwood
BRISTOL RD
PH
ST MARY'S GDNS
SAYS LA
Says Farm
BS40
Langford Court
LANGFORD LA
Copthorn Lane
GRANFIELD GDNS
Elmgrove Farm
Grange Farm
Pear Tree Ind Est
Langford Court Farm
Langford Green Farm
RUSHWAY A368
JEWS LA
Warren House
Nature Reserve
Limestone Link
The Lookout
Upper Langford
Springhead Farm
Langford Green
Burrington CE Prim Sch
LINK LA
B3134
THE SQUARE
RICKFORD LA
FRY'S LA
Burrington
Link
HAM LINK
59
Mendip Lodge Wood
Rock of Ages
THE COMBE
P
PH
Aveline's Hole
Dolebury Warren Nature Reserve
Hill Farm
Elephant's Hole
Burrington Combe
Read's Cavern
Rod's Pot
Sidcot Swallet
Rowberrow
School Farm
PH
BACK LA
ROWBERROW LA
SCHOOL LA
HILL LA
Rowberrow Bottom
BS25
Warren House
Rowberrow Cavern
Bos Swallet
Limestone Link
Goatchurch Cavern
Whitcombe's Hole
East Twin Swallet
B3134

Beam Mill
Leggs
HALE LA
BAKERS LA
Stepstones Farm
Mill Farm
MILL LA
Congresbury Yeo
HAVYATT RD
A38
Havyatt Farm
Havyatt Green
ASHEY LA

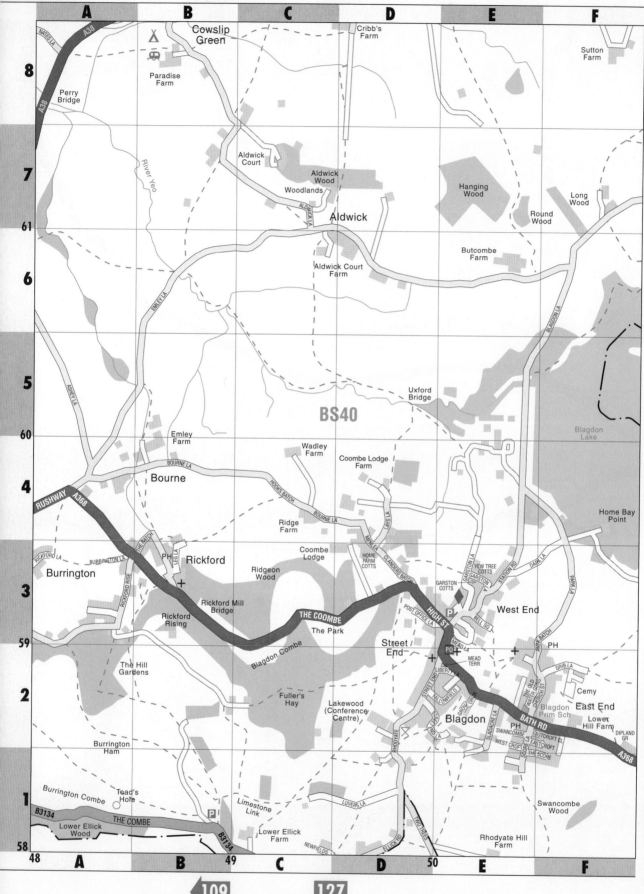

109
93

A B C D E F

8

7

61

6

5

60

4

59

3

2

1

58

48 A B 49 C D 50 E F

109
127

Cowslip Green

Cribb's Farm

Sutton Farm

Paradise Farm

Perry Bridge

NATE'S LA

A38

River Yeo

Aldwick Court

Aldwick Wood

Woodlands

ALDWICK LA

Aldwick

Hanging Wood

Long Wood

Round Wood

Aldwick Court Farm

Butcombe Farm

BLAGDON LA

EMLEY LA

Uxford Bridge

BS40

Blagdon Lake

Emley Farm

BOURNE LA

Bourne

Wadley Farm

Coombe Lodge Farm

Home Bay Point

ASHEY LA

A368

RUSHWAY

HOOKS BATCH

BOURNE LA

Ridge Farm

Coombe Lodge

LAYS LA

NYE LA

Home Farm Cotts

CLANDERS BATCH

GARSTON LA

Yew Tree Cotts

GARSTON LA

STATION RD

PARK LA

DARK LA

Rickford LA

BURRINGTON LA

THE BATCH

PH

LEG LA

Rickford

Ridgeon Wood

Garston Cotts

P

West End

Burrington

RICKFORD RISE

Rickford Mill Bridge

Rickford Rising

THE COOMBE

The Park

POST OFFICE LA

HIGH ST

BELL SQ

MEAD LA

PH

PARK BATCH

Blagdon Combe

The Hill Gardens

Fuller's Hay

Lakewood (Conference Centre)

Street End

PO

MEAD TERR

GRIB LA

Cemy

THE OLD WATER GDNS
CHURCH ST

LIBERTY LA

STREET END LA

FALLOWFIELD

Blagdon Prim Sch

East End

Lower Hill Farm

Burrington Ham

RHODYATE

CROSS LA

Blagdon

SLADACRE LA

SWANCOMBE

BATH RD

PH

EASTCROFT CL
EASTCROFT

A368

DIPLAND GR

WEST CROFT

THE SCORE

SCORE LA

Burrington Combe

Toad's Hole

Limestone Link

LUVERS LA

Swancombe Wood

B3134

THE COMBE

P

Lower Ellick Wood

Lower Ellick Farm

NEWFIELDS

TWO TREES

ELLICK RD

Rhodyate Hill Farm

B313A

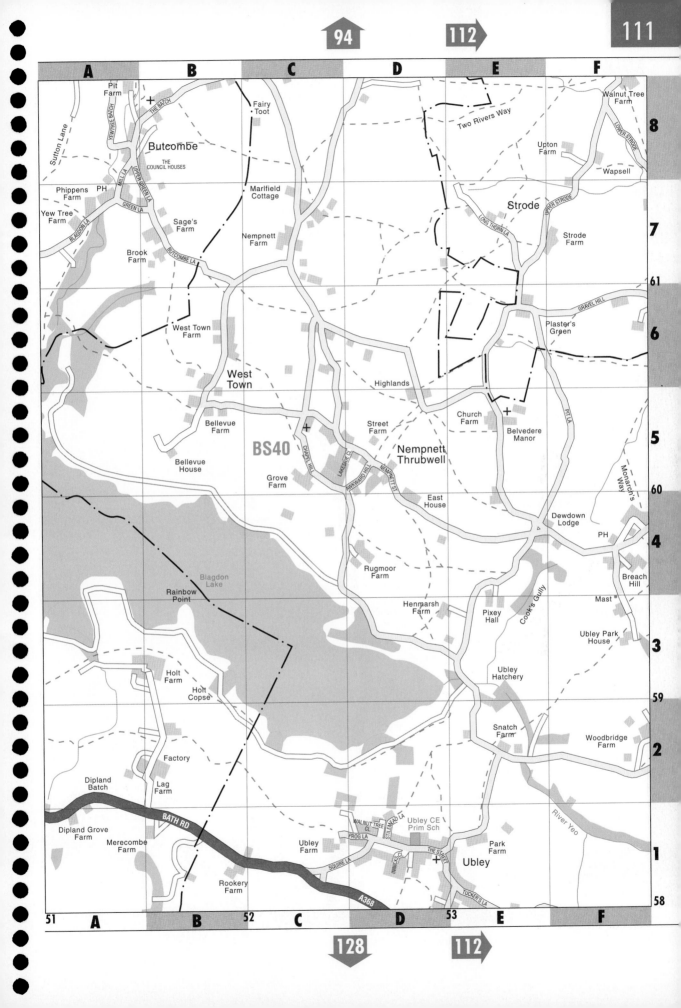

A | B | C | D | E | F

8

The Knoll

WHITLING ST

Lower Strode

Lower Strode Farm

Church Farm

SCOT LA

PH

CHURCH LA

PILGRIMS WAY

THE CEDARS

BLIND LA

B3114

Works

Chew Stoke CE Prim Sch

MILL LA

THE STREET

WEBBS MEAD

Chew Stoke

QUARRY HAY

BRISTOL RD

BILBIE RD

BILBIE CL

BUSHY THORN RD

WALLY COURT RD

WALLEY LA

HOME ORCH

SCHOOL LA

PO

CHAPEL LA

CHAPEL

Wallis Farm

Fairseat Ind Est

7

Manor Farm

LOWER STRODE

GRAVEL HILL

SHOREDITCH

Scornfield La

Stoke Hill House

STOKE HILL

Woodford Hill

61

Perry House Farm

BREACH HILL LA

Rose Cottage

6

Stoke Villice

Woodford Lodge

Obelisk

Rookery Farm

CAPEL LA

Manor Farm

BS40

5

KNIGSHILL LA

Breach Hill Common

60

Nunnery Copse

Breach Hill

Chew Valley Lake

4

Herons Green Farm

Herons Green

MORETON LA

Herons Green Bay

P

Moreton Point

3

59

Monarch's Way

Moat Farm

2

VILLICE LA

Bickfield Farm

BICKFIELD LA

NEWCLOSE LA

STRATFORD LA

1

River Yeo

Summerlea Farm

B3114

Oldbarn La

A368

58

54 | A | B | 55 | C | D | 56 | E | F

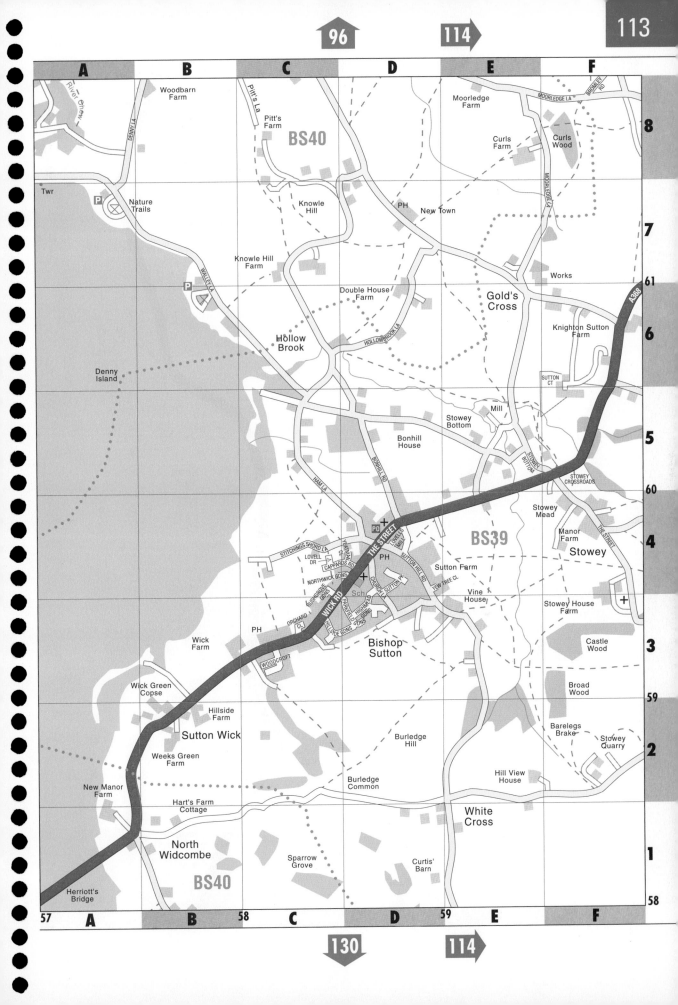

96
114

A B C D E F

8
7
61
6
5
60
4
59
3
2
1
58

River Chew

Twr

Woodbarn Farm

DENNY LA

P

Nature Trails

Pitt's La

Pitt's Farm

BS40

Knowle Hill

WALLEY LA

P

Knowle Hill Farm

Hollow Brook

Denny Island

Double House Farm

HOLLOWBROOK LA

PH

New Town

Moorledge Farm

MOORLEDGE LA

BROMLEY RD

Curls Farm

Curls Wood

MOORLEDGE LA

Works

Gold's Cross

Knighton Sutton Farm

A368

SUTTON CT

Mill

Stowey Bottom

Bonhill House

HAM LA

BONHILL RD

STOWEY BOTTOM

Stowey Crossroads

Stowey Mead

Manor Farm

THE STREET

BS39

Stowey

PO

THE STREET

LOVELL'S MILL

STITCHINGS SHORD LA

LOVELL DR

CAPPARDS RD

YEATMAN CL

NORTHWICK GDNS

RUSHGROVE GDNS

WICK RD

PH

SUTTON HILL RD

CHURCH LA

SUTTON PK

Sutton Farm

YEW TREE CL

Vine House

Stowey House Farm

Castle Wood

ORCHARD CL

PARKFIELD GDNS

HIGHMEAD

HILLSIDE GDNS

Sch

Bishop Sutton

PH

WOODCROFT

Wick Farm

Wick Green Copse

Hillside Farm

Sutton Wick

Weeks Green Farm

New Manor Farm

Hart's Farm Cottage

North Widcombe

BS40

Herriott's Bridge

Sparrow Grove

Burledge Common

Burledge Hill

Curtis' Barn

White Cross

Hill View House

Broad Wood

Barelegs Brake

Stowey Quarry

130
114

57 58 59

A B C D E F

A   B   C   D   E   F

8

Bromley Farm

Curl's Farm

Utcombe Farm

STANTON WICK LA

Stanton Wick

CHELWOOD RDBT

A37

A368

Chelwood House Hotel

Stanton Wick Farm

Park Farm

7

A368

Fry's Bottom

61

Round Hill

Salter's Brook

Red Hill

Breach

6

FEATHERED LA

Folly Wood

Honey Gaston

North End Farm

5

Folly Farm Nature Reserve

BS39

THE FLAT

North End

KING LA

60

Dowling's Wood

Taylor's Farm

LOWER BRISTOL RD

4

Cinderlands Brake

Tynemoor Wood

Hill Farm

3

Warwick Arms (PH)

Tynemore Farm

UPPER BRISTOL RD

TYNINGS WAY

WARWICK GDNS

ROGERS CL

BROOMHILL LA

FURMLEAZE LA

THE MEAD

MAYPOLE CL

Clutton Prim Sch

BATCH LA

BATCH CL

GREENRIDGE

STATION RD

PO

Clutton

CHURCH LA

VALLEY VIEW

VENUS LA

CARLTON CT

KINGS OAK MDW

CLUTTON HILL

59

Church Farm

MAYNARD TERR

Cholwell Farm

Sleight Farm

Cholwell House

Bendalls Bridge

2

Cholwell

Willow Farm

New Cholwell Farm

MARSH LA

NANNY HURN'S LA

1

Limestone Link

Paul Wood

Temple Cloud

THE SQUARE

ASHWAYS HO

PAULMONT RISE

PAULWOOD RD

PH

FAIRVIEW

ELM VIEW

OAKLANDS

ASHMEAD

CHARLOW

TEMPLE INN LA

MEADWAY

TILEDOWN

FALLODOWN

CLARK WAY

FIELDGARDENS RD

GOLDNEY

GOLDNEY WAY

CLAY HILL

HALT CL

GREYFIELD VIEW

Cameley C.E. Prim Sch

A37

58

60   A   B   **61**   C   D   **62**   E   F

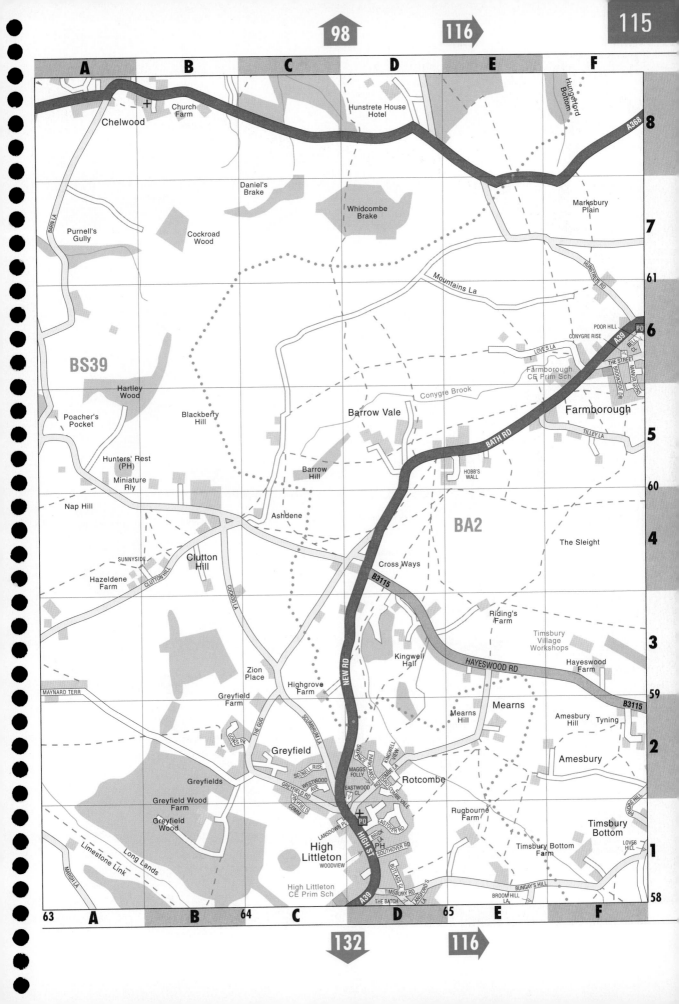

115
99

A B C D E F

8

A368
A39
Beech Tree Farm
The Brendons
Priston New Farm
Pendown Hill

7

Marksbury Plain
Mollifrend Ho
Conygre Brook
Pottern
Pottern Brake
PH

61

Old Inn
Sewage Works
Castle Farm
Priest Barrow

6

A39 BATH RD OLD LA
POOR HILL
THE STREET
BRIDGE GDNS
BELLIFANTS
FERENBERGE CL
MEADWAY
THE BATCH
THE CHURCH
RECTORY CE
THE MEAD
PH
LITTLE LA
TILLEY CL
TILLEY LA
Farmborough
Long Wood
MANOR GDNS

5

TILLEY LA
TIMSBURY RD
Tilley Farm
BA2
Farmborough Common

60

FOUNDRY COTTS
Wallmead House Farm
Lammas Field Farm
Priston Wood
PRISTON LA

4

Wallmead Farm
Wall Mead
BLOOMFIELD RD
Bloomfield
NORTHFIELD
THE WOODLANDS

3

Sleight Farm
BLOOMFIELD CL
BLOOMFIELD AVE
UPPER FURLONG
UPPIATT LA
BLOOMFIELD PARK RD
THE GLEBE
CROCOMBE LA
Crocombe
CROCOMBE
THE MEAD
St Mary's CE Prim Sch
PARKWAY LA
Tunley Farm
B3115
OVERDALE
The Sleight

59

B3115
HAYESWOOD RD
NORTH RD
LANSDOWN VIEW
LANSDOWN CRES
TUNLEY HILL
MEADGATE

2

Tyning
PRIORS HILL
THE AVENUE
SOMERSET FOLLY
ST MARY'S GN
NEWMANS LA
THE SQUARE
CONYGRE GN
PITFOUR TERR
HIGH ST
THE MEAD
HOMEFIELD
MAGGS LA
SOUTH RD
RECTORY
CHAPEL LA
CHURCH
HOOK HILL
Hook
PH
PARKWAY
Meadgate East
CAMERTON RD
MEADGATE
Bengrove Wood
ST MARY'S CL
SOV LA
CH LA
PO
BAKERS PAR
SOUTH VIEW

1

Loves Hill Farm
PRIORS HILL
LOVES HILL
GREENVALE
KELLY VIEW
LAUREL GDNS
GREENVALE CL
GREENVALE DR
ST JOHNS RD
BARTHOLOMEW ROW
Timsbury
MILL LA
RADFORD HILL
The Folly
Meadgate Farm
WEEKESLEY LA
RED HILL
Sheep House Farm
Limestone Link
ORCHARD COTTS
WHITEBROOK LA
Timsbury Bottom
Lynch Ho
Greenvale
NEW PIT COTTS
BRIDGE PLACE
WICK LA
Farmbrook

58

115
133

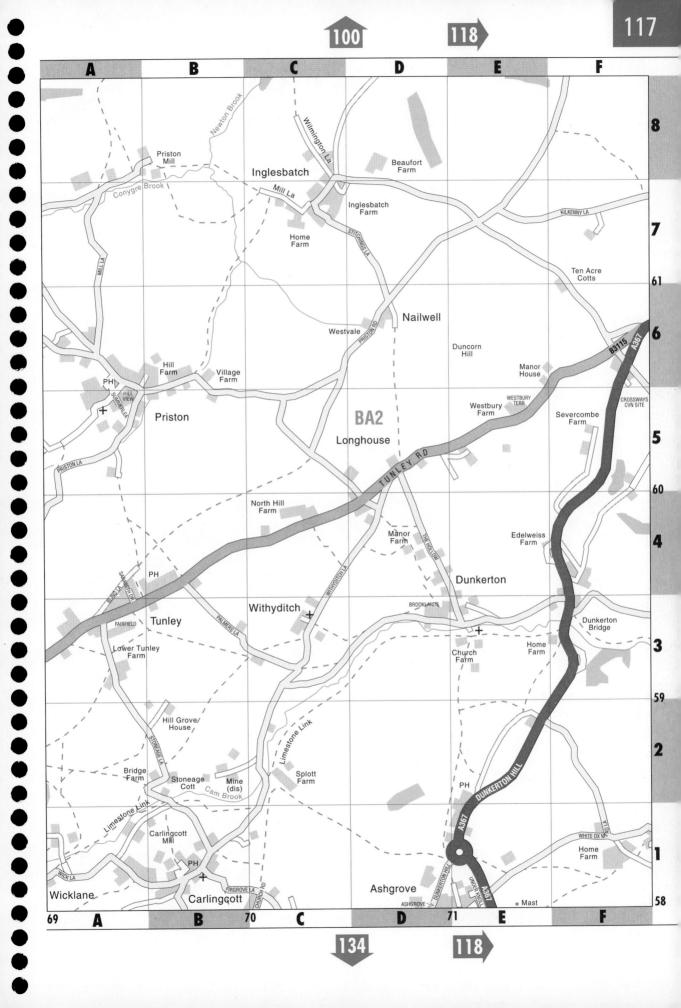

100

118

8

7

61

6

5

60

4

59

3

2

58

A B C D E F

Priston Mill

Conygre Brook

Newton Brook

Inglesbatch

Mill La

Wilmington La

Beaufort Farm

Inglesbatch Farm

Home Farm

STITCHINGS LA

Kilkenny La

Ten Acre Cotts

Nailwell

Westvale

PRISTON RD

Duncorn Hill

Manor House

B3115

A367

Hill Farm

Village Farm

PH

SHAMP LA

HILL VIEW

Priston

BA2

Longhouse

Westbury Farm

WESTBURY TERR

Severcombe Farm

CROSSWAYS CVN SITE

PRISTON LA

TUNLEY RD

North Hill Farm

Manor Farm

THE HOLLOW

Edelweiss Farm

PH

SAWPIT LA

BLIND LA

Tunley

FAIRFIELD

PALMERS LA

Withyditch

WITHYDITCH LA

Dunkerton

BROOKLANDS

Church Farm

Home Farm

Dunkerton Bridge

Lower Tunley Farm

Hill Grove House

STONEAGE LA

Limestone Link

Splott Farm

Bridge Farm

Stoneage Cott

Cam Brook

Mine (dis)

PH

DUNKERTON HILL

A367

WHITE OX MD

Home Farm

UNDER KNOLL

Limestone Link

Carlingcott Mill

PH

WICK LA

FIRGROVE LA

CHURCH RD

Ashgrove

A367

Mast

Wicklane

Carlingcott

ASHGROVE

DUNKERTON HILL

69 A B 70 C D 71 E F

134

118

117
101

| | A | B | C | D | E | F |

8

Middle Wood

Vernham Wood

BRISTOL VIEW 1
UPPER BLOOMFIELD RD 2
FOSSE WAY EST 3

WELLSWAY

OLD FOSSE RD

A367

LYMPSHAM GN
ABINGDON GDNS
MENDIP GDNS
HANWELL RD
FOSSE GDNS
GREGORYS GR
CARDINAL CL
PK CR RD
HEATHER DR

CRANMORE PL
RIDGE GREEN
GREEN CL CL
WILLOW CL
SPRUCE WAY
MEADOW PK
HOLLY DR
SULIS MANOR RD

FULLERS WAY

Wansdyke Sch

OLD FROME RD

MIDFORD RD

B3110

Odd Down

St Gregory's RC Coll

Mast

Hazel Way

ALDER WAY

SOUTHSTOKE LA

CRANLEIGH

Nurseries

Woodleaze

KILKENNY LA

P&R

BURNT HOUSE RD

Sulis Manor

PACK HORSE LA

7

Down Wood

West Wood

Works

VICTORIA COTTS

PH

Southstoke

COURTMEAD

THINGDON

61

Hodshill

A367

COMBE HAY LA

Rowley Wood

6

Fortnight Farm

Engine Wood

Fosse Farm

Week Farm

Limestone Link

5

Rowley House

Rowley Farm

Anchor Fafm

Cemy PH

60

Rainbow Wood

Manor House Farm

Cam Brooke

Combe Hay

Dunnyham Brake

Tut's Wood

Brake Wood

Upper Twinhoe Farm

Middle Twinhoe

4

BA2

Upper Twinhoe

3

Limestone Link

Underdown Wood

Twinhoe Green

59

TWINHOE LA

2

Manor Farm

BATH HILL

1

White Ox Mead Farm

Upper Hayes

Wellow

Weavers Orch

MANOR CL

FARM LA

BULL'S HILL

Church Farm

St Julian's CE Prim Sch

MILL HILL

FORD RD

HUNGERFORD TERR

HENLEY VIEW

HIGH ST

STATION RD

THE SQUARE

RAILWAY LA

58

Wellow Brook

| 72 | A | B | 73 | C | D | 74 | E | F |

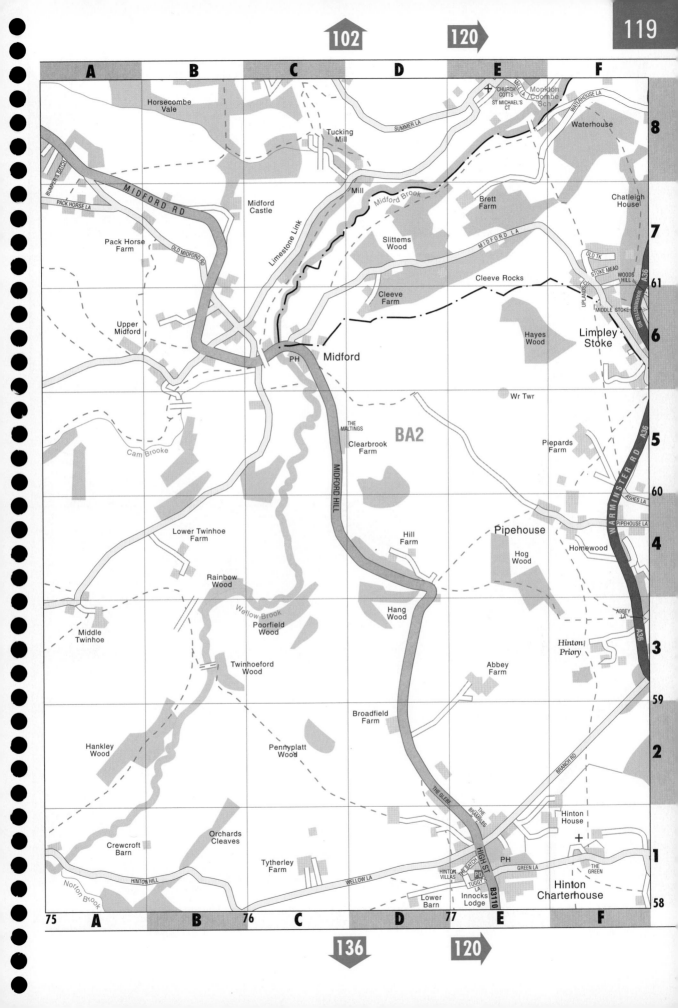

A   B   C   D   E   F

Horsecombe Vale

SUMMER LA

Tucking Mill

Church Cotts
St Michael's CT
Monkton Coombe Sch

Waterhouse LA
Waterhouse

8

MIDFORD RD

Midford Castle

PACK HORSE LA

BUMPER'S BATCH

OLD MIDFORD RD

Mill
Midford Brook

Brett Farm

Chatleigh House

7

Pack Horse Farm

Limestone Link

Slittems Wood

MIDFORD LA

Cleeve Rocks

OLD TK
STOKE MEAD

WOODS HILL

A36

61

Upper Midford

Cleeve Farm

UPLANDS

MIDDLE STOKE

WARMINSTER RD

PH

Midford

Hayes Wood

Limpley Stoke

6

Cam Brooke

Wr Twr

THE MALTINGS

MIDFORD HILL

BA2

Clearbrook Farm

Piepards Farm

5

Lower Twinhoe Farm

Hill Farm

Pipehouse

ASHES LA

60

PIPEHOUSE LA

Rainbow Wood

Hog Wood

Homewood

WARMINSTER RD

4

Wellow Brook

Poorfield Wood

Hang Wood

ABBEY LA

A36

3

Middle Twinhoe

Twinhoeford Wood

Abbey Farm

Hinton Priory

59

Hankley Wood

Pennyplatt Wood

Broadfield Farm

BRANCH RD

2

THE GLEBE

Crewcroft Barn

Orchards Cleaves

Tytherley Farm

WELLOW LA

HINTON HILL

Norton Brook

HINTON VILLAS
THE BATCH
PO
TUGGY'S LA
Lower Barn

Innocks Lodge

HIGH ST
PH
THE BRAMBLES
B3110

GREEN LA

Hinton House

THE GREEN

Hinton Charterhouse

1

75   A   B   76   C   D   77   E   F

58

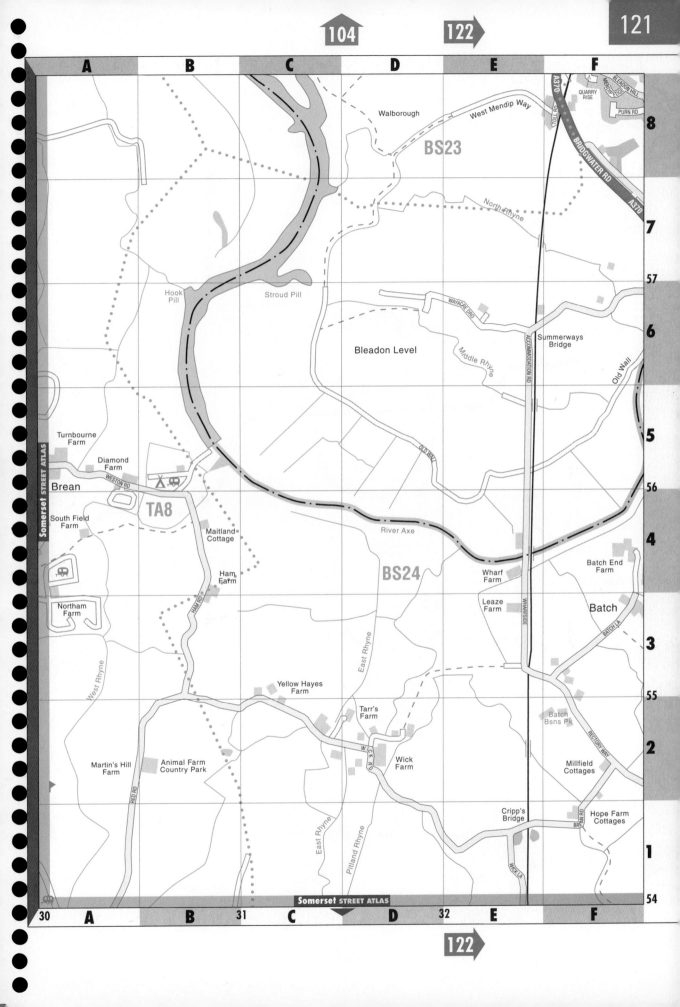

A | B | C | D | E | F

8

Walborough
West Mendip Way
BS23
North Rhyne

BLEADON HILL
MENDIP EDGE
QUARRY RISE
PURN RD
A370
BRIDGWATER RD
A370
TOLL RD

7

57

Hook Pill
Stroud Pill
WAYACRE DRO
Summerways Bridge
Old Wall

6

Bleadon Level
Middle Rhyne
ACCOMMODATION RD

OLD WAY

5

Turnbourne Farm
Diamond Farm
WESTON RD
Brean
TA8
South Field Farm
River Axe
56

Maitland Cottage
BS24
Wharf Farm
Batch End Farm

4

Ham Farm
HAM RD
Leaze Farm
Batch
WHARFSIDE

Northam Farm
BATCH LA

3

West Rhyne
East Rhyne
55

Yellow Hayes Farm
Batch Bsns Pk
RECTORY WAY

Tarr's Farm
RED RD

Martin's Hill Farm
Animal Farm Country Park
WICK RD
Wick Farm
Millfield Cottages

2

Cripp's Bridge
Hope Farm Cottages
BRN RD

East Rhyne
Pitland Rhyne
WICK LA

1

54

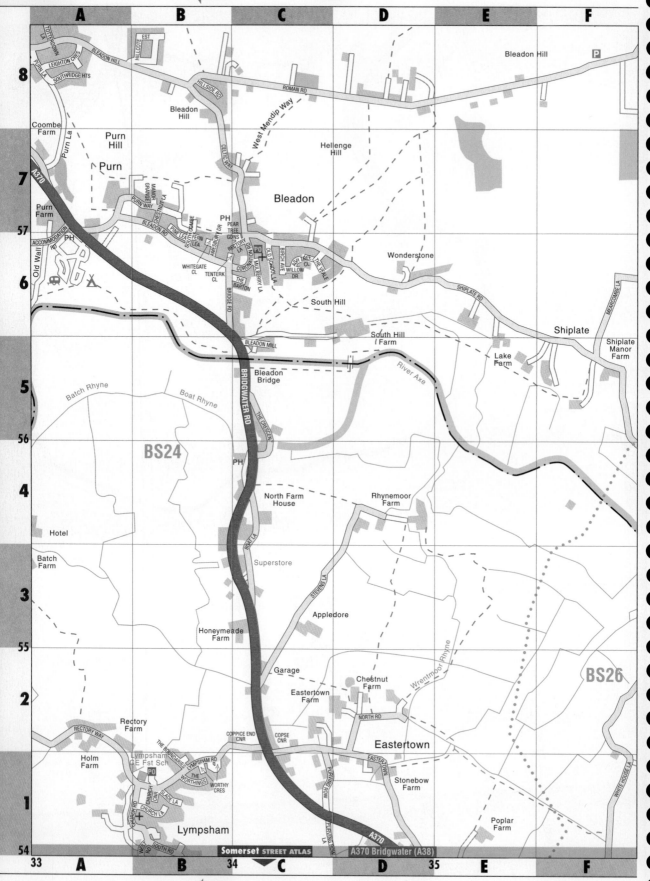

121
105

A   B   C   D   E   F

8

Bleadon Hill
P

BLEADON HILL
HILLCOTE EST
HILLSIDE RD
ROMAN RD

TOTTEROWN LA
LEIGHTON CRES
PURN LA
BLEADON HILL
SOUTHRIDGE HTS

Bleadon Hill

7

Coombe Farm
Purn Hill
Purn
A370
Purn La
West Mendip Way
CELTIC WAY
Hellenge Hill
Bleadon

57

Purn Farm
PH
ACCOMMODATION RD
Old Wall
PH
MANOR GRANGE LA
PURN WAY
CHESTNUT LA
BLEADON RD
PINE LEA
COOMBE
FERN LEA
AMESBURY DR
RECTORY LA
PEAR TREE GDNS
PH
PO
OLD SCHOOL LA
OLD MILL
MULBERRY LA
BIRCH AVE
ASH TREE CL
WILLOW DR
THE TITHE
Wonderstone
SHIPLATE RD
MEADCOMBE LA

6

WHITEGATE CL
TENTERK CL
THE BARTON
CORUM
BRIDGE RD
South Hill
South Hill Farm
Shiplate
Shiplate Manor Farm

BLEADON MILL
BRIDGWATER RD
Bleadon Bridge
River Axe
Lake Farm

5

Batch Rhyne
Boat Rhyne
THE CRESCENT
BS24

56

PH
4

North Farm House
Rhynemoor Farm

Hotel
BOAT LA

Batch Farm
Superstore

3

STEVENS LA
Appledore

55

Honeymeade Farm
Wrentmoor Rhyne
BS26

Garage

2

Rectory Way
Rectory Farm
COPPICE END CNR
COPSE CNR
Eastertown Farm
Chestnut Farm
NORTH RD
Eastertown
Stonebow Farm
EASTERTOWN

THE BOUNDARIES
Holm Farm
Lympsham CE Fst Sch
PO
LYMPSHAM RD
THE WORTHINGS
WORTHY CRES
PURVING ROW
WHITE HOUSE LA

1

CHURCH CNR
SLADE LA
Lympsham
CHURCH RD
WEST RD
SOUTH RD
A370
PURVING ROW LA
A370 Bridgwater (A38)
Poplar Farm

54

33   A   B   34   C   D   35   E   F

121

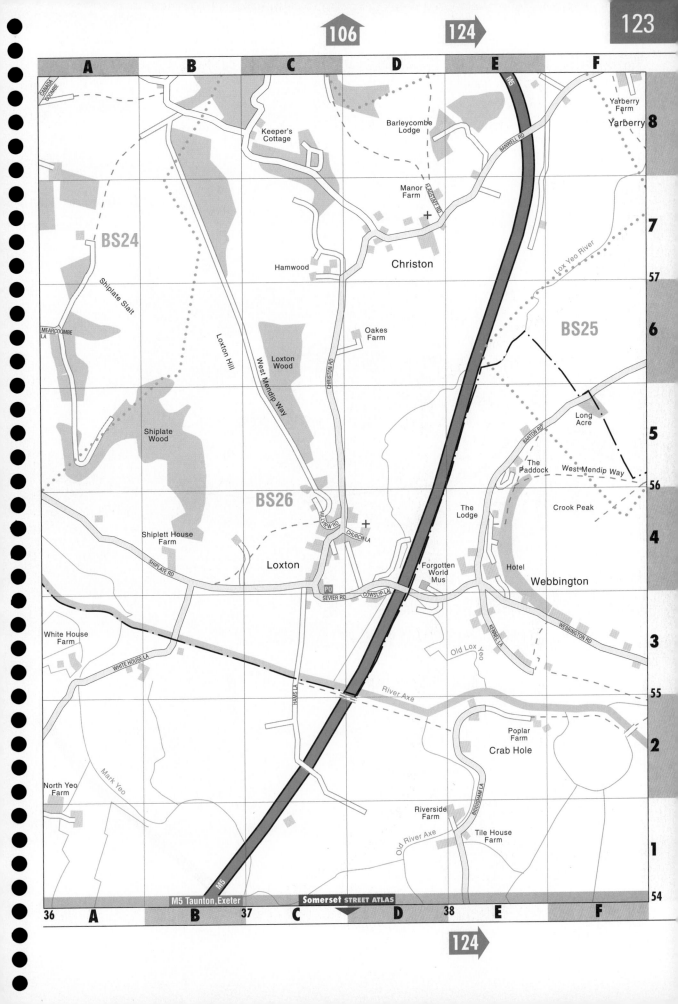

A B C D E F

8 7 57 6 5 56 4 3 55 2 1 54

CANADA COOMBE

BS24

Keeper's Cottage

Barleycombe Lodge

Yarberry Farm

Yarberry

Manor Farm

Christon

Shiplate Slait

Hamwood

Lox Yeo River

MEARCOOMBE LA

Loxton Hill

Oakes Farm

BS25

Loxton Wood

West Mendip Way

CHRISTON RD

Long Acre

Shiplate Wood

BARTON RD

The Paddock

West Mendip Way

Crook Peak

BS26

The Lodge

Shiplett House Farm

HILLVIEW RD

CHURCH LA

Loxton

Forgotten World Mus

Hotel

Webbington

SHIPLATE RD

PO

SEVIER RD

COWSLIP LA

KENNEL LA

WEBBINGTON RD

White House Farm

Old Lox Yeo

WHITE HOUSE LA

HANKS LA

River Axe

Poplar Farm

Crab Hole

North Yeo Farm

Mark Yeo

Riverside Farm

BIDDISHAM LA

Tile House Farm

Old River Axe

M5

36 A B 37 C D 38 E F

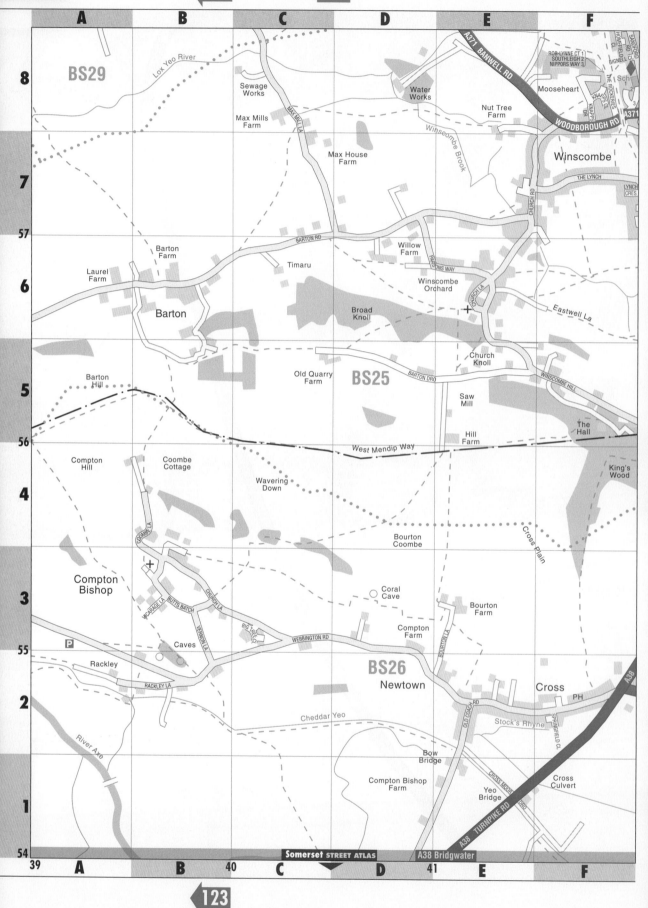

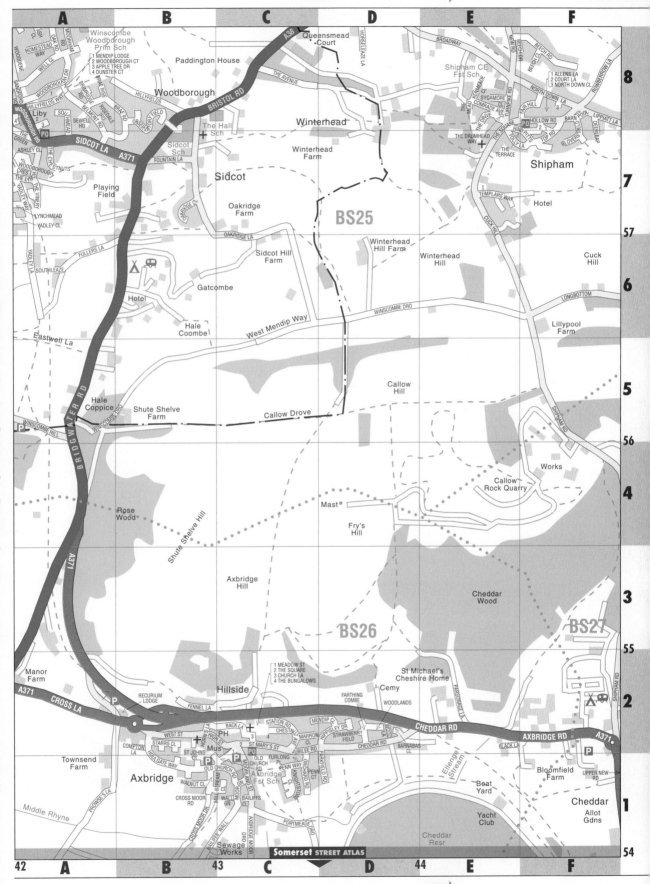

Somerset STREET ATLAS

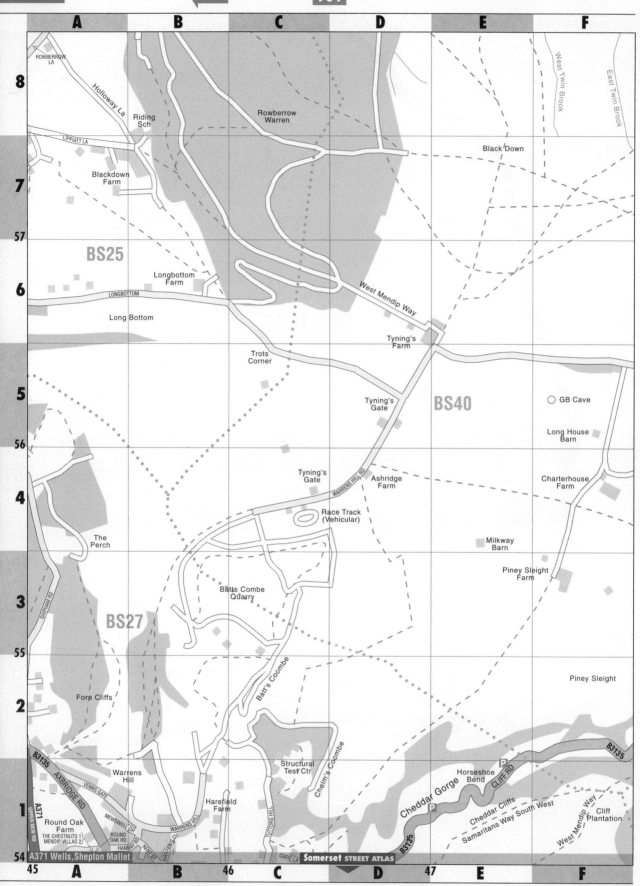

A   B   C   D   E   F

8

ROWBERROW LA

Holloway La

Riding Sch

Rowberrow Warren

West Twin Brook

East Twin Brook

Black Down

LIPPIATT LA

Blackdown Farm

7

57

BS25

Longbottom Farm

West Mendip Way

6

LONGBOTTOM

Long Bottom

Tyning's Farm

Trots Corner

Tyning's Gate

GB Cave

5

BS40

56

Long House Barn

Tyning's Gate

Ashridge Farm

Charterhouse Farm

4

WARRENS HILL RD

Race Track (Vehicular)

Milkway Barn

The Perch

Piney Sleight Farm

SHIPHAM RD

3

Batts Combe Quarry

55

BS27

Batt's Coombe

Piney Sleight

Fore Cliffs

2

Chelm's Coombe

Structural Test Ctr

B3135

Cheddar Gorge

Horseshoe Bend

CLIFF RD

B3135

AXBRIDGE RD

VENNS GATE

Warrens Hill

P

P

Cheddar Cliffs

Samaritans Way South West

West Mendip Way

Cliff Plantation

1

MEWSWELL DR

Harefield Farm

WARRENS HILL

TUTTORS HILL

A371

UPPER NEW RD

Round Oak Farm

THE CHESTNUTS 1
MENDIP VILLAS 2

ROUND OAK RD

KENT ST

HANNAY

CUFIC LA

54

A371 Wells, Shepton Mallet

Somerset STREET ATLAS

45   A   B   46   C   D   47   E   F

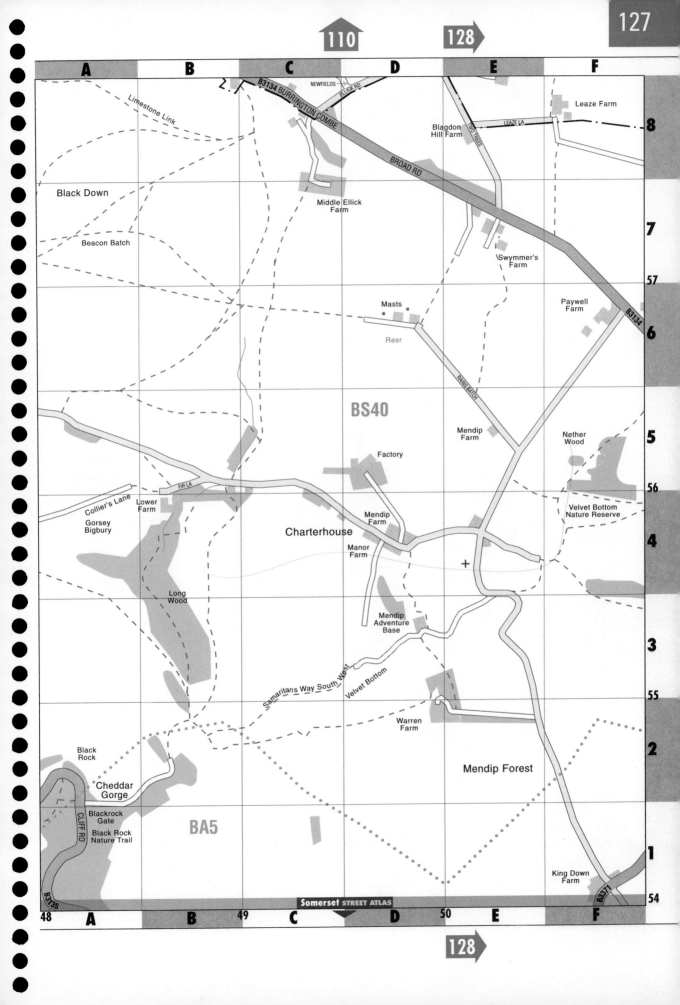

110
128

A　B　C　D　E　F

8

NEWFIELDS
ELLICK RD
B3134 BURRINGTON COMBE
Leaze Farm
Blagdon
Hill Farm
LEAZE LA
BROAD RD
TWO TREES

Limestone Link

Black Down

Middle Ellick
Farm

7

Beacon Batch

Swymmer's
Farm

57

Masts

Paywell
Farm

B3134

Resr

6

RAINS BATCH

BS40

Mendip
Farm

Nether
Wood

5

Factory

56

Collier's Lane

FIR LA

Lower
Farm

Mendip
Farm

Charterhouse

Velvet Bottom
Nature Reserve

Gorsey
Bigbury

Manor
Farm

4

Long
Wood

Mendip
Adventure
Base

3

Samaritans Way South West

Velvet Bottom

55

Warren
Farm

Black
Rock

Mendip Forest

2

Cheddar
Gorge

CLIFF RD

Blackrock
Gate

Black Rock
Nature Trail

BA5

1

King Down
Farm

B3371

B3135

54

48　A　B　49　C　D　50　E　F

128

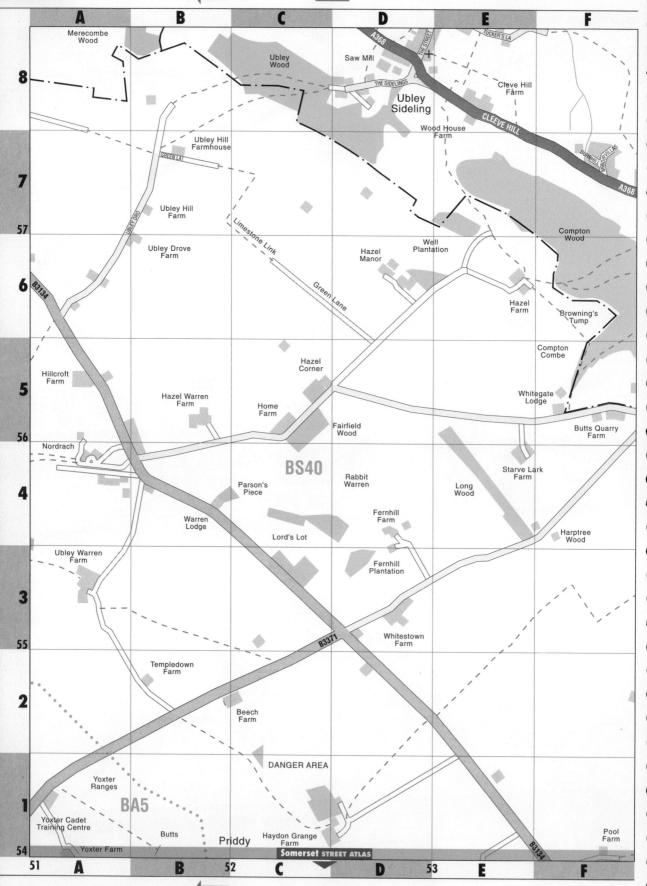

A   B   C   D   E   F

8

Merecombe Wood

Ubley Wood

Saw Mill

A368

THE STREET

TUCKER'S LA

Cleve Hill Farm

THE SIDELINGS

Ubley Sideling

Wood House Farm

CLEVE HILL

DURNHILL VILLAS

A368

7

Ubley Hill Farmhouse

GREEN LA

UBLEY DRO

Ubley Hill Farm

Limestone Link

Compton Wood

57

Ubley Drove Farm

Hazel Manor

Well Plantation

Green Lane

6

B3134

Hazel Farm

Browning's Tump

Compton Combe

Hazel Corner

5

Hillcroft Farm

Hazel Warren Farm

Home Farm

Fairfield Wood

Whitegate Lodge

56

Nordrach

BS40

Rabbit Warren

Starve Lark Farm

Butts Quarry Farm

4

Parson's Piece

Long Wood

Fernhill Farm

Harptree Wood

Warren Lodge

Lord's Lot

3

Ubley Warren Farm

Fernhill Plantation

55

B3371

Whitestown Farm

Templedown Farm

2

Beech Farm

DANGER AREA

1

Yoxter Ranges

BA5

Yoxter Cadet Training Centre

Butts

Priddy

Haydon Grange Farm

B3134

Pool Farm

54

Yoxter Farm

51   A   B   52   C   D   53   E   F

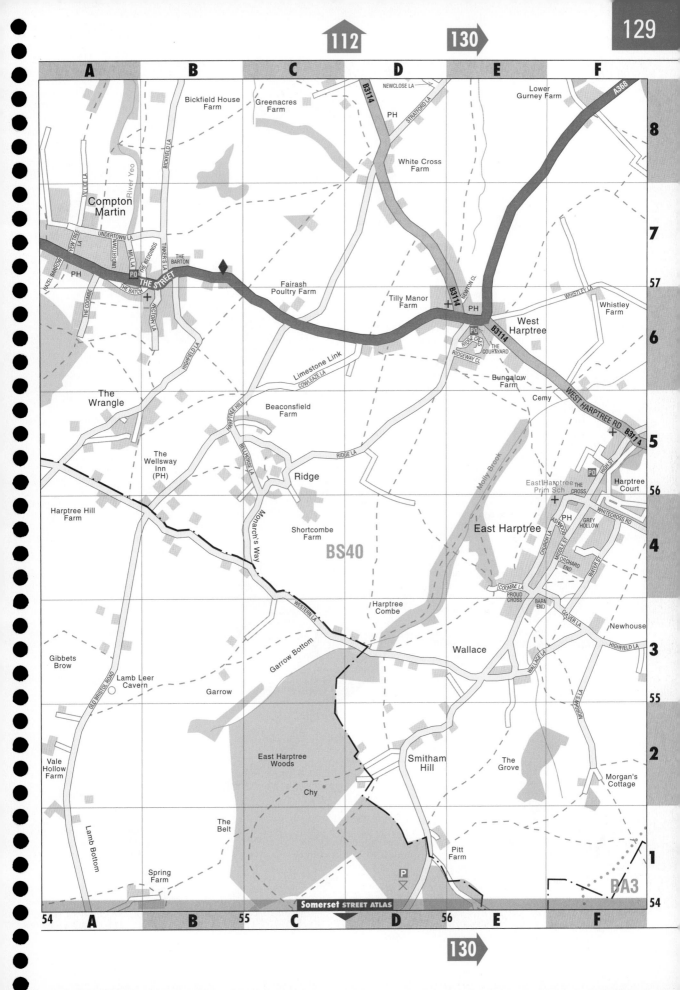

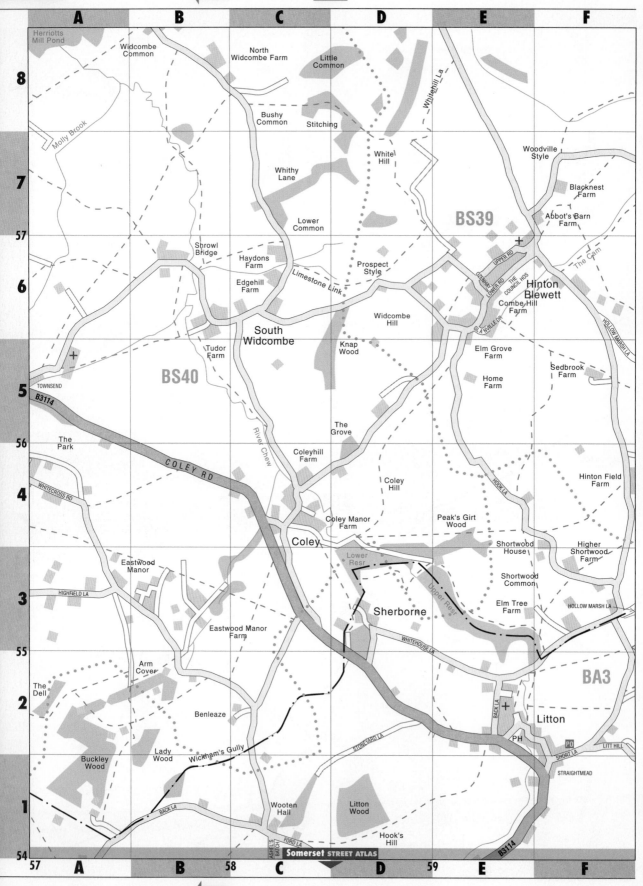

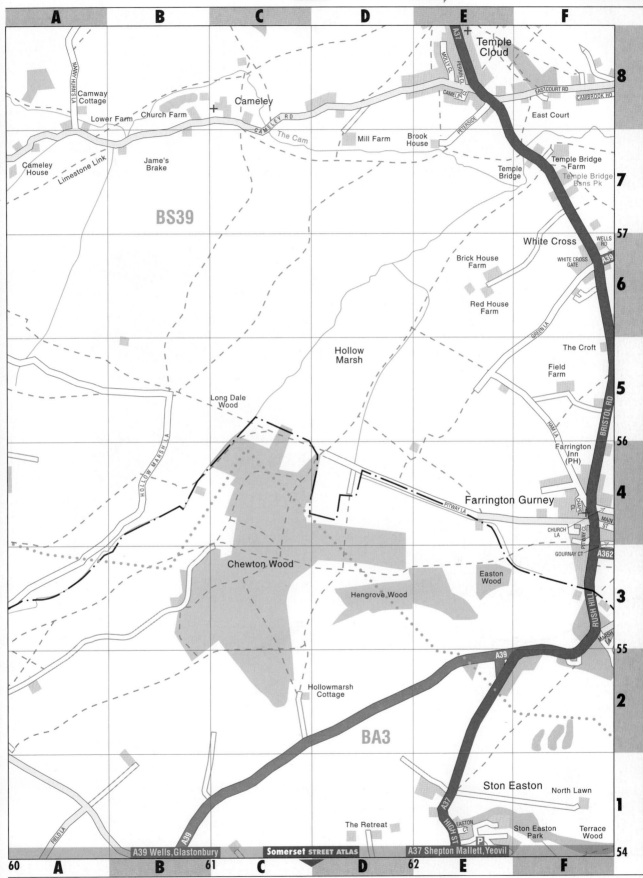

A   B   C   D   E   F

8

Temple Cloud

Camway Cottage

Cameley

East Court

EASTCOURT RD

CAMBROOK HO

Lower Farm   Church Farm

Mill Farm   Brook House

Temple Bridge Farm

7

Cameley House   Limestone Link   Jame's Brake

CAMELEY RD

The Cam

Temple Bridge

Temple Bridge Bsns Pk

BS39

White Cross   WELLS RD   57

Brick House Farm   WHITE CROSS GATE   A39   6

Red House Farm

GREEN LA

The Croft

Hollow Marsh

Field Farm   5

Long Dale Wood

HAM LA   56

Farrington Inn (PH)

BRISTOL RD

Farrington Gurney   4

PITWAY LA   CHAPEL CL

CHURCH LA   MAIN ST

Chewton Wood   Easton Wood   GOURNAY CT   A362

Hengrove Wood   RUSH HILL   3

MARSH   55

Hollowmarsh Cottage

A39

BA3   2

Ston Easton   North Lawn

1

The Retreat   A37   HIGH ST   EASTON CT   Ston Easton Park   Terrace Wood

P

54

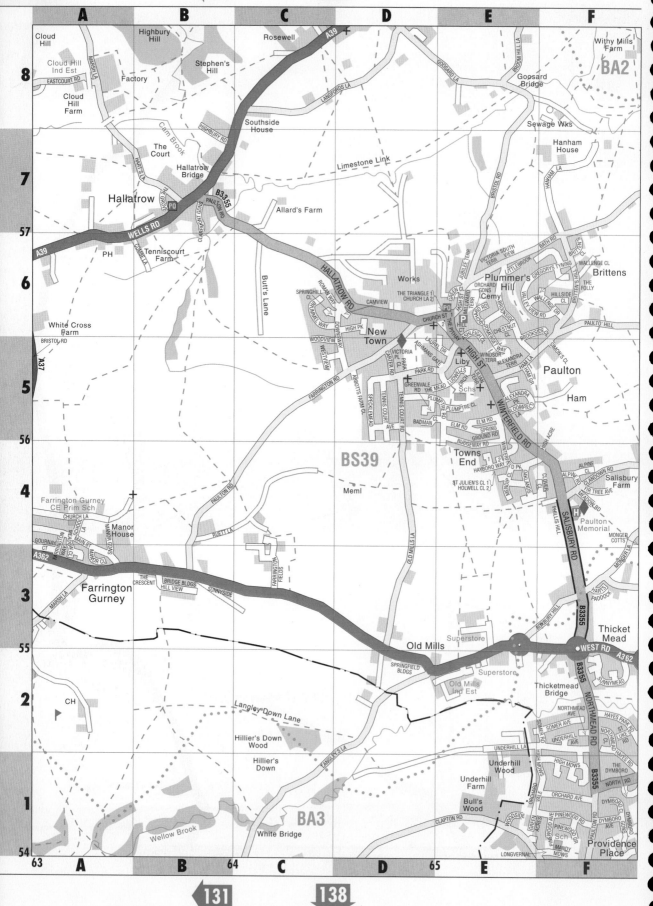

BA2

A · B · C · D · E · F

8

Cloud Hill

Cloud Hill Ind Est

EASTCOURT RD

Cloud Hill Farm

Highbury Hill

Stephen's Hill

Factory

Rosewell

A39

Withy Mills Farm

Southside House

Langfords La

GOOSARD LA

Goosard Bridge

BROOM HILL LA

Sewage Wks

Hanham House

HANHAM LA

BRISTOL RD

7

Cam Brook

The Court

Hallatrow Bridge

Hallatrow

HARTS LA

THE GROVE

PO

B3355

Allard's Farm

Limestone Link

Plummer's Hill

Cemy

Brittens

The Folly

57

WELLS RD

A39

PH

CORBETT LA

Tenniscourt Farm

CLAREMONT GDNS

PAULTON RD

HALLATROW RD

Works

JUBILEE TERR

VICTORIA SOUTH TERR

SOUTH VIEW

LITTLEBROOK

GREGORYS TYNING

BATH RD

WALLENGE CL

6

White Cross Farm

BRISTOL RD

Butt's Lane

SPRINGHILL CL

ROMAN WAY

TRAMMEL WAY

JOWNSWAY

HIGH PK

WOODVIEW

WESTVIEW

CAMVIEW

New Town

THE TRIANGLE

CHURCH LA

CHURCH ST

GREEN CL

HIGH ST

MILLWARD TERR

ORCHARD GDNS

VALLEY VIEW RD

PO

BROOKSIDE

CHESTNUT

BROOKSIDE

HILLSIDE

SIMON'S CL

PAULTO' HILL

A37

FARRINGTON RD

ABBOTTS FARM CL

SPECKLEMEAD

CARTER CL

VICTORIA PL

PARK CL

PARK RD

ASHMANS GATE

LAUREL DR

Victoria

Liby

THE PITHAY

P

ASHLEIGH CL

THE MEAD

WINDSOR TERR

ALEXANDRA TERR

HAM LA

SIMON'S CL

Paulton

5

GREENVALE RD

TENNIS COURT AVE

TENNIS COURT RD

LUDWELLS

ORCH LA

PLIMP RD

PLUMPTRE CL

BADMAN

ELM RD

ELM RD

SPRING GROUND RD

BLOOMPTRE

HIGH ACRE

WINTERFIELD RD

ALEXANDRA

Ham

56

Meml

BUDGEWAY RD

Towns End

HAYBORO WAY

ST JULIEN'S CL

HOLWELL CL

OAKLANDS

MENDIP CL

CLOVER

ALPINE

ALPINE

CLANDOWN RD

Salisbury Farm

FIR TREE AVE

4

Farrington Gurney CE Prim Sch

CHURCH LA

MEADOW CL

MEADOW DRIVE

MAIN ST

Manor House

PAULTON RD

RUETT LA

FARRINGTON FIELDS

OLD MILLS LA

PHILLIS HILL

SALISBURY RD

MEADOCK RD

H

Paulton Memorial

MONGER COTTS

MONGER LA

3

GOURNAY CT

MARSH LA

Farrington Gurney

THE CRESCENT

HILL VIEW

BRIDGE BLDGS

SONNYSIDE

Farrington Fields

B3355

BOXBURY HILL

HARTS PADDOCK

Thicket Mead

55

Old Mills

SPRINGFIELD BLDGS

Superstore

Superstore

Old Mills Ind Est

WEST RD

A362

B3355

SUNNYMEAD

Thicketmead Bridge

NORTHMEAD RD

2

CH

Langley Down Lane

Hillier's Down Wood

LANGLEYS LA

UNDERHILL LA

Thicketmead

NORTHMEAD AVE

SOMER AVE

UNDERHILL AVE

HIGH MDWS

HAYES PARK RD

NORTH ST

ST LUKE'S RD

HAYES RD

1

Hillier's Down

BA3

White Bridge

Underhill Wood

Underhill Farm

Bull's Wood

CLAPTON RD

HIGH MDWS

ORCHARD AVE

WOODSIDE

GREEN ACRES

PINEWOOD AVE

PINEWOOD GR

Sch

ORCHARD VALE

NORTH RD

THE DYMBORO

B3355

DYMBORO CL

DYMBORO GDNS

DYMBORO AVE

OLD DYMBORO WAY

North Rd

Providence Place

LONGVERNAL

MANDY MDWS

54

Wellow Brook

BS39

A · B · C · D · E · F

63 · 64 · 65

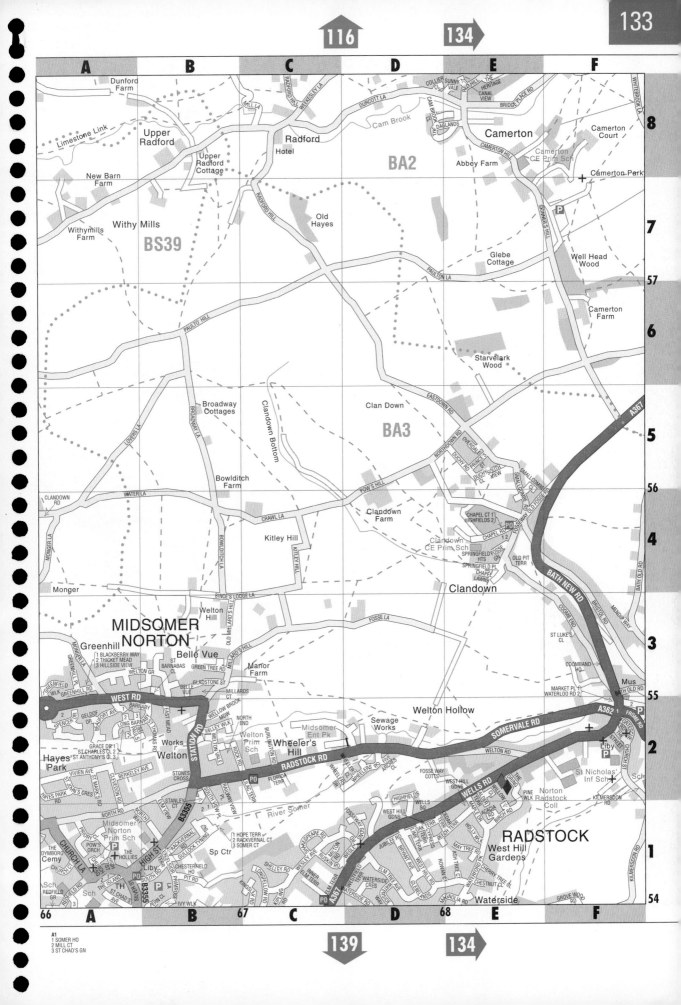

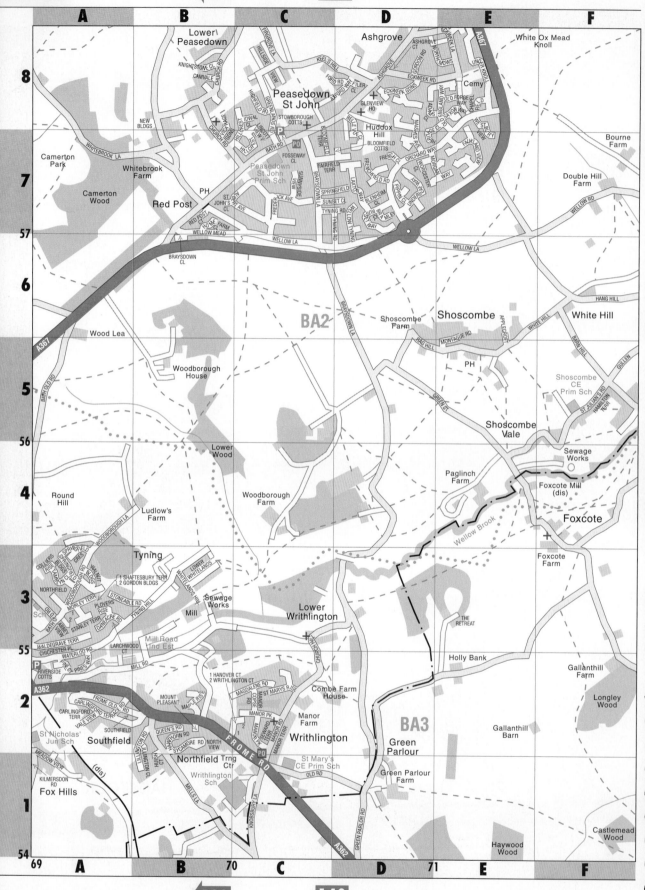

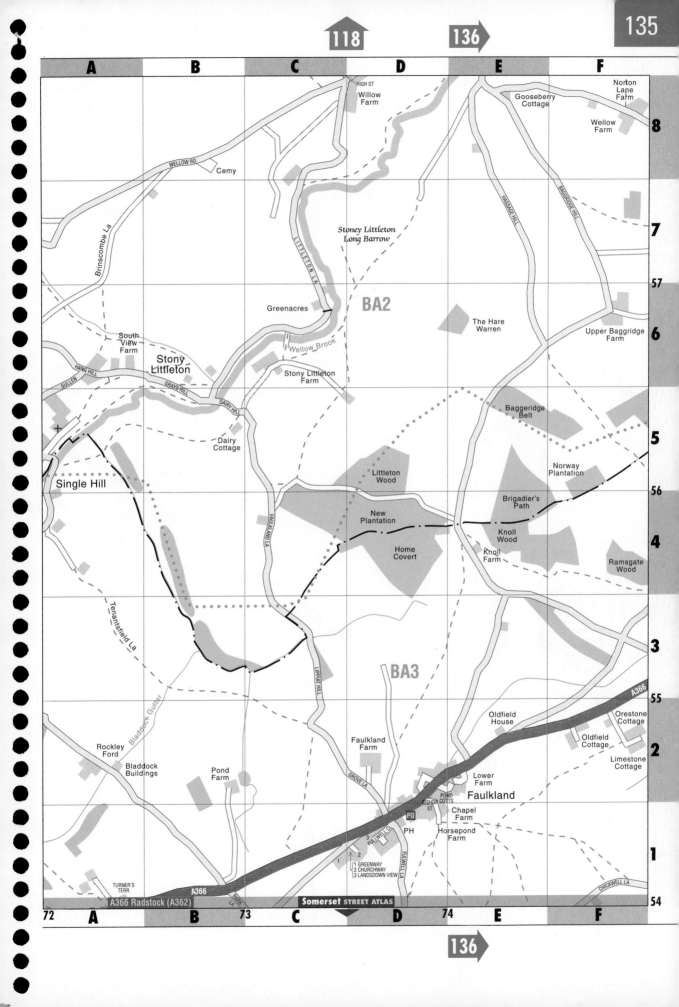

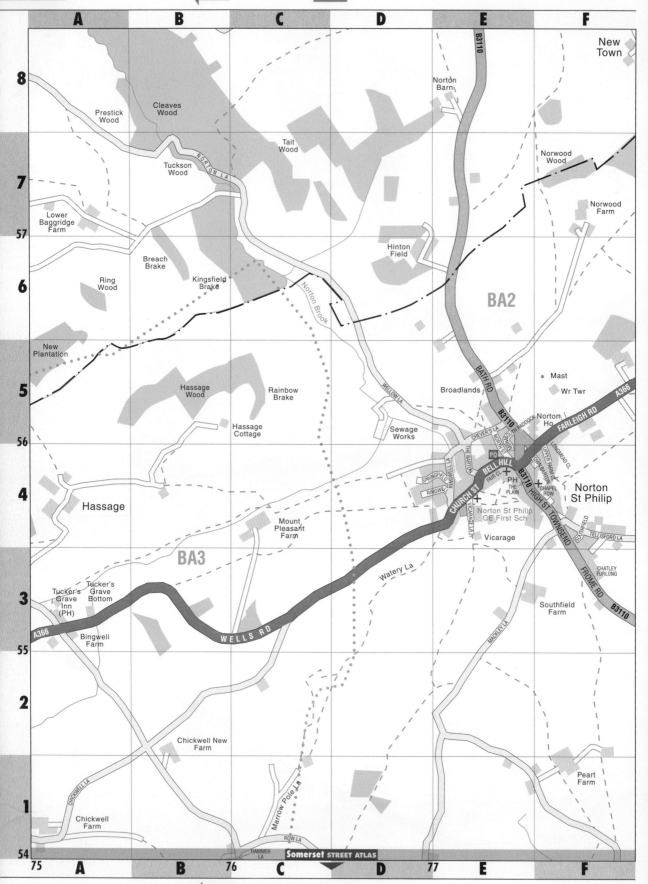

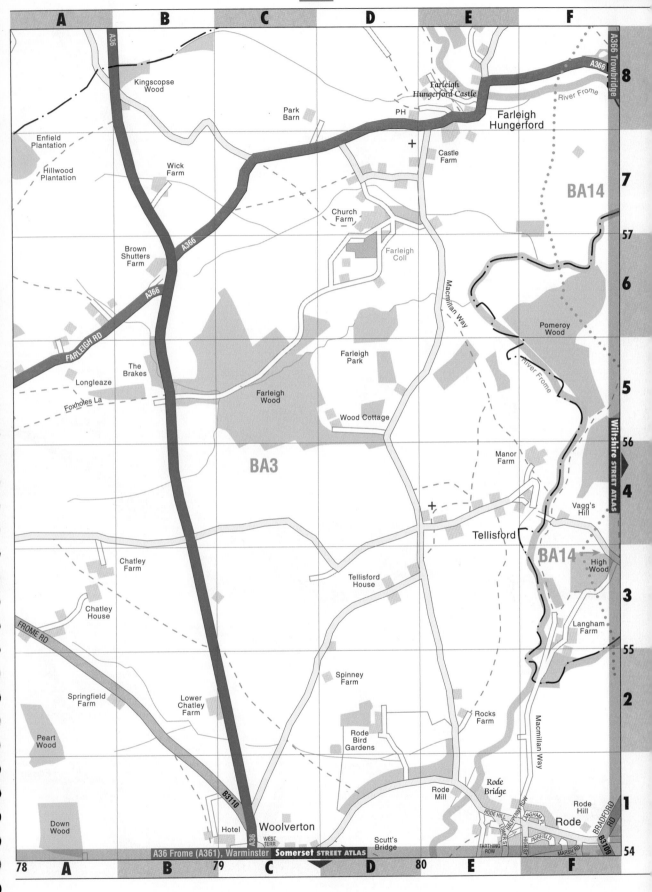

A B C D E F

8

Kingscope Wood

Park Barn

Farleigh Hungerford Castle

PH

Farleigh Hungerford

A366 Trowbridge

River Frome

BA14

Enfield Plantation

Hillwood Plantation

Wick Farm

Castle Farm

7

57

Brown Shutters Farm

Church Farm

Farleigh Coll

6

A366

Macmillan Way

Pomeroy Wood

River Frome

The Brakes

Longleaze

Foxholes La

Farleigh Wood

Farleigh Park

Wood Cottage

5

56

FARLEIGH RD

BA3

Manor Farm

Vagg's Hill

4

Chatley Farm

Tellisford House

Tellisford

BA14

High Wood

3

Chatley House

Langham Farm

55

FROME RD

Springfield Farm

Lower Chatley Farm

Spinney Farm

Rocks Farm

Macmillan Way

2

Peart Wood

Rode Bird Gardens

Rode Mill

Rode Bridge

Rode Hill

Rode

1

Down Wood

B3110

Hotel

A36

WEST TERR

Woolverton

Scutt's Bridge

RODE HILL

LOWER ST

FARTHING ROW

LANGHAM ROW

HIGH ST

FAIRFIELD

MARSH RD

Rode Hill

BRADFORD RD

B3109

54

78 A B 79 C D 80 E F

A366
Wiltshire STREET ATLAS

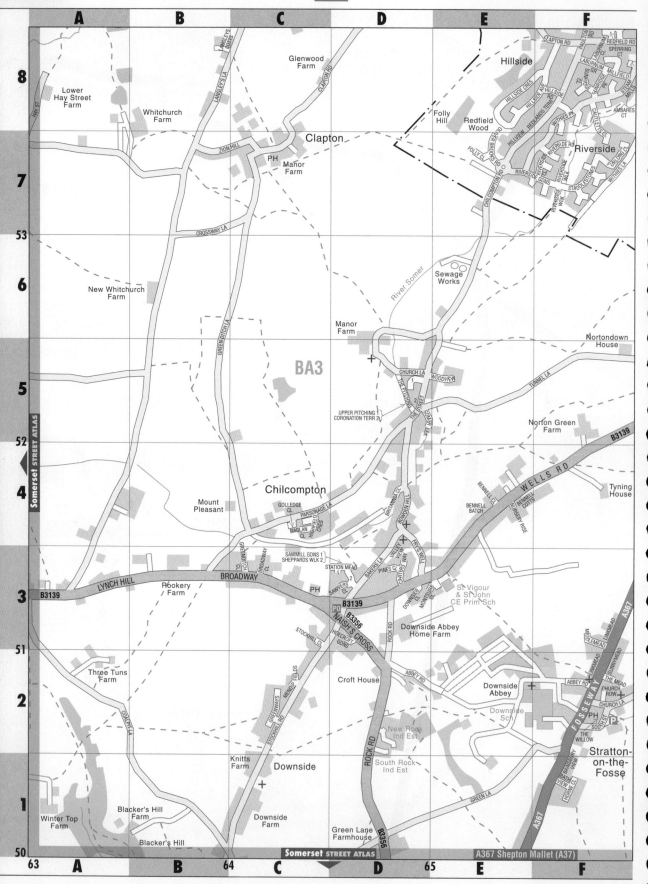

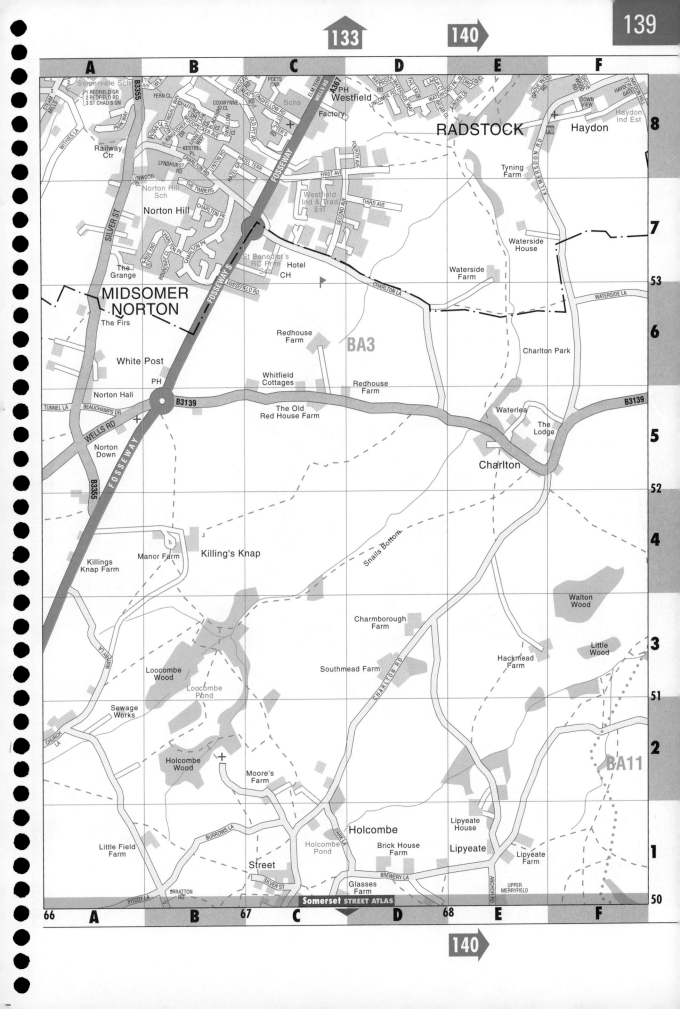

| A | B | C | D | E | F |

8

Haydon House

Huish House

HAYDON HILL

A366 Trowbridge

Haywood Wood

Peak's Wood

A362

FROME RD

TERRY HILL

Haywood Farm

A366

A366

AMMERDOWN TERR

7

Upper Lentney Farm

Upper Lentney Farm Cottage

Lentney Farm

KNOBSBURY LA

Upper Knobsbury

A366

B3139

Terry Hill Plantation

A362 Frome

A362

53

Lower Knobsbury

WATERSIDE LA

Tyning Farm

Kilmersdon CE Prim Sch

Home Farm

KNOBSBURY HILL

Gagman Coppice

Nap Wood

Ammerdown House

6

BA3

Sewage Works

AMES LA

Somerset STREET ATLAS

B3139 KILMERSDON HILL

PH
COLES GDNS

Kilmersdon

(dis)

Ammerdown Bridge

Ammerdown Park

Coldbath Plantation

5

P

Manor Farm

SILVER ST

Wedingham Copse

Hatchet Hill Coppice

The Column

52

Walton Farm

HOARE'S LA

Beatle's Wood

Babington Wood

Batch Farm

HATCHET HILL

4

South View

NEW RD

Upton's Piece

Kingsdown Wood

Lowerfield Farm

Babington Park

Cornish's Grave

Mells Down Farm

3

Babington

Works

51

BA11

Babington House

Lodge

Works

Jericho Bridge

2

Cherry Garden Farm

LUCKINGTON CROSS

DARK LA

Newbury House

CHARITY LA

White Cottage

Edney's Farm

1

Luckington Manor Farm

BA3

Newbury Farm

TINKER'S LA

POPLES LA

Newbury

Works

50

| 69 | A | B | 70 | C | D | 71 | E | F |

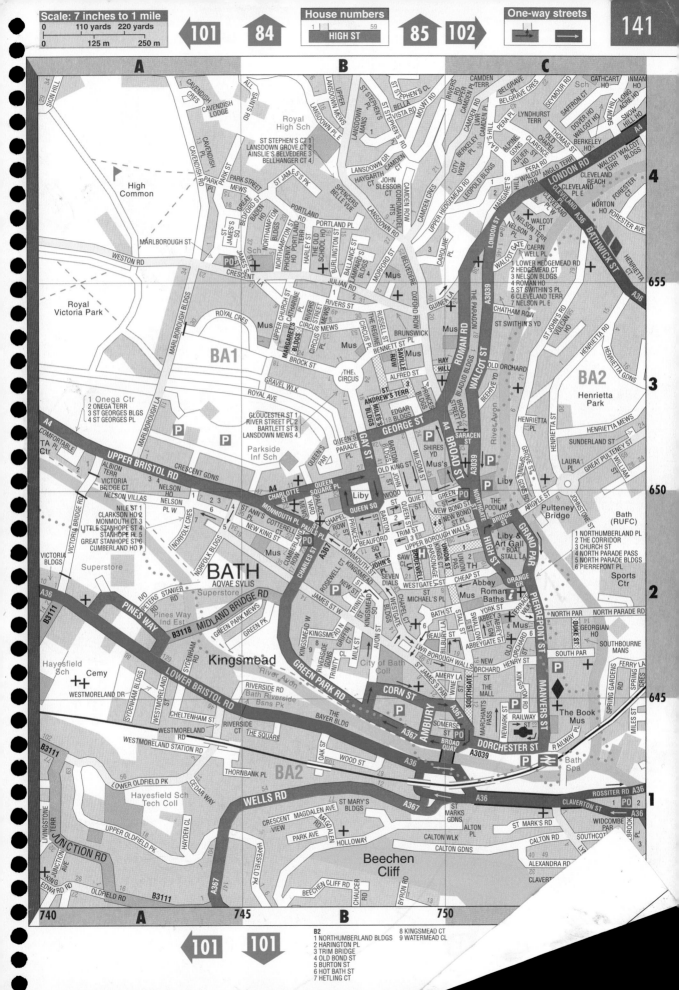

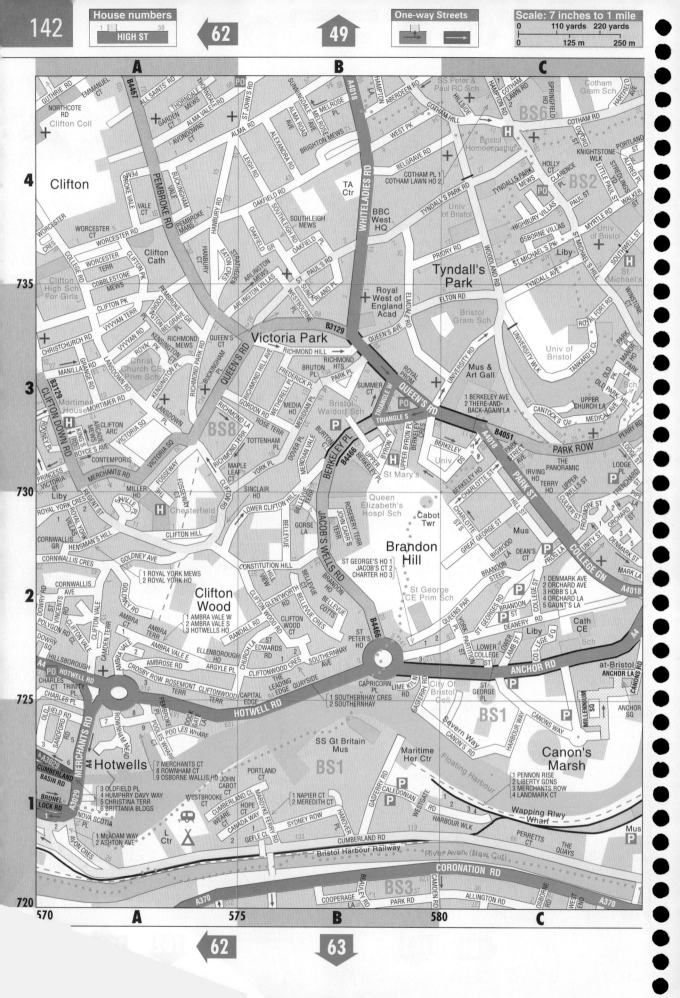

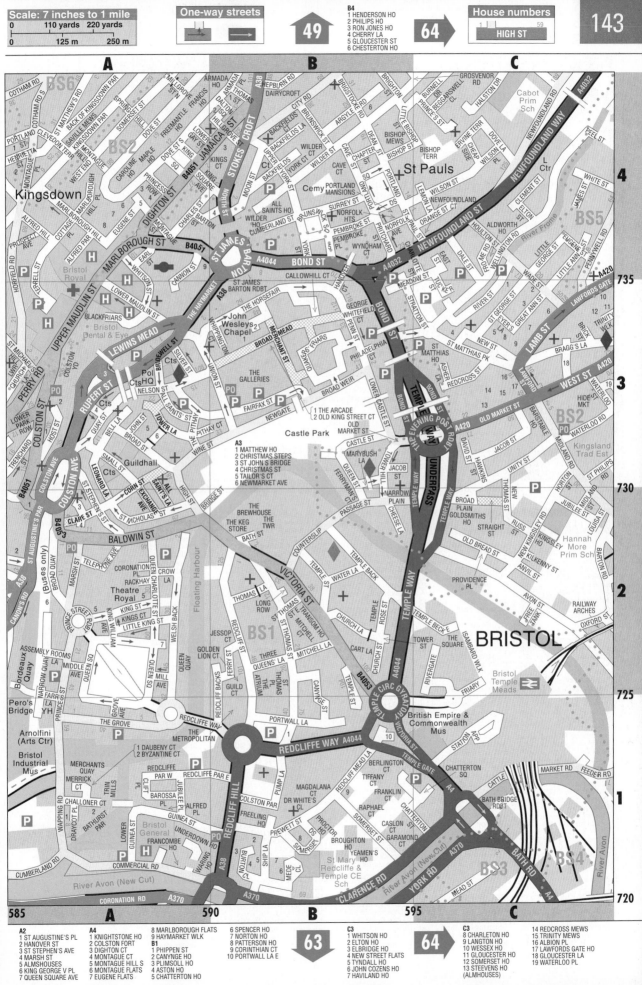

One-way streets

49

B4
1 HENDERSON HO
2 PHILIPS HO
3 RON JONES HO
4 CHERRY LA
5 GLOUCESTER ST
6 CHESTERTON HO

64

House numbers

1   59
HIGH ST

A3
1 MATTHEW HO
2 CHRISTMAS STEPS
3 ST JOHN'S BRIDGE
4 CHRISTMAS ST
5 TAILOR'S CT
6 NEWMARKET AVE

1 THE ARCADE
2 OLD KING STREET CT

1 DAUBENY CT
2 BYZANTINE CT

A2
1 ST AUGUSTINE'S PL
2 HANOVER ST
3 ST STEPHEN'S AVE
4 MARSH ST
5 ALMSHOUSES
6 KING GEORGE V PL
7 QUEEN SQUARE AVE

A4
1 KNIGHTSTONE HO
2 COLSTON FORT
3 DIGHTON CT
4 MONTAGUE CT
5 MONTAGUE HILL S
6 MONTAGUE FLATS
7 EUGENE FLATS

8 MARLBOROUGH FLATS
9 HAYMARKET WLK

B1
1 PHIPPEN ST
2 CANYNGE ST
3 PLIMSOLL HO
4 ASTON CT
5 CHATTERTON HO

6 SPENCER HO
7 NORTON HO
8 PATTERSON HO
9 CORINTHIAN CT
10 PORTWALL LA E

63

C3
1 WHITSON HO
2 ELTON HO
3 ELBRIDGE HO
4 NEW STREET FLATS
5 TYNDALL HO
6 JOHN COZENS HO
7 HAVILAND HO

64

C3
8 CHARLETON HO
9 LANGTON HO
10 WESSEX HO
11 GLOUCESTER HO
12 SOMERSET HO
13 STEEVENS HO
   (ALMSHOUSES)

14 REDCROSS MEWS
15 TRINITY MEWS
16 ALBION PL
17 LAWFORDS GATE HO
18 GLOUCESTER LA
19 WATERLOO PL

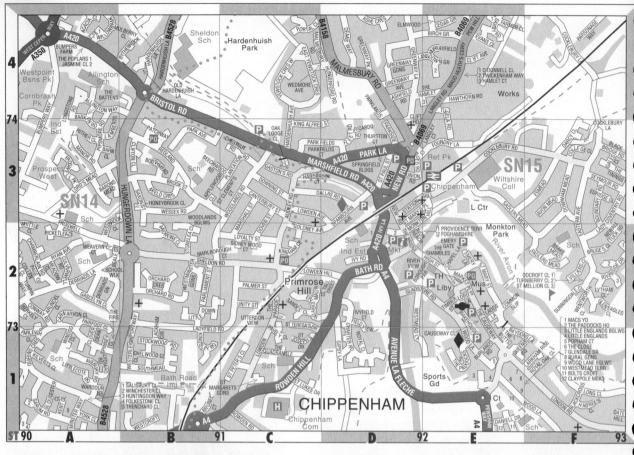

Chippenham

Acacia Cl SN14 . . . . A4
Allington Sch SN14 . . . . . A4
Allington Way SN14 . . . . A4
Andrews Cl SN14 . . . . . . B2
Applewood Cl SN14 . . . . B3
Arundel Cl SN14 . . . . . . A2
Ashe Cres SN15 . . . . D4
Ashfield Rd SN15 . . . . . . D4
Audley Cl SN14 . . . . A3
Avebury Rd SN14 . . . . . . A1
Avenue La
  Fleche SN15 . . . . D1
Avon Mead SN15 . . . . . . F3
Avon Reach SN15 . . . . . . D2
Bakehouse Cl SN15 . . . . E2
Barken Rd SN14 . . . . A4
Barn Cl SN14 . . . . A3
Barons Mead SN14 . . . . A3
Bath Rd SN15 . . . . D2
Bath Road
  Ind Est SN14 . . . . B1
Battens The SN14 . . . . . A4
Baydons La SN15 . . . . . . E1
Beale Ct SN14 . . . . A3
Beechwood Rd SN14 . . . C2
Berkely Cl SN14 . . . . A2
Birch Gr SN15 . . . . E4
Black Bridge Rd SN15 . . F3
Blackcross SN15 . . . . . . F1
Bolts Croft SN15 . . . . . . E1
Boothmead SN14 . . . . . . B3
Borough Par SN15 . . . . . F3
Boundary Rd SN15 . . . . . F3
Brake Mead SN15 . . . . . F2
Bridge The SN15 . . . . . . D2
Bristol Rd SN14,SN15 . . B4
Brook St SN14 . . . . B3
Bruges Cl SN15 . . . . E2
Brunel Ct SN14 . . . . B1
Bumpers Farm SN14 . . . A4
Bumpers Farm
  Ind Est SN14 . . . . A3
Bumpers Way SN14 . . . . A4
Burlands Rd SN15 . . . . . E1
Butts The SN15 . . . . E1
Bythebrook SN14 . . . . . . B4
Canterbury Cl SN14 . . . C3
Carnarvon Cl SN14 . . . . A2
Causeway Cl SN15 . . . . . E2
Causeway The SN15 . . . . E2
Cedar Gr SN15 . . . . E2

Chamberlain Rd SN14 . A2
Chapel La SN15 . . . . E2
Charter Prim Sch SN15 F1
Charter Rd SN15 . . . . . . D1
Chelwood Cl SN14 . . . . . B1
Chestnut Rd SN14 . . . . . C3
Chippenham Com
  Hospl SN14 . . . . C1
Claypole Mead SN15 . . . E1
Clift Ave SN15 . . . . E4
Clift Ho SN15 . . . . D3
Clifton Cl SN14 . . . . B3
Close The SN15 . . . . E1
Clover Dean SN15 . . . . . A1
Cocklebury La SN15 . . . F4
Cocklebury Rd SN15 . . . E3
College Cl SN15 . . . . F3
Collen Cl SN14 . . . . A2
Common Slip SN15 . . . . E2
Conway Rd SN14 . . . . . . A2
Cornbrash Pk SN14 . . . . A4
Culverwell Rd SN14 . . . A2
Dallas Rd SN15 . . . . D3
Daniell Dr SN15 . . . . E1
Darcy Cl SN15 . . . . F3
Deansway SN15 . . . . D4
Derriads Gn SN14 . . . . . A2
Derriads La SN14 . . . . . . A2
Dover St SN14 . . . . C2
Downham Mead SN15 . . F3
Downing St SN14 . . . . . . C3
Eastern Ave SN15 . . . . . F3
East Yewstock
  Cres SN14 . . . . C4
Edridge Cl SN15 . . . . . . F3
Elmwood SN15 . . . . E4
Emery Gate SN15 . . . . . E2
Emery La SN15 . . . . E2
Erleigh Dr SN15 . . . . C2
Esmead SN15 . . . . F3
Evans Cl SN15 . . . . E2
Fairfoot Cl SN14 . . . . . . A2
Farleigh Cl SN14 . . . . . . A1
Farmer Cl SN15 . . . . E4
Field View SN15 . . . . D2
Firs The SN14 . . . . A1
Fleet Rd SN15 . . . . D3
Foghamshire SN15 . . . . D2
Folkestone Cl SN14 . . . A1
Foundry La SN15 . . . . . . E3
Frogwell SN14 . . . . A2

Frogwell Pk SN14 . . . . . A3
Frogwell Sch SN14 . . . . A2
Gales Cl SN15 . . . . F3
Gascelyn Cl SN14 . . . . . A2
Gaston's Rd SN14 . . . . . C3
Gipsy La SN15 . . . . D1
Gladstone Rd SN15 . . . . D2
Glendale Dr SN15 . . . . . E1
Gleneagles Cl SN15 . . . F2
Goldney Ave SN14,SN15 C2
Greenway Ave SN15 . . . D4
Greenway Gdns SN15 . . D4
Greenway La SN15 . . . . D4
Greenway Pk SN15 . . . . D4
Habrel's Cl SN15 . . . . . . F1
Hamlet Ct SN15 . . . . E4
Hamlet The SN15 . . . . . . E4
Hardbrook SN14 . . . . . . C3
Hardenhuish Ave SN15 . C3
Hardenhuish La SN14 . . B4
Hathaway Ret Pk SN14 . C3
Hawthorn Rd SN15 . . . . E4
High St SN15 . . . . E2
Hither Cl SN15 . . . . A3
Honeybrook Cl SN14 . . . A2
Hungerdown La SN14 . . B3
Hungerford Rd SN15 . . . A3
Huntington Way SN14 . . A1
Ivyfield Ct SN15 . . . . . . D2
Ivy La SN15 . . . . E2
Ivy Lane Ind Est SN15 . . D2
Ivy Lane Prim
  Sch SN15 . . . . D2
Ivy Rd SN15 . . . . D2
Jasmine Cl SN14 . . . . . . A4
Kent Cl SN14 . . . . A1
Kilverts Cl SN14 . . . . . . A1
King Alfred St SN15 . . . C3
Kingham Cl SN14 . . . . . C2
Kingsley Rd SN14 . . . . . B1
Lackham Cir SN14 . . . . . B1
Ladds La SN15 . . . . E2
Lady Coventry Rd SN15 F3
Ladyfield Rd SN14 . . . . . B1
Lamberts SN15 . . . . A3
Langley Ct SN15 . . . . . . E4
Langley Rd SN15 . . . . . . E4
Lansdown Cl SN15 . . . . F1
Larkham Rise SN15 . . . F1
Littlecote Rd SN14 . . . . A1
Little Down SN15 . . . . . . E1
Little Englands
  Bglws SN15 . . . . E1

London Rd SN15 . . . . . . F1
Long Cl SN15 . . . . F1
Longstone Rd SN14 . . . A4
Lord's La SN15 . . . . A3
Lord's Mead SN14 . . . . . A3
Lowden SN15 . . . . C2
Lowden Ave SN15 . . . . . C3
Lowden Hill SN14,SN15 . C2
Loyalty St SN14 . . . . C2
Lydiard Rd SN14 . . . . . . A1
Lytham Cl SN15 . . . . E1
Macs Yd SN15 . . . . E1
Malmesbury Rd SN15 . . D4
Manor Rd SN14 . . . . A3
Market Pl SN15 . . . . E1
Marlborough Ct SN14 . . B2
Marshall St SN15 . . . . . . C2
Marshfield Rd SN15 . . . D3
Maud Heath's
  Cswy SN15 . . . . E4
Maur Cl SN15 . . . . C2
Meadow Cl SN14 . . . . . . A1
Minster Way SN14 . . . . . A1
Monkton Rd SN15 . . . . . D3
Monkton Park
  Prim Sch SN15 . . . . . F2
Mulberry Cl SN14 . . . . . A4
Murrayfield SN15 . . . . . D4
Neeld Cres SN14 . . . . . . B3
Newall Tuck Rd SN15 . . F2
New Rd SN15 . . . . D3
Oak Lodge Cl SN15 . . . . C1
Oate Hill SN15 . . . . F1
Odcroft Cl SN15 . . . . . . E4
O'Donnell Cl SN15 . . . . . D4
Old Hardenhuish
  La SN14 . . . . B4
Old Rd SN15 . . . . D3
Orchard Cres SN14 . . . . B2
Orchard Rd SN14 . . . . . B2
Paddocks Ho The SN15 . E1
Paddocks The SN15 . . . E1
Page Cl SN14 . . . . C2
Palmer St SN14 . . . . C2
Parade The SN15 . . . . . . C2
Park Ave SN14 . . . . B3
Park Fields SN15 . . . . . . D3
Parkfields Ct SN15 . . . . D3
Park La SN15 . . . . D3
Parklands SN15 . . . . D4
Parkside SN15 . . . . D3
Parliament St SN14 . . . . C2
Parsonage Way SN15 . . F4
Patchway SN14 . . . . B3
Pavely St SN15 . . . . C1

Pew Hill SN15 . . . . E4
Pewsham Way SN15 . . . E1
Picketleaze SN14 . . . . . A2
Pipsmore Rd SN14 . . . . A3
Plantation Rd SN15 . . . . C2
Popham Ct SN15 . . . . . . E1
Poplars The SN14 . . . . . A4
Portal Cl SN15 . . . . C4
Portway SN14 . . . . B1
Prospect West SN14 . . . A3
Providence Terr SN15 . . D2
Quadrangle The SN15 . . C1
Queens Cres SN14 . . . . A1
Queens Crescent
  Prim Sch SN14 . . . . . A1
Queens Sq SN15 . . . . . . E1
Redland SN14 . . . . C2
Redland Prim
  Sch SN14 . . . . B3
Ricardo Rd SN15 . . . . . . D3
Riverside Dr SN15 . . . . . F2
River View SN15 . . . . . . D2
Rowden Hill SN15 . . . . . C1
Rowden Rd SN15 . . . . . . C1
Royal Cl SN15 . . . . D1
Royal Oak Cl SN15 . . . . F1
Rural Gdns SN15 . . . . . . E1
Ryan Ave SN14 . . . . A2
Sadlers Mead SN15 . . . E3
St Clement's Ct SN14 . . C3
St Joseph's Dr SN15 . . . C1
St Lukes Dr SN15 . . . . . C1
St Margarets
  Gdns SN14 . . . . B2
St Mary's Pl SN15 . . . . . E2
St Mary's RC Prim
  Sch SN15 . . . . C1
St Mary St SN15 . . . . . . E2
St Mellion Cl SN15 . . . . F2
St Paul St SN15 . . . . E2
St Peter's CE Prim
  Sch SN14 . . . . A3
St Peter's Cl SN15 . . . . . C1
St Teresa's Dr SN15 . . . C2
Salisbury Cl SN14 . . . . . A1
Sandes Cl SN14 . . . . . . C2
Sarum Cl SN14 . . . . A1
Saxby Rd SN15 . . . . E4
Saxon St SN14 . . . . B3
School Wlk SN14 . . . . . . A2
Seymour Rd SN15 . . . . . F3
Shambles The SN15 . . . E2
Sheldon Rd SN15 . . . . . B2
Sheldon Sch SN14 . . . . B4
Sidney Wood Ct SN14 . . C2

Southmead SN14 . . . . . . B1
Spanbourn Ave SN15 . . D3
Spinney Cl SN14 . . . . . . A1
Springfield Bldgs
  SN15 . . . . D3
Station Hill SN15 . . . . . . D3
Stockwood Rd SN15 . . . B1
Stonelea Cl SN14 . . . . . B2
Sunningdale Cl SN15 . . F2
Tall Trees SN15 . . . . D2
Thurston Ct SN15 . . . . . D3
Timber St SN15 . . . . E2
Tinings The SN15 . . . . . . E3
Trenchard Cl SN14 . . . . A1
Tugela Rd SN15 . . . . E4
Turnberry Cl SN15 . . . . . C1
Turpin Way SN15 . . . . . . A2
Twickenham Way SN15 . E4
Union Rd SN15 . . . . D3
Unity St SN14 . . . . C2
Utterson View SN15 . . . C2
Villiers Cl SN15 . . . . F2
Wardour Rd SN14 . . . . . A1
Weavern Ct SN14 . . . . . . A2
Wedmore Ave SN15 . . . . C3
Wentworth Cl SN15 . . . . F2
Wessex Rd SN14 . . . . . . B3
Westbrook Cl SN14 . . . . A2
West Cepen Way SN14 . A4
Westcroft SN14 . . . . B1
Westerleigh Cl SN14 . . . B1
Westmead La SN15 . . . . D2
Westmead Terr SN15 . . . E1
Westminster Gdns
  SN14 . . . . B2
Westpoint Bsns Pk
  SN14 . . . . A4
Whittle Cl SN15 . . . . A2
Willowbank SN14 . . . . . A4
Wiltshire Coll SN15 . . . . E3
Winchester Cl SN14 . . . A1
Windsor Cl SN14 . . . . . . A1
Wood La SN15 . . . . E1
Woodlands Bglws
  SN14 . . . . B3
Woodlands Rd SN14 . . . C3
Wood Lane Bglws
  SN15 . . . . E1
Yelde Hall Mus★ SN15 . E2
Yewstock Cres W SN15 . C4
York Cl SN14 . . . . A1

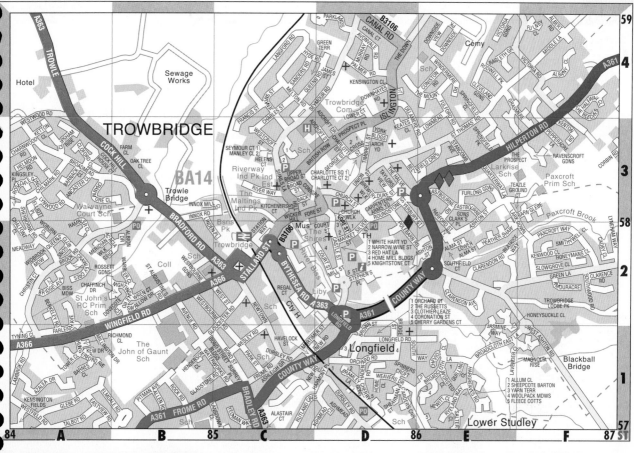

Trowbridge

Acacia Cres BA14 ..... B2
Adcroft Dr BA14 ...... D3
Adcroft St BA14 .... D3
Alastair Ct BA14 ...... C1
Albany Cl BA14 .... F4
Albion Dr BA14 .... E1
Allen Rd BA14 .... B1
Allum Cl BA14 .... E1
Alma St BA14 .... E2
Amouracre BA14 ...... F2
Ancaster Ct BA14 ..... A3
Arch Yd BA14 .... D3
Ashleigh Gr BA14 ..... C1
Ashmead BA14 .... D1
Ashmead Ct BA14 .... D1
Ashton St BA14 .... E3
Avenue Rd BA14 ...... B2
Avonvale Rd BA14 .... D4
Azalea Dr BA14 .... A1
Back St BA14 .... C3
Barnack Cl BA14 ...... A3
Barnes Cl BA14 .... A1
Barn Glebe BA14 ...... F3
Beatrice Way BA14 .... E2
Beeches The BA14 .... F4
Bellefield Cres BA14 .. E3
Berkeley Rd BA14 ..... A2
Biss Mdw BA14 .... A2
Bond St BA14 .... C1
Bond Street
  Bldgs C1
Bradford Rd BA14 ..... B2
Bradley Rd BA14 ...... C1
Bramley La BA14 ...... D1
Brewery Wlk BA14 .... D3
Bridge Ave BA14 ...... A2
Bridge St BA14 .... B2
British Row BA14 ..... D3
Broadcloth East
  La BA14 .... E1
Broadcloth La BA14 ... E1
Broadmead BA14 ..... A3
Broad St BA14 .... C3
Brook Rd BA14 .... A2
Brown St BA14 .... D1
Bryer Ash
  Bsns Pk BA14 ...... C2
Bythesea Rd BA14 .... C2
Cadby Cl BA14 .... F2
Canal Ct BA14 .... D4

Canal Rd BA14 .... D4
Carders Cnr BA14 .... D1
Carpenters Arms
  Yd BA14 .... D1
Castle St BA14 .... D2
Chaffinch Dr BA14 .... B2
Chalfont Cl BA14 ..... A2
Charles St BA14 ...... C4
Charlotte Ct BA14 .... D3
Charlotte Sq BA14 ... D3
Charlotte St BA14 .... D3
Charnwood Rd BA14 . A3
Cherry Gardens
  Ct BA14 .... D1
Cherry Gdns BA14 ... D1
Cheviot La BA14 ..... E1
Chilmark Rd BA14 .... A3
Christin Ct BA14 ..... A2
Church St BA14 ...... D3
Church Wlk BA14 .... D3
Clarence Rd BA14 .... F2
Clarendon Ave BA14 . E2
Clarendon Rd BA14 .. E2
Clarendon Sch
  The BA14 .... B1
Clark's Pl BA14 ...... E2
Cleveland Gdns BA14 . E4
Clipsham Rise BA14 .. A2
Cloford Cl BA14 ..... A3
Clothier Leaze BA14 .. D1
Cock Hill BA14 ...... A3
Cock Hill House
  Ct BA14 .... A3
Conigre BA14 .... D2
Coniston Rd BA14 ... E4
Corbin Rd BA14 ..... F3
Coronation St BA14 .. D1
County Way BA14 ... D2
Court St BA14 ...... D2
Cranmore Cl BA14 ... E1
Crawley Cres BA14 .. A2
Cross St BA14 ...... C4
Delamere Rd BA14 ... D3
Dovecote Cl BA14 ... B2
Downhayes Rd BA14 . D3
Downside Pk BA14 ... E4
Downside View BA14 . E4
Down The BA14 ..... D4
Duke St BA14 .... D1
Dursley Rd BA14 .... D1

Eastbourne Gdns BA14 E3
Eastbourne Rd BA14 . E3
Eastview Rd BA14 ... A1
Elliott Pl BA14 ...... A3
Elmdale Rd BA14 .... A1
Farleigh Ave BA14 ... A1
Farm Cl BA14 .... B3
Fleece Cotts BA14 ... E1
Fore St BA14 .... D3
Francis St BA14 ..... C4
Frome Rd BA14 ..... B1
Fulford Rd BA14 .... E4
Fulney Cl BA14 ..... F4
Furlong Gdns BA14 .. E3
George St BA14 ..... D3
Gladstone Rd BA14 .. C1
Glebe Rd BA14 ..... A1
Gloucester Rd BA14 . C2
Grasmere BA14 ..... E4
Green La BA14 ...... F2
Green Terr BA14 .... C4
Haden Rd BA14 ..... D1
Halfway Cl BA14 .... F4
Halve The BA14 ..... D3
Harford St BA14 .... E2
Harmony Pl BA14 ... D1
Havelock Cl BA14 ... C1
Heather Shaw BA14 . E2
Helens Ct BA14 ..... C3
Helmdon Rd BA14 .. A3
Henderson Cl BA14 . B1
Hewitt Cl BA14 ..... E1
Hill St BA14 .... C3
Hilperton Rd BA14 .. F3
Home Ct BA14 ..... D1
Home Mill Bldgs BA14 D1
Honeymans Cl BA14 . F2
Honeysuckle Cl BA14 . E1
Hungerford Ave BA14 . A1
Hyde Rd BA14 ..... C4
Innox Mill Cl BA14 .. B3
Innox Rd BA14 ..... B3
Islington BA14 ..... D4
James St BA14 ..... D4
Jasmine Way BA14 .. E1
Jenkins St BA14 .... C4
John of Gaunt Sch
  The BA14 .... B1
Keates Cl BA14 .... D3
Kensington Cl BA14 . C3
Kensington Fields
  BA14 .... A1
Kenton Dr BA14 .... F3
Kenwood Cl BA14 .. F2

Ketton Cl BA14 ...... A3
Kew Dr BA14 .... A1
Kingsley Pl BA14 ..... A3
Kitcheners Ct BA14 ... C3
Knightstone Ct BA14 . D2
Lambrok Rd BA14 .... A1
Langford Rd BA14 ... C4
Lansdown Cl BA14 ... B1
Lark Down BA14 ..... E4
Larkrise Sch BA14 ... E3
Lavender Cl BA14 .... E1
Linden Pl BA14 ...... B2
Longfield Rd BA14 ... D1
Longmeadow Prim Sch
  BA14 .... D1
Lower Alma St BA14 . E2
Lower Ct BA14 ...... E3
Lowmead BA14 ..... D3
Lyneham Way BA14 .. F2
Lynwood Rd BA14 ... A3
Magnolia Rise BA14 .. F1
Maltings Ind Pk
  The BA14 .... C3
Manley Cl BA14 .... C3
Margaret Stancomb
  Inf Sch BA14 ...... C3
Market St BA14 .... D2
Meadway BA14 ..... A2
Melton Rd BA14 .... C4
Meridian Wlk BA14 . D1
Middle La BA14 .... F4
Millington Dr BA14 . D2
Mill St BA14 ...... D2
Mortimer St BA14 .. C1
Mount The BA14 ... E4
Murray Rd BA14 ... D4
New Rd BA14 ..... D1
Newtown Com Prim Sch
Newtown BA14 ... C2
Newtown Com Prim
  Sch BA14 .... C1
Nightingale Rd BA14 . B1
Oak Tree Cl BA14 .. B3
Orchard Cl BA14 ... D1
Orchard Rd BA14 .. D1
Palmer Rd BA14 ... D4
Parklands BA14 .... D4
Park St BA14 ..... C1
Paxcroft Prim
  Sch BA14 .... F3
Paxcroft Way BA14 . F2
Pepperacre La BA14 . E2
Pitman Ave BA14 .. B1

Polebarn Rd BA14 ... D2
Prospect Pl BA14 .... D3
Prospect The BA14 .. E3
Quarterway La BA14 . E3
Queens Club
  Gdns BA14 .... A2
Queens Rd BA14 ... C1
Quilling Cl BA14 ... E1
Ragleth Gr BA14 ... E4
Rambler Cl BA14 ... A1
Ravenscroft Gdns BA14 F3
Red Hat La BA14 ... D2
Regal Ct BA14 ..... C2
Richmond Cl BA14 . A1
River Way BA14 ... C1
Riverway Ind Pk BA14 C3
Rock Rd BA14 ..... B1
Rodwell Pk BA14 .. E4
Rosedale Gdns BA14 . A3
Rossett Gdns BA14 . A2
Roundstone St BA14 . D3
Rutland Cres BA14 . C1
Ryeland Way BA14 . C1
St Augustine's RC Coll
  BA14 .... C2
St Augustine's Rd
  BA14 .... C2
St John's RC Prim
  Sch BA14 .... A2
St Stephen's Pl BA14 . D2
St Thomas' Rd BA14 . E3
Salter Cl BA14 .... E1
Sanders Rd BA14 .. C4
Seymour Ct BA14 .. C3
Seymour Rd BA14 . D4
Shails La BA14 .... C3
Shearman St BA14 . D1
Sheepcote Barton
  BA14 .... E1
Sherborne Rd BA14 . A2
Shires The BA14 .. D2
Silver St BA14 .... D2
Slowgrove Cl BA14 . F2
Smithywell Cl BA14 . E1
Snails Lane Ind
  Est BA14 .... C3
Southfield Ct BA14 . E2
South Way BA14 .. D1
Southwood Rd BA14 . D1
Spinners Croft BA14 . D1
Springfield Cl BA14 . E4
Springfield Pk BA14 . E3
Stallard St BA14 .. D2
Stancomb Ave BA14 . E3

Station Way BA14 ... C2
Surrey Pl BA14 ..... C1
Swallow Dr BA14 ... B2
Talbot Rd BA14 .... A1
Taylors View BA14 .. D3
Teazle Ground Ct BA14 E3
Timbrell St BA14 ... D3
Tower Cl BA14 ..... A1
Trowbridge Com
  Hospl BA14 ...... D4
Trowbridge Lodge Pk
  BA14 .... F2
Trowbridge Mus★
  BA14 .... C2
Trowbridge Parochial CE
  Jun Sch BA14 .... E4
Trowbridge Sta BA14 . C2
Trowle BA14 .... A4
Tyning Cl BA14 .... A1
Union St BA14 .... D3
Upper Broad St BA14 . C3
Victoria Gdns BA14 . E4
Victoria Rd BA14 .. F4
Walwayne Court Sch
  BA14 .... B3
Warbler Cl BA14 ... B2
Waterworks Rd BA14 . C1
Weavers Dr BA14 .. D1
Wesley Rd BA14 ... E1
West Ashton Rd BA14 . F1
Westbourne Gdns
  BA14 .... B2
Westbourne Rd BA14 . C2
Westcroft St BA14 . C3
Westfield Rd BA14 . A1
West St BA14 ..... C2
Westwood Rd BA14 . A4
White Hart Yd BA14 . D2
Wicker Hill BA14 .. D3
Widbrook Mdw BA14 . A2
Windermere Rd BA14 . E4
Wingfield Rd BA14 . B2
Woburn Cl BA14 .. A3
Woolpack Mdws BA14 . E1
Worsted Cl BA14 .. E1
Wren Ct BA14 .... B2
Yarn Terr BA14 ... E1
Yeoman Way BA14 . C1
Yerbury St BA14 .. D3
York Bldgs BA14 .. D3

Index

Church Rd ⑥ Beckenham BR2..........**53** C6

Place name	Location number	Locality, town or village	Postcode district	Page and grid square
May be abbreviated on the map	Present when a number indicates the place's position in a crowded area of mapping	Shown when more than one place has the same name	District for the indexed place	Page number and grid reference for the standard mapping

Public and commercial buildings are highlighted in magenta   **Places of interest** are highlighted in blue with a star★

Abbreviations used in the index

Acad	Academy	Comm	Common	Gd	Ground	L	Leisure	Prom	Prom
App	Approach	Cott	Cottage	Gdn	Garden	La	Lane	Rd	Road
Arc	Arcade	Cres	Crescent	Gn	Green	Liby	Library	Recn	Recreation
Ave	Avenue	Cswy	Causeway	Gr	Grove	Mdw	Meadow	Ret	Retail
Bglw	Bungalow	Ct	Court	H	Hall	Meml	Memorial	Sh	Shopping
Bldg	Building	Ctr	Centre	Ho	House	Mkt	Market	Sq	Square
Bsns, Bus	Business	Ctry	Country	Hospl	Hospital	Mus	Museum	St	Street
Bvd	Boulevard	Cty	County	HQ	Headquarters	Orch	Orchard	Sta	Station
Cath	Cathedral	Dr	Drive	Hts	Heights	Pal	Palace	Terr	Terrace
Cir	Circus	Dro	Drove	Ind	Industrial	Par	Parade	TH	Town Hall
Cl	Close	Ed	Education	Inst	Institute	Pas	Passage	Univ	University
Cnr	Corner	Emb	Embankment	Int	International	Pk	Park	Wk, Wlk	Walk
Coll	College	Est	Estate	Intc	Interchange	Pl	Place	Wr	Water
Com	Community	Ex	Exhibition	Junc	Junction	Prec	Precinct	Yd	Yard

Index of localities, towns and villages

Abbots Leigh 62 A8
Acton Turville 42 F6
Almondsbury 24 A5
Alveston 15 B4
Aust 13 A6
Avonmouth 33 D2
Axbridge 125 B1
Backwell 76 B6
Badminton 30 F2
Banwell 107 B3
Barrow Gurney 77 E5
Bath 101 E8
Bath 141 B2
Bathampton 85 F1
Batheaston 85 F4
Bathford 86 C1
Bevington 2 F6
Bishop Sutton 113 D3
Bitton 82 E8
Blagdon 110 E2
Bleadon 122 C7
Bradley Stoke 36 E8
Brean 121 A4
Bristol 143 C2
Bristol 63 F2
Brockley 75 C2
Burrington 109 F3
Burton 43 B3
Camerton 133 E8
Charfield 11 B4
Charlcombe 84 E3
Cheddar 125 F1
Chew Magna 96 C4
Chew Stoke 112 D8
Chilcompton 138 C4
Chipping Sodbury 28 D1
Churchill 108 F4
Churchill Green 108 D5

Clapton In Gordano . . .45 E1
Claverham 74 F1
Cleeve 92 B8
Clevedon 57 B3
Clutton 114 E3
Coalpit Heath 38 D6
Codrington 40 C2
Cold Ashton 68 F6
Colerne 70 F6
Compton Bishop 124 A3
Compton Dando 98 D6
Compton Martin 129 A7
Congresbury 91 E4
Corston 100 B7
Cromhall 10 A1
Doynton 54 A1
Dundry 78 D2
Dunkerton 117 E4
Dyrham 54 D4
Easter Compton 23 E2
East Harptree 129 E4
East Hewish 90 B6
Easton-in-Gordano 47 A4
Elberton 14 A6
Failand 61 C3
Falfield 9 E7
Farmborough 116 B6
Farrington Gurney 131 F4
Faulkland 135 E2
Felton 94 C8
Flax Bourton 76 F7
Frampton Cotterell 38 B8
Freshford 120 B5
Gaunt's Earthcott 25 B5
Hallen 34 C5
Hambrook 37 C2
Hawkesbury Upton 20 A3
Henbury 34 E2

Henfield 38 D3
High Littleton 115 C1
Hillesley 19 E8
Hinton 54 C6
Hinton Blewett 130 E6
Hinton Charterhouse . .119 E1
Holcombe 139 D1
Horton 29 B6
Hutton 105 E2
Iron Acton 26 D3
Kelston 83 C3
Kenn 73 F7
Keynsham 81 D2
Kilmersdon 140 B5
Kingsdown 86 F3
Kingston Seymour 73 C2
Kingswood 11 E4
Langford 109 C8
Langridge 84 E7
Leigh Woods 62 C6
Limpley Stoke 120 A4
Littleton-upon-Severn . .13 E8
Litton 130 F2
Locking 106 A4
Long Ashton 62 A1
Loxton 123 C4
Luckington 31 E4
Lympsham 122 B1
Marksbury 99 B1
Marshfield 69 E8
Midford 119 C6
Midsomer Norton 133 B3
Monkton Combe 102 F1
Monkton Farleigh 103 F7
Nailsea 59 E3
Newport 4 B7
Newton St Loe 100 D6
North End 73 F3

North Nibley 5 D4
Norton St Philip 136 F4
Olveston 14 B3
Paulton 132 F5
Peasedown St John . . .134 C8
Pensford 97 E4
Pill 47 C5
Pilning 22 D7
Pitt Court 5 F5
Portbury 46 D3
Portishead 45 B4
Priddy 128 B1
Priston 117 B5
Publow 97 F5
Pucklechurch 53 A5
Radstock 133 E1
Rangeworthy 27 A8
Redhill 93 D3
Rockhampton 8 E7
Rode 137 F1
Rowberrow 109 A1
Saltford 82 D2
Sandford 108 A3
Severn Beach 22 B6
Shipham 125 F7
Shirehampton 47 E7
Shockerwick 86 F5
Shoscombe 134 E6
Southstoke 118 E7
Stanton Drew 96 F1
Star 108 D1
Stone 3 F3
Ston Easton 131 E1
Stratton-on-the-Fosse 138 E1
Swainswick 85 C3
Temple Cloud 114 E1
Thornbury 8 E2
Tickenham 58 F4

Timsbury 116 B2
Tockington 14 C1
Tormarton 41 E2
Tortworth 10 C7
Tytherington 16 C5
Ubley 111 E1
Udley 92 C4
Upper Swainswick 85 B5
Upton Cheyney 83 B8
Wellow 118 D1
Westerleigh 39 B4
West Harptree 129 E6
West Hewish 90 A5
West Kington 56 F7
Weston 84 B1
Weston-super-Mare . .104 B8
West Town 75 F5
Westwood 120 E3
Whitchurch 80 D4
White Cross 131 F6
Wick 67 D6
Wick St Lawrence 89 B7
Wickwar 18 B5
Winford 94 F7
Winscombe 124 F7
Winsley 120 D7
Winterbourne 37 F6
Woodford 4 A4
Woolley 84 F5
Woolverton 137 C1
Wraxall 60 C3
Wrington 92 E1
Yate 27 C1
Yatton 91 C8

5

5C Bsns Ctr BS21 ......57 B1

A

Abbey Cl BS31 ....81 F6
Abbey Ct Bath BA2 ...102 B7
  Bristol BS4 ....64 F5
Abbey Gn BA1 ....141 C2
Abbey Ho **5** BS37 ....39 D7
Abbey La
  Hinton Charterhouse BA2 ..120 A4
  Thornbury BS35 ......15 D6
Abbey Mews GL12 .....11 F4
Abbey Pk BS31 ....81 F6
Abbey Rd Bristol BS9 ..48 F7
  Chilcompton BA3 ....138 D2
  Stratton-on-t-F BA3 .138 F2
Abbey Ret Pk BS34 ....36 C2
Abbey St BA1 ....141 C2
  Kingswood GL12 .....11 F5
Abbey View Bath BA2 ..102 B5
  Radstock BA3 ....134 A4
Abbey View Gdns BA2 .102 B5
Abbeydale BS36 ....37 E6
Abbeygate St BA1 ....141 C2
Abbeywood Dr BS9 ....48 C5
Abbeywood Pk BS34 ...36 C2
Abbot's Cl BS22 ......89 A3
Abbots Ave BS15 ......65 C4
Abbots Cl BS14 ....80 A3
Abbots Horn BS48 .....59 C1
Abbots Leigh Rd BS8 ..62 C7
Abbots Rd BS15 ....65 C2
Abbots Way BS9 ......49 E6
Abbotsbury Rd BS48 ..59 D1
Abbotsford Rd BS6 ....49 B1
Abbotswood Bristol BS15 ..65 D7
  Yate BS37 ....39 D7
Abbotswood Prim Sch
  BS37 ....39 D6
Abbott Rd BS35 ....22 A5
Abbotts Farm Cl BS39 ..132 D5
Aberdeen Rd BS6 .....142 B4
Abingdon Gdns BA2 ..118 D8
Abingdon Rd BS16 ....51 A3
Ableton La BS35 ......22 A5
Ableton Wlk BS9 ......48 C5
Abon Ho BS9 ....48 C4
Abraham Cl BS5 ......64 B8
Abraham Fry Ho BS15 .65 E7
Abson Rd BS16 ....53 C4
Acacia Ave Bristol BS16 ..51 D4
  Weston-S-M BS23 ...105 B8
Acacia Cl BS16 ....51 D3
Acacia Ct BS31 ....81 C4
Acacia Gr BA2 ....101 C3
Acacia Mews **3** BS16 ..51 D4
Acacia Rd Bristol BS16 ..51 D4
  Radstock BA3 ......133 E1
Accommodation Rd
  BS24 ....121 E6
Acid Rd BS11 ....33 C4
Aconite Cl BS22 ......89 B5
Acorn Gr BS13 ....78 E6
Acraman's Rd **7** BS3 ..63 C4
Acresbush Cl BS13 ...79 A5
Acton Rd BS16 ....51 A3
Adams Cl BA2 ....134 D8
Adams Ct **6** BS8 .....62 F6
Adams Hay **6** BS4 ...64 D1
Adastral Rd BS20 ....106 D4
Adderly Gate BS16 ...52 B7
Addicott Rd BS23 ...104 E6
Addiscombe Rd
  Bristol BS14 ....80 B5
  Weston-S-M BS23 ..104 E4
Addison Rd BS3 ......63 E3
Adelaide Pl
  Bristol,Fishponds BS16 ..50 F4
  12 Bristol,Upper Easton
    BS5 ....64 B8
Adelante Cl BS34 ....37 A4
Admiral Cl BS16 .....50 E7
Admiral's Wlk BS20 ..45 B5
Adryen Ct **6** BS5 ....64 C7
Aelfric Mdw BS20 ....45 F4
Agate St BS3 ....63 B3
Aiken St BS5 ....64 B6
Ainslie's Belvedere BA1 ..141 B4
Aintree Dr BS16 .....37 F1
Air Balloon Ct **1** BS5 ..65 A7
Air Balloon Hill Inf Sch
  BS5 ....65 A7
Air Balloon Hill Jun Sch
  BS5 ....65 A7
Air Balloon Rd BS5 ..65 A7
Airport Rd BS14 .....80 A8
Airport Rdbt BS24 ...105 E7
Airport View Caravan Pk
  BS24 ....105 E7
Aisecome Way BS22 ..105 C6
Akeman Way BS11 ...47 C8
Alanscourt BS30 .....66 B5
Alard Rd BS4 ....79 F7
Albany BS23 ....87 F1
Albany Gate BS34 ....36 E5
Albany Rd Bath BA2 ..101 C6
  Bristol BS6 ....49 F1
Albany St BS15 ......65 C8
Albany Way BS30 ....66 C5
Albemarle Row **10** BS8 ..62 F6
Albemarle Terr **2** BS8 ..62 F6
Albert Ave
  Peasedown St John BA2 ..134 C7

Albert Ave continued
  Weston-S-M BS23 ..104 E6
Albert Cres BS2 .....64 B5
Albert Ct BS23 ......104 E6
Albert Gr BS5 ....64 F8
Albert Gr S BS5 .....64 F8
Albert Par BS5 ......64 D8
Albert Pk BS6 ....49 F1
Albert Park Pl BS6 ..49 F1
Albert Pl Bath BA2 ..102 C1
  1 Bristol,Bedminster BS3 ..63 C3
  Bristol,Eastfield BS9 ..49 A7
  Portishead BS20 ....45 D4
Albert Quadrant BS23 ..104 E8
Albert Rd
  Bristol,Jefferies Hill BS15 ..65 D5
  Bristol, St Philip's Marsh
    BS2 ....64 A4
  Bristol,Staple Hill BS16 ..51 E4
  Clevedon BS21 ......57 C3
  Keynsham BS31 .....81 E5
  Portishead BS20 ....45 D5
  Severn Beach BS35 ..22 A6
  Weston-S-M BS23 ..104 E6
Albert St BS5 ....64 C8
Albert Terr Bath BA2 ..101 C6
  Bristol BS16 ....50 F4
Alberton Rd BS16 ....50 F6
Albion Cl BS16 ......51 F5
Albion Pl **16** BS2 ..143 C3
Albion Rd BS5 ......50 B1
Albion St **6** BS5 ...64 C8
Albion Terr Bath BA1 ..141 A3
  Bristol BS34 ....24 B1
Alburys BS40 ....92 D3
Alcove Rd BS16 .....50 B1
Alder Dr BS5 ....50 E1
Alder Terr BA3 .....133 E2
Alder Way BA2 .....118 D8
Aldercombe Rd BS9 ..48 C8
Alderdown Cl BS11 ..48 A8
Alderley Rd Bath BA2 ..101 B4
  Hillesley GL12 ......19 D1
Aldermoor Way BS30 ..65 E4
Alderney Ave BS4 ...64 F4
Alders The BS16 ....37 B1
Alderton Rd Bristol BS7 ..49 E8
  Burton SN14 ....43 D6
Aldwick Ave BS13 ...79 C3
Aldwick La BS40 ....110 C7
Aldworth Ho BS2 ...143 C4
Alec Ricketts Cl BA2 ..100 F5
Alexander Bldgs **12** BA1 ..85 B1
Alexander Hosea Prim Sch
  GL12 ....18 B5
Alexander Mews **5**
  BS23 ....104 E7
Alexander Pl BA2 ...120 C6
Alexander Way BS49 ..91 B7
Alexandra Cl BS16 ..51 D4
Alexandra Ct BS21 ..57 C4
Alexandra Gdns BS16 ..51 D4
Alexandra Par BS23 ..104 E7
Alexandra Pk
  Bristol,Fishponds BS16 ..50 F4
  Bristol,Redland BS6 ..49 C2
  Paulton BS39 ......132 E5
Alexandra Pl **1** Bath BA2 ..102 C1
  Bristol BS16 ....51 D4
Alexandra Rd Bath BA2 ..141 C1
  Bristol,Clifton BS8 ..142 B4
  Bristol,Eastfield BS9 ..49 C8
  Bristol,Highridge BS13 ..78 F7
  Bristol,Jefferies Hill BS15 ..65 D5
  Clevedon BS21 ......57 C4
  Coalpit Heath BS36 ..38 D7
Alexandra Terr BS39 ..132 E5
Alexandra Way BS35 ..8 B3
Alford Rd BS4 ......64 C2
Alfred Ct **4** BS23 ..104 E7
Alfred Hill BS2 .....143 A4
Alfred Lovell Gdns **7**
  BS30 ....66 A4
Alfred Par BS2 .....143 A4
Alfred Pl Bristol BS1 ..143 A1
  Bristol,Tyndall's Park
    BS2 ....142 C4
Alfred Rd
  Bristol,Westbury Park BS6 ..49 A4
  Bristol,Windmill Hill BS3 ..63 D3
Alfred St Bath BA1 ..141 B3
  Bristol,Moorfields BS5 ..64 D8
  Bristol,Newton BS2 ..64 A6
  Weston-S-M BS23 ..104 E8
Algars Dr BS37 .....26 E3
Algiers St BS3 ......63 D3
Alison Gdns BS48 ...76 A7
All Hallows Ct **11** BS5 ..64 B8
All Hallows Rd BS5 ..64 B8
All Saint's La BS1 ...143 A2
All Saints East Clevedon CE
  Prim Sch BS21 .....57 F4
All Saints Ho BS2 ..143 B4
All Saints La BS21 ..57 F4
All Saints Rd Bath BA1 ..141 B4
  Bristol BS8 ....142 A4
  Weston-S-M BS23 ..87 E1
All Saints' St BS1 ...143 A3
Allanmead Rd BS14 ..80 B8
Allengrove La SN14 ..31 C3
Allens La BS25 .....125 F8
Aller BS24 ....105 B2
Aller Par BS24 .....105 B2
Allerton Cres BS14 ..80 B4
Allerton Gdns BS14 ..80 B5
Allerton Rd BS14 ...80 B4

Allfoxton Rd BS7 ....50 A3
Allington Dr BS30 ...65 F4
Allington Gdns BS48 ..75 C8
Allington Rd BS3 ...142 C1
Allison Ave BS4 .....64 E4
Allison Rd BS4 .....64 E4
Alma Cl BS15 ......65 E8
Alma Ct BS8 ....49 B1
Alma Rd
  Bristol,Clifton BS8 ..142 B4
  Bristol,New Cheltenham
    BS15 ....51 E1
Alma Road Ave BS8 ..142 B4
Alma St Bristol BS8 ..49 B1
  Weston-S-M BS23 ..104 E7
Alma Vale Rd BS8 ..142 A4
Almeda Rd BS5 .....65 A6
Almond Cl BS22 ....89 A1
Almond Way BS16 ...51 F5
Almondsbury Bsns Ctr
  BS32 ....24 D3
Almondsbury CE Prim Sch
  BS32 ....24 A4
Almondsbury Intc BS32 ..24 C3
Almondsbury Rdbt BS32 ..24 B3
Almorah Rd BS3 ....63 E3
Almshouses
  5 Bristol BS1 ....143 A2
  Marshfield SN14 ....69 E8
Alpha Ctr The BS37 ..27 C3
Alpha Rd BS3 ....63 C4
Alpine Cl BS39 .....132 F4
Alpine Gdns BA1 ...141 C4
Alpine Rd Bristol BS5 ..50 C1
  Paulton BS39 ......132 F4
Alsop Rd **5** BS15 ..51 E1
Alton Pl BA2 ....141 C1
Alton Rd BS7 ....49 F5
Altringham Rd BS5 ..64 D8
Alverstoke BS14 ....79 F7
Alveston Hill BS35 ..15 A6
Alveston Rd BS32 ..14 D3
Alveston Wlk BS9 ..48 B7
Alwins Ct **3** BS30 ..65 F4
Ambares Ct BA3 ...138 B4
Amberey Rd BS23 ..104 F5
Amberlands Cl BS48 ..76 A7
Amberley Cl Bristol BS16 ..51 D7
  Bristol,Little Stoke BS34 ..36 B8
Amberley Gdns **3** BS48 ..59 D1
Amberley Rd
  Bristol,Downend BS16 ..51 D7
  Bristol,Little Stoke BS34 ..36 B8
Amberley Way GL12 ..18 B4
Amble Cl BS15 .....65 F7
Ambleside Ave BS10 ..35 B2
Ambleside Rd BA2 ..101 C2
Ambra Ct BS8 ......142 A2
Ambra Terr BS8 ....142 A2
Ambra Vale BS8 ....142 A2
Ambra Vale E BS8 ..142 A2
Ambra Vale S BS8 ..142 A2
Ambra Vale W BS8 ..142 A2
Ambrose Rd BS8 ...142 A2
Ambury BA1 ....141 B1
Amercombe Wlk BS14 ..80 E6
American Mus in Britain★
  BA2 ....103 A5
Amery La BA1 .....141 C2
Ames La BA3 ......140 B6
Amesbury Dr BS24 ..122 B6
Ammerdown Terr BA3 ..140 F7
Anchor Cl BS5 ......64 E6
Anchor La BS1 .....142 C2
Anchor Rd Bathford BA1 ..84 D1
  Bristol,Canon's Marsh
    BS1 ....142 C2
  Bristol,New Cheltenham
    BS15 ....52 A2
  Holcombe BA3 .....139 F1
Anchor Sq BS1 .....142 C2
Anchor Way BS20 ..47 D4
Ancliff Sq BA15 ....120 E4
Andereach Cl BS14 ..80 B8
Andover Rd BS4 ...63 F2
Andrew Millman Ct BS37 ..27 F1
Andruss Dr BS41 ...78 D2
Angels Gd BS4 .....64 F6
Angers Rd BS4 .....64 A4
Anglesea Pl **15** BS8 ..49 A2
Anglo Terr BA1 ....141 C4
Animal Farm Country Pk★
  TA8 ....121 B2
Annandale Ave BS22 ..88 E3
Annie Scoot Ct **1** BS16 ..51 A4
Anson Cl BS31 .....82 D2
Anson Rd Locking BS24 ..106 B5
  Weston-S-M BS22 ..88 D4
Anstey St BS5 .....50 B1
Anstey's Rd BS15 ..65 C5
Ansteys Cl BS15 ...65 B5
Anthea Rd BS5 ....50 E2
Antona Ct BS11 ...47 D7
Antona Dr BS11 ...47 D7
Antrim Rd BS9 ....49 B6
Anvil Rd BS49 .....74 F1
Anvil St BS2 ......143 C2
Apex Ct BS32 .....24 D3
Apperley Cl BS37 ..39 E8
Apple Tree Dr BS25 ..125 A8
Appleby Wlk BS4 ..79 D7
Applecroft BA2 ....134 E6
Appledore **4** BS22 ..88 A2
Appledore Cl BS14 ..80 B8
Applegate BS10 ...35 A3
Appleridge La GL13 ..3 C4
Appletree Ct BS22 ..89 B2
Appletree Mews BS22 ..89 B2

Applin Gn BS16 ....52 C6
Appsley Cl BS22 ...88 C1
Apseleys Mead BS32 ..24 C2
Apsley Rd Bath BA1 ..101 A7
  Bristol BS8 ....49 A1
Apsley St BS5 .....50 C3
Arbutus Dr BS9 ...48 C8
Arcade Mews BS8 ..142 A1
Arcade The BS1 ...143 B3
Arch Cl BS41 ......61 F1
Archer Ct Bristol BS30 ..65 F3
  Clevedon BS21 .....57 D4
Archer Wlk BS14 ..80 E6
Arches The **1** BS5 ..64 B7
Archfield Ct BS6 ..49 C1
Archfield Rd BS6 ..49 C1
Archgrove BS41 ..61 F1
Archway St BA2 ..102 B5
Ardagh Ct BS7 ....49 F7
Arden Cl Bristol BS32 ..36 E6
  Weston-S-M BS22 ..88 F3
Ardenton Wlk BS10 ..35 A3
Ardern Cl BS9 ....48 B8
Ardmore BS8 ......62 D6
Argus Ct BS3 ......63 C2
Argus Rd BS3 .....63 C2
Argyle Ave **6** Bristol BS5 ..50 C2
  Weston-S-M BS23 ..104 F4
Argyle Dr BS37 ...27 E4
Argyle Pl BS8 .....142 A2
Argyle Rd
  Bristol,Chester Park BS16 ..51 B2
  Bristol,St Pauls BS2 ..143 B4
  Clevedon BS21 .....57 D6
Argyle St **5** Bristol,Lower Easton
    BS5 ....50 C2
  6 Bristol,Southville BS3 ..63 C4
Argyle Terr BA2 ...101 C6
Arkells Ct GL12 ...18 A6
Arley Cotts **4** BS6 ..49 D1
Arley Hill BS6 .....49 D1
Arley Pk BS6 ......49 D1
Arley Terr BS5 ....50 E1
Arlingham Way BS34 ..23 F1
Arlington Mews BS8 ..142 B4
Arlington Rd Bath BA2 ..101 D5
  Bristol BS4 ....64 D5
Arlington Villas BS8 ..142 B3
Armada Ho BS2 ...143 A4
Armada Pl BS1 ....143 B4
Armada Rd BS14 ..80 A6
Armes Ct BA2 .....141 C1
Armidale Ave **2** BS6 ..49 E1
Armidale Cotts **3** BS6 ..49 E1
Armoury Sq BS5 ..64 A8
Armstrong Cl BS35 ..15 D7
Armstrong Ct BS37 ..27 C3
Armstrong Dr BS30 ..66 B5
Armstrong Way BS37 ..27 B2
Arnall Dr BS10 ....34 F1
Arncliffe BS10 ....49 C8
Arneside Rd BS10 ..35 C1
Arno's St BS4 .....64 A3
Arnold Ct BS37 ...28 B1
Arnold's Way BS49 ..74 A2
Arnolds Field Trad Est
  GL12 ....18 A5
Arnor Cl BS22 ....89 A4
Arrowfield Cl BS14 ..80 A2
Artemesia Ave BS22 ..105 E8
Arthur Skemp Cl BS5 ..64 B7
Arthur St
  7 Bristol,Moorfields BS5 ..64 C8
  Bristol,St Philip's Marsh
    BS2 ....64 A5
Arthurs Ct BS16 ..52 C6
Arthurswood Rd BS13 ..79 A4
Arundel Cl BS13 ..79 B5
Arundel Ct BS7 ...49 D3
Arundel Rd Bath BA1 ..85 A1
  Bristol BS7 ....49 D3
  Clevedon BS21 .....57 D3
Arundell Ct BS23 ..104 E8
Arundell Rd BS23 ..87 E1
Ascension Ho BA2 ..101 D4
Ascot Cl BS16 ....37 F1
Ascot Rd BS10 ....35 E2
Ash Cl
  Bristol,Hillfields BS16 ..51 C3
  Bristol,Little Stoke BS34 ..36 D7
  Weston-S-M BS22 ..89 D2
  Winscombe BS25 ..108 A1
  Yate BS37 ....27 D3
Ash Ct BS14 ....80 A6
Ash Gr Bath BA2 ..101 C4
  Bristol BS16 ....51 D3
  Clevedon BS21 .....57 E4
  Weston-S-M BS23 ..104 E2
Ash Hayes Dr BS48 ..59 E1
Ash Hayes Rd BS48 ..59 F1
Ash La BS32 ......23 D2
Ash Rd Banwell BS29 ..106 E4
  Bristol BS7 ....49 E5
Ash Ridge Rd BS32 ..24 B3
Ash Tree Cl BS24 ..122 C6
Ash Tree Ct BA3 ..133 E1
Ash Wlk BS10 ....34 F3
Ashbourne Cl **2** BS30 ..66 C6
Ashbrooke House Sch
  BS23 ....104 D6
Ashburton Rd BS10 ..35 C1
Ashbury Dr BS22 ..88 B2
Ashcombe Cl **1** BS30 ..66 C6
Ashcombe Cres BS30 ..66 C6
Ashcombe Gdns BS23 ..105 A8

Ashcombe Park Rd BS23 ..88 A1
Ashcombe Prim Sch
  BS23 ....105 A7
Ashcombe Rd BS23 ..104 F7
Ashcott BS14 ......79 F7
Ashcroft BS24 .....105 B2
Ashcroft Ave BS31 ..81 D5
Ashcroft Rd BS9 ..48 C7
Ashdene Ave BS5 ..50 D3
Ashdene Rd BS23 ..105 A8
Ashdown Ct BS9 ..48 F8
Ashdown Rd BS20 ..45 A6
Ashel's Batch BA3 ..130 C1
Asher La BS2 ......143 C3
Ashes La BA2 ......120 A4
Ashey La BS40 ....110 A5
Ashfield Pl BS6 ...49 F1
Ashfield Rd BS3 ..63 B3
Ashfield Terr **8** BS3 ..63 B3
Ashford Dr BS24 ..105 A1
Ashford Rd Bath BA2 ..101 D4
  Bristol BS34 ....36 A7
  Redhill BS40 ......93 C4
Ashford Way BS15 ..66 A7
Ashgrove
  Peasedown St John BA2 ..134 D8
  Thornbury BS35 ....8 C1
Ashgrove Ave
  Abbots Leigh BS8 ..62 B7
  Bristol BS7 ....49 F4
Ashgrove Ct BS7 ..49 F4
Ashgrove Ct BS34 ..134 D8
Ashgrove Rd
  Bristol,Ashley Down BS7 ..49 F4
  Bristol,Bedminster BS3 ..63 B3
Ashland Rd BS13 ..79 A4
Ashleigh Cl Paulton BS39 ..132 E6
  Weston-S-M BS23 ..105 A8
Ashleigh Cres BS49 ..91 B8
Ashleigh Rd
  Weston-S-M BS23 ..105 A8
  Yatton BS49 ....91 B8
Ashley BS15 ......65 F8
Ashley Ave BA1 ...101 C7
Ashley Cl Bristol BS7 ..49 F4
  Winscombe BS25 ..125 A7
Ashley Court Rd **2** BS7 ..49 F4
Ashley Ct BS7 ....49 F5
Ashley Down Jun & Inf Schs
  BS7 ....49 F5
Ashley Down Rd BS7 ..49 F4
Ashley Grove Rd
  6 Bristol BS2 ....49 F2
  1 Bristol BS2 ....50 A1
Ashley Hill BS6,BS7 ..49 F2
Ashley Ho BS34 ..23 F1
Ashley La BA15 ..120 F7
Ashley Par BS2 ..49 F2
Ashley Pk BS6 ...49 F3
Ashley Rd Bathford BA1 ..86 E3
  Bristol BS6 ....49 E1
  Clevedon BS21 .....57 B1
Ashley St BS2 ....50 A1
Ashley Terr BA1 ..101 C7
Ashley Trad Est **7** BS2 ..49 F2
Ashman Cl **5** BS5 ..64 A8
Ashman Ct **1** BS16 ..50 E3
Ashmans Ct BA1 ..101 B6
Ashmans Gate BS39 ..132 C5
Ashmans Yd BA1 ..101 B6
Ashmead BS39 ....114 E1
Ashmead Ho **12** BS5 ..64 C7
Ashmead Rd BS31 ..82 B5
Ashmead Road Ind Est
  BS31 ....82 B5
Ashmead Way **8** BS1 ..62 F5
Ashton BS16 ......37 C1
Ashton Ave BS1 ..142 A1
Ashton Cl BS21 ..57 B1
Ashton Court Est★ BS41 ..62 D4
Ashton Cres BS48 ..59 D1
Ashton Dr BS3 ...62 F2
Ashton Gate Prim Sch
  BS3 ....63 A4
Ashton Gate Rd BS3 ..63 A4
Ashton Gate Terr **3** BS3 ..63 A4
Ashton Gate Trad Est
  BS3 ....62 E3
Ashton Gate Underpass
  BS3 ....62 F4
Ashton Hill BA2 ..100 A7
Ashton Park Comp Sch
  BS3 ....62 E3
Ashton Rd
  Bristol,Ashton Gate BS3 ..62 F4
  Bristol,Bower Ashton BS3 ..62 D3
Ashton Vale Prim Sch
  BS3 ....62 F2
Ashton Vale Rd BS3 ..62 E3
Ashton Vale Trad Est
  BS3 ....62 E3
Ashton Way BS31 ..81 E6
Ashvale Cl BS48 ..60 A2
Ashville Rd BS3 ..63 A4
Ashways Ho BS39 ..114 E1
Ashwell Cl BS14 ..80 E6
Ashwicke BS14 ..80 A6
Ashwicke Rd SN14 ..70 B3
Ashwood BS40 ..129 F4
Aspen Cl SN14 ...70 F6
Aspen Park Rd BS22 ..105 E8
Aspley Cl BA1 ...101 B7
Assembly Rooms La
  BS1 ....143 A2
Aston Ho **4** BS1 ..143 B1

Astry Cl BS11 . . . . .34 A1
at-Bristol★ BS1 . . . . .142 C2
Atchley St **17** BS5 . . . . .64 B7
Atherston BS30 . . . . .66 D5
Athlone Wlk BS4 . . . . .63 E1
Atholl Cl BS22 . . . . .88 F3
Atkins Cl BS14 . . . . .80 E6
Atlantic Bsns Pk BS23 . . . .87 C1
Atlantic Rd Bristol BS11 . .47 C8
  Weston-S-M BS23 . . . . . . .87 C1
Atlantic Rd S BS23 . . . . . . .87 C1
Atlantic View Ct BS23 . . . .87 C1
Atlas Cl BS5 . . . . .51 A4
Atlas Rd BS3 . . . . .63 E3
Atlas St BS2 . . . . .64 B5
Atlay Ct BS49 . . . . .74 B1
Atrium The BS1 . . . . .143 B2
Attewell Ct BA2 . . . . .101 F4
Atwell Dr BS32 . . . . .24 B1
Atwood Dr BS11 . . . . .34 B2
Atyeo Cl BS3 . . . . .62 E1
Aubrey Ho **9** BS3 . . . . . . .63 B3
Aubrey Meads BS30 . . . . . .82 E8
Aubrey Rd BS3 . . . . .63 B3
Auburn Ave BS30 . . . . .66 B3
Auburn Rd BS6 . . . . .49 B1
Auckland Cl BS23 . . . . . . .104 F3
Audley Ave BA1 . . . . .101 D7
Audley Cl Bath BA1 . . . . .101 D7
  Rangeworthy BS37 . . . . . . .27 A8
Audley Gr BA1 . . . . .101 C7
Audley Park Rd BA1 . . . . .101 C7
Audrey Wlk BS9 . . . . .49 D7
Augusta Pl BA1 . . . . .101 D7
Augustine's Cl BS20 . . . . . .44 E4
Augustus Ho BS15 . . . . . . .65 B6
Aust La BS9 . . . . .49 A8
Aust Rd Olveston BS35 . . . .13 F5
  Pilning BS35 . . . . .12 D3
Austen Dr BS22 . . . . .89 B4
Austen Gr BS7 . . . . .50 A8
Austen Ho BS7 . . . . .50 A8
Autumn Mews BS24 . . . . .106 A8
Avalon Cl BS49 . . . . .74 A1
Avalon Ho BS48 . . . . .59 C1
Avalon La BS5 . . . . .65 B6
Avalon Rd BS5 . . . . .65 B6
Avebury Rd BS3 . . . . .62 F2
Avening Cl BS48 . . . . .76 A8
Avening Rd BS15 . . . . .65 A8
Avenue Pl BA2 . . . . .102 B1
Avenue The
  Backwell BS48 . . . . .76 A7
  Bath,Claverton Down BA2 .102 E5
  Bath,Combe Down BA2 . . .102 C1
  Bristol,Clifton BS8 . . . . . . .49 A1
  Bristol,Crew's Hole BS5 . . .64 F8
  Bristol,Harry Stoke BS16 . . .36 E1
  Bristol,Little Stoke BS34 . . .36 C6
  Bristol,Montpelier BS7 . . . .49 E3
  Bristol,Patchway BS34 . . . .24 D2
  Bristol,Sneyd Park BS9 . . . .48 E3
  Clevedon BS21 . . . . .57 E6
  Keynsham BS31 . . . . .81 B2
  Timsbury BA2 . . . . .116 B2
  Weston-S-M BS22 . . . . . . .89 C3
  Winscombe BS25 . . . . . . .125 C8
  Yate BS37 . . . . .27 D1
  Yatton BS49 . . . . .91 B8
Averay Rd BS16 . . . . .50 C4
Averill Ct BS21 . . . . .57 D4
Avon & Somerset Pol HQ
  BS20 . . . . .44 F3
Avon Bsns Pk BS16 . . . . . .51 A3
Avon Cl Bristol BS5 . . . . . .64 F6
  Keynsham BS31 . . . . .81 F6
  Weston-S-M BS23 . . . . . .104 F2
Avon Cres Bristol BS1 . . .142 A1
  Wickwar GL12 . . . . .18 B6
Avon Ct Batheaston BA1 . . .86 A4
  Bristol BS16 . . . . .51 B5
Avon Gorge Ind Est BS11 .47 C7
Avon Gorge Nature Reserve★
  BS8 . . . . .62 E7
Avon Gr BS9 . . . . .48 D2
Avon Hts BA2 . . . . .120 C6
Avon La BS31 . . . . .82 F5
Avon Meads BS2 . . . . .64 C5
Avon Mill La BS31 . . . . . . .81 F6
Avon Pk Bath BA1 . . . . . .101 A7
  Bristol BS5 . . . . .64 D7
Avon Prim Sch BS11 . . . . .47 D8
Avon Rd Bristol BS13 . . . . .79 A6
  Charfield GL12 . . . . .11 A4
  Keynsham BS31 . . . . .81 F5
  Pill BS20 . . . . .47 C5
Avon Ring Rd BS16 . . . . . .52 C4
Avon Rise SN14 . . . . .31 E4
Avon Riverside Est BS11 . .47 C7
Avon Ski Ctr★ BS25 . . . .108 C3
Avon St Bath BA1 . . . . . . .141 B2
  Bristol BS2 . . . . .143 C2
Avon Trad Est BS2 . . . . . . .64 A5
Avon Vale BS9 . . . . .48 D4
Avon Valley Bsns Pk BS4 . .64 E6
Avon Valley Ctry Pk★
  BS31 . . . . .82 D6
Avon Valley Rly BS30 . . . . .66 C3
Avon View BS15 . . . . .65 B3
Avon Way
  Bristol,Henleaze BS10 . . . . .49 D7
  Bristol,Stoke Bishop BS9 . . .48 C4
  Portishead BS20 . . . . .45 C5
  Thornbury BS35 . . . . .15 D7
Avonbank Ind Est BS11 . . .47 B7

Avonbridge Trad Est
  BS11 . . . . .47 C8
Avoncliff Halt BA15 . . . . .120 F5
Avondale Bldgs BA1 . . . . . .85 B2
Avondale Bsns Ctr **3**
  BS15 . . . . .51 C2
Avondale Ct Bath BA1 . . .101 B7
  Bristol,Oldland BS30 . . . . . .65 F3
  Bristol,Sneyd Park BS9 . . . .48 D3
Avondale Pl BA1 . . . . .85 F3
Avondale Rd BA1 . . . . . . .101 B6
Avondown Cl BS10 . . . . . . .35 D2
Avondown Ct BS3 . . . . .63 C2
Avonlea Bristol BS15 . . . . .65 C5
  Yate BS37 . . . . .39 D8
Avonlea Ct BS30 . . . . .66 A3
Avonleaze BS9 . . . . .48 B5
Avonleigh Ct **4** BS3 . . . . .63 B2
Avonleigh Rd BS3 . . . . .63 B2
Avonmouth CE Prim Sch
  BS11 . . . . .47 C8
Avonmouth Rd
  Avonmouth BS11 . . . . .33 B1
  Bristol BS11 . . . . .47 C8
Avonmouth Sta BS11 . . . . .33 B1
Avonmouth Way
  Avonmouth BS11 . . . . .33 D1
  Bristol BS10 . . . . .34 E3
Avonmouth Way W BS11 . .33 B1
Avonside Ind Est BS2 . . . . .64 C6
Avonside Rd BS2 . . . . .64 C6
Avonside Way BS4 . . . . . . .64 F6
Avonsmere Residential Pk
  BS34 . . . . .36 C3
Avonvale Rd BS5 . . . . .64 C7
Avonwood Cl BS11 . . . . . . .47 E6
Awdelett Cl BS11 . . . . .34 B1
Awkward Hill BS40 . . . . . .111 D5
Axbridge CE Fst Sch
  BS26 . . . . .125 C1
Axbridge Cl BS48 . . . . .75 E8
Axbridge Moor Dro
  BS26 . . . . .125 C1
Axbridge Mus★ BS26 . . . .125 C2
Axbridge Rd Bath BA2 . . .102 A2
  Bristol BS4 . . . . .63 F2
  Cheddar BS27 . . . . .125 F2
Axe Cl BS23 . . . . .105 A5
Axe Ct **4** BS35 . . . . .15 C8
Axford Way BA2 . . . . .134 D8
Axis The 79 D5
Aycote Cl BS22 . . . . .88 C2
Ayford La SN14 . . . . .69 F4
Aylesbury Cres BS3 . . . . . .63 B1
Aylesbury Rd BS3 . . . . .63 B1
Aylmer Cres BS14 . . . . .80 B6
Aylminton Wlk BS11 . . . . . .34 B2
Ayr St BA2 . . . . .101 D6
Azalea Rd BS22 . . . . .89 A5
Aztec Ctr The BS32 . . . . . .24 A2
Aztec W BS32 . . . . .24 A2
Azure The **7** BS6 . . . . . . .49 E1

B

Back La
  Axbridge BS26 . . . . .125 C2
  Keynsham BS31 . . . . .81 E6
  Kingston Seymour BS21 . . . .73 A5
  Litton BA3 . . . . .130 B1
  Litton BA3 . . . . .130 E2
  Marshfield SN14 . . . . .69 F8
  Pill BS20 . . . . .47 C5
  Pucklechurch BS16 . . . . . . .53 C4
  Rowberrow BS25 . . . . .109 A1
  Wickwar GL12 . . . . .18 A5
Back Of Kingsdown Par
  BS6 . . . . .143 A4
Back Rd BS3 . . . . .63 A4
Back St
  Hawkesbury Upton GL9 . . . .20 A3
  Weston-S-M BS23 . . . . . .104 E7
Back Stoke La BS9 . . . . . . .48 F6
Backfields BS2 . . . . .143 B4
Backfields Ct BS2 . . . . . . .143 B4
Backfields La BS2 . . . . . . .143 B4
Backwell Bow BS48 . . . . . .60 C1
Backwell CE Jun Sch
  BS48 . . . . .76 C5
Backwell Comm BS48 . . . . .76 B8
Backwell Hill Rd BS48 . . . .76 E5
Backwell Sch BS48 . . . . . . .76 B6
Backwell Wlk BS13 . . . . . . .78 F8
Baden Hill Rd GL12 . . . . . .16 C6
Baden Ho BA1 . . . . .141 B4
Baden Rd
  Bristol,Redfield BS5 . . . . . .64 C7
  Bristol,Warmley BS15 . . . . .66 A4
Badenham Gr BS11 . . . . . . .47 F8
Bader Cl BS37 . . . . .27 D3
Badger Cl BS30 . . . . .65 F3
Badger Rise BS20 . . . . .44 F3
Badger's La BS32 . . . . .23 C3
Badgers Cl BS32 . . . . .24 D3
Badgers Holt BS14 . . . . . . .80 C6
Badgers Rise BS10 . . . . . . .35 E4
Badgers The BS22 . . . . . . .89 C3
Badgers Way BS24 . . . . . .105 F8
Badgers Wlk BS4 . . . . .64 D2
Badgeworth BS37 . . . . .39 D6
Badman Cl BS39 . . . . .132 D5
Badminton BS16 . . . . .37 C1
Badminton Ctr The
  BS37 . . . . .27 C2
Badminton Gdns BA1 . . . .101 C8

Badminton Rd Bristol BS2 .49 F1
  Bristol,Downend BS16 . . . . .51 E7
  Chipping Sodbury BS37 . . . .41 B7
  Coalpit Heath BS16,BS36 . . .38 C6
Badminton Road Trad Est
  BS37 . . . . .27 B1
Badminton Sch BS9 . . . . . .49 A5
Badminton Wlk BS16 . . . . .51 E7
Badocks Wood Prim Sch
  BS10 . . . . .35 B1
Baggridge Hill BA2 . . . . . .135 F7
Baglyn Ave BS15 . . . . .51 F3
Bagnell Cl BS14 . . . . .80 E5
Bagnell Rd BS14 . . . . .80 E5
Bagstone Rd BS37,GL12 . . .16 F4
Bagworth Dr BS30 . . . . . . .65 F3
Bailbrook Coll BA1 . . . . . . .85 D2
Bailbrook Gr BA1 . . . . .85 C3
Bailbrook La BA1 . . . . .85 D3
Baildon Cres BS23 . . . . . .105 A4
Baildon Ct **2** BS23 . . . . .104 F4
Baildon Rd BS23 . . . . .105 A4
Bailey **?** BS22 . . . . .105 E8
Bailey's Court Prim Sch
  BS32 . . . . .36 F6
Baileys Court Rd BS32 . . . .36 F6
Baileys Ct BS32 . . . . .36 F6
Baileys Mead Rd BS16 . . . .50 C5
Bailiffs Cl BS26 . . . . .125 C1
Bailiffs' Wall BS26 . . . . . .125 B1
Bainsbury View BA3 . . . . .138 F1
Baker Cl **9** BS21 . . . . .57 B1
Baker St BS23 . . . . .104 E8
Baker's Bldgs BS40 . . . . . . .92 D2
Baker's Pk BS13 . . . . .79 B6
Bakers Ground BS34 . . . . . .37 A5
Bakers La
  Chilcompton BA3 . . . . . . .138 D3
  Langford BS40 . . . . .109 C8
Bakers Par BA2 . . . . .116 B2
Bakersfield BS30 . . . . .66 B3
Balaclava Ind Est BS16 . . . .50 F3
Balaclava Rd BS16 . . . . . . .50 F3
Baldwin St BS1 . . . . .143 A2
Balfour Rd BS3 . . . . .63 B3
Ballance St BA1 . . . . .141 B4
Ballast La BS11 . . . . .33 E2
Balls Barn La BS24 . . . . . . .90 A2
Balmain St BS4 . . . . .64 A4
Balmoral Cl BS34 . . . . .36 D4
Balmoral Ct BS16 . . . . .52 A5
Balmoral Mans **3** BS7 . . .49 F2
Balmoral Rd
  Bristol,Longwell Green
    BS30 . . . . .65 F2
  Bristol,Montpelier BS7 . . . .49 F2
  Keynsham BS31 . . . . .81 E4
Balmoral Way BS22 . . . . . .88 D2
Baltic Pl BS20 . . . . .47 D4
Bamfield BS14 . . . . .80 A6
Bampton **5** BS22 . . . . . . .88 F2
Bampton Cl
  Bristol,Emerson's Green
    BS16 . . . . .52 C6
  Bristol,Headley Park BS13 . .79 B7
Bampton Croft BS16 . . . . . .52 C6
Bampton Dr BS16 . . . . .37 D1
Banfield Cl BS11 . . . . .48 A8
Bangor Gr BS4 . . . . .64 F5
Bangrove Wlk BS11 . . . . . .47 E8
Banister Gr BS4 . . . . .79 D7
Bank Leaze Prim Sch
  BS11 . . . . .34 B2
Bank Pl BS20 . . . . .47 D4
Bank Rd
  Avonmouth BS11 . . . . .33 D7
  Bristol BS16 . . . . .65 D8
  Pilning BS35 . . . . .22 E6
Banks Cl BS21 . . . . .73 D8
Bankside BS16 . . . . .51 F4
Bankside Rd BS4 . . . . .64 D3
Banner Rd BS6 . . . . .49 E1
Bannerdown Cl BA1 . . . . . .86 B5
Bannerdown Dr BA1 . . . . . .86 A4
Bannerdown Rd BA1 . . . . . .86 C5
Bannerleigh La BS8 . . . . . .62 E6
Bannerleigh Rd BS8 . . . . . .62 E6
Bannerman Rd BS5 . . . . . . .64 B8
Bannerman Road Prim Sch
  BS5 . . . . .50 B1
Bannetts Tree Cres BS35 . .15 A5
Bantock Cl BS4 . . . . .79 D6
Bantry Rd BS4 . . . . .79 E8
Banwell Cl Bristol BS13 . . .79 A8
  Keynsham BS31 . . . . .82 A2
Banwell Cty Prim Sch
  BS29 . . . . .107 B3
Banwell Rd
  Banwell BS26,BS29 . . . . . .123 C8
  Bath BA2 . . . . .118 D8
  Bristol BS3 . . . . .63 A3
  Locking BS24 . . . . .106 B3
  Winscombe BS25, BS29 . . .107 E1
Banyard Rd BS20 . . . . .46 E5
Baptist St BS5 . . . . .50 A1
Baranwheel Ct BS5 . . . . . . .64 F6
Barberry Farm Rd BS49 . . .74 B1
Barbour Gdns BS13 . . . . . .79 D3
Barbour Rd BS13 . . . . .79 D3
Barcroft Cl BS15 . . . . .65 C8
Barker Ct **5** BS5 . . . . .64 C7
Barker Wlk BS5 . . . . .50 A1
Barkers Mead BS37 . . . . . .27 F4
Barkleys Hill BS16 . . . . . . .50 C5
Barlands Ho BS10 . . . . .34 F3
Barley Cl Bristol BS16 . . . . .52 A6
  Frampton Cotterell BS36 . . .38 C8

Barley Close Com Prim Sch
  BS16 . . . . .52 A6
Barley Croft BS9 . . . . .48 F5
Barley Cross BS22 . . . . . . .89 A5
Barley Wood Walled Gdn★
  BS40 . . . . .92 F2
Barn Cl BS16 . . . . .52 B6
Barn End
  East Harptree BS40 . . . . . .129 E3
  Marshfield SN14 . . . . .70 A8
Barn Hill BA2 . . . . .134 F5
Barn La BS39 . . . . .115 A7
Barn Owl Way BS34 . . . . . .36 F5
Barn Pool BS25 . . . . .125 F8
Barnabas Cl BS26 . . . . . . .125 D2
Barnabas St **12** BS2 . . . . .49 E1
Barnaby Cl BA3 . . . . .133 B2
Barnack Trad Est BS3 . . . . .63 C1
Barnard Wlk BS31 . . . . . . .81 D4
Barnard's Cl BS49 . . . . .91 C7
Barnes St BS5 . . . . .64 D8
Barnfield Way BA1 . . . . . . .86 B3
Barnhill Cl BS37 . . . . .28 A4
Barnhill Rd BS37 . . . . .28 B1
Barns Cl
  Barrow Gurney BS48 . . . . . .77 E4
  Nailsea BS48 . . . . .59 E2
Barns Ground BS21 . . . . . .73 E8
Barnstaple Ct BS4 . . . . .79 E8
Barnstaple Rd BS4 . . . . . . .79 E8
Barnstaple Wlk BS4 . . . . . .79 F8
Barnwood Ct BS48 . . . . . . .59 B1
Barnwood Rd BS37 . . . . . . .39 C7
Barossa Pl BS1 . . . . .143 A1
Barrack's La BS11 . . . . .47 D8
Barratt St BS5 . . . . .50 C1
Barrington Cl BS15 . . . . . . .51 F2
Barrington Ct
  11 Bristol,Knowle BS2 . . . .63 F4
  Bristol,New Cheltenham
    BS15 . . . . .51 E1
Barrow Court La BS19 . . . . .77 B5
Barrow Ct BS21 . . . . .58 F4
Barrow Hill BS30 . . . . .67 B5
Barrow Hill Cres BS11 . . . .47 C7
Barrow Hill Rd BS11 . . . . . .47 D6
Barrow Hospl BS48 . . . . . . .78 A6
Barrow La BS40,BS48 . . . . .77 F1
Barrow Rd Bath BA2 . . . . .101 C1
  Bristol BS2 . . . . .64 A7
  Hutton BS24 . . . . .105 E4
Barrow St BS48 . . . . .77 D5
Barrowmead Dr BS11 . . . . .47 F7
Barrows The BS22 . . . . . . .105 C2
Barrs Court Ave BS30 . . . . .66 A5
Barrs Court Prim Sch
  BS30 . . . . .65 F5
Barrs Court Rd BS30 . . . . . .66 A5
Barrs La GL11 . . . . .5 C4
Barry Cl Bristol BS30 . . . . .66 C1
  Weston-S-M BS24 . . . . . .105 A1
Barry Rd BS30 . . . . .66 C2
Barstable Ho BS2 . . . . . . .143 C3
Bartholomew Row BA2 . . .116 B2
Bartlett St BA1 . . . . .141 B3
Bartlett's Rd BS3 . . . . .63 C2
Bartletts Way BS24 . . . . . .106 B4
Bartley St BS3 . . . . .63 D4
Barton Bldgs BA1 . . . . . . .141 B3
Barton Cl Alveston BS35 . . .15 A5
  1 Bristol BS4 . . . . .64 F6
  Winterbourne BS36 . . . . . . .37 E5
Barton Ct BS5 . . . . .64 C6
Barton Dro BS25 . . . . .124 D5
Barton Hill Prim Sch
  BS5 . . . . .64 B6
Barton Hill Rd BS5 . . . . . . .64 B7
Barton Hill Trad Est **9**
  BS5 . . . . .64 C6
Barton Ho BS5 . . . . .64 C6
Barton Manor BS2 . . . . . . .64 A6
Barton Rd Bristol BS2 . . . .143 C2
  Winscombe BS25 . . . . . . .124 C6
Barton St Bath BA1 . . . . . .141 B2
  Bristol BS1 . . . . .143 A4
Barton The
  Bleadon BS24 . . . . .122 C6
  Bristol BS15 . . . . .65 C4
  Compton Martin BS40 . . . .129 B5
  Corston BA2 . . . . .100 A7
  Norton St Philip BA2 . . . . .136 E4
Barton Vale **6** BS2 . . . . . .64 A6
Bartonia Gr BS4 . . . . .64 F2
Barwick Ho BS11 . . . . .47 E1
Barwood Cl BS15 . . . . .65 F8
Batch Bsns Pk BS24 . . . . .121 F2
Batch La Clutton BS39 . . . .114 F3
  Lympsham BS24 . . . . .121 F3
Batch The
  Backwell BS48 . . . . .76 D1
  Batheaston BA1 . . . . .85 F3
  Blagdon BS40 . . . . .111 B8
  Burrington BS40 . . . . .110 B3
  Chew Magna BS40 . . . . . . .96 B3
  Churchill BS25 . . . . .108 F4
  Farmborough BA2 . . . . . . .116 A6
  High Littleton BS39 . . . . . .115 D1
  Hinton Charterhouse BA2 . .119 E1
  Saltford BS31 . . . . .82 D3
  Yatton BS49 . . . . .91 B7
Batches The BS3 . . . . .63 B2
Batchfield La BS16,BS37 . . .53 D8
Bates Cl BS5 . . . . .64 A8
Bath Abbey★ BA1 . . . . . .141 C2
Bath Bldgs BS6 . . . . .49 E1
Bath Bridge Rdbt BS1 . . . .143 C1
Bath Foyer The BA2 . . . . .101 A6

Bath Hill Keynsham BS31 . . .81 F5
  Wellow BA2 . . . . .118 D2
Bath New Rd BA3 . . . . . . .133 F4
Bath Old Rd BA3 . . . . .133 F4
Bath Postal Mus★ BA1 . . .141 C3
Bath Race Course★ BA1 . .84 A6
Bath Rd
  Bitton BA1,BA2,BS30 . . . . .82 F7
  Blagdon BS40 . . . . .111 B1
  Bristol BS3 . . . . .143 C1
  Bristol,Brislington BS4 . . . .64 F1
  Bristol,Hick Gates BS4,BS31 81 B8
  Bristol,Longwell Green
    BS30 . . . . .65 F3
  Bristol,North Common BS30 .66 D6
  Bristol,Totterdown BS4 . . . .64 B4
  Bristol,Upper Knowle BS4 . .64 B4
  Bristol,Willsbridge BS30 . . .66 C1
  Chipping Sodbury BS37,GL9 .41 C4
  Colerne SN14 . . . . .70 E2
  Farmborough BA2 . . . . . . .115 E5
  Kingsdown SN13 . . . . .86 F5
  Norton St Philip BA2 . . . . .136 E5
  Paulton BS39 . . . . .132 F6
  Peasedown St John BA2 . . .134 C7
  Saltford BS31 . . . . .82 D3
  Thornbury BS35 . . . . .15 B8
  Wick BS30 . . . . .67 E4
Bath Riverside Bsns Pk
  BA2 . . . . .141 B1
Bath Small Sch BA1 . . . . . .85 C2
Bath Spa Sta BA1 . . . . . . .141 C1
Bath Spa Univ Coll BA1 . . .84 C1
Bath Spa University Coll
  (Newton Park Campus)
  BA2 . . . . .100 B5
Bath St Bath BA1 . . . . . . .141 C2
  Bristol BS1 . . . . .143 B2
  Bristol,Ashton Gate BS3 . . .63 A4
  Bristol,Staple Hill BS16 . . .51 E4
Bath View BA3 . . . . .138 F1
Bathampton La BA2 . . . . . .85 E1
Bathampton Prim Sch
  BA2 . . . . .85 F2
Batheaston CE Prim Sch
  BA1 . . . . .85 F4
Bathford CE Prim Sch
  BA1 . . . . .86 C2
Bathford Hill Bathford BA1 .86 B2
  Compton Dando BS39 . . . . .98 E5
Bathford Manor BA1 . . . . . .86 B2
Bathings The **1** BS35 . . . . .15 C8
Bathurst Par BS1 . . . . .143 A1
Bathurst Rd BS22 . . . . . . .105 C8
Bathwell Rd BS4 . . . . .64 A3
Bathwick Hill BA2 . . . . . . .102 C6
Bathwick Rise BA2 . . . . . .102 B7
Bathwick St BA1,BA2 . . . .141 C4
Batley Ct BS30 . . . . .66 D4
Batstone Cl BA1 . . . . .85 B2
Batten Ct BS37 . . . . .28 C1
Batten's La BS5 . . . . .65 A6
Battenburg Rd BS5 . . . . . . .65 A7
Battens Rd BS5 . . . . .65 B7
Battersby Way BS10 . . . . . .34 E2
Battersea Rd BS5 . . . . .64 C8
Battery La BS20 . . . . .45 D7
Battery Rd BS20 . . . . .45 D6
Battle La BS40 . . . . .96 A3
Battson Rd BS14 . . . . .80 E4
Baugh Gdns BS16 . . . . .37 E1
Baxter Cl BS15 . . . . .65 F8
Bay Gdns BS5 . . . . .50 C2
Bay Rd BS21 . . . . .57 D6
Bay Tree Cl BS34 . . . . .35 F7
Bay Tree Rd Bath BA1 . . . . .85 B2
  Clevedon BS21 . . . . .57 E1
Bay Tree View BS22 . . . . . .88 D1
Bayer Bldg The BA2 . . . . .141 B1
Bayham Rd BS4 . . . . .64 A3
Bayleys Dr BS15 . . . . .65 C6
Baynham Ct **3** BS15 . . . . .65 B5
Baynton Ho **2** BS5 . . . . . .64 B7
Baynton Mdw BS16 . . . . . .52 C6
Baynton Rd BS3 . . . . .63 A4
Bayswater Ave BS6 . . . . . . .49 B3
Bayswater Rd BS7 . . . . .49 F7
Baytree Ct BS22 . . . . .88 D1
Baytree Rd BS22 . . . . .88 C1
Baytree Sch BS22 . . . . . . .105 C8
Baytree View BS22 . . . . . .105 C8
Beach Ave Clevedon BS21 . .57 C2
  Severn Beach BS35 . . . . . .22 A7
Beach Ct BS23 . . . . .104 D6
Beach End Rd BS23 . . . . . .104 C2
Beach Hill Bristol BS30 . . . .66 F3
  Portishead BS20 . . . . .45 C6
Beach La BS30 . . . . .67 C2
Beach Mews BS21 . . . . . . .57 C4
Beach Rd
  Severn Beach BS35 . . . . . .21 F7
  Weston-S-M BS23 . . . . . .104 D6
  Weston-S-M,Kewstoke
    BS22 . . . . .88 A5
Beach Rd E BS20 . . . . .45 D6
Beach Rd W BS20 . . . . .45 C6
Beach The BS21 . . . . .57 C4
Beachgrove Gdns BS16 . . .51 C2
Beachgrove Rd BS16 . . . . .51 B4
Beachley Wlk BS11 . . . . . . .47 D7
Beacon La BS36 . . . . .37 C6
Beacon Rd BA1 . . . . .85 A1
Beacon Rise Prim Sch
  BS15 . . . . .65 D6
Beaconlea BS15 . . . . .65 D6

Beaconsfield Rd
Bristol,Crew's Hole BS5 . . .64 E7
Bristol,Kensington Park BS4 64 B3
Bristol,Woolcott Park BS8 . .49 A1
Clevedon BS21 . . . . .57 E3
Weston-S-M BS23 . . . . . .104 E7
Beaconsfield St 6 BS5 . .64 B6
Beafort Cl BS24 . . . . . .106 C3
Beale Cl BS14 . . . . .80 E6
Beam St BS5 . . . . .64 C7
Bean Acre The BS11 . . . .47 D8
Bean St 11 BS5 . . . . .50 A1
Beanhill Cres BS35 . . . . .15 A5
Beanwood Pk BS37 . . . . .39 D3
Bearbridge Rd BS13 . . . . .78 F4
Beau St BA1 . . . . .141 B2
Beauchamp Rd BS7 . . . . .49 D4
Beauchamps Dr BA3 . . .139 A5
Beauford Sq BA1 . . . . . .141 B2
Beaufort BS16 . . . . .37 C1
Beaufort Ave
Midsomer Norton BA3 . . .133 A2
Yate BS37 . . . . .27 D2
Beaufort Bldgs 7 BS8 . . .62 F7
Beaufort Cl BS5 . . . . . . .64 D7
Beaufort Cres BS34 . . . . .36 E4
Beaufort Ct Bristol BS16 . .52 A8
Clevedon BS21 . . . . .57 C5
Beaufort E BA1 . . . . .85 C1
Beaufort Gdns 2 BS48 . .59 D1
Beaufort Ho 11 BS5 . . . . .64 B7
Beaufort Hts BS5 . . . . . .64 E7
Beaufort Mews
3 Bath BA1 . . . . .85 C1
Chipping Sodbury BS37 . . . .28 B1
Beaufort Pl Bath BA1 . . . .85 C1
Bristol,Frenchay BS16 . . . . .37 B1
Bristol,Upper Easton BS5 . .64 A8
Beaufort Rd
Bristol,Chester Park BS15 . .51 C1
Bristol,Horfield BS7 . . . . . .49 F6
Bristol,Pile Marsh BS5 . . . .64 E7
Bristol,Staple Hill BS16 . . .51 E5
Bristol,Vinney Green BS16 .52 A8
Bristol,Woolcott Park BS8 . .49 A1
Frampton Cotterell BS36 . . .38 A8
Weston-S-M BS23 . . . . . .104 F7
Yate BS37 . . . . .27 D2
Beaufort St
Bristol,Bedminster BS3 . . . .63 C2
4 Bristol,Upper Easton BS5 . . . . .64 A8
Beaufort Trad Pk BS16 . . .53 B4
Beaufort Villas 8 BA1 . . .85 B1
Beaufort W 11 BA1 . . . . .85 B1
Beaufort Way BS10 . . . . .49 D8
Beauley Rd BS3 . . . . .63 B4
Beaumont Cl Bristol BS30 66 A3
Weston-S-M BS23 . . . . . .104 F4
Beaumont St BS5 . . . . . . .64 A8
Beaumont Terr 6 BS5 . . .64 A8
Beaver Cl BS36 . . . . .37 F7
Beazer Cl 5 BS16 . . . . . .51 D3
Beck Cl BS16 . . . . .52 C7
Beck Ho BS34 . . . . .36 A8
Becket Dr BS22 . . . . . . .89 A3
Becket Prim Sch BS22 . . .89 A2
Becket Rd BS22 . . . . .89 A4
Becket's La BS48 . . . . . . .75 E8
Beckfield Farm BS37 . . . .26 F5
Beckford Ct BA2 . . . . . .102 B7
Beckford Gdns Bath BA2 102 B8
Bristol BS14 . . . . .80 A3
Beckford Rd BA2 . . . . . .102 B7
Beckford's Twr★ BA1 . . . .84 D4
Beckhampton Rd BA2 . .101 D5
Beckington BS24 . . . . . .105 A2
Beckington Rd BS3 . . . . . .63 F2
Beckington Wlk BS3 . . . .63 F2
Becks Bsns Pk BS23 . . . .105 A7
Beckspool Rd BS16 . . . . .37 C1
Bedford Cres BS7 . . . . . . .49 F5
Bedford Ct BA1 . . . . . . .102 B8
Bedford Rd BS23 . . . . . .104 E4
Bedford St BA1 . . . . . . .102 B8
Bedminster Down Rd
BS3,BS13 . . . . .63 B1
Bedminster Down Sch
BS13 . . . . .78 F7
Bedminster Par BS3 . . . .63 D4
Bedminster Pl 10 BS3 . . .63 D4
Bedminster Rd BS3 . . . . .63 C2
Bedminster Sta BS3 . . . . .63 D3
Bedwin Cl BS20 . . . . .44 F4
Beech Ave BA2 . . . . . . .102 E5
Beech Cl Alveston BS35 . . .15 A5
Bristol BS30 . . . . .66 A5
Shipham BS25 . . . . .125 F8
Beech Ct BS14 . . . . .80 A5
Beech Dr Nailsea BS48 . . .60 A3
Shipham BS25 . . . . .125 E8
Beech Gr BA2 . . . . .101 D4
Beech Ho BS16 . . . . .50 C5
Beech Leaze BS35 . . . . . .15 A5
Beech Rd Bristol BS7 . . . .49 E5
Saltford BS31 . . . . .82 E3
Shipham BS25 . . . . .125 F8
Yatton BS49 . . . . .91 C8
Beech Terr BA3 . . . . . . .133 E1
Beechacres BS35 . . . . .8 C1
Beechcroft BS41 . . . . . . .78 D2
Beechcroft Wlk BS7 . . . . .50 A8
Beechen Cliff Rd BA2 . . .141 B1
Beechen Cliff Sch BA2 . .102 A4
Beechen Dr BS16 . . . . . . .51 B3
Beeches Gr BS4 . . . . .64 D2
Beeches Ind Est BS37 . . . .27 B2
Beeches The Bath BA2 . . .101 D1

Beeches The *continued*
Bristol,Bradley Stoke BS32 .36 D8
Bristol,Frenchay BS16 . . . . .37 B1
Bristol,Oldland Common
BS30 . . . . .66 C2
Bristol,St Anne's BS4 . . . .64 E5
Sandford BS25 . . . . .108 B4
Beechfield Cl BS41 . . . . .62 C2
Beechfield Gr BS9 . . . . . .48 C8
Beechmont Cl BS24 . . . .104 F1
Beechmont Dr BS24 . . . .105 A1
Beechmount Ct BS14 . . . .80 B8
Beechmount Gr BS14 . . . .80 B8
Beechwood Ave
Bristol BS15 . . . . .65 D5
Locking BS24 . . . . .106 A5
Beechwood Cl BS14 . . . . .80 C8
Beechwood Dr BS20 . . . . .44 E5
Beechwood Rd Bath BA2 102 B1
Bristol BS16 . . . . .51 B4
Easton-in-G BS20 . . . . . . .47 A4
Nailsea BS48 . . . . .59 D2
Portishead BS20 . . . . .44 E5
Beehive Trad Est BS5 . . . .64 E7
Beehive Yd BA1 . . . . . . .141 C3
Beek's La SN14, BA1 . . . . .69 D5
Bees Ho BS21 . . . . .57 C2
Beesmoor Rd BS36 . . . . . .38 B6
Begbrook Dr BS16 . . . . . .50 F6
Begbrook La BS16 . . . . . .50 F6
Begbrook Pk BS16 . . . . . .51 A7
Begbrook Prim Sch BS16 50 F6
Beggar Bush La BS8 . . . . .62 B6
Beggarswell Cl BS2 . . . .143 C4
Belfast Wlk BS4 . . . . . . .79 E8
Belfry BS30 . . . . .66 B6
Belfry Ave BS5 . . . . .65 A8
Belgrave Cres BA1 . . . . .141 C4
Belgrave Hill 5 BS8 . . . . .49 A2
Belgrave Pl Bath BA1 . . .141 C4
Bristol BS8 . . . . .142 A3
Belgrave Rd Bath BA1 . . . .85 B1
Bristol BS8 . . . . .142 B4
Weston-S-M BS22 . . . . . .105 B8
Belgrave Terr 2 BA1 . . . .85 A1
Bell Barn Rd BS9 . . . . . . .48 D6
Bell Cl Bristol BS10 . . . . .49 E7
Farmborough BA2 . . . . . .115 F6
Bell Hill Bristol BS16 . . . . .50 C4
Norton St Philip BA2 . . . .136 E4
Bell Hill Rd BS5 . . . . .64 F8
Bell La BS1 . . . . .143 A3
Bell Pit Brow BS48 . . . . . .60 B2
Bell Rd BS36 . . . . .38 C6
Bell Sq Blagdon BS40 . . .110 E3
Marshfield SN14 . . . . .70 A8
Bell Wlk BS40 . . . . .92 E2
Bella Vista Rd BA1 . . . . .141 B4
Bellamy Ave BS13 . . . . . .79 C4
Bellamy Cl BS15 . . . . . . .65 A5
Belland Dr BS14 . . . . .79 F4
Belle Ct 7 BS2 . . . . .63 F4
Belle Vue BA3 . . . . .133 B3
Belle Vue Cl BA2 . . . . . .134 D8
Belle Vue Rd BS5 . . . . . . .50 C1
Bellevue BS8 . . . . .142 B2
Bellevue Cl BS15 . . . . . . .65 E7
Bellevue Cotts
Bristol,Clifton Wood BS8 . .142 B2
Bristol,Westbury on Trym
BS9 . . . . .49 A7
Bellevue Cres BS8 . . . . .142 B2
Bellevue Ct Bristol BS8 . .142 B2
Clevedon BS21 . . . . .57 D4
Bellevue Mans BS21 . . . .57 D4
Bellevue Pk BS4 . . . . . . .64 D2
Bellevue Rd
Bristol,Kingswood BS15 . . . .65 F7
Bristol,St George BS5 . . . .65 A8
6 Bristol,Windmill Hill BS2 .63 F4
Clevedon BS21 . . . . .57 D4
Bellevue Terr
Bristol,Brislington BS4 . . . .64 D2
Bristol,Clifton Wood BS8 . .142 B2
Bristol,Windmill Hill BS2 . . .63 F4
Bellfields La BS16 . . . . . .37 C1
Bellhanger Ct BA1 . . . . .141 B4
Bellhorse La BS40 . . . . .129 C5
Bellhouse Wlk BS11 . . . . .34 B1
Bellifants BA2 . . . . .116 A6
Bellotts Rd BA2 . . . . . . .101 C6
Belluton La BS39 . . . . . . .97 D5
Belluton Rd BS4 . . . . .64 A3
Belluton Villas BS39 . . . . .97 D5
Belmont Dr Bristol BS34 . .36 E5
Failand BS8 . . . . .61 B3
Belmont Hill BS48,BS8 . . .61 B1
Belmont Pk BS7 . . . . .35 F1
Belmont Rd Bath BA2 . . .102 C1
Bristol,Arno's Vale BS4 . . .64 C3
Bristol,Montpelier BS6 . . . .49 E2
Winscombe BS25 . . . . . . .125 A8
Belmont St BS5 . . . . .50 B1
Belmont The BS21 . . . . . .57 D3
Belmore Gdns BA2 . . . . .101 B3
Beloe Rd BS7 . . . . .49 E5
Belroyal Ave BS4 . . . . . . .64 F3
Belsher Dr BS15 . . . . . . .66 A6
Belstone Wlk BS4 . . . . . .79 C8
Belton Ct BA1 . . . . .84 B2
Belton Rd Bristol BS5 . . . .64 B8
Portishead BS20 . . . . .45 A6
Belvedere BA1 . . . . .141 B4
Belvedere Cres BS22 . . . .88 C1
Belvedere Rd BS6 . . . . . .49 B3
Belvoir Rd Bath BA2 . . . .101 D5
Bristol BS6 . . . . .49 E2
Bence Ct 2 BS15 . . . . . . .65 B5

Bences Cl SN14 . . . . .69 F8
Benches La BS40 . . . . .94 D3
Benford Cl BS16 . . . . .51 C6
Bennell Batch BA3 . . . . .138 E4
Bennell Cl BA3 . . . . .138 E4
Bennell Cotts BA3 . . . . .138 E4
Bennett La BA1 . . . . .85 A1
Bennett Rd BS5 . . . . .64 E7
Bennett St BA1 . . . . .141 B3
Bennett Way BS1,BS8 . . . .62 F5
Bennett's Ct BS37 . . . . . .28 A1
Bennett's Rd BA1 . . . . . . .85 C3
Bennetts Way BS21 . . . . .57 E5
Bensaunt Gr BS10 . . . . . .35 D4
Bentley Cl BS14 . . . . .79 F3
Bentley Rd BS22 . . . . .89 B3
Benville Ave BS9 . . . . . . .48 C8
Berchel Ho 4 BS3 . . . . . .63 D4
Berenda Dr BS30 . . . . . . .66 B3
Beresford Cl BS31 . . . . . .82 E2
Beresford Gdns BA1 . . . . .84 A3
Berkeley Ave
Bristol,Bishopston BS7 . . . .49 D3
Bristol,Brandon Hill BS8 . .142 C3
Midsomer Norton BA3 . . .133 A2
Berkeley Cl Bristol BS16 . .52 A8
Charfield GL12 . . . . .11 A5
Berkeley Cres
Bristol BS8 . . . . .142 B3
Weston-S-M BS23 . . . . . . .104 C2
Berkeley Ct Bath BA2 . . .102 C6
Bristol,Bishopston BS7 . . . .49 D3
Bristol,Patchway BS34 . . . .23 F1
Bristol,Upper Easton BS5 . .64 B7
Berkeley Gdns BS31 . . . . .81 E4
Berkeley Gn
Bristol,Frenchay BS16 . . . . .37 B1
Bristol,Lower Easton BS5 . .50 D2
Berkeley Green Rd BS5 . .50 C2
Berkeley Ho Bath BA1 . . .141 C4
Bristol,Brandon Hill BS1 . .142 C3
7 Bristol,Staple Hill BS16 .51 D5
Berkeley Pl Bath BA1 . . .141 C4
Bristol BS8 . . . . .142 B3
Berkeley Rd
Bristol,Bishopston BS7 . . . .49 D3
Bristol,Kingswood BS15 . . .65 D7
Bristol,Mayfield Park BS16 .51 B2
Bristol,Staple Hill BS16 . . .51 D5
Bristol,Westbury Park BS6 .49 B4
Berkeley Sq BS8 . . . . . . .142 B3
Berkeley St BS5 . . . . .50 C3
Berkeley Way BS16 . . . . .52 B7
Berkeleys Mead BS32 . . . .37 A6
Berkshire Rd BS7 . . . . . . .49 D3
Berlington Ct BS1 . . . . . .143 B1
Bernard Ireland Ho BA1 . .84 B1
Berners Cl BS4 . . . . .79 D7
Berrow Lodge 7 BS23 . .104 E5
Berrow Wlk BS3 . . . . .63 E2
Berrows Mead BS37 . . . . .27 A8
Berry Croft 5 BS3 . . . . . .63 D4
Berry Hill Cl BS10 . . . . . .35 D1
Berry La BS7 . . . . .49 F6
Berwick Cl BS10 . . . . .34 E8
Berwick Ct BS10 . . . . . . .34 B5
Berwick La BS10 . . . . . . .34 D7
Berwick Rd BS5 . . . . .50 B2
Beryl Gr BS14 . . . . .80 C8
Beryl Rd BS3 . . . . .63 B3
Besom La BS37 . . . . .39 D5
Bethel Rd BS5 . . . . .64 F8
Betjeman Ct 2 BS30 . . . .66 A5
Betts Gn BS16 . . . . .52 C7
Bevan Ct BS34 . . . . .35 F2
Beverley Ave BS16 . . . . . .37 F1
Beverley Cl BS5 . . . . .65 B6
Beverley Gdns BS9 . . . . . .48 D7
Beverley Rd BS7 . . . . .49 F8
Beverston Gdns BS11 . . . .34 B2
Beverstone BS15 . . . . . . .65 C8
Bevington Cl BS34 . . . . . .23 E1
Bevington La GL13 . . . . . . .2 F7
Bevington Wlk BS34 . . . . .23 E1
Bewdley Rd BA2 . . . . . . .102 B4
Bexley Rd BS16 . . . . .51 B3
Bhirraff Ct 14 BS6 . . . . . .49 B1
Bibstone BS15 . . . . .66 A8
Bibury Ave BS34 . . . . . . .36 B8
Bibury Cl Bristol BS9 . . . .49 D7
Nailsea BS48 . . . . .60 A1
Bibury Cres
Bristol,Hanham BS15 . . . . .65 C5
Bristol,Henleaze BS9 . . . . .49 D7
Bibury Ho BA1 . . . . .84 B2
Bickerton Cl BS10 . . . . . .34 F3
Bickfield La BS40 . . . . . .129 B8
Bickford Cl BS30 . . . . . . .66 A6
Bickley Cl BS15 . . . . .65 C2
Biddestone Rd BS7 . . . . . .35 E1
Biddisham Cl 6 BS48 . . . .59 E1
Biddisham La BS26 . . . . .123 E2
Biddle St BS49 . . . . .91 B7
Bideford Cres BS4 . . . . . .79 F8
Bideford Rd BS22 . . . . . . .88 F2
Bidwell Cl BS10 . . . . .35 B3
Bifield Cl BS14 . . . . .80 F5
Bifield Gdns BS14 . . . . . .80 E5
Bifield Rd BS14 . . . . .80 F5
Big Tree Cl BS26 . . . . . .124 C3
Bignell Cl BS25 . . . . . . .124 F8
Bigwood La BS1 . . . . . . .142 C2
Bilberry Cl BS9 . . . . .48 C8
Bilbie Cl Bristol BS10 . . . .49 E7
Chew Stoke BS40 . . . . . . .112 E8
Bilbie Rd
Chew Stoke BS40 . . . . . . .112 E8
Weston-S-M BS22 . . . . .89 B3

Bilbury La BA1 . . . . .141 B2
Billand Cl BS13 . . . . .78 E3
Bilsham La BS35 . . . . .12 F2
Bince's Lodge La BA3 . . .133 B3
Binces La BA2 . . . . .99 E3
Bindon Dr BS10 . . . . .35 D4
Binhay Rd BS49 . . . . .91 C7
Binley Gr BS14 . . . . .80 D5
Binmead Gdns 1 BS13 . . .79 B4
Birbeck Rd BS9 . . . . .48 E5
Birch Ave Bleadon BS24 . .122 C6
Clevedon BS21 . . . . .57 E4
Birch Cl Bristol BS34 . . . . .35 E7
Locking BS24 . . . . .106 B4
Birch Croft BS14 . . . . .80 A3
Birch Ct BS31 . . . . .81 C4
Birch Dr Alveston BS35 . . . .14 F4
Langford BS40 . . . . .109 A5
Pucklechurch BS16 . . . . . . .53 B5
Birch Gr BS20 . . . . .45 C4
Birch Ho BS16 . . . . .51 B5
Birch Rd
Bristol,Southville BS3 . . . . .63 B4
Bristol,Upper Soundwell
BS15 . . . . .51 E3
Radstock BA3 . . . . .133 E1
Yate BS37 . . . . .27 D2
Birchall Rd BS6 . . . . .49 C4
Birchdale Rd BS14 . . . . . .80 A8
Birchdene BS48 . . . . .60 A2
Birches The BS48 . . . . . . .60 A2
Birchills Trad Est BS4 . . . .64 F1
Birchwood Ave BS23 . . . .105 A7
Birchwood Ct BS4 . . . . . . .64 F6
Birchwood Dr BS8 . . . . . .61 B3
Birchwood La BS39 . . . . . .97 F2
Birchwood Rd BS4 . . . . . .64 F4
Birdale Cl BS10 . . . . .34 E3
Birdcombe Cl BS48 . . . . . .59 E3
Birdlip Cl BS48 . . . . .60 A1
Birdwell La BS41 . . . . . . .61 F1
Birdwell Prim Sch BS41 .78 A8
Birdwell Rd BS41 . . . . . . .61 F1
Birdwood BS15 . . . . .65 D6
Birgage Rd GL9 . . . . .19 F2
Birkbeck Ct BS23 . . . . . .104 D7
Birkdale Bristol BS30 . . . .66 B6
Yate BS37 . . . . .39 E8
Birkett Rd BS23 . . . . .87 B1
Birkin St 5 BS2 . . . . .64 A6
Birnbeck Rd BS23 . . . . . . .87 C1
Bisdee Rd BS24 . . . . . . .105 D2
Bishop Ave BS22 . . . . .89 A3
Bishop Manor Rd BS10 . . .49 D7
Bishop Mews BS2 . . . . . .143 B4
Bishop Rd
Bristol,Bishopston BS7 . . . .49 D4
Bristol,Emerson's Green
BS16 . . . . .52 C6
Bishop Road Prim Sch
BS7 . . . . .49 D4
Bishop St Bristol BS2 . . .143 B4
Faulkland BA3 . . . . .135 D2
Bishop Sutton Prim Sch
BS39 . . . . .113 D4
Bishop Terr BS2 . . . . . . .143 C4
Bishop's Wood BS32 . . . . .24 C6
Bishops Cl BS9 . . . . .48 E3
Bishops Cove BS13 . . . . . .78 F5
Bishops Knoll BS9 . . . . . .48 C3
Bishops Mead BS49 . . . . .92 A8
Bishops Rd BS49 . . . . . . .92 A8
Bishopsworth CE Jun Sch
BS13 . . . . .78 F6
Bishopsworth Rd BS13 . . .79 A7
Bishopthorpe Rd BS10 . . .49 E7
Bishport Ave BS13 . . . . . .79 C3
Bishport Cl BS13 . . . . . . .79 B4
Bishport Gn BS13 . . . . . . .79 C3
Bisley BS37 . . . . .39 C7
Bissex Mead BS16 . . . . . .52 B5
Bittern Cl BS22 . . . . .88 F1
Bitterwell Cl BS36 . . . . . .38 D3
Bittlemead BS13 . . . . . . .79 F4
Bitton Sta★ BS30 . . . . . . .66 B1
Black La BS26 . . . . .125 E2
Black Nore Point BS20 . . .44 E5
Black Rock Nature Trail★
BA5 . . . . .127 A1
Blackacre BS14 . . . . .80 C4
Blackberry Ave 5 BS16 . .50 E5
Blackberry Dr
Frampton Cotterell BS36 . . .38 C6
Weston-S-M BS22 . . . . .89 A2
Blackberry Hill BS16 . . . .50 E5
Blackberry Hill Hospl
BS16 . . . . .50 F5
Blackberry La
Portishead BS20 . . . . .44 F2
Winsley BA2,BA15 . . . . . .120 C8
Blackberry Way BA3 . . . .133 A3
Blackbird Cl BA3 . . . . . .139 B8
Blackdown Ct 8 BS14 . . . .80 B5
Blackdown Rd BS20 . . . . .45 B5
Blackfriars BS1 . . . . . . .143 A3
Blackfriars Rd BS48 . . . . .59 B1
Blackhorse Ct BS15 . . . . .65 C8
Blackhorse Hill BS35,
BS10 . . . . .35 B8
Blackhorse La BS16 . . . . .52 A8
Blackhorse Pl BS16 . . . . .52 A6
Blackhorse Prim Sch
BS16 . . . . .52 A8
Blackhorse Rd
Bristol,Kingswood BS15 . . .65 D8
Bristol,Vinney Green BS16 .52 A7
Blackmoor Clevedon BS21 .57 C1
Langford BS40 . . . . .109 C6

Blackmoor *continued*
3 Weston-S-M BS22 . . . . .88 F2
Blackmoor Cl BS40 . . . .109 C6
Blackmoor Rd BS8 . . . . . .47 E2
Blackmoors La BS3 . . . . . .62 E4
Blackmore Dr BA2 . . . . .101 C5
Blackrock La
Pensford BS14,BS39 . . . . .97 E7
Publow BS39 . . . . .97 E7
Blacksmith La BA1 . . . . . .85 B6
Blacksmith's La BA1 . . . . .83 B3
Blackswarth Ho 6 BS5 . .64 D7
Blackswarth Rd BS5 . . . . .64 D7
Blackthorn Cl BS13 . . . . . .79 D5
Blackthorn Dr
Bristol BS32 . . . . .36 D7
Portishead BS20 . . . . .45 E5
Blackthorn Gdns BS22 . . .89 A1
Blackthorn Rd BS13 . . . . .79 D5
Blackthorn Sq BS21 . . . . .57 D1
Blackthorn Terr BS22 . . . .89 A1
Blackthorn Way BS48 . . . .60 A2
Blackthorn Wlk BS15 . . . .51 E2
Bladen Cl BS20 . . . . .45 E4
Bladud Bldgs BA1 . . . . .141 C3
Blagdon Cl Bristol BS3 . . .63 E2
Weston-S-M BS24 . . . . . .104 F1
Blagdon La BS40 . . . . . .110 F6
Blagdon Pk BA2 . . . . . . .101 A4
Blagdon Prim Sch BS40 110 F2
Blagrove Cl BS13 . . . . . . .79 C3
Blagrove Cres BS13 . . . . .79 C3
Blaisdon
Weston-S-M BS22 . . . . . .105 D7
Yate BS37 . . . . .39 E7
Blaisdon Cl BS10 . . . . . . .35 A1
Blaise Castle Miniature Rly★
BS10 . . . . .34 E2
Blaise Castle Mus★ BS10 34 E2
Blaise Hamlet BS11 . . . . .34 D2
Blaise Prim Sch BS10 . . .34 F2
Blaise Wlk BS9 . . . . .48 C6
Blake End BS22 . . . . .88 E4
Blake Rd BS7 . . . . .50 B6
Blakeney Gr BS48 . . . . . .75 C8
Blakeney Mills BS37 . . . . .27 E1
Blakeney Rd
Bristol,Horfield BS7 . . . . . .50 A7
Bristol,Patchway BS34 . . . .23 E1
Blakes Rd BS35 . . . . .8 B1
Blanchards BS37 . . . . . . .40 D8
Blanchards Cotts BS37 . . .40 D8
Blandford Cl
2 Bristol BS9 . . . . .49 B6
Nailsea BS48 . . . . .59 E1
Blands Row BS35 . . . . . . .12 B1
Bleadon Hill BS24 . . . . .122 A8
Bleadon Mill BS24 . . . . .122 C5
Bleadon Rd BS24 . . . . . .122 B7
Blenham Ct BS23 . . . . . .105 A8
Blenheim Cl
Peasedown St John BA2 . .134 D7
Weston-S-M BS22 . . . . . . .89 A2
Blenheim Ct BS32 . . . . . . .24 D3
Blenheim Dr Bristol BS34 .36 B4
Yate BS37 . . . . .27 D3
Blenheim Gdns BA1 . . . . .85 A2
Blenheim Rd BS6 . . . . . . .49 B3
Blenheim St BS5 . . . . . . .50 A1
Blenheim Way BS20 . . . . .45 E5
Blenman Cl BS16 . . . . . . .51 A7
Blethwin Cl BS10 . . . . . . .34 F1
Blind La Bath BA1 . . . . . . .84 C2
Chew Stoke BS40 . . . . . . .112 E8
Congresbury BS49 . . . . . . .91 F6
Peasedown St John BA2 . .117 A4
Bloomfield BS24 . . . . . . .105 A2
Bloomfield Ave
Bath BA2 . . . . .101 E4
Timsbury BA2 . . . . .116 B3
Bloomfield Cl BA2 . . . . .116 B3
Bloomfield Cotts BA2 . . .134 D7
Bloomfield Cres BA2 . . . .101 D2
Bloomfield Dr BA2 . . . . .101 D2
Bloomfield Gr BA2 . . . . .101 E3
Bloomfield La BS39 . . . .132 E5
Bloomfield Park Rd
BA2 . . . . .116 B3
Bloomfield Pk BA2 . . . . .101 E3
Bloomfield Rd Bath BA2 .101 E3
Bristol BS4 . . . . .64 D4
Timsbury BA2 . . . . .116 B3
Bloomfield Rise BA2 . . . .101 D2
Bloomfield Rise N BA2 .101 D2
Bloomfield Road Link
BS4 . . . . .64 C4
Bloomfield Terr BA2 . . . .134 C7
Bloy Sq BS5 . . . . .50 C1
Bloy St BS5 . . . . .50 C1
Blue Falcon Rd BS15 . . . .51 E1
Blue Water Dr BS24 . . . .106 D3
Bluebell Cl Bristol BS9 . . .48 B6
Thornbury BS35 . . . . .8 D2
Bluebell Rd BS22 . . . . . . .89 A6
Bluebells The BS32 . . . . .36 F7
Blueberry Way BS22 . . . .88 F1
Blythe Gdns BS22 . . . . . .89 A3
Boat La BS24 . . . . .122 C3
Boat Stall La BA2 . . . . . .141 C2
Bobbin La BA15 . . . . . . .120 F3
Bockenem Cl BS35 . . . . . .15 D7
Bodey Cl BS30 . . . . .66 A5
Bodley Way BS24 . . . . . .105 E7
Bodmin Wlk BS4 . . . . . . .79 F8
Bodyce Rd 4 BS35 . . . . . .15 A5

Boiling Wells La BS2 50 A3
Bolton Rd BS7 49 E3
Bond St BS1 143 B3
Bond's La SN14 55 E1
Bonhill Rd BS39 113 D5
Bonnington Wlk BS7 50 B7
Bonville Bsns Ctr BS4 64 F2
Bonville Rd BS4 64 F2
Book Mus The★ BA1 141 C1
Boot La BS3 63 D4
Booth Rd BS3 63 C4
Bordesley Rd BS14 80 A3
Boreal Way BS24 105 F7
Borgie Pl BS22 88 F3
Borleyton Wlk BS13 78 F4
Borver Gr BS13 79 B4
Boscombe Cres BS16 51 F7
Boston Rd BS7 49 F8
Boswell Rd BA15 120 F3
Boswell St 4 BS5 50 C2
Botham Cl BS22 89 A4
Botham Dr BS4 64 E1
Boucher Pl 2 BS2 50 A2
Boulevard BS23 104 E8
Boulters Rd BS13 79 C4
Boulton's La 5 BS15 65 D8
Boulton's Rd 4 BS15 65 D8
Boundaries The BS24 122 B1
Boundary Cl
  Midsomer Norton BA3 139 B7
  Weston-S-M BS23 104 E3
Boundary Rd
  Avonmouth BS11 33 D3
  Coalpit Heath BS36 38 D7
  Weston-S-M BS24 106 A7
Bourchier Gdns BS13 79 B3
Bourne Cl Bristol BS15 65 B8
  Winterbourne BS36 37 E7
Bourne La Blagdon BS40 110 C4
  Bristol BS5 50 B2
  Burrington BS40 110 B4
Bourne Rd BS15 65 B8
Bourneville Rd BS5 64 D8
Bournville Com Inf Sch
  BS23 105 A4
Bournville Jun Sch
  BS23 104 F5
Bournville Rd BS23 104 F4
Boursland Cl BS32 24 D2
Bourton Ave BS34 36 C8
Bourton Cl BS34 36 C8
Bourton Combe BS48 76 F7
Bourton La
  Compton Bishop BS26 124 E3
  Weston-S-M BS22 89 D4
Bourton Mead
  Flax Bourton BS48 76 F8
  Long Ashton BS41 62 A1
Bourton Wlk BS13 79 A8
Bouverie St BS5 64 B8
Boverton Rd BS34 36 B4
Bowden Cl BS9 48 C8
Bowden Hill BA3 138 D4
Bowden Pl BS16 51 F7
Bowden Rd BS5 50 E1
Bowden Way BS8 61 B3
Bowen Rd BS24 106 C5
Bower Ashton Terr BS3 62 F4
Bower Ct BS3 63 A2
Bower Rd BS3 63 A3
Bower Wlk BS3 63 E3
Bowerleaze BS9 48 C5
Bowlditch La BA3 133 B4
Bowling Hill BS37 28 A1
Bowling Hill Bsns Pk
  BS37 28 A1
Bowling Rd BS37 40 B8
Bowmead 7 BS4 64 D1
Bowood BS16 37 C1
Bowring Cl BS13 79 C3
Bowsland BS32 24 E2
Bowsland Green Prim Sch
  BS32 24 E2
Bowsland Way BS32 24 D2
Bowstreet La BS35 35 A8
Box Bush La BS24 90 C1
Box Rd BA1 86 C3
Box Wlk BS31 81 C4
Boxbury Hill BS39 132 F3
Boxhedge Farm La BS36 38 E3
Boyce Cl BA2 100 F5
Boyce Dr BS2 50 A2
Boyce's Ave BS8 142 A3
Boyd Cl BS30 67 B7
Boyd Rd BS31 82 D3
Brabazon Rd BS34 36 B2
Bracewell Gdns BS10 35 C4
Bracey Dr BS16 51 C6
Brackenbury Dr BS34 36 F5
Brackendene BS32 24 C1
Brackenwood Gdns★
  BS20 44 F5
Brackenwood Rd BS21 57 E6
Bracton Dr BS14 80 A5
Bradeston Gr BS16 51 A7
Bradford Cl BS21 57 C1
Bradford Pk BA2 102 A2
Bradford Rd Bath BA2 102 A1
  Bathford BA1 86 B2
  Rode BA3 137 F1
  Winsley BA15 120 D6
  Winsley BA15 120 E7
Bradhurst St 7 BS5 64 B6
Bradley Ave Bristol BS11 47 E6
  Winterbourne BS36 37 E5
Bradley Cres BS11 47 E6
Bradley Ct BS16 51 C5
Bradley Pavilions 2
  BS32 24 C2
Bradley Rd Bristol BS34 23 F1
  Portbury BS20 46 E5
Bradley Stoke Way BS32 36 E7
Bradstone Rd BS36 37 D5
Bradville Gdns BS41 77 F8
Bradwell Gr BS10 49 C8
Brae Rd BS25 125 B8
Brae Rise BS25 125 A8
Braemar Ave BS7 35 F1
Braemar Cres BS7 35 F1
Braemor Ct BS9 49 A8
Bragg's La BS2 143 C3
Braikenridge Cl BS21 57 C1
Braikenridge Rd BS4 64 D4
Brainsfield BS9 48 F6
Brake Cl
  Bristol,Little Stoke BS32 36 E7
  Bristol,Woodstock BS15 65 F7
Brake The
  Coalpit Heath BS36 38 C5
  Yate BS37 27 E5
Brakewell Gdns BS14 80 A4
Bramble Dr BS9 48 D3
Bramble La BS9 48 C3
Bramble Rd BS22 88 E3
Bramble Way BA2 102 B1
Brambles The
  Hinton Charterhouse BA2 119 E1
  Keynsham BS31 81 D3
Bramblewood BS49 74 B1
Brambling Wlk BS16 50 F6
Bramley Cl
  Kingswood GL12 11 F4
  Locking BS24 106 A5
  Olveston BS35 14 A3
  Peasedown St John BA2 134 D7
  Pill BS20 47 C4
  Sandford BS25 108 A4
  Yatton BS49 91 B7
Bramley Ct 6 BS30 65 F4
Bramley Dr BS48 76 A5
Bramleys The
  Nailsea BS48 75 B8
  Portishead BS20 45 F5
Brampton Ho BS20 45 E4
Brampton Way BS20 45 E4
Bramshill Dr BS22 88 F3
Branch Rd BA2 119 F2
Branche Gr BS13 79 D3
Branches Cross BS40 92 E3
Brandash Rd BS37 28 C1
Brandon Ho BS8 142 B2
Brandon St BS1 142 C2
Brandon Steep BS1 142 C2
Brangwyn Gr BS7 50 B6
Brangwyn Sq BS22 88 F8
Branksome Cres BS34 36 B3
Branksome Dr
  Bristol BS34 36 B3
  Winterbourne BS36 37 E6
Branksome Rd BS6 49 B3
Bransby Way BS24 106 A8
Branscombe Ct BS3 63 B2
Branscombe Rd BS9 48 C4
Branscombe Wlk BS20 44 F3
Branwhite Cl BS7 50 B7
Brassknocker Hill BA2 102 F2
Brassmill Ent Ctr BA1 101 A7
Brassmill La BA1 101 A7
Brassmill Lane Trad Est
  BA1 101 A7
Bratton Rd BS4 79 D7
Braunton Rd BS3 63 C3
Braydon Ave BS32 36 D7
Brayne Ct BS30 65 F3
Braysdown Cl BA2 134 B6
Braysdown La BA2 134 C7
Breach Hill La BS40 112 C6
Breach La BS48 74 F4
Breach Rd BS3 63 A3
Breaches Gate BS32 36 F6
Breaches The BS20 47 B5
Brean Down Ave
  Bristol BS9 49 B5
  Weston-S-M BS23 104 E4
Brean Rd BS24 121 F1
Brecknock Rd BS4 64 A3
Brecon Cl BS9 49 B6
Brecon Rd BS9 49 B6
Brecon View BS24 105 A1
Bredon BS37 39 D7
Bredon Cl BS15 65 F6
Bredon Nook Rd BS10 49 C7
Bree Cl BS22 89 A4
Brendon Ave BS23 104 F8
Brendon Cl BS30 66 C4
Brendon Gdns 2 BS48 59 E1
Brendon Rd Bristol BS3 63 D3
  Portishead BS20 45 A5
Brenner St BS5 50 B2
Brent Cl BS24 105 B2
Brent Rd BS7 49 F5
Brentry Ave 5 BS5 64 B7
Brentry Hospl BS10 35 B2
Brentry La BS10 35 B3
Brentry Lodge BS10 35 A3
Brentry Prim Sch BS10 35 B4
Brentry Rd BS16 50 F3
Brereton Way BS30 66 B4
Brewerton Cl BS10 35 C3
Brewery Hill BS30 82 F7
Brewery La BA3 139 D1
Brewhouse The BS1 143 B2
Briar Cl Nailsea BS48 60 A2
Briar Cl *continued*
  Radstock BA3 139 D8
Briar Ct BS20 47 C4
Briar Mead BS49 74 A1
Briar Rd BS24 105 E3
Briar Way BS16 51 C3
Briar Wlk BS16 51 C3
Briarfield Ave BS15 65 C5
Briarleaze BS35 14 F2
Briars Ct BA2 101 A4
Briars The BS48 75 F7
Briarside Ho BS10 35 D3
Briarside Rd BS10 35 D3
Briarwood BS9 48 F6
Briarwood Sch BS16 51 B3
Briary Rd BS20 45 C5
Briavels Gr BS6 49 F2
Brick Cotts BS35 6 E1
Brick La BS39 115 D1
Brick St BS2 143 C3
Bridewell La Bath BA1 141 B2
  Hutton BS24,BS26,BS29 106 D1
Bridewell St BS1 143 A3
Bridge Bldgs BS39 132 B3
Bridge Cl BS14 80 C4
Bridge Farm Cl BS14 80 A3
Bridge Farm Inf Sch
  BS14 80 A4
Bridge Farm Jun Sch
  BS14 80 A4
Bridge Farm Sq BS49 91 D4
Bridge Gdns BA2 116 A6
Bridge Ho 11 Bath BA1 85 C1
  11 Clevedon BS21 57 C2
  Weston-S-M BS23 104 F6
Bridge Place Rd BA2 133 E8
Bridge Rd Bath BA2 101 C5
  Bleadon BS24 122 B6
  Bristol,Eastville BS5 50 B3
  Bristol,Mangotsfield BS15 52 A3
  Bristol,Shortwood BS16 52 C4
  Leigh Woods BS8 62 E6
  Weston-S-M BS23 104 F6
  Yate BS37 27 A2
Bridge St Bath BA2 141 C2
  Bristol BS1 143 A2
  Bristol,Lower Easton BS5 50 D2
Bridge Valley Rd BS8 62 E8
Bridge Way BS36 38 B8
Bridge Wlk BS7 50 A8
Bridgeleap Rd BS16 51 F8
Bridges Ct 2 BS16 51 B4
Bridges Dr BS16 51 C6
Bridgman Gr BS34 36 B3
Bridgwater Ct BS24 105 A3
Bridgwater Rd
  Dundry BS41,BS13,BS48 78 D6
  Lympsham BS24 122 C5
  Weston-S-M BS23,BS24 104 F2
  Winscombe BS25,BS26 125 A5
Bridle Way BS35 14 F4
Briercliffe Rd BS9 48 D7
Brierly Furlong BS34 36 D3
Briery Leaze Rd BS14 80 A4
Bright St
  Bristol,Kingswood BS15 65 D8
  Bristol,Russell Town BS5 64 B7
Brighton Cres BS3 63 B2
Brighton Mews BS8 142 B4
Brighton Pk 16 BS5 64 B8
Brighton Pl BS15 51 D1
Brighton Rd
  Bristol,Cribbs Causeway
  BS34 35 F8
  Bristol,Woolcott Park BS6 49 C1
  Weston-S-M BS23 104 E6
Brighton St 13 BS2 49 E1
Brighton Terr 9 BS3 63 B2
Brigstocke Rd BS2 143 B4
Brimbles The BS7 36 B2
Brimbleworth La BS22 89 C3
Brimridge Rd BS25 125 A8
Brimsham Green Sec Sch
  BS37 27 D4
Brimsham Park Sh Ctr
  BS37 27 F4
Brinkmarsh La GL12 9 D2
Brinkworthy Rd BS16 50 E6
Brinmead Wlk BS13 78 F3
Brins Cl BS34 36 F4
Brinsea Batch BS49 108 E8
Brinsea La BS49 108 F8
Brinsea Rd BS49 91 E2
Brinsham La BS37 28 A6
Brinsmead Cres BS20 47 D4
Briscoes Ave BS13 79 D4
Brislington Hill BS4 64 E2
Brislington Ret Pk BS4 64 E1
Brislington Sch BS4 80 F8
Brislington Trad Est BS4 64 F2
Bristol & Anchor Ho BS5 64 D8
Bristol Bsns Pk BS16 36 E1
Bristol Cathedral Sch
  BS1 142 C2
Bristol City Fball Gd BS3 62 F3
Bristol Dental Hospl
  BS1 143 A3
Bristol Eye Hospl BS1 143 A3
Bristol Gate 1 BS8 62 F5
Bristol Gateway Sch The
  BS2 50 A2
Bristol General Hospl
  BS1 143 A1
Bristol Gram Sch BS8 142 C3
Bristol Harbour Rly★
  BS1 142 B1
Bristol Hill BS4 64 D2
Bristol Homeopathic Hospl
  BS6 142 C4
Bristol Ind Mus★ BS1 143 A1
Bristol Old Vic Theatre Sch
  BS8 49 A1
Bristol Parkway N BS34 37 A5
Bristol Parkway Sta BS34 36 E4
Bristol Rd Bristol BS16 37 C2
  Chew Stoke BS40 112 E8
  Churchill BS25 109 A5
  Congresbury BS49 91 D5
  Cromhall GL12 17 B7
  Farrington Gurney BS39 131 F5
  Frampton Cotterell BS36,
  BS37 26 B3
  Keynsham BS31 81 E6
  Luckington SN14 31 E3
  Newton St Loe BA2 100 D7
  Paulton BS39 132 E7
  Pensford BS39 97 D6
  Portishead BS20 45 E4
  Radstock BA3 133 F3
  Redhill BS40 94 A3
  Thornbury BS35 15 B8
  Weston-S-M BS22 89 C2
  Whitchurch BS14 80 D3
  Winscombe BS25 125 C8
  Winterbourne BS16,BS36 37 D4
  Wraxall BS48 60 D4
Bristol Rd Lower BS23 87 F1
Bristol RFC BS7 49 F6
Bristol Road-Lower BS23 87 E1
Bristol Royal Infmy BS2 143 A4
Bristol Steiner Sch BS6 49 B2
Bristol Vale Ctr For Ind
  BS3 63 B1
Bristol View BA2 118 C8
Bristol Waldorf Sch
  BS8 142 B3
Bristol Zoo Gdns★ BS8 48 F1
Bristow Broadway BS11 33 C1
Bristowe Ho BS16 51 B5
Britannia Cl Bristol BS16 37 F1
  Chilcompton BA3 138 D4
Britannia Cres BS34 36 D5
Britannia Ct 1 BS16 51 D5
Britannia Rd
  Bristol,Cribbs Causeway
  BS34 35 E7
  Bristol,Kingswood BS15 65 C8
  Bristol,Whitehall BS5 50 C1
Britannia Way BS21 57 C1
British Empire &
  Commonwealth Mus★
  BS1 143 C1
British Rd BS3 63 C3
Brittan Pl BS20 46 E3
Brittania Bldgs BS8 142 A1
Britten Ct 10 BS30 65 F4
Britten's Cl BS39 132 F6
Britten's Hill BS39 132 F6
Brittons Pass SN14 69 F8
Brixham Rd BS3 63 C1
Brixton Rd BS5 64 B8
Brixton Road Mews 22
  BS5 64 B8
Broad Croft 3 BS32 24 C2
Broad La
  Coalpit Heath BS36 38 D5
  Westerleigh BS37 39 A4
  Yate BS37 27 C4
Broad Mead La BS40 95 A3
Broad Oak Rd BS13 78 F4
Broad Oaks BS8 62 E6
Broad Plain BS2 143 C2
Broad Quay Bath BA1 141 C1
  Bristol BS1 143 A2
Broad Rd Blagdon BS40 127 D8
  Bristol BS15 51 C1
Broad St Bath BA1 141 C3
  Bristol BS1 143 A3
  Bristol,Staple Hill BS16 51 F4
  Chipping Sodbury BS37 28 B1
  Congresbury BS49 91 D4
  Wrington BS40 92 D2
Broad Stones BA15 103 E7
Broad Street Pl BA1 141 C3
Broad Weir BS1 143 B3
Broad Wlk BS4 64 A2
Broadbury Rd BS4 79 E8
Broadcroft BS40 95 F3
Broadcroft Ave BS49 74 F1
Broadcroft Cl BS49 74 F1
Broadfield Ave BS15 51 C1
Broadfield Rd BS4 64 B1
Broadlands BS21 57 F3
Broadlands Ave BS31 81 D6
Broadlands Dr BS11 34 A1
Broadlands Sch BS31 81 D6
Broadleas BS13 79 C7
Broadleaze BS11 47 E7
Broadleaze Way BS25 107 F2
Broadleys Ave BS9 49 C7
Broadmead BS1 143 B3
Broadmead La BS31 82 A6
Broadmoor La BA1 84 A3
Broadmoor Pk BA1 84 B2
Broadmoor Vale BA1 84 A3
Broadoak Com Sch
  BS23 104 E3
Broadoak Hill BS41 78 F2
Broadoak Rd
  Langford BS40 109 A5
  Weston-S-M BS23 104 D3
Broadoak Wlk BS16 51 B4
Broadstone La BS21 72 F3
Broadstone Wlk BS13 79 D5
Broadwalk Sh Ctr BS4 64 B2
Broadway Bath BA2 102 B6
  Chilcompton BA3 138 C3
  Locking BS24 106 D4
  Saltford BS31 82 D3
  Shipham BS25 125 E8
  Weston-S-M BS24 105 A2
  Yate BS37 27 F2
Broadway Ave BS9 49 D6
Broadway Cl BA3 138 C3
Broadway Inf Sch BS37 27 F2
Broadway La BA3 133 B5
Broadway Rd
  Bristol,Bishopston BS7 49 D3
  Bristol,Bishopsworth BS13 78 F5
Broadway The GL11 5 F8
Broadways Dr BS16 50 F7
Brock End BS20 44 F3
Brock St BA1 141 B3
Brockeridge Inf Sch
  BS36 38 C7
Brockhurst Gdns BS15 65 A8
Brockhurst Rd BS15 65 A8
Brockley Cl Bristol BS34 36 C7
  Nailsea BS48 59 D1
  Weston-S-M BS24 104 F1
Brockley Combe Rd
  BS48 76 B1
Brockley Cres BS24 104 F1
Brockley La BS48 75 D4
Brockley Mini Farm★
  BS48 92 F7
Brockley Rd BS31 82 D3
Brockley Way BS49 75 B3
Brockley Wlk BS13 79 A8
Brockridge La BS36 38 C7
Brocks 4 BS4 64 D1
Brocks La BS41 61 F1
Brocks Rd BS13 79 C3
Brockway BS48 59 F2
Brockwood BA15 120 F7
Brockworth BS37 39 C6
Brockworth Cres BS16 50 F6
Bromfield Wlk BS16 52 B7
Bromley Dr BS16 51 D8
Bromley Heath Ave BS16 51 D8
Bromley Heath Jun & Inf
  Schs BS16 51 E8
Bromley Heath Rd BS16 51 D8
Bromley Heath Rdbt
  BS16 37 D1
Bromley Rd Bristol BS7 49 F5
  Stanton Drew BS39 96 F1
Bromley Sq BS49 91 E3
Brompton Cl BS15 66 A8
Brompton Rd BS24 105 A2
Broncksea Rd BS7 35 F1
Brook Cl BS41 62 B1
Brook Cotts BA2 100 B7
Brook Gate BS3 62 E1
Brook Hill BS6 49 F1
Brook Ho Bristol BS34 36 C8
  3 Thornbury BS35 15 C8
Brook La
  Bristol,Broomhill BS16 50 E6
  Bristol,Montpelier BS6 49 F1
Brook Lintons BS4 64 D3
Brook Office Pk BS16 38 B2
Brook Rd Bath BA2 101 D6
  Bristol,Crofts End BS5 50 F1
  Bristol,Hillfields BS16 51 B4
  Bristol,Mangotsfield BS16 51 F6
  Bristol,Montpelier BS6 49 F1
  Bristol,Southville BS3 63 D4
  Bristol,Warmley BS15 66 B8
Brook St Bristol BS5 64 C7
  Chipping Sodbury BS37 40 A8
Brook Way BS32 36 D8
Brookcote Dr BS34 36 D6
Brookdale Rd BS13 79 B6
Brookfield Ave BS7 49 D3
Brookfield Cl BS37 28 C2
Brookfield La 2 BS6 49 D2
Brookfield Pk BA1 84 B2
Brookfield Rd
  Bristol,Patchway BS34 36 B8
  3 Bristol,Redland BS6 49 D2
Brookfield Wlk
  Bristol BS30 66 C3
  Clevedon BS21 57 F3
Brookhouse La SN14 55 D1
Brookland Rd Bristol BS6 49 D5
  Weston-S-M BS22 105 B7
Brooklands BA2 117 D3
Brooklea BS30 66 B3
Brookleaze BS9 48 C5
Brookleaze Bldgs BA1 85 B2
Brooklyn BS40 92 D2
Brooklyn Rd Bath BA1 85 C2
  Bristol BS13 79 B8
Brookmead BS35 15 D7
Brookridge Ct 4 BS16 51 D4
Brookridge Ho BS10 34 F3
Brookside Paulton BS39 132 E6
  Pill BS20 47 D3
  Winford BS40 94 F7
Brookside Cl
  Batheaston BA1 85 F5
  Paulton BS39 132 E6
Brookside Dr
  Farmborough BA2 115 F6
  Frampton Cotterell BS36 38 B8
Brookside Ho BA1 84 B1
Brookside Rd BS4 64 E2
Brookthorpe BS37 39 D8
Brookthorpe Ave BS11 34 A1
Brookthorpe Ct BS37 39 D8
Brookview Wlk BS13 79 B7
Broom Farm Cl BS48 75 E8

Broom Hill BS16 ....50 E5
Broom Hill La BS39 ...132 E8
Broomground BA15 ....120 E7
Broomhill Jun & Inf Schs
   BS4 ....64 F3
Broomhill La BS39 .....114 E3
Broomhill Rd BS4 ....65 A2
Brooms The BS16 ....38 A1
Brotherswood Ct BS32 ..24 D4
Brougham Hayes BA2 ..101 D6
Brougham Pl 2 BA1 ....85 C2
Broughton Ho BS1 .....143 B1
Brow Hill Bathampton BA2 .85 F4
   Batheaston BA1 ....85 F4
Brow The
   Bath,Combe Down BA2 .102 C1
   Bath,South Twerton BA2 .101 B5
Browne Ct 5 BS8 ....62 F6
Browning Ct BS7 ....50 B8
Brownlow Rd BS23 .....104 E4
Browns Ct BS23 ....104 E6
Broxholme Wlk BS11 ....47 F8
Bruce Ave BS5 ....50 C1
Bruce Rd BS5 ....50 C1
Brue Cl BS23 ....105 A5
Brummel Way BS39 .....132 C6
Brunel Cl Bristol BS30 ..66 C7
   Weston-S-M BS24 .....104 E1
Brunel Ct BS37 ....27 C2
Brunel Ho BA2 ....101 A6
Brunel Lock Rd BS1 .....62 F5
Brunel Rd BS13 ....79 A4
   Nailsea BS48 ....59 B1
Brunel Way
   Bristol BS1,BS3 ....62 F4
   Thornbury BS35 ....62 F4
Brunswick Pl Bath BA1 .141 B3
   10 Bristol BS1 ....62 F5
Brunswick Sq BS2 .....143 B4
Brunswick St 1 Bath BA1 .85 B1
   Bristol,Redfield BS5 ...64 C7
   Bristol,St Pauls BS2 ..143 B4
Bruton BS24 ....105 A2
Bruton Ave Bath BA2 ..101 F4
   Portishead BS20 ....45 A5
Bruton Avenue Garages
   BA2 ....101 F4
Bruton Cl Bristol BS5 ...64 F8
   Nailsea BS48 ....75 E8
Bruton Pl BS8 ....142 B3
Bryansons Cl BS16 .....50 D6
Bryant Ave BA3 ....133 D1
Bryant Gdns BS21 ......57 C1
Bryant's Hill BS5 ....65 B6
Bryants Cl BS16 ....37 C1
Brynland Ave BS7 ......49 E4
Buckingham Ct BS32 ...24 D3
Buckingham Dr BS34 ...36 D5
Buckingham Gdns BS16 .51 E6
Buckingham Ho BS34 ...35 F2
Buckingham Par BS35 ...8 B1
Buckingham Pl
   Bristol,Mangotsfield BS16 .51 E6
   Bristol,Victoria Park BS8 .142 A3
Buckingham Rd
   Bristol BS4 ....64 D5
   Weston-S-M BS24 .....105 D5
Buckingham St BS3 .....63 C2
Buckingham Vale BS8 .142 A4
Buckland Gn BS22 ......89 A5
Bucklands Batch BS48 ..75 F8
Bucklands Dr BS48 .....76 A8
Bucklands End BS48 ....75 F8
Bucklands Gr BS48 .....75 F8
Bucklands La BS48 .....75 F8
Bucklands View BS48 ...76 A8
Bucklewell Cl BS11 .....47 F6
Bude Ave BS5 ....65 A8
Bude Cl BS48 ....60 B1
Bude Rd BS34 ....36 B4
Building of Bath Mus ★
   BA1 ....141 C3
Bull La Bristol BS5 .....64 F6
   Pill BS20 ....47 C4
Bull's Hill BA2 ....118 E1
Bullens Cl BS32 ....24 D2
Buller Rd BS4 ....64 C2
Bullocks La BS21 ....73 C4
Bully La BS37 ....17 D1
Bumper's Batch BA2 ..119 A8
Bungalows The BS26 ..125 C2
Bungay's Hill BA2,BS39 .115 E1
Bunting Ct BS22 ....88 E1
Burbank Cl BS30 ....66 A3
Burchells Ave BS15 ....51 B1
Burchells Green Cl BS15 .51 B1
Burchells Green Rd BS15 .51 B1
Burchill Cl BS39 ......114 F3
Burcombe Cl BS36 .....38 D6
Burcott Rd BS11 ....33 D5
Burden Cl BS32 ....36 F6
Burfoot Rd BS14 ....80 E4
Burfoote Gdns BS14 ...80 E4
Burford Ave BS34 ......36 C8
Burford Cl Bath BA2 ..101 B3
   Portishead BS20 ....45 E4
Burford Gr BS11 ....47 F5
Burgage Cl BS37 ....40 B8
Burgess Green Cl BS4 ..64 E7
Burghill Rd BS10 ....35 A1
Burghley Ct BS36 ......37 E5
Burghley Rd BS6 ....49 E2
Burgis Rd BS14 ....80 D6
Burleigh Gdns BA1 ....101 A8
Burleigh Way GL12 .....18 B5
Burley Ave BS16 ....51 F5
Burley Crest BS16 .....51 F5
Burley Gr BS16 ....51 F5

Burlington Ct 9 BS6 ...49 B2
Burlington Rd Bristol BS6 .49 B2
   Midsomer Norton BA3 .133 C2
Burlington St Bath BA1 .141 B4
   16 Weston-S-M BS23 ..104 E8
Burltons The GL12 .....10 B2
Burnbush Cl BS14 ......80 E6
Burnbush Prim Sch BS14 .80 D5
Burnell Dr BS2 ....143 C4
Burnett Bsns Pk BS31 ..82 B1
Burnett Hill BS31 ......99 B8
Burney Way BS30 ......66 A3
Burnham Cl Bristol BS15 .51 F1
   Weston-S-M BS24 ....104 F1
Burnham Dr Bristol BS15 .51 F1
   Weston-S-M BS24 ....104 F1
Burnham Rd Bath BA2 .101 C6
   Bristol BS11 ....47 D6
Burnside Cl BS10 ....35 C2
Burnt House Rd BA2 ..118 D8
Burrington Ave BS24 ..104 F1
Burrington CE Prim Sch
   BS40 ....109 F3
Burrington Cl
   Nailsea BS48 ....59 E1
   Weston-S-M BS24 ....104 F1
Burrington Combe ★
   BS40 ....110 A1
Burrington La BS40 ...110 A3
Burrough Wlk BS13 ....79 A8
Burrows Way BS36 .....37 E6
Burrows La BA3 ....139 D1
Burrows The BS22 .....89 D3
Burton Cl BS1 ....143 B1
Burton Ct
   2 Bristol,Ridgeway BS16 .50 E3
   3 Bristol,Victoria Park BS8 .142 B3
Burton Rd GL9 ....42 F6
Burton St 5 BA1 ......141 B3
Burwalls Rd BS8 ....62 E6
Bury Hill BS36 ....37 F3
Bury Hill La BS37 ......28 A8
Bury Hill View BS16 ....37 E1
Bury La BS30 ....67 F7
Bury The BS24 ....106 A3
Burycourt Cl BS11 .....34 A1
Bush Ave BS34 ....36 D5
Bush Ct Alveston BS35 ..14 F5
   10 Bristol BS4 ....63 F4
Bush Ind Est BS5 ......64 D8
Bushes La BS37 ....29 A6
Bushy Ho BS2 ....63 F3
Bushy Pk BS2 ....63 F3
Bushy Thorn Rd BS40 .112 E8
Business Pk The BS13 ..79 E3
Butcombe BS24 ....105 A2
Butcombe La BS40 ....111 B7
Butcombe Wlk BS14 ...80 B5
Butham La
   Chew Magna BS40 .....96 A4
   Chew Magna BS40 .....96 A3
Butlass Cl BS39 ....115 D1
Butler Ho BS5 ....64 F8
Butlers Cl BS5 ....64 F7
Butlers Wlk 3 BS5 .....64 F6
Butt La BS35 ....8 C3
Butt's Batch BS40 .....92 D1
Butt's La SN14 ....55 B4
Buttercliffe Rise BS41 ..62 C3
Butterfield Cl BS10 ....49 E7
Butterfield Pk BS21 ....57 C1
Butterfield Rd BS10 ....49 E7
Butterfield Cl BS36 ....38 B6
Buttermere Rd BS23 ..105 A5
Butterworth Ct BS4 ....79 D7
Button Cl BS14 ....80 A6
Butts Batch BS26 .....124 B3
Butts Orch BS40 ....92 D1
Buxton Wlk BS7 ....50 A8
Bye Mead BS16 ....52 B8
Byfield BA2 ....102 B1
Byfields GL12 ....73 C8
Byron Cl BS24 ....106 A4
Byron Ct BS23 ....104 F8
Byron Pl
   Bristol,Brandon Hill BS8 .142 B3
   Bristol,Staple Hill BS16 .51 E4
Byron Rd Bath BA2 ...101 F4
   Locking BS24 ....106 A4
   Weston-S-M BS23 ....105 A4
Byron St
   Bristol,Moorfields BS5 ..64 C7
   5 Bristol,St Pauls BS5 .50 A1
Byways Cvn Pk BS21 ...57 C1
Byzantine Ct BS1 .....143 A1

C

Cabot Cl Bristol BS15 ..65 C7
   Chipping Sodbury BS37 .27 F1
   Saltford BS31 ....82 D2
Cabot Ct BS7 ....35 F1
Cabot Gn BS5 ....64 B7
Cabot Ho 6 BS15 ......15 C8
Cabot Prim Sch BS2 ..143 C4
Cabot Rise BS20 ....45 A5
Cabot Way Bristol BS8 ..62 F5
   Pill BS20 ....47 D3
   Weston-S-M BS22 .....89 A3
Cabstand BS20 ....45 D6
Cadbury Camp La BS20 .59 D6
Cadbury Camp La W
   BS21 ....58 C5
Cadbury Farm Rd BS49 .91 C7
Cadbury Halt BS20 .....44 F1

Cadbury Heath Cty Prim Sch
   BS30 ....66 B6
Cadbury Heath Rd BS30 .66 B5
Cadbury Ho BS20 ......45 E4
Cadbury La BS20 ....44 F1
Cadbury Rd
   Keynsham BS31 ....82 A2
   Portishead BS20 ......45 E4
Cadbury Sq BS49 ......91 E3
Cadby Ho BA2 ....101 A6
Caddick Cl BS15 ....51 F2
Cade Cl
   Bristol,Gee Moor BS15 .65 F6
   Bristol,Great Stoke BS34 .36 E5
Cadmium Rd BS11 .....33 C4
Cadogan Rd BS14 .....80 A8
Caen Rd BS3 ....63 D3
Caernarvon Rd BS31 ...81 C4
Caine Rd BS7 ....49 F7
Cains Cl BS15 ....65 E6
Cairn Cl BS48 ....60 A1
Cairn Gdns BS36 ....37 E4
Cairns Cl BS6 ....49 C4
Cairns Rd BS6 ....49 C4
Cairns' Cres 11 BS2 ...49 F1
Cala Trad Est BS3 .....62 F3
Calcott Rd BS4 ....64 A3
Caldbeck Cl BS10 ......35 D2
Calder Cl BS31 ....82 A4
Caldicot Cl
   Bristol,Lawrence Weston
     BS11 ....34 C2
   Bristol,Willsbridge BS30 .66 B2
Caledonia Mews BS8 ..62 F6
Caledonia Pl BS8 ......62 F6
Caledonian Rd Bath BA2 .101 D6
   Bristol BS1 ....142 B1
California Rd BS30 .....66 B3
Callicroft Inf Sch BS34 .35 F8
Callicroft Jun Sch BS34 .35 F8
Callicroft Rd BS34 .....36 A7
Callington Rd BS4 .....64 A1
Callowhill Ct BS1 .....143 B3
Calluna Cl BS22 ....89 A5
Calton Gdns BA2 .....141 C1
Calton Rd BA2 ....141 C1
Calton Wlk BA2 ....141 B1
Cam Brook Cl BA2 ...133 D8
Camberley Dr BS36 ....37 F8
Camberley Rd BS4 .....79 D8
Camberley Wlk BS22 ..105 E8
Camborne Rd BS7 .....50 A7
Cambrian Dr BS37 .....27 E3
Cambridge Cres BS9 ...49 A7
Cambridge Gr BS21 ....57 D5
Cambridge Pk BS6 .....49 B3
Cambridge Pl BS23 ...104 D8
Cambridge Rd Bristol BS7 .49 E4
Cambridge St
   8 Bristol,Redfield BS5 .64 C7
   Bristol,Windmill Hill BS3 .63 F4
Cambridge Terr BA2 ..102 B5
Cambrook Ho BS39 ..131 F8
Camden Cres BA1 ....141 B4
Camden Rd Bath BA1 ..85 A1
   Bristol BS3 ....142 B1
Camden Row BA1 ....141 B4
Camden Terr Bath BA1 .141 C4
   Bristol BS8 ....142 A2
   Weston-S-M BS23 ....104 E7
Cameley CE Prim Sch
   BS39 ....114 E1
Cameley Cl BS39 .....131 E8
Cameley Gn BA2 .....100 F6
Cameley Rd BS39 ....131 C8
Camelford Rd BS5 .....50 D1
Cameron Wlk BS7 .....50 C6
Cameroons Cl BS31 ...81 E4
Camerton CE Prim Sch
   BA2 ....133 E8
Camerton Cl BS31 .....82 E3
Camerton Hill BA2 ...133 E8
Camerton Rd Bristol BS5 .50 C1
   Timsbury BA2 ....116 C1
Camp La SN14 ....55 C4
Camp Rd Bristol BS8 ..62 F7
   Thornbury BS35 ....7 B6
   Weston-S-M BS23 .....87 C1
Camp View Nailsea BS48 .59 D2
   Winterbourne BS36 ....37 E4
Campbell Ct BS11 .....33 F1
Campbell Farm BS11 ..33 F1
Campbell Farm Dr BS11 .33 F1
Campbell St BS2 ....49 E1
Campian Wlk BS4 .....79 D6
Campion Cl Thornbury BS35 .8 D2
   Weston-S-M BS22 ....105 D7
Campion Dr BS32 ......24 D2
Camplins BS21 ....57 C1
Camvale BA2 ....134 B8
Camview BS39 ....132 D6
Camwal Ind Est BS2 ...64 A5
Camwal Rd BS2 ....64 A5
Canada Coombe BS24 .106 A1
Canada Way BS1 .....142 B1
Canal Terr BA2 ....85 F1
Canal View BA2 ....133 E8
Canberra Cres BS24 ..106 B6
Canberra Gr BS34 .....36 C7
Canberra Rd BS23 ....104 F3
Candy Ct BS4 ....64 D5
Canford La BS9 ....48 E6
Canford Rd BS9 ....48 E8
Cann La BS30 ....66 E6

Cannans Cl BS36 ......37 E7
Cannon St
   Bristol,Kingsdown BS1 .143 A4
   Bristol,Southville BS3 ..63 C4
Cannons Gate BS21 ....73 C8
Canon St BS5 ....64 C8
Canon's Rd BS1 ......142 C1
Canon's Wlk BS15 .....51 F2
Canons Cl BA2 ....101 B2
Canons Rd BS1 ......142 C2
Canons Way BS1 .....142 C1
Canons Wlk BS22 .....88 D2
Canowie Rd BS6 ......49 B3
Cantell Gr BS14 ....80 F5
Canterbury Cl
   Weston-S-M BS22 .....89 B3
   Yate BS37 ....27 E3
Canterbury Ct BS16 ...50 E6
Canterbury Rd BA2 ...101 D5
Canterbury St 5 BS5 ..64 B6
Canters Leaze GL12 ...18 B4
Cantock's Cl BS8 ....142 C3
Canvey Cl BS10 ....49 E7
Canynge Ho 2 BS1 ..143 B1
Canynge Rd BS8 ......62 F8
Canynge Sq BS8 ......62 F8
Canynge St BS1 .....143 B2
Capel Cl BS15 ....66 B8
Capel Rd BS11 ....34 B1
Capell Cl BS22 ....105 B8
Capenor Cl BS20 ......45 C4
Capgrave Cl BS4 ......65 A3
Capgrave Cres BS4 ....65 A3
Capital Edge BS8 ....142 B2
Caple La BS40 ....112 B5
Cappards Rd BS39 ...113 C4
Capri Villas BS23 ......87 C2
Capricorn Pl BS1 .....142 B2
Caraway Gdns BS5 ....50 C2
Carberry View 7 BS24 .106 A8
Cardigan Cres BS22 ..105 C8
Cardigan Mews BS9 ...49 B5
Cardigan Rd BS9 ......49 B6
Cardill Cl BS13 ....79 A8
Cardinal Cl BA2 ......118 D8
Carditch Dro BS49 ...108 B8
Carey Developments 1
   BS21 ....57 C1
Carey's Cl BS21 ....57 F4
Carfax Ct BS6 ....49 A3
Carice Gdns BS21 .....73 D8
Carisbrooke Rd BS4 ...79 D7
Carlingford Terr BA3 .134 A3
Carlingford Terrace Rd
   BA3 ....134 A2
Carlow Rd BS4 ....79 E8
Carlton Cl BS39 ......114 F3
Carlton Ct
   Bristol,Ashley Down BS7 .49 F4
   3 Bristol,Westbury on Trym
     BS9 ....49 A7
Carlton Ho 2 BS9 .....49 A7
Carlton Mans BS23 ..104 D7
Carlton Pk BS5 ....64 C8
Carlton St BS23 ......104 D7
Carlyle Rd BS5 ....50 C1
Carmarthen Cl BS37 ..27 E4
Carmarthen Gr BS30 ..66 B1
Carmarthen Rd BS9 ...49 A5
Carnarvon Rd BS6 ....49 D2
Caroline Bldgs BA2 ..102 B5
Caroline Cl
   Chipping Sodbury BS37 .28 B2
   Keynsham BS31 ....81 C4
Caroline Ho BS2 .....143 A4
Caroline Pl BA1 ......141 B4
Carpenter Cl BS23 ...105 A7
Carpenters La BS31 ...81 E5
Carr Ho Bath BA2 ....101 A6
   3 Bristol BS2 ....49 F1
Carre Gdns BS22 ......88 F4
Carrick Ho 8 BS8 .....62 F6
Carrington Rd BS3 ....63 A3
Carroll Ct BS16 ....36 E1
Carsons Rd BS16 ......52 B2
Cart La BS1 ....143 B2
Carter Rd BS39 ......132 D5
Carter Wlk BS32 ......36 D8
Carters Way BA3 ....138 D3
Cartledge Rd 6 BS5 ..50 C1
Cary Ct 2 BS2 ....49 F1
Cashmore Ho 8 BS5 ..64 B7
Casion Ct BS1 ....143 B1
Cassell Rd BS16 ......51 C5
Cassey Bottom La BS5 .65 A7
Casson Dr BS16 ......51 C5
Castle Batch Com Prim Sch
   BS22 ....89 A5
Castle Cl Bristol BS10 .34 E2
   Flax Bourton BS48 ....76 F7
Castle Coombe BS30 ...8 C1
Castle Ct
   Bristol,Arno's Vale BS4 .64 C4
   Bristol,Stoke Gifford BS34 .37 A4
   Thornbury BS35 ....8 B1
Castle Farm La BS41 ...78 B2
Castle Farm Rd BS15 ..65 C2
Castle Gdns BA2 .....101 E3
Castle Hill BS29 .....107 C2
Castle La SN14 ....55 E2
Castle Prim Sch BS31 .81 D4
Castle Rd
   Bristol,Hopewell Hill BS15 .51 D2
   Bristol,Oldland Common
     BS30 ....66 D3
   Clevedon BS21 ....57 E6
   Pucklechurch BS16 ....53 C6
   Weston-S-M BS22 .....88 E3

Castle Sch The BS35 ...8 B2
Castle Sixth Form Ctr
   BS35 ....8 B1
Castle St Bristol BS1 .143 A3
   Thornbury BS35 ....8 B1
Castle View BS24 ....105 F8
Castle View Rd BS21 ..57 D5
Castlegate Ho BS4 ....64 E3
Castlewood Cl BS21 ...57 D4
Caswell Hill BS20 .....46 B1
Caswell La BS20 ......46 B2
Catbrain Hill BS10 .....35 B6
Catbrain La BS10 ......35 B6
Catchpot La BS37 .....41 A6
Catemead BS21 ....73 C8
Cater Rd BS13 ....79 B6
Catharine Pl BA1 ....141 B3
Cathcart Ho BA1 ....141 C4
Cathedral Church of The Holy
   & Undivided Trinity ★
   BS1 ....142 C2
Catherine Ct 10 BS6 ..49 E1
Catherine Hill BS35 ...13 F2
Catherine Mead St BS3 .63 D4
Catherine St BS11 .....47 C8
Catherine Way BA1 ...86 A5
Catley Gr BS41 ....62 B2
Cato St BS5 ....50 B2
Cattistock Dr BS5 .....65 A6
Cattle Market Rd BS1 .143 C1
Cattybrook Rd BS16 ...52 D5
Cattybrook St 6 BS5 ..64 B7
Caulfield Rd BS22 .....89 B4
Causeway BS48 ....59 B3
Causeway The
   Coalpit Heath BS36 ...38 D7
   Congresbury BS49 .....91 D4
   Nailsea BS48 ....59 F8
   Yatton BS49 ....91 C7
Causeway View BS48 ..59 C2
Causley Dr BS30 ......66 A5
Cautletts Cl BA3 ....138 F8
Cavan Wlk BS4 ....63 D1
Cave Ct BS2 ....143 B4
Cave Dr BS16 ....51 D6
Cave Gr BS16 ....52 B7
Cave St BS2 ....143 B4
Cavell Ct BS21 ....57 C1
Cavendish Cl
   Saltford BS31 ....82 D2
   Tormarton GL9 ....41 E2
Cavendish Cres BA1 ..141 A4
Cavendish Gdns BS9 ..48 C4
Cavendish Lodge BA1 .141 A4
Cavendish Pl BA1 ....141 A4
Cavendish Rd Bath BA1 .141 A4
   Bristol,Henleaze BS9 ..49 A5
   Bristol,Patchway BS34 .35 F8
Caveners Ct BS22 .....88 B1
Caversham Dr BS48 ...60 A2
Caves Cotts BS16 .....51 E7
Cecil Ave BS5 ....50 F1
Cecil Rd Bristol,Clifton BS8 .62 F8
   Bristol,Kingswood BS15 .65 D8
   Weston-S-M BS23 .....87 C1
Cedar Ave BS22 ....88 C1
Cedar Cl
   Bristol,Cadbury Heath BS30 .66 B4
   Bristol,Patchway BS34 .35 F7
   Long Ashton BS41 .....61 F1
Cedar Ct
   Bristol,Combe Dingle BS9 .48 D7
   Bristol,Mangotsfield BS16 .51 E6
   Bristol,Sneyd Park BS9 .48 C4
   Bristol,Westbury on Trym
     BS9 ....48 F8
Cedar Dr BS31 ....81 D4
Cedar Gr Bath BA2 ...101 D3
   Bristol BS9 ....48 D5
Cedar Hall BS16 ......51 D8
Cedar Pk BS9 ....48 D5
Cedar Row BS11 ......47 F6
Cedar Terr BA3 ......133 D2
Cedar Way Bath BA2 .141 A1
   Nailsea BS48 ....60 A2
   Portishead BS20 ......45 C4
   Pucklechurch BS16 ....53 C5
   Winterbourne BS36 ....37 D5
Cedarhurst Rd BS20 ..44 E4
Cedarn Ct BS22 ....88 B4
Cedars The BS40 ....112 D8
Cedern Ave BS24 ....106 C4
Cedric Cl BA1 ....101 C7
Cedric Rd BA1 ....101 C8
Celandine Cl BS35 .....8 D2
Celestine Rd BS37 ....27 C3
Celia Terr BS4 ....64 F6
Celtic Way BS24 .....122 B7
Cemetery Rd BS4 .....64 A3
Cennick Ave BS15 ....51 E1
Centaurus Rd BS34 ...35 D7
Central Ave Bristol BS15 .65 C5
   Severn Beach BS10 ....22 A3
Central Pk BS14 ....80 B7
Central Trad Est BS4 ..64 B4
Central Way Bristol BS10 .49 E8
   Clevedon BS21 ....57 E1
Centre Dr BS29 ......106 E4
Centre The
   Keynsham BS31 ....81 E5
   10 Weston-S-M BS23 .104 E7
Ceres Cl BS30 ....66 D5
Cerney Gdns BS48 ....60 A2
Cerney La BS11 ....47 E5
Cesson Cl BS37 ....40 C8

Chadleigh Gr BS4 79 D7
Chaffinch Dr BA3 139 B8
Chaffins The BS21 57 E2
Chaingate La BS37 27 A6
Chakeshill Cl BS10 35 C3
Chakeshill Dr BS10 35 C4
Chalcombe Cl BS34 36 C8
Chalcroft Ho [1] BS3 63 A4
Chalcroft Wlk BS13 78 E4
Chalet The BS10 34 F3
Chalfield Cl BS31 82 A2
Chalfont Rd BS22 105 C8
Chalford Cl BS37 39 D8
Chalk Farm Cl BS39 97 A7
Chalks Rd BS5 64 D8
Chalks The BS40 96 B3
Challender Ave BS10 34 F2
Challoner Ct BS1 143 A1
Challow Dr BS22 88 B2
Champion Rd BS15 52 A2
Champneys Ave [3] BS10 34 F3
Champs Sur Marne BS32 36 E8
Chancel Cl Bristol BS9 48 D3
Nailsea BS48 59 D1
Chancellor's Pound BS40 93 D3
Chancery St BS5 64 B7
Chandag Inf Sch BS31 82 A4
Chandag Jun Sch BS31 82 A4
Chandag Rd BS31 82 A4
Chandler Cl BA1 84 B1
Chandos Ct BS23 104 D6
Chandos Rd Bristol BS6 49 C1
Keynsham BS31 81 E7
Chandos Trad Est BS2 64 A5
Channel Ct BS22 88 B3
Channel Hts BS24 104 F1
Channel Rd BS21 57 E5
Channel View Cres BS20 45 B5
Channel View Rd BS20 45 B5
Channell's Hill BS9 49 A8
Channon's Hill BS16 50 F4
Chantry Cl BS48 59 C1
Chantry Dr BS22 89 A4
Chantry Gr BS11 34 C2
Chantry La BS16 37 F1
Chantry Mead Rd BA2 101 E3
Chantry Rd Bristol BS8 49 B1
Thornbury BS35 8 B2
Chapel Barton
[7] Bristol BS3 63 B2
Nailsea BS48 59 C2
Chapel Cl Bristol BS15 66 B8
Chew Stoke BS40 112 E8
Farrington Gurney BS39 131 F4
Nailsea BS48 59 E2
Winford BS40 95 A6
Chapel Ct Bath BA1 141 B2
Bristol,Brentry BS10 35 D3
Bristol,St Philip's Marsh BS2 64 A5
Radstock BA3 133 E4
Clevedon BS21 57 D3
Chapel Field BA2 134 E8
Chapel Gdns BS10 35 A1
Chapel Green La BS6 49 B2
Chapel Hill Backwell BS48 76 D7
Clevedon BS21 57 D3
Newport GL13 4 B7
Ubley BS40 111 C5
Wrington BS40 92 D3
Chapel La
Acton Turville GL9 43 A6
Bristol,Clay Hill BS5 50 E2
Bristol,Frenchay BS16 51 C7
Bristol,Lawrence Weston BS11 34 C2
Bristol,Warmley BS15 66 B8
Chew Stoke BS40 112 D8
Chipping Sodbury BS37 41 A7
Claverham BS49 91 F8
Cleeve BS49 92 B7
Hillesley GL12 19 E8
Hinton SN14 54 C5
Thornbury GL12 9 A1
Winford BS40 95 A6
Chapel Lawns BA3 133 E4
Chapel Pill La BS20 47 E4
Chapel Rd
Bristol,Bishopsworth BS13 79 A6
Bristol,Jefferies Hill BS15 65 C5
[2] Bristol,Lower Easton BS5 50 B1
Radstock BA3 133 E4
Thornbury BS35 7 C5
Chapel Row Bath BA1 141 B2
Bathford BA1 86 C2
Luckington SN14 31 E4
Norton St Philip BA2 136 F4
Pill BS20 47 C4
Chapel St Bristol BS2 64 A5
Thornbury BS35 15 B8
Chapel Way BS4 64 E6
Chapel Wlk BA2 116 C2
Chaplains Wood BS20 44 E5
Chaplin Rd BS5 50 B1
Chapter St BS2 143 B4
Charbon Gate BS34 36 F5
Charborough Ct BS34 36 A2
Charborough Rd BS34 35 F2
Charborough Road Prim Sch BS34 35 F2
Charbury Wlk BS11 47 E5
Chard Cl BS48 75 F8
Chard Ct BS14 80 B6
Chard Rd BS21 57 E1
Chardstock Ave BS9 48 D8
Chardyke Dr BS39 114 E1
Charfield [4] BS15 66 A8
Charfield Prim Sch GL12 10 F5
Charfield Rd Bristol BS10 35 D1
Kingswood GL12 11 E5
Chargrove [3] Bristol BS30 66 C6
Yate BS37 39 D7
Charis Ave BS10 49 C7
Charity La BA3 140 C1
Charlcombe La BA1 84 F3
Charlcombe Rise BA1 84 F2
Charlcombe View Rd BA1 85 A2
Charlcombe Way BA1 84 F2
Charlecombe Ct BS9 48 F6
Charlecombe Rd BS9 48 F6
Charles Ave BS34 36 E4
Charles Cl BS35 8 C3
Charles Ct BS8 142 A2
Charles England Ho BS34 35 F7
Charles Pl BS8 142 A2
Charles Rd BS34 36 B3
Charles St Bath BA1 141 B2
Bristol BS1 143 A4
Charleton Ho [8] BS2 143 C3
Charlock Cl BS22 105 D7
Charlock Rd BS22 105 D7
Charlotte St Bath BA1 141 B2
Bristol,Brandon Hill BS1 142 C3
Bristol,St Pauls BS2 143 C4
Charlotte St S BS1 142 C2
Charlton Ave Bristol BS34 35 F2
Weston-S-M BS23 104 D4
Charlton Ct BS34 23 F1
Charlton Dr BS48 60 C7
Charlton Gdns BS10 35 A3
Charlton La Bristol BS10 35 A3
Radstock BA3 139 D6
Charlton Mead Ct BS10 35 D4
Charlton Mead Dr BS10 35 D3
Charlton Pk
Keynsham BS31 81 D5
Midsomer Norton BA3 139 B7
Charlton Pl BS10 35 D4
Charlton Rd
Bristol,Brentry BS10 35 C3
Bristol,Chester Park BS15 51 B1
Holcombe BA3 139 D3
Keynsham BS31,BS14 81 C3
Midsomer Norton BA3 139 B8
Weston-S-M BS23 104 D4
Charlton St [16] BS5 64 B7
Charlton View BS20 45 C5
Charminster Rd BS16 51 B3
Charmouth Ct BS3 63 D1
Charmouth Rd BA1 101 B7
Charnell Rd BS16 51 E4
Charnhill Brow BS16 52 A4
Charnhill Cres BS16 51 F4
Charnhill Dr BS16 51 F4
Charnhill Ridge BS16 52 A4
Charnhill Vale BS16 51 F4
Charnwood BS16 52 A4
Charnwood Rd BS14 80 B4
Charter Ho BS1 142 B2
Charter Rd BS22 105 B8
Charter Wlk BS14 80 A6
Charterhouse Cl BS48 59 F1
Charterhouse Rd BS5 64 D8
Chartley BS9 48 D2
Chase La GL12 18 C6
Chase Rd BS15 51 D2
Chase The BS16 51 C3
Chasefield La [1] BS16 51 B4
Chatcombe BS37 39 E7
Chatham Pk BA2 102 C6
Chatham Row BA1 141 C3
Chatley Furlong BA2 136 F3
Chatsworth Pk BS35 8 C3
Chatsworth Rd
Bristol,Arno's Vale BS4 64 C4
Bristol,Hillfields BS16 51 B3
Chattenden Ho BS9 48 E3
Chatterton Gn BS14 79 F3
Chatterton Ho [5] BS1 143 B1
Chatterton Rd BS37 27 D1
Chatterton Sq BS1 143 C1
Chatterton St BS1 143 C1
Chaucer Rd Bath BA2 101 F4
Midsomer Norton BA3 139 B8
Weston-S-M BS23 105 A4
Chaundey Gr BS13 79 B5
Chavenage BS15 52 A1
Cheap St BA1 141 C2
Cheapside BS2 143 C4
Cheapside St [8] BS3 63 F4
Cheddar Cl BS48 75 F8
Cheddar Gorge★ BS27 126 E1
Cheddar Gr BS13 79 A8
Cheddar Grove Prim Sch BS13 79 A8
Cheddar Rd BS26 125 E2
Chedworth Bristol BS15 51 F3
Yate BS37 39 B7
Chedworth Cl BA2 102 F3
Chedworth Rd BS7 50 A6
Cheese La BS2 143 B2
Chelford Gr BS34 36 B8
Chelmer Gr BS31 81 F4
Chelmsford Wlk BS4 64 F5
Chelscombe BA1 84 B1
Chelsea Cl BS31 82 A5
Chelsea Pk BS5 64 C8
Chelsea Rd Bath BA1 101 C7
Bristol BS5 50 B1
Chelsfield BS48 76 A7
Chelston Rd BS4 79 D7
Chelswood Ave BS22 105 C8
Chelswood Gdns BS22 105 D8
Cheltenham Cres [2] BS6 49 D1
Cheltenham La BS6 49 D2
Cheltenham Rd BS6 49 E1
Cheltenham St BA2 141 A1
Chelvey Batch BS48 75 F3
Chelvey La BS48 75 E4
Chelvey Rd BS48 75 D5
Chelvey Rise BS48 60 A1
Chelvy Cl BS13 79 D3
Chelwood BS23 104 F8
Chelwood Dr BA2 101 D1
Chelwood Rd Bristol BS11 47 D7
Saltford BS31 82 E4
Chelwood Rdbt BS39 114 E8
Chepstow Pk BS16 37 F1
Chepstow Rd BS4 79 D8
Chepstow Wlk BS31 81 D5
Chequers Cl BS30 66 C3
Chequers Ct BS32 37 A6
Cherington Bristol BS15 65 B5
Yate BS37 39 D6
Cherington Rd
Bristol BS10 49 D7
Nailsea BS48 60 A2
Cheriton Pl
Bristol,Eastfield BS9 49 B7
Bristol,Warmley Tower BS30 66 C6
Cherry Ave BS21 57 E2
Cherry Cl BS49 91 B8
Cherry Garden La BS30 66 B2
Cherry Garden Prim Sch BS30 66 C2
Cherry Garden Rd BS30 66 C1
Cherry Gdns BS30 66 C1
Cherry Gr Bristol BS16 52 A6
Yatton BS49 91 B8
Cherry Hay BS21 57 D1
Cherry La [4] BS1 143 B4
Cherry Orchard La
[4] Bristol BS5 64 F8
Luckington SN14 31 C5
Cherry Rd
Chipping Sodbury BS37 28 A1
Long Ashton BS41 61 F1
Nailsea BS48 59 D1
Cherry Tree Cl
Bristol BS16 51 C2
Keynsham BS31 81 C4
Radstock BA3 133 E1
Cherry Wood BS30 66 B2
Cherrytree Cres BS16 51 C2
Cherrytree Ct BS16 53 C5
Cherrytree Rd BS16 51 C2
Cherrywood Rd BS22 88 F2
Cherrywood Rise BS22 88 F2
Chertsey Rd BS6 49 B1
Cherwell Cl BS35 15 C7
Cherwell Rd BS31 82 A4
Chescombe Rd BS49 91 B7
Chesham Rd N BS22 105 B8
Chesham Rd S BS22 105 B8
Chesham Way BS15 51 D1
Cheshire Cl BS37 27 E3
Chesle Cl BS20 44 E3
Chesle Way BS20 44 E3
Cheslefield BS20 44 E3
Chesley Hill BS30 66 F7
Chessel Cl BS32 24 C2
Chessel Ct [6] BS3 63 B2
Chessel St BS3 63 B3
Chessell Ave BS35 22 C7
Chessington Ave BS14 80 B5
Chester Cl BS24 106 A8
Chester Ct [4] BS5 64 C7
Chester Park Jun & Inf Schs BS16 51 A3
Chester Park Rd BS16 51 B2
Chester Pk BS5 50 E1
Chester Rd BS5 50 E1
Chester St BS5 50 B2
Chesterfield Ave BS6 49 E2
Chesterfield Cl BS29 106 F3
Chesterfield Ho BA3 133 B1
Chesterfield Hospl BS8 142 A2
Chesterfield Rd
Bristol,Mangotsfield BS16 51 E5
Bristol,Montpelier BS6 49 E2
Chestermaster Cl BS32 24 A5
Chesters BS30 66 A4
Chesterton Dr BS48 60 A2
Chesterton Ho [6] BS2 143 B4
Chestertons The BA2 102 F8
Chestnut Ave
Axbridge BS26 125 C2
Weston-S-M BS22 89 A1
Chestnut Chase BS48 60 A3
Chestnut Cl
Acton Turville GL9 43 A6
Banwell BS29 107 A3
Bristol BS14 80 F5
Congresbury BS49 91 D4
Paulton BS39 132 E6
Radstock BA3 133 E1
Chestnut Ct BS16 52 A5
Chestnut Dr
Chipping Sodbury BS37 28 A1
Claverham BS49 74 F1
Thornbury BS35 8 C1
Chestnut Gr Bath BA2 101 C4
Clevedon BS21 57 E4
Westwood BA15 120 F4
Chestnut Ho BS13 79 D3
Chestnut La BS24 122 B7
Chestnut Park Est GL12 11 F4
Chestnut Rd
Bristol,Lower Soundwell BS15 51 F3
Bristol,Mangotsfield BS16 51 D6
Long Ashton BS41 62 B2
Chestnut Way BS15 51 F3
Chestnut Wlk Bristol BS13 79 A6
Saltford BS31 82 E3
Chestnuts The
Cheddar BS27 126 A1
Winscombe BS25 125 A7
Chetwode Cl BS10 35 D3
Chetwood Ho BS5 64 C6
Chevening Cl BS34 36 D4
Chever's La BA2 136 E5
Cheviot Dr BS35 15 E8
Cheviot Way BS30 66 C5
Chew Cotts BS31 81 F5
Chew Ct BS40 113 D4
Chew Hill BS40 96 A4
Chew La BS40 95 F1
Chew Magna Prim Sch BS40 96 B3
Chew Rd BS40 95 C5
Chew St BS40 96 A3
Chew Stoke CE Prim Sch BS40 112 D8
Chew Valley Lake Nature Trails★ BS40 113 A7
Chew Valley Sch BS40 95 F1
Chewton Cl BS16 51 B3
Chewton Rd BS31 81 F2
Cheyne Rd BS9 48 D6
Chichester Ho BS4 64 F6
Chichester Pl BA3 134 A2
Chichester Way
[4] Weston-S-M BS24 106 A8
Yate BS37 27 D3
Chickwell La BA3 136 A1
Chilcompton Rd BA3 138 E7
Chillwood Cl BS37 26 E3
Chillyhill La BS40 95 F2
Chiltern Cl
Bristol,Cadbury Heath BS30 66 C5
Bristol,Whitchurch BS14 80 B4
Chiltern Pk BS35 15 E8
Chilton Ct [7] BA1 85 B1
Chilton Rd Bath BA1 85 B1
Bristol BS4 80 A8
Chimes The BS48 75 C8
Chine The BS16 50 D5
Chine View BS16 51 F8
Chiphouse Rd BS15 51 F3
Chippenham Rd SN14 70 A8
Chipperfield Dr BS15 51 F1
Chipping Cross BS21 73 C8
Chipping Edge Est BS37 28 C1
Chipping Sodbury Sch BS37 40 B8
Chipping The GL12 11 F4
Chippings The BS16 50 D5
Chisbury St BS5 50 C3
Chittening Ind Est BS11 33 D7
Chittening Rd BS11 33 E7
Chock La BS9 49 A7
Christ Church CE Inf Sch BS16 51 D5
Christ Church CE Jun Sch BS16 51 D5
Christ Church CE Prim Sch
Bristol,Hanham BS15 65 B4
Bristol,Victoria Park BS8 142 A3
Weston-S-M BS23 104 E8
Christ the King RC Prim Sch BS35 8 D1
Christchurch Ave BS16 51 D5
Christchurch Cl [1] BS48 59 E2
Christchurch La BS16 51 D5
Christchurch Path S [13] BS23 104 E8
Christchurch Rd BS8 142 A3
Christian Cl BS22 89 A3
Christina Terr BS8 142 A1
Christmas St [4] BS1 143 A3
Christmas Stps [2] BS1 143 A3
Christmas Tree BS34 35 D6
Christon Rd
Banwell BS29 107 A1
Loxton BS26 123 C6
Christon Terr BS23 104 F2
Chubb Cl BS30 65 F5
Church Ave
Bristol,Bridge Yate BS30 66 D7
[3] Bristol,Lower Easton BS5 50 B1
Bristol,Sneyd Park BS9 48 E4
Falfield GL12 9 E7
Church Cl Bathampton BA2 85 F2
Bathford BA1 86 B2
Bristol BS10 34 E2
Clevedon BS21 57 A2
Frampton Cotterell BS36 38 B8
Portishead BS20 45 D5
Yatton BS49 91 C7
Church Cnr BS24 122 B1
Church Cotts BA2 119 E8
Church Ct [3] Bristol BS16 51 D3
Midsomer Norton BA3 133 A1
Redhill BS40 93 D3
Church Dr Bristol BS5 64 E8
Congresbury BS49 91 D4
Church Farm Bsns Pk BA2 100 A7
Church Farm Cl BA2 99 B1
Church Farm Rd BS16 52 C6
Church Hayes Cl BS48 75 E8
Church Hayes Dr BS48 75 E8
Church Hill Bristol BS4 64 E2
Church Hill *continued*
Burton SN14 43 B3
Freshford BA2 120 B5
Olveston BS35 13 F3
Radstock BA3 134 C3
Timsbury BA2 116 B2
Church Ho BS7 49 F8
Church La Axbridge BS26 125 C2
Backwell BS48 76 C5
Badminton GL9 30 E5
Bath BA2 102 C4
Batheaston BA1 85 F4
Bishop Sutton BS39 113 D4
Bitton BS30 82 E7
Bristol BS1 143 B2
Bristol,Bromley Heath BS16 37 F1
Bristol,Clifton Wood BS8 142 B2
Bristol,Henbury BS10 34 E2
Bristol,Southville BS3 63 D3
Chew Stoke BS40 112 D8
Chilcompton BA3 138 D5
Chipping Sodbury BS37 41 B8
Churchill BS25 108 D5
Clutton BS39 114 E3
Coalpit Heath BS36 38 C6
Compton Bishop BS26 124 B3
Compton Dando BS39 98 D6
Cromhall GL12 10 A1
East Harptree BS40 129 E4
Farmborough BA2 116 A6
Farrington Gurney BS39 132 A4
Flax Bourton BS48 76 F7
Hambrook BS16 37 E2
Hutton BS24 105 E2
Limpley Stoke BA2 120 A5
Long Ashton BS41 62 C2
Loxton BS26 123 D4
Lympsham BS24 122 B1
Marshfield SN14 70 A8
Midsomer Norton BA3 133 A1
Nailsea BS48 59 C1
Nailsea,Stone-edge Batch BS21 59 C4
Paulton BS39 132 E6
Portbury BS20 46 E3
Rangeworthy BS37 16 F1
Stratton-on-t-F BA3 138 F2
Timsbury BA2 116 B2
Whitchurch BS14 80 B3
Wickwar GL12 18 A6
Winscombe BS25 124 E6
Winterbourne BS36 37 C6
Yatton BS49 91 C7
Church Lane End BS48 76 F8
Church Leaze BS11 47 D6
Church Mdws BS14 80 C4
Church Par BS4 64 E2
Church Pl BS20 47 C4
Church Rd
Abbots Leigh BS8 62 A8
Almondsbury BS32 24 A5
Alveston BS35 15 A1
Bath,Combe Down BA2 102 C1
Bath,Weston Park BA1 84 C1
Bitton BS30 82 E7
Bristol,Bedminster BS3 63 C3
Bristol,Bishopsworth BS13 79 A6
Bristol,Filton BS34 36 A3
Bristol,Frenchay BS16 51 C7
Bristol,Golden Hill BS7 49 E5
Bristol,Jefferies Hill BS15 65 B5
Bristol,Kingswood BS15 65 E8
Bristol,Moorfields BS5 64 D8
Bristol,Sneyd Park BS9 48 D3
Bristol,Stoke Gifford BS34 36 E4
Bristol,Upper Soundwell BS16 51 E3
Bristol,Westbury-on-Trym BS9 49 A7
Doynton BS30 54 A1
Dundry BS41 78 D2
Easter Compton BS35 23 A1
Easton-in-G BS20 47 A4
Frampton Cotterell BS36 38 C8
Leigh Woods BS8 62 D6
Luckington SN14 31 F4
Lympsham BS24 122 A1
Peasedown St John BA2 134 B8
Pensford BS39 97 A7
Pilning BS35 22 B7
Redhill BS40 93 D3
Severn Beach BS35 22 A6
Thornbury BS35 8 B2
Thornbury,Oldbury-on-Severn BS35 7 B5
Weston-S-M BS22 88 E2
Whitchurch BS14 80 C4
Wick BS30 67 B6
Winford BS40 95 A7
Winscombe BS25 124 E7
Winterbourne BS36 37 E4
Yate BS37 27 F2
Yate,Goose Green BS37 27 E3
Yatton BS49 91 C7
Church Rd N BS20 45 D5
Church Rd S BS20 45 D4
Church Rise BS40 95 A7
Church Row BA3 138 F2
Church Sq Clutton BS39 114 E2
Midsomer Norton BA3 133 A1
Church St Banwell BS29 107 B3
Bath BA1 141 C2
Bath,Weston Park BA1 84 B1
Bath,Widcombe BA2 102 B4
Bathford BA1 86 B2
Blagdon BS40 110 F2
Bristol BS1 143 B2
Bristol,Lower Easton BS5 50 B1

Church St continued
Bristol,Russell Town BS5 . . . . .64 B6
Norton St Philip BA2 . . . . .136 E4
Paulton BS39 . . . . .132 D6
Pensford BS39 . . . . .97 D4
Radstock BA3 . . . . .133 F2
Woolley BA1 . . . . .84 F6
Church Town BS48 . . . . .76 C5
Church View
Almondsbury BS32 . . . . . . .23 F4
Bristol,Filton BS34 . . . . . . .36 A3
Bristol,Staple Hill BS16 . . . .51 D5
Hillesley GL12 . . . . .19 D8
Newport GL13 . . . . .4 C8
Thornbury GL13 . . . . .8 E7
Wraxall BS48 . . . . .60 B2
Church Wlk Pill BS20 . . . .47 C4
Wrington BS40 . . . . .92 D2
Churchdown Wlk BS11 . . .47 E5
Churchend La GL12 . . . . .10 F3
Churchfarm Cl BS37 . . . . .27 F3
Churchfield Cl BS15 . . . .105 A7
Churchill Ave BS21 . . . . .57 C2
Churchill Bsns Pk BS34 . .105 A7
Churchill CE Prim Sch
BS40 . . . . .109 A5
Churchill Cl Bristol BS30 . .66 A5
7 Clevedon BS21 . . . . . . .57 C2
Churchill Com Sch
BS25 . . . . .108 D5
Churchill Dr BS9 . . . . .48 D7
Churchill Gate BS25 . . . .108 F4
Churchill Gn BS25 . . . . .108 D5
Churchill Rd Bristol BS4 . . .64 C4
Weston-S-M BS23 . . . . . .105 A7
Churchland Way BS24 . . .106 B8
Churchlands Rd **8** BS3 . . .63 B2
Churchpath Rd BS20 . . . . .47 C4
Churchside BS16 . . . . .51 B7
Churchward Cl **9** BS15 . . .65 B6
Churchward Rd
Weston-S-M BS22 . . . . . . .89 B3
Yate BS37 . . . . .27 B3
Churchway BA3 . . . . . . .135 D1
Churchways BS14 . . . . . . .80 C4
Churchways Ave BS7 . . . . .49 E6
Churchways Cres BS7 . . . .49 E6
Churston Cl BS14 . . . . . . .80 A3
Circle The BA2 . . . . .101 B3
Circuit 32 BS5 . . . . .64 B8
Circular Rd BS9 . . . . .48 E2
Circus Mews BA1 . . . . . .141 B3
Circus Pl BA1 . . . . .141 B3
Circus The BA1 . . . . .141 B3
City Academy Bristol The
BS5 . . . . .64 C8
City Bsns Pk BS5 . . . . . . .64 A8
City Mus & Art Gal★
BS8 . . . . .142 C3
City of Bath Coll BA1 . . . .141 B2
City of Bristol Coll
(Bedminster Ctr) BS3 . . . .63 E2
City of Bristol Coll (College
Green Ctr) BS1 . . . . . . .142 C2
City of Bristol Coll (Hartcliffe
Ctr) BS13 . . . . .79 D4
City of Bristol Coll (Lawrence
Weston Ctr) BS11 . . . . . . .34 B1
City of Bristol Coll Brunel Ctr
BS7 . . . . .49 E4
City of Bristol Coll Downend
Ctr BS16 . . . . .52 B4
City Rd BS2 . . . . .143 B4
City View BA1 . . . . .141 C4
Clamp The BS30 . . . . .66 C3
Clanage Rd BS3 . . . . .62 E4
Clanders Batch BS40 . . . .110 D3
Clandown CE Prim Sch
BA3 . . . . .133 E4
Clandown Rd BS39 . . . . . .132 F4
Clapton Dro BS20 . . . . . . .45 D1
Clapton La BS20 . . . . .45 E2
Clapton Rd BA3 . . . . . . .132 E1
Clapton Wlk BS9 . . . . .48 C5
Clare Ave BS7 . . . . .49 C3
Clare Gdns BA2 . . . . . . .101 D1
Clare Rd
Bristol,Chester Park BS15 . .51 C2
Bristol,Cotham BS6 . . . . . .49 C2
Bristol,Lower Easton BS5 . . .50 B2
Clare St Bristol BS1 . . . . .143 A2
Bristol,Moorfields BS5 . . . .64 C8
Clare Wlk BS35 . . . . .8 B2
Claremont Ave BS7 . . . . . .49 D3
Claremont Bldgs BA1 . . . .85 A1
Claremont Cres BS23 . . . .87 B1
Claremont Ct BS9 . . . . . . .49 C5
Claremont Gdns
Clevedon BS21 . . . . .57 E1
Paulton BS39 . . . . .132 B7
4 Nailsea BS48 . . . . .59 D1
Claremont Pl **14** BA1 . . . . .85 A1
Claremont Rd Bath BA1 . . .85 B1
Bristol BS7 . . . . .49 D3
Claremont Sch BS9 . . . . . .49 C5
Claremont St BS5 . . . . . . .50 A1
Claremont Terr **10** BS5 . . . .64 C8
Claremont Wlk BA1 . . . . . .85 A1
Clarence Ave BS16 . . . . . .51 E5
Clarence Ct BS15 . . . . . . .51 E5
Clarence Gdns BS16 . . . . .51 E5
Clarence Grove Rd
BS23 . . . . .104 E5
Clarence Pl Bath BA1 . . . .101 B6
Bristol BS2 . . . . .142 C4
Clarence Rd Bristol BS1 . .143 B1
Bristol,Chester Park BS15 . .51 B1
Bristol,Newton BS2 . . . . . .64 A7
Bristol,Staple Hill BS16 . . . .51 E5

Clarence Rd E BS23 . . . .104 E5
Clarence Rd N BS23 . . . .104 D5
Clarence Rd S BS23 . . . .104 D5
Clarence St BA1 . . . . . . .141 C4
Clarence Terr BA2 . . . . . .102 E4
Clarendon Rd Bath BA2 . .102 B5
Bristol BS6 . . . . .49 C2
Weston-S-M BS23 . . . . . .104 F8
Clarendon Villas BA2 . . . .102 B5
Clark Cl BS48 . . . . .60 B2
Clark Dr BS16 . . . . .50 F7
Clark St BS5 . . . . .64 A8
Clarke St BS3 . . . . .63 D4
Clarken Cl BS48 . . . . .59 E1
Clarken Coombe BS41 . . . .62 B3
Clarkson Ave BS22 . . . . . .88 C1
Clarkson Ho BA1 . . . . . . .141 A1
Clatworthy Dr BS14 . . . . . .80 A7
Claude Ave BA2 . . . . . . .101 C5
Claude Terr BA2 . . . . . . .101 C5
Clavell Rd BS10 . . . . .34 A3
Claverham Cl BS49 . . . . . .91 D7
Claverham Dro BS49 . . . . .74 D5
Claverham Pk BS49 . . . . . .91 F8
Claverham Rd
Bristol BS16 . . . . .51 A5
Yatton BS49 . . . . .91 E8
Claverton Bldgs BA2 . . . .141 C1
Claverton Ct BA2 . . . . . . .102 E4
Claverton Down Rd BA2 . .102 F3
Claverton Dr BA2 . . . . . . .102 F3
Claverton Pumping Sta★
BA2 . . . . .103 C5
Claverton Rd BS31 . . . . . .82 E2
Claverton Rd W BS31 . . . . .82 D3
Claverton St BA2 . . . . . . .141 C1
Clay Bottom BS5 . . . . .50 E2
Clay Hill BS5 . . . . .50 E2
Clay La Bitton BS30 . . . . . .82 D8
Bristol,Bitton BS30 . . . . . .66 D1
Bristol,Little Stoke BS34 . . .36 C7
Thornbury BS35 . . . . .8 E1
Clay Pit Rd BS6 . . . . .49 A3
Claydon Gn BS14 . . . . . . .79 F3
Clayfield BS37 . . . . .27 E5
Clayfield Rd BS4 . . . . .64 E3
Claymore Cres BS15 . . . . .51 B1
Claypiece Rd BS13 . . . . . .79 A4
Claypool Rd BS15 . . . . . . .65 E7
Clayton Cl BS20 . . . . .45 E4
Clayton St
Avonmouth BS11 . . . . .33 A1
21 Bristol BS5 . . . . .64 B8
Cleave St BS2 . . . . .50 A2
Cleeve Ave BS16 . . . . .51 E7
Cleeve Dr BS49 . . . . .92 B8
Cleeve Gdns BS16 . . . . . . .51 D7
Cleeve Gn BA2 . . . . .101 A6
Cleeve Gr BS31 . . . . .81 D5
Cleeve Hill Bristol BS16 . . .51 D7
Compton Martin BS40 . . . .128 E8
Cleeve Hill Extension
BS16 . . . . .51 E6
Cleeve Hill Rd BS40 . . . . . .92 C7
Cleeve La BS30 . . . . .53 D1
Cleeve Lawns BS16 . . . . . .51 D7
Cleeve Lodge Cl BS16 . . . .51 E6
Cleeve Lodge Rd BS16 . . . .51 E6
Cleeve Park Rd BS16 . . . . .51 E7
Cleeve Pl BS48 . . . . .60 A1
Cleeve Rd Bristol BS4 . . . .64 B3
Bristol,Frenchay BS16 . . . .51 C8
Bristol,Mangotsfield BS16 . .51 E6
Yate BS37 . . . . .27 E1
Cleeve Wood Rd BS16 . . . .51 D7
Cleevedale Rd BA2 . . . . . .102 A1
Clement St BS2 . . . . .143 C4
Cleve Ct
4 Bristol,Clifton Wood BS8 . .62 F6
Bristol,Filton BS34 . . . . . . .36 A4
Cleve House Sch BS4 . . . . .64 B3
Cleve Rd BS34 . . . . .36 A4
Clevedale BS16 . . . . .51 D7
Clevedale Ct BS16 . . . . . . .51 D7
Clevedon Com Sch BS21 . .57 F5
Clevedon Craft Ctr★
BS21 . . . . .58 A2
Clevedon Ct★ BS21 . . . . .58 A4
Clevedon Hospl BS21 . . . . .57 E3
Clevedon La BS21 . . . . . . .59 C7
Clevedon Min Rly★ BS21 . .57 B2
Clevedon Pier★ BS21 . . . . .57 C4
Clevedon Rd Bristol BS7 . . .49 D3
Midsomer Norton BA3 . . . .133 C2
Nailsea BS21 . . . . .59 C4
Nailsea,West Hill BS48 . . . .60 B4
Nailsea,Wraxall BS48 . . . . .60 D6
Portishead BS20 . . . . .45 D3
Weston-S-M BS23 . . . . . .104 E6
Wraxall,Flax Bourton BS48 . .60 F2
Clevedon Terr BS6 . . . . . .143 A4
Clevedon Wlk **2** BS48 . . . .59 E2
Cleveland Cl BS35 . . . . . . .15 E8
Cleveland Ct BA2 . . . . . . .102 C6
Cleveland Pl BA1 . . . . . . .141 C4
Cleveland Pl E BA1 . . . . . .141 C4
Cleveland Pl W BA1 . . . . .141 C4
Cleveland Reach BA1 . . . .141 C4
Cleveland Row BA1 . . . . . .102 B8
Cleveland Terr BA1 . . . . . .141 C4
Cleveland Wlk BA2 . . . . . .102 C6
Clewson Rise BS14 . . . . . .79 F3
Cliff Court Dr BS16 . . . . . .51 B7
Cliff Rd
Cheddar BS27,BS40 . . . . .126 E1
Weston-S-M BS22 . . . . . . .88 A2
Cliffe Dr BA2 . . . . .120 A6

Clifford Gdns BS11 . . . . . .47 E6
Clifford Rd BS16 . . . . .51 C4
Clift House Rd BS3 . . . . . .63 A4
Clift House Spur BS3 . . . . .62 F4
Clift Pl BS1 . . . . .143 A1
Clift Rd BS3 . . . . .63 A4
Clifton Arc BS8 . . . . .142 A3
Clifton Ave BS23 . . . . . . .104 E5
Clifton Cath★ BS8 . . . . . .142 A4
Clifton Cl **1** BS8 . . . . . . .62 F7
Clifton Coll BS8 . . . . .142 A4
Clifton College Prep Sch
BS8 . . . . .48 F1
Clifton Ct **12** BS21 . . . . . .57 C2
Clifton Down BS8 . . . . . . .62 F7
Clifton Down Rd BS8 . . . .142 A3
Clifton Down Sh Ctr BS8 . .49 B1
Clifton Down Sta BS8 . . . .49 B1
Clifton High Gr BS9 . . . . . .48 E5
Clifton High Sch BS8 . . . .142 A4
Clifton Hill BS8 . . . . .142 A2
Clifton Metro **10** BS8 . . . . .49 B1
Clifton Park BS8 . . . . .62 F8
Clifton Pk BS8 . . . . .142 A3
Clifton Pl BS5 . . . . .64 A8
Clifton Rd Bristol BS8 . . . .142 A2
Weston-S-M BS23 . . . . . .104 E5
Clifton St
Bristol,Bedminster BS3 . . . .63 C3
Bristol,Upper Easton BS5 . . .64 A8
Portishead BS20 . . . . .45 C2
Clifton Suspension Bridge★
BS8 . . . . .62 F7
Clifton Vale BS8 . . . . .142 A2
Clifton Vale Cl BS8 . . . . . .142 A2
Clifton View **1** BS3 . . . . . .63 F4
Clifton Wood Ct BS8 . . . . .142 B2
Clifton Wood Rd BS8 . . . .142 B2
Cliftonwood Cres BS8 . . . .142 B2
Cliftonwood Terr BS8 . . . .142 A2
Clinton Rd BS3 . . . . .63 C2
Clive Rd BS14 . . . . .80 C8
Clockhouse Mews BS20 . . .45 D6
Cloisters Rd BS16 . . . . . . .37 F6
Clonmel Rd BS4 . . . . .63 D1
Close The
Bristol,Catbrain BS10 . . . . .35 A5
Bristol,Little Stoke BS34 . . .36 C6
Bristol,Patchway BS32 . . . .24 C1
Bristol,Upper Soundwell
BS16 . . . . .51 D3
Coalpit Heath BS36 . . . . . .38 C6
Portishead BS20 . . . . .44 F1
Thornbury BS35 . . . . .15 B8
Closemead BS21 . . . . .57 D1
Clothier Rd BS4 . . . . .64 F2
Cloud Hill Ind Est BS39 . .132 A8
Clouds Hill Ave BS5 . . . . . .64 F8
Clouds Hill Rd BS5 . . . . . .64 F8
Clovelly Cl BS5 . . . . .64 F8
Clovelly Rd Bristol BS5 . . . .64 F8
Weston-S-M BS22 . . . . . . .89 A2
Clover Cl Clevedon BS21 . . .57 F3
Paulton BS39 . . . . .132 E4
Clover Ct BS22 . . . . .105 D7
Clover Ground BS9 . . . . . .49 B7
Clover Leaze BS32 . . . . . .36 D6
Cloverdale Dr BS30 . . . . . .66 A3
Cloverlea Bsns Ctr BS36 . .38 C3
Cloverlea Rd BS30 . . . . . . .66 C5
Clutton Hill BS39 . . . . . . .115 B4
Clutton Prim Sch BS39 . . .114 E3
Clyde Ave BS31 . . . . .81 F4
Clyde Ct **2** BS3 . . . . .63 C3
Clyde Gdns Bath BA2 . . . .101 B6
Bristol BS5 . . . . .65 B6
Clyde Gr BS34 . . . . .35 F2
Clyde Ho **7** BS35 . . . . . . .15 C8
Clyde La BS6 . . . . .49 C2
Clyde Mews **3** BS6 . . . . . .49 C2
Clyde Pk BS6 . . . . .49 B2
Clyde Rd
Bristol,Totterdown BS4 . . . .64 A3
Bristol,Woolcott Park BS6 . .49 B2
Frampton Cotterell BS36 . . .38 B7
Clyde Terr
3 Bristol,Bedminster BS3 . .63 C3
Bristol,Totterdown BS4 . . . .64 A3
Clydesdale Cl BS14 . . . . . .80 A6
Clynder Gr BS21 . . . . .57 E6
Co-Operation Rd BS5 . . . . .50 C1
Coach House Mews
BS23 . . . . .87 D1
Coalbridge Cl BS22 . . . . . .88 F2
Coaley Rd BS11 . . . . .47 D5
Coalpit La BA3 . . . . .138 A2
Coalpit Rd BA1 . . . . .86 A4
Coalsack La BS36 . . . . .38 B3
Coalville Rd BS36 . . . . . . .38 D7
Coape Rd BS14 . . . . .80 F5
Coates Est BS48 . . . . .59 F3
Coates Gr BS48 . . . . .60 A2
Coates Wlk BS4 . . . . .79 D6
Cobblestone Mews BS8 . .142 A4
Cobden Ctr The BS16 . . . . .38 A2
Cobden St BS5 . . . . .64 C7
Coberley BS15 . . . . .65 C6
Cobhorn Dr BS13 . . . . .78 F4
Cobley Croft BS21 . . . . . . .73 C8
Cobourg Rd BS6 . . . . .49 F2
Cobthorn Way BS49 . . . . . .91 B5
Coburg Villas **12** BA1 . . . . .85 A1
Cock & Yew Tree Hill
BS40 . . . . .95 A2
Cock La SN14 . . . . .54 D5

Cock Rd BS15 . . . . .65 F6
Cockers Hill BS39 . . . . . . .98 C5
Codrington Pl BS8 . . . . . .142 A3
Codrington Rd BS7 . . . . . .49 D3
Cody Ct **1** BS15 . . . . .65 B5
Cogan Rd BS16 . . . . .51 E3
Cogsall Rd BS14 . . . . .80 F6
Coker Rd BS22 . . . . .89 B2
Colbourne Rd BA2 . . . . . .101 D1
Colchester Cres BS4 . . . . .79 D7
Coldharbour La
Bristol BS16 . . . . .50 E8
Weston-S-M BS23 . . . . . .104 D3
Coldharbour Rd BS6 . . . . .49 B4
Coldpark Gdns BS13 . . . . .78 E5
Coldpark Rd BS13 . . . . . . .78 E5
Coldrick Cl BS14 . . . . .79 F3
Cole Rd BS2 . . . . .64 B6
Colebrook Rd BS15 . . . . . .65 C8
Coleford Rd BS10 . . . . .35 D1
Colehouse La BS21 . . . . . .73 C8
Colemead BS13 . . . . .79 B5
Coleridge Ho BS34 . . . . . .24 A1
Coleridge Rd Bristol BS5 . . .50 C3
Clevedon BS21 . . . . .57 C3
Weston-S-M BS23 . . . . . .105 A4
Coleridge Vale Rd E **1**
BS21 . . . . .57 D2
Coleridge Vale Rd N
BS21 . . . . .57 C2
Coleridge Vale Rd S
BS21 . . . . .57 D2
Coleridge Vale Rd W **4**
BS21 . . . . .57 C2
Coles Gdns BA3 . . . . .140 B5
Colesborne Cl BS37 . . . . . .39 E8
Coleshill Dr BS13 . . . . .79 B5
Coley Rd BS40 . . . . .130 B4
Colin Cl BS35 . . . . .8 C1
Collard Ho **2** BS16 . . . . . . .50 F4
College Ave BS16 . . . . .51 A5
College Ct BS16 . . . . .51 A5
College Fields BS8 . . . . . . .62 F8
College Gn BS1 . . . . .142 C2
College Park Dr BS10 . . . . .34 F1
College Rd Bath BA1 . . . . .84 E1
Bristol,Clifton BS8 . . . . . . .62 F8
Bristol,Eastfield BS9 . . . . . .49 A7
Bristol,Fishponds BS16 . . . .51 A5
College Sq BS1 . . . . .142 C2
College St BS1 . . . . .142 C2
College View **19** BA1 . . . . . .85 A1
College Way BS34 . . . . . . .36 A4
Collet Cl BS22 . . . . .89 C4
Collett Cl BS15 . . . . .65 B5
Collett Way BS37 . . . . .27 C3
Collier Cl BA2 . . . . .133 D8
Colliers Break BS16 . . . . . .52 B5
Colliers La BA1 . . . . .84 F4
Colliers Rise BA3 . . . . . . .134 A3
Colliers Wlk **4** BS48 . . . . .59 E2
Collin Rd BS4 . . . . .64 D4
Collingwood Ave BS15 . . . .51 E1
Collingwood Cl
Saltford BS31 . . . . .82 E2
Weston-S-M BS22 . . . . . . .88 E3
Collingwood Rd **4** BS6 . . . .49 B1
Collins Ave BS34 . . . . .36 C6
Collins Dr BS35 . . . . .22 C3
Collins St BS11 . . . . .47 B8
Collinson Rd BS13 . . . . . . .79 B5
Colliter Cres BS3 . . . . .63 B2
Collum La BS22 . . . . .88 E6
Coln Sq BS35 . . . . .15 C8
Colne Gn BS31 . . . . .82 A4
Colombo Cres BS23 . . . . .104 E3
Colston Ave BS1 . . . . .143 A2
Colston Cl Bristol BS16 . . . .51 D4
Winterbourne BS36 . . . . . .37 E4
Colston Ct BS7 . . . . .49 D3
Colston Dale BS16 . . . . . . .50 E4
Colston Fort **2** BS2 . . . . . .143 A4
Colston Hill BS16 . . . . .50 D4
Colston Mews BS6 . . . . . . .49 E1
Colston Par BS1 . . . . .143 B1
Colston Rd BS5 . . . . .50 C1
Colston St
Bristol,Kingsdown BS1 . . . .143 A3
Bristol,Upper Soundwell
BS16 . . . . .51 D3
Colston Yd BS1 . . . . .143 A3
Colston's Collegiate Lower
Sch BS16 . . . . .50 D5
Colston's Collegiate Sch
BS16 . . . . .50 D4
Colston's Prim Sch BS6 . . .49 D1
Colstone Cl **3** BS16 . . . . . .50 E3
Colstons Girls' Sch BS6 . . .49 E1
Colthurst Dr BS15 . . . . . . .65 E5
Colts Gn BS37 . . . . .40 E8
Columbus Ho BA2 . . . . . . .102 D8
Colwyn Rd **2** BS5 . . . . . . .50 C1
Colyton **11** BS22 . . . . .89 A2
Colyton Ct BS3 . . . . .63 D1
Comb Paddock BS9 . . . . . .49 B7
Combe Down CE Prim Sch
BA2 . . . . .102 B1
Combe Fields BS20 . . . . . .45 C6
Combe Gr BA1 . . . . .101 B8
Combe Hay La BA2 . . . . . .118 B6
Combe Ho BS15 . . . . .65 B5
Combe La BS39 . . . . .132 B6
Combe Pk BA1 . . . . .101 C8
Combe Rd BA2 . . . . .102 B1
Portishead BS20 . . . . .45 D5
Combe Road Cl BA2 . . . . .102 B1
Combe Side BS48 . . . . .76 A2

Combe The BS40 . . . . . . .109 F2
Combermere BS35 . . . . . . .15 D8
Combeside BA2 . . . . .102 A3
Combfactory La **13** BS5 . . . .64 B8
Comfortable Pl BA1 . . . . . .141 A3
Commercial Rd BS1 . . . . .143 A1
Common (East) The
BS32 . . . . .24 C1
Common La
Easton-in-G BS20 . . . . . . .47 B2
Easton Green BS25 . . . . . .108 B5
Common Mead La BS16 . . .37 A1
Common Rd Bristol BS15 . . .65 B3
Winterbourne BS36 . . . . . .37 F7
Common The
Bristol,Frenchay BS16 . . . .51 B7
Bristol,Patchway BS32 . . . .24 C1
Olveston BS35 . . . . .13 F3
Commonfield Rd BS11 . . . .34 B1
Commonmead La BS37 . . . .40 F8
Compton Dr Bristol BS9 . . .48 C7
Weston-S-M BS24 . . . . . .105 A2
Compton Gn BS31 . . . . . . .81 E4
Compton La BS26 . . . . . . .125 B2
Compton Lodge **3** BS6 . . . .49 B1
Compton St BS5 . . . . .64 C7
Comrade Ave BS25 . . . . . .125 E8
Comyn Wlk BS16 . . . . .51 A5
Concorde Dr Bristol BS10 . .35 B1
Clevedon BS21 . . . . .57 B1
Concorde Rd BS34 . . . . . . .35 F2
Condor Cl BS22 . . . . .105 D8
Condor Ho BS7 . . . . .50 C7
Condover Rd BS4 . . . . .65 A3
Conduit Pl **2** BS2 . . . . . . .50 A1
Conduit Rd BS2 . . . . .50 A1
Cone The BS10,BS34 . . . . .35 C6
Coneygree BS13 . . . . .78 F6
Conference Ave BS20 . . . . .45 F4
Conference Cl BS20 . . . . . .45 F4
Congleton Rd BS5 . . . . . . .64 D8
Conham Hill BS15 . . . . . . .65 A5
Conham Rd BS4,BS5,BS15 . .64 F5
Conham Vale BS15 . . . . . . .65 A5
Conifer Cl Bristol BS16 . . . .51 D6
Frampton Cotterell BS36 . . .26 A1
Conifer Way BS24 . . . . . . .105 E5
Coniston Ave BS9 . . . . .48 E6
Coniston Cl BS30 . . . . .66 D6
Coniston Cres BS23 . . . . .104 F4
Coniston Prim Sch BS34 . . .23 F1
Coniston Rd BS34 . . . . . . .23 F1
Connaught Pl BS23 . . . . . .104 D8
Connaught Prim Sch
BS4 . . . . .79 E8
Connaught Rd BS4 . . . . . . .79 E8
Connection Rd BA2 . . . . . .101 A6
Constable Cl BS31 . . . . . . .81 F6
Constable Dr BS22 . . . . . . .88 E3
Constable Rd BS7 . . . . .50 B6
Constantine Ave BS34 . . . .36 F5
Constitution Hill BS8 . . . . .142 B2
Contemporis BS8 . . . . . . .142 A3
Convent Cl BS10 . . . . .34 D3
Convocation Ave BA2 . . . .102 F5
Conway Gn BS31 . . . . .82 A3
Conway Rd BS4 . . . . .64 C4
Conygar Cl BS21 . . . . .57 F5
Conygre Gn BA2 . . . . .116 B2
Conygre Gr BS34 . . . . .36 C3
Conygre Rd BS34 . . . . .36 B3
Conygre Rise BA2 . . . . . . .115 F6
Conygre Terr BA2 . . . . . . .102 E6
Cook Cl BS30 . . . . .66 C4
Cook St BS11 . . . . .47 C8
Cook's Folly Rd BS9 . . . . . .48 D3
Cook's La Banwell BS29 . . .107 A4
Clevedon BS21 . . . . .58 B2
Cooke's Dr BS35 . . . . .23 A1
Cooks Bridle Path BS48 . . .93 D8
Cooks Cl BS32 . . . . .24 D3
Cooks Gdns BS48 . . . . .60 A2
Cooks La BS36 . . . . .38 D3
Cooksley Rd BS5 . . . . .64 C8
Cookworthy Cl **2** BS5 . . . . .64 B6
Coomb End BA3 . . . . .133 F3
Coomb Rocke BS9 . . . . . . .48 D5
Coomband Ho BA3 . . . . . .133 F3
Coombe Ave BS35 . . . . .8 B2
Coombe Bridge Ave BS9 . .48 D6
Coombe Cl BS10 . . . . .34 D3
Coombe Dale
Backwell BS48 . . . . .94 A8
Bristol BS9 . . . . .48 C6
Coombe Gdns BS9 . . . . . . .48 E6
Coombe La Bristol BS9 . . . .48 E6
Compton Bishop BS26 . . . .124 B4
East Harptree BS40 . . . . . .129 E4
Easton-in-G BS8 . . . . .47 A1
Coombe Rd Bristol BS5 . . . .50 C2
Nailsea BS48 . . . . .59 E1
Weston-S-M BS23 . . . . . . .87 E1
Coombe The
Blagdon BS40 . . . . .110 C3
Compton Martin BS40 . . . .129 A6
Coombe Way BS10 . . . . . . .34 F1
Coombes Way BS30 . . . . . .66 D4
Cooper Rd Bristol BS9 . . . . .48 F7
Thornbury BS35 . . . . .15 B7
Cooperage La BS3 . . . . . . .142 B1
Cooperage Rd BS5 . . . . . . .64 D7
Coopers Dr BS37 . . . . .27 F5
Coots The BS14 . . . . .80 E6
Cope Pk BS32 . . . . .24 C5
Copeland Dr **3** BS14 . . . . . .80 B5

Copford La BS41 62 B1
Copley Ct BS15 65 E5
Copley Gdns Bristol BS7 50 B6
Weston-S-M BS22 88 F2
Coppack Ho 8 BS21 57 C2
Copperfield Dr BS22 88 F4
Coppice End Cnr BS24 122 C2
Coppice The
Bristol,Bishopsworth BS13 78 E4
Bristol,Little Stoke BS32 36 E7
Copse Cl BS24 105 A1
Copse Cnr BS24 122 C2
Copse End BS25 107 F2
Copse Rd Bristol BS4 64 B6
Clevedon BS21 57 C4
Keynsham BS31 82 C4
Copseland BA2 102 D5
Copthorne Cl 1 BS14 80 B5
Coralberry Dr BS22 88 F1
Corbet Cl BS11 34 C2
Corbett Cl BS37 27 F4
Corbett Ho 11 BS5 64 C7
Cordwell Wlk BS10 49 D7
Corey Cl 5 BS2 49 F1
Corfe Cl BS48 59 D1
Corfe Cres BS31 81 E4
Corfe Pl BS30 66 B1
Corfe Rd BS4 79 D7
Coriander Dr BS32 37 A7
Coriander Wlk BS5 50 C2
Corinthian Ct 9 BS1 143 B1
Corinum Cl BS16 52 C6
Cork Pl BA1 101 D7
Cork St BA1 101 D7
Cork Terr BA1 101 D7
Corker's Hill 9 BS5 64 F6
Cormorant Cl BS22 88 F1
Corn St Bath BA1 141 B2
Bristol BS1 143 A2
Corner Croft BS21 57 D1
Cornfield Cl BS32 24 C1
Cornfields The BS22 88 F5
Cornhill Dr BS14 80 A7
Cornish Gr BS14 80 E6
Cornish Rd BS14 80 E6
Cornish Wlk BS14 80 E6
Cornleaze BS13 79 A5
Cornwall Cres BS37 27 F3
Cornwall Rd BS7 49 D4
Cornwallis Ave
Bristol BS8 142 A2
Weston-S-M BS22 88 F4
Cornwallis Cres BS8 62 F6
Cornwallis Gr BS8 142 A2
Coromandel Hts BA1 141 B4
Coronation Ave
Bath BA2 101 C4
Bristol BS16 51 A4
Keynsham BS31 81 D4
Coronation Cl BS30 66 A5
Coronation Est BS23 104 F3
Coronation Pl BS1 143 A2
Coronation Rd
Banwell BS29 107 A3
Bath BA1 101 D7
Bleadon BS24 122 C6
Bristol,Cadbury Heath BS30 66 B5
Bristol,Mangotsfield BS16 51 E5
Bristol,Southville BS3 142 C1
Bristol,Warmley BS15 66 A7
Weston-S-M BS22 88 E2
Coronation Terr BA3 138 D5
Corondale Rd BS22 105 D8
Corpus Christi RC Prim Sch BS23 104 D6
Corridor The BA1 141 C2
Corsley Wlk BS4 79 F8
Corston BS24 105 A2
Corston Dr BA2 100 B6
Corston La BA2 100 A8
Corston View BA2 101 C2
Corston Wlk BS11 47 D7
Cossham Cl BS35 8 C2
Cossham Meml Hospl BS16 51 C2
Cossham Rd BS5 64 D7
Cossham St BS16 52 B5
Cossham Wlk BS5 51 A1
Cossington Rd BS4 79 F8
Cossins Rd BS6 49 B3
Costers Cl BS35 15 A5
Costiland Dr BS13 78 F6
Cote Dr BS9 49 A4
Cote House La BS9 49 A5
Cote La BS9 49 A5
Cote Lea Pk BS9 49 B7
Cote Paddock BS9 48 F4
Cote Pk BS9 48 E6
Cote Rd BS9 49 A4
Cotham Brow BS6 49 D1
Cotham Gdns 15 BS6 49 B1
Cotham Gr BS6 49 D1
Cotham Gram Sch BS6 142 C4
Cotham Hill BS6 142 C4
Cotham Lawn Ho BS6 142 C4
Cotham Lawn Rd BS6 49 C1
Cotham Pk BS6 49 C1
Cotham Pk N BS6 49 C1
Cotham Pl BS6 142 C4
Cotham Rd BS6 142 C4
Cotham Rd S BS6 143 A4
Cotham Sch (Charnwood Annexe) BS6 49 C1
Cotham Side BS6 49 D1
Cotham Vale BS6 49 C1
Cotman Wlk Bristol BS7 50 B6
1 Weston-S-M BS22 88 F2
Cotrith Gr BS10 34 E3
Cotswold Cl BS20 45 E4
Cotswold Ct BS37 28 B1
Cotswold Education Ctr BS16 52 A5
Cotswold La BS37 41 A8
Cotswold Rd Bath BA2 101 E4
Bristol BS3 63 D3
Chipping Sodbury BS37 40 B8
Cotswold Terr BA2 102 E6
Cotswold View Bath BA2 101 B5
Bristol,Filton BS34 36 A3
Bristol,Hopewell Hill BS15 51 D2
Charfield GL12 11 B5
Wickwar GL12 18 B6
Cottage Gdns BS5 65 A7
Cottage Pl 3 Bath BA1 85 C2
Bristol BS2 143 A4
Cottages The BS40 92 D2
Cotterell Ct BA1 141 B2
Cottington Ct BS15 65 E5
Cottisford Rd BS5 50 B4
Cottle Gdns BS14 80 F6
Cottle Rd BS14 80 F6
Cottles La BA15 120 F6
Cotton Mead BA2 100 B7
Cottonwood Dr BS30 66 A3
Cottrell Ave BS15 51 C2
Cottrell Rd BS5 50 C3
Coulson Dr BS22 89 B3
Coulson Wlk BS15 51 C2
Coulson's Cl BS14 80 A3
Coulson's Rd BS14 80 A3
Council Hos BS22 89 B8
Council Hos The BS39 130 E6
Council Houses The BS40 111 B8
Counterpool Rd BS15 65 C7
Counterslip BS1 143 B2
Counterslip Gdns BS14 80 C6
Countess Wlk BS16 50 D6
County St BS4 64 A4
County Way BS34 37 A4
Court Ave Bristol BS34 36 F5
Yatton BS49 91 C7
Court Cl Backwell BS48 76 C5
Bristol BS7 49 E7
Portishead BS20 45 D4
Court Dr BS25 108 B4
Court Farm Pk* BS29 106 F5
Court Farm Rd
Bristol,Longwell Green BS30 65 E2
Bristol,Whitchurch BS14 79 F3
Court Gdns
Batheaston BA1 86 A4
Yate BS37 39 E8
Court Hay BS20 47 A4
Court Hill BS39 98 D5
Court La Bathford BA1 86 B2
Clevedon BS21 58 A3
Shipham BS25 125 F8
Wick BS30 67 B6
Court Mdw GL13 3 E3
Court Mead GL13 3 E3
Court Pl BS22 88 F2
Court Rd
Bristol,Horfield BS7 49 F6
Bristol,Kingswood BS15 65 D7
Bristol,Oldland Common BS30 66 C3
Frampton Cotterell BS36 37 F8
Weston-S-M BS22 88 A5
Court View BS30 67 C6
Court View Cl BS32 24 A5
Court-de-Wyck CE Prim Sch BS49 74 F1
Courtenay Cres BS4 79 D7
Courtenay Rd BS31 82 B2
Courtenay Wlk BS22 89 A3
Courtfield Gr BS16 51 A4
Courtlands Bristol BS32 24 C1
Keynsham BS31 81 E5
Courtlands La BS3 62 E4
Courtmead BA2 118 F7
Courtney Prim Sch BS15 65 F7
Courtney Rd BS15 65 E7
Courtney Way BS15 66 A7
Courtside Mews BS6 49 C1
Courtyard The BS40 129 E6
Courville Cl BS35 15 A4
Cousins Cl BS10 34 D3
Cousins La BS5 64 F8
Cousins Mews BS4 64 F6
Cousins Way BS16 52 B8
Couzens Cl BS37 28 B2
Couzens Pl BS34 36 F5
Coventry Wlk BS4 64 F6
Cowdray Rd BS4 79 D7
Cowhorn Hill BS30 66 C4
Cowleaze La BS40 129 C6
Cowler Wlk BS13 78 F4
Cowling Dr BS14 80 C5
Cowling Rd BS14 80 D5
Cowper Rd BS6 49 C1
Cowper St BS5 64 C7
Cowship La GL12 17 D6
Cowslip La BS26 123 D3
Cox Ct BS30 65 F4
Cox's Gn BS40 92 E1
Coxgrove Hill BS16 52 F7
Coxley Dr BA1 85 B2
Coxway BS21 57 F2
Coxwynne Cl BA3 139 C8
Crabtree Cl BS41 78 D1
Crabtree La BS41 78 D2
Crabtree Wlk BS5 50 D2
Cradock Cl BS30 66 B4
Craftes Ct BS5 50 E1
Cranberry Wlk BS9 48 C8
Cranbourne Chase BS23 88 A1
Cranbourne Rd BS34 35 F7
Cranbrook Rd BS6 49 C3
Crandale Rd BA2 101 D5
Crandell Cl BS10 34 F4
Crane Cl BS15 66 B8
Cranford Cl BS22 88 D1
Cranford Ct 1 BS9 49 B6
Cranham BS37 39 C7
Cranham Cl BS15 51 F2
Cranham Dr BS34 24 C1
Cranham Rd BS10 49 C8
Cranhill Rd BA1 101 D8
Cranleigh BA2 118 F8
Cranleigh Court Inf Sch BS37 27 D3
Cranleigh Court Rd BS37 27 D2
Cranleigh Gdns BS9 48 E4
Cranleigh Rd BS14 80 B5
Cranmoor Gn BS35 22 D7
Cranmore BS24 105 A2
Cranmore Ave BS31 81 E6
Cranmore Cres BS10 35 D1
Cranmore Pl BA2 118 E8
Cranside Ave BS6 49 C4
Cransley Cres BS9 49 C7
Crantock Ave BS13 79 B8
Crantock Dr BS32 24 B5
Crantock Rd BS37 27 D1
Cranwell Gr BS14 80 A5
Cranwell Rd BS24 106 C5
Cranwells Pk BA1 101 D8
Crates Cl BS15 65 E8
Craven Cl BS30 65 F5
Craven Way BS30 65 F5
Crawford Cl 1 BS21 57 B1
Crawl La BA3 133 C4
Craydon Gr BS14 80 D4
Craydon Rd BS14 80 D5
Craydon Wlk BS14 80 D5
Crediton 5 BS22 89 A2
Crediton Cres BS4 63 F1
Crescent Gdns BA1 141 A3
Crescent La BA1 141 B4
Crescent Rd BS16 51 C6
Crescent The
Backwell BS48 76 A6
Bristol,Frenchay BS16 36 F1
Bristol,Henleaze BS9 49 C6
Bristol,Sea Mills BS9 48 C6
Bristol,Upper Soundwell BS16 51 D3
Farrington Gurney BS39 132 B3
Lympsham BS24 122 C5
Olveston BS32 14 D4
Stanton Drew BS39 96 F1
Weston-S-M BS22 88 B1
Wick BS30 67 C7
Crescent View BA2 141 B1
Crescent View Ct BS22 88 B1
Creslands Ind Units BS24 105 A3
Cresswell Cl BS22 89 A2
Crest The Bristol BS4 64 C2
West Kington SN14 56 F3
Creswicke Ave BS15 65 C5
Creswicke Rd BS4 79 E7
Crew's Hole Rd BS5 64 E7
Crewkerne Cl BS48 60 B1
Cribb's La BS40 93 D1
Cribbs Causeway Ctr BS34 35 A6
Cribbs Cswy BS10 35 A6
Crickback La BS40 96 A3
Cricket Field Gn BS48 59 D2
Cricklade Ct BS48 60 A1
Cricklade Rd BS7 49 E4
Cripps Rd BS3 63 C3
Crispin La 4 BS35 8 B1
Crispin Way BS15 51 F2
Crockerne CE Prim Sch BS20 47 C4
Crockerne Dr BS20 47 C3
Crockerne Ho BS20 47 D4
Crocombe BA2 116 C3
Crocombe La BA2 116 C3
Croft Ave BS16 50 C4
Croft Cl BS30 82 D8
Croft Rd BA1 85 B1
Croft The Backwell BS48 76 A7
Bath BA2 102 E1
Bristol,Mangotsfield BS16 51 F5
Bristol,Oldland Common BS30 66 C3
Clevedon BS21 57 F4
Hutton BS24 105 E3
Westwood BA15 120 F3
Croft View BS9 49 C6
Crofters Wlk BS32 36 D8
Crofton Ave BS7 49 F6
Crofton Fields BS36 37 E6
Crofts End Ind Est BS5 50 E1
Crofts End Rd BS5 50 E1
Crokeswood Wlk BS11 34 A1
Crome Rd BS7 50 B7
Cromer Ct BS21 57 D5
Cromer Rd Bristol BS5 50 C2
Weston-S-M BS23 104 E5
Cromhall La GL12 9 D1
Cromwell Ct BS15 65 E5
Cromwell Dr BS22 89 A4
Cromwell Rd
Bristol,Montpelier BS6 49 E2
Bristol,St George BS5 65 A8
Cromwell St BS3 63 C3
Cromwell View BS6 49 E2
Cromwells Hide BS16 50 F5
Crook's La BS22 88 A4
Croomes Hill BS16 51 D6
Cropthorne Rd BS7 36 A1
Cropthorne Rd S BS7 50 A8
Crosby Row BS8 142 A2
Cross Combe Wlk BS13 79 B3
Cross Elms La BS9 48 E5
Cross Hands Rd BS35 22 D7
Cross La BS26 125 A2
Cross Lanes BS20 47 C4
Cross Moor Dr BS26 125 B1
Cross Moor Dro BS26 124 E1
Cross Moor Rd BS26 125 B1
Cross St Bristol BS15 51 D1
Keynsham BS31 81 F7
3 Weston-S-M BS23 104 E7
Cross The BS40 129 F4
Cross Tree Gr BS32 36 D8
Cross Wlk BS14 80 A6
Crosscombe Dr BS13 79 C3
Crossfield Rd BS16 51 E3
Crossleaze Rd BS15 65 C3
Crossley Cl BS36 37 F7
Crossman Ave BS36 37 E5
Crossman Wlk BS21 57 F2
Crosspost La BA2 99 B4
Crossway La BA3 138 B7
Crossways Cvn Site BA2 117 F5
Crossways Jun & Inf Sch BS35 8 D1
Crossways Rd Bristol BS4 64 A1
Thornbury BS35 8 D1
Crow La Bristol BS1 143 A2
Henbury BS10 34 F2
Crow Mdw GL12 11 F4
Crowe Hill BA2 120 B5
Crowe La BA2 120 B5
Crowley Way BS11 33 B1
Crown Gdns BS30 66 B7
Crown Glass Pl 5 BS48 59 E2
Crown Hill Bath BA1 84 C1
Bristol BS5 64 F8
Winford BS40 95 A5
Crown Hill Wlk BS5 50 F1
Crown Ho BS48 59 C1
Crown Ind Est BS30 66 C7
Crown Rd Bath BA1 84 B1
Bristol,Hopewell Hill BS15 51 D2
Bristol,Warmley Tower BS30 66 C6
Crowndale Rd BS4 64 A3
Crownleaze BS16 51 D3
Crows Gr BS32 24 D3
Crowther Pk BS7 50 A4
Crowther Rd BS7 50 A4
Crowther St 4 BS3 63 B3
Crowthers Ave BS37 27 E3
Croydon Ho 1 BS5 64 B8
Croydon St BS5 64 B8
Crunnis The BS32 36 E6
Crusty La BS20 47 C5
Crystal Way BS32 36 E8
Cuck Hill BS25 125 E7
Cuckoo La
High Littleton BS39 115 B3
Winterbourne BS36 37 F3
Wraxall BS48 60 A6
Cuffington Ave BS4 64 D4
Cufic La BS27 126 C1
Culleysgate La BS30 67 F6
Culver La BS40 129 F3
Culver St BS1 142 C2
Culverhay BS39 98 D6
Culverhay Sch BA2 101 B2
Culverhill Rd BS37 28 A1
Culverhill Sch BS37 39 D7
Culvers Cl BS31 81 E6
Culvers Rd BS31 81 E6
Culvert Ave BS37 27 B1
Culvert The BS32 36 D8
Culverwell Rd BS13 79 A4
Cumberland Basin Rd BS8 62 F5
Cumberland Cl BS1 142 A1
Cumberland Gr 5 BS6 49 F2
Cumberland Ho BA1 141 A2
Cumberland Pl 7 BS8 62 F6
Cumberland Rd
Bristol,Canon's Marsh BS1 142 B1
9 Bristol,Clifton Wood BS8 62 F5
Cumberland Row BA1 141 B2
Cumberland St BS2 143 B4
Cumbria Cl BS35 8 E1
Cunningham Gdns BS16 51 B5
Curland Gr 6 BS14 80 B5
Curlew Cl BS16 50 F6
Curlew Gdns BS22 88 F1
Currells La BS40 77 B1
Curtis La BS34 37 A4
Custom Cl BS14 80 A7
Cutler Rd BS13 78 F6
Cutsheath Rd GL12 16 C8
Cutters Row BS3 63 E4
Cygnet Cres BS22 88 F1
Cynder Way BS16 38 A1
Cynthia Rd BA2 101 D5
Cypress Ct BS9 48 D3
Cypress Gdns BS8 62 E6
Cypress Gr BS9 49 C6
Cypress Terr BA3 133 D1
Cypress Wlk SN14 70 F6
Cyrus Ct BS16 52 B7

D

Dafford St BA1 85 C2
Dafford's Bldgs BA1 85 C2
Daglands The BA2 133 E8
Daines Ct 4 BS16 50 E3
Dairy Hill BA2 135 B5
Dairycroft BS2 143 B4
Daisey Bank BA2 102 B4
Daisy Green La GL12 5 D2
Daisy Rd BS5 50 C2
Dakin Cl BS4 63 E1
Dakota Dr BS14 80 A4
Dalby Ave BS3 63 D4
Daldry Gdns BS35 14 A3
Dale St
Bristol,St George BS5 64 F8
Bristol,St Pauls BS2 143 C4
Daley Cl BS22 89 B3
Dalkeith Ave BS15 51 C1
Dalrymple Rd 11 BS2 49 E1
Dalston Rd BS3 63 B4
Dalton Sq BS2 143 B4
Dalwood 12 BS22 89 A2
Dame Court Cl BS22 88 F4
Damery La Stone GL13 4 A3
Woodford GL13 4 A4
Woodford,Damery GL13 4 B2
Dampier Rd BS3 63 A3
Damson Rd BS22 105 E7
Danbury Cres BS10 35 C1
Danbury Wlk BS10 35 C1
Danby Ho BS7 50 A5
Dancey Mead BS13 78 F6
Dandy's Mdw BS20 45 E4
Dane Cl BA15 120 E7
Dane Rise BA15 120 E7
Daneacre Rd BA3 134 A3
Dangerfield Ave BS13 78 F6
Daniel Cl BS21 57 F3
Daniel Mews BA2 102 B7
Daniel St BA2 102 B7
Dano View Gdns BS20 45 C5
Dapps Hill BS31 81 F5
Dapwell La BS14,BS31 81 A1
Dark La Backwell BS48 76 B5
Banwell BS29 107 C2
Blagdon BS40 110 E3
Chew Magna BS40 95 F3
Freshford BA2 120 B5
Holcombe BA3 139 C1
Kilmersdon BA3 140 A1
Darley Cl BS10 34 D3
Darlington Mews BA2 102 B7
Darlington Pl BA2 102 B6
Darlington Rd BA2 102 B8
Darlington St BA2 102 B7
Darmead BS24 89 B1
Darnley Ave BS7 49 F6
Dart Cl BS35 15 B8
Dart Rd BS21 57 D1
Dartmoor St BS3 63 B3
Dartmouth Ave BA2 101 C5
Dartmouth Cl BS22 89 A2
Dartmouth Wlk BS31 81 D4
Daubeny Cl BS16 51 B5
Daubeny Ct BS1 143 A1
Daventry Rd BS4 63 F1
Davey St BS2 49 F1
Davey Terr 7 BS2 49 F1
David St BS2 143 C3
David's La BS35 15 A4
David's Rd Bristol BS14 80 C6
Thornbury BS35 8 C1
Davids Cl BS35 15 A4
Davies Dr BS4 64 F5
Davin Cres BS20 47 C3
Davis Cl BS30 65 F5
Davis Ct BS35 8 C2
Davis La BS21 73 F8
Davis St BS11 47 B8
Davonport Cl BS30 66 A2
Davron Ct BS3 63 E4
Dawes Cl BS21 57 D1
Dawes Ct 3 BS8 62 F6
Dawley Cl BS36 37 E7
Dawlish Rd BS3 63 D2
Dawn Rise BS15 52 A1
Daws Ct BS16 51 B4
Day Cres BA2 100 F6
Day House La GL12 19 C8
Day's Rd BS2 64 A6
Days Road Commercial Ctr BS2 64 A7
De Clifford Rd BS11 34 C2
De La Warre Ct 11 BS4 64 F6
De Verose Ct BS15 65 E4
Deacon Cl BS36 37 E5
Deacons Cl BS22 88 E2
Deacons Ct BS22 88 C1
Deadmill La BA1 85 C3
Dean Ave BS35 8 C2
Dean Cl Bristol BS15 65 B4
Weston-S-M BS22 89 B3
Dean Cres 8 Bristol BS3 63 C4
1 Bristol BS3 63 D4
Dean Ct BS37 27 C3
Dean La BS3 63 C4
Dean Rd Avonmouth BS11 33 C5
Yate BS37 27 C3
Dean St
Bristol,Southville BS3 63 C4
Bristol,St Pauls BS2 143 B4
Dean's Ct BS1 142 C2
Dean's Dr BS5 51 A2
Deanery Cl BS15 66 B8

Deanery Rd
Bristol,Warmley BS15 . . . . .66 B8
BristolBrandon Hill BS1 . . . .142 C2
Deanery Road Rdbt BS15 66 B7
Deanery Wlk BA2 . . . . . . .120 C6
Deanhill La BA1 . . . . .84 A2
Deanna Ct BS16 . . . . .51 E6
Deans Mead BS11 . . . . . . .48 A8
Deans The BS20 . . . . .45 B4
Debecca's La BS20 . . . . . . .47 B4
Deep Coombe Rd BS3 . . . . .63 A2
Deep Pit Rd BS5 . . . . .50 F2
Deer Mead BS21 . . . . .57 B1
Deerhurst Bristol BS15 . . . .51 E3
Yate BS37 . . . . .39 C8
Deering Cl BS11 . . . . .34 B1
Deerleap BS25 . . . . .125 F8
Deers Wood Prim Sch
BS15 . . . . .52 A2
Deerswood BS15 . . . . .52 A2
Delabere Ave BS16 . . . . . . .51 B5
Delapre Rd BS23 . . . . .104 D3
Delius Gr BS4 . . . . .79 D7
Dell The
Bristol,Bradley Stoke BS32 . .36 E7
Bristol,Cadbury Heath BS16 66 C5
Bristol,Westbury on Trym
BS9 . . . . .48 F5
Nailsea BS48 . . . . .59 D2
Weston-S-M BS22 . . . . .88 E4
Delvin Rd BS10 . . . . .49 C8
Denbigh St BS2 . . . . .49 F1
Dene Cl BS31 . . . . .81 F3
Dene Rd BS14 . . . . .80 C4
Denleigh Cl BS14 . . . . .80 A4
Denmark Ave BS1 . . . . . . .142 C2
Denmark Pl BS7 . . . . .49 E3
Denmark Rd BA2 . . . . .101 D6
Denmark St BS1 . . . . .142 C2
Denning Ct BS22 . . . . .89 B4
Dennisworth BS16 . . . . .53 B5
Dennor Pk BS14 . . . . .80 B7
Denny Cl BS20 . . . . .45 A5
Denny Isle Dr BS35 . . . . . . .22 A6
Denny La BS40 . . . . .96 B1
Denny View BS20 . . . . .45 A5
Dennyview Rd BS8 . . . . .61 F8
Denston Dr BS20 . . . . .45 E4
Denston Wlk BS13 . . . . .79 A7
Denton Patch BS16 . . . . . . .52 B7
Dentwood Gr BS9 . . . . .48 B8
Denys Ct BS35 . . . . .14 A3
Derby Rd BS7 . . . . .49 E3
Derby St BS5 . . . . .64 D7
Derham Cl BS49 . . . . .91 B8
Derham Ct BS49 . . . . .91 B8
Derham Pk BS49 . . . . .91 B8
Derham Rd BS13 . . . . .79 A5
Derhill Terr BA2 . . . . .102 E6
Dermot St BS5 . . . . .49 F1
Derrick Rd BS15 . . . . .65 D8
Derricke Rd BS14 . . . . .80 F6
Derry Rd BS3 . . . . .63 B2
Derwent Cl BS34 . . . . .36 A8
Derwent Ct BS35 . . . . .15 D8
Derwent Gr BS31 . . . . .82 A5
Derwent Rd Bristol BS5 . . . .50 F1
Weston-S-M BS23 . . . . .105 A5
Devaney Cl BS4 . . . . .64 F5
Deveron Gr BS31 . . . . .82 A4
Devil's La GL12 . . . . .11 A2
Devon Gr BS5 . . . . .64 C8
Devon Rd BS5 . . . . .50 C1
Devon Road Trad Est [1]
BS5 . . . . .50 C1
Devonshire Bldgs
Bath BA2 . . . . .101 E4
Bristol BS3 . . . . .63 E4
Devonshire Ct BS23 . . . . . .104 E4
Devonshire Dr BS20 . . . . . . .44 F5
Devonshire Mews BA2 . . . .101 F3
Devonshire Pl BA2 . . . . . . .101 F4
Devonshire Rd
Bathampton BA2 . . . . .85 E1
Bristol BS6 . . . . .49 B4
Weston-S-M BS23 . . . . .104 E4
Devonshire Villas BA2 . . . .101 F3
Dewfalls Dr BS32 . . . . .24 D1
Dial Hill Rd BS21 . . . . .57 D4
Dial La Bristol BS16 . . . . . . .51 D6
Felton BS40,BS48 . . . . .77 D1
Diamond Batch BS24 . . . . . .89 B1
Diamond Rd BS5 . . . . .64 F7
Diamond St BS3 . . . . .63 C3
Diamonite Ind Pk BS16 . . . .51 A3
Diana Gdns BS32 . . . . .36 E8
Dibden Cl BS16 . . . . .52 A8
Dibden La BS16 . . . . .52 B7
Dibden Rd BS16 . . . . .52 A7
Dickens Cl BS7 . . . . .50 A8
Dickenson Rd BS23 . . . . . .104 E6
Dickenson's Gr BS49 . . . . . .91 E3
Didsbury Cl BS10 . . . . .34 F1
Dighton Ct [3] BS2 . . . . . . .143 A4
Dighton Gate BS34 . . . . . . .36 E5
Dighton St BS2 . . . . .143 A4
Dillon Ct [17] BS5 . . . . .64 D7
Dinder Cl BS48 . . . . .75 E8
Dinghurst Rd BS25 . . . . . . .108 E4
Dingle Cl BS9 . . . . .48 C6
Dingle Rd BS13 . . . . .78 F7
Dingle Rd BS9 . . . . .48 D7
Dingle The Bristol BS9 . . . . .48 D7
Winterbourne BS36 . . . . .37 D4
Yate BS37 . . . . .27 F4
Dingle View BS9 . . . . .48 C7
Dinglewood Cl BS9 . . . . .48 D7
Dings Wlk [4] BS2 . . . . .64 A6

Dipland Gr BS40 . . . . .110 F2
District Ctr BS32 . . . . .36 E8
Dixon Bsns Ctr BS4 . . . . . . .64 F2
Dixon Gdns BA1 . . . . .84 F1
Dixon Rd BS4 . . . . .64 F2
Dock Gate La BS8 . . . . .142 A1
Dodington Ash BS37 . . . . . . .41 B2
Dodington La BS37 . . . . .40 D5
Dodington Rd BS37 . . . . .40 D5
Dodisham Wlk BS16 . . . . . . .51 B6
Doleberrow BS25 . . . . .108 F3
Dolebury Warren Nat Res *
BS25 . . . . .109 B3
Dolemoor La
Congresbury BS49 . . . . .91 A4
Congresbury BS49 . . . . .91 C3
Dolman Cl BS10 . . . . .34 F3
Dolphin Sq BS23 . . . . .104 D7
Dominion Rd Bath BA2 . . . .101 A6
Bristol BS16 . . . . .50 F3
Donald Rd BS13 . . . . .78 F7
Doncaster Rd BS10 . . . . .49 C8
Doncombe Hill SN14 . . . . . . .70 F7
Doncombe La SN14 . . . . .70 F7
Donegal Rd BS4 . . . . .63 D1
Dongola Ave BS7 . . . . .49 E4
Dongola Rd BS7 . . . . .49 E4
Donnington Wlk BS31 . . . . . .81 D4
Doone Rd BS7 . . . . .49 F8
Dorcas Ave BS34 . . . . .36 F5
Dorchester Cl [6] BS48 . . . . .59 D1
Dorchester Rd BS7 . . . . .50 A7
Dorchester St BA1 . . . . . . .141 C1
Dorester Cl BS10 . . . . .35 C4
Dorian Cl BS7 . . . . .49 E7
Dorian Rd BS7 . . . . .49 E7
Dorian Way BS7 . . . . .49 E8
Dormeads View BS24 . . . . .105 F7
Dormer Cl BS36 . . . . .38 D6
Dormer Rd BS5 . . . . .50 B3
Dorset Cl BA2 . . . . .101 D6
Dorset Gr [9] BS2 . . . . .50 A2
Dorset Ho BA2 . . . . .101 D3
Dorset Rd
Bristol,Eastfield BS9 . . . . . . .49 B6
Bristol,Hopewell Hill BS15 . . .51 D1
Dorset St Bath BA2 . . . . . . .101 D6
[6] Bristol BS3 . . . . .63 B3
Dorset Way BS37 . . . . .28 A3
Douglas Ct BS23 . . . . .104 F5
Douglas Rd
Bristol,Horfield BS7 . . . . .49 F7
Bristol,Kingswood BS15 . . . . .65 D7
Weston-S-M BS23 . . . . .104 F5
Douglas Rd Ind Pk BS15 . . . .65 D7
Doulton Way BS14 . . . . .80 B5
Dove La
Bristol,Russell Town BS5 . . . .64 C7
Bristol,St Pauls BS2 . . . . . .143 A4
Dove St BS2 . . . . .143 A4
Dove St S BS2 . . . . .143 A4
Dovecote BS37 . . . . .39 F7
Dovedale BS35 . . . . .15 D8
Dover Ho BA1 . . . . .141 C4
Dover Pl [6] Bath BA1 . . . . . .85 A1
Bristol BS8 . . . . .142 B3
Dovercourt Rd BS7 . . . . .50 A6
Dovers La BA1 . . . . .86 C2
Dovers Pk BA1 . . . . .86 C2
Doveswell Gr BS13 . . . . .79 A4
Dovetail Dr BS23 . . . . .105 A7
Doveton St [9] BS3 . . . . .63 D4
Dovey Ct BS30 . . . . .66 C5
Dowdeswell Cl [1] BS10 . . . . .34 F3
Dowding Cl BS37 . . . . .28 C2
Dowding Rd BA1 . . . . .85 B1
Dowland [13] BS22 . . . . .89 A2
Dowland Gr BS4 . . . . .79 D6
Dowling Rd BS13 . . . . .79 D3
Down Ave BA2 . . . . .102 A1
Down Cl BS20 . . . . .44 F4
Down Farm Ho BS36 . . . . . . .37 D6
Down La BA2 . . . . .85 F1
Down Leaze [2] BS35 . . . . . .15 A5
Down Rd Alveston BS35 . . . . .15 A5
Marshfield SN14 . . . . .56 C2
Portishead BS20 . . . . .44 F4
Winterbourne BS36 . . . . .37 F4
Down The Alveston BS35 . . . .14 F5
Tockington BS32 . . . . .14 D3
Down View Bristol BS7 . . . . .49 F3
Radstock BA3 . . . . .139 F3
Downend Comp Sch
Bristol BS16 . . . . .51 F5
Bristol BS16 . . . . .51 F7
Downend Park Rd BS16 . . . . .51 D5
Downend Pk BS7 . . . . .49 F5
Downend Rd
Bristol,Fishponds BS16 . . . . .51 C5
Bristol,Hopewell Hill BS15 . . .51 D1
Bristol,Horfield BS7 . . . . .49 F5
Downend Bristol BS9 . . . . . . .48 C7
Keynsham BS31 . . . . .81 D5
Downfield Cl [1] BS35 . . . . . .15 A5
Downfield Dr BS36 . . . . .38 B8
Downfield Lodge BS8 . . . . . .49 A1
Downfield Rd BS8 . . . . .49 A1
Downland Cl [5] BS48 . . . . . .59 D1
Downleaze
Bristol,Downend BS16 . . . . . .51 D8
Bristol,Sneyd Park BS9 . . . . .48 F3
Portishead BS20 . . . . .45 A5
Downleaze Dr BS37 . . . . .40 B8
Downleaze Rd BS9 . . . . .48 F3
Downman Rd BS7 . . . . .50 A4
Downs Cl
[3] Alveston BS35 . . . . .15 A5
Weston-S-M BS22 . . . . .88 F1

Downs Cote Ave BS9 . . . . . .48 F6
Downs Cote Dr BS9 . . . . . . .48 F6
Downs Cote Gdns BS9 . . . . .49 A6
Downs Cote Pk BS9 . . . . . . .49 A6
Downs Cote View BS9 . . . . .49 A6
Downs Ct BS9 . . . . .49 B6
Downs Pk E BS6 . . . . .49 A4
Downs Pk W BS6 . . . . .49 A4
Downs Rd Bristol BS9 . . . . . .49 A6
Downside BS41 . . . . .78 D2
Downs The
Portishead BS20 . . . . .45 B4
Wickwar GL12 . . . . .17 F7
Downside BS20 . . . . .45 C5
Downside Abbey * BA3 . . . .138 E2
Downside Cl
Bathampton BA2 . . . . .85 F1
Bristol BS30 . . . . .65 F5
Chilcompton BA3 . . . . .138 D3
Downside Cvn Pk BS48 . . . . .76 D1
Downside Rd
Backwell BS48 . . . . .93 E8
Bristol BS8 . . . . .49 A1
Weston-S-M BS23 . . . . .104 F4
Downside Sch BA3 . . . . .138 F2
Downsview Ct BS8 . . . . .49 A1
Downsway BS9 . . . . .132 D6
Downton Rd BS4 . . . . .63 D1
Dowry Pl [3] BS8 . . . . .62 F5
Dowry Rd BS8 . . . . .142 A1
Dowry Sq BS8 . . . . .142 A2
Doynton La BS30,SN14 . . . . .54 B3
Dr White's Cl BS1 . . . . .143 B1
Dragon Rd BS31 . . . . .50 E1
Dragon Rd BS36 . . . . .37 D5
Dragon Wlk BS5 . . . . .50 F8
Dragons Hill Cl BS31 . . . . . .81 F5
Dragons Hill Ct BS31 . . . . . .81 F5
Dragons Hill Gdns BS31 . . . .81 F5
Dragonswell Rd BS10 . . . . . .35 A2
Drake Ave BA2 . . . . .101 F2
Drake Cl Saltford BS31 . . . . .82 D2
Weston-S-M BS22 . . . . .88 F4
Drake Rd BS3 . . . . .63 A3
Drakes Way BS20 . . . . .45 B5
Dramway Rd BS16 . . . . .52 C6
Dransfield Way BA2 . . . . . .101 C4
Draper Ct [3] BS5 . . . . .64 C7
Draycot Pl BS1 . . . . .143 A1
Draycott Rd BS7 . . . . .49 F5
Draydon Rd BS4 . . . . .79 D8
Drayton BS24 . . . . .105 A2
Drayton Cl BS14 . . . . .80 B8
Drayton Rd BS9 . . . . .48 C8
Drifton Hill SN14 . . . . .56 F7
Dring The BA3 . . . . .133 E2
Drive The
Bristol,Hengrove BS14 . . . . . .80 C6
Bristol,Henleaze BS9 . . . . . . .49 B5
Churchill BS25 . . . . .108 E4
Shipham BS25 . . . . .125 E8
Stanton Drew BS39 . . . . .96 F1
Weston-S-M BS23 . . . . .104 F8
Drove Ct BS48 . . . . .59 E3
Drove Rd BS23 . . . . .104 F5
Drove The BS20 . . . . .46 D6
Drove Way BS24,BS25 . . . . .107 E7
Druetts Cl BS10 . . . . .49 E6
Druid Cl BS9 . . . . .48 E5
Druid Hill BS9 . . . . .48 E5
Druid Rd BS9 . . . . .48 D4
Druid Stoke Ave BS9 . . . . . .48 D5
Druid Woods BS9 . . . . .48 C5
Drumhead Way The
BS25 . . . . .125 E8
Drummond Ct BS30 . . . . .65 F4
Drummond Rd
Bristol,Ridgeway BS16 . . . . . .50 F3
Bristol,St Pauls BS2 . . . . . . .49 E1
Dryleaze Keynsham BS31 . . .27 E5
Yate BS37 . . . . .27 E5
Dryleaze Rd BS16 . . . . .50 F6
Drysdale Cl BS22 . . . . .88 D1
Dubbers La BS5 . . . . .50 E2
Dublin Cres BS9 . . . . .49 B6
Duchess Rd BS8 . . . . .49 A1
Duchess Way BS16 . . . . .50 D6
Duchy Cl BA3 . . . . .133 E5
Duchy Rd BA3 . . . . .133 E5
Ducie Rd
Bristol,Russell Town BS5 . . . .64 B7
Bristol,Staple Hill BS16 . . . . .51 F5
Duck La Kenn BS21 . . . . .74 A6
Langford BS40 . . . . .109 A8
Duck St Churchill BS25 . . . .108 C5
Tytherington GL12 . . . . .16 C5
Duckmoor Rd BS3 . . . . .63 A3
Duckmoor Road Ind Est
BS3 . . . . .63 A4
Dudley Cl BS31 . . . . .81 E4
Dudley Ct [3] BS30 . . . . .65 F4
Dudley Gr BS7 . . . . .50 A8
Dugar Wlk BS6 . . . . .49 C3
Duke St BA2 . . . . .141 C2
Dulverton Rd BS7 . . . . .49 D4
Dumaine Ave BS34 . . . . .36 E5
Dumfries Pl BS23 . . . . .104 E5
Dumpers La BS40 . . . . .96 B3
Duncan Gdns BA1 . . . . .84 A3
Duncombe La BS15 . . . . .51 B2
Duncombe Rd BS15 . . . . .51 B1
Dundas Cl BS10 . . . . .34 C2
Dundonald Rd BS6 . . . . .49 B3
Dundridge Gdns BS5 . . . . . .65 A6
Dundridge La BS5 . . . . .65 A6

Dundry CE Prim Sch
BS41 . . . . .78 D2
Dundry Cl BS15 . . . . .65 D6
Dundry La Dundry BS41 . . . . .78 C3
Winford BS40 . . . . .95 A7
Dundry View BS4 . . . . .64 A1
Dunedin Way BS22 . . . . .89 C4
Dunford Rd BS3 . . . . .63 D3
Dunkeld Ave BS34 . . . . .35 F2
Dunkerry Rd BS3 . . . . .63 D3
Dunkerton Hill BA2 . . . . . . .117 C2
Dunkery Cl BS48 . . . . .59 E1
Dunkery Rd BS23 . . . . .87 F1
Dunkirk Rd BS16 . . . . .50 F8
Dunmail Prim Sch BS10 . . . .35 C2
Dunmail Rd BS10 . . . . .35 C2
Dunmore St [3] BS2 . . . . . . .63 F4
Dunsdown La SN14 . . . . .55 B5
Dunsford Pl BA2 . . . . .102 B6
Dunster Cres BS24 . . . . . . .105 A2
Dunster Ct BS25 . . . . .125 A8
Dunster Gdns Bristol BS30 66 B2
[5] Nailsea BS48 . . . . .59 E1
Dunster Ho BA2 . . . . .102 A2
Dunster Rd Bristol BS4 . . . . .79 F8
Keynsham BS31 . . . . .81 E4
Dunsters Rd BS49 . . . . .74 B1
Durban Rd BS34 . . . . .35 F8
Durban Way BS49 . . . . .74 B1
Durbin Park Rd BS21 . . . . . .57 D5
Durbin Wlk BS5 . . . . .64 A8
Durcott La BA2 . . . . .133 D8
Durdham Ho BS6 . . . . .49 A3
Durdham Pk BS6 . . . . .49 A3
Durham Gr BS31 . . . . .81 F4
Durham Rd [10] Bristol BS2 50 A2
Charfield GL12 . . . . .11 A5
Durleigh Cl BS13 . . . . .79 A7
Durley Hill BS31 . . . . .81 C7
Durley La BS31 . . . . .81 D7
Durley Pk BA2 . . . . .101 E4
Durnford Ave BS3 . . . . .63 A4
Durnford St BS3 . . . . .63 A4
Durnhill BS40 . . . . .128 F7
Dursley Cl BS37 . . . . .27 E1
Dursley Rd BS11 . . . . .47 E5
Durston BS24 . . . . .105 A2
Durville Rd BS13 . . . . .79 B6
Durweston Wlk BS14 . . . . . .80 C8
Dutton Cl BS14 . . . . .80 D6
Dutton Rd BS14 . . . . .80 D6
Dutton Wlk BS14 . . . . .80 D6
Dye House Rd GL12 . . . . . . .11 F5
Dyer's La BS37 . . . . .27 A4
Dyers Cl BS13 . . . . .79 D4
Dylan Thomas Ct [4]
BS30 . . . . .66 A5
Dymboro Ave BA3 . . . . .132 F1
Dymboro Cl BA3 . . . . .132 F1
Dymboro Gdns BA3 . . . . . . .132 F1
Dymboro The BA3 . . . . .132 F1
Dyrham BS16 . . . . .37 C1
Dyrham Cl
Bristol,Henleaze BS9 . . . . . . .49 D6
Bristol,Kingswood BS15 . . . . .65 F8
Pucklechurch BS16 . . . . .53 C4
Thornbury BS35 . . . . .8 C3
Dyrham Par BS34 . . . . .36 C8
Dyrham Park (Deer Park) *
SN14 . . . . .54 F5
Dyrham Rd BS15 . . . . .65 F8
Dyson Cl BS49 . . . . .91 B8

E

Eagle Cl BS22 . . . . .105 D8
Eagle Cres BS16 . . . . .53 C5
Eagle Dr BS34 . . . . .35 E8
Eagle Pk BA1 . . . . .85 F5
Eagle Rd Batheaston BA1 . . .85 F5
Bristol BS4 . . . . .64 D2
Eagles The BS49 . . . . .91 B8
Eagles Wood BS32 . . . . .24 D3
Eagles Wood Bsns Pk
BS32 . . . . .24 C3
Earl Russell Way BS5 . . . . . .64 B7
Earl St BS1 . . . . .143 A4
Earlesfield BS48 . . . . .59 C1
Earlham Gr BS23 . . . . .105 A2
Earlsmead BS16 . . . . .50 E4
Earlstone Cl BS30 . . . . .66 A4
Earlstone Cres BS30 . . . . . . .66 A4
Early Way BS7 . . . . .49 E8
Earthcott Rd BS35 . . . . .15 F1
Easedale Cl BS10 . . . . .35 D2
East Cl BA2 . . . . .101 A2
East Clevedon Triangle
BS21 . . . . .57 F3
East Croft BS9 . . . . .49 C7
East Ct BS3 . . . . .62 F3
East Dundry La BS41 . . . . . . .79 A1
East Dundry Rd BS13,
BS14 . . . . .79 F2
East End SN14 . . . . .70 A8
East Gr BS6 . . . . .49 F1
East Harptree Prim Sch
BS40 . . . . .129 F4
East Hill BS9 . . . . .49 B7
East Lea Rd BA1 . . . . .101 A8
East Mead BA3 . . . . .133 B2
East Par BS9 . . . . .48 C6
East Park Dr BS5 . . . . .50 C2
East Park Bristol BS5 . . . . . .50 C2
Bristol BS5 . . . . .50 D1
East Priory Cl BS9 . . . . .49 A7
East Ridge Dr BS13 . . . . .78 F5
East Shrubbery [3] BS6 . . . . .49 B2

East St Avonmouth BS11 . . . .33 A1
Banwell BS29 . . . . .107 C3
Bristol,Southville BS3 . . . . . .63 D4
Bristol,St Pauls BS2 . . . . . .143 C4
East View BS16 . . . . .51 F4
East Way BA2 . . . . .101 A5
East Wlk BS37 . . . . .27 E1
East Wood Pl BS20 . . . . .45 E7
Eastbourne Ave BA1 . . . . . . .85 B1
Eastbourne Rd [9] BS5 . . . . .64 B8
Eastbury Cl BS35 . . . . .8 C1
Eastbury Rd Bristol BS16 . . .51 A4
Thornbury BS35 . . . . .8 C1
Eastcliff BS20 . . . . .45 E7
Eastcombe Gdns BS23 . . . . .87 F1
Eastcombe Rd BS23 . . . . . . .87 F1
Eastcote Pk BS14 . . . . .80 B5
Eastcourt Rd BS39 . . . . . . .131 F8
Eastcroft BS40 . . . . .110 F2
Eastcroft Cl BS40 . . . . .110 E2
Eastdown Rd BA3 . . . . .133 D5
Easter Ct BS37 . . . . .27 B1
Eastermead La BS29 . . . . . .107 C3
Eastern Ho BS23 . . . . .87 E1
Eastertown BS24 . . . . .122 D1
Eastfield BS9 . . . . .49 B7
Eastfield Ave BA1 . . . . .84 B2
Eastfield Dr BS37 . . . . .27 E4
Eastfield Gdns BS23 . . . . . . .87 F1
Eastfield Pk BS23 . . . . .87 F1
Eastfield Rd
Bristol,Eastfield BS9 . . . . . . .49 A7
Bristol,Eastfield BS9 . . . . . . .49 B7
Bristol,Redland BS6 . . . . .49 D2
Hutton BS24 . . . . .105 E2
Eastfield Terr BS9 . . . . .49 B6
Eastgate Ctr BS5 . . . . .50 B3
Eastgate Office Ctr BS5 . . . .50 B3
Eastlake Cl BS7 . . . . .50 B7
Eastland Ave BS35 . . . . .8 C2
Eastland Rd BS35 . . . . .8 C2
Eastlea BS21 . . . . .57 B1
Eastleigh Cl BS16 . . . . .51 E4
Eastleigh Rd
Bristol,Southmead BS10 . . . .35 D1
Bristol,Upper Soundwell
BS16 . . . . .51 E3
Eastley Cl GL12 . . . . .9 C7
Eastlyn Rd BS13 . . . . .79 B8
Eastmead Ct BS9 . . . . .48 E4
Eastmead La BS9 . . . . .48 E4
Eastnor Rd BS14 . . . . .80 A3
Easton Bsns Ctr BS5 . . . . . .64 B8
Easton CE Prim Sch BS5 64 A8
Easton Ct BA3 . . . . .131 E1
Easton Hill Rd BS35 . . . . .8 D1
Easton Ho [9] BA1 . . . . .85 C1
Easton Rd
Bristol,Newton BS5 . . . . .64 A7
Bristol,Upper Easton BS5 . . .64 B8
Pill BS20 . . . . .47 C4
Easton Way BS5 . . . . .64 A8
Eastover Cl BS9 . . . . .49 A8
Eastover Gr BA2 . . . . .101 C1
Eastover Rd BS39 . . . . .115 D7
Eastville BA1 . . . . .85 B1
Eastway BS48 . . . . .59 D3
Eastway Cl BS48 . . . . .59 D2
Eastway Sq BS48 . . . . .59 E3
Eastwood BA2 . . . . .102 F6
Eastwood Cl BS39 . . . . .115 C1
Eastwood Cres BS4 . . . . .64 F5
Eastwood Rd BS4 . . . . .64 F4
Eastwoods BA1 . . . . .86 B3
Eaton Cl
Bristol,Hillfields BS16 . . . . . .51 E4
Bristol,Stockwood BS14 . . . .80 B5
Eaton Cres BS8 . . . . .142 A4
Eaton St [14] BS3 . . . . .63 C3
Ebden Lo [15] BS22 . . . . .89 A2
Ebdon La BS22 . . . . .89 C5
Ebdon Rd BS22 . . . . .88 F4
Ebenezer La BS9 . . . . .48 E5
Ebenezer St BS5 . . . . .64 D7
Eccleston Ho [1] BS5 . . . . . . .64 B6
Eckweek Gdns BA2 . . . . . . .134 E8
Eckweek La BA2 . . . . .134 E8
Eckweek Rd BA2 . . . . .134 D8
Eclipse Ct [1] BS16 . . . . .51 C4
Eclipse Office Pk [2]
BS16 . . . . .51 C4
Eden Gr BS7 . . . . .36 A1
Eden Park Cl BA1 . . . . .86 A4
Eden Park Dr BA1 . . . . .86 A4
Eden Terr BA1 . . . . .85 B2
Eden Villas [1] BA1 . . . . .85 C2
Edgar Bldgs BA1 . . . . .141 B3
Edgarley Ct BS21 . . . . .57 C5
Edgecombe Ave BS22 . . . . . .88 D2
Edgecombe Cl BS15 . . . . . . .51 F1
Edgecombe Mews BA1 . . . . .84 B1
Edgecorner La SN14 . . . . . . .43 A3
Edgecumbe Rd BS6 . . . . .49 D2
Edgefield Cl BS14 . . . . .79 F3
Edgefield Rd BS14 . . . . .79 F3
Edgehill Rd BS21 . . . . .57 D6
Edgeware Rd
Bristol,Southville BS3 . . . . . .63 C4
Bristol,Staple Hill BS16 . . . . .51 D4
Edgewood Cl
Bristol,Hengrove BS14 . . . . . .80 B8
Bristol,Oldland BS30 . . . . . . .66 A3
Edgeworth BS37 . . . . .39 C6
Edgeworth Rd BA2 . . . . . . .101 C2
Edinburgh Pl [1] BS23 . . . . .104 E8

Edinburgh Rd BS31 .....81 E4
Edington Gr BS10 .....35 A2
Edmund Cl BS16 .....51 D6
Edmund Ct BS16 .....53 B6
Edna Ave BS4 .....64 E3
Edward Bird Ho BS7 .....50 B6
Edward Ct BS31 .....81 F4
Edward Rd
  Bristol,Kingswood BS15 .....65 E8
  Bristol,Totterdown BS4 .....64 B4
  Clevedon BS21 .....57 E5
Edward Rd S BS21 .....57 E5
Edward Rd W BS21 .....57 E6
Edward St Bath BA2 .....102 B7
  Bath,Lower Weston BA1 .....101 C7
  Bristol,Lower Easton BS5 .....50 C4
  Bristol,Moorfields BS5 .....64 C7
Edwards Ct **10** BS5 .....64 D7
Edwin Short Cl BS30 .....82 E8
Effingham Rd BS6 .....49 E2
Egerton Brow BS7 .....49 D4
Egerton Rd Bath BA2 .....101 E4
  Bristol BS7 .....49 D4
Eggshill La BS37 .....27 D1
Eglin Croft BS13 .....79 B4
Eighth Ave
  Bristol,Hengrove BS14 .....80 A7
  Bristol,Northville BS7 .....36 B1
Eirene Terr BS20 .....47 D4
Elberton BS15 .....66 A8
Elberton Rd Bristol BS9 .....48 B7
  Elberton BS35 .....13 F5
Elborough Ave BS49 .....91 B8
Elborough Gdns BS24 .....106 C3
Elbridge Ho **3** BS2 .....143 C3
Elbury Ave BS15 .....51 C2
Elbury View GL12 .....11 B5
Elderberry Wlk
  Bristol BS10 .....35 C3
  Weston-S-M BS22 .....88 F1
Elderwood Dr BS30 .....66 A3
Elderwood Rd BS14 .....80 B7
Eldon Pl BA1 .....85 B2
Eldon Terr BS3 .....63 D3
Eldon Way BS4 .....64 C5
Eldonwall Trad Est BS4 .....64 C7
Eldred Cl BS9 .....48 D5
Eleanor Cl BA2 .....101 A5
Eleanor Cotts BA2 .....101 A6
Eleventh Ave BS7 .....36 B1
Elfin Rd BS16 .....51 A5
Elgar Cl Bristol BS4 .....79 D6
  Clevedon BS21 .....57 E1
Elgin Ave BS7 .....35 F1
Elgin Pk BS6 .....49 B2
Elgin Rd BS16 .....51 B2
Eliot Cl Bristol BS7 .....36 A1
  Weston-S-M BS23 .....105 A3
Elizabeth Cl Hutton BS24 105 D3
  Thornbury BS35 .....15 C8
Elizabeth Cres BS34 .....36 E4
Elizabeth Ho BS20 .....47 D4
Elizabeth Way BS16 .....52 B3
Elizabeths Mews **12** BS4 .....64 F6
Elkstone Wlk BS30 .....66 C2
Ellacombe Rd BS30 .....65 F2
Ellan Hay Rd BS34 .....37 A6
Ellbridge Cl BS9 .....48 D5
Ellen Ho BA2 .....101 A5
Ellenborough Cres
  BS23 .....104 E6
Ellenborough Ct BS23 .....104 E6
Ellenborough Ho BS8 .....142 A2
Ellenborough Park Rd
  BS23 .....104 E6
Ellenborough Pk N
  BS23 .....104 D6
Ellenborough Pk S
  BS23 .....104 D6
Ellercroft Rd GL12 .....11 F8
Ellesmere BS35 .....15 C8
Ellesmere Rd
  1 Bristol BS4 .....64 D1
  Weston-S-M BS23 .....104 D2
Ellfield Cl BS13 .....78 F6
Ellick Rd BS40 .....110 D1
Ellicks Cl BS32 .....24 E2
Ellicott Rd BS7 .....49 F5
Ellinghurst Cl BS10 .....35 A2
Elliott Ave BS16 .....37 C1
Elliott Ho BS7 .....50 A3
Ellis Ave BS13 .....79 A8
Ellis Pk BS22 .....89 C4
Elliston Dr BA2 .....101 B4
Elliston La BS6 .....49 C2
Elliston Rd BS31 .....49 C2
Ellsbridge Cl BS31 .....82 B5
Ellsbridge Ho Norton
  Radstock Coll BS31 .....82 B5
Ellsworth Rd BS10 .....34 F2
Ellyott Ct **5** BS16 .....50 E3
Elm Cl Banwell BS29 .....106 E4
  Bristol,Lawrence Weston
  BS11 .....33 F1
  Bristol,Little Stoke BS34 .....36 D7
  Chipping Sodbury BS37 .....28 A1
  Nailsea BS48 .....59 C1
  Star BS25 .....108 D1
  Yatton BS49 .....91 B7
Elm Ct
  Bristol,Hengrove BS14 .....80 A6
  Bristol,Redland BS6 .....49 B2
  Keynsham BS31 .....81 C4
Elm Farm BS48 .....60 A2
Elm Gr Bath BA2 .....101 C4

Elm Gr continued
  Locking BS24 .....105 F4
  Swainswick BA1 .....85 C2
Elm Hayes BS13 .....78 F6
Elm La BS6 .....49 B2
Elm Lodge Rd BS48 .....60 B2
Elm Park Prim Sch BS36 .....37 C6
Elm Pk BS34 .....36 A2
Elm Pl BA2 .....101 F4
Elm Rd
  Bristol,Golden Hill BS7 .....49 E5
  Bristol,Mount Hill BS15 .....65 E6
  Paulton BS39 .....132 E5
Elm Terr BA3 .....139 C8
Elm Tree Ave
  Nailsea BS21 .....59 A4
  Radstock BA3 .....133 D1
Elm Tree Pk BS20 .....46 D3
Elm Tree Rd
  Clevedon BS21 .....57 D2
  Locking BS24 .....106 A4
Elm View
  Midsomer Norton BA3 .....133 B1
  Temple Cloud BS39 .....114 E1
Elm Wlk Portishead BS20 .....45 C4
  Yatton BS49 .....91 B7
Elm Wood BS37 .....39 E8
Elmcroft Cres BS7 .....50 A4
Elmdale Cres BS35 .....8 C1
Elmdale Gdns **2** BS16 .....51 A4
Elmdale Rd
  Bristol,Bedminster BS3 .....63 B2
  Bristol,Tyndall's Park BS8 .....142 B3
Elmfield BS15 .....65 E6
Elmfield Cl BS15 .....65 E6
Elmfield Rd BS9 .....49 A8
Elmfield Sch for Deaf
  Children BS9 .....49 B8
Elmgrove Ave **10** BS5 .....64 B8
Elmgrove Dr BS37 .....27 F2
Elmgrove Pk **1** BS6 .....49 D1
Elmgrove Rd
  Bristol,Cotham BS6 .....49 D1
  Bristol,Upper Eastville BS16 .....50 E3
Elmham Way BS24 .....89 B1
Elmhirst Gdns BS37 .....28 A2
Elmhurst Ave BS5 .....50 D3
Elmhurst Est BA1 .....86 A4
Elmhurst Gdns BS41 .....77 F8
Elmhurst Rd BS24 .....105 E2
Elmhyrst Rd BS23 .....104 F8
Elming Down Cl BS32 .....36 D6
Elmlea Ave BS9 .....48 F5
Elmlea Jun & Inf Schs
  BS9 .....48 F5
Elmleigh Ave BS16 .....52 B5
Elmleigh Cl BS16 .....52 B5
Elmleigh Rd BS16 .....52 B5
Elmore Bristol BS15 .....51 F2
  Yate BS37 .....39 D8
Elmore Rd
  Bristol,Horfield BS7 .....50 A6
  Bristol,Patchway BS34 .....23 F1
Elms Gr BS34 .....24 B1
Elms The Banwell BS29 .....107 A4
  Bristol,Frenchay BS16 .....37 C1
  Bristol,Henbury BS10 .....34 F2
Elmsleigh Rd BS23 .....104 E4
Elmsley La BS22 .....88 C5
Elmswood BS23 .....104 F8
Elmtree Ave BS16 .....52 A7
Elmtree Cl BS15 .....51 D1
Elmtree Dr BS13 .....78 F5
Elmtree Way BS15 .....51 D1
Elmvale Dr BS24 .....105 F3
Elsbert Dr BS13 .....78 E6
Elstree Rd BS5 .....50 E1
Elton Ho **2** BS2 .....143 C3
Elton La BS7 .....49 D2
Elton Rd
  Bristol,Redland BS7 .....49 D2
  Bristol,Two Mile Hill BS15 .....51 C1
  Bristol,Tyndall's Park
  BS8 .....142 B3
  Clevedon BS21 .....57 C3
  Weston-S-M BS22 .....89 A4
Elton St BS2 .....143 C4
Elvard Cl BS13 .....79 A4
Elvard Rd BS13 .....79 A4
Elvaston Rd BS3 .....63 E3
Elwell La BS40 .....78 A1
Ely Gr BS9 .....48 B7
Elysian Vills **2** BS15 .....65 B8
Embassy Rd BS5 .....50 E1
Embassy Wlk BS5 .....50 E1
Embercourt Dr BS48 .....76 A6
Embleton Prim Sch BS10 .....35 C2
Embleton Rd BS10 .....35 C2
Emerald Pk BS16 .....38 B1
Emerson Green Prim Sch
  BS16 .....52 B7
Emerson Sq BS7 .....50 A8
Emersons Green La BS16 .....52 B6
Emersons Way BS16 .....52 C7
Emery Gate BS29 .....107 B3
Emery Rd BS4 .....64 F1
Emet Gr BS16 .....52 B6
Emet La BS16 .....52 B6
Emley La BS40 .....110 B6
Emlyn Cl **6** BS22 .....89 B4
Emlyn Rd BS5 .....50 C2
Emma-Chris Way BS34 .....36 C2
Emmanuel Ct BS8 .....142 A4
Emmett Wood BS14 .....80 B3
Empire Cres BS15 .....65 E4
Empress Menen Gdns
  BA1 .....101 A8
Emra Cl BS5 .....50 F1

Emra Ho BS5 .....64 B8
Enderleigh Gdns BS25 .....108 F4
Enfield Rd BS16 .....51 A3
Engine Common La BS37 27 C5
Engine La BS48 .....75 B8
England's Cres BS36 .....37 E7
Englishcombe La BA2 .....101 D3
Englishcombe Rd BS13 .....79 C3
Englishcombe Tithe Barn★
  BA2 .....100 F2
Englishcombe Way BA2 101 E3
Enmore BS24 .....105 A2
Ennerdale Cl BS23 .....105 A5
Ennerdale Rd BS10 .....35 D2
Enterprise Trad Ctr BS4 .....79 E7
Entry Hill BA2 .....101 F2
Entry Hill Dr BA2 .....101 F3
Entry Hill Gdns BA2 .....101 F3
Entry Hill Pk BA2 .....101 F2
Entry Rise BA2 .....101 F1
Epney Cl BS34 .....23 F1
Epsom Cl BS16 .....37 F1
Epworth Rd BS10 .....35 A3
Equinox BS32 .....24 C3
Erin Wlk BS4 .....79 D8
Ermine Way BS11 .....47 C7
Ermleet Rd **1** BS6 .....49 C2
Ernest Barker **14** BS5 .....64 B7
Ernestville Rd BS16 .....50 F3
Ervine Terr BS2 .....143 C4
Esgar Rise BS22 .....88 E3
Eskdale BS35 .....15 D7
Eskdale Cl BS22 .....105 D8
Esmond Gr BS21 .....57 D4
Esplanade Rd BS20 .....45 C7
Essery Rd BS5 .....50 C2
Esson Rd BS15 .....51 B1
Estcourt Gdns BS16 .....50 D5
Estcourt Gdns BS16 .....50 D5
Estoril BS37 .....27 F1
Estune Wlk BS41 .....62 A2
Etloe Rd BS6 .....49 A4
Eton La BS29 .....106 E7
Eton Rd BS4 .....64 D3
Etonhurst BS23 .....104 D6
Ettlingen Way BS21 .....57 F2
Ettricke Dr BS16 .....51 B5
Eugene Flats **7** BS2 .....143 A4
Eugene St
  Bristol,Kingsdown BS2 .....143 A4
  Bristol,St Pauls BS2,BS5 .....143 C4
Evans Cl BS4 .....64 F5
Evans Rd BS6 .....49 B2
Eve Rd BS5 .....50 B1
Evelyn Rd Bath BA1 .....101 B8
  Bristol BS10 .....49 C7
Evelyn Terr **15** BA1 .....85 A1
Evening Post Rdbt The
  BS2 .....143 C3
Evenlode Gdns BS11 .....47 F5
Evenlode Way BS31 .....82 A3
Evercreech Rd BS14 .....80 B4
Everest Ave BS16 .....50 E4
Everest Rd BS16 .....50 E4
Evergreen Cl BS25 .....107 F1
Ewart Rd BS22 .....105 C8
Ewell Rd BS14 .....80 B6
Exbourne **10** BS22 .....89 A2
Excelsior St BA2 .....102 B5
Excelsior Terr BA3 .....133 B1
Exchange Ave BS1 .....143 A2
Exchange Ct BS15 .....65 E8
Exeter Bldgs BS6 .....49 B2
Exeter Rd Bristol BS4 .....63 B4
  Portishead BS20 .....45 E4
  Weston-S-M BS23 .....104 E5
Exford Cl BS23 .....104 F2
Exley Cl BS30 .....66 D5
Exmoor Rd BA2 .....101 F2
Exmoor St BS3 .....63 B3
Exmouth Rd BS4 .....63 F1
Exton Cl **5** BS14 .....80 B5
Eyer's La BS2 .....143 C3

F

Faber Gr BS13 .....79 C4
Fabian Dr BS34 .....36 E5
Factory Rd BS36 .....37 F7
Failand Cres BS9 .....48 C5
Failand La BS20 .....46 F2
Failand Wlk BS9 .....48 C6
Fair Cl BA2 .....136 E4
Fair Furlong BS13 .....79 A4
Fair Furlong Prim Sch
  BS13 .....79 B4
Fair Hill BS25 .....125 F8
Fair Lawn BS30 .....66 B4
Fair View Dr BS6 .....49 C2
Fairacre Cl Bristol BS7 .....50 B5
  Locking BS24 .....106 B4
Fairacres Cl BS31 .....81 F5
Fairfax St BS1 .....143 B3
Fairfield
  Peasedown St John BA2 .....117 A3
  Rode BA3 .....137 F1
Fairfield Ave BA1 .....85 A2
Fairfield Cl Backwell BS48 76 D7
  Marshfield SN14 .....70 A8
  Weston-S-M BS22 .....88 B1
Fairfield High Sch BS6 .....49 F2
Fairfield Mead BS40 .....76 D7
Fairfield Park Rd BA1 .....85 A2
Fairfield Pl BS3 .....63 B4
Fairfield Pneu Sch BS48 .....76 C6
Fairfield Rd Bath BA1 .....85 B1

Fairfield Rd continued
  Bristol,Montpelier BS6 .....49 F2
  Bristol,Southville BS3 .....63 B4
Fairfield Terr Bath BA1 .....85 A1
  Peasedown St John BA2 .....134 C7
Fairfield View BA1 .....85 A2
Fairfield Way BS48 .....76 C6
Fairfoot Rd BS4 .....64 A3
Fairford Cl BS15 .....51 F2
Fairford Cres BS34 .....36 C8
Fairford Rd BS11 .....47 D7
Fairhaven BS37 .....27 F1
Fairhaven Rd BS6 .....49 C4
Fairlawn BS16 .....51 D4
Fairlawn Ave BS34 .....36 A3
Fairlawn Rd BS6 .....49 F2
Fairlyn Dr BS15 .....51 F3
Fairoaks BS30 .....66 A3
Fairseat Ind Est BS40 .....112 E7
Fairview BS22 .....88 F4
Fairview Ho BS9 .....48 F8
Fairview Rd BS15 .....65 F8
Fairway BS4 .....64 D1
Fairway Cl Bristol BS30 .....66 B4
  Weston-S-M BS22 .....88 B2
Fairway Ind Ctr BS34 .....35 F3
Fairways BS31 .....82 E2
Fairy Hill BS39 .....98 D6
Falcon Cl
  Bristol,Patchway BS34 .....35 E8
  Bristol,Westbury on Trym
  BS9 .....48 F8
  Portishead BS20 .....45 D4
Falcon Cres BS22 .....105 D8
Falcon Ct BS9 .....49 A7
Falcon Dr BS34 .....35 E8
Falcon Way BS35 .....8 D2
Falcon Wlk BS34 .....23 E1
Falcondale Rd BS9 .....48 F7
Falcondale Wlk BS9 .....49 A8
Falconer Rd BA1 .....84 A3
Falconride Prim Sch
  BS15 .....51 F1
Falfield Rd BS4 .....64 C3
Falfield Wlk BS10 .....49 C8
Falkland Rd **4** BS6 .....49 F2
Fallodon Ct BS9 .....49 B5
Fallodon Way BS9 .....49 B5
Fallowfield Blagdon BS40 110 E2
  Bristol BS30 .....66 D5
  Weston-S-M BS22 .....88 F3
Falmouth Cl BS48 .....60 A1
Falmouth Rd BS7 .....49 E4
Fane Cl BS10 .....35 A3
Fanshawe Rd BS14 .....80 A7
Far Handstones BS30 .....66 A4
Faraday Rd **2** BS8 .....62 F5
Farendell Rd BS16 .....38 B1
Farington Rd BS10 .....49 D7
Farlands BS16 .....53 B6
Farleigh Hungerford Castle★
  BA3 .....137 E8
Farleigh La GL12 .....10 C2
Farleigh Rd Backwell BS48 76 C6
  Clevedon BS21 .....57 B1
  Keynsham BS31 .....81 D4
  Norton St Philip BA2 .....136 F5
Farleigh Rise BA15 .....86 E1
Farleigh View BA15 .....120 F3
Farleigh Wlk BS13 .....79 A8
Farler's End BS48 .....75 F8
Farley Cl BS34 .....36 C7
Farm Cl BS16 .....52 B6
Farm Ct BS16 .....51 E7
Farm La
  Easter Compton BS35 .....22 E2
  Wellow BA2 .....118 C1
Farm Lees GL12 .....11 A6
Farm Rd Bristol BS16 .....51 E7
  Hutton BS24 .....105 E2
  Weston-S-M BS22 .....88 B1
Farmborough CE Prim Sch
  BA2 .....115 F6
Farmcote GL12 .....19 D8
Farmer Rd BS13 .....78 E4
Farmhouse Cl **7** BS48 .....59 E2
Farmhouse Ct **1** BS48 .....59 E1
Farmwell Cl BS13 .....79 B5
Farnaby Cl BS4 .....79 C7
Farnborough Rd BS24 .....106 C4
Farndale BS5 .....65 A6
Farndale Rd BS22 .....105 D8
Farne Cl BS9 .....49 B5
Farr St BS11 .....47 B8
Farr's La BS1 .....143 A2
Farrant Cl BS4 .....79 D6
Farrington Fields BS39 .....132 C3
Farrington Gurney CE Prim
  Sch BS39 .....132 A4
Farrington Rd BS39 .....132 C5
Farrington Way BS39 .....132 B3
Farrs La BA2 .....102 B2
Farthing Combe BS26 .....125 D2
Farthing Row BA3 .....137 E1
Faukland View BA2 .....134 E7
Faulkland La BA2,BA3 .....135 C4
Faulkland Rd BA2 .....101 D5
Faversham Dr BS24 .....105 A1
Fawkes Cl BS15 .....66 B8
Fearnville Est BS21 .....57 C2
Featherbed La
  Chew Stoke BS40 .....95 A3
  Clutton BS39 .....114 C6
  Thornbury BS35 .....7 B6
Featherstone Rd **4** BS16 50 F4
Feddon Village BS21 .....44 F5
Feeder Rd BS2 .....64 A5

Felix Rd BS5 .....64 B8
Felstead Rd BS10 .....35 E1
Feltham Ct BS16 .....35 F2
Feltham Rd BS16 .....53 C6
Felton Gr BS13 .....79 A8
Felton La BS40 .....94 E7
Felton St BS40 .....94 E5
Feniton **6** BS22 .....89 A2
Fennel Dr BS32 .....37 A2
Fennel La BS26 .....125 B2
Fennel Gr BS10 .....35 A2
Fenners BS22 .....89 B4
Fenshurst Gdns BS41 .....77 F8
Fenswood Cl BS41 .....61 E1
Fenswood Mead BS41 .....61 E1
Fenswood Rd BS41 .....61 E1
Fenton Cl BS31 .....82 D3
Fenton Ct BS7 .....49 D4
Fenton Rd BS7 .....49 D4
Ferenberge Cl BA2 .....116 A6
Fermaine Ave BS4 .....64 F4
Fern Cl
  Bristol,Brentry BS10 .....35 B3
  Midsomer Norton BA3 .....133 B1
Fern Gr Bristol BS32 .....36 D8
  Nailsea BS48 .....75 C8
Fern Lea BS24 .....122 B6
Fern Lodge BS23 .....104 D6
Fern Rd BS16 .....51 D5
Fern St BS2 .....49 F1
Fernbank Ct **2** BS6 .....49 C2
Fernbank Rd BS6 .....49 C2
Fernbrook Cl BS16 .....37 B1
Ferndale Ave BS30 .....66 A3
Ferndale Cl BS32 .....24 D7
Ferndale Rd Bath BA1 .....85 C3
  Bristol BS7 .....36 A2
  Portishead BS20 .....45 D6
Ferndene BS32 .....24 C2
Ferndown BS37 .....27 E1
Ferndown Cl BS11 .....48 A7
Fernhill BS32 .....24 C7
Fernhill Ct
  Almondsbury BS32 .....24 C7
  Bristol BS11 .....34 B1
Fernhill La BS11 .....34 B1
Fernhurst Rd BS5 .....50 F1
Fernlea Gdns BS20 .....47 B4
Fernlea Rd BS22 .....105 C7
Fernleaze BS36 .....38 C6
Fernleigh Ct **1** BS6 .....49 B2
Fernside BS48 .....76 A7
Fernsteed Rd BS13 .....78 F6
Ferry Ct BA2 .....102 B6
Ferry La BA2 .....102 B6
Ferry Rd BS15 .....65 D1
Ferry St BS1 .....143 B2
Ferry Steps Ind Est BS2 .....64 A4
Ferryman's Ct BS2 .....143 B2
Fiddes Rd BS6 .....49 C4
Fiddlers Wood La BS32 .....36 E8
Field Farm Cl BS34 .....36 F4
Field La Bristol BS30 .....65 F3
  Dyrham SN14 .....54 F6
  Littleton-U-S BS35 .....14 A8
  Litton BA3 .....131 A1
  Tytherington BS35 .....15 C3
Field Rd BS15 .....51 C1
Field View BS5 .....64 A8
Field View Dr BS16 .....51 C6
Fielders The BS22 .....89 B4
Fieldgardens Rd BS39 .....114 F1
Fielding Ho BA2 .....101 A6
Fielding's Rd BA2 .....101 C6
Fieldins BA15 .....120 E7
Fieldway BS25 .....108 B4
Fiennes Cl BS16 .....51 E4
Fifth Ave
  Bristol,Hengrove BS14 .....80 B7
  Bristol,Northville BS7 .....36 A1
Fifth Way BS11 .....33 E2
Filby Dr BS34 .....36 C8
Filer Cl BA2 .....134 D8
Filton Abbey Wood Sta
  BS7 .....36 B1
Filton Ave
  Bristol BS7,BS34 .....50 A7
  Bristol,Filton BS34 .....36 B3
Filton Avenue Jun & Inf Schs
  BS7 .....50 A7
Filton Coll N BS34 .....36 A4
Filton Coll S BS34 .....36 A4
Filton Gr BS7 .....49 F6
Filton High Sch BS34 .....36 D3
Filton Hill Prim Sch
  BS34 .....36 B4
Filton La BS34 .....36 D2
Filton Rd
  Bristol,Frenchay BS16 .....37 B1
  Bristol,Harry Stoke BS16 .....36 F2
  Bristol,Harry Stoke BS34,
  BS16 .....36 D2
  Bristol,Horfield BS7 .....49 F8
Filwood Broadway BS4 .....79 E8
Filwood Ct BS16 .....51 B3
Filwood Dr BS15 .....65 F8
Filwood Ho BS15 .....65 F8
Filwood Rd BS16 .....51 A3
Finch Cl Thornbury BS35 .....8 C2
  Weston-S-M BS22 .....105 E8
Finch Rd BS37 .....40 A8
Finmere Gdns BS22 .....89 A4
Fir La BS40 .....127 B5
Fir Leaze BS48 .....59 B1
Fir Rd SN14 .....70 F6
Fir Tree Ave
  Paulton BS39 .....132 F4
  Weston-S-M BS24 .....105 E4

Fir Tree Cl BS34 ....35 F7
Fir Tree La BS5 ....65 A7
Fircliff Pk BS20 ....45 D7
Fire Engine La BS36 ....38 D7
Fire Station La BS11 ....33 D4
Firework Cl BS15 ....66 B8
Firfield St BS4 ....64 A4
Firgrove Cres BS37 ....28 A2
Firgrove La BA2 ....117 B1
Firs Ct BS31 ....81 C4
Firs The Bath BA2 ....102 B1
Bristol BS16 ....51 E6
Limpley Stoke BA2 ....120 A5
First Ave Bath BA2 ....101 E4
Bristol,Hengrove BS14 .....80 A7
Bristol,St Anne's BS4 .....64 E5
Portbury BS20 ....46 E5
Radstock BA3 ....139 C8
First Way BS11 ....33 C1
Fisher Ave BS15 ....52 A1
Fisher Rd BS15 ....52 A1
Fishponds Rd BS5 ....50 D3
Fishponds Trad Est BS5 ..50 E2
Fishpool Hill BS10 ....35 B4
Fitchett Wlk 2 BS10 .....34 F3
Fitzgerald Rd BS3 ....63 F3
Fitzharding Rd BS20 .....47 E3
Fitzroy Rd BS16 ....51 B2
Fitzroy St BS4 ....64 A4
Fitzroy Terr 7 BS6 ....49 B2
Five Acre Dr BS16 ....51 A7
Five Arches Cl BA3 ....133 D2
Flagstaff Rd BS26 ....123 D7
Flamingo Cres BS22 .....105 E8
Flat The BS39 ....114 D5
Flatwoods Cres BA2 .....102 F3
Flatwoods Rd BA2 ....102 F3
Flax Bourton CE Prim Sch
BS48 ....76 F8
Flax Bourton Rd BS8 .....61 B3
Flaxman Cl BS7 ....50 B6
Flaxpits La BS36 ....37 E5
Florence Brown Com Sch
The BS4 ....79 D4
Florence Gr BS22 ....105 E8
Florence Pk
Almondsbury BS32 ....24 C5
Bristol BS6 ....49 B4
Florence Rd BS16 ....51 E3
Florida Terr BA3 ....133 C2
Flowerdown Bridge
BS22 ....105 D7
Flowerdown Rd BS24 ....106 D4
Flowers Hill BS4 ....64 E1
Flowers Hill Cl BS4 ....64 E1
Flowers Hill Trad Est
BS4 ....64 E1
Flowerwell Rd BS13 .....79 B5
Folleigh Cl BS41 ....62 B2
Folleigh Dr BS41 ....62 B2
Folleigh La BS41 ....62 B2
Folliot Cl BS16 ....51 A7
Folly Bridge Cl BS37 ....27 D2
Folly Brook Rd BS16 .....38 B1
Folly Cl BA3 ....138 D2
Folly Farm Nature Reserve★
BS39 ....114 B5
Folly La Bristol BS2 ....64 A6
Shipham BS25 ....125 E2
Weston-S-M BS23 ....104 E1
Folly Rd BS37 ....26 A5
Folly The Bristol BS16 ....51 F7
Cold Ashton SN14 ....68 F6
Paulton BS39 ....132 F6
Saltford BS31 ....82 F2
Fontana Cl BS30 ....66 B3
Fonthill Prim Sch BS10 ..35 E2
Fonthill Rd Bath BA1 .....84 E2
Bristol BS10 ....35 D2
Fonthill Way BS30 ....66 C2
Fontmell Ct BS14 ....80 D7
Fontwell Dr BS16 ....37 F1
Footes La BS36 ....38 B7
Footshill Cl BS15 ....65 C6
Footshill Dr BS15 ....65 C7
Footshill Gdns BS15 .....65 C6
Footshill Rd BS15 ....65 C6
Forbes Fraser Hospl
BA1 ....101 B8
Ford La Bristol BS16 .....52 B6
Litton BA3 ....130 C1
Ford Rd
Peasedown St John BA2 ..134 D8
Wellow BA2 ....118 F1
Ford St BS5 ....64 C6
Forde Cl BS30 ....65 F5
Fordell Pl BS4 ....64 A3
Forefield Pl BA2 ....141 C1
Forefield Rise BA2 ....102 B4
Forehills BS20 ....45 C4
Forelands BS23 ....87 B1
Forest Ave BS16 ....51 B3
Forest Dr
Bristol,Brentry BS10 .....35 C3
Weston-S-M BS23 ....88 A1
Forest Edge BS15 ....65 C4
Forest Hills BS32 ....24 B5
Forest Rd
Bristol,Hillfields BS16 ....51 B4
Bristol,Kingswood BS15 ..65 D7
Forest Wlk
Bristol,Hillfields BS16 ....51 B4
Bristol,Kingswood BS15 ..65 C7
Forester Ave BA2 ....102 B8
Forester Ct BA2 ....141 C4
Forester La BA2 ....102 B8
Forester Rd Bath BA2 ....102 B8
Portishead BS20 ....45 D4

Forge End BS20 ....46 E3
Forgotten World Mus★
BS26 ....123 D4
Fortescue Rd BA3 ....133 F2
Fortfield Rd BS14 ....80 B5
Forty Acre La BS35 ....15 B3
Foss Ct 8 BS5 ....64 F8
Foss La BS35 ....7 E6
Fosse Barton BS48 ....59 D2
Fosse Cl BS48 ....59 C2
Fosse Gdns BA2 ....118 D8
Fosse Gn BA3 ....133 D3
Fosse La Batheaston BA1 ..86 A4
Nailsea BS48 ....59 D2
Radstock BA3 ....133 D3
Fosse Way BS48 ....59 C2
Fosse Way Cotts BA3 ....133 D2
Fosse Way Sch BA3 .....139 C8
Fossedale Ave BS14 .....80 C6
Fossefield Rd BA3 ....139 B6
Fosseway Clevedon BS21 ..57 C2
Midsomer Norton BA3 ....139 A5
Radstock BA3 ....139 C8
Radstock,Clandown BA3 ..133 E4
Fosseway Cl BA2 ....134 B7
Fosseway Ct BS8 ....142 A2
Fosseway Gdns BA3 .....133 D1
Fosseway Jun Sch BA2 ..101 D1
Fosseway S BS37 ....139 B7
Fosseway The BS8 ....142 A3
Foster St BS5 ....50 B2
Foundry Cotts BA2 .....116 B4
Foundry La BS5 ....50 F2
Fountain Ct Bristol BS32 ..24 C3
2 Yate BS37 ....39 D7
Fountain La BS25 ....125 D3
Fountaine Ct 3 BS5 .....50 C2
Fountains Dr BS30 ....65 F6
Four Acre Ave BS16 .....51 E8
Four Acre Cres BS16 .....37 E1
Four Acre Rd BS16 ....51 E8
Four Acres BS13 ....78 E4
Four Acres Cl Bristol BS13 78 F4
Nailsea BS48 ....75 E8
Four Acres Prim Sch
BS13 ....78 E4
Four Seasons Sq BS37 ....27 E1
Fourth Ave
Bristol,Hengrove BS14 ....80 B7
Bristol,Northville BS7 .....36 A1
Radstock BA3 ....139 D8
Fourth Way BS11 ....33 C1
Fowey Cl BS48 ....76 A8
Fowey Rd BS22 ....89 A4
Fox & Hounds La BS31 ....81 F5
Fox Ave BS37 ....27 C2
Fox Cl Bristol BS4 ....64 F5
Hawkesbury Upton GL9 ...19 F2
Fox Ct BS30 ....65 F3
Fox Den Rd BS34 ....36 D3
Fox Hill BA2 ....102 A2
Fox Ho BS4 ....64 E3
Fox Rd BS5 ....64 C7
Foxborough Gdns BS32 ..24 D2
Foxcombe Rd Bath BA1 ..101 B7
Bristol BS14 ....80 B4
Foxcote BS15 ....65 F7
Foxcote Rd BS3 ....63 A3
Foxcroft Cl BS32 ....36 F6
Foxcroft Rd BS5 ....64 D8
Foxe Rd BS36 ....38 B8
Foxfield Ave BS32 ....24 D2
Foxglove Cl Bristol BS16 ..50 E5
Thornbury BS35 ....8 D2
Weston-S-M BS22 ....89 A5
Foxhill Ho BA2 ....102 A1
Foxholes La BS32 ....14 C4
Foye Ho BS8 ....62 E6
Fraley Rd BS9 ....49 A8
Frampton Cotterell CE Prim
Sch BS36 ....38 A8
Frampton Cres BS16 .....51 C4
Frampton Ct
8 Bristol,Cadbury Heath
BS30 ....65 F4
15 Bristol,Pile Marsh BS5 ..64 D7
Frampton End Rd BS36,
BS37 ....26 D2
France La GL9 ....20 B2
Frances Greeves Ct BS10 34 F1
Francis Ct BS5 ....64 F7
Francis Fox Rd 7 BS23 ..104 E7
Francis Ho BS2 ....143 A4
Francis Pl BS30 ....65 F4
Francis Rd
Bristol,Bedminster BS3 ....63 C2
Bristol,Eastfield BS10 .....49 C8
Francis Way BS30 ....66 D6
Francombe Gr BS10 .....49 E6
Francombe Ho BS1 .....143 A1
Frankcom Ho BA2 ....102 B7
Frankland Cl BA1 ....84 B1
Frankley Bldgs BA1 .....85 B1
Frankley Terr 6 BA1 .....85 B1
Franklin Ct BS1 ....143 B1
Franklin's Way BS49 .....74 F1
Franklyn Ct 6 BS16 .....50 E3
Franklyn La 9 BS2 ....49 F1
Franklyn St BS2 ....49 F1
Fraser Cl BS22 ....88 F4
Fraser St BS3 ....63 D3
Frayne Rd BS3 ....63 A4
Frederick Ave BA2 ....134 C2
Frederick Pl BS8 ....142 B3
Fredericks Way SN14 ....43 B3
Fredrick St BS4 ....64 A4
Free Tank BS2 ....143 C2
Freeland Bldgs 1 BS5 ...50 C2

Freeland Pl BS8 ....62 F6
Freelands BS21 ....73 C8
Freeling Ho BS1 ....143 B1
Freemans La BS48 ....77 B2
Freemantle Gdns BS5 ....50 C3
Freemantle Ho BS2 .....143 A4
Freemantle Rd BS5 .....50 C3
Freestone Rd BS2 ....64 A6
Freeview Rd BA2 ....101 A5
Freezinghill La BS30 .....68 B4
Fremantle La 8 BS6 .....49 D1
Fremantle Rd BS6 ....49 D1
Fremantle Sq BS6 ....49 D1
French Cl Nailsea BS48 ...59 F3
Peasedown St John BA2 ..134 D7
Frenchay CE Prim Sch
BS16 ....51 B7
Frenchay Cl BS16 ....51 B7
Frenchay Hill BS16 ....51 C7
Frenchay Hospl BS16 .....51 B8
Frenchay Park Rd BS16 ..50 F6
Frenchay Rd Bristol BS16 51 C6
Weston-S-M BS22 ....104 E4
Frenchay Village Mus★
BS16 ....51 A8
Frenchfield Rd BA2 .....134 D7
Freshford CE Prim Sch
BA2 ....120 B5
Freshford La BA2 ....120 A4
Freshford Sta BA2 ....120 C5
Freshland Way BS15 .....65 B8
Freshmoor 6 BS21 ....57 F3
Friar Ave BS22 ....88 E3
Friars Ho 4 BS37 ....39 D7
Friary BS1 ....143 C2
Friary Cl Clevedon BS21 ..57 C5
Westwood BA15 ....120 E4
Friary Grange Pk BS36 ...37 E6
Friary Rd Bristol BS7 .....49 D4
Portishead BS20 ....45 B5
Friendly Row BS20 ....47 C5
Friendship Gr 3 BS48 ....59 F1
Friendship Rd Bristol BS4 64 A2
Nailsea BS48 ....59 F3
Friezewood Rd BS3 ....63 A4
Fripp Cl BS5 ....64 B6
Frith La GL12 ....17 F3
Frobisher Ave BS20 .....45 B5
Frobisher Cl
Portishead BS20 ....45 A5
Weston-S-M BS22 ....88 E4
Wrington BS40 ....92 E2
Frobisher Rd BS3 ....63 A3
Frog La Bristol BS1 .....142 C2
Coalpit Heath BS36 ....38 E7
Felton BS40 ....94 C8
North Nibley GL11 ....5 C5
Ubley BS40 ....111 D1
Winford BS40 ....94 F5
Frogmore St BS1 ....142 C2
Frome Ct BS35 ....15 C8
Frome Glen BS36 ....37 E4
Frome Old Rd BA3 ....134 A2
Frome Pl 1 BS16 ....50 E5
Frome Rd Bath BA2 .....101 D1
Bristol BS2 ....143 C4
Chipping Sodbury BS37 ..28 C1
Norton St Philip BA2 ....136 F3
Radstock BA3 ....134 B2
Frome Valley Rd BS16 ....50 F6
Frome View BS36 ....38 B7
Frome Villas BS16 ....51 C7
Frome Way BS36 ....37 E5
Fromebank Jun Sch
BS37 ....27 D3
Fromeside Pk BS16 ....51 B7
Front St BS25 ....108 E4
Froomshaw Rd BS16 .....51 A7
Frost & Reed Ho 3 BS5 ..64 F8
Frost Hill BS49 ....91 D7
Fry Ct 2 BS3 ....63 C4
Fry's Cl BS16 ....50 D4
Fry's Hill BS4 ....64 D3
Fry's La BS40 ....109 F3
Fry's Well BA3 ....138 D3
Frys Hill BS15 ....51 E2
Frys Leaze BA1 ....85 B2
Fryth Ho BS48 ....60 B3
Fryth Way BS48 ....59 F3
Fuddlebrook Cotts SN14 ..69 F6
Fulford Rd BS13 ....79 C5
Fulford Wlk BS13 ....79 B5
Fullens Cl BS22 ....105 D2
Fuller Rd BA1 ....85 C2
Fullers La BS25 ....125 A6
Fullers Way BA2 ....118 D8
Fullwell Cl BA3 ....135 D1
Fulmar Cl BS35 ....8 D1
Fulmar Rd BS22 ....88 F1
Fulwell La BA3 ....135 D1
Furber Ct BS5 ....65 B6
Furber Rd BS5 ....65 B6
Furber Ridge BS5 ....65 B6
Furber Vale BS5 ....65 B6
Furland Rd BS22 ....88 C2
Furlong Cl BA3 ....138 F7
Furlong Pl BS26 ....125 C1
Furlong The BS6 ....49 D6
Furnleaze BS39 ....114 E3
Furnwood BS5 ....65 A6
Furze Cl BS22 ....88 B2
Furze Rd Bristol BS16 ....51 C3
Weston-S-M BS22 ....88 A3
Furzewood Rd BS15 .....65 F8
Fussell Ct BS15 ....65 F8
Fylton Croft BS14 ....80 B3

G

Gable Cl BS35 ....23 A2
Gable Rd 7 BS5 ....50 A1
Gables Cl BS29 ....107 B3
Gadshill Dr BS34 ....36 E5
Gadshill Rd BS5 ....50 C2
Gages Cl BS15 ....65 F7
Gages Rd BS15 ....65 F7
Gainsborough Cl BA1 ....84 B1
Gainsborough Dr BS22 ...88 F3
Gainsborough Gdns
BA1 ....101 C8
Gainsborough Rd BS31 ..81 F5
Gainsborough Sq BS7 ....50 B7
Galingale Way BS20 .....45 F5
Galleries The BS1 ....143 B3
Gallivan Cl BS34 ....36 B8
Galway Rd BS4 ....63 E1
Gambril La GL12 ....9 F5
Gander Cl BS13 ....79 B5
Gannet Rd BS22 ....88 F1
Garamond Ct BS1 ....143 B1
Garden Cl Bristol BS9 ....48 C5
Weston-S-M BS22 ....88 E2
Garden Ct BS8 ....142 A4
Gardeners Wlk BS41 .....62 B1
Gardens Rd BS21 ....57 C4
Gardens The BS16 ....36 F1
4 Bristol,Upper Soundwell
BS16 ....51 D3
Gardner Ave BS13 ....78 F7
Gardner Rd BS20 ....45 D6
Garfield Rd BS5 ....64 F8
Garfield Rd BS5 ....65 A8
Garfield Terr 4 BA1 .....85 C2
Garland Ho 9 BS21 .....57 C2
Garner Ct 4 BS22 ....89 B4
Garnet St BS3 ....63 B3
Garnett Pl BS16 ....51 F7
Garonor Way BS20 ....46 F5
Garre Ho BA2 ....100 F5
Garrett Dr BS32 ....36 D7
Garrick Rd BA2 ....100 F5
Garsdale Rd BS22 .....105 D8
Garston La BS40 ....110 E3
Garston La BS40 ....110 E3
Garstons Bathford BA1 ...86 D2
8 Clevedon BS21 ....57 B1
Wrington BS40 ....92 E2
Garstons Cl Backwell BS48 75 E4
Wrington BS40 ....92 E2
Garstons Orch BS40 .....92 D1
Garstons The BS20 ....45 D4
Garth Rd BS13 ....79 A8
Garton Ho 3 BS16 ....51 D5
Garvey Ho 14 BS5 ....64 C7
Gas La BS2 ....64 A6
Gasferry Rd BS1 ....142 B1
Gaskins The BS7 ....50 A7
Gaston Ave BS31 ....81 F6
Gastons The BS11 ....48 A8
Gatcombe Dr BS34 ....36 E4
Gatcombe Rd BS13 ....79 B5
Gatehouse Ave BS13 .....79 A5
Gatehouse Cl BS13 ....79 A5
Gatehouse Ct BS13 ....79 B5
Gatehouse Sh Ctr BS13 ..79 B5
Gatehouse Way BS13 ....79 A5
Gatesby Mead BS34 .....36 E5
Gathorne Cres BS37 .....27 D2
Gathorne Rd BS3 ....63 B4
Gatton Rd BS2 ....50 A1
Gaunt's La BS1 ....142 C2
Gaunts Cl BS20 ....44 F4
Gaunts Earthcott La
BS32 ....25 B5
Gaunts Rd BS37 ....40 B8
Gay Ct BA1 ....85 E3
Gay Elms Prim Sch BS13 79 A4
Gay Elms Rd BS13 ....79 A4
Gay St BA1 ....141 B3
Gay's Hill BA1 ....141 C4
Gays Rd BS15 ....65 B4
Gaywood Ho 7 BS3 .....63 B3
Gazelle Rd BS24 ....105 B3
Gazzard Cl BS36 ....37 E7
Gazzard Rd BS36 ....37 E7
Gee Moors BS15 ....65 F7
Gefle Cl BS1 ....142 B1
Geldof Dr BA3 ....133 A2
General Hospl BS23 .....104 E2
Geoffrey Cl BS13 ....78 E6
George & Dragon La 11
BS5 ....64 D7
George Cl BS48 ....76 D7
George Ct BS6 ....49 B1
George Ho BA2 ....102 B6
George Jones Rd BS2 ....64 A6
George La SN14 ....55 C1
George St Bath BA1 .....141 B3
Bath,Bathwick BA2 ....102 B6
Bristol BS5 ....64 C8
Portishead BS20 ....45 C2
Weston-S-M BS23 ....104 E7
George Whitefield Ct
BS1 ....143 B3
George's Pl BA2 ....102 B6
George's Pl BA1 ....85 A1
Georges Bldgs BA1 .....85 C3
Georgian Ho BA2 ....141 C2
Georgian House Mus★
BS1 ....142 C2
Georgian View BA2 .....101 C2
Gerald Rd BS3 ....63 A3
Gerard Rd BS23 ....104 F8

Gerrard Bldgs BA2 .....102 B7
Gerrard Cl BS4 ....79 D7
Gerrish Ave
Bristol,Mangotsfield BS16 ..51 F5
Bristol,Moorfields BS5 ....64 C8
Gibbet La BS14 ....80 D1
Gibbs Ct 14 BS5 ....64 D7
Gibbsfold Rd BS13 ....79 C4
Gibson Rd BS6 ....49 D1
Giffard Ho BS34 ....36 D6
Gifford Cl BS37 ....27 A8
Gifford Cres BS34 ....36 C6
Gifford Ct BS37 ....36 D2
Gifford Rd BS10 ....34 F4
Giffords Pl BS13 ....79 A7
Gilbeck Rd BS48 ....59 C2
Gilbert Rd
Bristol,Hopewell Hill BS15 51 D1
Bristol,Moorfields BS5 ....64 C8
Gilberyn Dr BS22 ....89 A3
Gilda Cl BS14 ....80 C5
Gilda Cres BS14 ....80 B6
Gilda Par BS14 ....80 C5
Gilda Sq W BS14 ....80 B5
Gill Ave BS16 ....51 B6
Gill Mews BS22 ....89 B4
Gillard Cl BS15 ....65 B8
Gillard Rd BS15 ....65 B8
Gillebank Cl BS14 ....80 D5
Gillham Ho BS7 ....49 D2
Gillingham Hill 6 BS5,
BS15 ....65 B5
Gillingham Terr 3 BA1 ...85 B1
Gillingstool BS35 ....15 C8
Gillingstool Prim Sch
BS35 ....15 B8
Gillmore Cl BS22 ....88 D1
Gillmore Rd BS22 ....88 D1
Gillray Cl BS7 ....50 B6
Gillson Cl BS24 ....105 D2
Gilpin Cl BS15 ....51 F1
Gilroy Cl BS30 ....66 B3
Gilslake Ave BS10 ....35 B3
Gilton Ho BS4 ....64 E2
Gimblet Rd BS22 ....89 B4
Gingell's Gn 4 BS5 .....65 A8
Gipsy Patch La BS34 ....36 C6
Glades The BS5 ....50 E2
Gladstone Ct Bath BA2 ..102 C2
Bristol BS16 ....51 E4
Gladstone Dr BS16 ....51 E3
Gladstone La BS36 ....38 C7
Gladstone Pl BA2 ....102 C2
Gladstone Rd Bath BA2 ..102 C2
Bristol,Hengrove BS14 ....80 B6
2 Bristol,Hopewell Hill
BS15 ....51 D1
Gladstone St
Bristol,Bedminster BS3 ....63 D4
12 Bristol,Pile Marsh BS5 ..64 D7
Bristol,Upper Soundwell
BS16 ....51 D3
Midsomer Norton BA3 ....133 B3
Glaisdale Rd BS16 ....51 A5
Glanville Dr BS39 ....130 E6
Glanville Gdns BS15 .....65 E7
Glass House La BS2 ......64 B5
Glastonbury Cl
Bristol BS30 ....65 F5
Nailsea BS48 ....60 B1
Glastonbury Way BS22 ...89 A2
Glebe Ave BS20 ....45 E4
Glebe Cl BS41 ....62 C2
Glebe Field BS32 ....24 A5
Glebe Ho Bath BA2 .....102 B5
Weston-S-M BS22 ....88 F3
Portishead BS20 ....45 E4
Glebe Inf Sch The BS49 ..91 B8
Glebe Rd Bath BA2 .....101 B4
Bristol BS5 ....64 E8
Clevedon BS21 ....57 C2
Long Ashton BS41 ....62 C2
Portishead BS20 ....45 E4
Weston-S-M BS23 ....104 E8
Glebe The Freshford BA2 120 B4
Hinton Charterhouse BA2 119 D2
Pilning BS35 ....22 C7
Timsbury BA2 ....116 B3
Wrington BS40 ....92 D2
Glebe Wlk BS31 ....81 C4
Glebelands BA3 ....133 D1
Glebelands Rd BS34 .....36 A3
Glebes The BS5 ....64 E8
Gledemoor Dr BS36 .....38 D7
Glen Ave BS8 ....61 F8
Glen Brook BS9 ....48 D4
Glen Dr BS9 ....48 D5
Glen Hospl The BS6 .....49 A2
Glen La BS4 ....64 E2
Glen Park Gdns BS5 .....65 A8
Glen Pk
Bristol,Eastville BS5 .....50 C2
Bristol,St George BS5 ....65 A8
Glen The
Bristol,Hanham BS15 ....65 B4
Bristol,Westbury Park BS6 ..49 A3
Saltford BS31 ....82 F1
Weston-S-M BS22 ....88 B2
Yate BS37 ....27 E2
Glen Yeo Terr BS49 .....91 C4
Glena Ave BS4 ....64 B2
Glenarm Rd BS4 ....64 E2
Glenarm Wlk BS4 ....64 E2
Glenavon Ct BS9 ....48 C4
Glenavon Pk BS9 ....48 C4

Glenburn Rd BS15 ......51 B1
Glencairn Ct BA2 .....102 B6
Glencoe Bsns Pk BS23 ..105 A7
Glencoyne Sq BS10 ....35 C2
Glencroft Way BS22 ....88 E3
Glendale 18 Bristol BS8 ..62 F6
 Bristol,Downend BS16 ..51 E8
 Bristol,Hillfields BS16 ..51 C3
Glendare St BS5 ....64 C6
Glendevon Rd BS14 ....80 A3
Gleneagles BS37 ......27 E1
Gleneagles Cl
 Nailsea BS48 ....60 A1
 Weston-S-M BS22 .....88 F3
Gleneagles Dr BS10 ....34 D3
Gleneagles Rd BS30 ...66 B6
Glenfall BS37 ....39 D7
Glenfrome Prim Sch BS5 ..50 B4
Glenfrome Rd BS2 .....50 B3
Glenview Ho BA2 .....134 D8
Glenview Rd BS4 ......64 D2
Glenwood BS16 ....51 C6
Glenwood Dr BS30 .....66 B4
Glenwood Mans BS23 ..87 D1
Glenwood Rd BS10 .....49 C7
Glenwood Rise BS20 ...44 F5
Glevum Cl BS16 ....52 C7
Gloster Ave BS5 ......50 D3
Gloucester Cl BS34 ....36 D5
Gloucester Ho 11 BS2 ..143 C3
Gloucester La 18 BS2 ..143 C3
Gloucester Rd
 Almondsbury BS32,BS35 ..24 C6
 Avonmouth BS11 ......33 A1
 Bath BA1 ....85 C3
 Bristol,Ashley Down BS7 ..49 E4
 Bristol,Little Stoke BS34 ..36 B7
 Bristol,Upper Soundwell
  BS16 ....51 E3
 Stone GL13 ....3 E3
 Thornbury BS35 ....8 C3
 Upper Swainswick BA1 ..85 A7
Gloucester Rd N BS7,
 BS34 ....36 A4
Gloucester Row
 6 Bristol BS8 ....62 F7
 Kingswood GL12 ......11 F8
Gloucester St Bath BA1 ..141 B3
 8 Bristol,Clifton BS8 ..62 F7
 Bristol,Lower Easton BS5 ..50 D3
 5 Bristol,St Pauls BS2 ..143 B4
 Weston-S-M BS23 ....104 D7
Gloucestershire County
 Cricket Gd BS7 ......49 E3
Glovers Field BS25 ...125 F7
Glyn Vale BS3 ....63 E1
Goddard Dr BS22 .....89 B4
Godfrey Ct 3 BS30 ....65 F4
Godwin Dr BS48 ......59 C3
Goffenton Dr BS16 ....51 B6
Goldcrest Rd BS37 .....39 F7
Golden Hill BS6 ......49 C5
Golden La GL12 ....11 F4
Golden Lion Ct BS1 ...143 B2
Golden Valley La BS30 ..66 F2
Golden Valley Prim Sch
 BS48 ....59 F2
Goldfinch Way BS16 ...53 C4
Goldney Ave
 Bristol,Clifton Wood BS8 ..142 A2
 Bristol,Warmley BS30 ..66 C7
Goldney Cl BS39 .....114 F1
Goldney Ct 7 BS16 ....50 E3
Goldney Rd BS8 .....142 A2
Goldney Way BS39 ...114 F1
Goldsbury Wlk BS11 ..34 A1
Goldsmiths Ho BS2 ...143 C3
Golf Club La BS31 .....82 E2
Golf Course La BS34 ..35 F3
Golf Course Rd BA2 ..102 D6
Golledge Cl BA3 .....138 C4
Gooch Ct BS30 ....66 C3
Gooch Way BS22 ......89 B3
Good Shepherd Cl BS7 ..49 C4
Goodeve Pk BS9 ......48 D3
Goodeve Rd BS9 ......48 D3
Goodhind St BS5 ......64 A8
Goodneston Rd BS16 ..51 A3
Goodrich Cl BS37 .....27 B1
Goodring Hill BS11 ....34 A1
Goodwin Dr BS14 .....79 F4
Goodwood Gdns BS16 ..37 F1
Goold Cl BA2 ....100 A8
Goolden St BS4 ....64 A3
Goosard La BS39 .....132 E8
Goose Acre BS32 ......36 F6
Goose Gn BS30 ....66 C3
 Frampton Cotterell BS36 ..38 C8
 Yate BS37 ....28 C1
Goose Green Way BS37 ..27 E4
Gooseham Mead BS49 ..91 D4
Gooseland Cl BS14 ....79 F3
Goosey La BS22 ....89 C2
Gordano Gdns BS20 ...47 B4
Gordano Rd BS20 .....46 D7
Gordano Sec Sch BS20 ..45 D3

Gordano Way BS20 ....46 F5
Gordon Ave BS5 ......50 E1
Gordon Bldgs BA3 ...134 A3
Gordon Cl BS5 ....50 E1
Gordon Rd Bath BA2 ..102 B5
 13 Bristol,Montpelier BS2 ..49 F1
 Bristol,Rose Green BS5 ..50 D1
 Bristol,Victoria Park BS8 ..142 B3
 Peasedown St John BA2 ..134 D8
 Weston-S-M BS23 ....104 F7
Gore Rd BS3 ....63 A3
Gore's Marsh Rd BS3 ..63 A2
Gores Pk BS39 ....115 B2
Gorham Cl BS11 ......34 C2
Gorlands Rd BS37 .....28 C1
Gorlangton Cl BS14 ....80 A7
Gorse Cover Rd BS35 ..22 A7
Gorse Hill BS16 ......51 C3
Gorse La Bristol BS8 ..142 B2
 Cold Ashton BS30,SN14 ..68 D7
Gosforth Cl BS10 .....35 B1
Gosforth Rd BS10 .....35 B1
Goslet Rd BS14 ....80 E5
Goss Barton BS48 .....59 C1
Goss Cl BS48 ....59 C1
Goss La BS48 ....59 C1
Goss View BS48 ......59 C1
Gotley Rd BS4 ....64 D2
Gott Dr BS4 ....64 D5
Goulston Rd BS13 .....79 A5
Goulston Wlk BS13 ....79 A5
Goulter St BS5 ....64 B6
Gournay Ct BS39 .....132 A3
Gourney Cl BS11 ......34 B2
Gover Rd BS15 ....65 C3
Governors Ho BA2 ...101 D6
Govier Way BS35 ......22 C4
Grace Cl
 Chipping Sodbury BS37 ..28 C1
 Yatton BS49 ....91 B8
Grace Ct BS16 ....51 D6
Grace Dr Bristol BS15 ..66 A8
 Midsomer Norton BA3 ..133 A2
Grace Park Rd BS4 ....64 D1
Grace Rd Bristol BS16 ..51 C5
 Weston-S-M BS22 .....89 B4
Gradwell Cl BS22 .....89 B3
Graeme Cl BS16 ......51 A4
Graham Rd
 4 Bristol,Bedminster BS3 ..63 C4
 21 Bristol,Lower Easton
  BS5 ....50 B1
 Bristol,Mangotsfield BS16 ..51 F6
 Weston-S-M BS23 ....104 E7
Grainger Ct BS11 .....47 E7
Graitney Cl BS49 ......92 A8
Grampian Cl BS30 .....66 C4
Granby Ct 16 BS8 .....62 F6
Granby Hill BS8 ......62 F6
Grand Par BA2 ......141 C2
Grand Pier* BS23 ...104 D7
Grandmother's Rock La
 BS30 ....67 D2
Granfield Gdns BS40 ..109 A5
Grange Ave
 Bristol,Hanham BS15 ..65 D5
 Bristol,Little Stoke BS34 ..36 C6
Grange Cl
 Bristol,Patchway BS32 ..24 C2
 Bristol,Stoke Gifford BS34 ..37 A4
 Weston-S-M BS23 ....104 C1
Grange Cl N BS9 ......49 B6
Grange Court Rd BS9 ..49 A6
Grange Ct Bristol BS15 ..65 D5
 Bristol,Henleaze BS9 ..49 B6
 Bristol,Westbury-on-Trym
  BS9 ....49 A8
Grange Dr BS16 ......51 C6
Grange End BS2 ......88 B2
Grange Farm Rd BS49 ..74 A1
Grange Pk
 Bristol,Eastfield BS9 ..49 B6
 Bristol,Frenchay BS16 ..51 C8
Grange Rd
 Bristol,Bishopsworth BS13 ..79 A5
 Bristol,Victoria Park BS8 ..142 A3
 Saltford BS31 ....82 C3
 Weston-S-M BS23 ....104 C1
Grange Sch & Sports Coll
 The BS30 ....66 B7
Grange The Bristol BS9 ..48 D7
 Flax Bourton BS48 ....76 F7
Grangeville Cl BS30 ...66 B3
Grangewood Cl BS16 ..51 C6
Granny's La BS15 .....65 E6
Grantham Ct 11 BS15 ..65 C8
Grantham Ho BS15 ....51 C1
Grantham La BS15 ....65 C8
Grantham Rd BS15 ....51 C1
Grantson Cl BS4 ......64 F2
Granville Chapel 5 BS8 ..62 F5
Granville Cl BS15 .....65 B3
Granville Rd BA1 .....84 E4
Granville St BS5 ......64 C6
Grasmere Cl BS10 .....49 A8
Grasmere Dr BS23 ...104 F4
Grass Meers Dr BS14 ..80 A4
Grassington Dr BS37 ..40 A8
Grassmere Gdns BS30 ..66 D6
Grassmere Rd BS49 ...91 B8
Gratitude Rd BS5 .....50 C1
Gravel Hill BS40 .....112 B7
Gravel Hill Rd N BS37 ..28 A5
Gravel Wlk BA1 .....141 B3
Graveney Cl BS4 ......64 D1
Gray Cl BS10 ....34 E2
Gray Hollow BS40 ...129 F4
Grayle Rd BS10 ....35 A2

Grayling Ho BS9 ......48 F7
Grays Hill BA2 ......135 B5
Great Ann St BS2 ....143 C3
Great Bedford St BA1 ..141 B4
Great Brockeridge BS9 ..48 F6
Great Dowles BS30 ....66 A4
Great George St
 Bristol,Brandon Hill BS1 ..142 C2
 Bristol,St Pauls BS2 ..143 C3
Great Hayles Rd BS14 ..80 A6
Great Leaze BS30 .....66 A4
Great Mdw BS2 ....37 A6
Great Meadow Rd BS32 ..36 F6
Great Park Rd BS32 ...24 C3
Great Pulteney St BA2 ..141 C2
Great Stanhope St BA1 ..141 A2
Great Stoke BS32 .....37 A5
Great Stoke Way
 Bristol,Great Stoke BS34 ..37 A5
 Bristol,Harry Stoke BS34 ..36 D3
Great Western Bsns Pk
 BS37 ....27 B3
Great Western La BS5 ..64 C6
Great Western Rd BS21 ..57 D2
Great Wood Cl BS13 ...79 C4
Greatstone La BS40 ...94 F5
Green Acre Rd BS14 ...80 A3
Green Cl Bristol BS7 ..50 A8
 Paulton BS39 ....132 E6
Green Cotts BA2 ....102 C2
Green Croft BS5 ......51 A1
Green Ct BS35 ....14 A2
Green Dell Cl BS10 ....34 D3
Green Ditch La BA3 ..138 B6
Green Dragon Rd BS36 ..37 D5
Green La Avonmouth BS11 ..33 B1
 Blagdon BS40 ....111 A7
 Easter Compton BS35 ..22 C1
 Failand BS8 ....61 C4
 Farrington Gurney BS39 ..131 F6
 Felton BS40 ....94 C3
 Freshford BA2 ......120 B2
 Hinton Charterhouse BA2 ..119 E1
 Marshfield SN14 .....69 E8
 Priddy BS40 ....128 B7
 Rangeworthy BS37,GL12 ..17 B2
 Severn Beach BS35 ....22 B8
 Stratton-on-t-F BA3 ..138 E1
 Tytherington GL12 ....16 B8
 Winsley BA15 ....120 F6
 Winterbourne BS36 ...37 C7
Green Park Mews BA1 ..141 A2
Green Park Rd BA1 ...141 B2
Green Parlor Rd BA3 ..134 D1
Green Pastures Rd BS48 ..60 B2
Green Pk BA1 ....141 B2
Green Side BS16 ......52 A6
Green St Bath BA1 ...141 C2
 Bristol BS3 ....63 F4
 Peasedown St John BA2 ..134 E5
Green The Backwell BS48 ..76 A5
 Bath BA2 ....101 D1
 Bristol,Lower Soundwell
  BS15 ....51 E2
 Bristol,Shirehampton BS11 ..47 E6
 Chipping Sodbury BS37 ..41 A8
 Compton Dando BS39 ..98 D5
 Cromhall GL12 ....17 B8
 Hinton Charterhouse BA2 ..119 F1
 Locking BS24 ....106 A4
 Luckington SN14 .....31 E4
 Olveston BS35 ....14 A2
 Pill BS20 ....47 D4
 Winscombe BS25 ....125 A7
Green Tree Rd BA3 ...133 B3
Green Wlk BS4 ....64 A1
Greenacre BS22 ......88 B2
Greenacres Bath BA1 ..84 B3
 Bristol BS9 ....48 E7
 Midsomer Norton BA3 ..132 F1
Greenacres Park Homes
 BS36 ....38 E5
Greenbank Ave BS5 ...50 C1
Greenbank Ave W BS5 ..50 C1
Greenbank Gdns BA1 ..84 B1
Greenbank Rd
 Bristol,Lower Easton BS5 ..50 D2
 Bristol,Mount Hill BS15 ..65 D5
 Bristol,Southville BS3 ..63 A4
Greenbank View BS5 ..50 D2
Greendale Rd
 Bristol,Lower Knowle BS3 ..63 E2
 Bristol,Westbury Park BS6 ..49 B3
Greenditch Ave BS13 ..79 C5
Greenditch Cl BA3 ...138 C3
Greenditch St BS35 ...13 C1
Greendown BS5 ......65 A7
Greendown Pl BA2 ...102 A1
Greenfield Ave BS10 ..49 D8
Greenfield Cres BS48 ..59 E3
Greenfield Pk BS20 ...45 C3
Greenfield Pl BS23 ...104 C8
Greenfield Rd BS10 ...35 D1
Greenfield Wlk BA3 ..133 A3
Greenfields Ave BS29 ..107 A2
Greengage Cl BS22 ..105 E8
Greenhaven 5 BS5 ....50 C1
Greenhayes BS37 .....40 C8
Greenhill BS35 ....15 A4
Greenhill Cl Nailsea BS48 ..59 D2
 Weston-S-M BS22 .....89 A3
Greenhill Croft BS25 ..108 B4
Greenhill Down BS35 ..15 A5
Greenhill Gdns BS35 ..15 A4
Greenhill Gr BS3 ......63 A2

Greenhill La
 Alveston BS35 ....14 F4
 Bristol BS11 ....34 C1
 Sandford BS25 ......108 B4
Greenhill Par 5 BS35 ..15 A5
Greenhill Pl BA3 ....133 A3
Greenhill Rd
 Alveston BS35 ....15 A5
 Midsomer Norton BA3 ..133 A3
 Sandford BS25 ......108 B4
Greenland Rd BS22 ...88 D1
Greenlands Rd BA2 ..134 C8
Greenlands Way BS10 ..34 F4
Greenleaze BS4 ......64 B1
Greenleaze Ave BS16 ..37 D1
Greenleaze Cl BS16 ...37 D1
Greenmore Rd BS4 ...64 B2
Greenore BS15 ....65 C7
Greenpark Rd BS10 ...35 C1
Greenridge BS39 ....114 F3
Greenridge Cl BS13 ...78 E4
Greenside Cl BS10 ....34 D3
Greenslade Gdns BS48 ..59 D3
Greenslade Inf Sch BS48 ..59 D3
Greensplott Rd BS11 ..33 E7
Greenvale BA3 ......116 B1
Greenvale Cl BA2 ....116 B1
Greenvale Dr BA2 ...116 B1
Greenvale Rd BS39 ..132 D5
Greenview BS30 ......66 A2
Greenway BA3 ......135 C1
Greenway Bush La BS3 ..63 B4
Greenway Ct BA2 ...101 F4
Greenway Dr BS10 ....49 D8
Greenway Ho 10 BS6 ..49 B2
Greenway La Bath BA2 ..102 A4
 Cold Ashton SN14 ....68 D5
Greenway Pk Bristol BS10 ..49 D8
 3 Clevedon BS21 ....57 F3
Greenway The BS16 ...51 C3
Greenways Bristol BS15 ..52 A1
 Chilcompton BA3 ....138 C2
Greenways Rd BS37 ..27 E3
Greenwell La BS40 ...109 C7
Greenwood Cl BS7 ...49 E7
Greenwood Dr BS35 ..14 F4
Greenwood Rd
 Bristol BS4 ....64 A1
 Weston-S-M BS22 .....88 E2
Gregory Cl BS30 ......66 A6
Gregory Mead BS49 ..74 A1
Gregorys Gr BA2 ....118 D8
Gregorys Tyning BS39 ..132 F6
Greinton BS24 ......105 A2
Grenville Ave BS24 ..106 A4
Grenville Cl BS5 .....64 F8
Grenville Pl 7 BS1 ....62 F5
Grenville Rd BS6 .....49 E3
Greve Ct 5 BS30 .....65 F4
Greville Rd BS3 ......63 B4
Greville St BS3 ....63 C4
Greyfield Comm BS39 ..115 C2
Greyfield Rd BS39 ...115 C2
Greyfield View BS39 ..114 F1
Greylands Rd BS13 ...78 F7
Greystoke Ave BS10 ..35 C1
Greystoke Gdns BS10 ..49 A8
Greystones BS16 .....37 C1
Grib La BS40 ....110 F2
Griffen Rd BS24 .....105 E7
Griffin Cl BS22 ....89 B2
Griffin Ct BA1 ......141 B2
Griffin Rd BS21 ......57 E3
Griggfield Wlk BS14 ..80 A7
Grimsbury Rd BS15 ...66 A7
Grindell Rd BS5 ......64 D7
Grinfield Ave BS13 ...79 C4
Grinfield Cl 11 BS13 ..79 C4
Grinfield Ct BS13 .....79 C4
Grittleton Rd BS7 ....49 E8
Grosvenor Bridge Rd
 BA1 ....85 C1
Grosvenor Ct 2 BS6 ..49 B1
Grosvenor Pk BA1 ...85 C1
Grosvenor Pl BA1 ....85 C1
Grosvenor Rd BS2 ...49 F1
Grosvenor Terr BA1 ..85 C2
Grosvenor Villas 9 BA1 ..85 B1
Grove Ave Bristol BS1 ..143 A1
 Bristol,Coombe Dingle BS9 ..48 C7
 3 Bristol,Upper Eastville
  BS16 ....50 F4
Grove Bank BS16 .....37 C5
Grove Ct BS9 ....48 E5
Grove Dr BS22 ....88 D1
Grove Ind Est The BS34 ..36 B8
Grove Jun Sch BS48 ..75 D8
Grove La Faulkland BA3 ..135 D2
 Hinton SN14 ....54 C6
 Weston-S-M BS23 ....104 D8
Grove Leaze BS11 ....47 D6
Grove Orch BS40 ....110 E2
Grove Park Ave BS4 ..64 D2
Grove Park Ct BS23 ...87 D1
Grove Park Rd Bristol BS4 ..64 D2
 Weston-S-M BS23 .....87 D1
Grove Park Terr BS16 ..50 F4
Grove Pk
 Bristol,Brislington BS4 ..64 D2
 Bristol,Redland BS6 ..49 C3
Grove Rd Bristol,Coombe Dingle BS9 ..48 D8
 Bristol,Redland BS6 ..49 A2
 Bristol,Ridgeway BS16 ..50 F4
 Weston-S-M BS23 ....104 D8
 Weston-S-M,Milton BS22 ..88 C1
Grove St BA2 ....141 C3

Grove The Bath BA1 ...84 C1
 Bristol,Cadbury Heath BS30 ..66 A4
 Bristol,Canon's Marsh
  BS1 ....143 A1
 Bristol,Little Stoke BS34 ..36 B7
 Paulton BS39 ....132 E7
 Rangeworthy BS37 ....27 A8
 Winscombe BS25 ....107 F1
 Wraxall BS48 ....60 C3
Grove View BS16 .....50 E6
Grove Wood Rd BA3 ..133 F1
Groves The BS13 .....79 D4
Grovesend Rd
 Thornbury BS35 ......15 D8
 10 Thornbury BS35 ....8 B1
Guernsey Ave BS4 ...64 F4
Guest Ave BS16 ......52 B7
Gug The BS39 ......115 C2
Guild Ct BS1 ....143 B2
Guildford Rd BS4 ....64 E6
Guinea La Bath BA1 ..141 C3
 Bristol BS16 ....51 A4
 Bristol BS16 ....51 A5
Guinea St BS1 ......143 A1
Gullen BA2 ....135 A6
Gulliford's Bank BS21 ..57 F2
Gullimores Gdns BS13 ..79 B4
Gullivers Pl BS37 .....40 A8
Gullock Tyning BA3 ..133 B1
Gullon Wlk BS13 .....78 F5
Gullons Cl BS13 ......79 A6
Gully La GL13 ....8 E7
Gully The BS36 ......37 F7
Gullybrook La 3 BS5 ..64 B6
Gunning Cl BS15 .....65 D6
Gunter's Hill BS5 ....65 A6
Guthrie Rd BS8 .....142 A4
Gwilliam St BS3 ......63 D3
Gwyn St BS2 ....49 E1
Gypsy La Keynsham BS31 ..99 B8
 Marshfield SN14 .....69 F7

H

Haberfield Hill BS20,BS8 ..47 E2
Haberfield Ho 1 BS8 ..62 F6
Habron Ct BS3 ....63 C3
Hacket Hill BS35 .....15 F8
Hacket La BS35 ......15 F8
Hadley Ct BS30 ......66 B6
Hadley Rd BA2 ......102 B2
Hadrian Cl BS9 ......48 C4
Hadrians Wlk BS16 ...52 C6
Haig Cl BS9 ....48 B7
Halbrow Cres BS16 ...51 C5
Haldon Cl BS3 ....63 D1
Hale Cl BS15 ....65 D8
Hales Horn Cl BS32 ..36 D6
Half Yd BS40 ....109 D8
Halfacre Cl BS14 .....80 A3
Halfacre La BS14 .....80 B4
Halfpenny Row BA3 ..137 E1
Halifax Rd BS37 .....27 D4
Hall End La BS37 .....17 D2
Hall La
 Cold Ashton,Lower Hamswell
  BA1 ....68 B3
 Cold Ashton,Tadwick BA1,
  SN14 ....68 E2
 Horton BS37 ....29 E5
Hall Sch The BS25 ...125 B8
Hall St BS3 ....63 C2
Hallam Ct BS21 ......57 C4
Hallam Rd BS21 ......57 C4
Hallards Cl BS11 .....47 F8
Hallatrow Rd BS39 ..132 C6
Hall La
 Bristol,Henbury BS10 ..34 D3
 Bristol,Mangotsfield BS16 ..52 C5
Hallen Cl
 Bristol,Henbury BS10 ..34 D3
 Bristol,Mangotsfield BS16 ..52 C5
Hallen Dr BS9 ....48 C5
Hallen Ind Est BS10 ..34 A7
Hallen Rd BS10 ......34 D4
Halletts Way BS20 ...45 D5
Halliwell Rd BS20 ....44 D4
Halls Gdns BS34 .....37 A4
Halls Rd BS15 ....65 D8
Halsbury Rd BS6 .....49 B4
Halstock Ave BS16 ...50 F3
Halston Dr BS2 .....143 C4
Halswell Gdns BS13 ..79 B4
Halswell Rd BS21 ....57 D1
Halt End BS14 ....80 C3
Halwyn Cl BS9 ....48 D5
Ham Cl BS39 ....114 F1
Ham Farm La BS16 ...52 B6
Ham Gn BS20 ....47 D3
Ham Gr BS39 ....132 E5
Ham La
 Bishop Sutton BS39 ..113 C5
 Bristol BS16 ....50 E6
 Doynton BS30 ....53 E1
 Dundry BS41 ....78 D3
 Farrington Gurney BS39 ..131 F5
 Kingston Seymour BS21 ..73 B2
 North End BS49 ......74 A3
 Paulton BS39 ....132 E5
 Thornbury BS35 ....7 C1
 Wraxall BS48 ....60 B4
 Yatton BS49 ....74 A3
Ham Link BS40 .....109 F3
Ham Rd BS24,TA8 ...121 B3
Ham Wood Cl BS24 ..105 B2
Hamble Cl BS35 ......15 C8
Hambledon Rd BS22 ..89 C4
Hambrook La BS16 ...37 A3
Hambrook Prim Sch
 BS16 ....37 D3

Ham – Hig 159

Hamilton Ho BA1 84 E3
Hamilton Rd Bath BA1 84 E2
Bristol,Southville BS3 63 B4
Bristol,Upper Easton BS5 64 B8
Weston-S-M BS23 87 C1
Hamilton Terr BA2 134 F5
Hamlet The BS48 60 A3
Hammer La BA3 136 C1
Hammersmith Rd BS5 64 D8
Hammond Cl BS4 64 E1
Hammond Gdns BS9 48 E7
Hampden Cl BS37 27 D4
Hampden Rd Bristol BS4 64 B3
Weston-S-M BS22 88 E2
Hampshire Way BS37 27 F4
Hampstead Rd BS4 64 C3
Hampton Cl BS30 66 A5
Hampton Cnr
Bristol,Shirehampton BS11 47 E6
[12] Bristol,Woolcott Park BS6 49 B1
Hampton Ct BS6 49 B1
Hampton Ho [10] BA1 85 C1
Hampton La [17] BS6 49 B1
Hampton Pk BS6 49 B1
Hampton Rd BS6 49 B1
Hampton Row BA2 102 B8
Hampton St BS15 51 D1
Hampton View BA1 85 B1
Hams La BS26 123 C3
Hams Rd BS31 81 F7
Hanbury Cl BS15 65 D5
Hanbury Ct BS8 142 A4
Hanbury Rd BS8 142 A4
Handel Ave [2] BS5 64 D7
Handel Rd BS31 81 E5
Handford Way BS30 66 B3
Hanford Ct BS14 80 D7
Hang Hill BA2 135 A6
Hanham Abbots Jun Sch BS15 65 C4
Hanham Bsns Pk BS15 65 B5
Hanham Hall Hospl BS15 65 D4
Hanham High Sch BS15 65 C4
Hanham La BS39 132 F7
Hanham Mills BS15 65 D1
Hanham Rd BS15 65 D7
Hanham Way BS48 59 B2
Hanna Cl BA2 101 B6
Hannah More Cl BS40 92 E2
Hannah More Inf Sch BS48 75 D8
Hannah More Prim Sch BS1 143 C2
Hannah More Rd BS48 75 C8
Hannay Rd BS27 126 B1
Hanny's La BS40 96 B3
Hanover Cl BS22 89 A4
Hanover Ct Bath BA1 85 B2
Bristol,Filton BS34 36 A3
Bristol,St Pauls BS1 143 B3
Radstock BA3 134 C2
Hanover Ho BS2 64 A7
Hanover Pl Bath BA1 102 B8
Bristol BS1 142 B1
Hanover St [2] Bath BA1 85 B1
[2] Bristol BS1 143 A2
Bristol,Russell Town BS5 64 C7
Hanover Terr [5] BA1 85 B1
Hans Price Cl BS23 104 E8
Hans Price Ho [14] BS23 104 E8
Hansford Cl BA2 101 E1
Hansford Mews BA2 101 F1
Hansford Sq BA2 101 E1
Hanson's Way [6] BS21 57 C2
Hantone Hill BA2 102 F8
Happerton La BS20 47 D2
Hapsburg Cl BS22 89 A4
Harbour Rd BS20 45 E6
Harbour Road Trad Est BS20 45 F6
Harbour Wall BS9 48 B4
Harbour Way BS1 142 C1
Harbour Wlk BS1 142 C1
Harbury Rd BS9 49 C7
Harbutts BA2 85 F1
Harcombe Hill BS36 37 E4
Harcombe Rd BS36 37 D5
Harcourt Ave BS5 65 A6
Harcourt Cl BS31 82 E2
Harcourt Gdns BA1 84 B2
Harcourt Hill BS6 49 C3
Harcourt Rd BS6 49 B3
Harden Rd BS14 80 E5
Hardenhuish Rd BS4 64 D5
Harding Pl BS31 82 B5
Hardington Dr BS31 82 A2
Hardwick Cl
Bristol,Broom Hill BS4 64 E3
Bristol,North Common BS30 66 D5
Hardwick Rd BS20 47 C5
Hardwicke BS37 39 C7
Hardy Ave BS3 63 A4
Hardy Ct BS30 65 F5
Hardy La BS32 14 A1
Hardy Rd BS3 63 B2
Hareclive Prim Sch BS13 79 C4
Hareclive Rd BS13 79 C4
Harefield Cl BS15 65 C2
Harescombe BS37 39 E7
Harewood Ho BS6 49 A3
Harewood Rd BS5 51 A1
Harford Cl BS9 48 C7
Harford Dr BS16 37 C1
Harford Sq BS40 96 B3
Harington Pl [2] BA1 141 B2
Harlech Way BS30 66 B2
Harleston St [1] BS5 64 A8
Harley Ct [3] BS8 62 F7
Harley La BS21 58 C6
Harley Mews [2] BS8 62 F7
Harley Pl [4] BS8 62 F7
Harley St BA1 141 B4
Harmer Cl BS10 34 F3
Harmony Dr BS20 44 F4
Harnhill Cl [2] BS13 79 B4
Harolds Way BS15 65 C6
Harptree BS24 105 A2
Harptree Cl BS48 75 D8
Harptree Ct [5] BS30 66 A4
Harptree Gr BS3 63 B2
Harptree Hill BS40 129 B5
Harrier Path BS22 105 E8
Harrington Ave BS14 80 E6
Harrington Cl BS30 82 E8
Harrington Gr BS14 80 E6
Harrington Rd BS14 80 E6
Harrington Wlk BS14 80 E6
Harris Barton BS36 38 B7
Harris Ct BS30 65 F4
Harris La BS8 61 F8
Harrison Cl BS16 52 B6
Harrow Rd BS4 64 D3
Harrowdene Rd BS4 64 B3
Harry Stoke Rd BS34 36 E2
Hart Cl BS20 47 E4
Hart's La BS39 132 B7
Hartcliffe Rd BS4 79 E8
Hartcliffe Sec Sch BS13 79 E4
Hartcliffe Way BS3, BS4, BS13 79 C7
Hartcliffe Wlk BS4 79 F8
Hartfield Ave BS6 142 C4
Hartgill Cl BS13 79 B3
Hartington Pk BS6 49 C2
Hartland [14] BS22 89 A2
Hartland Ho BS5 64 C6
Hartley Cl BS37 28 C1
Harts Croft BS37 27 F4
Harts Paddock BA3 132 F3
Harvest Cl BS32 24 D1
Harvest La BS24 106 B8
Harvest Way BS22 89 A5
Harvey Cl BS22 89 A4
Harvey's La [6] BS5 64 F8
Harwood Gdns BS22 88 E4
Harwood Ho [13] BS5 64 B7
Haselbury Gr BS31 82 E2
Haskins Ct [4] BS30 66 A4
Haslands BS48 75 D8
Haslemere Ind Est BS11 33 C2
Hassage Hill BA2 135 E7
Hassell Dr BS2 64 A7
Hastings Cl BS3 63 C1
Hastings Rd BS3 63 C1
Hatchet Hill BA3,BA11 140 E4
Hatchet La BS34 36 E4
Hatchet Rd BS34 36 E5
Hatchmere BS35 15 D8
Hatfield Bldgs BA2 102 B5
Hatfield Rd Bath BA2 101 F3
Weston-S-M BS23 105 A8
Hatherley BS37 39 E7
Hatherley Rd BS7 49 E4
Hathway Wlk BS5 64 A8
Hatters' La BS37 28 C1
Havage Dro BS24 107 D8
Haven The BS15 51 E1
Haversham Cl BS22 88 D1
Haverstock Rd BS4 64 A3
Haviland Gr BA1 84 B3
Haviland Ho [7] BS2 143 C3
Haviland Pk BA1 84 B2
Havory BA1 85 C1
Havyat Rd BS40 109 E8
Havyat Road Trad Est BS40 92 E1
Haw La BS35 14 B3
Hawarden Terr BA1 85 B1
Hawburn Cl BS4 64 D2
Haweswater Cl BS30 66 D6
Hawke Rd BS22 88 E4
Hawkesbury CE Prim Sch GL9 19 F3
Hawkesbury Grange GL9 20 A2
Hawkesbury Rd
Bristol BS16 50 E3
Hillesley GL12 19 D6
Hawkesley Dr BS34 36 D6
Hawkesworth Rd BS37 27 C3
Hawkfield Bsns Pk BS14 79 D5
Hawkfield Cl BS14 79 D5
Hawkfield Rd BS13 79 D5
Hawkfield Way BS14 79 D5
Hawkins Cl BS30 66 C5
Hawkins Cres BS32 36 E8
Hawkins St BS2 143 C3
Hawkley Dr BS32 24 D3
Hawkmoor La BS16 50 E8
Hawkridge Dr BS16 53 C5
Hawksmoor Cl BS14 80 A6
Hawksworth Dr
Bristol BS15 65 B5
Weston-S-M BS22 89 C4
Hawthorn Ave BS15 65 B5
Hawthorn Cl Bristol BS34 35 E7
Charfield GL12 11 A4
Portishead BS20 44 F5
Hawthorn Coombe BS22 88 E3
Hawthorn Cres
Thornbury BS35 8 C2
Yatton BS49 74 A2
Hawthorn Gdns BS22 88 D2
Hawthorn Gr BA2 102 A1
Hawthorn Hill BS22 88 E2
Hawthorn Hts BS22 88 D3
Hawthorn Pk BS22 88 E3
Hawthorn Rd BA3 134 B2
Hawthorn Way
Bristol BS34 36 E5
Nailsea BS48 60 A2
Hawthorne Cl BS16 53 C5
Hawthorne Gdns BS16 51 F4
Hawthorne Rise BS10 35 C3
Hawthorne St BS4 64 A3
Hawthornes The BS16 51 F4
Hawthorns La BS31 81 E5
Hawthorns The BS21 57 C3
Hay Hill BA1 141 B3
Hay La BS40 94 D6
Hay Leaze BS37 27 D4
Hay St
Farrington Gurney BA3 138 A8
Marshfield SN14 70 A8
Hayboro Way BS39 132 E4
Haycombe BS14 79 F6
Haycombe Dr BA2 101 A4
Haycombe La BA2 101 A3
Haycroft La GL13 4 C6
Haycroft Rd BS34 36 A3
Hayden Cl BA2 141 A1
Haydock Cl BS16 37 F1
Haydon Ct [12] BS8 49 A2
Haydon Gate BA3 139 F8
Haydon Gdns BS7 50 B5
Haydon Hill BA3 140 A8
Haydon Ind Est BA3 139 F8
Haye's La GL9 30 F2
Hayeley Dr BS32 36 E6
Hayes Cl BS2 64 A7
Hayes Ct BS34 36 A7
Hayes Park Rd BA3 132 F2
Hayes Rd BA3 132 F1
Hayesfield Pk BA2 141 B1
Hayesfield Sch Tech Coll BA2 101 D6
Hayesfield School Tech Coll BA2 141 A1
Hayeswood Rd BA2 115 E3
Hayfield SN14 70 A8
Haygarth Ct BA1 141 B4
Hayleigh Ho BS13 79 C4
Haymarket The BS1 143 A3
Haymarket Wlk [9] BS1 143 A4
Haynes Ho [1] BS16 51 D4
Haynes La BS16 51 D5
Hayter Ct BS10 35 D3
Haythorn Ct BS16 51 F5
Haythorne Ct [8] BS16 50 E3
Haytor Pk BS9 48 D6
Hayward Cl BS21 57 C1
Hayward Ind Est [1] BS16 51 D3
Hayward Rd
Bristol,Russell Town BS5 64 C7
Bristol,Upper Soundwell BS16 51 D3
Haywood Cl BS24 105 A1
Haywood Gdns BS24 105 B1
Hazel Ave BS6 49 B2
Hazel Barrow BS40 129 A7
Hazel Cote Rd BS14 80 B4
Hazel Cres BS35 8 D1
Hazel Gdns BS35 15 A4
Hazel Gr Bath BA2 101 D4
Bristol BS7 50 A8
Midsomer Norton BA3 139 B8
Hazel La Alveston BS35 14 F2
Tockington BS35 14 E3
Hazel Terr BA3 139 C8
Hazel Way BA2 118 D8
Hazelbury Dr BS30 66 C6
Hazelbury Rd Bristol BS14 80 C7
Nailsea BS48 59 D1
Hazeldene Rd
Bristol BS34 36 A7
Weston-S-M BS23 105 A8
Hazelgrove BS36 37 E5
Hazell Cl BS21 57 E1
Hazelton Rd BS7 49 D3
Hazelwood Ct BS9 48 D3
Hazelwood Rd BS9 48 D3
Hazleton Gdns BA2 102 F3
Head Croft BS48 77 B8
Headford Ave BS5 65 B7
Headford Rd BS4 63 D1
Headington Cl BS15 65 D4
Headley Ct BS13 79 B6
Headley La BS13 79 B7
Headley Park Ave BS13 79 B7
Headley Park Prim Sch BS13 79 B6
Headley Park Rd BS13 79 A7
Headley Rd BS13 79 A6
Headley Wlk BS13 79 B7
Healey Dr SN14 54 C6
Heart Meers [2] BS14 80 B5
Heath Cl BS36 37 E6
Heath Ct BS16 51 D7
Heath Gates [2] BS48 59 F2
Heath Gdns Bristol BS16 51 D8
Coalpit Heath BS36 38 C5
Heath House La BS7,BS16 50 C5
Heath House Priory Hospl BS16 50 B4
Heath Rd
Bristol,Downend BS16 51 D8
Bristol,Eastville BS5 50 B3
Bristol,Hanham BS15 65 B4
Nailsea BS48 59 F2
Nailsea BS48 59 F3
Heath Ridge BS41 62 A2
Heath Rise BS30 66 B5
Heath St BS5 50 C3
Heath Wlk BS16 51 D7
Heathcharts BS24 105 A3
Heathcote Dr BS36 38 D7
Heathcote La BS36 38 D7
Heathcote Rd
Bristol,Chester Park BS16 51 B2
Bristol,Staple Hill BS16 51 E5
Heathcote Wlk BS16 51 C2
Heather Ave BS36 38 B6
Heather Cl BS15 65 B8
Heather Dr BA2 118 D8
Heatherdene BS14 79 F7
Heathfield Cl Bath BA1 84 A3
Keynsham BS31 81 C5
Heathfield Cres BS14 80 B4
Heathfield Rd BS48 59 E3
Heathfield Way BS48 59 E2
Heathfields BS16 51 D8
Heathgate BS49 91 B8
Heathgates BS23 104 D4
Hebden Rd BA15 120 F3
Heber St BS5 64 C7
Hebron Rd [9] BS3 63 C3
Hedgemead Cl BS16 50 D5
Hedgemead Ct BA1 141 C4
Hedgemead View BS16 50 E5
Hedges Cl [3] BS21 57 B1
Hedges The BS22 89 C3
Hedwick Ave BS5 64 E7
Hedwick St BS5 64 E7
Heggard Cl BS13 79 A5
Helens Rd BS25 108 B4
Hellier Wlk BS13 79 C3
Helston Rd BS48 60 A1
Hemming Way BS24 105 E3
Hemmings Par [4] BS5 64 B7
Hemplow Cl BS14 80 D7
Hempton La BS32 24 B2
Hen La BS40 94 E3
Henacre Rd BS11 47 F8
Henbury Court Prim Sch BS10 34 F3
Henbury Ct BS10 34 E3
Henbury Gdns BS10 34 E2
Henbury Hill BS9 34 F1
Henbury Rd Bristol BS15 65 B5
Bristol,Henbury BS10 34 F2
Bristol,Westbury on Trym BS9 49 A8
Henbury Road Henbury Hill BS9 48 F8
Henbury Sch BS10 34 E3
Hencliffe Rd BS14 80 D7
Hencliffe Way BS15 65 B3
Henderson Ho [1] BS2 143 B4
Henderson Rd BS15 65 B5
Hendre Rd BS3 63 A2
Heneage La GL12 9 F8
Henfield Bsns Pk BS36 38 D2
Henfield Cres BS30 66 B3
Henfield Rd BS36 38 C4
Hengaston St BS3 63 B2
Hengrove Ave BS14 80 B8
Hengrove La BS14 80 B8
Hengrove Rd BS4 64 A2
Hengrove Sch BS14 80 B7
Hengrove Way
Bristol,Hartcliffe BS13 79 C5
Bristol,Novers Park BS14 79 E6
Henleaze Ave BS9 49 A5
Henleaze Gdns BS9 49 A5
Henleaze Jun & Inf Schs BS9 49 C5
Henleaze Park Dr BS9 49 C6
Henleaze Pk BS9 49 C5
Henleaze Rd BS9 49 B6
Henleaze Terr BS9 49 B7
Henley Gr BS9 49 B5
Henley Grove Ct BS9 49 B5
Henley La BS49 91 D7
Henley Lodge Bath BA1 101 C8
Yatton BS49 91 D7
Henley Pk BS49 91 C7
Henley View BA2 118 D1
Hennessy Cl BS14 79 F3
Henrietta Ct BA2 141 C4
Henrietta Gdns BA2 141 C3
Henrietta Mews BA2 141 C3
Henrietta Pl BA2 141 C3
Henrietta Rd BA2 141 C3
Henrietta St Bath BA2 141 C3
Bristol,Kingsdown BS2 143 A4
[5] Bristol,Lower Easton BS5 50 B1
Henry Butt Ho [12] BS23 104 E8
Henry St Bath BA1 141 C2
Bristol BS3 63 F4
Henry Williamson Ct [1] BS30 66 A5
Henshaw Cl BS15 51 C2
Henshaw Rd BS15 51 C2
Henshaw Wlk BS15 51 C2
Hensley Gdns BA2 101 E4
Hensley Rd BA2 101 E3
Hensman's Hill BS8 142 A2
Hepburn Rd BS2 143 B4
Herald Cl BS9 48 D5
Herapath St BS5 64 C6
Herbert Cres BS5 50 D3
Herbert Rd Bath BA2 101 D5
Clevedon BS21 57 D4
Herbert St
Bristol,Moorfields BS5 64 C8
Bristol,Southville BS3 63 D4
Hercules Cl BS34 36 D6
Hereford Rd BS2 50 A2
Hereford St BS3 63 D3
Heritage Cl BA2 134 D8
Heritage The BA2 133 E8
Herkomer Cl BS7 50 B7
Herluin Way BS22,BS23 105 B6
Hermes Cl BS31 82 D2
Hermitage Cl BS11 47 E7
Hermitage Rd Bath BA1 84 E1
Bristol BS16 51 E5
Hern La BS48 77 E5
Heron Cl BS22 105 E8
Heron Ct BS21 57 C2
Heron Gdns BS20 45 E4
Heron Rd BS5 50 B1
Heron Way BS37 40 A8
Herridge Cl BS13 79 B4
Herridge Rd BS13 79 B4
Hersey Gdns BS13 78 E3
Hesding Cl BS15 65 C3
Hester Wood BS37 27 F4
Hestercombe Rd BS13 79 B6
Hetling Ct [7] BA1 141 B2
Hewish Ct BS23 104 E8
Hewland Ct BS11 34 C2
Heyford Ave BS5 50 B4
Heyron Wlk BS13 79 B4
Heywood Rd BS20 47 C4
Heywood Terr BS20 47 C4
Hibbs Cl SN14 69 F8
Hicking Ct [9] BS15 51 D1
Hicks Ave BS16 52 B8
Hicks Common Rd BS36 37 E5
Hicks Ct BS30 65 F4
Hide Mkt BS2 143 C3
High Acre BS39 132 F4
High Bannerdown BA1 86 B4
High Down Jun & Inf Schs BS20 45 A4
High Elm BS15 65 E6
High Gr BS9 48 B7
High Littleton CE Prim Sch BS39 115 C1
High Mdws BA3 132 F1
High Mead Gdns BS39 113 D3
High Pk Bristol BS14 64 B1
Paulton BS39 132 D6
High St Axbridge BS26 125 B2
Badminton GL9 30 E2
Banwell BS29 107 A2
Bath BA1 141 C2
Bath,Twerton BA2 101 B6
Bath,Weston BA1 84 B1
Bathampton BA2 85 F1
Batheaston BA1 85 F3
Bathford BA1 86 D2
Bitton BS30 82 E8
Blagdon BS40 110 E3
Bristol BS1 143 A2
Bristol,Jefferies Hill BS15 65 C5
Bristol,Kingswood BS15 65 E8
Bristol,Lower Easton BS5 50 B1
Bristol,Oldland Common BS30 66 D4
Bristol,Redland BS8 49 A2
Bristol,Shirehampton BS11 47 E6
Bristol,Staple Hill BS16 51 D4
Bristol,Warmley BS15 66 B8
Bristol,Westbury on Trym BS9 49 A7
Chew Magna BS40 96 A3
Chipping Sodbury BS37 28 B1
Claverham BS49 74 F1
Congresbury BS49 91 D4
Doynton BS30 53 F1
Dyrham SN14 54 D4
East Harptree BS40 129 F5
Freshford BA2 120 B5
Hawkesbury Upton GL9 19 F3
High Littleton BS39 115 D1
Hillesley GL12 19 D8
Hinton Charterhouse BA2 119 E1
Iron Acton BS37 26 D4
Keynsham BS31 81 E6
Kingswood GL12 11 F4
Marshfield SN14 69 F8
Midsomer Norton BA3 133 B1
Nailsea BS48 59 F3
Norton St Philip BA2 136 F4
Paulton BS39 132 E5
Paulton,Plummer's Hill BS39 132 E6
Pensford BS39 97 E4
Portbury BS20 46 E3
Portishead BS20 45 D5
Rode BA3 137 F1
Saltford BS31 82 F3
Ston Easton BA3 131 E1
Thornbury BS35 15 B8
Timsbury BA2 116 B2
Wellow BA2 118 D1
Weston-S-M BS23 104 D8
Weston-S-M,Worle BS22 88 E2
Wick BS30 67 D6
Wickwar GL12 18 A5
Winford BS40 95 A7
Winterbourne BS36 37 D6
Woolley BA1 84 F6
Wrington BS40 92 D2
Yatton BS49 91 C8
High View BS20 45 A4
Higham St [4] BS2 63 F4
Highbury Cotts [9] BA1 85 A1
Highbury Par BS23 87 C1
Highbury Pl BA1 85 A1
Highbury Rd
Bristol,Bedminster BS3 63 C2
Bristol,Horfield BS7 49 F7
Paulton BS39 132 B7

Highbury Rd continued
Weston-S-M BS23 ....87 C1
Highbury Terr 11 BA1 ...85 A1
Highbury Villas
10 Bath BA1 ....85 A1
Bristol BS2 ....142 C4
Highcroft 4 Bristol BS30 .66 C6
Weston-S-M BS3 ....87 F1
Highcroft Jun Sch BS36 .38 C8
Highdale Ave BS21 ......57 E3
Highdale Cl BS14 ....80 B4
Highdale Rd BS21 ....57 E3
Highett Dr BS5 ....50 A1
Highfield Ave BS15 ......65 D5
Highfield Cl BA2 ....101 B5
Highfield Cres BA3 .....138 C4
Highfield Dr BS20 ....44 E3
Highfield Gdns BS30 ....66 C2
Highfield Gr BS7 ....49 D5
Highfield La
Compton Martin BS40 ...129 B6
East Harptree BS40 ....130 A3
Horton BS37 ....29 E7
Highfield Rd
Chipping Sodbury BS37 ..28 A1
Keynsham BS31 ....81 F2
Peasedown St John BA2 .134 C8
Weston-S-M BS24 ....105 A1
Highfields
Hawkesbury Upton GL9 ...19 F2
Midsomer Norton BA3 ...133 D2
Radstock BA3 ....133 E4
Stanton Drew BS39 .....96 F1
Highfields Cl BS34 ......36 E3
Highgrove St BS4 ....64 A4
Highland Cl BS22 ....88 B2
Highland Cres 3 BS8 ....49 A2
Highland Pl 13 BS8 ......49 A2
Highland Rd BA2 ....101 B5
Highland Sq 4 BS8 ......49 A2
Highland Terr BA2 ......101 D6
Highlands Dr GL11 ....5 E4
Highlands La BS24 ......106 A8
Highlands Rd
Long Ashton BS41 ....62 A2
Portishead BS20 ....45 B5
Highleaze Rd BS30 ......66 C4
Highmead Gdns BS13 ....78 E4
Highmore Ct BS7 ....50 B7
Highmore Gdns BS7 .....50 C7
Highnam Cl BS34 ....24 B1
Highridge Cres BS13 ....78 F5
Highridge Gn BS13 ......78 E6
Highridge Inf Sch BS13 .78 F6
Highridge Pk BS13 ......78 F6
Highridge Rd
Bristol,Bedminster BS3 ..63 B2
Bristol,Bishopsworth BS13,
BS41 ....78 E4
Highridge Wlk BS13 .....78 E7
Highview Rd BS15 ....51 F2
Highwall La BS14,BS31 ..80 F1
Highway BS37 ....27 F2
Highwood Bsns Pk BS34 .35 E7
Highwood Rd BS10,BS34 .35 D7
Highwood Rd BS34 ......35 F7
Highworth Cres BS37 ....39 D8
Highworth Rd BS4 ....64 D6
Hildesheim Bridge
BS23 ....104 F7
Hildesheim Cl BS23 ....104 F6
Hildesheim Ct 9 BS23 ..104 F7
Hilhouse BS9 ....48 C6
Hill Ave Bath BA2 ......101 F1
Bristol BS3 ....63 E3
Hill Burn BS9 ....49 C6
Hill Cl BS16 ....52 B8
Hill Crest BS4 ....64 B1
Hill Ct BS39 ....132 E6
Hill Dr BS8 ....61 C3
Hill End Dr BS10 ....34 D3
Hill Gay Cl BS20 ....44 F4
Hill Gr BS9 ....49 C6
Hill House Rd BS16 .....51 F5
Hill La
Chipping Sodbury BS37 ..41 B7
Clevedon BS21 ....58 C4
Portishead BS20 ....44 F1
Rowberrow BS25 ....109 A1
Thornbury BS35,GL13 ....2 A2
Hill Lawn BS4 ....64 D3
Hill Moor BS21 ....57 E2
Hill Pk BS49 ....91 E5
Hill Rd Clevedon BS21 ..57 D4
Dundry BS41 ....78 D2
Sandford BS25 ....108 A3
Weston-S-M BS23 ....104 F8
Weston-S-M,Worle BS22 ..88 E2
Hill Rd E BS22 ....88 E2
Hill St
Bristol,Brandon Hill BS1 .142 C2
Bristol,Kingswood BS15 ..65 F8
Bristol,St George BS5 ...64 F8
Bristol,Windmill Hill BS3 .63 F4
Hill The Almondsbury BS32 .24 B4
Freshford BA3 ....120 C5
Hill Top BS20 ....45 A4
Hill View Bristol BS8 ...142 B2
Bristol,Filton BS34 ....36 A3
Bristol,Henleaze BS9 ...49 C6
Bristol,New England BS16 .52 A8
Bristol,Upper Soundwell
BS16 ....51 D2
Farrington Gurney BS39 .132 B3
Marksbury BA2 ....99 B1

Hill View continued
Priston BA2 ....117 A5
Hill View Cl BS30 ....66 C5
Hill View Ct BS22 ......105 D8
Hill View Rd Bath BA1 ...85 B2
Weston-S-M BS23 ....105 A7
Hill's Barton BS13 ......63 A1
Hillbrook Rd 5 BS35 ....15 D8
Hillburn Rd BS5 ....65 A8
Hillcote Est BS24 ......122 B8
Hillcrest
Peasedown St John BA2 .134 C7
Pensford BS39 ....97 E3
Thornbury BS35 ....8 B1
Hillcrest Cl BS48 ....59 E1
Hillcrest Dr BA2 ....101 C4
Hillcrest Rd Nailsea BS48 .59 E1
Portishead BS20 ....44 E4
Hillcroft Cl Bristol BS15 .65 E4
Weston-S-M BS22 ....88 A2
Hilldale Rd BS48 ....76 B5
Hillesley CE Prim Sch
GL12 ....19 E8
Hillesley Rd GL12 ....11 F4
Hillfields Ave BS16 .....51 C3
Hillfields Prim Sch BS16 .51 C2
Hillgrove St BS2 ....143 B4
Hillgrove Terr BS23 ....104 D1
Hillier's La BS25 ....108 C4
Hillmead BS40 ....109 A5
Hillmer Rise BS29 ......106 F3
Hillpath BS29 ....107 B2
Hills Cl BS31 ....82 A5
Hillsborough BS8 ......142 A2
Hillsborough Ho BS3 ...105 A4
Hillsborough Rd BS4 ....64 C4
Hillsdon Rd BS9 ....48 F8
Hillside
Bristol,Mangotsfield BS16 .52 A5
Bristol,Tyndall's Park
BS6 ....142 C4
Burton SN14 ....43 A4
Portbury BS20 ....46 E3
Hillside Ave Bristol BS15 .65 C8
Midsomer Norton BA3 ...138 F8
Hillside Cl
Frampton Cotterell BS36 .38 C7
Paulton BS39 ....132 F6
Hillside Cres BA3 ......138 E8
Hillside Fst Sch BS22 ...88 E2
Hillside Gdns
Bishop Sutton BS39 ....113 C3
Weston-S-M BS22 ....88 B1
Hillside Ho 5 BS6 ....49 D1
Hillside La BS36 ....38 C7
Hillside Rd Backwell BS48 .76 A4
Bath BA2 ....101 D4
Bleadon BS24 ....122 B8
Bristol BS5 ....65 A7
Clevedon BS21 ....57 D3
Long Ashton BS41 ......62 B2
Midsomer Norton BA3 ..138 F8
Portishead BS20 ....44 D4
Hillside St BS4 ....64 A4
Hillside View
Midsomer Norton BA3 ...133 A3
Peasedown St John BA2 .134 C8
Hillside W BS24 ....105 A4
Hilltop Gdns
Bristol,St George BS5 ...65 A7
Bristol,Upper Soundwell
BS16 ....51 D2
Hilltop Rd BS16 ....51 D2
Hilltop View BS5 ....65 A7
Hillview
Midsomer Norton BA3 ...138 E7
Timsbury BA2 ....116 B1
Hillview Ave BS21 ....57 D2
Hillview Gdns BS40 .....94 C8
Hillview Park Homes
BS22 ....105 D8
Hillview Rd Loxton BS26 .123 C4
Pucklechurch BS16 .....53 C5
Hillyfield Rd BS13 ......79 A6
Hillyfields BS25 ....125 B8
Hillyfields Way BS25 ...125 A8
Hilton Ct 5 BS5 ....64 B8
Hinckley Cl BS22 ....89 C4
Hind Pitts BS25 ....125 F7
Hinton BS24 ....105 A4
Hinton Cl Bath BA2 ....100 F6
Saltford BS31 ....82 E3
Hinton Dr BS30 ....66 C6
Hinton Hill BA2 ....119 A1
Hinton La 13 BS8 ....62 F6
Hinton Rd
Bristol,Fishponds BS16 ..51 A4
Bristol,Lower Easton BS5 .50 C1
Hinton Villas BA2 ......119 E1
Hippisley Dr BS26 ......125 D2
Hiscocks Dr BA2 ....101 E4
Hitchen Cl SN14 ....69 F8
Hither Bath Bridge BS4 .64 C1
Hither Gn BS21 ....57 F2
Hither Green Ind Est
BS21 ....57 F2
Hither Mead BS36 ....37 E6
Hiways Pk Cvn Pk BS10 .34 A4
Hoare's La BA3,BA11 ...140 B3
Hobart Rd BS23 ....104 F3
Hobb's La BS1 ....142 C2
Hobb's Wall BS39 ......115 D5
Hobbiton Rd BS22 ....89 A4
Hobbs Cl 1 BS48 ....59 F2
Hobbs La
Barrow Gurney BS48 ....77 E3

Hobbs La continued
Bristol BS30 ....52 B1
Hobhouse Cl BS9 ....49 C7
Hobwell La BS41 ....62 C2
Hockeys La BS16 ....51 A4
Hockley Ct BA1 ....84 D1
Hoddon La BS16 ....53 D5
Hodshill BA2 ....118 F6
Hoecroft Gdns BA3 .....138 D3
Hogarth Mews BS22 .....89 A3
Hogarth Wlk Bristol BS7 .50 C7
Weston-S-M BS22 ....89 A3
Hogues Wlk 5 BS13 .....79 B4
Holbeach Way BS14 .....80 A2
Holbrook Cres BS13 .....79 D4
Holbrook La BS30 ....67 B7
Holcombe BS14 ....80 A5
Holcombe Cl BA2 ....85 F1
Holcombe Gn BA1 ....84 B2
Holcombe Gr BS31 ....81 D5
Holcombe La BA2 ....85 F1
Holcombe Vale BA2 ......85 F1
Holdenhurst Rd BS15 ....51 C1
Holders Wlk BS41 ....77 F8
Holford Cl BS48 ....59 E1
Holford Ct BS14 ....80 B5
Holland Ct BS23 ....105 A8
Holland Rd Bath BA1 ....85 B1
Clevedon BS21 ....57 B1
Holland St BS23 ....105 A8
Hollidge Gdns 3 BS3 ....63 D4
Hollies La BA1 ....86 A6
Hollies The Bristol BS15 .65 E6
Midsomer Norton BA3 ...133 A1
Hollis Ave BS20 ....45 C3
Hollis Cl BS41 ....78 A8
Hollis Cres BS20 ....45 C3
Hollis Gdns SN14 ....31 E4
Hollister's Dr BS13 .....79 D4
Hollow La BS22 ....88 F3
Hollow Marsh La BA3,
BS39 ....131 B4
Hollow Rd
Almondsbury BS32 ....24 A4
Bristol BS15 ....65 E8
Shipham BS25 ....125 F8
Hollow The Bath BA2 ...101 B4
Peasedown St John BA2 .117 D4
Holloway BA2 ....141 B1
Holloway Hill SN14 ......56 F7
Holloway Rd BS5 ....22 C4
Hollowbrook La BS39,
BS40 ....113 D6
Hollowmead BS49 ....91 E8
Hollowmead Cl BS49 ....91 F8
Hollows The BS36 ....38 C2
Hollway Cl BS14 ....80 E5
Hollway Rd BS14 ....80 E5
Holly Cl Alveston BS35 ..14 F4
Bristol BS5 ....51 A2
Nailsea BS48 ....60 A3
Pucklechurch BS16 .....53 C5
Weston-S-M BS22 ....89 A1
Holly Cres BS15 ....51 A2
Holly Ct BS2 ....142 C4
Holly Dr Bath BA2 ......118 D8
Colerne SN14 ....70 F6
Holly Gn BS15 ....52 A1
Holly Gr BS16 ....51 C3
Holly Hill BS37 ....26 E3
Holly Hill Rd BS15 ......51 F1
Holly Ho BS11 ....34 C2
Holly La BS21 ....57 F6
Holly Lodge Cl BS5 ......51 A2
Holly Lodge Rd BS5 .....50 F2
Holly Ridge BS20 ....45 A5
Holly Wlk Keynsham BS31 .81 D4
Radstock BA3 ....133 E1
Hollybush Cl
Acton Turville GL9 ......43 A6
Winsley BA15 ....120 E7
Hollybush La Bristol BS9 .48 E5
Bristol BS9 ....48 F4
Hollyguest Rd BS15 .....65 E6
Hollyleigh Ave BS34 ....35 F2
Hollyman Wlk 5 BS21 ...57 F3
Hollymead La BS9 ....48 E4
Hollyridge BS14 ....80 C6
Hollywood La BS10,BS35 .35 A4
Hollywood Rd BS4 ....64 D2
Holm La BS35 ....13 B2
Holm Rd BS24 ....105 E2
Holm-mead La BS30 .....82 C7
Holmdale Rd BS34 ....36 C3
Holmes Ct BS9 ....49 B5
Holmes Gr BS9 ....49 B5
Holmes Hill Rd BS5 .....64 F8
Holmes St BS5 ....64 B6
Holmesdale Rd BS3 ......63 E3
Holmlea BS20 ....45 F5
Holmoak Rd BS31 ....81 C4
Holms Rd BS23 ....105 A5
Holmwood BS15 ....65 C5
Holmwood Cl BS36 ......37 D6
Holmwood Gdns BS9 ....49 B8
Holroyd Ho BS3 ....63 D3
Holsom Cl BS14 ....80 F6
Holsom Rd BS14 ....80 F6
Holst Gdns BS4 ....79 D7
Holton Rd BS7 ....50 A6
Holtsdown La BA1 ....85 F7
Holwell Cl BS39 ....132 E4
Holy Cross RC Prim Sch
BS3 ....63 C4
Holy Family RC Prim Sch
BS34 ....36 B8

Holy Trinity Prim Sch
BS32 ....24 C2
Holy Well Cl BS4 ....64 E6
Holymead Inf Sch BS4 ..64 D2
Holymead Jun Sch BS4 ..64 D2
Holyrood Cl BS34 ....36 D4
Home Cl Bristol BS10 ...35 C2
Wrington BS40 ....92 E3
Home Farm Cl BA2 ......85 F1
Home Farm Cotts BS40 .110 D3
Home Farm Rd BS8 ......62 B8
Home Farm Way BS35 ....23 A1
Home Field Cl BS16 .....52 B6
Home Gdns BS6 ....49 A2
Home Ground
Bristol,Eastfield BS9 ....49 B7
Bristol,Shirehampton BS11 .47 D7
Home Mead
Bristol,Cadbury Heath BS30 .66 A4
Bristol,Novers Park BS4 .79 E7
Home Orch
Chew Stoke BS40 ......112 D8
Yate BS37 ....27 D2
Homeapple Hill BS30 ....66 F6
Homeavon Ho BS31 ......81 F5
Homefield
Congresbury BS49 ......91 E3
Locking BS24 ....106 A5
Thornbury BS35 ....15 D8
Timsbury BA2 ....116 C2
Yate BS37 ....27 C2
Homefield Cl
Locking BS24 ....106 A5
Saltford BS31 ....82 F3
Winscombe BS25 ......107 F1
Homefield Dr BS16 ......51 A5
Homefield Ind Est BS24 .106 A5
Homefield Rd
Pucklechurch BS16 .....53 B5
Saltford BS31 ....82 F3
Homeground Bristol BS16 .52 B6
Clevedon BS21 ....57 F2
Homelea Pk E BA1 ......101 A7
Homelea Pk W BA1 .....101 A7
Homeleaze Rd BS10 .....35 D3
Homemead BA2 ....100 A8
Homemead Dr BS4 ....64 D1
Homestead BS20 ....44 E3
Homestead Cl BS36 ......38 D7
Homestead Gdns BS16 ..51 B8
Homestead Rd BS34 .....36 A3
Homestead The
Clevedon BS21 ....57 C3
Keynsham BS31 ....81 F2
Homestead Way BS25 ..125 A8
Honey Garston Cl 6
BS13 ....79 B4
Honey Garston Rd BS13 .79 B4
Honey Hill Rd BS15 .....65 F8
Honey Suckle La BS16 ...50 E5
Honey Way BS15 ....65 F8
Honeyborne Way GL12 ..18 B5
Honeyhall La BS49 .....108 D7
Honeylands BS20 ....45 C3
Honeymead BS14 ....80 D6
Honeysuckle Cl BS32 ...24 E2
Honeysuckle Pl 3 BS24 .106 A5
Honeywick Cl BS3 ....63 C2
Honister Ho BS34 ....36 A8
Honiton BS22 ....89 A2
Honiton Rd Bristol BS16 .51 A3
Clevedon BS21 ....57 E1
Hook Hill BA2 ....116 D2
Hook La BA3,BS39 ......130 E4
Hooks Batch BS40 ......110 C4
Hooper Rd BS14 ....80 D5
Hope Ct BS1 ....142 B1
Hope Rd Bristol BS3 ....63 C2
Yate BS37 ....27 A2
Hope Sq BS8 ....62 F6
Hope Terr BA3 ....133 A1
Hopechapel Hill 11 BS8 .62 F6
Hopetoun Rd BS2 ....49 F3
Hopewell Gdns BS11 ....47 F7
Hopkin Cl BS35 ....15 D7
Hopkins Ct 13 BS6 ......49 B1
Hopkins St BS23 ....104 E8
Hopland Cl BS30 ....66 B3
Hopp's Rd BS15 ....65 D7
Horesham Gr BS13 ......79 C5
Horfield CE Prim Sch
BS10 ....49 D7
Horfield Rd BS7 ....49 E4
Horfield Rd BS2 ....143 A4
Horley Rd BS2 ....50 A2
Horn's La BS26 ....125 B2
Hornbeam Rd BS16 ......51 C6
Hornbeam Wlk BS31 .....81 C3
Hornbeams The BS16 ....37 B1
Horne Cl BA3 ....138 F1
Horse La BS35 ....8 D5
Horse Race La BS8 ......61 A6
Horse St BS37 ....28 C1
Horsecastle Cl BS49 ....74 A1
Horsecastle Farm Rd
BS49 ....74 A1
Horsecombe Brow BA2 .102 A1
Horsecombe Gr BA2 ....102 A1
Horsecombe Vale BA2 ..102 A1
Horsecroft Gdns BS30 ..66 A6
Horsefair The BS1 ......143 B3
Horseleaze La BS25 ....108 D1
Horsepool La BS30 ....67 F8
Horsepool Rd BS13 ......78 E3
Horseshoe Ct BS36 ......38 D7
Horseshoe Dr BS9 ....48 C4
Horseshoe La BS37 ......28 B1
Horseshoe Wlk BA2 ....102 B5

Horsford Rd GL12 ....11 B5
Horstmann Cl BA1 ......101 B7
Hortham La BS32 ....24 E5
Horton CE Prim Sch
BS37 ....29 C5
Horton Ct★ BS37 ....29 D7
Horton Hill BS37 ....29 C5
Horton Ho BA2 ....141 C4
Horton Rd
Chipping Sodbury BS37 ..28 C2
Chipping Sodbury,Little
Sodbury End BS37 .....28 D4
Horton St BS2 ....143 C3
Horwood Ct 3 BS30 .....66 A4
Horwood La GL12 ....18 B4
Horwood Rd BS48 ....59 F1
Hosey Wlk BS13 ....79 A5
Host St BS1 ....143 A3
Hot Bath St 6 BA1 .....141 B2
Hot Water La BS15 ......52 A3
Hottom Gdns BS7 ....50 A7
Hotwell Rd
Bristol,Clifton BS8 .....62 F6
Bristol,Clifton Wood BS8 .142 B1
Hotwells Ho BS8 ....142 A2
Hotwells Prim Sch BS8 .62 F6
Houlgate Way BS26 ....125 B1
Houlton St BS2 ....143 C4
Hounds Cl BS37 ....28 B1
Hounds Rd BS37 ....28 B1
How Hill BA2 ....101 A6
Howard Ave BS5 ....64 E8
Howard Cl BS31 ....82 D3
Howard Rd
Bristol,Henleaze BS6 ....49 B4
Bristol,Southville BS3 ..63 C4
Bristol,Staple Hill BS16 .51 D4
Thornbury BS35 ....8 C2
Howard St BS5 ....50 E1
Howard Wlk BS30 ....66 D7
Howecroft Ct BS9 ....48 E4
Howecroft Gdns BS9 ....48 E4
Howells Mead BS16 .....52 B7
Howes Cl BS30 ....66 A6
Howett Rd 16 BS5 ....64 C7
Howsmoor La
Bristol,Lyde Green BS16 .52 C8
Bristol,New England BS16 .52 B8
Hoylake BS37 ....39 E8
Hoylake Dr BS30 ....66 B6
Huckford La BS36 ....38 A4
Huckford Rd BS36 ....37 E5
Huckley Way BS32 ......36 F6
Hudd's Hill Rd BS5 ......64 F8
Hudd's Vale Rd BS5 .....64 E8
Hudson Cl BS37 ....39 F8
Hughenden Rd
Bristol,Golden Hill BS7 ..49 E5
Bristol,Redland BS8 ....49 A2
Weston-S-M BS23 .....105 A8
Huish Ct BA3 ....134 B2
Hulbert Cl BS4 ....65 A2
Hulse Rd BS4 ....64 D1
Humber Way BS11 ......33 D5
Humberstan Wlk BS11 ..47 D8
Humphry Davy Way 6
BS8 ....62 F5
Humphrys Barton BS4 ..64 F5
Hung Rd BS11 ....47 E5
Hungerford Cl BS4 ......80 E8
Hungerford Cres BS4 ...64 E1
Hungerford Gdns BS4 ...80 E8
Hungerford Rd Bath BA1 .101 C7
Bristol BS4 ....80 E8
Hungerford Terr BA2 ...118 D1
Hungerford Wlk BS4 ....64 E1
Hunstrete Rd BA2 ......115 F7
Hunt's La BS49 ....91 E8
Hunter's Way BS34 .....36 B3
Hunters Cl BS15 ....65 C5
Hunters Dr BS15 ....51 F1
Hunters Mead GL9 ......20 A2
Hunters Rd BS15 ....65 C5
Hunters Rd E BS15 .....65 C4
Hunters' Rest Miniature Rly★
BS39 ....115 A5
Huntingham Rd BS13 ...78 F4
Huntley Gr BS48 ....60 A1
Hunts Ground Rd BS34 ..36 F4
Hunts La BS7 ....49 E6
Hurle Cres BS8 ....49 B1
Hurle Rd BS8 ....49 B1
Hurlingham Rd BS7 .....49 F2
Hurn La BS31 ....82 A3
Hurn Rd BS21 ....57 F2
Hursley Hill BS14,BS39 .97 D8
Hursley La BS14 ....80 E1
Hurst Rd Bristol BS4 ....79 F8
Weston-S-M BS23 .....105 A6
Hurst Wlk BS4 ....79 F8
Hurston Rd BS4 ....79 D7
Hurstwood Rd BS16 .....51 D6
Hutton CE Prim Sch
BS24 ....105 E2
Hutton Cl Bristol BS9 ...48 E7
Keynsham BS31 ....82 A2
Hutton Hill BS24 ....105 F2
Hutton Moor La BS22,
BS24 ....105 C6
Hutton Moor Rd BS22 ..105 C7
Hutton Park Caravan Pk
BS24 ....105 C6
Huyton Rd BS5 ....50 E3
Hyatts Wood Rd BS48 ..76 E1
Hyde Ave BS35 ....8 B3
Hyde The BS21 ....73 C8
Hyde's La SN14 ....69 A6
Hyland Gr BS9 ....48 F8

I

Ida Rd 2 BS5 .64 C8
Iddesleigh Rd BS6 .49 B3
Idstone Rd BS16 .51 B4
Idwal Cl BA2 .134 C8
Iford Cl BS31 .82 E3
Iford Hill BA15 .120 E2
Iford La BA2,BA15 .120 C3
Ilchester Cres BS13 .63 B1
Ilchester Rd BS13 .79 B8
Iles Cl BS15 .65 D4
Ilex Ave BS21 .57 E2
Ilex Cl BS13 .78 F6
Ilex La BS25 .107 F1
Ilminster BS24 .105 A2
Ilminster Ave BS4 .79 F8
Ilminster Avenue Prim Sch BS4 .80 A8
Ilminster Cl
Clevedon BS21 .57 E2
Nailsea BS48 .75 D8
Ilsyn Gr BS14 .80 D7
Imber Court Cl BS14 .80 B8
Imperial Arc BS3 .63 D4
Imperial Pk BS13 .79 C6
Imperial Rd
Bristol,Hengrove BS14 .80 C8
8 Bristol,Woolcott Park BS6 .49 B1
Imperial Wlk BS14 .64 B1
Inchalloch 8 BA1 .85 A1
Inclosures The BS24 .105 F8
Ingleside Rd BS15 .51 C1
Inglestone Rd GL12 .18 B5
Ingleton Dr BS22 .89 A4
Ingmire Rd BS5 .50 B3
Ingst Hill BS35 .13 B3
Ingst Rd BS35 .13 D4
Inkerman Cl BS7 .49 E7
Inman Ho BA1 .141 C4
Inn Cotts BS11 .48 A7
Inner Down The BS32 .14 D3
Inner Elm Terr BA3 .133 C1
Innicks Cl BS40 .111 D1
Innocks Est GL11 .5 D4
Innox Gdns BS13 .79 A5
Innox Gr BA2 .100 F2
Innox La BA1 .85 B5
Innox Rd BA2 .101 B5
Inns Court Ave BS4 .79 D7
Inns Court Dr BS4 .79 D6
Inns Ct Gn BS4 .79 D7
Instow 7 BS22 .89 A2
Instow Rd BS4 .79 E8
Instow Wlk BS4 .79 E8
International Helicopter Mus★ BS24 .105 E5
International Sch of Choueifat SN14 .70 C4
International Trad Est BS11 .33 B2
Interplex 16 BS32 .24 C3
Inverness Rd BA2 .101 C6
IO Ctr BS10 .33 F5
Ipswich Dr BS4 .64 E6
Irby Rd BS3 .63 A3
Irena Rd BS16 .50 F3
Ireton Rd BS3 .63 B3
Iron Acton CE Prim Sch BS37 .26 E4
Iron Acton Way BS37 .27 B3
Iron Hogg La GL12 .9 C3
Ironchurch Rd BS11 .33 C5
Ironmould La BS4,BS31 .65 A1
Irving Cl Bristol BS16 .51 E4
Clevedon BS21 .57 F3
Irving Ho BS1 .142 C3
Isambard Wlk BS1 .143 C2
ISF Rd BS11 .33 C3
Island Gdns BS16 .50 C4
Island The BA3 .133 A1
Island Trad Pk BS11 .33 C1
Isleys Ct BS30 .65 F3
Islington Rd BS3 .63 C4
Ison Hill Rd BS10 .34 D3
Itchington Rd
Alveston BS35 .15 F4
Tytherington GL12 .16 B4
Ivo Peters Rd BA2 .141 A2
Ivor Rd BS5 .64 C8
Ivy Ave BA2 .101 C4
Ivy Bank Pk BA2 .101 F2
Ivy Cl BS48 .59 D1
Ivy Ct BS20 .44 F5
Ivy Gr BA2 .101 C4
Ivy House Cotts BS29 .106 D7
Ivy La Bristol BS16 .51 A3
Weston-S-M BS24 .106 A8
Ivy Pl BA2 .101 C4
Ivy Terr BS37 .39 B4
Ivy Wlk Banwell BS29 .106 E4
Midsomer Norton BA3 .139 B8
Ivybridge 8 BS22 .89 A2
Ivywell Rd BS9 .48 E3
Iwood La BS40 .92 A2

J

Jack Knight Ho BS7 .49 F5
Jackson Cl BS35 .22 D7
Jacob St BS2 .143 C3
Jacob's Ct BS1 .142 B2
Jacob's Wells Rd BS8 .142 B2
Jacobs Mdw BS20 .45 F4
Jamaica St BS2 .143 B4
James Cl BS16 .51 E4
James Rd BS16 .51 E3
James St
Bristol,Baptist Mills BS2 .50 A2
Bristol,St Pauls BS5 .143 C4
James St W BA1 .141 B2
Jane St BS5 .64 B7
Jarvis St BS5 .64 B6
Jasmine Cl BS22 .89 A1
Jasmine Ct 9 BS23 .104 E8
Jasmine Gr BS11 .34 C2
Jasmine La BS49 .74 F2
Jasmine Way BS24 .89 A1
Jasper St BS3 .63 B3
Jays The GL12 .16 B6
Jean Rd BS4 .64 E2
Jefferies Hill Bottom BS15 .65 B5
Jeffery Ct BS30 .66 B6
Jeffreys Ct 9 BS16 .50 E3
Jellicoe Ave BS16 .50 E7
Jellicoe Ct BS22 .88 E4
Jena Ct BS31 .82 D3
Jenner Cl BS37 .40 D8
Jersey Ave BS4 .64 F4
Jesmond Rd
Clevedon BS21 .57 C3
Weston-S-M BS22 .89 C4
Jesse Hughes Ct BA1 .85 C2
Jessop Ct BS1 .143 B2
Jessop Underpass BS3 .62 F4
Jews La Bath BA2 .101 C6
Churchill BS25 .108 F4
Jim O'Neil Ho BS11 .47 D7
Jocelin Dr BS22 .88 F4
Jocelyn Rd BS7 .49 F7
Jockey La BS5 .65 A7
John Cabot Ct BS1 .142 A1
John Cabot Cty Tech Coll BS15 .65 C7
John Carr's Terr BS8 .142 B2
John Cozens Ho 6 BS2 .143 C3
John James Ct BS7 .50 B7
John Repton Gdns BS10 .35 B2
John Slessor Ct BA1 .141 B4
John St Bath BA1 .141 B3
Bristol BS1 .143 A3
Bristol,Baptist Mills BS2 .50 A2
Bristol,St George BS15 .65 C8
John Wesley Rd BS5 .65 B6
John Wesleys Chapel BS1 .143 B3
Johnson Dr BS30 .65 F5
Johnson Rd BS16 .52 C5
Johnsons La BS5 .50 D1
Johnsons Rd
1 Bristol,Moorfields BS5 .64 C8
Bristol,Whitehall BS5 .50 C1
Johnstone St BA2 .141 C2
Jones Cl BS49 .74 A1
Jordan Wlk BS32 .36 D8
Jorrocks Ind Est BS37 .39 C4
Joy Hill BS8 .62 F6
Jubilee Cres BS16 .52 A6
Jubilee Dr Failand BS8 .61 B4
Thornbury BS35 .8 D1
Jubilee Gdns BS37 .28 A2
Jubilee Ho BS34 .36 C8
Jubilee La Cromhall GL12 .17 B7
Langford BS40 .109 A6
Jubilee Path BS22 .88 C1
Jubilee Pl Bristol BS1 .143 A1
Bristol,Warmley BS15 .66 A7
Clevedon BS21 .57 D1
Jubilee Rd
Axbridge BS26 .125 C2
Bristol,Baptist Mills BS2 .50 A1
Bristol,Crew's Hole BS5 .64 F7
Bristol,Upper Knowle BS4 .64 C2
Bristol,Upper Soundwell BS15 .51 E3
Radstock BA3 .133 D1
Weston-S-M BS23 .104 E7
Jubilee St BS2 .143 C2
Jubilee Terr BS39 .132 E6
Jubilee Way
Avonmouth BS11 .33 B2
Weston-S-M BS22 .89 C3
Julian Cl BS9 .48 E3
Julian Ct BS9 .48 E3
Julian Rd Bath BA1 .141 B3
Bristol BS9 .48 E3
Julier Ho BA1 .141 C4
Julius Cl BS16 .52 C6
Julius Rd BS7 .49 D3
Junction Ave BA2 .141 A1
Junction Rd Bath BA2 .141 A1
Bristol BS4 .64 C4
Juniper Ct 2 BS5 .50 C2
Juniper Pl BS22 .88 F4
Juniper Way BS32 .37 A7
Jupiter Rd BS34 .35 E7
Justice Ave BS31 .82 E3
Justice Rd BS16 .51 A3
Jutland Rd BS11 .33 B1

K

Karelean Ct BS10 .35 D3
Karen Cl BS48 .76 A4
Karen Dr BS48 .76 A5
Katharine Lady Berkeley's Sch GL12 .11 F6
Kathdene Gdns BS7 .49 F3
Katherine Dr GL12 .11 A5
Kaynton Mead BA1 .101 B7
Keats Ho 4 BS23 .104 F4
Keats Rd BA3 .139 C8
Keble Ave BS13 .78 F5
Keeds La BS41 .61 F1
Keedwell Hill BS41 .61 F1
Keel Cl BS5 .64 F6
Keel's Hill BA2 .134 C8
Keen's Gr BS35 .22 C7
Keene's Way BS21 .57 C2
Keep The Bristol BS30 .66 D5
Weston-S-M BS22 .89 A3
Keg Store The BS1 .143 B2
Keinton Wlk BS10 .35 A2
Kelbra Cres BS36 .38 B6
Kellaway Ave BS7 .49 D5
Kellaway Cres BS9 .49 D6
Kellaway Ct BS6 .49 D5
Kellways BS48 .76 A4
Kelso Pl BA1 .101 D7
Kelston Cl Saltford BS31 .82 D4
Yate BS37 .39 D7
Kelston Gdns Bristol BS10 49 D8
Weston-S-M BS22 .89 B5
Kelston Gr BS15 .65 E6
Kelston Rd Bath BA1 .83 E1
Bristol BS10 .49 D8
Keynsham BS31 .81 D5
Weston-S-M BS22 .89 B5
Kelston View BA2 .101 A5
Kelston Wlk BS16 .51 C4
Kelting Gr BS21 .57 F2
Kemble Cl Bristol BS15 .65 E6
Nailsea BS48 .60 A1
Kemble Gdns BS11 .47 F5
Kemble Ho BS34 .23 F1
Kempe Way BS24 .105 E7
Kempe's Cl BS41 .62 A2
Kemperleye Way BS32 .36 D7
Kempton Cl Bristol BS16 .37 F1
Thornbury BS35 .8 B3
Kencot Wlk BS13 .79 B3
Kendal Rd BS7 .50 A7
Kendall Gdns BS16 .51 D4
Kendall Rd BS16 .51 D4
Kendon Dr BS10 .49 D7
Kendon Way BS10 .49 D8
Kenilworth BS37 .39 F8
Kenilworth Cl BS31 .81 D4
Kenilworth Ct BA1 .102 B8
Kenilworth Dr BS30 .66 B2
Kenilworth Rd BS6 .49 C1
Kenmare Rd BS4 .63 E1
Kenmeade Cl BS25 .125 E8
Kenmore Cres BS7 .35 E1
Kenmore Dr BS7 .35 E1
Kenmore Gr BS7 .35 E1
Kenn Bsns Pk BS21 .73 E7
Kenn Cl BS23 .105 A5
Kenn Ct BS4 .79 E7
Kenn Est BS21 .73 E5
Kenn Moor Dr BS21 .57 E1
Kenn Moor Rd BS49 .74 B1
Kenn Rd Bristol BS5 .65 A7
Clevedon BS21 .73 F6
Kenn St BS21 .73 F7
Kennard Cl BS15 .65 C7
Kennard Rd BS15 .65 C8
Kennard Rise BS15 .65 C8
Kennaway Rd BS21 .57 E2
Kennedy Ho BS37 .27 F1
Kennedy Way BS37 .27 F1
Kennel Dr GL9 .30 E2
Kennel La BS26 .123 E3
Kennel Lodge Rd BS3 .62 E4
Kennet Pk BA2 .85 E1
Kennet Rd BS31 .82 A4
Kennet Way 4 BS35 .15 D8
Kenneth Rd BS4 .64 D2
Kennford 6 BS22 .88 F2
Kennington Ave
Bristol,Ashley Down BS7 .49 F4
4 Bristol,Hopewell Hill BS15 .51 D1
Kennington Rd BA1 .101 B7
Kennion Rd BS5 .65 A7
Kennmoor Cl BS30 .66 A6
Kennmoor Rd BS21 .74 A6
Kensal Ave BS3 .63 E3
Kensal Rd BS3 .63 E3
Kensington Cl BS35 .8 B2
Kensington Ct Bath BA1 .85 B1
Bristol BS8 .142 A3
Kensington Gdns BA1 .85 B1
Kensington Park Rd BS4 64 C2
Kensington Pk 12 BS5 .50 A1
Kensington Pl Bath BA1 .85 B1
Bristol BS8 .142 A3
Kensington Rd
3 Bristol BS5 .65 A8
5 Bristol,Staple Hill BS16 .51 D4
Bristol,Woolcott Park BS6 .49 C1
Weston-S-M BS23 .104 F5
Kent Ave BS37 .27 F3
Kent Cl BS34 .36 D4
Kent Mews BS16 .50 E7
Kent Rd Bristol BS7 .49 E4
Congresbury BS49 .91 D5
Kent St Bristol BS3 .63 C3
Cheddar BS27 .126 B1
Kent Way BS22 .89 B4
Kenton Ho BS34 .23 F1
Kenton Mews BS9 .49 C5
Kents Gn BS15 .51 E2
Kentshare La BS40 .95 B6
Keppel Cl BS31 .82 D2
Kerry Rd BS4 .63 E1
Kersteman Rd BS6 .49 C3
Kestrel Cl Bristol BS34 .35 E8
Chipping Sodbury BS37 .39 F8
Kestrel Cl *continued*
Thornbury BS35 .8 D2
Kestrel Dr
Pucklechurch BS16 .53 C4
Weston-S-M BS22 .88 E1
Kestrel Pl BA3 .139 B8
Keswick Wlk BS10 .35 C2
Ketch Rd BS3 .63 F3
Kew Rd BS23 .87 E1
Kew Wlk BS4 .80 C8
Kewside BS22 .88 B4
Kewstoke Prim Sch BS22 88 B3
Kewstoke Rd Bath BA2 .102 A2
Bristol BS9 .48 E4
Weston-S-M BS22 .88 C3
Keyes Path BS22 .88 F4
Keyhaven Bglws BS22 .88 A4
Keynsham By-Pass BS31 .81 E7
Keynsham Hospl BS31 .81 F4
Keynsham Prim Sch BS31 .81 D5
Keynsham Rd BS30,BS31 .82 A8
Keynsham Sta BS31 .81 E6
Keys Ave BS7 .49 F7
Kidney Hill BS37 .39 A3
Kielder Dr BS22 .88 F3
Kilbirnie Rd BS14 .80 A3
Kilburn Ct 17 BS5 .64 B8
Kilburn St 19 BS5 .64 B8
Kildare BA2 .102 B7
Kildare Rd BS4 .63 D1
Kilkenny La BA2 .118 B8
Kilkenny Pl BS20 .45 C6
Kilkenny St BS2 .143 C2
Killcott Rd GL12 .19 E8
Kilmersdon CE Prim Sch BA3 .140 A6
Kilmersdon Hill BA3 .140 A5
Kilmersdon Rd
Bristol BS13 .79 B4
Radstock BA3 .139 E8
Kilminster Cl BS34 .36 D6
Kilminster Rd BS11 .47 D7
Kiln Cl BS15 .51 B2
Kiln Ct BS5 .64 B8
Kiln Pk BS23 .105 A6
Kilnhurst Cl BS30 .65 F2
Kilve BS24 .105 A2
Kilvert Cl BS4 .64 D5
Kimberley Ave BS16 .51 C5
Kimberley Cl BS16 .51 F7
Kimberley Cres BS16 .51 C5
Kimberley Rd
Bristol,Hopewell Hill BS15 .51 D1
Bristol,Staple Hill BS16 .51 C5
Clevedon BS21 .57 C2
Kinber Cl BA1 .84 A3
Kinema Ho BS4 .64 C4
King Alfred Way BA15 .120 D7
King Dick's La 7 BS5 .64 F8
King Edmund Com Sch BS37 .27 E1
King Edward Cl BS14 .80 A6
King Edward Rd BA2 .101 D5
King Edward's Pre-Prep Sch BA1 .101 C8
King Edward's Sch BA2 102 C7
King George V Pl 6 BS1 .143 A2
King George's Rd
Bath BA2 .101 C6
Bristol BS13 .78 F5
King John's Rd BS15 .51 B2
King La Clutton BS39 .114 F4
Horton BS37 .29 A7
King Rd Bristol BS4 .64 C1
Churchill Green BS49 .108 E6
King Road Ave BS11 .33 B2
King Sq BS2 .143 A4
King Square Ave BS2 .143 A4
King St Avonmouth BS11 .33 A1
Bristol BS1 .143 A2
Bristol,Burchells Green BS15 .65 B8
Bristol,Whitehall BS5 .50 C1
King William Ave BS1 .143 A2
King William St BS3 .63 B4
King's Ave BS6,BS7 .49 C4
King's Dr BS7 .49 C4
King's Head La BS13 .78 F7
King's La Clevedon BS21 .57 D5
7 Weston-S-M BS23 .104 E8
King's Parade Ave 1 BS8 .49 B1
King's Parade Mews BS8 49 A1
King's Rd
Bristol,Kensington Park BS4 64 C3
Bristol,Victoria Park BS8 .142 A3
Clevedon BS21 .57 D5
Portishead BS20 .44 F4
Kingcott Mill Farm Cvns BS48 .77 B8
Kingdown Rd BS40 .94 C5
Kingfisher Cl Bristol BS32 .24 E2
Thornbury BS35 .8 D2
Kingfisher Ct BA2 .120 C6
Kingfisher Dr Bristol BS16 50 E6
Midsomer Norton BA3 .139 B8
Kingfisher Rd
Chipping Sodbury BS37 .40 A8
Weston-S-M BS22 .105 F8
Kingrove Cres BS37 .40 C8
Kingrove La BS37 .40 C7
Kings Ave BS15 .65 B4
Kings Chase Sh Ctr BS15 65 D8
Kings Court Prim Sch BS37 .39 E8
Kings Ct Bath BA1 .141 B2
Kings Ct *continued*
Bristol,Canon's Marsh BS1 .143 A2
Bristol,Kingsdown BS1 .143 B4
Bristol,Little Stoke BS34 .36 C6
Kings Dr
Bristol,Hanham BS15 .65 B4
Bristol,Stoke Gifford BS34 .37 A4
Kings Oak Mdw BS39 .114 E2
Kings Park Ave BS2 .64 C6
Kings Rd BS40 .92 D1
Kings Sq BS30 .82 D8
Kings Weston Ave BS11 .47 E8
Kings Weston La
Avonmouth BS11 .33 E3
Bristol BS11 .48 A8
Kings Weston Rd BS11, BS10 .34 C1
Kings Wlk BS13 .78 E7
Kingscote BS37 .39 D6
Kingscote Pk BS5 .65 B6
Kingscourt Cl BS14 .80 A4
Kingsdown Gr SN13 .86 F3
Kingsdown Par BS6 .143 A4
Kingsdown View 17 BA1 .85 A1
Kingsfield BA2 .101 C3
Kingsfield La
Bristol,Mount Hill BS15 .65 E5
Bristol,Stone Hill BS30 .65 E4
Kingsfield Sch BS15 .66 A8
Kingsgate Ct BS37 .39 E8
Kingshill BS48 .59 C2
Kingshill Gdns BS48 .59 C1
Kingshill Ho BS4 .64 B1
Kingshill La BS40 .112 C4
Kingshill Rd BS4 .64 B1
Kingsholm Rd BS10 .49 D8
Kingsholme Ct BS23 .87 E1
Kingsholme Rd BS15 .51 D1
Kingsland Cl 1 BS2 .64 A6
Kingsland Rd BS2 .64 A6
Kingsland Road Bridge 3 BS2 .64 A6
Kingsland Trad Est BS2 .64 A7
Kingsleigh Ct BS15 .65 F7
Kingsleigh Gdns BS15 .65 F7
Kingsleigh Pk BS15 .65 F7
Kingsley Ho Bristol BS2 .143 C2
Bristol,Westbury on Trym BS9 .49 A8
Kingsley Pl 1 BS3 .63 C4
Kingsley Rd
Bristol,Lower Easton BS5 .50 C1
Bristol,Montpelier BS6 .49 D2
Clevedon BS21 .57 D2
Radstock BA3 .133 C1
Weston-S-M BS23 .104 F3
Kingsmarsh Ho 3 BS5 .64 B7
Kingsmead BS48 .59 C2
Kingsmead Ct 8 BA1 .141 B2
Kingsmead N BA1 .141 B2
Kingsmead Rd BS5 .51 A1
Kingsmead Sq BA1 .141 B2
Kingsmead St BA1 .141 B2
Kingsmead W BA1 .141 B2
Kingsmead Wlk BS5 .51 A1
Kingsmill BS9 .48 D5
Kingston Ave
Clevedon BS21 .57 E3
Saltford BS31 .82 C3
Kingston Cl BS16 .52 A7
Kingston Dr Bristol BS16 .52 A7
Nailsea BS48 .75 C8
Kingston La BS40 .94 F8
Kingston Mead BS40 .94 F7
Kingston Rd Bath BA1 .141 C2
Bristol BS3 .63 C4
Nailsea BS48 .75 C8
Kingston Way BS48 .75 C8
Kingstree St BS4 .64 A4
Kingsway Bath BA2 .101 C3
Bristol,Little Stoke BS34 .36 C6
Bristol,St George BS5 .65 B7
Portishead BS20 .44 F4
Kingsway Ave BS15 .65 B8
Kingsway Cres BS15 .65 C8
Kingsway Sh Prec BS5 .65 B7
Kingswear 3 BS22 .89 A2
Kingswear Rd BS3 .63 D2
Kingsweston Down Nature Res★ BS9,BS11 .34 C1
Kingsweston Sch BS11 .48 A8
Kingswood Abbey Gatehouse★ GL12 .11 F5
Kingswood Day Prep Sch BA1 .84 E1
Kingswood Heritage Mus★ BS30 .66 B6
Kingswood Prim Sch GL12 .11 F5
Kingswood Rd GL12 .19 D8
Kingswood Sch BA1 .84 E2
Kingswood Trad Est 7 BS15 .51 D1
Kington La BS35 .7 E1
Kington Rd BS35 .7 E3
Kingwell View BS39 .115 D2
Kinsale Rd BS14 .80 C7
Kinsale Wlk BS4 .63 E1
Kinvara Rd BS4 .79 E8
Kipling Ave BA2 .101 F4
Kipling Rd Bristol BS7 .36 B1
Radstock BA3 .133 C1
Weston-S-M BS23 .105 A3
Kirkby Rd BS11 .34 A1

Kirkstone Gdns BS10 ....35 C2
Kirkstone Ho BS34 ....36 A8
Kirtlington Rd BS5 ....50 B3
Kite Hay Cl BS16 ....50 E5
Kite Wlk BS22 ....105 E8
Kites Cl BS34 ....24 C2
Kitland La BS40 ....109 B8
Kitley Hill BA3 ....133 C4
Knapp La GL12 ....10 B3
Knapp Rd BS35 ....8 D1
Knapp Rd E BS35 ....8 E2
Knapp The BS37 ....27 F5
Knapps Cl BS25 ....124 F8
Knapps Dr BS25 ....124 F8
Knapps La BS5 ....50 E2
Kneller Cl BS11 ....48 A8
Knight Cl BS22 ....89 A5
Knightcott BS29 ....106 F3
Knightcott Gdns BS29 ....106 F3
Knightcott Ind Est BS29 106 F3
Knightcott Pk BS29 ....107 A3
Knightcott Rd
  Abbots Leigh BS8 ....61 F8
  Banwell BS29 ....106 C3
Knighton Rd BS10 ....35 E1
Knights Cl BS9 ....49 B6
Knightsbridge Pk BS13 ..79 E4
Knightstone Cl
  Axbridge BS26 ....125 C1
  Peasedown St John BA2 ..134 B8
Knightstone Cswy BS23 104 C8
Knightstone Ct
  Bristol BS5 ....50 D2
  Clevedon BS21 ....57 D1
  Weston-S-M BS23 ....87 D1
Knightstone Gdns BS4 ..64 B2
Knightstone Ho
  1 Bristol BS2 ....143 A4
  Weston-S-M BS23 ....104 D8
Knightstone Mount BS5 ..65 A6
Knightstone Pk **4** BS13 .64 B2
  Bristol BS15 ....65 B2
  7 Weston-S-M BS22 ....88 F2
Knightstone Rd BS23 ....104 C8
Knightstone Rise **5** BS5 .64 F8
Knightstone Sq BS14 ....80 C5
Knightstone Wlk BS5 ..142 C4
Knightwood Rd BS34 ....36 F5
Knobsbury Hill BA3 ....140 D6
Knobsbury La BA3 ....140 C7
Knole Cl BS32 ....23 F4
Knole La BS10 ....35 B3
Knole Pk BS32 ....23 F3
Knoll Cl BS9 ....48 D3
Knoll Hill BS9 ....48 D3
Knoll The BS20 ....45 D7
Knovill Cl BS11 ....34 B2
Knowle Park Jun & Inf Schs
  BS4 ....64 A1
Knowle Rd BS2 ....63 F3
Knowles Rd BS21 ....57 C2
Knowles Rd Est **1** BS21 .57 C2
Knowsley Rd BS16 ....50 E3
Kyght Cl BS15 ....66 A8
Kylross Ave BS14 ....80 B5
Kynges Mill Cl BS16 ....51 A7
Kyngstone Ct **10** BS16 ....50 E3
Kyrle Gdns BA1 ....85 F3

L

La Maison BS5 ....51 A2
Labbott The BS31 ....81 E5
Laburnum Cl BA3 ....138 E8
Laburnum Ct BS23 ....105 B7
Laburnum Gr Bristol BS16 51 B4
  Midsomer Norton BA3 ....138 F8
Laburnum Rd Bristol BS15 65 C5
  Weston-S-M BS23 ....105 B7
Laburnum Wlk BS31 ....81 C3
Lacey Rd BS14 ....80 F6
Lacock Dr BS30 ....65 F5
Ladd Cl BS15 ....65 F7
Ladden Ct BS35 ....15 C8
Ladies Mile BS8 ....48 F1
Ladman Gr BS14 ....80 E6
Ladman Rd BS14 ....80 E5
Ladycroft **4** BS21 ....57 B1
Ladye Bay BS21 ....57 D7
Ladye Wake BS22 ....88 F4
Ladymead La BS40 ....108 F5
Ladymeade BS48 ....76 A7
Ladysmith Rd BS6 ....49 B4
Ladywell BS40 ....92 D2
Laggan Gdns BA1 ....84 E1
Lake Rd Bristol BS10 ....49 C8
  Portishead BS20 ....45 D7
Lake View Rd BS5 ....64 D8
Lakemead Gdns BS13 ..78 F4
Lakemead Gr BS13 ....78 F6
Lakeside BS16 ....50 E3
Lakeside Cl BS40 ....111 D5
Lakewood Cres BS10 ....49 B8
Lakewood Rd BS10 ....49 B8
Lamb Hill BS5 ....64 F7
Lamb Ho BS34 ....36 A8
Lamb St BS2 ....143 C3
Lambert Pl BS4 ....79 D6
Lambley Rd BS5 ....64 E8
Lambourn Cl BS3 ....63 D3
Lambourn Rd BS31 ....82 A4
Lambourne Way BS20 ..45 F5

Lambridge **6** BA2 ....85 C1
Lambridge Bldgs **1** BA1 .85 C1
Lambridge Mews **5** BA1 85 C1
Lambridge Pl BA1 ....85 C1
Lambridge St BA1 ....85 C1
Lambrook Rd BS16 ....51 A4
Lamington Cl BS13 ....78 F6
Lamont Ho **7** BA1 ....85 C1
Lamord Gate BS34 ....36 E5
Lampard's Bldgs BA1 ..141 B4
Lampeter Rd BS9 ....49 A7
Lampley Rd BS21 ....73 D2
Lampton Ave BS13 ....79 E3
Lampton Gr BS13 ....79 E3
Lampton Rd BS41 ....61 F1
Lanaway Rd BS16 ....51 B6
Lancashire Rd BS7 ....49 E3
Lancaster Cl BS34 ....36 D4
Lancaster House Sch
  BS23 ....104 F8
Lancaster Rd Bristol BS2 .50 A2
  Yate BS37 ....27 E3
Lancaster St **10** BS5 ....64 C7
Lancelot Rd BS16 ....50 E8
Land The BS36 ....38 C7
Landemann Cir BS23 ....87 E1
Landemann Circ BS23 ..104 E8
Landemann Path **3**
  BS23 ....104 E8
Landmark Ct BA1 ....142 C1
Landsdown View BA3 ..135 D3
Landseer Ave BS7 ....50 B7
Landseer Cl BS22 ....88 F3
Landseer Rd BA2 ....101 B6
Lane The BS35 ....22 F2
Lanercost Rd BS10 ....35 C2
Lanes End BS4 ....64 C1
Lanesborough Rise BS14 80 D7
Laneys Dro BS24 ....105 E5
Langdale Ct BS34 ....36 A8
Langdale Rd BS16 ....50 F4
Langdon Rd BA2 ....101 B4
Langdon Ct BS14 ....80 E5
Langfield Cl BS10 ....34 E3
Langford La BS40 ....109 E5
Langford Rd Bristol BS13 .78 F8
  Langford BS40 ....109 C6
  Weston-S-M BS23 ....105 A6
Langford Way BS15 ....65 E2
Langford's La BS39 ....115 D1
Langfords La BS39 ....132 C8
Langham Pl BA3 ....137 F1
Langham Rd BS4 ....64 B2
Langhill Ave BS4 ....79 D7
Langley Cres BS3 ....62 E1
Langley Mow BS16 ....52 B7
Langley's La BA3,BS39 ..132 C1
Langleys Cotts BA3 ....138 B8
Langport Gdns BS48 ....75 C8
Langport Rd BS23 ....104 E5
Langridge La BA1 ....84 D8
Langsdown Ho **6** BS2 ..49 F1
Langthorn Cl BS36 ....38 C7
Langton Court Rd BS4 ..64 D5
Langton Ct **1** BS16 ....50 E3
Langton Ho **9** BS2 ....143 C3
Langton Pk BS3 ....63 C4
Langton Rd BS4 ....64 D5
Langton Way BS4 ....64 F6
Lansdown BS37 ....39 E8
Lansdown Cl BS15 ....51 D2
Lansdown Cres Bath BA1 84 F1
  Timsbury BA2 ....116 C2
Lansdown Ct BS23 ....104 F8
Lansdown Gdns BS22 ....89 B5
Lansdown Gr BA1 ....141 B4
Lansdown Grove Ct
  BA1 ....141 B4
Lansdown Ho BS15 ....51 D2
Lansdown Hts BA1 ....84 F1
Lansdown La BA1 ....84 B4
  Upton Cheyney BS30 ....67 C1
Lansdown Mans BA1 ..141 B4
Lansdown Mews BA1 ..141 B3
Lansdown Pk BA1 ....84 E3
Lansdown Pl Bristol BS8 142 A3
  High Littleton BS39 ....115 D1
Lansdown Pl E BA1 ....141 B4
Lansdown Pl W BA1 ....84 F1
Lansdown Rd Bath BA1 ..84 E2
  Bristol,Hopewell Hill BS15 .51 D2
  6 Bristol,Upper Easton
  BS5 ....64 B8
  Bristol,Victoria Park BS8 .142 A3
  Bristol,Woolcott Park BS6 .49 C1
  Pucklechurch BS16 ....53 C6
  Saltford BS31 ....82 E3
Lansdown Terr Bath BA1 .84 C1
  Bristol BS6 ....49 D5
Lansdown View
  Bath BA2 ....101 C5
  Bristol BS15 ....65 F8
  Timsbury BA2 ....116 C2
Lansdowne BS16 ....37 C1
Lansdowne Ct **2** BS5 ..64 B8
Lanthony Cl **1** BS24 ..106 A8
Lapdown La GL9 ....41 D1
Laphams Ct **11** BS30 ..65 F4
Lapwing Cl BS32 ....24 D2
Lapwing Gdns
  Bristol BS16 ....50 F6
  Weston-S-M BS22 ....88 F1
Larch Cl Langford BS40 ..109 A5
  Nailsea BS48 ....60 A2
Larch Ct BA3 ....139 D8
Larch Dr Bristol BS15 ....51 E3
  Colerne SN14 ....70 F6
Larch Way BS34 ....35 E7

Larches The BS22 ....89 A3
Larchgrove Cres BS22 ..88 F1
Larchgrove Wlk BS22 ..88 F1
Larchwood Ct BA3 ....134 A3
Lark Cl BA3 ....139 B8
Lark Pl BA1 ....101 D7
Lark Rd BS22 ....88 F1
Lark's Field BS16 ....50 E5
Lark's La BS37 ....26 B7
Larkfield BS36 ....38 D7
Larkhall Pl BA1 ....85 C2
Larkhall Terr BA1 ....85 C2
Larkhill Rd BS24 ....106 B6
Larksleaze Rd BS30 ....65 F2
Larkspur Cl BS35 ....8 D1
Lasbury Gr BS13 ....79 C5
Latchmoor Ho BS13 ....79 A8
Late Broads BS20 ....45 B4
Latimer Cl BS4 ....64 E4
Latteridge La
  Iron Acton BS35,BS37 ....26 A7
  Tytherington BS35 ....15 F1
Latteridge Rd BS37 ....26 D4
Latton Rd BS7 ....49 F8
Launceston Ave BS15 ....65 B5
Launceston Rd BS15 ....51 B1
Laura Pl BA2 ....141 C3
Laurel Dr Colerne SN14 ..70 F6
  Nailsea BS48 ....59 F2
  Paulton BS39 ....132 E5
  Weston-S-M BS23 ....104 E2
Laurel Gdns
  Timsbury BA2 ....116 B1
  Yatton BS49 ....74 B1
Laurel St BS15 ....65 D8
Laurel Terr BS49 ....74 B1
Laurels The
  Bristol,Catbrain BS10 ....35 A6
  Bristol,Mangotsfield BS16 ..52 A6
  Churchill BS25 ....108 F4
  Weston-S-M BS23 ....104 E2
  Westwood BA15 ....120 F3
Laurie Cres BS9 ....49 D6
Laurie Lee Ct **3** BS30 ..66 A5
Lavender Cl
  Thornbury BS35 ....8 D1
  Weston-S-M BS22 ....89 A5
Lavender Ct BS5 ....50 F1
Lavender Way BS32 ....36 F7
Lavenham Rd BS37 ....27 B2
Lavers Cl BS15 ....65 E6
Lavington Cl BS21 ....57 B1
Lavington Rd BS5 ....65 B6
Lawford Ave BS34 ....36 C6
Lawford St BS2 ....143 C3
Lawfords Gate BS2 ....143 C3
Lawfords Gate Ho **17**
  BS2 ....143 C3
Lawn Ave BS16 ....51 B5
Lawn Rd BS16 ....51 B5
Lawns Rd BS37 ....27 F2
Lawns The Bristol BS11 ..47 E7
  Weston-S-M BS22 ....89 B3
  Yatton BS49 ....74 A1
Lawnside BS48 ....76 B5
Lawnwood Ind Units **14**
  BS5 ....64 B8
Lawnwood Rd **15** BS5 ..64 B8
Lawrence Ave BS5 ....50 B1
Lawrence Cl BS15 ....52 A2
Lawrence Dr BS37 ....27 B2
Lawrence Gr BS9 ....49 B5
Lawrence Hill BS5 ....64 B7
Lawrence Hill Ind Pk
  BS5 ....64 B8
Lawrence Hill Rdbt BS5 ..64 A7
Lawrence Hill Sta BS5 ..64 B7
Lawrence Mews BS22 ..88 E2
Lawrence Rd
  Weston-S-M BS22 ....88 E2
  Wrington BS40 ....92 E2
Lawrence Weston Rd
  Avonmouth BS11 ....33 F4
  Bristol,Lawrence Weston
  BS11 ....34 A3
  Bristol,Lawrence Weston
  BS11 ....34 B1
Lawson Cl BS31 ....82 C2
Laxey Rd BS7 ....49 F7
Laxton Cl BS35 ....14 A3
Laxton Dr GL12 ....11 F4
Laxton Way BA2 ....134 D7
Lays Dr BS31 ....81 C5
Lays Farm Bsns Ctr BS31 81 C4
Lays Farm Trad Est BS31 .81 C4
Lays La BS40 ....110 D4
Lea Croft BS13 ....79 A4
Lea Grove Rd BS21 ....57 C4
Leach Cl BS21 ....57 D1
Leading Edge The BS8 ..142 B2
Leafy Way BS24 ....106 B4
Leaholme Gdns BS14 ....80 A3
Leaman Cl BS37 ....28 B1
Leap Vale BS16 ....52 A8
Leap Valley Cres BS16 ..52 A8
Lear Cl BS30 ....66 B5
Leawood Ct BS23 ....87 C1
Leaze La BS40 ....110 A3
Leaze The Radstock BA3 .139 D8
  Yate BS37 ....27 D2
Leda Ave BS14 ....80 A7
Ledbury Rd BS16 ....51 C4
Lee Cl BS34 ....35 F8
Leechpool Way BS37 ....27 E5
Leedham Rd BS24 ....106 C5
Leeming Way BS11 ....47 C8
Lees Ct BS15 ....51 E1

Lees Hill BS15 ....51 E2
Lees La BS30 ....66 D5
Leeside BS20 ....45 C5
Leewood Rd BS23 ....87 C1
Leg La BS40 ....110 B3
Leicester Sq BS16 ....51 D3
Leicester St **6** BS3 ....63 D4
Leicester Wlk BS4 ....64 F5
Leigh Cl BA1 ....85 A2
Leigh Court Bsns Ctr
  BS8 ....48 A2
Leigh La Cold Ashton BA1 ..69 B3
  Westerleigh BS37 ....39 B1
Leigh Rd BS8 ....142 B4
Leigh St BS3 ....63 A4
Leigh View Rd BS20 ....45 E7
Leigh Woods Forest Walks★
  BS8 ....48 C1
Leighton Cres BS24 ....122 A8
Leighton Rd Bath BA1 ....84 A3
  Bristol,Southville BS3 ....63 B4
  Bristol,Upper Knowle BS4 ..64 B2
Leighwood Dr BS48 ....59 B1
Leighwoods Ho BS8 ....62 D6
Leinster Ave BS4 ....79 D8
Leisure Rd BS5 ....65 E5
Lemon La BS2 ....143 C4
Lena Ave **3** BS5 ....50 C1
Lena St BS5 ....50 C1
Lennox Way BS11 ....33 B1
Lenover Gdns **3** BS13 ..79 B4
Leonard La BS1 ....143 A3
Leonard Rd BS5 ....64 D7
Leonards Ave BS5 ....50 C1
Leopold Bldgs BA1 ....141 C4
Leopold Rd BS6 ....49 E2
Lescren Way BS11 ....33 C1
Leslie Rise BA15 ....120 F3
Lester Dr BS22 ....89 A3
Lewin St **9** BS5 ....64 D7
Lewington Rd BS16 ....51 C4
Lewins Mead BS1 ....143 A3
Lewis Cl
  Bristol,Mangotsfield BS16 ..52 B5
  Bristol,North Common BS30 66 D5
Lewis Rd BS13 ....79 A8
Lewis St BS2 ....64 C5
Lewisham Gr BS23 ....105 A8
Lewton La BS36 ....37 E7
Ley La BS35 ....13 D3
Leyland Wlk BS13 ....78 F4
Leys The BS21 ....57 B1
Leyton Villas BS6 ....49 B2
Liberty Gdns BS1 ....142 C1
Liberty La BS40 ....110 E2
Lichfield Rd BS4 ....64 E6
Lilac Cl BS10 ....35 C1
Lilac Ct BS31 ....81 C4
Lilac Terr BA3 ....133 C2
Lilac Way BS22 ....89 A5
Lilian Terr BS39 ....132 E5
Lillian St **5** BS5 ....64 C8
Lillington Cl BA3 ....134 B2
Lillington Rd BA3 ....134 B2
Lilliput Ave BS37 ....40 A8
Lilliput Ct BS37 ....40 B8
Lillypool Farm (Cheese &
  Cider)★ BS25 ....125 F6
Lilstock Ave BS7 ....49 F4
Lilton Wlk BS13 ....63 A1
Lilymead Ave BS4 ....64 A3
Lime Ave GL9 ....42 B8
Lime Cl
  Bristol,Brentry BS10 ....35 B3
  Locking BS24 ....106 A6
  Weston-S-M BS22 ....89 A1
Lime Croft BS37 ....27 F4
Lime Ct BS31 ....81 C4
Lime Gr Alveston BS35 ....14 F4
  Bath BA2 ....102 B6
Lime Grove Gdns BA2 ..102 B6
Lime Grove Specl Sch
  BA2 ....102 B6
Lime Kiln Cl BS34 ....36 D3
Lime Kiln Gdns BS32 ....24 D2
Lime Kiln La BS21 ....57 D3
Lime Kiln Rd BS1 ....142 B2
Lime Rd
  Bristol,Conham BS15 ....65 A5
  Bristol,Southville BS3 ....63 B4
Lime Terr BA3 ....133 D1
Lime Tree Gr BS20 ....47 D3
Lime Trees Rd BS9 ....49 D6
Limebreach Wood BS48 ..59 D3
Limeburn Hill BS40 ....95 E5
Limekiln La BA2 ....102 F4
Limekiln Rd BS37,GL12 ..17 C2
Limekilns Cl BS31 ....81 F5
Limerick Rd BS6 ....49 C2
Limes The Badminton GL9 30 C2
  Bristol BS16 ....37 B1
Limpley Stoke Rd BA15 .120 D6
Lincoln Cl BS31 ....81 C4
Lincoln Cl BS16 ....50 D6
Lincoln St BS5 ....64 B7
Lincombe Ave BS16 ....51 D6
Lincombe Rd Bristol BS16 51 C6
  Radstock BA3 ....139 D8
Lincott View BA2 ....134 C4
Linden Ave BS23 ....105 B8
Linden Cl
  Bristol,Mayfield Park BS16 .51 A2
  Bristol,Stockwood BS14 ....80 E6
  Colerne SN14 ....70 F6
  Radstock BA3 ....139 D8
  Winterbourne BS36 ....37 E6
Linden Ct BS21 ....57 D4

Linden Dr BS32 ....36 E8
Linden Gdns BA1 ....101 D8
Linden Ho BS16 ....50 C5
Linden Rd Bristol BS6 ....49 B4
  Clevedon BS21 ....57 D4
Lindens The BS22 ....88 E4
Lindisfarne Cl BA15 ....120 E6
Lindon Ho BS4 ....64 E3
Lindrea St **3** BS3 ....63 B3
Lindsay Rd BS7 ....50 A4
Lindsey Cl BS20 ....44 F4
Linemere Cl BS48 ....76 D6
Lines Way BS14 ....80 C3
Lingfield Pk BS16 ....37 F2
Link La Burrington BS40 ..109 F3
  Monkton Farleigh BA15 ....103 F8
Link Rd Bristol BS34 ....35 F3
  Nailsea BS48 ....59 F2
  Portishead BS20 ....45 C5
  Yate BS37 ....27 F1
Linkmead BA3 ....138 F2
Links Cl BS23 ....104 D4
Links Rd BS23 ....104 C5
Linkside BS21 ....57 E6
Linley Cl BA2 ....101 A5
Linleys The BA1 ....101 C7
Linne Ho BA2 ....101 A5
Linnell Cl BS7 ....50 B6
Linnet Cl Bristol BS34 ....35 E8
  Weston-S-M BS22 ....88 E1
Linnet Way BS4 ....139 B8
Lintern Cres BS30 ....66 B6
Lintham Dr BS15 ....65 F6
Lion Cl BS48 ....59 D2
Lipgate Pl BS20 ....45 D3
Lippiat Hill BA3 ....135 C3
Lippiatt La Shipham BS25 125 E8
  Timsbury BA2 ....116 B3
Lisburn Rd BS4 ....63 E1
Lisle Rd BS22 ....89 B4
Lister Gr BA15 ....120 F3
Litfield Pl BS8 ....62 F7
Litfield Rd BS8 ....62 F8
Litt Hill BA3 ....130 F2
Little Ann St BS2,BS5 ..143 C4
Little Birch Croft BS14 ..80 A3
Little Bishop St BS2 ....143 B4
Little Bristol Cl GL12 ....11 B4
Little Bristol La GL12 ....11 B4
Little Caroline Pl **4** BS8 .62 F5
Little Dowles BS30 ....66 A4
Little George St
  Bristol BS2 ....143 C4
  Weston-S-M BS23 ....104 E7
Little Green La BS35 ....22 A7
Little Halt BS20 ....44 E4
Little Ham BS21 ....73 C8
Little Hayes BS16 ....51 B6
Little Headley Cl BS13 ..79 B7
Little King St BS1 ....143 A2
Little La BA2 ....116 A6
Little Mdw BS32 ....37 A6
Little Mead BS11 ....34 B1
Little Mead Cl BS24 ....105 E3
Little Meadow End BS48 .75 E8
Little Orch BS23 ....104 D1
Little Paradise BS3 ....63 D4
Little Parr Cl BS16 ....50 C5
Little Paul St BS2 ....142 C4
Little Stanhope St BA1 ..141 A2
Little Stoke La BS34 ....36 D6
Little Stoke Prim Sch
  BS34 ....36 D6
Little Stoke Rd BS9 ....48 E4
Little Withey Mead BS9 ..48 F5
Littlebrook BS39 ....132 E6
Littlecross Ho BS3 ....63 B4
Littledean BS37 ....39 E7
Littlefields Ave BS29 ....107 B3
Littlefields Rd BS29 ....107 B3
Littlefields Rise BS29 ....107 B3
Littleton Ct BS34 ....23 F1
Littleton Drew La GL9 ....43 A6
Littleton La Wellow BA2 ..135 C7
  Winford,Littleton BS40 ....95 B5
  Winford,Upper Littleton
  BS40,BS41 ....95 B5
Littleton Rd BS3 ....63 D2
Littleton St **4** BS5 ....50 C1
Littlewood La BS49 ....75 C2
Litton BS24 ....105 A2
Livingstone Mews BS3 ..63 C3
Livingstone Rd BA2 ....101 D5
Livingstone Terr **3** BA2 141 A1
Llanarth Villas **3** BS6 ..49 D1
Llewellyn Ct BS9 ....49 A8
Llewellyn Way BS22 ....89 B3
Lock Gdns BS13 ....78 E2
Lock's Acre BS35 ....15 B6
Lock's La BS37 ....25 C4
Lockemor Rd BS13 ....79 F4
Locking Farm Ind Est
  BS24 ....106 A5
Locking Head Dro BS24 106 A6
Locking Moor Rd
  Locking BS24 ....106 A6
  Weston-S-M BS22 ....105 D8
Locking Prim Sch BS24 106 B4
Locking Rd BS22,BS23 ..105 D7
Lockingwell Rd BS31 ....81 D5
Lockleaze Rd BS7 ....50 A6
Lockleaze Sch BS7 ....50 C7
Locksbrook Ct BA1 ....101 B6
Locksbrook Rd Bath BA1 101 C6
  Weston-S-M BS22 ....89 B5
Locksbrook Trad Est
  BA1 ....101 B6

Lodge Causeway Trad Ctr
BS16 . . . . .50 F3
Lodge Cl BS49 . . . . .91 B8
Lodge Cswy BS16 . . . . . .51 A3
Lodge Crt BS9 . . . . .48 E4
Lodge Dr Bristol BS30 . . .66 C2
  Long Ashton BS41 . . . . . .62 B2
  Weston-S-M BS23 . . . . . .88 A1
Lodge Gdns BA2 . . . . . .101 D1
Lodge Hill BS15 . . . . . . .51 C2
Lodge La BS48 . . . . .60 B2
Lodge Pl BS1 . . . . .142 C3
Lodge Rd Bristol BS15 . . .51 C1
  Wick BS30 . . . . .53 B1
  Yate,Engine Common BS37 .27 A3
  Yate,Nibley BS37 . . . . . . .27 A3
Lodge St BS1 . . . . .142 C3
Lodge Wlk BS16 . . . . . . .51 D6
Lodgeside Ave BS15 . . . .51 C1
Lodgeside Gdns BS15 . . .51 C1
Lodore Rd BS16 . . . . . . .50 F3
Lodway BS20 . . . . .47 C4
Lodway Cl BS20 . . . . . . .47 C5
Lodway Gdns BS20 . . . . .47 C4
Lodway Rd BS4 . . . . . . .64 C2
Logan Rd BS7 . . . . .49 D3
Logus Ct 14 BS30 . . . . . .65 F4
Lombard St BS3 . . . . . . .63 D4
Lombardy Cl BS22 . . . . .105 E8
Lomond Rd BS7 . . . . . . .35 F1
London Rd Bath BA1 . . .141 C4
  Bristol,Bridge Yate BS30 . .66 D7
  Bristol,St Pauls BS2 . . . . .49 F1
  Wick BS30 . . . . .67 E6
London Rd E BA1 . . . . . .86 A3
London Rd W BA1 . . . . . .85 E2
London St Bath BA1 . . . .141 C4
  Bristol BS15 . . . . .65 D8
Long Acre Ho BA1 . . . . .141 C4
Long Acre Rd BS14 . . . . .80 A3
Long Acres Cl BS9 . . . . .48 D7
Long Ashton Rd BS41 . . .62 B2
Long Ave BS21 . . . . .57 B2
Long Barnaby BA3 . . . . .133 A2
Long Beach Rd BS30 . . . .66 B3
Long Cl
  Bristol,Frenchay BS16 . . . .51 C6
  Bristol,Little Stoke BS32 . . .36 E6
Long Croft BS37 . . . . . . .27 D4
Long Cross Bristol BS11 . .34 D7
  Felton BS40 . . . . .94 D7
Long Eaton Dr BS14 . . . .80 B7
Long Fox Manor BS4 . . . .65 A1
Long Handstones BS30 . . .66 A4
Long Hay Cl BA2 . . . . . .101 B5
Long La Backwell BS48 . . .76 C2
  Felton BS40 . . . . .94 B5
  Wrington BS40 . . . . .93 B2
Long Mdw BS16 . . . . . . .50 D6
Long Mead BS37 . . . . . . .27 E5
Long Rd BS16 . . . . .52 A5
Long Row BS1 . . . . .143 B2
Long Thorn La BS40 . . . .111 E7
Long Valley Rd BA2 . . . .100 F5
Long-Thorn BS48 . . . . . .75 F6
Longacre BS21 . . . . .73 B8
Longbottom BS25 . . . . .126 A6
Longbrook Trad Est BS3 .62 E3
Longcross GL12 . . . . . . .10 B1
Longden Rd BS16 . . . . . .51 F6
Longdown Dr BS22 . . . . .89 B4
Longfellow Ave BA2 . . . .101 F4
Longfellow Rd BA3 . . . .139 C8
Longfield Rd BS7 . . . . . .49 E3
Longford BS37 . . . . .39 C8
Longford Ave BS10 . . . . .49 D8
Longlands Ho 13 BS5 . . .64 C7
Longleat Cl BS9 . . . . . . .49 C5
Longleaze Gdns BS24 . .105 F3
Longmead Ave BS7 . . . . .49 D5
Longmead Cl BA2 . . . . .136 F4
Longmead Croft BS13 . . .78 F4
Longmead Rd BS16 . . . . .38 B1
Longmeadow Rd BS31 . . .81 C4
Longmoor Ct BS3 . . . . . .63 A2
Longmoor Rd BS3 . . . . . .63 A2
Longney Pl BS34 . . . . . . .23 F1
Longreach Gr BS14 . . . . .80 D6
Longridge Way
  Weston-S-M BS24 . . . . .105 E7
  Weston-S-M BS24 . . . . .106 A8
Longs Dr BS37 . . . . .27 C2
Longs View BS37 . . . . . .11 A5
Longton Grove Rd 4
  BS23 . . . . .104 E8
Longton Ind Est BS23 . .104 F6
Longvernal BA3 . . . . . . .132 F1
Longvernal Prim Sch
  BA3 . . . . .132 F1
Longway Ave BS13, BS14 .79 F4
Longwell Green Prim Sch
  BS30 . . . . .65 F3
Longwell Ho BS30 . . . . . .65 F3
Longwood BS4 . . . . .65 A2
Longwood Ho BS8 . . . . . .61 D4
Longwood La BS41 . . . . .61 F4
Lons Ct BS30 . . . . .66 C1
Lonsdale Ave BS23 . . . .104 F4
Lonsdale Bsns Ctr 4
  BS15 . . . . .51 C2
Lorain Wlk BS10 . . . . . . .34 F2
Lorne Rd BA2 . . . . .101 D6
Lorton Cl BS10 . . . . .35 D1
Lorton Rd BS10 . . . . . . .35 B1
Lotts' Ave BS48 . . . . . . .76 B5
Lotus Ct BS22 . . . . .88 C1
Loughman Rd BS15 . . . . .65 E8
Louisa St BS2 . . . . .143 C2

Louise Ave BS16 . . . . . . .52 A5
Love La
  Chipping Sodbury BS37 . . .40 A8
  Yate BS37 . . . . .28 A4
Love's La BA2 . . . . .115 F6
Lovelinch Gdns BS41 . . . .61 F1
Lovell Ave BS30 . . . . . . .66 D4
Lovell Dr BS39 . . . . .113 C4
Lovell's Hill BS15 . . . . . .65 B5
Lovells Mill BS39 . . . . . .113 C4
Lovells The BS20 . . . . . . .47 B4
Loveringe Cl BS10 . . . . . .34 F4
Lovers La BA3, BS39 . . . .133 A5
Lovers' Wlk BS23 . . . . . .104 D8
Loves Hill BS39 . . . . . . .116 A1
Lowbourne BS14 . . . . . . .79 F6
Lower Ashley Rd
  Bristol,Baptist Mills BS2,
  BS5 . . . . .50 A1
  12 Bristol,St Pauls BS2 . . .49 F1
Lower Batch BS40 . . . . . .96 B3
Lower Borough Walls
  BA1 . . . . .141 C2
Lower Bristol Rd
  Bath BA2 . . . . .141 A2
  Bath,Locksbrook BA2 . . . .101 B6
  Clutton BS39 . . . . .114 F4
Lower Burlington Rd
  BS20 . . . . .45 E6
Lower Camden Pl BA1 . .141 C4
Lower Castle St BS1 . . . .143 B3
Lower Chapel La BS36 . . .38 C7
Lower Chapel Rd BS15 . . .65 C5
Lower Cheltenham Pl
  BS6 . . . . .49 F1
Lower Church La BS2 . . .143 A3
Lower Church Rd BS23 . .104 D8
Lower Claverham BS49 . . .74 F3
Lower Clifton Hill BS8 . .142 B2
Lower Cock Rd BS15 . . . .65 F7
Lower College St BS1 . . .142 C2
Lower Court Rd BS32 . . . .24 A5
Lower Down Rd BS20 . . . .45 B5
Lower East Hayes BA1 . .102 B8
Lower Fallow Cl BS14 . . .79 F3
Lower Farm La BA2 . . . .100 B7
Lower Gay St BS2 . . . . .143 A4
Lower Grove Rd BS16 . . . .50 F4
Lower Guinea St BS1 . . .143 A1
Lower Hanham Rd BS15 . .65 C6
Lower Hedgemead Rd
  BA1 . . . . .141 C4
Lower High St BS11 . . . . .47 D7
Lower House Cres BS34 . .36 B4
Lower Kingsdown Rd
  SN13 . . . . .86 F3
Lower Knole La BS10 . . . .35 A3
Lower Knowles Rd BS21 . .57 C2
Lower Lamb St BS1 . . . . .142 C2
Lower Linden Rd BS21 . . .57 D3
Lower Maudlin St BS1 . .143 A3
Lower Moor Rd BS37 . . . .27 E4
Lower Northend BA1 . . . .85 F5
Lower Norton La
  Weston-S-M,Norton BS22 . .88 C4
  Weston-S-M,Worle Hill
  BS22 . . . . .88 E4
Lower Oldfield Pk BA2 . .141 A1
Lower Parade Ground Rd
  BS24 . . . . .106 C5
Lower Park Row BS1 . . .143 A3
Lower Queen's BS21 . . . .57 D3
Lower Rd BS39 . . . . .130 E6
Lower Redland Mews 2
  BS6 . . . . .49 B2
Lower Redland Rd BS6 . . .49 B2
Lower Sidney St BS3* . . .63 A4
Lower St BA3 . . . . .137 C1
Lower Station Rd
  4 Bristol,Ridgeway BS16 . .51 A4
  Bristol,Staplehill BS16 . . . .51 C4
Lower Stoke BA2 . . . . . .120 A8
Lower Stone Cl BS36 . . . .38 C7
Lower Strode BS40 . . . . .112 A7
Lower Strode Rd BS21 . . .73 A7
Lower Thirlmere Rd
  BS34 . . . . .36 A8
Lower Tockington Rd
  BS32 . . . . .14 A1
Lower Whitelands BA3 . .134 B3
Lowerhouse La GL11 . . . . .5 D5
Lowlis Cl BS10 . . . . .34 F3
Lowther Rd BS10 . . . . . . .35 C2
Loxley Gdns BA2 . . . . . .101 C4
Loxton Dr BA2 . . . . .101 B6
Loxton Rd BS23 . . . . . . .104 F2
Loxton Sq BS14 . . . . .80 A6
Lucas Ct BS4 . . . . .64 D1
Luccombe Hill BS6 . . . . .49 B2
Luckington Court Gdns★
  SN14 . . . . .31 F5
Luckington Cross BA1 . .140 B2
Luckington Prim Sch
  SN14 . . . . .31 E5
Luckington Rd BS7 . . . . .49 E8
Lucklands Rd BA1 . . . . . .84 C1
Luckley Ave BS13 . . . . . .79 C5
Luckwell Prim Sch BS3 . .63 A3
Luckwell Rd BS3 . . . . . . .63 B3
Lucky La BS3 . . . . .63 D4
Ludlow Cl
  Bristol,St Pauls BS2 . . . . .49 F1
  Bristol,Willsbridge BS30 . . .66 B2
  Keynsham BS31 . . . . .81 D5
Ludlow Ct BS30 . . . . .66 B1
Ludlow Rd BS7 . . . . .50 A4
Ludwell Cl BS36 . . . . . . .37 D5
Ludwells Orch BS39 . . . .132 E5

Luggard's Cross BS21 . . .59 C4
Lullington Rd BS4 . . . . . .64 B2
Lulsgate Rd BS13 . . . . . .79 A8
Lulworth Cres BS16 . . . . .51 F8
Lulworth Rd BS31 . . . . . .81 E4
Lunty Mead BS48 . . . . . .75 F6
Lurgan Wlk BS4 . . . . . . .63 D1
Lutyens Cl BS16 . . . . . . .50 E8
Luvers La BS40 . . . . . . .110 D1
Lux Furlong BS9 . . . . . . .48 B7
Luxton St BS5 . . . . .64 B8
Lychgate Pk BS24 . . . . .106 A4
Lydbrook Cl BS37 . . . . . .39 D8
Lyddington Rd BS7 . . . . .49 F8
Lyddon Rd BS22 . . . . . . .89 B3
Lyddyieth Ct BA15 . . . . .120 E7
Lyde Green Rdbt BS16 . . .52 B8
Lydford Wlk BS3 . . . . . . .63 C2
Lydiard Croft BS15 . . . . .65 C3
Lydney Rd
  Bristol,Southmead BS10 . .35 D1
  Bristol,Staple Hill BS16 . . .51 E4
Lydstep Terr BS3 . . . . . . .63 C4
Lye Cross Rd BS40 . . . . .93 C1
Lye Hole La BS40 . . . . . .93 D2
Lye Mead BS40 . . . . .95 A6
Lyefield Rd BS22 . . . . . . .88 E4
Lyes The BS49 . . . . .91 D3
Lyme Gdns BA1 . . . . . . .101 B4
Lyme Rd BA1 . . . . .101 B4
Lymore Ave BA2 . . . . . .101 C5
Lymore Gdns BA2 . . . . .101 C5
Lymore Terr BA2 . . . . . .101 C4
Lympsham CE Fst Sch
  BS24 . . . . .122 B1
Lympsham Gn BA2 . . . . .118 D8
Lympsham Rd BS24 . . . .122 B1
Lynbrook BS41 . . . . .61 F1
Lynbrook La BA2 . . . . . .101 F3
Lynch Cl BS22 . . . . .88 F3
Lynch Cres BS25 . . . . . .124 F7
Lynch Ct BS30 . . . . .65 F4
Lynch Hill BA3 . . . . .138 A3
Lynch The BS25 . . . . . . .124 F7
Lynchmead BS25 . . . . . .125 A7
Lyncombe Hill BA2 . . . . .141 C1
Lyncombe Vale BA2 . . . .102 B4
Lyncombe Vale Rd BA2 . .102 A4
Lyncombe Wlk BS16 . . . .51 B2
Lyndale Ave BS9 . . . . . . .48 D5
Lyndale Rd Bristol BS5 . . .64 D8
  Yate BS37 . . . . .27 D1
Lynde Cl BS13 . . . . .79 B4
Lyndhurst Rd Bath BA2 . .101 C6
  Bristol BS9 . . . . .48 F7
  Keynsham BS31 . . . . .81 F3
  Midsomer Norton BA3 . . .139 B8
  Weston-S-M BS23 . . . . . .104 E4
Lyndhurst Terr BA1 . . . .141 C4
Lynfield Pk BA1 . . . . . . .84 C1
Lynmouth Cl BS22 . . . . . .89 A2
Lynmouth Rd 3 BS2 . . . .50 A2
Lynn Rd BS16 . . . . .50 D5
Lynton 3 BS15 . . . . .66 A8
Lynton Cl BS20 . . . . .45 E4
Lynton Pl 9 BS5 . . . . . . .64 C8
Lynton Rd Bristol BS3 . . .63 D2
  Midsomer Norton BA3 . . .139 B8
Lynton Way BS16 . . . . . .37 B1
Lynwood Cl BA3 . . . . . . .139 A8
Lynwood Rd BS3 . . . . . . .63 B2
Lynx Cres BS24 . . . . . . .105 B2
Lyons Court Rd BS14 . . . .80 D7
Lyons Ct BS23 . . . . .104 F7
Lyppiatt Rd BS5 . . . . . . .64 D8
Lyppincourt Rd BS10 . . . .35 A3
Lypstone Cl 9 BS24 . . . .106 A8
Lysander Rd BS10, BS34 . .35 C6
Lysander Wlk BS34 . . . . .36 E5
Lytchet Dr BS16 . . . . . . .51 F8
Lytes Cary Rd BS31 . . . . .82 A3
Lytton Gdns BA2 . . . . . .101 B4
Lytton Gr Bristol BS7 . . . .50 A8
  Keynsham BS31 . . . . .82 A5
Lyveden Gdns BS13 . . . . .79 B5
Lyvedon Way BS41 . . . . .62 B1

M

Mabberley Cl BS16 . . . . .52 C5
Macaulay Bldgs BA2 . . . .102 C4
Macaulay Rd BS7 . . . . . .50 A8
Macdonald Wlk 2 BS15 . .65 D8
Macey's Rd BS13 . . . . . . .79 D3
Machin Cl BS10 . . . . .34 F3
Machin Gdns BS10 . . . . . .35 A3
Machin Rd BS10 . . . . . . .35 A3
Macies The BA1 . . . . . . .84 B3
Mackie Ave BS34 . . . . . .36 B2
Mackie Gr BS34 . . . . . . .36 B2
Mackie Rd BS34 . . . . . . .36 B2
Mackley La BA2 . . . . . . .136 E3
Macleod Cl BS21 . . . . . . .57 A2
Macquarie Farm Cl BS49 .74 A1
Macrae Ct BS15 . . . . . . .65 E8
Macrae Rd BS20 . . . . . . .47 E4
Madam La
  Weston-S-M BS22 . . . . . .89 A3
  Weston-S-M BS22 . . . . . .89 A4
  Weston-S-M,Worle BS22 . .88 F3
Madam's Paddock BS40 . .96 B3
Madeira Ct BS23 . . . . . .104 C8
Madeira Rd
  Clevedon BS21 . . . . .57 D3
  Weston-S-M BS23 . . . . . .87 C1
Madeline Rd BS16 . . . . . .50 F2
Madison Cl BS37 . . . . . . .27 D2

Maesbury BS15 . . . . .65 E6
Maesbury Rd BS39 . . . . .132 E4
Maesknoll La BS14, BS39 . .97 B8
Maesknoll Rd BS4 . . . . . .64 A2
Magdalana Ct BS1 . . . . .143 B1
Magdalen Ave BA2 . . . .141 B1
Magdalen Rd BA2 . . . . .141 B1
Magdalen Way BS22 . . . .89 A3
Magdalene Pl BS2 . . . . . .49 F1
Magdalene Rd BA3 . . . .134 C2
Magellan Cl BS22 . . . . . .88 F4
Maggs Cl BS10 . . . . .35 C3
Maggs Folly BS39 . . . . .115 D2
Maggs Hill BA2 . . . . . . .116 B2
Maggs La Bristol BS5 . . . .50 A4
  Whitchurch BS14 . . . . . . .80 C4
Magnolia Ave BS22 . . . . .89 A1
Magnolia Cl BS22 . . . . .105 E2
Magnolia Rd BA3 . . . . . .133 E1
Magpie Bottom La
  Bristol,Jefferies Hill BS5 . .65 B6
  Bristol,St George BS15 . . .65 C6
Magpie Cl BS22 . . . . . . .105 E8
Maiden Way BS11 . . . . . .47 C8
Maidenhead Rd BS13 . . . .79 D3
Maidstone Gr BS24 . . . . .105 A4
Maidstone St BS3 . . . . . .63 F3
Main Rd Bristol BS16 . . . .52 D5
  Brockley BS49 . . . . .75 D2
  Flax Bourton BS48 . . . . . .76 F7
  Hutton BS24 . . . . .105 E2
Main St BS39 . . . . .132 A4
Main View BS36 . . . . . . .38 D7
Maisemore BS37 . . . . . . .39 E6
Maisemore Ave BS34 . . . .24 B1
Makin Cl BS30 . . . . .66 C5
Malago Rd BS3 . . . . .63 D3
Malago Vale Est BS3 . . . .63 D3
Malago Wlk BS13 . . . . . .78 E4
Maldowers La 2 BS5 . . . .65 A8
Mall Sh Ctr The BS34 . . .35 D6
Mall The Bath BA1 . . . . .141 C2
  Bristol BS8 . . . . .62 F7
Mallard Cl
  Bristol,Crofts End BS5 . . . .50 F1
  Bristol,Patchway BS32 . . . .24 D2
  Chipping Sodbury BS37 . . .40 A8
Mallard Wlk BS22 . . . . .105 E8
Mallow Cl Clevedon BS21 . .57 E2
  Thornbury BS35 . . . . .8 D2
Malmains Dr BS16 . . . . . .37 B1
Malmesbury Cl
  Bristol,Bishopston BS6 . . . .49 C4
  Bristol,Mount Hill BS30 . . .65 F5
Maltings Ind Est The
  BA1 . . . . .101 B6
Maltings The
  Midford BA2 . . . . .119 C5
  Weston-S-M BS22 . . . . . .88 F2
Maltlands BS22 . . . . . . .105 D8
Malvern Bldgs BA1 . . . . .85 A3
Malvern Ct BS5 . . . . .64 F7
Malvern Dr Bristol BS30 . .66 C5
  Thornbury BS35 . . . . .15 D8
Malvern Rd
  Bristol,Crew's Hole BS5 . . .64 F7
  Bristol,Kensington Park BS4 .64 D3
  Weston-S-M BS23 . . . . . .104 E5
Malvern Terr 4 BA1 . . . .85 A1
Malvern Villas 3 BA1 . . .85 A1
Mancroft Ave BS11 . . . . .47 F7
Mandy Mdws BA3 . . . . .132 F1
Mangotsfield CE Prim Sch
  BS16 . . . . .52 B6
Mangotsfield Rd BS16 . . .52 A5
Mangotsfield Sch BS16 . .52 B4
Manilla Cres BS23 . . . . . .87 C1
Manilla Pl BS23 . . . . . . .87 C1
Manilla Rd BS8 . . . . . . .142 A3
Manmoor La BS21 . . . . . .58 A1
Manor Cl
  Coalpit Heath BS36 . . . . . .38 C6
  Easton-in-G BS20 . . . . . . .47 A4
  Farrington Gurney BS39 . .132 A3
  Portishead BS20 . . . . .45 A5
  Tockington BS32 . . . . .14 C1
  Wellow BA2 . . . . .118 D1
Manor Cl The BS8 . . . . . .61 F8
Manor Coalpit Heath CE Prim
  Sch The BS36 . . . . .38 D6
Manor Copse Rd BA3 . . .134 C2
Manor Cotts GL11 . . . . . .5 F5
Manor Court Dr BS7 . . . .49 E7
Manor Ct Backwell BS48 . .76 A5
  9 Bristol,Baptist Mills BS5 . .50 A1
  Bristol,Stapleton BS16 . . . .50 E4
  Locking BS24 . . . . .106 B4
  Weston-S-M BS23 . . . . . .105 A8
Manor Dr BA1 . . . . .86 C2
Manor Farm BS32 . . . . . .36 D8
Manor Farm Cl BS24 . . . .105 B2
Manor Farm Cres
  Bristol BS32 . . . . .24 D1
  Weston-S-M BS24 . . . . . .105 B2
Manor Gardens Ho BS16 .50 F5
Manor Gdns
  Farmborough BA2 . . . . . .115 F6
  Farrington Gurney BS39 . .132 A3
  Locking BS24 . . . . .106 A4
  Weston-S-M BS22 . . . . . .88 B2
Manor Gr
  Bristol,Mangotsfield BS16 . .52 A4
  Bristol,Patchway BS34 . . . .24 B2
Manor Grange BS24 . . . .122 B2
Manor Ho
  6 Bristol,Baptist Mills BS5 .50 B1
  Bristol,Kingsdown BS2 . . .142 C4
Manor La Abbots Leigh BS8 .61 F8

Manor La continued
  Charfield GL12 . . . . .11 A4
  Winterbourne BS36 . . . . . .37 F7
Manor Pk Bath BA1 . . . .101 B8
  Bristol BS6 . . . . .49 B3
  Radstock BA3 . . . . .134 C2
  Tockington BS32 . . . . . . .14 C1
Manor Pl
  Bristol,Frenchay BS16 . . . .37 C1
  Bristol,Stoke Gifford BS34 . .37 A4
Manor Rd
  Abbots Leigh BS8 . . . . . . .61 F7
  Bath BA1 . . . . .85 C1
  Bristol,Ashley Down BS7 . .49 E4
  Bristol,Fishponds BS16 . . . .51 A5
  Bristol,Highridge BS13 . . . .79 A6
  Bristol,Mangotsfield BS16 . .52 A4
  Radstock BA3 . . . . .134 C2
  Rangeworthy BS37 . . . . . .27 A7
  Saltford BS31 . . . . .82 C2
  Weston-S-M BS23 . . . . . .105 A8
  Wick BS30 . . . . .67 C5
Manor Terr BA3 . . . . . . .134 C2
Manor Valley BS23 . . . . . .88 A1
Manor Villas BA1 . . . . . .84 C1
Manor Way
  Chipping Sodbury BS37 . . .28 C2
  Failand BS8 . . . . .61 C4
  Weston-S-M BS35 . . . . . . .8 B3
Manorbrook Prim Sch
  BS35 . . . . .8 C2
Mansel Cl BS31 . . . . .82 C3
Mansfield Ave BS23 . . . .105 B8
Mansfield St BS3 . . . . . . .63 C2
Manston Cl BS14 . . . . . . .80 C7
Manvers St BA1 . . . . . . .141 C1
Manworthy Rd BS4 . . . . .64 D3
Manx Rd BS7 . . . . .49 F8
Maple Ave Bristol BS16 . . .51 C3
  Thornbury BS35 . . . . .8 C1
Maple Cl
  Bristol,Cadbury Heath BS30 .66 B4
  Bristol,Little Stoke BS34 . . .36 C7
  Bristol,Stockwood BS14 . . .80 D5
  Weston-S-M BS23 . . . . . .105 A8
Maple Ct Bristol BS9 . . . .48 F8
  6 Bristol BS15 . . . . .51 D1
Maple Dr BA3 . . . . .133 E1
Maple Gdns BA2 . . . . . .101 E4
Maple Gr BA2 . . . . .101 E4
Maple Ho BS2 . . . . .143 A4
Maple Leaf Ct BS8 . . . . .142 A3
Maple Rd
  Bristol,Golden Hill BS7 . . .49 E5
  Bristol,St Anne's BS4 . . . . .64 D5
Maple Rise BA3 . . . . . . .134 B2
Maple Wlk
  Keynsham BS31 . . . . .81 D4
  Pucklechurch BS16 . . . . . .53 C5
Mapleleaze BS4 . . . . . . .64 D3
Maplemeade BS7 . . . . . .49 C4
Mapleridge La BS37 . . . . .28 D7
Maples The BS48 . . . . . . .59 C1
Maplestone Rd BS14 . . . .80 A3
Mapstone Cl BS16 . . . . . .37 B3
Marbeck Rd BS10 . . . . . .35 B1
Marchants Pass BA1 . . .141 C1
Marchfields Way BS23 . .105 A5
Marconi Cl BS23 . . . . . .105 B7
Marconi Rd BS20 . . . . . .44 F5
Mardale Cl BS10 . . . . . . .35 C2
Marden Rd BS31 . . . . . . .82 A4
Mardon Rd BS4 . . . . .64 D6
Mardyke Ferry Rd BS1 . .142 B1
Margaret Rd BS13 . . . . . .78 F4
Margaret's Bldgs BA1 . .141 B3
Margaret's Hill BA1 . . . .141 C4
Margate St BS3 . . . . .63 F3
Marguerite Rd BS13 . . . . .78 F7
Marigold Wlk BS3 . . . . . .63 A2
Marina Gdns BS16 . . . . . .50 E3
Marindrin Dr BS22 . . . . . .89 B4
Marine Hill BS21 . . . . . . .57 C4
Marine Par Clevedon BS21 .57 C4
  Pill BS20 . . . . .47 C5
  Weston-S-M BS23 . . . . . .104 D6
  Weston-S-M BS23 . . . . . .87 B1
Mariner's Cl BS22 . . . . . .88 D1
Mariner's Way BS20 . . . . .47 C5
Mariners Cl BS48 . . . . . .76 A6
Mariners Dr
  Backwell BS48 . . . . .76 A6
  Bristol BS9 . . . . .48 C3
Mariner's Path BS9 . . . . .48 E3
Marion Rd BS15 . . . . . . .65 B3
Marion Wlk BS5 . . . . . . .65 A7
Marissal Cl BS10 . . . . . . .34 E3
Marissal Rd BS10 . . . . . .34 E3
Mariston Way BS30 . . . . .66 C6
Marjoram Pl BS32 . . . . . .36 F7
Mark La BS1 . . . . .142 C2
Market Ave BS22 . . . . . . .89 C3
Market Ind Est BS49 . . . .74 B1
Market La BS23 . . . . . . .104 D8
Market Pl Marshfield SN14 .70 A8
  Radstock BA3 . . . . .133 F2
  Winford BS40 . . . . .94 F7
Market Sq BS16 . . . . . . .51 C3
Marketside BS2 . . . . .64 B4
Marklands BS9 . . . . .48 E3
Marksbury CE Prim Sch
  BA2 . . . . .99 B2
Marksbury Rd BS3 . . . . . .63 D2
Marlborough Ave 13
  BS16 . . . . .50 E3

Marlborough Bldgs
BA1 ....141 A3
Marlborough Dr
Bristol BS16 ....37 B1
Weston-S-M BS22 .....89 B2
Marlborough Flats 8
BS2 ....143 A4
Marlborough Hill BS2 .143 A4
Marlborough Hill Pl
BS2 ....143 A4
Marlborough La BA1 ..141 A3
Marlborough St
Bath BA1 ....141 A4
Bristol,Kingsdown BS2 .143 A4
Bristol,Upper Eastville BS5 .50 E3
Marle Pits BS48 ....76 A6
Marlepit Gr BS13 ......78 F6
Marlfield Wlk BS13 ....78 E7
Marling Rd BS5 ....64 F8
Marlowe Ho 3 BS23 ...104 F4
Marlwood Dr BS10 .....35 A3
Marlwood Sch BS35 ....14 F5
Marmaduke St BS3 .....63 F3
Marmion Cres BS10 ....34 F3
Marne Cl BS14 ....80 D5
Marron Cl BS26 ....125 C2
Marsden Rd BA2 ......101 B3
Marsh Cl BS36 ....37 E5
Marsh Common Rd BS35 22 D6
Marsh La
Bristol,Ashton Vale BS3 ..63 B2
Bristol,Barton Hill BS5 ...64 C6
Burton SN14,GL9 ......43 C4
Farrington Gurney BS39 .132 A3
Portbury BS20 ....46 F6
Temple Cloud BS39 ....115 A1
Marsh Lane Ind Est BS20 46 F7
Marsh Rd Bristol BS3 ...62 F3
Rode BA3 ....137 F1
Yatton BS49 ....91 B8
Marsh St Avonmouth BS11 .47 C8
4 Bristol BS1 ....143 A2
Marshacre La BS35 .....13 F6
Marshall Ho 1 BS16 ...50 F8
Marshall Wlk BS4 ......79 D7
Marsham Way BS30 .....65 F4
Marshfield CE Prim Sch
SN14 ....70 B8
Marshfield La BS30 .....67 D1
Marshfield Rd
Bristol,Frenchay BS16 ...51 C8
Bristol,Hillfields BS16 ...51 C4
Tormarton GL9 ....41 E1
Marshfield Way BA1 ....85 A1
Marshwall La BS32 .....23 E6
Marson Rd BS21 ....57 D3
Marston Rd BS4 ....64 B3
Mart The 6 BS23 ......104 E7
Martcombe Rd BS20 ....47 C2
Martin Cl BS34 ....35 E8
Martin Ct 12 BS16 .....50 E4
Martin St 2 BS3 ....63 B3
Martin's Rd BS15 ....65 C5
Martindale Ct BS22 ....105 D8
Martindale Rd BS22 ....105 D8
Martingale Rd BS4 ......64 D4
Martins Cl BS15 ....65 C5
Martins Gr BS22 ....88 E2
Martlock Cres BS3 ......63 C1
Martock BS24 ....104 F2
Martock Rd Bristol BS3 ..63 C2
Keynsham BS31 ....82 A3
Martor Ind Est SN14 ....56 A2
Marwood Rd BS4 ....79 E4
Mary Carpenter Pl 14
BS2 ....49 F1
Mary Ct BS5 ....64 D8
Mary Elton Prim Sch
BS21 ....57 B1
Mary St BS5 ....64 D8
Marybush La BS2 ......143 B3
Marygold Leaze BS30 ...66 A4
Mascot Rd BS3 ....63 D3
Masefield Ho BS23 ....105 A4
Masefield Way BS7 .....50 A6
Maskelyne Ave BS10 ....49 D7
Masons View BS36 .....37 F7
Matchells Cl BS4 ....64 E6
Materman Rd BS14 .....80 E5
Matford Cl Bristol BS10 ..35 A4
Winterbourne BS36 ....37 E5
Matford La GL13 ....3 F4
Matthew Ho 1 BS1 ....143 A3
Matthew's Rd 17 BS5 ..64 C7
Matthews Cl BS14 ......80 F6
Maules La BS16 ....36 F2
Maunsell Rd BS11 ......34 B2
Maurice Rd BS6 ....49 E2
Mautravers Cl BS32 .....36 D7
Mawdeley Ho 11 BS3 ...63 C4
Max Mill La BS25 ......124 C8
Maxse Rd BS4 ....64 B2
May Gr GL12 ....11 B5
May Park Prim Sch BS5 .50 C2
May St BS15 ....51 C1
May Tree Cl BS48 ......59 C1
May Tree Rd BA3 ......133 E1
May Tree Wlk BS31 .....81 C3
May's La BS24 ....90 C3
Maybank Rd BS37 ......27 D1
Maybec Gdns BS5 ......65 A6
Maybourne BS4 ....65 A2
Maybrick Rd BA2 ......101 D5
Maycliffe Pk BS6 ....49 F2
Mayfair Ave BS48 ......59 F1

Mayfield Ave Bristol BS16 .51 A2
Weston-S-M BS22 .....88 E1
Mayfield Ct BS16 ....51 A3
Mayfield Pk BS16 ......51 A3
Mayfield Pk N BS16 ....51 A2
Mayfield Pk S BS16 ....51 A2
Mayfield Rd BA2 ......101 D5
Mayfields BS31 ....81 E5
Mayflower Gdns BS48 ..60 A2
Maynard Cl Bristol BS13 .79 C5
4 Clevedon BS21 .....57 F3
Maynard Rd BS13 ......79 C5
Mayors Bldgs BS16 .....51 B5
Maypole Cl Clutton BS39 .114 E3
Hawkesbury Upton GL9 ..20 A3
Maypole Ct BS15 ....65 B5
Maysfield Cl BS20 ......45 D3
Maysgreen La BS24 ....90 B3
Maysmead La BS40 ....109 C6
Maytree Ave BS13 ......79 B7
Maytree Cl BS13 ....79 B7
Mayville Ave BS34 .....36 A3
Maywood Ave 3 BS16 ..51 B4
Maywood Cres BS16 ....51 B4
Maywood Rd BS16 ......51 C4
Maze St BS5 ....64 B6
McAdam Way BS1 ......62 F5
McCrae Rd BS24 ......106 B5
McLaren Rd BS11 ......33 B1
Mead Cl Bath BA2 .....101 E3
Bristol BS11 ....47 E6
Mead Ct Bsns Pk BS35 .15 B8
Mead La Blagdon BS40 ..110 E3
Saltford BS31 ....82 F4
Sandford BS25 ....107 E4
Tockington BS35 ......13 D2
Mead Rd Bristol BS34 ...36 F5
Chipping Sodbury BS37 ..28 C1
Portishead BS20 ......45 C2
Mead Rise BS3 ....63 F4
Mead St BS3 ....143 C1
Mead Terr BS40 ....110 E2
Mead The Alveston BS35 .15 A5
Bristol BS34 ....36 B4
Clutton BS39 ....114 E3
Dundry BS41 ....78 D2
Farmborough BA2 .....116 A6
Paulton BS39 ....132 E5
Shipham BS25 ....125 E8
Stratton-on-t-F BA3 ...138 F2
Timsbury BA2 ....116 C3
Winsley BA15 ....120 E7
Mead Vale BS22 ......105 E8
Mead Vale Com Prim Sch
BS22 ....88 E1
Mead Way BS35 ....15 B7
Meade Ho BA2 ....101 A5
Meadgate Bristol BS16 ..52 B7
Camerton BA2 ....116 E2
Meadlands BA2 ....100 B7
Meadow Cl Backwell BS48 .76 B6
Bristol BS16 ....51 F7
Farrington Gurney BS39 .132 A3
Nailsea BS48 ....59 E3
Portishead BS20 ......44 F5
Meadow Court Dr BS30 .66 C3
Meadow Croft BS24 ....105 B2
Meadow Dr Bath BA2 ..118 D8
Locking BS24 ....106 B4
Portishead BS20 ......44 F1
Meadow Gdns BA1 .....84 A1
Meadow Gr BS11 ......47 D7
Meadow La BA2 ....85 D1
Meadow Mead
Frampton Cotterell BS36 .38 B8
Yate BS37 ....27 F5
Meadow Pk BA1 ....86 B3
Meadow Rd
Chipping Sodbury BS37 ..28 A1
Clevedon BS21 ....57 D3
Cromhall GL12 ....10 B4
Paulton BS39 ....132 F4
Meadow St
Avonmouth BS11 .....33 A1
Axbridge BS26 ......125 C2
Bristol BS2 ....143 C4
Weston-S-M BS23 ....104 E7
Meadow Vale BS5 ......51 A1
Meadow View
Coalpit Heath BS36 ....38 D7
Radstock BA3 ....134 A1
Meadow View Cl BA1 ..101 A4
Meadow Villas 15 BS23 .104 E8
Meadow Way BS32 .....36 E7
Meadowbank BS22 .....88 F3
Meadowbrook Prim Sch
BS32 ....36 E8
Meadowcroft BS16 .....52 A8
Meadowland BS49 ......74 A1
Meadowland Rd BS10 ..34 E4
Meadowlands BS22 .....89 C2
Meadows End BS25 ....108 D4
Meadows Prim Sch The
BS30 ....82 D8
Meadows The
Bristol BS15 ....65 D4
Luckington SN14 ......31 F4
Meadowside 2 BS35 ....15 D8
Meadowside Dr BS14 ...80 A3
Meadowsweet Ave BS34 .36 B3
Meads The Bristol BS16 ..51 F7
Burton SN14 ....43 B3
Meadway Bristol BS9 ...48 C6
Farmborough BA2 .....116 A6
Temple Cloud BS39 ...114 E1
Meadway Ave BS48 .....59 D2
Mearcombe La BS24 ...122 F6
Meardon Rd BS14 ......80 E6

Meare BS24 ....104 F2
Meare Rd BA2 ....102 A2
Mede Cl BS1 ....143 B1
Media Ho BS8 ....142 B3
Medical Ave BS2,BS8 ..142 C3
Medina Ho BS35 ....15 C7
Medway Cl BS31 ....82 A3
Medway Ct BS35 ....15 D8
Medway Dr
Frampton Cotterell BS36 .38 B7
Keynsham BS31 ......82 A3
Meere Bank BS11 ......34 B1
Meetinghouse La BS49 ..75 A1
Meg Thatcher's Gdns
BS5 ....65 B7
Meg Thatchers Gn BS5 .65 B7
Melbourne Dr BS37 .....28 C1
Melbourne Rd BS7 .....49 D4
Melbourne Terr 2 BS21 .57 D2
Melbury Rd BS4 ....64 A2
Melcombe Ct BA2 .....101 D4
Melcombe Rd BA2 .....101 D4
Melita Rd BS6 ....49 E3
Mellent Ave BS13 ......79 C3
Mells Cl BS31 ....82 A2
Mells La BA3 ....134 B1
Melrose Ave Bristol BS8 .142 B4
Yate BS37 ....28 A2
Melrose Cl BS37 ....28 A2
Melrose Gr BA2 ....101 B3
Melrose Pl BS8 ....142 B4
Melrose Terr BA1 ....85 A2
Melton Cres BS7 ....50 A7
Melville Rd BS6 ....49 B1
Melville Terr BS3 ....63 C3
Melvin Sq BS4 ....63 E1
Memorial Cl BS15 ......65 B4
Memorial Rd Bristol BS15 .65 B4
Wrington BS40 ....92 E2
Memorial Stadium (Bristol
Rovers FC) BS7 ......49 F6
Mendip Ave BS22 ......88 F2
Mendip Cl Axbridge BS26 125 D2
Keynsham BS31 ....81 D5
3 Nailsea BS48 ......59 E1
Paulton BS39 ....132 E4
Yatton BS49 ....91 B7
Mendip Cres BS16 .....52 A8
Mendip Edge BS24 ....121 F8
Mendip Fields BA3 ....138 C2
Mendip Gdns Bath BA2 .118 D8
Yatton BS49 ....91 B7
Mendip Green Fst Sch
BS22 ....88 E1
Mendip Lodge BS25 ...125 A8
Mendip Rd Bristol BS3 ...63 D3
Locking BS24 ....106 D4
Portishead BS20 ......45 B5
Weston-S-M BS23 ....105 A7
Yatton BS49 ....91 B7
Mendip Rise BS24 .....106 B4
Mendip View BS30 .....67 C7
Mendip View Ave BS16 .51 A3
Mendip Villas
Cheddar BS27 ....126 A1
Compton Martin BS40 ..128 F7
Mendip Way BA3 ......133 F3
Menhyr Gr BS10 ....35 B3
Menlea BS40 ....110 D3
Mercer Ct BS14 ....80 B8
Merchant St BS1 ......143 B3
Merchants Ct BS8 .....142 A1
Merchants Quay BS1 ..143 A1
Merchants Rd
Bristol,Hotwells BS8 ...142 A1
Bristol,Victoria Park BS8 .142 A3
Merchants Row BS1 ...143 A1
Merchants The SN14 ...31 E4
Merchants Trad Pk BS2 .64 C6
Mercia Dr BS2 ....50 A2
Mercier Cl BS37 ....27 F2
Meredith Ct BS1 ......142 A1
Merfield Rd BS4 ....64 B2
Meriden BA1 ....101 D8
Meridian Pl BS8 ......142 B3
Meridian Rd BS6 ....49 C1
Meridian Vale BS8 ....142 B3
Meriet Ave BS13 ....79 B4
Merioneth St BS3 ......63 F3
Meriton St BS2 ....64 B5
Merlin Cl Bristol BS9 ....48 F8
Weston-S-M BS22 ....105 E8
Merlin Ct BS10 ....49 B7
Merlin Pk BS20 ....45 A4
Merlin Rd BS10,BS34 ...35 C6
Merlin Ridge BS16 .....53 C4
Merlin Way BS37 ....39 F8
Merrett Ct BS7 ....50 B6
Merrick Ct BS1 ....143 A1
Merrimans Rd BS11 ....47 D8
Merryfield Rd BS24 ...106 B6
Merryholes La BS32 ....14 D3
Merryweathers BS4 ....64 E2
Merrywood Cl 5 BS3 ...63 B4
Merrywood Rd BS4 .....64 B2
Mersham Rd BS3 ....63 C4
Merstham Rd 12 BS2 ...50 A2
Merton Dr BS24 ......106 A8
Merton Rd BS7 ....49 E5
Mervyn Rd BS7 ....49 E4
Meryl Ct BS6 ....49 C3
Metford Gr BS6 ....49 B3
Metford Pl BS6 ....49 C3
Metford Rd BS6 ....49 C3
Methwyn Cl BS22 .....105 C7
Metropolitan The BS1 ..143 B1
Mews The BA1 ....101 A8

Mewswell Dr BS27 ....126 B1
Michaels Mead BA1 ....84 B2
Middle Ave BS1 ....143 A2
Middle La
Kingston Seymour BS21 ..72 F4
Middle Rd BS15 ....51 F3
Middle St BS40 ....129 F4
Middle Stoke BA2 .....120 A6
Middle Yeo Gn BS48 ...59 D3
Middledown Rd SN14 ..55 C1
Middleford Ho 3 BS13 ..79 C4
Middlemead BA3 ......138 F4
Middlepiece La BA2,BS31 99 B7
Middleton Rd BS11 .....47 E8
Midford BS24 ....104 F2
Midford Hill BA2 ......119 C5
Midford La BA2 ....119 E7
Midford Rd BA2 ....119 B7
Midhaven Rise BS22 ....88 E4
Midland Bridge Rd BA1,
BA2 ....141 A2
Midland Rd Bath BA1 ..101 D7
Bristol,Newton BS2 ...143 C3
Bristol,Upper Soundwell
BS16 ....51 D4
Midland Road Bsns Pk
BS16 ....51 D4
Midland St BS2 ....143 C2
Midland Terr BS16 .....50 F3
Midland Way BS35 .....15 C7
Midsomer Ent Pk BA3 ..133 C2
Midsomer Norton Prim Sch
BA3 ....133 B1
Midsomer Norton Railway Ctr
BA3 ....139 A8
Midsummer Bldgs BA1 .85 B2
Milbourne Cl BA15 ....120 D7
Milburn Rd BS23 ......104 F7
Milbury Gdns BS22 .....88 C2
Mildred St BS5 ....64 C7
Mile Wlk BS14 ....80 A6
Miles Cl BS20 ....47 E3
Miles Ct BS30 ....65 F4
Miles Rd BS8 ....49 A1
Miles St BA2 ....141 C1
Miles's Bldgs BA1 .....141 B3
Milestone Ct BS22 .....89 D2
Milford Ave BS30 ......67 B7
Milford St BS3 ....63 C4
Milk St BA1 ....141 B2
Mill Ave BS1 ....143 A2
Mill Cl
Frampton Cotterell BS36 .38 C7
Portbury BS20 ....46 D2
Mill Cres BS37 ....39 B4
Mill Ct 2 BA3 ....133 A1
Mill Hill BA2 ....118 E1
Mill Ho 10 BS5 ....50 A1
Mill La Bath BA2 .....101 B6
Bathampton BA2 ......85 F2
Bitton BS30 ....82 E8
Bristol,Cadbury Heath BS30 66 C5
Bristol,Southville BS3 ...63 D4
Chew Stoke BS40 ....112 D8
Chipping Sodbury BS37 ..40 E6
Compton Martin BS40 ..129 A7
Congresbury BS49 ....91 A4
Doynton BS30 ....53 F1
Falfield GL12 ....9 F7
Frampton Cotterell BS36 ..26 B1
Monkton Combe BA2 ..119 E8
Portbury BS20 ....46 E3
Priston BA2 ....117 A7
Redhill BS40 ....111 A8
Timsbury BA2 ....116 B1
Tockington BS32 ......14 B1
Upton Cheyney BS30 ...66 F1
Wrington BS40 ......109 F8
Mill Leg BS49 ....91 D4
Mill Rd Radstock BA3 .134 D2
Winterbourne BS36 ....37 D4
Mill Road Ind Est BA3 .134 B3
Mill Stps BS36 ....37 F4
Mill Stream Ct BS26 ..125 C1
Millard Cl BS10 ....35 D2
Millard's Hill BA3 .....133 C3
Millards Ct BA3 ......133 B3
Millards Hill BA3 .....133 B3
Millbank Cl BS4 ....64 E3
Millbook Ct 1 BS6 .....49 E1
Millbrook Ave BS4 .....64 F3
Millbrook Cl BS30 .....66 C6
Millbrook Ct BA2 .....141 C1
Millbrook Pl BA2 .....141 C1
Millbrook Rd BS37 .....27 B2
Millcross BS21 ....73 C8
Millennium Cl BS36 ....38 D7
Millennium Sq BS1 ...142 C1
Miller Cl BS23 ....104 F8
Miller Ho BS8 ....142 A2
Miller Wlk BA2 ....85 F1
Millers Cl BS20 ....47 C4
Millers Dr BS30 ....66 D5
Millers Rise BS22 ......89 A4
Millfield
Midsomer Norton BA3 ..138 F8
Thornbury BS35 ....8 C2
Millfield Dr BS30 ......66 C6
Millground Rd BS13 ....78 F5
Millgrove St N BS2 ....143 A4
Millier Rd BS49 ....92 B3
Milliman Cl BS13 ......79 C5
Millmead Ho 2 BS13 ...79 C4
Millmead Rd BA2 .....101 C5
Millpill Cl BS9 ....48 D5
Millpond Prim Sch BS5 .50 A1
Millpond St 9 BS5 ....50 A1
Millpool Ct BS10 ....35 B1

Millpool Ct EPD BS9 ...49 B8
Millward Gr BS16 ......51 C4
Millward Terr BS39 ....132 E6
Milner Gn BS30 ....66 A5
Milner Rd BS7 ....49 F5
Milsom St Bath BA1 ..141 B3
Bristol BS5 ....64 A8
Milton Ave Bath BA2 ..101 F4
Weston-S-M BS23 ....105 A8
Milton Brow BS22 ......88 B2
Milton Cl Nailsea BS48 ..59 E3
Yate BS37 ....27 D2
Milton Ct BS23 ....105 A8
Milton Gn BS22 ....88 C1
Milton Hill BS22 ....88 C1
Milton Jun & Inf Schs
BS22 ....88 C1
Milton Park Rd BS22 ...88 C1
Milton Pk 1 BS5 ....64 C7
Milton Rise BS22 ....88 C1
Miltons Cl BS13 ....79 D4
Milverton BS24 ....104 F2
Milverton Gdns BS6 ....49 F2
Milward Rd BS31 ......81 E6
Mina Rd BS2 ....50 A2
Minehead Rd BS4 ......63 F1
Miners Cl BS41 ....61 F2
Minerva Gdns BA2 ....101 C4
Minor's La BS10 ....34 A8
Minsmere Rd BS31 .....82 A4
Minster Cl 1 BS37 .....39 D7
Minster Way BA2 .....102 C8
Minto Rd BS2 ....50 A2
Minto Road Ind Ctr 8
BS2 ....50 A2
Minton Cl BS14 ....80 B5
Mission Rd BS37 ....27 B4
Mitchell Ct BS1 ....143 B2
Mitchell La BS1 ....143 B2
Mitchell Wlk BS30 .....66 D6
Mitford-Slade Ct BS49 ..91 C7
Mivart St BS5 ....50 B2
Mizzymead Cl 1 BS48 ..59 D1
Mizzymead Rd BS48 ...59 E1
Mizzymead Rise BS48 ..59 E1
Modecombe Gr BS10 ...34 F3
Mogg St BS2 ....50 A2
Molesworth Cl BS13 ...79 A4
Molesworth Dr BS13 ...79 A4
Molly Cl BS39 ....131 E8
Monarch Ct BS16 ......38 A1
Monger Cotts BS39 ...132 F4
Monger La
Midsomer Norton BA3 ..133 A3
Paulton BS39 ....133 A4
Monk Rd BS7 ....49 D4
Monk's Park Ave BS7 ..49 E8
Monks Ave BS15 ......65 B8
Monks Hill BS22 ....88 B3
Monks Ho 3 BS37 .....39 D7
Monks Park Sch BS7 ...49 D8
Monks Park Way BS7 ..49 E8
Monksdale Rd BA2 ....101 C4
Monkton Ave BS24 ....105 A2
Monkton Combe Jun Sch
BA2 ....102 C1
Monkton Combe Sch
BA2 ....102 E1
Monkton Farleigh CE Prim
Sch BA15 ....103 E7
Monkton Rd BS15 .....65 B5
Monmouth Cl BS20 ....44 F4
Monmouth Ct Bath BA1 .141 A2
Pill BS20 ....47 C5
Monmouth Hill BS32 ...23 C1
Monmouth Paddock
BA2 ....136 E5
Monmouth Pl BA1 ....141 B2
Monmouth Rd Bristol BS7 49 D4
Keynsham BS31 ....81 D5
Pill BS20 ....47 C5
Monmouth St Bath BA1 .141 B2
Bristol BS3 ....63 F3
Monsdale Cl BS10 ......35 A3
Monsdale Dr BS10 .....35 A2
Montague Cl BS34 .....36 E5
Montague Ct 4 BS2 ...143 A4
Montague Flats 6 BS2 .143 A4
Montague Hill BS2 ....143 A4
Montague Hill S 5 BS2 143 A4
Montague Ho 8 BA1 ...85 C2
Montague Pl BS6 .....143 A4
Montague Rd
Peasedown St John BA2 .134 C5
Saltford BS31 ....82 D2
Montague St BS1 .....143 A4
Montepelier BS23 .....104 F8
Montgomery St BS3 ....63 F3
Montpelier Ct BS6 .....49 E2
Montpelier E BS23 .....87 F1
Montpelier Sta BS6 ....49 E2
Montreal Ave BS7 .....50 A8
Montreaux Ho 2 BS5 ..65 A7
Montrose Ave BS6 .....49 C1
Montrose Cotts BA1 ....84 C1
Montrose Dr BS30 .....66 B6
Montrose Pk BS4 ......64 D2
Montroy Cl BS9 ....49 D7
Montsurs Cl BA3 .....138 E3
Moon St BS2 ....143 B4
Moor Croft Dr BS30 ....65 F3
Moor Croft Rd BS24 ...105 A2
Moor End Spout BS48 ..59 D2
Moor Gn BS26 ....125 C1

Moo – Nor 165

Moor Gr BS11 .... 48 A8
Moor La Backwell BS48 ... 75 F6
Clapton In Gordano BS20 .. 45 E1
Clevedon BS21 .... 58 A2
Clevedon,East Clevedon BS21 .... 57 E2
Clevedon,Walton in Gordano BS21 .... 58 C6
Hutton BS24 .... 105 D3
Tickenham BS21 .... 58 F4
Tockington BS32 .... 24 A8
Weston-S-M BS24 .... 105 F7
Moor Pk BS21 .... 57 E2
Moor Rd Banwell BS29 .. 107 B5
Yatton BS49 .... 74 B2
Moordell Cl BS37 .... 27 D1
Moorend Farm Ave BS10 33 E5
Moorend Gdns BS11 ..... 47 F7
Moorend Rd BS16 .... 37 D3
Moorfield Rd BS48 ...... 76 A6
Moorfields Cl BA2 ..... 101 D3
Moorfields Ct BS48 ...... 59 D2
Moorfields Ho Bristol BS5 64 C7
Nailsea BS48 .... 59 D2
Moorfields Rd Bath BA2 101 D4
Nailsea BS48 .... 59 D2
Moorgrove Ho BS9 ..... 48 C7
Moorham Rd BS25 ..... 108 A1
Moorhill St 17 BS5 ...... 50 B1
Moorhouse La BS10 ..... 34 B4
Moorings The Bath BA2 . 102 B6
Pill BS20 .... 47 C4
Moorland Rd Bath BA2 .. 101 D5
Weston-S-M BS23 ...... 104 E4
Yate BS37 .... 27 D1
Moorland St BS26 ..... 125 C1
Moorlands Cl BS48 ...... 59 D2
Moorlands Dr BA2 ..... 120 B6
Moorlands Inf Sch BA2 . 101 D4
Moorlands Jun Sch BA2 .... 101 D3
Moorlands Rd
Bristol,Mayfield Park BS16 . 51 A2
Bristol,Ridgeway BS16 .... 50 F3
Moorlands The BA2 .... 101 D3
Moorlay Cres BS40 ...... 94 F8
Moorledge La BS39, BS40 .... 113 F7
Moorledge Rd BS40 ..... 96 B1
Moorpark Ave BS37 ..... 27 D1
Moorside BS49 .... 74 B1
Moorside Ct BS21 .... 57 E2
Moorside Villas BS21 .... 57 E2
Moorslade La GL12 .... 3 D1
Moravian Ct 3 BS15 .... 65 D8
Moravian Rd BS15 ...... 65 D8
Morden Wlk BS14 .... 80 D7
Moreton Cl BS14 .... 80 A4
Moreton La BS40 ...... 112 E2
Morford St BA1 .... 141 B4
Morgan Cl Saltford BS31 .. 82 D2
Weston-S-M BS24 ...... 106 B8
Morgan Pl BS48 .... 77 B8
Morgan St BS2 .... 49 F1
Morgan Way BA2 ...... 134 E7
Morgan's La BS40 ..... 129 F2
Morgans Bldgs BS20 .... 59 F8
Morgans Hill Cl BS48 .... 75 D8
Morley Ave BS16 .... 52 A4
Morley Cl
Bristol,Little Stoke BS34 .. 36 C7
Bristol,Upper Soundwell BS16 .... 51 D4
Morley Rd
Bristol,Southville BS3 ..... 63 C4
Bristol,Upper Soundwell BS16 .... 51 D3
Morley Sq BS7 .... 49 E4
Morley St
Bristol,Baptist Mills BS2 ... 49 F1
Bristol,Russell Town BS5 ... 64 B7
Morley Terr Bath BA2 ... 101 D6
1 Bristol BS15 .... 51 D1
Radstock BA3 .... 134 A3
Mornington Rd 14 BS8 .. 49 A2
Morpeth Rd BS4 .... 79 D8
Morris La BA1 .... 86 B3
Morris Rd BS7 .... 50 A5
Morse Rd BS5 .... 64 C7
Mortimer Cl BA1 .... 84 B2
Mortimer House Hospl BS8 .... 142 A3
Mortimer Rd
Bristol,Newleaze BS34 .... 36 B2
Bristol,Victoria Park BS8 . 142 A3
Morton Mill BS35 .... 8 C3
Morton St Bristol BS5 .... 64 B7
Thornbury BS35 .... 8 C4
Morton Way BS35 .... 8 D1
Moseley Gr BS23 ...... 104 E2
Motorway Distribution Ctr BS11 .... 33 C2
Mount Beacon BA1 ...... 85 A1
Mount Beacon Pl BA1 ... 84 F1
Mount Cl BS36 .... 37 F8
Mount Cres BS36 .... 37 E5
Mount Gdns BS15 .... 65 D6
Mount Gr BA2 .... 101 B3
Mount Hill Rd BS15 ..... 65 D6
Mount Pleasant
Bath BA2 .... 102 D1
Hallen BS10 .... 34 C4
Pill BS20 .... 47 D4
Radstock BA3 .... 134 B2
Mount Pleasant Terr BS3 .... 63 C4
Mount Rd BA1 .... 141 B4
Mount The BS49 .... 91 C8
Mount View
1 Bath,Beacon Hill BA1 ... 85 A1
Bath,Southdown BA2 .... 101 B3
Mountain Ash BA1 .... 84 D1
Mountain Mews 5 BS5 ... 65 A7
Mountain Wood BA1 .... 86 C2
Mountain's La BA2 ..... 115 E6
Mountbatten Cl
Weston-S-M BS22 .... 88 E4
Yate BS37 .... 27 D3
Mounteney's La GL12 .... 18 D7
Mow Barton Bristol BS13 . 78 F6
Yate BS37 .... 27 D2
Mowbray Rd BS14 ...... 80 C7
Mowcroft Rd BS13 ...... 79 D4
Moxham Dr BS13 .... 79 C4
MTC Bsns Pk BS24 ..... 105 A3
Mud La BS49 .... 74 D2
Muddy La BS22 .... 89 A8
Muirfield Bristol BS30 .... 66 A6
Yate BS37 .... 39 E8
Mulberry Ave BS20 ...... 45 E5
Mulberry Cl
Backwell BS48 .... 76 A6
Bristol BS15 .... 65 E8
Portishead BS20 .... 45 F5
Weston-S-M BS22 .... 89 A1
Mulberry Dr BS15 .... 51 F1
Mulberry La BS24 ...... 122 C6
Mulberry Rd BS49 .... 91 E3
Mulberry Wlk BS9 .... 48 C8
Mule St GL13 .... 4 B3
Muller Ave BS7 .... 49 F4
Muller Rd BS5,BS7 ...... 50 B3
Mulready Cl BS7 .... 50 C6
Mumbleys Hill BS35 ..... 14 E7
Mumbleys La
Thornbury,Alveston Down BS35 .... 14 E6
Thornbury,Kington BS35 ... 14 E8
Murford Ave BS13 .... 79 B4
Murford Wlk BS13 ...... 79 B4
Murhill BA2 .... 120 C6
Murray St 9 BS3 .... 63 C4
Mus of Bath at Work★ BA1 .... 141 B4
Mus Of Costume★ BA1 . 141 B3
Mus of East Asian Art★ BA1 .... 141 B3
Musgrove Cl BS11 ...... 34 C2
Myrtle Dr BS11 .... 47 E5
Myrtle Gdns BS49 .... 91 C8
Myrtle Hill BS20 .... 47 C5
Myrtle Rd BS2 .... 142 C4
Myrtle St BS3 .... 63 B3
Myrtle Tree Cres BS22 ... 88 A6
Myrtleberry Mead BS22 . 89 A5
Myrtles The BS24 ...... 105 D2

N

Nags Head Hill BS5 ..... 65 A7
Nailsea & Backwell Sta BS48 .... 75 F7
Nailsea Christ Church CE Jun Sch BS48 .... 59 D3
Nailsea Cl BS13 .... 79 A7
Nailsea Moor La BS48 ... 74 F7
Nailsea Park Cl 4 BS48 . 59 F2
Nailsea Pk BS48 .... 59 F2
Nailsea Sch BS48 .... 59 E1
Nailsea Wall BS21 ...... 74 C8
Nailsea Wall La BS48 .... 74 E7
Nailsworth Ave BS37 .... 27 E1
Naish Hill BS20 .... 45 F1
Naish Ho BA2 .... 101 A6
Naish La BS48 .... 77 D3
Naish's Cross BA3 ..... 138 D3
Naishcombe Hill BS30 ... 67 C7
Naishes Ave BA2 ...... 134 D7
Naite The BS35 .... 7 D6
Nanny Hurn's La BS39 . 114 A1
Napier Ct BS1 .... 142 B1
Napier Ho BS6 .... 49 B2
Napier Miles Rd BS11 ... 48 A8
Napier Rd
Avonmouth BS11 .... 33 B1
Bath BA1 .... 84 A3
Bristol,Baptist Mills BS5 ... 50 B2
Bristol,Woolcott Park BS6 .. 49 B2
Napier Sq BS11 .... 33 A1
Napier St BS5 .... 64 B6
Narrow La BS16 .... 51 E4
Narrow Plain BS2 ...... 143 B2
Narrow Quay BS1 ...... 143 A2
Narroways Rd BS2 ...... 50 A3
Naseby Wlk BS5 .... 50 F1
Nash Cl BS31 .... 82 A5
Nash Dr BS7 .... 50 C7
Nates La BS40 .... 92 F1
Naunton Way BS22 ...... 88 B2
Neads Dr BS30 .... 66 C5
Neale Way BS11 .... 33 C1
Neate Ct BS34 .... 36 C8
Neath Rd BS5 .... 64 D8
Nelson Bldgs BA1 ...... 141 C4
Nelson Ct BS22 .... 88 E4
Nelson Ho Bath BA1 .... 141 A3
8 Bristol BS16 .... 51 D5
Nelson Par 11 BS3 ...... 63 D4
Nelson Pl BA1 .... 141 C4
Nelson Pl E BA1 .... 141 C4
Nelson Pl W BA1 .... 141 A2
Nelson Rd 2 Bristol BS16 51 D4
Bristol BS16 .... 51 D5
Nelson St Bristol BS1 ... 143 A3
Bristol,Ashton Vale BS3 ... 63 A2
Nelson Terr BA1 .... 141 C4
Nelson Villas BA1 ...... 141 A2
Nempnett St BS40 ..... 111 D5
Neston Wlk BS4 .... 79 F8
Netham Gdns BS5 ...... 64 D7
Netham Park Ind Est BS5 .... 64 D6
Netham Rd BS5 .... 64 D6
Netham View Ind Pk BS5 64 D7
Netherton Wood La BS48 75 A6
Netherways BS21 .... 57 B1
Nettlestone Cl BS10 ..... 34 E4
Nettleton & Burton CE Prim Sch SN14 .... 43 B2
Nettleton Rd SN14 ...... 43 B2
Neva Rd BS23 .... 104 E6
Nevalan Dr BS5 .... 65 A6
Nevil Rd BS7 .... 49 E4
Neville Rd BS15 .... 51 E2
New Bldgs Bristol BS16 ... 50 F4
Peasedown St John BA2 .. 134 B8
New Bond St BA1 ...... 141 C2
New Bond Street Pl BA1 .... 141 C2
New Bristol Rd BS22 .... 88 E1
New Brunswick Ave BS5 . 65 B7
New Charlotte St BS3 ... 63 D4
New Cheltenham Rd BS15 .... 51 E1
New Church Rd BS23 .. 104 D2
New Cut Bow BS21 ...... 73 A6
New Fosseway Rd BS14 . 80 B6
New Fosseway Sch BS14 80 B6
New John St 15 BS3 .... 63 C3
New King St BA1 ...... 141 B2
New Kingsley Rd BS2 .. 143 C2
New La BS35 .... 15 C5
New Leaze BS32 .... 24 C3
New Mdws BS14 .... 80 B6
New Mills La GL12 ...... 19 E8
New Orchard St BA1 ... 141 C2
New Park Ho BS21 ...... 57 D5
New Pit Cotts BA2 ..... 116 F1
New Queen St
Bristol,Burchells Green BS15 .... 65 B8
Bristol,Windmill Hill BS3 ... 63 E4
New Rd Banwell BS29 ... 106 E4
Bathford BA1 .... 86 D2
Bristol,Filton BS34 .... 35 F3
Bristol,Harry Stoke BS34 .. 36 D3
Churchill BS25 .... 108 F4
Clevedon BS21 .... 57 D2
Freshford BA2 .... 120 B5
High Littleton BS39 ..... 115 C3
Kilmersdon BA3 .... 140 E4
Kingswood GL12 .... 11 F6
North Nibley GL11 .... 5 E4
Olveston BS35 .... 14 A2
Pensford BS39 .... 97 D3
Pill BS20 .... 47 C4
Rangeworthy BS37 .... 27 A8
Rangeworthy,Hall End BS37 17 C1
Redhill BS40 .... 94 A4
Shipham BS25 .... 108 E1
Tytherington GL12 .... 16 C6
New Rock Ind Est BA3 . 138 D2
New Siblands Sch BS35 ... 8 D1
New St Bath BA1 .... 141 B2
Bristol BS2 .... 143 C3
Charfield GL12 .... 11 A6
New Stadium Rd BS5 .... 50 B2
New Station Rd BS16 .... 51 A4
New Station Way BS16 .. 51 A4
New Street Flats 4 BS2 .... 143 C3
New Thomas St BS2 ... 143 C2
New Tyning La BS37 .... 29 C4
New Walls BS41 .... 63 F4
New Wlk BS15 .... 65 B5
Newark St BA1 .... 141 C1
Newbolt Cl BS23 ...... 105 B4
Newbourne Rd BS22 ... 105 C8
Newbrick Rd BS34 ...... 37 A5
Newbridge Cl BS4 ...... 64 D5
Newbridge Ct BA1 ..... 101 B7
Newbridge Gdns BA1 .. 101 A8
Newbridge Hill BA1 .... 101 B7
Newbridge Ho BS9 ...... 48 C4
Newbridge Jun Sch BA1 .... 101 B7
Newbridge Rd
Bath BA1,BA2 .... 101 B7
Bristol BS4 .... 64 E6
Newbridge St John's Inf Sch BA1 .... 101 B7
Newbridge Trad Est BS4 64 D5
Newbury Rd BS7 .... 50 A7
Newclose La BS40 ..... 112 D1
Newcombe Dr BS9 ...... 48 C4
Newcombe Rd BS9 ...... 48 F7
Newditch La BS40 ...... 77 C1
Newent Ave BS15 .... 65 C7
Newfields BS40 .... 127 C8
Newfoundland Ct BS2 .. 143 C4
Newfoundland Rd BS2 . 143 C4
Newfoundland St BS2 .. 143 C4
Newfoundland Way BS2 .... 143 C4
Newgate BS1 .... 143 B3
Newhaven Pl BS20 ...... 44 E4
Newhaven Rd BS20 ..... 44 D4
Newland Dr BS13 .... 79 A4
Newland Ho BA1 .... 84 F1
Newland Hts BS6 .... 49 F2
Newland Rd Bristol BS13 . 79 A3
Weston-S-M BS23 ...... 104 F6
Newland Wlk BS13 ...... 79 A3
Newlands Ave BS36 ..... 38 C7
Newlands Cl BS20 .... 45 C5
Newlands Gn BS21 ...... 57 E1
Newlands Hill BS20 ..... 45 C4
Newlands Rd BS31 ...... 81 D4
Newlands The BS16 ..... 51 B7
Newleaze BS34 .... 36 A2
Newlyn Ave BS9 .... 48 D5
Newlyn Way BS37 .... 27 F2
Newlyn Wlk BS4 .... 64 B1
Newman Cl BS37 .... 39 B4
Newmans La BA2 ...... 116 B2
Newmarket Ave 6 BS1 . 143 A3
Newnham Cl BS14 ...... 80 D7
Newnham Pl BS34 ...... 23 F1
Newpit La BS30 .... 66 F2
Newport Cl Clevedon BS21 57 C2
Portishead BS20 .... 44 F4
Newport Rd BS20 .... 47 C5
Newport St BS3 .... 63 E3
Newquay Rd BS4 .... 63 F1
Newry Wlk BS4 .... 63 E1
Newsome Ave BS20 ..... 47 C4
Newton Cl Bristol BS15 ... 52 A1
West Harptree BS40 ..... 129 E6
Newton Dr BS30 .... 66 A5
Newton Gn BS48 .... 75 C8
Newton Rd Bath BA2 ... 100 F6
Bristol BS30 .... 66 A5
Weston-S-M BS23 ...... 104 E6
Newton St BS5 .... 64 A8
Newton's Rd
Weston-S-M BS22 .... 88 E3
Weston-S-M BS22 .... 88 E4
Newtown GL12 .... 11 A5
Niblett Cl BS15 .... 65 F6
Niblett's Hill BS5 .... 65 A6
Nibley La BS37 .... 26 F3
Nibley Rd BS11 .... 47 E5
Nichol's Rd BS20 .... 44 F5
Nicholas La BS5 .... 65 A6
Nicholas Rd BS5 .... 50 B1
Nicholas St BS3 .... 63 E4
Nicholettes BS30 .... 66 D5
Nicholls Ct BS36 .... 37 E7
Nicholls La BS36 .... 37 E6
Nigel Pk BS11 .... 47 E7
Nightingale Cl Bristol BS4 64 E6
Frampton Cotterell BS36 ... 38 A6
Thornbury BS35 .... 8 D2
Weston-S-M BS22 .... 88 E1
Nightingale Ct BS4 ..... 64 D3
Nightingale Gdns BS48 .. 59 D2
Nightingale La BS36 .... 38 A8
Nightingale Rise BS20 ... 44 F3
Nightingale Way BA3 .. 139 B8
Nile St BA1 .... 141 A2
Nine Tree Hill 6 BS1 .... 49 E1
Ninth Ave BS7 .... 36 B1
Nippors Way BS25 ..... 124 F8
Nithsdale Rd BS23 ..... 104 E4
Nixon Trad Units BS24 . 105 A3
No 1 Royal Cres Mus★ BA1 .... 141 B3
Noble Ave BS30 .... 66 C4
Nomis Pk BS49 .... 91 E2
Nore Gdns BS20 .... 45 C6
Nore Park Dr BS20 ...... 44 F5
Nore Rd BS20 .... 45 A6
Norfolk Ave
Bristol,Montpelier BS6 .... 49 E2
Bristol,St Pauls BS2 ..... 143 B4
Norfolk Bldgs BA1 ..... 141 A2
Norfolk Cres BA1 ...... 141 A2
Norfolk Gr BS31 .... 81 C4
Norfolk Hts BS2 .... 143 B4
Norfolk Pl BS3 .... 63 C3
Norfolk Rd
Portishead BS20 .... 45 E4
Weston-S-M BS23 ...... 104 F5
Norland Rd BS8 .... 62 F8
Norley Rd BS7 .... 49 F7
Norman Gr BS15 .... 51 D2
Norman Rd
Bristol,Baptist Mills BS2 ... 50 A2
Bristol,Warmley BS30 .... 66 B8
Saltford BS31 .... 82 E3
Normanby Rd 20 BS5 .... 50 B1
Normans The BA2 .... 85 F1
Normans Way BS20 ..... 46 E7
Normanton Rd 16 BS8 ... 49 A2
Norrisville Rd 5 BS6 .... 49 E1
North Chew Terr BS40 ... 96 B3
North Croft BS30 .... 66 D4
North Ct BS32 .... 24 D3
North Devon Rd BS16 ... 51 A5
North Down Cl BS25 ... 125 F8
North Down La BS25 .. 125 F8
North Dro BS48 .... 59 A2
North East Rd BS35 ...... 8 C2
North End
Midsomer Norton BA3 .. 133 B2
Yatton BS49 .... 74 A2
North End Rd BS49 ..... 73 F3
North Gr BS20 .... 47 C4
North Green St 12 BS8 .. 62 F6
North Hills Cl BS24 ... 105 B2
North La Bath BA2 ..... 102 D5
Nailsea BS48 .... 59 B1
2 Weston-S-M BS23 .... 104 E7
North Leaze BS41 .... 62 B2
North Mdws BA2 ...... 134 E8
North Nibley CE Prim Sch GL11 .... 5 D5
North Par Bath BA2 .... 141 C2
Yate BS37 .... 27 E2
North Parade Bldgs BA1 .... 141 C2
North Parade Pas BA1 . 141 C2
North Parade Rd BA2 .. 102 B6
North Pk BS15 .... 51 E1
North Rd Banwell BS29 .. 107 A3
Bath,Bathwick BA2 ..... 102 C6
Bath,Fox Hill BA2 ...... 102 B2
6 Bristol BS3 .... 63 A4
Bristol,Montpelier BS6 .... 49 E2
Bristol,Stoke Gifford BS34 . 36 F4
Leigh Woods BS8 .... 62 D7
Lympsham BS24 .... 122 D2
Midsomer Norton BA3 .. 133 A1
Thornbury BS35 .... 8 C2
Timsbury BA2 .... 116 C2
Winterbourne BS36 ...... 37 F7
Yate BS37 .... 27 B3
Yate,Engine Common BS37 . 27 B5
North Side Rd BS48 ..... 93 F8
North Somerset Junc BS5 .... 64 B6
North St
Bristol,Mangotsfield BS16 . 51 E5
Bristol,Oldland Common BS30 .... 66 C4
Bristol,Southville BS3 ..... 63 B3
Bristol,St Pauls BS1 ..... 143 B4
Nailsea BS48 .... 59 B1
Norton St Philip BA2 .... 136 E4
Weston-S-M BS23 ...... 104 E8
Wickwar GL12 .... 18 A6
North Stoke La BS30 .... 83 B8
North View Bristol BS6 ... 49 A4
Bristol,Mangotsfield BS16 . 51 E5
Bristol,Upper Soundwell BS16 .... 51 D4
Radstock BA3 .... 134 B2
North View Cl BA2 .... 101 B5
North View Dr BS29 ... 107 A2
North Way Bath BA2 ... 101 A5
Bristol BS34 .... 36 B4
Midsomer Norton BA3 .. 133 A1
North Wlk BS37 .... 27 E1
Northampton Bldgs BA1 .... 141 B4
Northampton Ho BS48 ... 60 D3
Northampton St BA1 ... 141 B4
Northavon Bsns Ctr BS37 27 C3
Northbridge Bsns Ctr BS37 .... 27 B2
Northcote Rd
Bristol,Clifton BS8 .... 48 F1
Bristol,Crew's Hole BS5 ... 64 E7
Bristol,Mangotsfield BS16 . 51 F6
Northcote St 18 BS5 .... 50 B1
Northdown Rd BA3 .... 133 E5
Northend BA1 .... 85 F5
Northend Ave BS15 ..... 51 D2
Northend Gdns BS15 .... 51 D2
Northend Rd BS15 ...... 51 E1
Northern Path BS21 ..... 57 F3
Northern Way BS21 ..... 57 F3
Northfield Radstock BA3 . 134 A3
Timsbury BA2 .... 116 C3
Winsley BA15 .... 120 F7
Yate BS37 .... 39 D8
Northfield Ave BS15 ..... 65 D5
Northfield Ho Bath BA1 .. 84 F1
10 Bristol BS3 .... 63 C4
Northfield La SN14 ...... 55 F1
Northfield Rd Bristol BS5 . 65 B7
Portishead BS20 .... 44 E3
Northfields BA1 .... 84 F1
Northfields Cl BA1 ...... 84 F1
Northgate St BA1 ...... 141 C2
Northleach Wlk BS11 .... 47 F5
Northleaze CE Prim Sch BS41 .... 62 B2
Northleigh Ave BS22 .... 88 C1
Northmead Ave BA3 ... 132 F2
Northmead Cl BA3 .... 132 F2
Northmead La BS37 ..... 26 D6
Northmead Rd BA3 .... 132 F2
Northover Ct BS35 ...... 22 E6
Northover Rd BS9 .... 35 A1
Northumberland Bldgs 1 BA1 .... 141 B2
Northumberland Pl BA1 .... 141 C2
Northumberland Rd BS6 49 D2
Northumbria Dr BS9 .... 49 B4
Northville Rd BS7 .... 36 A1
Northwick Gdns BS39 .. 113 D4
Northwick Rd Bristol BS7 . 49 F8
Chew Magna BS39,BS41 ... 96 D7
Pilning BS35 .... 12 E1
Northwood Pk BS36 ..... 37 B7
Northwoods Wlk BS10 ... 35 D3
Norton Cl Bristol BS15 ... 65 F7
Chew Magna BS40 .... 96 B3
Norton Hill Sch BA3 ... 139 B8
Norton Ho 7 Bristol BS1 143 B1
Bristol,Patchway BS34 .... 23 F1
Norton La
Chew Magna BS39,BS40 .. 96 D5
Wellow BA2 .... 136 B7
Weston-S-M BS22 .... 88 C4
Whitchurch BS14 .... 80 C2
Norton Radstock Coll BA3 .... 133 F2
Norton Rd BS4 .... 64 A3
Norton St Philip CE First Sch BA2 .... 136 E4
Nortons Wood La BS21 .. 58 A5
Norwich Dr BS4 .... 64 E6
Norwood Ave BA2 ..... 102 E5

Norwood Farm★ BA2 ..136 F7
Norwood Gr BS20 ....44 F5
Notgrove Cl BS22 ....88 B2
Nottingham Rd BS7 .....49 E3
Nottingham St BS3 ......63 F3
Nova Scotia Pl BS1 ....142 A1
Nova Way BS11 ....33 B1
Novers Cres BS4 ....79 C8
Novers Hill BS4 ....79 C8
Novers Hill Trad Est BS3 .63 C1
Novers La BS4 ....79 D7
Novers Lane Inf Sch BS4 79 C7
Novers Lane Jun Sch
BS4 ....79 C7
Novers Park Dr BS4 .....79 C8
Novers Park Rd BS4 ....79 D8
Novers Rd BS4 ....79 C8
Nowhere La BS48 ....60 A1
Nugent Hill BS6 ....49 D1
Nunney Cl BS31 ....82 A2
Nupdown Rd BS35 ....1 E5
Nurseries The GL12 .....16 B5
Nursery Gdns BS10 .....35 A3
Nursery Rise BA3 ......138 E4
Nursery The BS3 ....63 B3
Nutfield Gr BS34 ....36 B2
Nutgrove Ave BS3 ....63 E3
Nutgrove La BS40 ....96 A4
Nuthatch Dr BS16 ....50 F6
Nuthatch Gdns BS16 .....51 A6
Nutwell Rd BS22 ....88 E2
Nutwell Sq BS22 ....88 E2
Nye Dro BS24 ....107 E8
Nye Rd BS25 ....107 F5
Nympsfield BS15 ....51 E2

O

Oak Ave BA2 ....101 C3
Oak Cl Bristol BS34 ......36 D7
Yate BS37 ....27 D3
Oak Ct Bristol BS14 ......80 A5
Weston-S-M BS22 ....89 C3
Oak Dr BS20 ....45 B4
Oak Gr BS20 ....47 C5
Oak Ho BS13 ....79 D4
Oak La BS5 ....50 F2
Oak Lodge BS37 ....39 D8
Oak Rd Bristol BS7 ......49 E5
Colerne SN14 ....70 F5
Winscombe BS25 ....125 A8
Oak St BA2 ....141 B1
Oak Terr BA3 ....133 D1
Oak Tree Caravan Pk
BS24 ....105 E5
Oak Tree Cl BS15 ....65 C3
Oak Tree Wlk BS31 ......81 D3
Oakdale Ave BS16 ....51 D8
Oakdale Cl BS16 ....51 E8
Oakdale Ct BS16 ....51 D7
Oakdale Gdns BS22 .....88 F2
Oakdale Rd
Bristol,Downend BS16 .....51 E8
Bristol,Hengrove BS14 ....80 A8
Oakdene Ave BS5 ....50 D3
Oakenhill Rd BS4 ....64 E2
Oakenhill Wlk BS4 ....64 E2
Oakes La GL9 ....42 B5
Oakfield Bsns Pk BS15 ..65 D7
Oakfield Cl BA1 ....101 D8
Oakfield Gr BS8 ....142 B4
Oakfield Pl BS8 ....142 B4
Oakfield Rd
Bristol,Kingswood BS15 ...65 D7
Bristol,Victoria Park BS8 ..142 B4
Keynsham BS31 ....81 F2
Oakford Ave BS23 ......104 F8
Oakford La SN14 ....70 B2
Oakhanger Dr BS11 .....34 B1
Oakhill BS24 ....105 A2
Oakhill Ave BS30 ....66 C2
Oakhill Cl BS48 ....60 B1
Oakhill La BS10 ....34 C4
Oakhill Rd BA2 ....101 F2
Oakhurst Rd BS9 ....48 F5
Oakland Bsn Pk BS37 ...27 B3
Oakland Dr BS24 ....105 E3
Oakland Rd
Bristol,Crew's Hole BS5 ...64 E8
6 Bristol,Woolcott Park
BS6 ....49 B1
Oaklands Clevedon BS21 ..57 C4
Paulton BS39 ....132 E4
Temple Cloud BS39 ......114 E1
Oaklands Cl BS16 ....52 B5
Oaklands Dr
Almondsbury BS32 ....24 A4
Bristol,Broomhill BS16 ....51 A7
Bristol,Oldland Common
BS30 ....66 C2
Oaklands Rd BS16 ......52 A5
Oakleaze BS36 ....38 D7
Oakleaze Rd BS35 ....8 C1
Oakleigh Ave BS5 ....50 D1
Oakleigh Cl BS48 ....76 B5
Oakleigh Gdns BS30 .....66 C2
Oakley Bath BA2 ....102 E5
7 Clevedon BS21 ....57 B1
Oakley Rd BS7 ....49 F7
Oakmeade Pk BS4 ....64 B2
Oakridge Cl Bristol BS15 .66 A7
Winscombe BS25 ....125 B7
Oakridge La BS25 ......125 C6
Oaks The Nailsea BS48 ...60 A2
Oaks The *continued*
Winford BS40 ....94 F7
Oaksey Gr BS48 ....60 A1
Oaktree Ave BS16 ....53 B4
Oaktree Cres BS32 ......24 C2
Oaktree Ct BS11 ....47 E7
Oaktree Gdns BS13 .....78 F4
Oaktree Pl BS22 ....89 C3
Oakwood Ave BS9 ....49 C6
Oakwood Bsns Pk BS24 105 A3
Oakwood Gdns BS36 .....38 E7
Oakwood Rd BS9 ....49 B6
Oatfield BS48 ....76 F1
Oatlands Ave BS14 ......80 A6
Oatley Trad Est 3 BS15 ..51 D1
Oberon Ave BS5 ....50 E2
Observatory Field BS25 .125 B8
Odins Rd BA2 ....101 D1
Okebourne Cl BS10 ......35 B4
Okebourne Rd BS10 ......35 B4
Old Acre Rd BS14 ....80 A3
Old Ashley Hill BS6 ......49 F2
Old Aust Rd BS32 ....24 C6
Old Banwell Rd BS24 ...106 B4
Old Barn La BS40 ....94 A5
Old Barrow Hill BS11 .....47 D7
Old Bond St 4 BA1 .....141 B2
Old Bread St BS2 ....143 C2
Old Brewery The BS20 ...47 C4
Old Brewhouse The BA1 .84 B2
Old Bristol Rd
Priddy BS40 ....129 A3
Weston-S-M BS22 ....89 A2
Old Chapel BA1 ....141 C4
Old Chelsea La BS8 .....61 C4
Old Church Rd
Axbridge BS26 ....125 C1
Clevedon BS21 ....57 C3
Nailsea BS48 ....75 D8
Weston-S-M BS23 ....104 D2
Old Coach Rd BS26 .....124 E2
Old Down Hill BS32 ......14 B2
Old Down Rd GL9 ....42 C8
Old England Way BA2 ..134 E8
Old Farm La BS5 ....65 B6
Old Ferry Rd BA2 ....101 C6
Old Forge Way BA2 .....134 E8
Old Fosse Rd Bath BA2 .101 C1
Radstock BA3 ....133 E4
Old Frome Rd BA2 .....118 E8
Old Gloucester Rd
Alveston BS35 ....15 B5
Bristol,Hambrook BS16 ....37 B2
Bristol,Stoke Gifford BS16 ..37 B4
Frampton Cotterell BS36 ..25 D3
Thornbury GL12 ....9 B2
Old Hill Winford BS40 ....94 D6
Wrington BS40 ....92 F3
Old Junction Rd BS23 ..105 B5
Old King St BA1 ....141 B3
Old King Street Ct BS1 .143 B3
Old La Bristol BS16 ......52 C6
Farmborough BA2 ....116 A6
Nailsea BS21 ....59 C4
Old Manor Cl GL12 ......11 A5
Old Market St BS2 ......143 B3
Old Midford Rd BA2 ....119 B7
Old Mill Cl BS37 ....39 B4
Old Mill Rd BS20 ....45 D5
Old Mill Way BS24 ......106 A8
Old Millard's Hill BA3 ..133 B3
Old Mills Ind Est BS39 ..132 E2
Old Mills La BS39 ....132 D3
Old Mixon Rd BS24 .....105 C2
Old Newbridge Hill BA1 101 A8
Old Orch BA1 ....141 C3
Old Orchard St BA1 ....141 C2
Old Park Hill BS2 ....142 C3
Old Park Rd Bristol BS11 .47 D7
Clevedon BS21 ....57 E4
Old Pit Rd BA3 ....139 C8
Old Pit Terr BA3 ....133 E4
Old Pk BS2 ....142 C3
Old Police Sta The BS4 ..64 A3
Old Post Office La BS23 104 D8
Old Priory Rd BS20 ......47 B4
Old Quarry BA2 ....101 D2
Old Quarry Rd BS11 ......47 E7
Old Quarry Rise BS11 .....47 E7
Old Rd BA3 ....134 C1
Old Rectory Rd GL12 ....11 F4
Old School Ho BS4 ....64 B2
Old School Ho The BA1 .141 B4
Old School La BS24 .....122 C6
Old Sneed Ave BS9 ....48 D4
Old Sneed Cotts BS9 ....48 E4
Old Sneed Pk BS9 ....48 D4
Old Sneed Rd BS9 ....48 D4
Old Sodbury CE Prim Sch
BS37 ....41 B8
Old St BS21 ....57 E3
Old Station Cl BS40 .....92 D1
Old Tarnwell BS39 ....97 B2
Old Tk BA2 ....119 F7
Old Vicarage Ct BS14 ....80 C4
Old Vicarage Gn BS31 ...81 E6
Old Vicarage Pl BS8 ......49 A1
Old Vicarage The
Bristol BS6 ....49 E1
Olveston BS35 ....14 A3
Old Wall BS24 ....121 D5
Old Water Gdns The
BS40 ....110 E2
Old Wells Rd BA2 ....101 F3
Old Weston Rd
Congresbury BS49 ....91 B5
Flax Bourton BS48 ....77 B8
Oldbridge Rd BS14 ......80 C3
Oldbury Chase BS30 .....66 A2
Oldbury Court Dr BS16 ..51 B6
Oldbury Court Prim Sch
BS16 ....51 C7
Oldbury Court Rd BS16 ..51 A5
Oldbury La Thornbury BS35 .8 B4
Wick BS30 ....67 D5
Oldbury Power Station
Visitor Ctr★ BS35 ....1 B1
Oldbury-on-Severn CE Prim
Sch BS35 ....7 B5
Oldfield BS21 ....57 E1
Oldfield Girls Sch BA1 ...83 F1
Oldfield La BA2 ....101 E4
Oldfield Park Halt BA2 .101 D6
Oldfield Park Inf Sch
BA2 ....101 D6
Oldfield Park Jun Sch
BA2 ....101 C4
Oldfield Pl BS8 ....62 F5
Oldfield Rd Bath BA2 ....141 A1
Bristol,Hotwells BS8 .....142 A1
Oldfields La BS35 ....25 D7
Oldlands Ave BS36 ....38 C6
Oldmead Wlk BS13 ....78 E7
Oldmixon Cres BS24 ...105 A3
Oldmixon Prim Sch
BS24 ....105 A2
Oldmixon Rd BS24 ......105 B1
Oldown Ctry Pk★ BS32 ..14 B4
Oldville Ave BS21 ....57 D2
Oldwood La BS37 ....27 B8
Olive Gdns BS35 ....14 F4
Oliver Brooks Rd BA3 ..138 E7
Olveston CE Prim Sch
BS35 ....14 A3
Olveston Rd BS7 ....49 E5
Olympus Cl BS34 ....36 D6
Olympus Rd BS34 ....35 D7
Onega Ctr BA1 ....141 A3
Onega Terr BA1 ....141 A3
Oolite Gr BA2 ....101 D1
Oolite Rd BA2 ....101 D1
Oram Ct BS30 ....65 F4
Orange Gr BA1 ....141 C2
Orange St BS2 ....143 C4
Orchard Ave Bristol BS1 .142 C2
Midsomer Norton BA3 ....132 F1
Portishead BS21 ....58 E4
Thornbury BS35 ....8 D1
Orchard Bvd BS30 ....66 B4
Orchard Cl Banwell BS29 107 B3
Bishop Sutton BS39 .....113 C3
Bristol,Kingswood BS15 ...65 E8
Bristol,Stoke Bishop BS9 ..48 F5
Charfield GL12 ....11 A5
Congresbury BS49 ....91 D4
Felton BS40 ....94 C8
Flax Bourton BS48 ....77 A8
Keynsham BS31 ....81 D6
Portishead BS20 ....45 D5
Weston-S-M,Kewstoke
BS22 ....88 B3
Weston-S-M,Worle BS22 ..88 F2
Westwood BA15 ....120 F3
Winterbourne BS36 ....37 E5
Wrington BS40 ....92 E2
Yate BS37 ....27 F2
Orchard Cl The BS24 ..105 F4
Orchard Cotts
10 Bristol BS16 ....51 D5
Timsbury BA2 ....116 F1
Orchard Cres BS11 ......47 D7
Orchard Ct
Bristol,Northville BS34 ....36 A2
18 Bristol,Pile Marsh BS5 ..64 D7
Claverham BS49 ....74 F1
Yate BS37 ....27 B3
Orchard Dr Aust BS35 ...13 A7
Bristol BS13 ....79 A6
Sandford BS25 ....108 A4
Orchard End BS40 ......129 F4
Orchard Gate BS32 ......24 C2
Orchard Gdns Bristol BS15 65 F8
Paulton BS39 ....132 E6
Orchard Grange BS35 ....8 B2
Orchard Ho 2 BS5 ....64 F8
Orchard La BS1 ....142 C2
Orchard Lea
6 Alveston BS35 ....15 A5
Pill BS20 ....47 D4
Orchard Pl 1 BS23 .....104 E7
Orchard Rd
Axbridge BS26 ....125 C1
Backwell BS48 ....76 A6
Bristol,Ashley Down BS7 ..49 E4
Bristol,Crew's Hole BS5 ...64 F8
Bristol,Kingswood BS15 ...65 E8
Clevedon BS21 ....57 D2
Coalpit Heath BS36 ......38 D7
Hutton BS24 ....105 E2
Long Ashton BS41 ....61 F1
Nailsea BS48 ....59 D1
Paulton BS39 ....132 E6
Pucklechurch BS16 ....53 B5
Orchard Rise BS35 ......14 A3
Orchard Sq BS5 ....64 D7
Orchard St Bristol BS1 ..142 C2
Weston-S-M BS23 ....104 E8
Orchard Terr BA2 ......101 B6
Orchard The
Bath,Combe Down BA2 ...102 B1
Bath,Newbridge BA1 ....101 A7
Bristol BS34 ....36 F5
Frampton Cotterell BS36 ..38 C8
Freshford BA2 ....120 C5
Locking BS24 ....106 A5
Pensford BS39 ....97 E4
Orchard The *continued*
Pill BS20 ....47 C4
Stanton Drew BS39 ....97 A2
Tytherington GL12 ....16 B5
8 Weston-S-M BS24 ....106 A8
Orchard Vale Bristol BS15 .65 F7
Midsomer Norton BA3 ....132 F1
Orchard Way BA2 ......134 D7
Orchard Wlk
Churchill BS25 ....108 E4
Kingswood GL12 ....11 F4
Orchards The
Bristol,Kingswood BS15 ....65 F7
Bristol,Shirehampton BS11 .47 E6
Oriel Gdns BA1 ....85 C2
Oriel Gr BA2 ....101 B4
Orion Dr BS34 ....36 D6
Orland Way BS30 ....66 A3
Orlebar Gdns BS11 ......34 B2
Orme Dr BS21 ....57 D5
Ormerod Rd BS9 ....48 E5
Ormonds Cl BS32 ....24 E1
Ormsley Cl BS34 ....36 C8
Orpen Gdns BS7 ....50 B5
Orpen Pk BS32 ....24 B3
Orpheus Ave BS34 ....36 D6
Orwell Dr BS31 ....82 A4
Orwell St BS3 ....63 E3
Osborne Ave Bristol BS7 ..49 F3
Weston-S-M BS23 ....104 F7
Osborne Cl BS34 ....36 D4
Osborne Rd Bath BA1 ...101 B7
Bristol,Redland BS8 ....49 A1
Bristol,Southville BS3 .....63 C4
Severn Beach BS35 ....22 A7
Weston-S-M BS23 ....104 F7
Osborne Terr 10 BS3 ....63 B2
Osborne Villas BS2 .....142 C4
Osborne Wallis Ho BS8 .142 A1
Oslings La BA1 ....86 B2
Osprey Ct BS14 ....79 D5
Osprey Gdns BS22 ....88 F1
Osprey Pk BS35 ....8 D3
Osprey Rd 15 BS5 ....64 C7
Otago Terr 5 BA1 ....85 C2
Ottawa Rd BS23 ....104 F3
Otter Rd 1 BS21 ....57 E1
Otterford Cl BS14 ....80 B5
Ottery Cl BS11 ....34 A1
Ottrells Mead BS32 ......24 C3
Our Lady of Lourdes RC Prim
Sch BS15 ....65 E7
Our Lady of the Rosary Cath
Prim Sch BS11 ....48 A8
Our Lady of the Rosary RC
Prim Sch BS11 ....34 A1
Oval The BA2 ....101 C4
Over La BS32 ....23 D2
Overdale
Peasedown St John BA2 ..116 F3
Radstock BA3 ....133 E5
Overhill BS20 ....47 D4
Overndale Rd BS16 ......51 C6
Overndale Sch BS37 .....41 A7
Overnhill Ct BS16 ....51 D5
Overnhill Rd BS16 ....51 D5
Overnhurst Ct 2 BS16 ...51 D5
Overton 5 BS4 ....64 D1
Overton Rd BS6 ....49 E2
Owen Dr BS8 ....61 B4
Owen Gr BS9 ....49 B5
Owen St 18 BS5 ....64 B8
Owls Head Rd BS15 ......65 E6
Oxbarton BS34 ....36 F5
Oxen Leaze BS32 ....24 E2
Oxford Pl
14 Bristol,Baptist Mills BS5 .50 B1
21 Bristol,Clifton Wood BS8 .62 F6
Weston-S-M BS23 ....104 D7
Oxford Row BA1 ....141 B3
Oxford Sq BS24 ....106 B6
Oxford St Bristol BS2 ....143 C2
7 Bristol,Redfield BS5 ....64 C7
Bristol,The Dings BS2 .....64 A6
Bristol,Tyndall's Park
BS2 ....142 C4
Bristol,Windmill Hill BS3 ..63 F4
Weston-S-M BS23 ....104 D7
Oxhouse Ind Est BS22 ...89 A5
Oxhouse La Failand BS8 ..61 B6
Winford BS40 ....94 D6
Oxleaze BS13 ....79 D4
Oxleaze La BS41 ....78 E3
Ozenhay BS39 ....130 E6
Ozleworth BS15 ....66 A8

P

Pack Horse La BA2 ....118 F7
Paddock Cl
Bristol,Mangotsfield BS16 ..52 C6
Bristol,Patchway BS32 ....24 E2
Paddock Gdn BS14 ....79 F4
Paddock Gdns BS35 .....15 A5
Paddock Park Homes
BS22 ....89 B2
Paddock The
Banwell BS29 ....107 A3
Clevedon BS21 ....57 D2
Corston BA2 ....100 B7
Portishead BS20 ....45 D4
Paddock Woods BA2 ...102 D2
Paddocks The Bath BA2 .102 B1
Sandford BS25 ....108 C4
Thornbury BS35 ....8 D1
Weston-S-M BS23 ....104 D2
Padfield Cl BA2 ....101 B5
Padleigh Hill BA2 ......101 B2
Padmore Ct 7 BS5 ....64 D7
Padstow Rd BS4 ....79 F8
Pagans Hill BS40 ....95 D2
Page Ct BS16 ....51 F4
Page Rd BS16 ....51 D4
Page's Ct BS49 ....91 C8
Pages Mead BS11 ....47 C8
Painswick Ave BS34 .....36 B8
Painswick Dr BS37 ....27 E1
Palace Yard Mews BA1 .141 B2
Palmdale Cl BS30 ....66 A3
Palmer Ave BS35 ....22 C3
Palmer Row 8 BS23 ....104 E8
Palmer St BS23 ....104 E8
Palmer's Elm BS24 ....90 B4
Palmer's Way BS24 .....105 D2
Palmers Cl BS30 ....66 A6
Palmers La BA2 ....117 B3
Palmers Leaze BS32 .....37 A6
Palmerston Rd BS6 ......49 C4
Palmerston St 6 BS3 ....63 C3
Palmyra Rd BS3 ....63 B2
Panoramic The BS1 ....142 C3
Paquet Ho BS20 ....47 D5
Parade Ct BS5 ....50 F2
Parade The
Bristol,Bishopsworth BS13 .79 A6
Bristol,Patchway BS34 ....23 F1
Bristol,Shirehampton BS11 .47 E6
Chipping Sodbury BS37 ...28 A1
Paradise Row BS39 ......98 A6
Paragon Ct BS23 ....87 C1
Paragon Rd BS23 ....87 C1
Paragon Sch The BA2 ..102 A3
Paragon The Bath BA1 ..141 C3
Bristol BS8 ....62 F6
Parbrook Ct BS14 ....80 B5
Parfitt's Hill 8 BS5 ......64 F6
Parish Brook Rd BS48 ...59 B2
Parish Wharf Est BS20 ...45 D6
Park Ave Bath BA2 ......141 B1
Bristol,Patchway BS32 ....24 A2
Bristol,Rose Green BS5 ...64 E8
Bristol,Upper Eastville BS5 50 D3
Bristol,Windmill Hill BS3 ..63 E3
Frampton Cotterell BS36 ..38 B6
Winterbourne BS36 ....37 E7
Yatton BS49 ....74 B1
Park Batch BS40 ....110 F3
Park Cl
Bristol,Cadbury Heath BS30 66 B5
Bristol,Kingswood BS15 ...65 E7
Keynsham BS31 ....81 D5
Paulton BS39 ....132 D5
Park Cres
Bristol,Cadbury Heath BS30 66 B5
Bristol,Frenchay BS16 .....37 C1
Bristol,Rose Green BS5 ...64 E8
Park Ct 5 BS23 ....104 E5
Park End BS29 ....106 E4
Park Farm Ct 13 BS30 ...65 F4
Park Farm Village Gn
BS36 ....38 B6
Park Gdns BA1 ....101 D8
Park Gr BS9 ....49 C5
Park Hill BS11 ....47 F6
Park La Bath BA1 ....101 D7
Blagdon BS40 ....110 F3
Bristol BS2 ....142 C3
Faulkland BA3 ....135 B1
North Nibley GL11 ....5 E7
Winterbourne BS36 ....38 B6
Park Leaze BS34 ....23 E1
Park Mews BS49 ....91 D3
Park Pl Bath BA1 ....141 A4
Bristol,Clay Hill BS5 ......50 E3
Bristol,Tyndall's Park
BS2 ....142 C3
Bristol,Victoria Park BS8 ..142 B3
Weston-S-M BS23 ....104 D8
Park Prim Sch The BS15 .65 E8
Park Rd Bath BA1 ....101 B7
Bristol,Brandon Hill BS3 ..142 B1
Bristol,Cadbury Heath BS30 66 B5
Bristol,Kingswood BS15 ...65 D8
Bristol,Northville BS7 .....36 A1
Bristol,Shirehampton BS11 .47 F6
Bristol,Staple Hill BS16 ....51 E5
Bristol,Stapleton BS16 ....50 D5
Clevedon BS21 ....57 D4
Congresbury BS49 ....91 E3
Cromhall GL12 ....10 B4
Keynsham BS31 ....81 E4
Paulton BS39 ....132 D5
Thornbury BS35 ....8 B2
Park Row Bristol BS1 ...142 C3
Frampton Cotterell BS36 ..38 A8
Park St Bath BA1 ....141 A4
Bristol,Brandon Hill BS1 ..142 C3
Bristol,Crew's Hole BS5 ...64 F8
Bristol,Totterdown BS4 ....64 A3
Hawkesbury Upton GL9 ...20 A2
Iron Acton BS37 ....26 D4
Park Street Ave BS1 ...142 C3
Park Street Mews BA1 .141 A4
Park The
Bristol,Frenchay BS16 .....37 B1
Bristol,Kingswood BS15 ...65 E8
Bristol,Patchway BS32 ....24 C3
Bristol,Willsbridge BS30 ..66 B1
Keynsham BS31 ....81 E6
Portishead BS20 ....45 F5
Yatton BS49 ....74 B1
Park View Bath BA2 ....101 D6
Bristol BS15 ....65 E7
Yate BS37 ....39 E8
Park View Ave BS35 ......8 C2

Park View Ct BS16 ......51 E5
Park View Terr BS5 ......64 E8
Park Villas BS23 ......104 D8
Park Way Bristol BS30 ......66 B5
  Midsomer Norton BA3 ...139 A8
Park Wood Cl BS14 ......79 F4
Parker St BS3 ......63 B3
Parkers Ave BS30 ......67 C7
Parkers Barton BS5 ......64 B6
Parkes Barton BS10 ......35 E4
Parkes Rd BS24 ......106 C5
Parkfield Ave 3 BS5 ......64 D7
Parkfield Gdns BS39 ...113 D3
Parkfield Rd
  Axbridge BS26 ......125 D1
  Pucklechurch BS16 ......53 A6
Parkhurst Ave BS16 ...51 B4
Parkhurst Rd BS23 ...105 A7
Parkland Way BS35 ......8 C3
Parklands Bristol BS15 ...65 E8
  High Littleton BS39 ...115 D2
Parklands Ave BS22 ...89 A4
Parklands Rd BS3 ......62 A4
Parkside BS36 ......37 E6
Parkside Gdns BS5 ......50 B4
Parkside Inf Sch BA1 ...141 B3
Parkstone Ave BS7 ......49 F6
Parkwall Cres BS30 ...65 F4
Parkwall Rd BS30 ......66 A4
Parkway Bristol BS34 ...37 A4
  Camerton BA2 ......116 E2
Parkway La BA2 ......116 D3
Parkway N BS34 ......37 A4
Parkway Trad Est 8 BS2 ...49 F2
Parkwell Cty Prim Sch
  BS30 ......66 A4
Parliament St BS4 ......64 A4
Parnall Cres BS37 ......27 C2
Parnall Rd BS16 ......51 A3
Parnall Road Ind Est
  BS16 ......51 A3
Parnell Rd Bristol BS16 ...50 E7
  Clevedon BS21 ......57 D3
Parry Cl BA2 ......101 B4
Parry's Cl BS9 ......48 E5
Parry's La BS9 ......48 F5
Parrys Gr BS9 ......48 E5
Parslow Barton 4 BS5 ...65 A7
Parson St BS3 ......63 B2
Parson Street Prim Sch
  BS3 ......63 C2
Parson Street Sta BS3 ...63 B2
Parsonage Cl BS40 ......94 F6
Parsonage La
  Axbridge BS26 ......125 E2
  Bath BA1 ......141 B2
  Chilcompton BA3 ......138 C4
  Pensford BS39 ......97 D6
  Winford BS40 ......94 F6
Parsonage Rd BS41 ......62 C2
Parsons Ave BS34 ......36 F5
Parsons Gn Clevedon BS21 73 C8
  Weston-S-M BS22 ......89 A3
Parsons Mead BS48 ......76 F7
Parsons Paddock BS14 ...80 A7
Parsons Way BS25 ......124 E6
Parsons Wlk BS30 ......66 D7
Partis Coll BA1 ......101 A8
Partis Way BA1 ......101 A8
Partition St BS1 ......142 C2
Partridge Cl BS22 ......88 F1
Partridge Dr BS16 ......51 C6
Partridge Rd BS16 ......53 C4
Passage Leaze BS11 ......47 D6
Passage Rd Aust BS35 ...12 F7
  Bristol,Eastfield BS9 ......49 A8
  Bristol,Henbury BS10 ...34 F3
Passage Road Brentry Hill
  BS9,BS10 ......35 A2
Passage St BS2 ......143 B2
Pastures Ave BS22 ......89 C3
Pastures The BA15 ......120 E3
Patch Croft BS21 ......73 C8
Patch Ct BS16 ......52 B4
Patch Elm La BS37 ......26 F7
Patch La BS37 ......27 C1
Patchway BS34 ......36 B8
Patchway Brook BS32 ...24 C2
Patchway CE Prim Sch
  BS34 ......24 C1
Patchway High Sch BS32 24 B1
Patchway Sta BS34 ......36 C6
Patchway Trad Est BS34 ...35 E7
Patridge Cl BS37 ......27 F4
Patterson Ho 8 BS1 ...143 B1
Paul St BS2 ......142 C4
Paul's Cswy BS49 ......91 D4
Paulman Gdns BS41 ......77 F8
Paulmont Rise BS39 ...114 E1
Paulton Dr BS7 ......49 C4
Paulton Inf Sch BS39 ...132 E5
Paulton Jun Sch BS39 ...132 E5
Paulton La BA2,BA3 ...133 D7
Paulton Meml Hospl
  BS39 ......132 F4
Paulton Rd
  Farrington Gurney BS39 ...132 B4
  Midsomer Norton BA3 ...132 F1
  Paulton BS39 ......132 B7
Paultow Ave BS3 ......63 E3
Paultow Rd BS3 ......63 E3
Paulwood Rd BS39 ......114 E1
Pavey Cl BS13 ......79 C4
Pavey Rd BS13 ......79 C4
Pavilions The BS4 ......64 C1
Pawlett BS24 ......105 A2

Pawlett Rd BS13 ......79 C3
Pawlett Wlk BS13 ......79 C3
Paxton BS16 ......50 E8
Paybridge Rd BS13 ......78 F4
Payne Dr BS5 ......64 B7
Payne Rd BS24 ......105 D2
Peache La BS16 ......51 E6
Peache Rd BS16 ......51 F6
Peacocks La BS15 ......65 C7
Pear Tree Gdns BS24 ...122 C6
Pear Tree Hey BS37 ......27 E5
Pear Tree Ind Est BS40 ...109 C4
Pear Tree Rd BS32 ......24 C2
Pearces Hill BS16 ......51 B7
Pearl St BS3 ......63 B3
Pearsall Rd BS30 ......65 C2
Pearse Cl BS22 ......89 B5
Peart Cl BS13 ......78 E5
Peart Dr BS13 ......78 E4
Peartree Cl BS13 ......79 B4
Peartree Field BS20 ......45 F5
Peartree La
  Bristol,Lower Soundwell
  BS15 ......51 F2
  Bristol,St George BS5 ......65 B6
Peasedown St John Prim Sch
  BA2 ......134 C7
Pedder Rd BS21 ......57 D1
Peel St BS5 ......143 C4
Peg Hill BS37 ......27 F4
Pegasus Pk BS34 ......36 C6
Pegasus Rd BS34 ......35 D7
Pelican Cl BS22 ......105 F8
Pemberton Ct BS16 ......51 C5
Pembery Rd BS3 ......63 B3
Pembroke Ave BS11 ......47 D6
Pembroke Ct BS21 ......57 C4
Pembroke Gate BS8 ......49 A1
Pembroke Gr BS8 ......142 A3
Pembroke Mans BS8 ......142 A4
Pembroke Pl
  Bristol,Hotwells BS8 ......142 A1
  Bristol,St Pauls BS1 ......143 B4
Pembroke Rd
  Bristol,Clifton BS8 ......142 A4
  Bristol,Shirehampton BS11 ...47 E6
  Bristol,Southville BS3 ...63 C4
  Bristol,Upper Soundwell
  BS15 ......51 E2
  Portishead BS20 ......44 E4
  Weston-S-M BS23 ......104 F4
Pembroke St BS2 ......143 B4
Pembroke Vale BS8 ......142 A4
Pen Park Rd BS10 ......35 D3
Penard Way BS15 ......65 F7
Penarth Dr BS24 ......105 A1
Pendennis Ave BS16 ......51 D4
Pendennis Ho 5 BS16 ...51 D5
Pendennis Pk BS4 ......64 D2
Pendennis Rd BS16 ......51 D5
Pendlesham Gdns BS23 ...88 A1
Pendock Cl BS30 ......66 C1
Pendock Ct BS16 ......52 B7
Pendock Rd Bristol BS16 ...51 C6
  Winterbourne BS36 ......37 E5
Penfield Rd BS2 ......50 A2
Penlea Ct BS11 ......47 D7
Penn Ct BS26 ......125 C1
Penn Dr BS16 ......37 C1
Penn Gdns BA1 ......101 A8
Penn Hill Rd BA1 ......84 A1
Penn Lea Ct BA1 ......101 B8
Penn Lea Rd BA1 ......101 B8
Penn St BS1 ......143 B3
Penn Way BS26 ......125 C1
Pennard BS24 ......105 A2
Pennard Ct BS14 ......80 B5
Pennard Gn BA2 ......101 A6
Penngrove BS30 ......66 A3
Pennine Gdns BS23 ......88 A1
Pennine Rd BS30 ......66 C4
Pennlea BS13 ......79 C7
Pennon Rise BS1 ......142 C1
Penns The BS21 ......57 C2
Pennycress BS22 ......105 D7
Pennyquick BA2 ......100 D6
Pennyquick View BA2 ...100 F6
Pennyroyal Gr BS16 ......50 E4
Pennywell Ct 3 BS5 ......64 A8
Pennywell Est 3 BS2 ......57 D2
Pennywell Rd BS5 ......64 A8
Penpole Ave BS11 ......47 E6
Penpole Cl BS11 ......47 D7
Penpole La BS11 ......47 E7
Penpole Pk BS11 ......47 E7
Penpole Pl BS11 ......47 E6
Penrice Cl BS22 ......88 C2
Penrith Gdns BS10 ......49 D8
Penrose BS14 ......79 F7
Penrose Dr BS32 ......36 D7
Pensford Ct BS14 ......80 D5
Pensford Cty Prim Sch
  BS39 ......97 D4
Pensford Hill BS39 ......97 D5
Pensford La BS39 ......97 A3
Pensford Old Rd BS39 ...97 E3
Pentagon The BS9 ......48 B5
Penthouse Hill BA1 ......85 F3
Pentire Ave BS13 ......79 A6
Pentland Ave BS35 ......15 C8
Peppershells La BS39 ...98 C6
Pepys Cl BS31 ......82 D2
Pera Pl BA1 ......141 C4
Pera Rd BA1 ......141 C4
Percival Rd BS8 ......62 F8
Percy Pl 13 BA1 ......85 A1
Percy St 8 BS3 ......63 D4

Percy Walker Ct BS16 ...51 C6
Peregrine Cl BS22 ......88 F1
Perfect View BA1 ......85 A1
Perrett Way BS20 ......47 E4
Perretts Ct BS1 ......142 C1
Perrin Cl BS39 ......131 E8
Perrings The BS48 ......75 E8
Perrinpit Rd BS36 ......25 E2
Perrott Rd BS15 ......52 A1
Perry Court Inf Sch BS14 80 A6
Perry Court Jun Sch
  BS14 ......80 A6
Perry Rd BS1 ......143 A3
Perry St BS5 ......64 A8
Perrycroft Ave BS13 ......79 A6
Perrycroft Rd BS13 ......79 A6
Perrymans Cl BS16 ......51 A6
Perrymead Bath BA2 ...102 B3
  Weston-S-M BS22 ......89 B5
Perrymead Ct BA2 ......102 B4
Perrys Lea BS32 ......24 D2
Pesley Cl BS13 ......79 A4
Peter's Terr BS5 ......64 B7
Petercole Dr BS13 ......79 A6
Peterside BS39 ......131 E8
Peterson Sq BS13 ......79 C3
Petersway Gdns BS5 ......65 A6
Petherbridge Way BS7 ...50 A5
Petherton Cl BS15 ......65 C5
Petherton Gdns BS14 ...80 B7
Petherton Rd BS14 ......80 B7
Petherton Road Inf Sch
  BS14 ......80 B7
Pethick Ho BS4 ......79 F8
Peto Garden at Iford Manor
  The ★ BA15 ......120 E3
Peto Gr BA15 ......120 F3
Pettigrove Gdns BS15 ...65 E7
Pettigrove Rd BS15 ......65 E6
Pevensey Wlk BS4 ......79 D7
Peverell Cl BS10 ......34 F3
Peverell Dr BS10 ......34 F3
Pheonix Bsns Pk BS3 ...63 A2
Philadelphia Ct BS1 ...143 B3
Philip St
  Bristol,St Philip's Marsh
  BS2 ......64 B5
  Bristol,Windmill Hill BS3 ...63 D4
Philippa Cl BS14 ......80 A7
Philips Ho 2 BS2 ......143 B4
Phillips Rd BS23 ......105 A6
Phillis Hill BS39 ......132 F4
Phippen St 1 BS1 ......143 B1
Phipps Barton BS15 ......65 B8
Phipps St BS3 ......63 B4
Phoenix Gr BS6 ......49 C5
Phoenix Ho Bath BA1 ...141 B4
  Bristol BS5 ......64 B6
Pickedmoor La BS35 ......7 E5
Pickwick Rd BA1 ......85 A2
Picton Mews 8 BS6 ......49 E1
Picton St BS6 ......49 E1
Pier Cl BS20 ......45 E7
Pier Rd BS20 ......45 E7
Pierrepont Pl BA1 ......141 C2
Pierrepont St BA1 ......141 C2
Pigeon House Dr BS13 ...79 D4
Pigeon La BS40 ......93 E1
Pigott Ave BS13 ......79 A4
Pilemarsh BS5 ......64 D7
Pilgrims Way Bristol BS16 51 D8
  Chew Stoke BS40 ......112 D8
  Shirehampton BS11 ......47 C7
  Weston-S-M BS22 ......88 E3
Pilgrims Wharf BS4 ......64 E7
Pilkington Cl BS34 ......36 C2
Pill Rd Abbots Leigh BS8 ...47 F1
  Pill BS20,BS8 ......47 E2
Pill St BS20 ......47 D4
Pill Way BS21 ......57 B2
Pillingers Gdns BS6 ......49 B2
Pillingers Rd BS15 ......65 C7
Pilning St BS35 ......23 C8
Pilning Sta BS35 ......22 F5
Pimm's La BS22 ......88 B2
Pimms La BS22 ......88 B2
Pimpernel Mead BS32 ...36 E7
Pinchay La BS40 ......95 A4
Pincots La GL12 ......18 B3
Pine Cl Thornbury BS35 ......8 C1
  Weston-S-M BS22 ......88 D2
Pine Ct Chew Magna BS40 ...96 B3
  Keynsham BS31 ......81 C4
  Radstock BA3 ......134 A2
Pine Gr BS7 ......36 A1
Pine Grove Pl BS7 ......49 D3
Pine Hill BS22 ......88 D2
Pine Lea BS24 ......122 B6
Pine Rd BS10 ......35 B3
Pine Ridge Cl BS9 ......48 C4
Pine Wlk BA3 ......133 E1
Pinecroft Bristol BS14 ...79 F7
  Portishead BS20 ......44 F6
Pinefield Sch BS9 ......49 B7
Pines Cl BA3 ......138 D3
Pines La BS32 ......14 D3
Pines Rd BS30 ......66 C1
Pines Way Bath BA2 ...141 A2
  Radstock BA3 ......134 A2
Pines Way Ind Est BA2 ...141 A2
Pinetree Rd BS24 ......106 D4
Pinewood BS15 ......51 F1
Pinewood Ave BA3 ......132 F1
Pinewood Cl BS9 ......49 B7
Pinewood Gr BA3 ......132 F1
Pinewood Rd BA3 ......132 F1

Pinewood Way SN14 ......70 F7
Pinhay Rd BS13 ......79 B6
Pinkers Mead BS16 ......52 C6
Pinkhams Twist BS14 ...80 A5
Pinnell Gr BS16 ......52 C7
Pinnell Gr BS16 ......52 C7
Pioneer Ave BA2 ......101 F1
Pioneer Pk BS4 ......64 C5
Pipe La BS1 ......142 C2
Pipehouse La BA2 ......119 F4
Piper Rd BS37 ......27 C1
Pippin Cl BA2 ......134 D7
Pippin Ct 4 BS30 ......65 F4
Pit La BS40 ......111 F5
Pit Rd BA3 ......133 B1
Pitch & Pay La BS9 ......48 E3
Pitch & Pay Pk BS9 ......48 E3
Pitch La BS6 ......49 D1
Pitchcombe BS37 ......39 C7
Pitchcombe Gdns BS9 ...48 D7
Pitching The BA3 ......138 D5
Pitfour Terr BA2 ......116 B2
Pitlochry Cl BS7 ......35 F1
Pitman Ct BA1 ......85 C2
Pitman Ho BA2 ......101 D4
Pitman Rd BS23 ......104 E6
Pitt Rd BS7 ......49 E5
Pitt's La BS40 ......96 B1
Pittville Cl BS35 ......8 C3
Pittville Pl 16 BS6 ......49 B1
Pitway Cl BS39 ......131 E4
Pitway La BS39 ......131 E4
Pixash Bsns Ctr BS31 ...82 B5
Pixash La BS31 ......82 C5
Pizey Ave BS21 ......57 B2
Pizey Ave Ind Est 2
  BS21 ......57 C2
Pizey Cl BS21 ......57 B2
Plain The
  Norton St Philip BA2 ...136 E4
  Thornbury BS35 ......8 B1
Players St BS16 ......37 B3
Playford Gdns BS11 ......47 E8
Pleasant Ho 4 BS16 ......51 D5
Pleasant Pl BA1 ......86 C2
Pleasant Pl BA1 ......86 C2
Pleshey Cl BS22 ......88 D2
Plimsoll Ho
  3 Bristol BS1 ......143 B1
  5 Bristol,Woolcott Park
  BS6 ......49 B1
Ploughed Paddock BS48 59 D1
Plover Cl
  Weston-S-M BS22 ......88 F1
  Yate BS37 ......27 C2
Plovers Rise BA3 ......134 A3
Plowright Ho 7 BS15 ...65 B5
Plum Tree Rd BS22 ......105 E8
Plumers Cl 4 BS21 ......57 C1
Plumley Cres BS24 ......106 A4
Plumley Cl BS23 ......104 C4
Plummer's Hill BS5 ......64 E8
Plumpton Ct BS16 ......37 F1
Plumptre Cl BS39 ......132 E5
Plumptre Rd BS39 ......132 E5
Plumtree Cl BS25 ......108 A1
Plunder St BS49 ......92 B7
Plumption Ct BA2 ......115 B4
Podgers Dr BA1 ......84 B2
Podium The BA1 ......141 C2
Poets Cnr BA3 ......139 C8
Poets' Cl BS5 ......64 D8
Polar Gdns SN14 ......31 E4
Polden Cl BS48 ......59 E1
Polden Ho BS3 ......63 D3
Polden Rd
  Portishead BS20 ......45 B5
  Weston-S-M BS23 ......104 F8
Polestar Way 5 BS24 ...106 A4
Pollard Rd BS22 ......89 B4
Polly Barnes Cl 4 BS15 ...65 B5
Polly Barnes Hill BS15 ...65 B5
Polygon Rd BS8 ......142 A2
Polygon The
  Avonmouth BS11 ......33 D1
  17 Bristol BS8 ......62 F6
Pomfrett Gdns BS14 ......80 E5
Pomphrey Hill BS16 ......52 C4
Pond Cotts BA2 ......135 D2
Ponsford Rd BS4 ......64 B1
Ponting Cl BS5 ......51 A1
Pool Cnr BS32 ......14 B2
Pool Ho BS34 ......36 A8
Pool La BS40 ......95 A2
Pool Rd BS15 ......51 E3
Poole Court Dr BS37 ...27 E2
Poole Ho BA2 ......100 F5
Poole St BS11 ......47 B8
Pooles Wharf BS8 ......142 A1
Pooles Wharf Ct BS8 ...142 A1
Poolmead Rd BA2 ......100 F5
Poor Hill BA2 ......115 F4
Pope's Wlk BA2 ......102 B3
Poplar Ave BS9 ......48 D6
Poplar Cl Bath BA2 ......101 D4
  Bristol BS30 ......66 C6
Poplar Dr BS16 ......53 B5
Poplar Fields BS36 ......66 D6
Poplar Gardens Ho BS15 65 E8
Poplar La GL12 ......18 B4
Poplar Pl Bristol BS16 ...51 A3
  17 Weston-S-M BS23 ...104 E8
Poplar Rd Bath BA2 ......118 D8
  Bristol,Crofts End BS5 ......50 F1
  Bristol,Mangotsfield BS13 ...78 F7
  Bristol,North Common BS30 66 D6
  Bristol,St George BS15 ...65 A5

Poplar Terr BS15 ......65 F8
Poplar Way SN14 ......70 F5
Poplar Way E BS15 ......33 F4
Poplar Way W BS10,BS11 33 D6
Poplar Wlk BS24 ......105 E5
Poplars The
  Easton-in-G BS20 ......47 B4
  Weston-S-M BS22 ......89 A1
Pople's La BA3 ......140 F1
Poppy Cl BS22 ......89 A5
Poppy Mead BS32 ......36 E7
Porlock Cl
  3 Clevedon BS21 ......57 E1
  Weston-S-M BS23 ......104 F2
Porlock Gdns BS48 ......59 E1
Porlock Rd Bath BA2 ...102 A1
  Bristol BS3 ......63 D3
Port Elizabeth Ho BS10 ...35 E1
Port Side Cl 5 BS5 ......64 F6
Port View BS20 ......47 C5
Portal Rd BS24 ......106 D4
Portbury Comm BS20 ...45 F4
Portbury Gr BS11 ......47 D6
Portbury Hundred The
  BS20 ......46 C4
Portbury La BS20 ......60 E7
Portbury Way BS20 ......46 E5
Portbury Wlk BS11 ......47 D6
Portishead Bsns Pk BS20 45 E5
Portishead Lo BS20 ......45 D4
Portishead Prim Sch
  BS20 ......45 C5
Portishead Rd BS22 ......89 B4
Portishead Way BS3 ......62 E3
Portland Cl BS48 ......59 D1
Portland Ct Bristol BS1 ...142 B1
  2 Bristol,Upper Soundwell
  BS16 ......51 D3
Portland Dr BS20 ......45 E4
Portland Mans BS2 ......143 B4
Portland Pl Bath BA1 ...141 B4
  Bristol BS16 ......51 D3
Portland Rd BA1 ......141 B4
Portland Sq BS2 ......143 B4
Portland St
  Bristol,Clifton BS8 ......62 F7
  Bristol,Upper Soundwell
  BS16 ......51 D3
Portland Terr BA1 ......141 B4
Portmeade Dro BS26 ...125 C1
Portmeirion Cl BS14 ......80 B5
Portview Rd BS11 ......47 B8
Portwall La BS1 ......143 B1
Portwall La E 10 BS1 ...143 B1
Portway
  Bristol,Shirehampton BS11 47 C6
  Bristol,Sneyd Park BS9 ...48 C3
Portway La BS37 ......28 E2
Portway Rdbt BS11 ......47 C8
Post Office La
  Blagdon BS40 ......110 D3
  Flax Bourton BS48 ......76 F7
Post Office Rd BS24 ...106 C5
Poston Way BA15 ......120 E7
Pottery Cl BS23 ......105 A6
Potts Cl BA1 ......85 F3
Pound Dr BS16 ......50 F5
Pound La Bristol BS16 ...50 F4
  Nailsea BS48 ......59 D3
Pound Mead BS40 ......94 C8
Pound Rd BS15 ......51 F2
Pound The
  Almondsbury BS32 ......24 A5
  Redhill BS40 ......93 D3
  Thornbury BS35 ......7 B6
Pountney Dr BS5 ......64 B8
Pow's Hill BA3 ......133 D5
Pow's Orch BA3 ......133 A1
Pow's Rd BS15 ......65 D7
Powis Cl BS22 ......88 C2
Powlett Ct BA2 ......102 B7
Powlett Rd BA2 ......102 B8
Poyntz Ct BS30 ......65 F3
Poyntz Rd BS4 ......79 F8
Preacher Cl BS5 ......65 B6
Preanes Gn BS22 ......89 A2
Precinct The BS20 ......45 D5
Preddy's La BS5 ......65 A6
Prescot Cl BS22 ......88 B2
Prescott BS37 ......39 D8
Press Moor Dr BS30 ...65 F4
Prestbury BS37 ......39 D8
Preston Wlk BS4 ......64 A1
Prestwick Cl BS4 ......64 D1
Pretoria Rd BS34 ......35 F8
Prewett St BS1 ......143 B1
Priddy Cl BA2 ......101 B5
Priddy Ct BS14 ......80 B5
Priddy Dr BS14 ......80 B5
Priests Way BS22 ......88 D2
Priestwood Cl BS10 ......35 D4
Primrose
  Bristol,Patchway BS32 ...24 D2
  Bristol,Two Mile Hill BS15 ...65 C8
Primrose Dr BS35 ......8 D2
Primrose La Bristol BS15 ...51 C1
  Midsomer Norton BA3 ...133 B1
Primrose Terr BS15 ......51 C1
Prince St BS1 ......143 A1
Prince Street Rdbt BS1 143 A2
Prince's Bldgs 19 BS8 ...62 F6
Prince's Rd BS21 ......57 D3
Prince's St Bristol BS2 ...143 C4

Prince's St *continued*
Radstock BA3 .... 133 E5
Princes Bldgs BA1 .... 141 B3
Princes Ct BS30 .... 65 F4
Princes St BA1 .... 141 B2
Princes' La BS8 .... 62 F6
Princes' Pl BS7 .... 49 E3
Princess Cl BS31 .... 81 E4
Princess Gdns BS16 .... 50 D6
Princess Row BS2 .... 143 A4
Princess St
Bristol,Newton BS2 .... 64 A7
Bristol,Windmill Hill BS3 .... 63 E4
Princess Victoria St BS8 .... 62 F6
Prinknash Ct 6 BS37 .... 39 D7
Prior Park Bldgs BA2 .... 102 B5
Prior Park Coll BA2 .... 102 C2
Prior Park Cotts BA2 .... 141 C1
Prior Park Gdns BA2 .... 102 B5
Prior Park Landscape Gdn★ BA2 .... 102 C3
Prior Park Rd BA2 .... 102 B4
Prior's Hill 11 BS6 .... 49 D1
Priors Hill BA2 .... 116 A2
Priors Lea BS37 .... 27 E1
Priory Ave BS9 .... 49 A7
Priory Cl Bath BA2 .... 102 B2
Midsomer Norton BA3 .... 133 A1
Priory Com Sch BS22 .... 89 B3
Priory Court Rd BS9 .... 49 A7
Priory Ct
Bristol,Hanham Green BS15 .... 65 C3
Bristol,Upper Knowle BS4 .... 64 B2
Priory Dene BS9 .... 49 A7
Priory Farm Trad Est BS20 .... 46 D3
Priory Gdns
Bristol,Henleaze BS7 .... 49 F8
Bristol,Shirehampton BS11 .... 47 D7
Easton-in-G BS20 .... 47 B4
Priory Mews BS23 .... 105 B7
Priory Rd
Bristol,Shirehampton BS8 .... 47 D6
Bristol,Tyndall's Park BS8 .... 142 C4
Bristol,Upper Knowle BS4 .... 64 B2
Easton-in-G BS20 .... 47 B4
Keynsham BS31 .... 81 E7
Portbury BS20 .... 46 D3
Weston-S-M BS23 .... 105 A7
Priory Wlk BS20 .... 46 D3
Priston Cl BS22 .... 89 B5
Priston La BA2 .... 117 A5
Priston Mill★ BA2 .... 117 B8
Priston Rd BA2 .... 117 D6
Pritchard St BS2 .... 143 B4
Probyn Cl BS16 .... 51 A7
Proctor Cl BS4 .... 64 D1
Proctor Ho BS1 .... 143 B1
Promenade The BS7 .... 49 D2
Prospect Ave
Bristol,Chester Park BS15 .... 51 B1
Bristol,Kingsdown BS2 .... 143 A4
Prospect Cl
Easter Compton BS35 .... 23 A2
Frampton Cotterell BS36 .... 37 F8
Winterbourne BS36 .... 37 E4
Prospect Cres BS15 .... 51 F2
Prospect Gdns BA1 .... 85 F1
Prospect La BS36 .... 37 F8
Prospect Pl
Bath,Beacon Hill BA1 .... 85 A1
Bath,Weston BA1 .... 84 C2
Bathford BA1 .... 86 D2
7 Bristol,Bedminster BS3 .... 63 C3
1 Bristol,Montpelier BS6 .... 49 D2
Bristol,Moorfields BS5 .... 64 C8
10 Weston-S-M BS23 .... 104 E8
Prospect Rd Bath BA2 .... 102 C4
Severn Beach BS35 .... 22 A5
Proud Cross BS40 .... 129 E4
Providence La BS41 .... 61 F2
Providence Pl BS2 .... 143 C2
Providence View BS41 .... 62 A1
Prowse Cl BS35 .... 8 C1
Prowse's La BS26 .... 125 A1
Prudham St 7 BS5 .... 50 C1
Publow La BS39 .... 97 E5
Pucklechurch CE Prim Sch BS16 .... 53 C6
Pucklechurch Trad Est BS16 .... 53 B4
Pudding Pie Cl BS40 .... 109 A5
Pudding Pie La BS40 .... 109 A6
Puffin Cl BS22 .... 105 F8
Pullin Ct BS30 .... 66 D4
Pullins Gn 3 BS35 .... 8 B1
Pulteney Ave BA2 .... 102 B6
Pulteney Gdns BA2 .... 102 B6
Pulteney Gr BA2 .... 102 B6
Pulteney Mews BA2 .... 102 B7
Pulteney Rd BA2 .... 102 B6
Pulteney Terr BA2 .... 102 B6
Pump La Bathford BA1 .... 86 B2
Bristol BS1 .... 143 B1
Redhill BS40 .... 93 D2
Tockington BS32 .... 14 D4
Pump Sq BS20 .... 47 D5
Purcell Wlk BS4 .... 79 D7
Purdown Rd BS7 .... 49 F5
Purdue Cl BS22 .... 89 B3
Purlewent Dr BA1 .... 84 C1
Purn La BS24 .... 122 A8
Purn Rd BS24 .... 121 F8
Purn Way BS24 .... 122 B7
Pursey Dr BS32 .... 36 F6
Purton Cl BS15 .... 65 E6
Purton Rd BS7 .... 49 D2
Purving Row BS24 .... 122 C1
Purving Row La BS24 .... 122 C1
Puttingthorpe Dr BS22 .... 105 C7
Puxley Cl BS14 .... 80 E6
Puxton La BS24 .... 90 D3
Puxton Moor La BS24 .... 90 E2
Puxton Rd BS24 .... 90 C2
Pye Cnr BS25 .... 108 D4
Pye Croft BS32 .... 24 E3
Pyecroft Ave BS9 .... 49 C7
Pyghtell The SN14 .... 31 E5
Pylewell La BS25 .... 108 D1
Pylle Hill Cres BS3 .... 63 F4
Pyne Point BS21 .... 57 C3
Pynne Cl BS14 .... 80 F5
Pynne Rd BS14 .... 80 F5
Pyracantha Wlk BS14 .... 80 A6

Q

Quadrangle The BS37 .... 39 C4
Quadrant BS32 .... 24 B3
Quadrant E BS16 .... 51 C3
Quadrant The
Bristol,Patchway BS32 .... 24 B2
Bristol,Westbury Park BS6 .... 49 B3
Quadrant W BS16 .... 51 C3
Quaker Cl 1 BS35 .... 8 B1
Quaker La BS35 .... 8 B1
Quaker's Cl BS16 .... 51 D8
Quaker's Rd BS16 .... 51 E8
Quakers' Friars BS1 .... 143 B3
Quantock Cl BS30 .... 66 C5
Quantock Rd Bristol BS3 .... 63 D3
Portishead BS20 .... 45 B5
Weston-S-M BS23 .... 104 E4
Quantock Terr BA2 .... 102 E2
Quantocks BA2 .... 102 A1
Quarries The BS32 .... 24 C6
Quarrington Rd BS7 .... 49 E5
Quarry Barton BS16 .... 37 C4
Quarry Cl Bath BA2 .... 101 F1
Limpley Stoke BA2 .... 120 D6
Quarry Hay BS40 .... 112 D8
Quarry La Bristol BS11 .... 34 C1
Winterbourne BS36 .... 37 E4
Quarry Mead BS35 .... 14 F5
Quarry Rd Alveston BS35 .... 14 F5
Bath BA2 .... 102 D6
Bristol,Frenchay BS16 .... 51 C7
Bristol,Jefferies Hill BS15 .... 65 D6
Chipping Sodbury BS37 .... 28 A1
Sandford BS25 .... 108 A2
Quarry Rise BS24 .... 121 F8
Quarry Rock Gdns Residential Pk BA2 .... 102 D4
Quarry Stps 8 BS8 .... 49 A2
Quarry The BS11 .... 34 C1
Quarry Vale Cotts BA2 .... 102 B1
Quarry Way Bristol BS16 .... 38 A1
Bristol,Fishponds BS16 .... 50 E5
Nailsea BS48 .... 59 D2
Quarrymans Ct BA2 .... 102 B1
Quay St BS1 .... 143 A3
Quays Ave BS20 .... 45 E5
Quays The BS1 .... 142 C1
Quayside BS8 .... 142 B2
Quayside La 4 BS5 .... 64 F6
Quebec BA2 .... 101 A6
Quedgeley BS37 .... 39 C8
Queen Ann Rd BS5 .... 64 B6
Queen Charlotte St BS1 .... 143 A2
Queen Charlton La BS14 .... 80 E2
Queen Elizabeth's Hospital Sch BS8 .... 142 B3
Queen Quay BS1 .... 143 A2
Queen Sq Bath BA1 .... 141 B2
Bristol BS1 .... 143 A2
Saltford BS31 .... 82 F3
Queen Square Ave 7 BS1 .... 143 A2
Queen Square Pl BA1 .... 141 B3
Queen St Avonmouth BS11 .... 33 A1
Bath BA1 .... 141 B2
Bristol BS2 .... 143 B3
Bristol,Lower Easton BS5 .... 50 D3
Bristol,St George BS15 .... 65 B8
Queen Victoria Rd BS6 .... 49 A4
Queen Victoria St BS2 .... 64 A6
Queen's Ave Bristol BS8 .... 142 B3
Portishead BS20 .... 45 C5
Queen's Ct BS8 .... 142 B3
Queen's Dr Bath BA2 .... 102 A2
Bristol BS7 .... 49 C5
Queen's Par BA1 .... 141 B3
Queen's Parade Pl BA1 .... 141 B3
Queen's Rd
Bristol,Ashley Down BS7 .... 49 F5
Bristol,Bishopsworth BS13, BS41 .... 78 F4
Bristol,Cadbury Heath BS30 .... 66 B4
Bristol,Crew's Hole BS5 .... 64 F7
Bristol,Victoria Park BS8 .... 142 B3
Clevedon BS21 .... 57 D3
Pucklechurch BS16 .... 53 B5
Radstock BA3 .... 134 B2
Weston-S-M BS23 .... 87 D1
Queen's Way BS22 .... 88 F4
Queens Down Ct BS4 .... 64 C3
Queens Down Gdns BS4 .... 64 C3
Queens Dr BS15 .... 65 B4
Queens Gate BS9 .... 48 D5
Queens Par BS1 .... 142 C2
Queens Rd Banwell BS29 .... 107 A3
Queens Rd *continued*
Bristol BS4 .... 64 C2
Keynsham BS31 .... 81 D4
Nailsea BS48 .... 59 D1
Portishead BS20 .... 44 E4
Queens Way BS20 .... 44 E4
Queens Wlk BS35 .... 8 B3
Queenscote BS20 .... 45 F5
Queensdale Cres BS4 .... 64 A1
Queensdown Gdns BS4 .... 64 C2
Queenshill Rd BS4 .... 64 A1
Queensholm Ave BS16 .... 37 E1
Queensholm Cl BS16 .... 37 E1
Queensholm Cres BS16 .... 37 E1
Queensholm Dr BS16 .... 37 E1
Queensway BS34 .... 36 D6
Queensway Ctr BS22 .... 89 B2
Queenwood Ave BA1 .... 85 A1
Queen's Pl BA2 .... 102 B5
Quickthorn Cl BS14 .... 80 A6
Quiet St BA1 .... 141 B2
Quilter Gr BS4 .... 79 D7

R

Raby Mews BA2 .... 102 B7
Raby Pl BA2 .... 102 B7
Rackfield Pl BA2 .... 101 B6
Rackham Cl BS7 .... 50 B6
Rackhay BS1 .... 143 A2
Rackley La BS26 .... 124 B2
Rackvernal Ct BA3 .... 133 B1
Rackvernal Rd BA3 .... 133 B1
Radford Hill
Peasedown St John BA2, BA3 .... 133 C7
Timsbury BA2 .... 116 C1
Radley Rd BS16 .... 51 B4
Radnor Bsns Ctr BS7 .... 49 E5
Radnor Rd
Bristol,Golden Hill BS7 .... 49 E5
Bristol,Henleaze BS9 .... 49 B5
Radstock Inf Sch BA3 .... 134 A3
Radstock Mus★ BA3 .... 133 F2
Radstock Rd BA3 .... 133 C2
Raeburn Rd BS5 .... 65 B6
Rag Hill BA2 .... 134 D5
Rag La GL12 .... 17 D5
Raglan Cl BA3 .... 138 C4
Raglan La Bristol BS5 .... 65 A7
Winford BS40 .... 94 E7
Raglan Pl Bristol BS7 .... 49 D3
Thornbury BS35 .... 15 B8
Weston-S-M BS23 .... 87 C1
Raglan Rd BS7 .... 49 D3
Raglan Terr BA1 .... 85 A2
Raglan Wlk BS31 .... 81 D4
Ragland La BA1 .... 85 A2
Ragland St BA1 .... 85 A2
Raikes Ct BS20 .... 47 D4
Railton Jones Cl BS34 .... 36 E3
Railway Arches BS2 .... 143 C2
Railway Cotts BS37 .... 40 E8
Railway La BA2 .... 118 D1
Railway Pl BA1 .... 141 C1
Railway St BA1 .... 141 C1
Railway Terr BS16 .... 51 C4
Railway View Pl BA3 .... 133 B2
Rainbow Ct BS37 .... 27 B3
Rainham Ct BS23 .... 87 C1
Rains Batch BS40 .... 127 E6
Raleigh Cl BS31 .... 82 D2
Raleigh Ct 3 BS23 .... 104 E5
Raleigh Rd BS3 .... 63 B4
Raleigh Rise BS20 .... 45 B6
Ralph Allen Dr BA2 .... 102 B3
Ralph Allen Sch BA2 .... 102 E2
Ralph Rd BS7 .... 49 F4
Ram Hill BS36 .... 38 D4
Ram Hill Bsns Pk BS36 .... 38 D5
Ramsay Cl BS22 .... 88 E4
Ramscombe La BA1 .... 85 F6
Ramsey Rd BS7 .... 49 F7
Ranchways BS20 .... 44 F4
Randall Cl BS15 .... 51 F2
Randall Rd BS8 .... 142 B2
Randolph Ave
Bristol BS13 .... 79 B5
Yate BS37 .... 27 D4
Randolph Cl BS13 .... 79 B5
Rangers Wlk BS15 .... 65 C4
Rangeworthy CE Prim Sch BS37 .... 16 F1
Rankers La BS39 .... 98 C5
Rannoch Rd BS7 .... 35 F1
Ranscombe Ave BS22 .... 88 D2
Ransford BS21 .... 57 B1
Raphael Ct BS1 .... 143 B1
Ratcliffe Dr BS34 .... 36 E5
Rathbone Cl BS36 .... 38 C5
Raven Cl BS22 .... 88 E1
Raven Ct BS9 .... 48 F8
Ravendale Dr BS30 .... 66 B2
Ravenglass Cres BS10 .... 35 D2
Ravenhead Dr BS14 .... 80 B8
Ravenhill Ave BS3 .... 63 F2
Ravenhill Rd BS3 .... 63 F3
Ravenscourt Rd BS34 .... 36 B7
Ravenswood BS30 .... 66 B3
Ravenswood Rd BS6 .... 49 C1
Ravenswood Sch BS48 .... 59 D3
Rawlins Ave BS22 .... 89 A5
Rawnsley Ho 13 BS5 .... 50 A1
Rayens Cl BS41 .... 61 F1
Rayens Cross Rd BS41 .... 61 F1
Rayleigh Rd BS9 .... 48 E7
Raymend Rd BS3 .... 63 E3
Raymend Wlk BS3 .... 63 E2
Raymill BS4 .... 65 A2
Raymond Ho BS16 .... 51 F4
Raymore Rise BS41 .... 61 F1
Raynes Rd BS3 .... 63 A3
Rayneswood BS23 .... 104 F8
Raysfield Inf Sch BS37 .... 39 F8
Raysfield Jun Sch BS37 .... 39 F8
Read's Row GL12 .... 19 D7
Reading Ct 1 BS15 .... 65 B8
Rector's Way BS23 .... 104 F6
Rectory Cl
Farmborough BA2 .... 116 A6
Nailsea BS48 .... 60 A2
Yate BS37 .... 27 F3
Rectory Dr BS49 .... 91 C7
Rectory Gdns BS10 .... 34 E2
Rectory La Bleadon BS24 .... 122 C6
Bristol BS34 .... 36 A3
Compton Martin BS40 .... 129 B6
Cromhall GL12 .... 17 A8
Timsbury BA2 .... 116 B2
Rectory Rd
Easton-in-G BS20 .... 47 B3
Frampton Cotterell BS36 .... 38 A8
Rectory Way
Lympsham BS24 .... 121 F2
Yatton BS49 .... 91 C7
Recurium Lodge BS26 .... 125 B2
Red Hill
Peasedown St John BA2 .... 116 E1
Redhill BS40 .... 93 D2
Red House La
Almondsbury BS32 .... 24 B4
Bristol BS9 .... 48 E6
Red Maids Sch The BS9 .... 49 A6
Red Post Ct BA2 .... 134 B7
Red Rd TA8 .... 121 A2
Redacre BS40 .... 93 D3
Redcar Ct BS16 .... 37 F1
Redcatch Rd BS4 .... 63 F2
Redcliff Backs BS1 .... 143 B2
Redcliff Cres BS3 .... 63 E4
Redcliff Hill BS1 .... 143 B1
Redcliff Mead La BS1 .... 143 B1
Redcliff St BS1 .... 143 B2
Redcliffe Cl BS20 .... 44 E3
Redcliffe Par E BS1 .... 143 A1
Redcliffe Par W BS1 .... 143 A1
Redcliffe Way BS1 .... 143 B1
Redcroft BS40 .... 93 D3
Redcross Mews 14 BS2 .... 143 C3
Redcross St BS2 .... 143 C3
Redding Pit La BS40 .... 94 E4
Reddings The Bristol BS15 .... 51 F2
Compton Martin BS40 .... 129 B7
Redfield Edge Prim Sch BS30 .... 66 D4
Redfield Gr BA3 .... 139 A8
Redfield Hill BS30 .... 66 E3
Redfield Rd Bristol BS34 .... 36 B7
Midsomer Norton BA3 .... 139 A8
Redford Cres BS13 .... 78 F3
Redford La BS16 .... 53 D4
Redford Wlk BS13 .... 78 F3
Redham La BS35 .... 22 F8
Redhill Cl BS16 .... 50 E3
Redhill Dr BS16 .... 50 E3
Redhill La BS35 .... 13 E6
Redland Court Rd BS6 .... 49 C2
Redland Gr BS6 .... 49 C2
Redland Green Rd BS6 .... 49 B3
Redland High Sch BS6 .... 49 C2
Redland Hill BS6 .... 49 B2
Redland Pk Bath BA2 .... 100 F6
Bristol BS6 .... 49 B2
Redland Rd Bristol BS6 .... 49 C2
Portbury BS20 .... 46 F6
Redland Sta BS6 .... 49 C2
Redland Terr 8 BS6 .... 49 B2
Redlands Terr BA3 .... 138 F8
Redlynch La BS31 .... 81 D2
Redshard La BS40 .... 109 B7
Redshelf Wlk BS10 .... 35 C3
Redwick & Northwick CE Prim Sch BS35 .... 12 D2
Redwick Cl BS11 .... 34 C2
Redwick Gdns BS35 .... 22 C7
Redwick Rd BS35 .... 22 C8
Redwing Dr BS22 .... 88 F1
Redwing Gdns BS16 .... 50 E6
Redwood Cl Bristol BS30 .... 66 A3
Nailsea BS48 .... 60 A2
Radstock BA3 .... 139 E8
Redwood Ho BS13 .... 79 D3
Redwood La BS48 .... 77 C7
Reed Cl BS10 .... 49 D6
Reed Ct BS30 .... 65 F3
Reed Way BS22 .... 89 C3
Reed's Row GL12 .... 19 D7
Reedley Rd BS9 .... 48 F5
Reedling Cl BS16 .... 50 E6
Regency Dr BS4 .... 65 A2
Regent Rd BS3 .... 63 D4
Regent St
Bristol,Clifton Wood BS8 .... 142 A2
Bristol,Kingswood BS15 .... 65 D8
Weston-S-M BS23 .... 104 E7
Regents Cl BS35 .... 8 B2
Regil La BS40 .... 95 A6
Regil Rd BS40 .... 94 F3
Regine The BA1 .... 141 B3
Remenham Dr BS9 .... 49 B5
Remenham Pk BS9 .... 49 B5
Rendcomb Cl BS22 .... 88 B2
Rendle Ho BS16 .... 51 F4
Rene Rd 12 BS5 .... 50 B1
Rennison Ct BS23 .... 104 E4
Repton Rd BS4 .... 64 D3
Retford Ho BA2 .... 102 E4
Retort Rd BS11 .... 33 C3
Retreat The BA3 .... 134 E3
Reubens Ct BS22 .... 88 F3
Reynold's Wlk BS7 .... 50 A7
Reynolds Cl BS31 .... 82 A5
Rhode Cl BS31 .... 82 A3
Rhodyate BS40 .... 110 D2
Rhodyate Hill BS49 .... 91 F6
Rhodyate La BS49 .... 92 A7
Rhodyate The BS29 .... 107 C1
Rhyne Terr BS23 .... 104 D2
Rhyne View BS48 .... 59 B1
Ribblesdale BS35 .... 15 D8
Richards Cl BS22 .... 89 B4
Richeson Cl BS10 .... 34 F2
Richeson Wlk BS10 .... 34 F2
Richmond Ave
Bristol,Great Stoke BS34 .... 36 E5
Bristol,Montpelier BS6 .... 49 F2
Richmond Cl Bath BA1 .... 84 F1
Keynsham BS31 .... 81 D4
Portishead BS20 .... 45 E5
Richmond Ct
11 Bristol,Hengrove BS14 .... 80 B5
7 Bristol,Redland BS8 .... 49 A2
2 Bristol,Windmill Hill BS3 .... 63 F4
Richmond Dale 6 BS8 .... 49 A2
Richmond Gn BS48 .... 59 F1
Richmond Hill Bath BA1 .... 84 F1
Bristol BS8 .... 142 B3
Richmond Hill Ave BS8 .... 142 B3
Richmond Hts Bath BA1 .... 84 F2
Bristol BS8 .... 142 B3
Richmond La Bath BA1 .... 84 F1
Bristol BS8 .... 142 B3
Richmond Mews BS8 .... 142 A3
Richmond Park Rd BS8 .... 142 A3
Richmond Pl BA1 .... 84 F1
Richmond Rd Bath BA1 .... 84 F1
Bristol,Mangotsfield BS16 .... 52 A5
Bristol,Montpelier BS6 .... 49 E1
Bristol,Pile Marsh BS5 .... 64 E7
Richmond St Bristol BS3 .... 63 F4
Weston-S-M BS23 .... 104 D7
Richmond Terr
Avonmouth BS11 .... 33 B1
Bristol BS8 .... 142 A3
Ricketts La BS22 .... 89 A2
Rickford La BS40 .... 110 A3
Rickford Rd BS48 .... 59 F1
Rickford Rise BS40 .... 110 A3
Rickyard Rd BS40 .... 92 E2
Ride The BS15 .... 52 A2
Ridge Cl BS20 .... 45 A4
Ridge Cres BS40 .... 129 E6
Ridge Green Cl BA2 .... 118 D8
Ridge Jun Sch The BS37 .... 27 F2
Ridge La BS40 .... 129 D5
Ridge The Bristol BS11 .... 47 E7
Coalpit Heath BS36 .... 38 C7
Yatton BS49 .... 91 B8
Ridgehill BS9 .... 49 C6
Ridgemeade BS14 .... 80 B4
Ridgeview BS41 .... 62 B2
Ridgeway
Coalpit Heath BS36 .... 38 D7
Nailsea BS48 .... 59 C1
Yate BS37 .... 28 A2
Ridgeway Ave BS23 .... 104 E6
Ridgeway Cl BS40 .... 129 E6
Ridgeway Ct BS10 .... 35 A1
Ridgeway Gdns BS14 .... 80 C5
Ridgeway Ind Ctr BS5 .... 50 E2
Ridgeway La BS14 .... 80 B5
Ridgeway Par BS5 .... 50 E3
Ridgeway Rd Bristol BS16 .... 50 F3
Long Ashton BS41 .... 62 A2
Ridgeway The
Bristol BS10 .... 35 A1
Weston-S-M BS22 .... 88 B2
Ridgewood BS9 .... 48 D3
Riding Barn Hill BS30 .... 67 A6
Ridingleaze BS11 .... 34 A1
Ridings Cl BS37 .... 28 D1
Ridings High Sch The BS36 .... 37 D6
Ridings Rd BS36 .... 38 C6
Ridings The Bristol BS13 .... 78 E4
Coalpit Heath BS36 .... 38 C6
Ringspit La BS14,BS39 .... 97 E8
Ringswell Gdns BA1 .... 85 B1
Ringwell BA2 .... 136 E4
Ringwell La BA2 .... 136 E4
Ringwood Cres BS10 .... 35 D1
Ringwood Gr BS23 .... 88 A1
Ringwood Rd BA2 .... 101 C5
Ripley Rd BS5 .... 51 A1
Ripon Ct BS16 .... 37 F2
Ripon Rd BS4 .... 64 E6
Ripple The BS21 .... 59 D4
Rippleside BS20 .... 45 C5
Rippleside Rd BS21 .... 57 E5
Risdale Rd BS3 .... 62 F1
Risedale BS15 .... 65 D5
Risedale Rd BS25 .... 125 A8
Rivendell BS22 .... 89 A4
River Mead Clevedon BS21 .... 73 D8
Yate BS37 .... 27 C3
River Pl BA2 .... 101 B6
River Rd
Chipping Sodbury BS37 .... 28 A1
Portbury BS20 .... 46 F8
River St BS2 .... 143 C3
River Street Pl BA1 .... 141 B3
River Terr BS31 .... 81 F5
River View BS16 .... 50 E5

Rivergate BS1 . . . . 143 C2
Riverland Dr BS13 . . . . . . .78 F5
Riverlea Bristol BS9 . . . . . .48 C5
Portishead BS20 . . . . .44 F6
Rivers Rd BA1 . . . . 141 C4
Rivers St BA1 . . . . .141 B3
Rivers Street Mews
BA1 . . . . .141 B3
Riverside BS29 . . . . .107 B5
Riverside Bsns Pk BS4 . . . .64 D6
Riverside Cl Bristol BS11 . . .47 F5
Clevedon BS21 . . . . .57 B1
Midsomer Norton BA3 . . . .138 F7
Weston-S-M BS22 . . . . . . .89 C3
Riverside Cotts
Bristol BS15 . . . . .65 B1
Radstock BA3 . . . . .134 A2
Riverside Ct Bath BA2 . . . .141 B1
2 Bristol BS4 . . . . .64 F6
Riverside Dr Cvn Site
BS16 . . . . .51 C7
Riverside Gdns Bath BA1 141 B2
Midsomer Norton BA3 . . . .138 F7
Riverside Mews 64 F6
Riverside Pk BS35 . . . . . . .21 F6
Riverside Rd Bath BA2 . . . 141 B1
Midsomer Norton BA3 . . . .138 F7
Riverside Stps BS4 . . . . . .64 E7
Riverside Way BS15 . . . . . .65 C3
Riverside Wlk
6 Bristol BS5 . . . . .64 F6
Midsomer Norton BA3 . . . .138 F7
Riverway BS48 . . . . .59 F3
Riverwood Rd BS16 . . . . . .37 C1
Riviera Cres BS16 . . . . . . .51 E4
Riviera Way BS34 . . . . . . .37 A4
Roach's La GL9 . . . . .30 D2
Road Hill SN13 . . . . .86 E8
Road Two BS10 . . . . .22 A3
Roath Rd BS20 . . . . .45 D5
Rob-Lynne Ct BS25 . . . . .124 F8
Robbins Cl Bristol BS32 . . .36 F6
Marshfield SN14 . . . . .69 F8
Robbins Ct BS16 . . . . .52 B6
Robel Ave BS36 . . . . .38 A8
Robert Ct Bristol BS16 . . . .52 B7
Leigh Woods BS8 . . . . .62 D6
Robert St
Bristol,Baptist Mills BS5 . . .50 B2
15 Bristol,Russell Town
BS5 . . . . .64 B7
Robertson Dr BS4 . . . . . . .64 F6
Robertson Rd BS5 . . . . . . .50 C2
Robin Cl
Bristol,Brentry BS10 . . . . . .35 B2
Bristol,Stockwood BS14 . . . .80 D6
Midsomer Norton BA3 . . . .139 B8
Weston-S-M BS22 . . . . . .105 E8
Robin Dr BS24 . . . . .105 E2
Robin La BS21 . . . . .57 D5
Robin Way BS37 . . . . .40 A7
Robinia Wlk BS14 . . . . . . .80 A7
Robinson Cl BS48 . . . . . . .76 A5
Robinson Dr BS5 . . . . .64 A8
Robinson Way BS48 . . . . . .76 A5
Rochester Cl BS24 . . . . . .105 A1
Rochester Rd BS4 . . . . . . .64 F5
Rochfort Ct BA1 . . . . .102 B8
Rock Ave BS48 . . . . .59 C2
Rock Cl BS4 . . . . .64 E2
Rock Cotts BS20 . . . . .47 E4
Rock Hall Cotts BA2 . . . . .102 B1
Rock Ho BS10 . . . . .35 C3
Rock La Bath BA2 . . . . . . .102 B1
Bristol BS34 . . . . .36 E8
Rock Rd Chilcompton BA3 138 D2
Keynsham BS31 . . . . .81 E5
Midsomer Norton BA3 . . . .133 B2
Wick BS30 . . . . .67 D8
Yatton BS49 . . . . .91 C7
Rock St BS35 . . . . .15 B8
Rock The BS4 . . . . .64 E8
Rock Villas BS20 . . . . .45 B1
Rockeries The BS25 . . . . .124 F8
Rockhall La BA2 . . . . .102 B1
Rockhill Est BS31 . . . . . . .81 F4
Rockingham Gdns BS11 . . .48 A8
Rockingham Gr BS23 . . . . .88 A1
Rockingham Rdbt BS11 . . .33 C6
Rockland Gr BS16 . . . . . . .50 D5
Rockland Rd BS16 . . . . . . .51 D7
Rockleaze Bristol BS9 . . . . .48 E2
9 Thornbury BS35 . . . . . . .8 B1
Rockleaze Ave BS9 . . . . . .48 E3
Rockleaze Ct BS9 . . . . . . .48 E3
Rockleaze Mans BS23 . . . .87 C1
Rockleaze Rd BS9 . . . . . . .48 E3
Rockliffe Ave BA2 . . . . . . 102 B8
Rockliffe Rd BA2 . . . . 102 B8
Rocks La BS40 . . . . .77 E1
Rockside Ave BS16 . . . . . .51 F8
Rockside Dr BS9 . . . . .49 C6
Rockside Gdns
Bristol BS16 . . . . .51 F8
Frampton Cotterell BS36 . . . .38 C8
Rockstowes Way BS10 . . . .35 D3
Rockwell Ave BS11 . . . . . .34 B1
Rockwood Ho BS37 . . . . . .28 A4
Rodborough BS37 . . . . . . .39 C7
Rodborough Way BS15 . . . .66 A7
Rodbourne Rd BS10 . . . . . .49 E6
Rode Bird Gdns* BA3 . . .137 D2
Rode Hill BA3 . . . . .137 E1
Rodford Way BS37 . . . . . . .39 D7
Rodfords Mead BS14 . . . . .80 A7
Rodmead Wlk BS13 . . . . . .79 A4
Rodmoor Rd BS20 . . . . . . .45 D6

Rodney BS24 . . . . .105 A2
Rodney Ave BS15 . . . . . . .65 A8
Rodney Cres BS34 . . . . . . .36 A4
Rodney Ho BA2 . . . . .101 A6
Rodney Pl BS8 . . . . .142 A3
Rodney Rd Backwell BS48 . .76 A6
Bristol BS15 . . . . .65 A8
Saltford BS31 . . . . .82 E2
Rodney Wlk BS15 . . . . . . .51 A1
Rodway Ct BS16 . . . . .52 A6
Rodway Hill BS16 . . . . . . .52 B3
Rodway Hill Rd BS16 . . . . .52 A4
Rodway Rd
Bristol,Cribbs Causeway
BS34 . . . . .35 F7
Bristol,Mangotsfield BS16 . . .52 A5
Rodway View BS15 . . . . . .51 F3
Roebuck Cl BS22 . . . . .89 B4
Roegate Dr BS4 . . . . .64 E6
Roegate Ho BS5 . . . . .51 A1
Rogers Cl Bristol BS30 . . . .66 B5
Clutton BS39 . . . . .114 E3
Rogers Ct BS37 . . . . .28 C1
Rogers Wlk BS30 . . . . .66 D7
Rokeby Ave BS6 . . . . .49 C1
Roman Baths The*
BA1 . . . . .141 C2
Roman Farm Ct BS11 . . . . .34 C2
Roman Farm Rd BS4 . . . . .79 E7
Roman Ho BA1 . . . . .141 C4
Roman Rd Bath BA1 . . . . .141 C3
Bleadon BS24 . . . . .122 C8
Bristol BS5 . . . . .50 B1
Sandford BS25 . . . . .107 F4
Roman Way
Bristol,Great Stoke BS34 . . . .36 E5
Bristol,Kensington Park BS4 64 C3
Paulton BS39 . . . . .132 C6
Roman Wlk
Bristol,Great Stoke BS34 . . .36 E5
Bristol,Kensington Park BS4 64 C3
Romney Ave BS7 . . . . .50 B6
Romney Avenue Inf Sch
BS7 . . . . .50 B6
Romney Avenue Jun Sch
BS7 . . . . .50 B6
Romo Ct 3 BS16 . . . . .51 C4
Ron Jones Ho 3 BS1 . . . . 143 B4
Ronald Rd BS16 . . . . .50 F6
Ronaldson BS30 . . . . .66 C2
Ronayne Wlk BS16 . . . . . .51 C6
Rookery Cl BS22 . . . . .88 E3
Rookery La Pilning BS35 . . .23 A6
Pucklechurch BS16,SN14 . . .53 F4
Rookery Rd BS4 . . . . .64 A3
Rookery Way BS14 . . . . . . .79 F4
Rooksbridge Wlk BA2 . . . 101 B4
Rosary Rdbt The BS16 . . . .52 C7
Rosary The BS16 . . . . .52 D7
Roper's La BS40 . . . . .92 E3
Rosary Rdbt The BS16 . . . .52 C7
Rose Acre BS10 . . . . .35 A3
Rose Cl BS36 . . . . .37 E4
Rose Cotts BS22 . . . . .89 C2
Rose Gdns BS22 . . . . .89 B4
Rose Green Cl BS5 . . . . . . .50 E2
Rose Green Rd BS5 . . . . . .50 D2
Rose Hill BA1 . . . . .85 C3
Rosea BS36 . . . . .38 C4
Rose Mead BS7 . . . . .50 A8
Rose Meare Gdns BS13 . . .78 E7
Rose Oak Dr BS36 . . . . . . .38 D7
Rose Oak Gdns BS36 . . . . .38 D7
Rose Oak La BS36 . . . . . . .38 D7
Rose Rd BS5 . . . . .64 E7
Rose Terr Bath BA2 . . . . . .102 C2
Bristol BS8 . . . . .142 B3
Rose Tree Ho BS16 . . . . . .51 F4
Rose Wlk BS16 . . . . .51 C3
Rosebay Mead BS16 . . . . . .50 E5
Roseberry Pk BS5 . . . . . . .64 D8
Roseberry Pl BA2 . . . . . . .101 C6
Roseberry Rd Bath BA2 . . .101 C6
Bristol BS5 . . . . .64 C7
Rosebery Ave BS2 . . . . . . .50 A1
Rosebery Terr BS8 . . . . . .142 B2
Rosedale Ave BS23 . . . . . 105 A7
Rosedale Rd BS16 . . . . . . .51 C3
Roselarge Gdns BS10 . . . . .35 A2
Rosemary Cl BS32 . . . . . . .36 F7
Rosemary La Bristol BS5 . . .50 B1
Freshford BA2 . . . . .120 B4
Rosemont Terr BS8 . . . . . .142 A2
Rosemount Ct BS15 . . . . . .65 B8
Rosemount La BA2 . . . . . .102 B4
Rosemount Rd BS48 . . . . . .77 B8
Rosery Cl BS9 . . . . .49 A8
Rosery The BS16 . . . . .51 C3
Rosevear BS2 . . . . .64 A7
Roseville Ave BS30 . . . . . .66 A2
Rosewarn Cl BA2 . . . . . . .101 A4
Rosewell Ct BA1 . . . . .141 B2
Rosewood Ave BS35 . . . . . .8 C3
Roshni Gar E 16 BS5 . . . . .50 B1
Roshni Gar W 15 BS5 . . . . .50 B1
Rosling Rd BS7 . . . . .49 E6
Roslyn Ave BS22 . . . . .88 C1
Roslyn Rd BS6 . . . . .49 C1
Ross Cl BS37 . . . . .28 B1
Rossall Ave BS34 . . . . .36 C6
Rossall Rd BS4 . . . . .64 D3
Rossendale Cl BS22 . . . . . .88 F3
Rossiter Rd BA2 . . . . .141 C1
Rossiter Wood Ct BS11 . . . .34 B2
Rossiter's La BS5 . . . . .65 A6
Rosslyn Rd BA1 . . . . .101 B7
Rosslyn Way BS35 . . . . . . .8 C3
Rotcombe La BS39 . . . . . .115 D2
Rotcombe Vale BS39 . . . . .115 D2
Rounceval St BS37 . . . . . . .28 A1

Round Oak Rd BS27 . . . . .126 A1
Roundhill Gr BA2 . . . . . . .101 B3
Roundhill Pk BA2 . . . . . . .101 A4
Roundmoor Cl BS31 . . . . . .82 D3
Roundmoor Gdns BS14 . . . .80 D7
Roundways BS36 . . . . .38 D6
Rousham Rd BS5 . . . . .50 A3
Row La BA2,BA3 . . . . 136 C1
Row Of Ashes La BS40 . . . .93 F4
Row The BS35 . . . . .13 A7
Rowacres Bath BA2 . . . . . .101 B3
Bristol BS14 . . . . .79 F5
Rowan Cl Bristol BS16 . . . .51 A2
Nailsea BS48 . . . . .60 A2
Rowan Ct 8 Bristol BS5 . . .64 B7
Radstock BA3 . . . . .133 E1
Rowan Ho BS13 . . . . .79 D4
Rowan Pl BS24 . . . . .89 B1
Rowan Tree Ho BS16 . . . . .51 F4
Rowan Way BS15 . . . . .65 B8
Langford BS40 . . . . .109 A5
Rowan Wlk BS31 . . . . .81 C4
Rowans The Bristol BS16 . . .37 C4
Portishead BS20 . . . . .45 C4
Rowberrow BS14 . . . . .79 F7
Rowberrow La
Rowberrow BS25 . . . . .108 F2
Shipham BS25 . . . . .125 F8
Rowberrow Way BS48 . . . . .59 E1
Rowland Ave BS16 . . . . . . .50 D4
Rowlands Cl BA1 . . . . .86 B2
Rowlandson Gdns BS7 . . . .50 B6
Rowley St BS3 . . . . .63 C3
Rownham Cl BS3 . . . . .62 E4
Rownham Ct BS8 . . . . . . .142 A1
Rownham Hill BS8 . . . . . . .62 E6
Rownham Mead BS8 . . . . .142 A1
Rows The BS22 . . . . .88 E2
Roy King Gdns BS30 . . . . . .66 C6
Royal Albert Rd BS6 . . . . . .49 A4
Royal Ave BA1 . . . . .141 B3
Royal Cl BS10 . . . . .34 D3
Royal Cres Bath BA1 . . . . .141 A3
Weston-S-M BS23 . . . . . . .104 D8
Royal Ct BS23 . . . . .104 D4
Royal Fort Rd BS2,BS8 . . .142 C3
Royal High Sch
Bath BA1 . . . . .141 B4
Bath,Landsdown BA1 . . . . .84 F2
Royal National Hospl for
Rheumatic Diseases
BA1 . . . . .141 B2
Royal Pk BS8 . . . . .142 A3
Royal Portbury Dock Rd
BS20 . . . . .46 E5
Royal Prom BS8 . . . . .142 B3
Royal Rd BS16 . . . . .52 A6
Royal Sands BS23 . . . . . .104 D4
Royal United Hospl BA1 101 B8
Royal Victoria Pk BS10 . . . .35 B2
Royal West of England Acad
BS8 . . . . .142 B3
Royal York Cres BS8 . . . . .62 F6
Royal York Ho BS8 . . . . . .142 A2
Royal York Mews BS8 . . . .142 A2
Royal York Villas BS8 . . . .142 A2
Royate Hill BS5 . . . . .50 D2
Roycroft Rd BS34 . . . . . . .36 B2
Royston Lodge BS23 . . . . .104 D6
Royston Wlk BS10 . . . . . . .35 D3
Rozel Rd BS7 . . . . .49 E5
Rubens Cl BS31 . . . . .82 A5
Ruby St BS3 . . . . .63 B3
Ruddymead BS21 . . . . .57 D2
Rudford Cl BS34 . . . . .24 B1
Rudge Cl BS15 . . . . .51 F2
Rudgeway Pk BS35 . . . . . .14 F1
Rudgeway Rd BS39 . . . . . .132 E4
Rudgewood Cl BS13 . . . . . .79 D4
Rudgleigh Ave BS20 . . . . . .47 C4
Rudgleigh Rd BS20 . . . . . .47 C4
Rudhall Gn BS22 . . . . .89 B3
Rudhall Gr BS10 . . . . .49 E7
Rudmore Pk BA1 . . . . .101 A7
Rudthorpe Rd BS7 . . . . . . .49 E5
Ruett La BS39 . . . . 132 E4
Ruffet Rd BS36 . . . . .38 B4
Rugby Rd BS4 . . . . .64 D3
Runnymead Ave BS4 . . . . .64 D2
Runnymede BS15 . . . . .51 F1
Runswick Rd BS4 . . . . .64 C3
Rupert St
Bristol,Kingsdown BS1 . . . .143 A3
Bristol,Redfield BS5 . . . . . .64 C7
Rush Cl BS32 . . . . .24 D2
Rush Hill Bath BA2 . . . . . .101 C2
Farrington Gurney BS39 . . .131 F3
Rusham BS13 . . . . .78 F4
Rushgrove Gdns BS39 . . . .113 C4
Rushmead La SN14 . . . . . .55 F2
Rushmoor BS21 . . . . .57 A1
Rushmoor Gr BS48 . . . . . .76 A5
Rushmoor La BS48 . . . . . . .76 A5
Rushton Dr BS36 . . . . .38 D7
Rushway BS40 . . . . .109 A4
Rushy BS30 . . . . .66 A4
Rushy Way BS16 . . . . .38 A1
Ruskin Gr BS7 . . . . .50 A8
Ruskin Ho BS34 . . . . .36 A8
Ruskin Rd BA3 . . . . .133 C1
Russ La BS21 . . . . .73 E4
Russ St BS2 . . . . .143 C2
Russell Ave BS15 . . . . .65 E7
Russell Cl BS40 . . . . .95 A6

Russell Gr BS6 . . . . .49 C5
Russell Rd
Bristol,Chester Park BS16 . .51 B2
Bristol,Henleaze BS6 . . . . .49 A4
Clevedon BS21 . . . . .57 C3
Locking BS24 . . . . .106 C6
Russell St BA1 . . . . .141 B3
Russell Town Ave BS5 . . . .64 B8
Russell Town Ind Pk 18
BS5 . . . . .64 C7
Russet Cl BS35 . . . . .14 A3
Russet Ct GL12 . . . . .11 F4
Russet Way BA2 . . . . .134 D7
Russets The BS20 . . . . . . .45 F4
Russett Cl BS48 . . . . .76 B6
Russett Gr BS48 . . . . .75 C8
Russetts Cotts BS48 . . . . . .76 B8
Rustic Pk BS35 . . . . .22 A6
Rutherford Cl BS30 . . . . . .66 A3
Ruthven Rd BS4 . . . . .79 E8
Rutland Ave BS30 . . . . . . .66 A2
Rutland Cl BS22 . . . . .105 C8
Rutland Rd BS7 . . . . .49 E3
Rydal Ave BS24 . . . . .106 A4
Rydal Ho BS34 . . . . .36 A8
Rydal Rd BS23 . . . . .104 F4
Ryde Rd BS4 . . . . .64 B2
Rye Cl BS13 . . . . .78 E6
Ryecroft Ave BS22 . . . . . . .88 E2
Ryecroft Rd BS36 . . . . .38 C7
Ryecroft Rise BS41 . . . . . . .62 B1
Ryedown La BS30 . . . . . . .66 D2
Ryland Pl 1 BS2 . . . . .50 A2
Rylestone Cl BS36 . . . . . . .37 F8
Rylestone Gr BS9 . . . . .48 F5
Rysdale Rd BS9 . . . . .48 F6

S

Sabrina Way BS9 . . . . .48 C4
Sacred Heart Prep Sch
BS40 . . . . .96 A3
Sadbury Cl BS22 . . . . .89 B4
Sadlier Cl BS11 . . . . .48 A8
Saffron Ct BA1 . . . . .141 C4
Saffron Ho 11 BS23 . . . . .104 E8
Saffrons The 7 BS22 . . . . .89 B4
Sage Cl BS20 . . . . .44 E4
Sages Mead BS32 . . . . . . .36 E8
Saint Way BS34 . . . . .37 A4
SS Gt Britain* BS1 . . . . . .142 B1
SS Peter & Paul RC Sch
BS8 . . . . .142 C4
St Agnes Ave BS4 . . . . . . .63 F2
St Agnes Cl BS48 . . . . .60 A1
St Agnes Gdns BS4 . . . . . .63 F2
St Agnes Wlk BS4 . . . . . . .63 F2
St Aidan's Cl BS5 . . . . .65 B6
St Aidan's Rd BS5 . . . . . . .65 B6
St Alban's Rd BS6 . . . . . . .49 B4
St Aldams Dr BS16 . . . . . .53 B5
St Aldwyn's Cl BS7 . . . . . . .49 F8
St Andrew's CE Jun Sch
BS49 . . . . .91 C4
St Andrew's CE Prim Sch
BA1 . . . . .141 B4
St Andrew's CE Prim Sch
GL12 . . . . .10 A1
St Andrew's Cl BS49 . . . . .91 C4
St Andrew's Dr BS21 . . . . .57 A2
St Andrew's Par 1
BS23 . . . . .104 F4
St Andrew's Rd
Avonmouth BS11 . . . . .33 B1
Avonmouth BS11 . . . . .33 B4
Bristol BS6 . . . . .49 E2
St Andrew's Terr BA1 . . . .141 B3
St Andrews Bristol BS30 . . .66 B6
Yate BS37 . . . . .27 F1
St Andrews Cl
Nailsea BS48 . . . . .60 A1
Weston-S-M BS22 . . . . . . .88 F3
St Andrews Gate Rdbt
BS11 . . . . .33 B2
St Andrews Mews BS6 . . . .49 B3
St Andrews Rd BS48 . . . . .76 B5
St Andrews Road Sta
BS11 . . . . .33 B4
St Andrews Trad Est
BS11 . . . . .33 C2
St Ann's Pl BA1 . . . . .141 B2
St Ann's Way BA2 . . . . . . .102 C6
St Anne's Ave BS31 . . . . . .81 D6
St Anne's CE Prim Sch
BS30 . . . . .66 C3
St Anne's CE Prim Sch
BS24 . . . . .90 B5
St Anne's Cl BS30 . . . . . . .66 B4
St Anne's Ct BS31 . . . . . . .81 D6
St Anne's Dr
Coalpit Heath BS36 . . . . . .38 C5
Wick BS30 . . . . .67 B7
St Anne's Inf & Jun Sch
BS4 . . . . .64 D5
St Anne's Park Prim Sch
BS4 . . . . .64 E5
St Anne's Park Rd BS4 . . . .64 E5
St Anne's Rd
Bristol,St Anne's Park BS4 . .64 D6
Bristol,St George BS5 . . . . .65 B6
St Anne's Terr BS4 . . . . . . .64 E5
St Annes Cl 7 BS5 . . . . . .64 F6
St Annes Ct BS4 . . . . .64 D5
St Annes Dr BS30 . . . . . . .67 B7
St Anthony's Cl BA3 . . . . .133 A2
St Anthony's Dr BS30 . . . . .67 B7

St Aubin's Ave BS4 . . . . . .64 F3
St Aubyn's Ave BS23 . . . . 104 D2
St Augustine of Canterbury
Sch BS16 . . . . .51 F7
St Augustine's Par BS1 . 143 A2
St Augustine's Pl 1
BS1 . . . . .143 A2
St Austell Cl BS48 . . . . . . .76 A8
St Austell Rd BS22 . . . . . .105 B8
St Barnabas CE Prim Sch
Bristol,Montpelier BS6 . . . .49 F1
Bristol,Warmley Tower
BS30 . . . . .66 C6
Portishead BS20 . . . . .45 B3
St Barnabas Cl
Bristol,Bridge Yate BS30 . . .66 C6
Bristol,Lower Knowle BS4 . .63 F1
Midsomer Norton BA3 . . . .133 B3
St Barnabas Ho BS30 . . . . .66 C7
St Bartholomew's Rd
BS7 . . . . .49 F3
St Bede's RC Sch BS11 . . .34 B2
St Bede's Rd BS15 . . . . . . .51 D2
St Benedict's RC Prim Sch
. . . . .139 C7
St Bernadette RC Prim Sch
BS14 . . . . .80 B6
St Bernadette RC Sec Sch
BS14 . . . . .80 B6
St Bernard's RC Sch
BS11 . . . . .47 E6
St Bernard's Rd BS11 . . . .47 E6
St Bonaventure's RC Prim
Sch BS7 . . . . .49 D4
St Brandon's Sch BS21 . . .57 B3
St Brelades Gr BS4 . . . . . .64 F5
St Brendan's Sixth Form Coll
BS4 . . . . .65 A1
St Brendan's Way BS11 . . .33 B1
St Brendans Rdbt BS11 . . .33 C1
St Briavels Dr BS37 . . . . . .39 D8
St Bridges Ct BS22 . . . . . .88 A6
St Cadoc Ho BS31 . . . . . . .81 F5
St Catherine's Cl BA2 . . . .102 C6
St Catherine's Ind Est
. . . . .63 D3
St Catherine's Mead
BS20 . . . . .47 D3
St Catherine's Terr BS3 . . .63 D3
St Catherines Pl 7 BS3 . . .63 D4
St Chad's Ave BA3 . . . . . .133 A8
St Chad's Gn BA3 . . . . . . .139 A8
St Charles Cl BA3 . . . . . . .133 A2
St Christopher's Ct 57 C5
St Christopher's Sch BS6 49 B4
St Christophers Cl BA2 . . .102 C8
St Clements Ct Bath BA1 .84 C1
6 Bristol BS16 . . . . .51 D3
Clevedon BS21 . . . . .57 C4
Keynsham BS31 . . . . .81 E4
2 Weston-S-M BS22 . . . . .89 A2
St Clements Rd BS31 . . . . .81 F4
St David's Ave BS30 . . . . . .66 B5
St David's Cl BS22 . . . . . . .88 B2
St David's Cres BS4 . . . . . .64 F6
St Dunstan's Rd BS3 . . . . .63 C2
St Dunstans BS31 . . . . . . .81 E6
St Edward's Rd BS8 . . . . .142 B2
St Edyth's Rd BS9 . . . . . . .48 C6
St Fagans Ct BS30 . . . . . . .66 B2
St Frances RC Sch BS48 .59 F1
St Francis Dr Wick BS30 . . .67 B7
Winterbourne BS36 . . . . . .37 F6
St Francis Rd
6 Bristol BS3 . . . . .63 A4
Keynsham BS31 . . . . .81 D6
St Gabriel's Bsns Pk 28
BS5 . . . . .64 B8
St Gabriel's Rd BS5 . . . . . .64 B8
St George CE Prim Sch
BS1 . . . . .142 B2
St George Pl BS1 . . . . . . .142 C2
St George's Hill
Bath BA2 . . . . .102 D8
Easton-in-G BS20 . . . . . . .47 A3
St George's Ho BS1 . . . . .142 B2
St George's Rd
Keynsham BS31 . . . . .81 D6
Portbury BS20 . . . . .46 E7
St Georges Ave 10 BS5 . . .64 F6
St Georges Blgs BA1 . . . .141 A3
St Georges Ho BS5 . . . . . .64 B8
St Georges Ind Est BS11 . .33 B3
St Georges Pl BA1 . . . . . .141 A3
St Georges Rd BS1 . . . . .142 C2
St Giles Barton GL12 . . . . .19 D8
St Gregory's RC Coll
BA2 . . . . .118 D8
St Gregory's Rd BS7 . . . . .49 F8
St Helen's Wlk BS5 . . . . . .51 A1
St Helena Rd BS6 . . . . . . .49 B3
St Helens CE Prim Sch
BS35 . . . . .15 A4
St Helens Dr Bristol BS30 . .66 C2
Wick BS30 . . . . .67 C7
St Helier Ave BS4 . . . . . . .64 F3
St Hilary Cl BS9 . . . . .48 D5
St Ivel Way BS30 . . . . .66 C6
St Ives Cl BS48 . . . . .60 A1
St Ives Rd BS23 . . . . .105 A5
St James Cl Bristol BS16 . .52 A5
Thornbury BS35 . . . . .8 C3
St James Ct BS32 . . . . . . .24 C3
St James Pl BS16 . . . . . . .52 A5
St James St Bristol BS16 . .52 A5

St James St continued
Weston-S-M BS23 ....104 D7
St James' Barton BS1 ..143 B4
St James' Barton Rdbt BS1 ....143 B4
St James's Ct 11 BS6 ....49 B1
St James's Par BA1 ....141 B2
St James's Pk BA1 ....141 B4
St James's Sq BA1 ....141 A4
St James's St BA1 ....141 B4
St John St
Hawkesbury Upton GL9 ....20 A3
2 Thornbury BS35 ....8 B1
St John the Evangelist CE Prim Sch BS21 ....57 C1
St John's Ave BS21 ....57 D3
St John's Bridge 3 BS1 143 A3
St John's CE Prim Sch BS8 ....49 A2
St John's CE Prim Sch BS31 ....81 E5
St John's CE Prim Sch BA3 ....133 A1
St John's Cl
Peasedown St John BA2 ..134 B7
Weston-S-M BS23 ....87 D1
St John's Cres Bristol BS3 63 E2
Midsomer Norton BA3 ...133 A2
St John's Ho BS5 ....64 D8
St John's La BS3 ....63 E2
St John's Mead CE Prim Sch BS37 ....28 B1
St John's Pl BA1 ....141 B2
St John's RC Prim Sch BA2 ....102 B6
St John's RC Prim Sch (Annexe) BA2 ....101 D4
St John's Rd
Backwell BS48 ....76 B5
Bath BA2 ....141 C3
Bath,Lower Weston BA1 ..101 C7
Bristol BS8 ....49 A1
Bristol,Bedminster BS3 ....63 C3
Clevedon BS21 ....57 D3
St John's St BS3 ....63 C3
St Johns Ct
Axbridge BS26 ....125 B2
Bristol,Bedminster BS3 ....63 D2
Bristol,Mayfield Park BS16 .51 A3
Keynsham BS31 ....81 E6
St Johns Rd BA2 ....116 B1
St Johns Way BS37 ....28 C2
St Joseph's RC Prim Sch
Bristol BS16 ....51 B3
Portishead BS20 ....45 C6
St Joseph's Rd
Bristol BS10 ....35 B3
Weston-S-M BS23 ....87 E1
St Jude's Terr BS22 ....88 C1
St Julian's CE Prim Sch BA2 ....118 E1
St Julian's Rd BA2 ....134 F5
St Julien's Cl BS39 ....132 E4
St Katherine's Sch BS20 .47 E3
St Keyna Ct BS31 ....81 F5
St Keyna Rd BS31 ....81 E5
St Kilda's Rd BA2 ....101 D5
St Ladoc Rd BS31 ....81 D6
St Laud Cl BS9 ....48 D5
St Leonard's Rd
Bristol,Golden Hill BS7 ....49 E5
Bristol,Lower Easton BS5 ..50 C2
St Loe Cl BS13 ....79 F3
St Lucia Cl BS7 ....49 E7
St Lucia Cres BS7 ....49 E7
St Luke St 12 BS5 ....64 B7
St Luke's Cl BA3 ....133 F3
St Luke's Cres BS3 ....63 F4
St Luke's Ct BS3 ....63 E4
St Luke's Gdns BS4 ....64 E2
St Luke's Mews BS4 ....64 E2
St Luke's Rd Bath BA2 ..101 F3
Bristol BS3 ....63 E4
Midsomer Norton BA3 ....132 F2
St Lukes Cl BS16 ....52 C7
St Margaret's Cl BS31 ....81 D6
St Margaret's Dr BS9 ....49 C5
St Margaret's La BS48 ....76 A5
St Margaret's Terr BS23 ....104 D8
St Margarets Cl BS48 ....76 A5
St Mark's Ave 1 BS5 ....50 B1
St Mark's Ecumenical CE/Methodist Prim Sch BS22 ....88 F4
St Mark's Gr 8 BS5 ....50 B1
St Mark's Rd Bath BA2 .141 C1
Bristol BS5 ....50 B1
Midsomer Norton BA3 ...133 A2
Weston-S-M BS22 ....89 A3
St Mark's Sch BA1 ....85 B2
St Mark's Terr 11 BS5 ....50 B1
St Marks Church Ho 4 BS5 ....50 B1
St Marks Cl BS31 ....81 E6
St Marks Gdns BA2 ....141 C1
St Marks Ho 13 BS5 ....50 B1
St Martin's CE Jun Sch BS22 ....88 D2
St Martin's Ct BA2 ....101 E1
St Martin's Gdns BS4 ....64 B1
St Martin's La SN14 ....69 F8
St Martin's Pk SN14 ....69 F8
St Martin's Rd BS4 ....64 B2
St Martin's Wlk BS4 ....64 B1
St Martins BS21 ....57 C5
St Martins Cl BS4 ....64 B1
St Martins Ct BS22 ....88 E3
St Martins Hospl BA2 ..101 E1
St Mary CE Prim Sch BA2 ....102 C8
St Mary Redcliffe & Temple CE Sch BS1 ....143 B1
St Mary Redcliffe CE Prim Sch BS3 ....63 E4
St Mary St BS35 ....15 B8
St Mary's Bldgs BA2 ...141 B1
St Mary's CE Prim Sch BS20 ....46 E3
St Mary's CE Prim Sch
Radstock BA3 ....134 C1
Thornbury BS35 ....8 A2
St Mary's CE Prim Sch
Timsbury BA2 ....116 C3
Yate BS37 ....27 E2
St Mary's Cl Bath BA2 ...102 B6
Timsbury BA2 ....116 B2
St Mary's Ct BS24 ....105 A1
St Mary's Gdns BS40 ...109 B5
St Mary's Gn BA2 ....116 B2
St Mary's Gr BS48 ....75 C8
St Mary's Hospl BS8 ...142 B3
St Mary's Park Rd BS20 .45 C4
St Mary's Pk BS48 ....75 C8
St Mary's RC Prim Sch BA1 ....84 B1
St Mary's Rd Bristol BS11 .47 D7
Hutton BS24 ....105 D2
Leigh Woods BS8 ....62 D6
Portishead BS20 ....45 C4
St Mary's St BS26 ....125 C2
St Mary's Way BS37 ....27 F2
St Mary's Wlk BS11 ....47 D6
St Marys Cl BS24 ....105 D2
St Marys RC Prim Sch BS32 ....37 A7
St Marys Rise BA3 ....134 C2
St Marys Way 6 BS35 ....8 B1
St Mathew's Pl BA2 ....102 B5
St Mathias Ho BS2 ....143 C3
St Matthew's Ave 10 BS6 49 D1
St Matthew's Cl BS23 ....87 D1
St Matthew's Rd BS6 ....143 A4
St Matthias & Dr Bell's CE Prim Sch BS16 ....51 A4
St Matthias Pk BS2 ....143 C3
St Michael On The Mount CE Prim Sch BS2 ....142 C3
St Michael's Ave
Clevedon BS21 ....57 D1
Weston-S-M BS22 ....89 A3
St Michael's CE Jun Sch BA2 ....101 A6
St Michael's CE Prim Sch BS34 ....36 E5
St Michael's Cl BS36 ....37 E7
St Michael's Ct BA2 ....119 E8
St Michael's Hill BS2 ....142 C4
St Michael's Hospl BS2 142 C4
St Michael's Pk BS2 ....142 C4
St Michael's Pl BA1 ....141 B2
St Michael's Rd BA1 ....101 D7
St Michaels CE Prim Sch BS36 ....37 E6
St Michaels Cl BS7 ....49 E4
St Michaels Ct BS15 ....65 B8
St Michaels Rd BA2 ....101 A5
St Nicholas Chantry CE Prim Sch BS21 ....57 E3
St Nicholas Cl BA15 ....120 D7
St Nicholas Ct BA2 ....85 F1
St Nicholas Inf Sch BA3 133 F2
St Nicholas of Tolentine RC Prim Sch BS5 ....64 A8
St Nicholas Pk 10 BS5 ....50 B1
St Nicholas Rd
Weston-S-M BS23 ....104 D2
Whitchurch BS14 ....80 C4
St Nicholas St BS1 ....143 A2
St Nicholas Way BS48 ...75 D2
St Nicholas' Rd BS2 ....49 F1
St Oswald's Ct BS13 ....79 A8
St Oswald's Ct BS6 ....49 B3
St Oswald's Rd BS6 ....49 B3
St Patrick's Ct BA2 ....102 B6
St Patrick's RC Prim Sch BS5 ....64 D7
St Patricks Ct BS31 ....81 E5
St Paul St BS2 ....143 B4
St Paul's RC Prim Sch BS37 ....39 E8
St Paul's Rd
2 Bristol,Southville BS3 ..63 D4
Bristol,Victoria Park BS8 .142 B4
Weston-S-M BS23 ....104 E5
St Pauls Pl Bath BA1 ....141 B2
Midsomer Norton BA3 ....133 A2
St Peter's Ave BS23 ....87 D1
St Peter's Cres BS36 ....38 B8
St Peter's Ho BS8 ....142 B2
St Peter's Rd BA3 ....139 C8
St Peter's Rise BS13 ....79 B7
St Peter's Terr BA2 ....101 D6
St Peter's Wlk 3 BS9 ....49 B6
St Peters CE Prim Sch BS20 ....45 D4
St Peters Rd BS20 ....45 D4
St Philip's CE Prim Sch BA2 ....101 D2
St Philip's Marsh Sch BS2 ....64 B5
St Philips Central BS2 ..64 A5
St Philips Cswy BS2 ....64 B5
St Philips Trad Pk BS2 ....64 B4
St Phillips Rd BS2 ....64 A7
St Pierre Dr BS30 ....66 B6
St Pius X RC Prim Sch BS13 ....79 A5
St Ronan's Ave BS6 ....49 C1
St Saviour's Inf Sch BA1 .85 B2
St Saviour's Jun Sch BA1 ....85 B2
St Saviour's Rd BA1 ....85 C2
St Saviour's Rise BS36 ..38 B6
St Saviour's Terr 10 BA1 .85 B1
St Saviours Way 4 BA1 .85 C1
St Stephen's Ave 3 BS1 ....143 A2
St Stephen's CE Jun Sch BS15 ....51 D2
St Stephen's CE Prim Sch BA1 ....84 F1
St Stephen's Cl BA1 ....84 F1
St Stephen's Ct BA1 ...141 B4
St Stephen's Pl BA1 ....141 B4
St Stephen's Rd
Bath BA1 ....141 B4
Bristol BS16 ....51 D2
St Stephen's St BS1 ...143 A2
St Stephens Bsns Ctr BS30 ....66 C5
St Stephens Cl BS16 ....51 E3
St Swithin's Pl BA1 ....141 C4
St Swithin's Yd BA1 ....141 C3
St Teresa's RC Prim Sch BS7 ....35 E1
St Thomas More RC Sec Sch BS7 ....50 A3
St Thomas Pl BS1 ....143 B2
St Thomas Rd BA3 ....133 B2
St Thomas St BS1 ....143 B2
St Thomas St E BS1 ....143 B2
St Ursula's High Sch BS9 49 A6
St Vigour & St John CE Prim Sch BA3 ....138 E3
St Vincent's Hill 1 BS6 ..49 A2
St Vincent's Rd BS8 ...142 A2
St Vincents Rock BS8 ....62 F6
St Vincents Trad Est BS2 .64 D6
St Werburgh's Pk BS2 ..50 A2
St Werburgh's Prim Sch BS5 ....50 A2
St Werburgh's Rd BS2 ...49 F2
St Whytes Rd BS4 ....79 D8
St Winifreds Dr BA2 ...102 D2
Salcombe Gdns BS22 ....89 A2
Salcombe Rd BS4 ....64 A1
Salem Rd BS36 ....37 F7
Salisbury Ave BS15 ....65 B8
Salisbury Dr BS16 ....51 E6
Salisbury Gdns BS16 ....51 E5
Salisbury Pk BS16 ....51 E6
Salisbury Rd Bath BA1 ...85 B2
Bristol,Mangotsfield BS16 .51 E6
Bristol,Redland BS6 ....49 D2
Bristol,St Anne's BS4 ....64 D5
Paulton BS39 ....132 F4
Weston-S-M BS22 ....88 C1
Salisbury St
Bristol,Pile Marsh BS5 ....64 E7
Bristol,Russell Town BS5 ..64 B6
Salisbury Terr BS23 ....104 D7
Sally Barn Cl BS30 ....65 E2
Sally Hill BS20 ....45 E7
Sally In The Wood BA1, BA15 ....103 D6
Sally Lunn's Kitchen Mus* BA1 ....141 C2
Sallys Way BS36 ....37 F7
Sallysmead Cl 4 BS13 ...79 B4
Salmon Cl BS35 ....22 A6
Salmons Way BS16 ....52 B8
Saltford CE Prim Sch BS31 ....82 E2
Saltford Ct BS31 ....82 E3
Salthouse Ct BS21 ....57 B2
Salthouse Farm Pk BS35 22 A7
Salthouse Rd BS21 ....57 B2
Salthrop Rd BS7 ....49 E4
Saltings Cl BS21 ....57 B2
Saltmarsh Dr BS11 ....34 A1
Saltwell Ave BS14 ....80 C5
Salway Cl BS40 ....95 E1
Sambourne La BS20 ....47 C4
Samian Way BS34 ....36 E5
Sampson House Bsns Pk BS10 ....34 D7
Sampsons Rd BS13 ....79 D4
Samuel St 3 BS5 ....64 C8
Samuel White Rd BS15 ..65 C4
Samuel White's Inf Sch BS15 ....65 C4
Samuel Wright Cl BS30 ..66 D5
San Andreas BS34 ....35 E6
Sanctuary Gdns BS9 ....48 D3
Sand Farm La BS22 ....88 A6
Sand Hill BS4 ....64 C4
Sand Rd BS22 ....88 B5
Sandbach Rd BS4 ....64 D4
Sandbed Rd BS2 ....50 A2
Sandburrows Rd BS13 ..78 F6
Sandburrows Wlk BS13 ..78 F6
Sandcroft BS14 ....79 F6
Sandcroft Ave BS23 ....104 D2
Sandford Cl 2 BS21 ....57 B1
Sandford Prim Sch BS25 ....108 B4
Sandford Rd Bristol BS8 .142 A1
Weston-S-M BS23 ....105 A7
Winscombe BS25 ....107 F1
Sandgate Rd BS4 ....64 D3
Sandholme Cl BS16 ....51 E8
Sandholme Rd BS4 ....64 D4
Sandhurst BS37 ....39 D8
Sandhurst Cl BS34 ....24 B1
Sandhurst Rd BS4 ....64 D4
Sandling Ave BS7 ....50 A7
Sandmead Rd BS25 ....108 A4
Sandown Cl BS16 ....37 F1
Sandown Rd
Bristol,Filton BS34 ....36 C3
Bristol,Kensington Park BS4 64 D4
Sandpiper Dr BS22 ....88 F1
Sandpits La GL9 ....20 A2
Sandringham Ave BS16 ..51 E8
Sandringham Ct BS23 ..104 F5
Sandringham Pk BS16 ...51 E8
Sandringham Rd
Bristol,Kensington Park BS4 64 D4
Bristol,Longwell Green BS30 ....65 F2
Bristol,Stoke Gifford BS34 .36 D4
Weston-S-M BS23 ....104 F5
Sands Hill SN14 ....54 E3
Sands La BS36 ....25 F1
Sandstone Rise BS36 ....37 E4
Sandwich Rd BS4 ....64 D4
Sandy Cl BS32 ....36 E6
Sandy La Aust BS35 ....13 A7
Aust BS35 ....13 A8
Bristol BS5 ....50 C3
Easton-in-G BS8 ....61 A8
Failand BS8 ....61 C7
Stanton Drew BS39,BS40 ..96 E3
Sandy Lodge BS37 ....39 E8
Sandy Park Rd BS4 ....64 C3
Sandyleaze BS9 ....48 E7
Sarabeth Dr BA2 ....117 A4
Saracen St BA1 ....141 C3
Sarah St BS5 ....64 B7
Sargent St BS3 ....63 E4
Sarum Cl BS16 ....52 C6
Sarum Cres BS10 ....35 C1
Sassoon Ct BS30 ....65 F5
Satchfield Cl BS10 ....34 F2
Satchfield Cres BS10 ....34 F2
Satellite Bsns Pk BS5 ..64 D6
Sates Way BS9 ....49 C6
Saunders Rd BS16 ....51 E4
Saunton Wlk BS4 ....79 E8
Savages Wood Rd BS32 .36 D8
Savernake Rd BS22 ....88 F3
Saville Cres BS22 ....105 C8
Saville Gate Cl BS9 ....48 F4
Saville Mews BS6 ....143 A4
Saville Pl BS8 ....142 A2
Saville Rd Bristol BS9 ...48 F3
Weston-S-M BS22 ....105 C8
Saville Row BA1 ....141 B3
Savoy Rd BS4 ....64 D4
Saw Cl BA1 ....141 B2
Saw Mill La 5 BS35 ....8 B1
Sawmill Gdns BA3 ....138 D3
Sawyers Cl
Chilcompton BA3 ....138 D3
Nailsea BS48 ....60 A2
Sawyers Ct BS21 ....57 E3
Saxby Cl Clevedon BS21 ..57 B1
Weston-S-M BS22 ....89 B4
Saxon Ct BS22 ....89 D3
Saxon Rd Bristol BS2 ....50 A2
Weston-S-M BS22 ....105 C8
Saxon St BS40 ....109 D6
Saxon Way Bristol BS32 ..24 C1
Peasedown St John BA2 ..134 E8
Winsley BA15 ....120 F7
Say Wlk BS30 ....66 D7
Says La BS40 ....109 B4
SBI Ctr BS15 ....65 B5
Scafell Cl BS23 ....88 A1
Scandrett Cl BS10 ....34 E2
Scantleberry Cl BS16 ....51 D8
Scaurs The BS22 ....88 F2
School Cl Banwell BS29 ..107 B3
Bristol,Clay Hill BS5 ....50 D2
Bristol,Little Stoke BS34 ...36 C8
Bristol,Whitchurch BS14 ...79 F4
Hillesley GL12 ....19 E8
School Ct BS34 ....37 A4
School La Badminton GL9 .30 E2
Barrow Gurney BS48 ....77 D5
Batheaston BA1 ....85 F4
2 Bristol BS16 ....50 E5
Chew Stoke BS40 ....112 D8
Farrington Gurney BS39 ..132 A4
Rowberrow BS25 ....109 A1
School of Christ the King RC Prim Sch BS4 ....79 E8
School Rd Bristol BS15 ...65 C8
Bristol,Broom Hill BS4 ....64 E3
Bristol,Cadbury Heath BS30 66 A4
Bristol,Oldland Common BS30 ....66 C3
Bristol,Totterdown BS4 ....64 A3
Frampton Cotterell BS36 ...38 A8
Wrington BS40 ....92 E2
School View BS48 ....60 B1
School Way BS35 ....22 A6
School Wlk Bristol BS5 ...50 D1
Yate BS37 ....27 E2
Scobell Rise BS39 ....115 C2
Scop The BS32 ....24 B5
Score La BS40 ....110 E2
Score The BS40 ....110 E2
Scot Elm Dr BS24 ....89 D1
Scot La BS40 ....95 D1
Scotch Horn Cl 7 BS48 ..59 F2
Scotch Horn Way BS48 ...59 F2
Scotland La BS4,BS14 ....81 A7
Scots Pine Ave 5 BS48 ..59 F2
Scott Ct BS30 ....65 F5
Scott Lawrence Cl BS16 .51 A7
Scott Rd BS23 ....105 A4
Scott Way BS37 ....39 F8
Scott Wlk BS30 ....66 D7
Scumbrum La BS39 ....115 C2
Sea Bank Rd BS20 ....32 E1
Sea Mills Inf Sch BS9 ...48 C7
Sea Mills Jun Sch BS9 ..48 B5
Sea Mills La BS9 ....48 C5
Sea Mills Sta BS9 ....48 B4
Seabrook Rd BS22 ....88 D1
Seagry Cl BS10 ....35 E1
Searle Court Ave BS4 ....64 E4
Searle Cres BS23 ....105 A6
Searle Ct BS21 ....57 E2
Seaton Ct BS3 ....63 D1
Seaton Rd BS5 ....50 C1
Seavale Mews BS21 ....57 C4
Seavale Rd BS21 ....57 C4
Seaview Rd
Portishead,Redcliffe Bay BS20 ....44 F4
Portishead,West Hill BS20 ..44 F6
Seawalls BS9 ....48 D2
Seawalls Rd BS9 ....48 D2
Second Ave Bath BA2 ...101 D5
Bristol BS14 ....80 B7
Radstock BA3 ....139 C7
Second Way BS11 ....33 D1
Seddon Rd 4 BS2 ....50 A2
Sedgefield Gdns BS16 ...37 F1
Sedgemoor Cl BS48 ....75 E8
Sedgemoor Rd Bath BA2 101 F2
Weston-S-M BS23 ....87 F1
Sedgwick Ho BS11 ....47 E7
Sefton Park Jun & Inf Schs BS7 ....49 F3
Sefton Park Rd BS7 ....49 F3
Sefton Sq BS24 ....106 A8
Selborne Rd BS7 ....49 F5
Selbourne Cl BA1 ....101 A8
Selbourne Rd BS23 ....104 E4
Selbrooke Cres BS16 ....51 C6
Selby Rd BS5 ....50 F1
Selden Rd BS14 ....80 E5
Selkirk Rd BS15 ....51 C1
Selley Wlk BS13 ....79 A5
Selway Ct BA2 ....102 B2
Selwood Cl BS22 ....105 C7
Selworthy BS15 ....65 E7
Selworthy Cl BS31 ....81 D5
Selworthy Gdns 4 BS48 .59 E1
Selworthy Ho BA2 ....101 F2
Selworthy Rd Bristol BS4 .64 B2
Weston-S-M BS23 ....105 A4
Selworthy Terr BA2 ....101 F2
Seneca Pl 1 BS5 ....64 D7
Seneca St BS5 ....64 D7
Septimus Bldgs BS14 ....79 D5
Serbert Cl BS20 ....45 E5
Serbert Rd BS20 ....45 E5
Serbert Way BS20 ....45 E5
Sercombe Pk BS21 ....57 E1
Serlo Ct BS22 ....89 A4
Serridge La BS36 ....38 D4
Seven Acres La BA1 ....85 F5
Seven Acres The BS24 ..105 F7
Seven Dials BA1 ....141 B2
Seventh Ave
Bristol,Hengrove BS14 ....80 A7
Bristol,Northville BS7 ....36 B1
Severn Ave BS23 ....104 E5
Severn Beach Prim Sch BS35 ....22 A6
Severn Beach Sta BS35 ..22 A6
Severn Cl GL12 ....11 A4
Severn Dr BS35 ....8 B2
Severn Grange BS10 ....34 D3
Severn La GL13 ....2 F8
Severn Rd
Avonmouth BS11 ....33 C4
Bristol BS11 ....47 D6
Hallen BS10 ....34 A7
Pill BS20 ....47 C5
Portishead BS20 ....45 C5
Severn Beach BS10 ....21 F3
Weston-S-M BS23 ....104 E5
Severn View BS11 ....34 C1
Severn View Rd BS35 ....8 C2
Severn Way Bristol BS34 ..23 F1
Keynsham BS31 ....82 A5
Severnleigh Gdns BS9 ...48 F3
Severnmeade BS20 ....44 F5
Severnside Trad Est BS11 ....33 C5
Severnwood Gdns BS35 ..22 A5
Sevier Rd BS26 ....123 C3
Sevier St BS2 ....49 F2
Seville Ct BS20 ....45 E7
Seville Rd BS20 ....45 E7
Seward Terr BA3 ....134 C2
Sewell Ho BS25 ....125 A8
Seymour Ave BS7 ....49 E4
Seymour Cl Clevedon BS21 57 E3
Weston-S-M BS22 ....88 F4
Seymour Rd Bath BA1 ..141 C4
Bristol,Ashley Down BS7 ...49 E4
Bristol,Baptist Mills BS5 ...50 A1
Bristol,Staple Hill BS16 ....51 E4
Bristol,Two Mile Hill BS15 ..51 C1
Seyton Wlk BS34 ....36 E5
Shackel Hendy Mews BS16 ....52 B5
Shackleton Ave BS37 ....39 F8
Shadow Wlk BS24 ....106 C3
Shadwell Rd BS7 ....49 D3

Shaft Rd Bath BA2 ......102 E1
Severn Beach BS35 .....22 A8
Shaftesbury Ave
Bath BA1 ....101 C7
Bristol BS6 ....49 E1
Shaftesbury Cl BS48 ....75 D8
Shaftesbury Mews BA2 .101 D5
Shaftesbury Rd
Bath BA2 ....101 D5
Weston-S-M BS23 ......105 B8
Shaftesbury Terr
8 Bristol BS5 ....64 D7
Radstock BA3 ....134 A3
Shakespeare Ave
Bath BA2 ....101 F4
Bristol BS7 ....50 A8
Shakespeare Rd BA3 ...133 C1
Shaldon Rd BS7 ....50 A4
Shallowbrooks La SN14 ..31 F8
Shallows The BS31 ......82 F3
Sham Castle La BA2 ....102 C7
Shamrock Rd BS5 ....50 D3
Shanklin Dr BS34 ....36 B3
Shannon Ct BS35 ....15 D8
Shapcott Cl BS4 ....64 B1
Shaplands BS9 ....48 F4
Sharland Cl BS9 ....48 A4
Sharland Gr **4** BS13 ...79 C4
Shaw Cl
Bristol,Mangotsfield BS16 .52 B3
3 Bristol,Upper Easton
BS5 ....64 B8
Shaw Gdns BS14 ....80 A8
Shaws Way BA2 ....100 F5
Shaymoor La BS35 ......23 A4
Shearmore Cl BS7 ......50 A7
Sheene Ct **18** BS3 .....63 C3
Sheene La BS3 ....63 C3
Sheene Way BS3 ....63 C3
Sheepfair La SN14 ......69 F6
Sheephouse Caravan Pk
BS20 ....46 E7
Sheeps Croft BS13 .....79 A5
Sheepwash The BS35 ....7 D5
Sheepway BS20 ....46 B5
Sheepway La BS20 .....46 C5
Sheepwood Cl BS10 ....35 A2
Sheepwood Rd BS10 ...35 A2
Sheiling Sch BS35 ......8 B2
Sheldare Barton BS5 ....65 B7
Sheldon Cl BS21 ....57 F2
Sheldrake Dr BS16 .....50 E6
Shellard Rd BS34 ......36 A2
Shellards La BS35 ......15 E2
Shellards Rd BS30 .....65 F3
Shelley Ave BS21 ......57 D2
Shelley Cl BS5 ....64 F8
Shelley Ho BS34 ....24 A1
Shelley Rd Bath BA2 ...101 F4
Radstock BA3 ....133 C1
Weston-S-M BS23 ......105 A4
Shelley Way BS7 ....50 A8
Shellmor Ave BS34 .....24 B1
Shellmor Cl BS32 ......24 D1
Shepherds Cl BS16 .....51 E5
Sheppard Rd BS16 .....51 C6
Sheppards Gdns BA1 ...84 B1
Sheppards Wlk BA3 ....138 D3
Shepperdine Rd BS35 ...1 D2
Sheppy's Mill BS49 .....91 D5
Shepton BS24 ....105 A2
Shepton Wlk BS3 ......63 C2
Sherbourne Ave BS32 ..36 E7
Sherbourne Cl BS15 ....51 F2
Sherbourne St BS5 .....64 D7
Sherbourne's Brake
BS32 ....36 E6
Sheridan Rd Bath BA2 .100 F5
Bristol BS7 ....50 A8
Sheridan Way BS30 ....66 A2
Sherrin Way BS13 ......78 E3
Sherrings The BS34 .....36 B8
Sherston Cl Bristol BS16 .51 B5
Nailsea BS48 ....60 A1
Sherston Rd Bristol BS7 .49 E8
Luckington SN14 ....31 F5
Sherwell Rd BS4 ......64 E1
Sherwood Cl BS31 .....81 E5
Sherwood Cres BS22 ...88 F3
Sherwood Rd Bristol BS15 51 B1
Keynsham BS31 ....81 E5
Shetland Rd BS10 .....35 D1
Shetland Way BS48 ....60 A1
Shickle Gr BA2 ....101 D1
Shield Ret Ctr BS34 ....36 A3
Shield Road Prim Sch
BS7 ....36 A1
Shields Ave BS7 ....36 A1
Shiels Dr BS32 ....36 D7
Shilton Cl BS15 ....65 F7
Shimsey Cl BS16 ......51 C6
Shiners Elms BS49 .....91 B8
Ship La BS1 ....143 B1
Shipham CE Fst Sch
BS25 ....125 E8
Shipham Cl
10 Bristol BS14 ......80 B5
Nailsea BS48 ....75 F8
Shipham La BS25 ......108 B1
Shipham Rd
Cheddar BS27 ....126 A3
Shipham BS25,BS27 ...125 F1
Shiplate Rd BS24,BS26 .122 E6
Shipley Mow BS16 .....52 B6
Shipley Rd BS9 ....49 A8
Shipman Ct BS16 ......51 E4
Shire Gdns BS11 ......47 D8
Shire Hill SN14 ....56 A7

Shire Way BS37 ....39 D6
Shirehampton Prim Sch
BS11 ....47 D6
Shirehampton Rd BS9 ..48 C6
Shirehampton Sta BS11 .47 D5
Shires Yd BA1 ....141 B3
Shockerwick La BA1 ....86 D4
Shop La GL9 ....30 E2
Shophouse Rd BA2 ....101 B5
Shopland Ho **10** BS21 .57 C2
Shorland Ho BS8 ......49 A1
Short La Litton BA3 ....130 F2
Long Ashton BS41 .....62 A2
Short St BS2 ....64 A5
Short Way Failand BS8 .61 B4
Thornbury BS35 ....15 B7
Shorthill Rd BS37 .....39 C4
Shortlands La BS11 ....34 A1
Shortwood Hill BS16 ...52 E4
Shortwood Rd
Bristol BS13 ....79 E3
Pucklechurch BS16 ....53 A4
Shortwood View BS15 ..65 D5
Shortwood Wlk BS13 ..79 E3
Shoscombe CE Prim Sch
BA2 ....134 F5
Showering Cl BS14 ....80 D5
Showering Rd BS14 ....80 D5
Shrewsbury Bow BS24 .106 A8
Shrubbery Ave BS23 ...87 D1
Shrubbery Cotts **4** BS6 .49 B2
Shrubbery Ct **6** BS16 .51 D5
Shrubbery Rd
Bristol BS16 ....51 D5
Weston-S-M BS23 ......87 D1
Shrubbery Terr BS23 ...87 C1
Shrubbery Wlk BS23 ...87 D1
Shrubbery Wlk W BS23 .87 D1
Shuter Rd BS13 ....78 E5
Sibland BS35 ....15 D8
Sibland Cl **3** BS35 ....15 D8
Sibland Rd BS35 ......15 D8
Sibland Way BS35 .....15 D8
Sidcot BS4 ....65 A2
Sidcot La BS25 ....125 A7
Sidcot Sch BS25 ......125 B7
Sideland Cl BS14 ......80 E6
Sidelands Rd BS16 ....51 C6
Sidelings The BS40 ....128 D8
Sidings The Bristol BS34 .36 C2
Charfield GL12 ....11 B5
Sidmouth Ct BS3 ......63 D1
Sidmouth Gdns BS3 ...63 D2
Sidmouth Rd BS3 .....63 E2
Sidney Hill Cottage Homes
BS25 ....108 E4
Signal Rd BS16 ....51 F4
Silbury Rd BS3 ....62 E2
Silbury Rise BS31 .....82 A2
Silcox Rd BS13 ....79 C4
Silver Birch Cl BS34 ...36 D7
Silver Ct BS48 ....59 C2
Silver Mead BS49 .....91 D2
Silver Moor La BS29 ...106 F7
Silver St Bristol BS1 ...143 A3
Chew Magna BS40 ....96 B3
Congresbury BS49 .....91 D2
Holcombe BA3 ....139 C1
Kilmersdon BA3 ....140 B5
Midsomer Norton BA3 .139 A7
Nailsea BS48 ....59 D2
Portishead BS20 ......44 F1
7 Thornbury BS35 ....8 B1
Wrington BS40 ....92 E2
Silverberry Rd BS22 ...89 A1
Silvercombe **1** BS23 ..104 E5
Silverhill Brake BS35 ..14 E1
Silverhill Rd BS10 .....34 E4
Silverhill Sch BS36 ....37 E7
Silverlow Rd BS48 ....59 D2
Silverstone Way BS49 .91 D3
Silverthorne La BS2 ...64 B6
Silverthorne Wharf BS2 .64 B6
Silverton Ct BS4 ......63 F1
Simmonds View BS34 ..36 F5
Simon's Cl BS39 ......132 F5
Simons Cl BS22 ....89 A2
Simplex Ind Est The
BS30 ....66 D4
Sinclair Ho
Bristol,Clifton Wood BS8 .142 A2
Bristol,Newleaze BS34 ..36 A2
Singapore Rd BS23 ....104 E3
Sion Hill Bath BA1 .....84 E1
Bristol BS8 ....62 F7
Sion Hill Pl BA1 ....84 E1
Sion La BS8 ....62 F7
Sion Pl Bath BA2 ......102 B6
Bristol BS8 ....62 F7
Sion Rd Bath BA1 .....84 E1
10 Bristol BS3 ....63 C3
Sir Bernard Lovell Sch
BS30 ....66 C4
Sir Bernard Lovell Sch
(annexe) BS30 ......66 D5
Sir Bevil Grenville's Mon★
BA1 ....85 E7
Sir John's La Bristol BS5 .50 B4
Bristol BS7 ....50 B5
Siskin Wlk BS22 ......105 F8
Siston Cl BS15 ....52 A2
Siston Comm
Bristol,Goose Green BS30 .52 B3
Bristol,New Cheltenham
BS15 ....52 A2
Siston Ctr The BS15 ...52 A2

Siston Hill BS30 ....52 B1
Siston Hill Rdbt BS16 ..52 B2
Siston La BS30 ....52 F2
Siston Pk BS15 ....52 A2
Six Streams BA1 ......84 B2
Six Ways BS21 ....57 C4
Sixpence BS39 ....115 D2
Sixth Ave
Bristol,Hengrove BS14 .80 A7
Bristol,Northville BS7 ..36 B1
Sixty Acres Cl BS8 ....61 B4
Skinner's Hill BA2 .....133 F7
Skinners La BS25 .....108 F4
Skippon Ct BS15 ......65 E5
Sladacre La BS40 .....110 E2
Slade La
Barrow Gurney BS48 ...77 C4
Lympsham BS24 ....122 B1
Slade Rd BS20 ....45 D5
Sladebrook Ave BA2 ..101 C3
Sladebrook Ct BA2 ...101 C3
Sladebrook Rd BA2 ...101 B4
Slades Ct BS48 ......76 A6
Slate La BS39 ....98 B7
Sleep La BS14 ....80 D3
Slimbridge Cl BS37 ...39 F7
Sloan St BS5 ....64 D8
Sloe Cl BS22 ....105 D8
Slough La BS40 ......92 E2
Slymbridge Ave BS10 ..35 A3
Small Down End BS25 .107 F2
Small La BS16 ....50 E5
Small St Bristol BS1 ...143 A3
Bristol,St Philip's Marsh
BS2 ....64 A5
Smallbrook La BS39 ...98 B6
Smallcombe Cl BA3 ...133 E5
Smallcombe Rd BA3 ..133 E4
Smallway BS49 ....91 D5
Smarts Gn BS37 ......40 C8
Smeaton Rd BS1 .....62 F5
Smith's Forge Ind Est
BS49 ....73 F3
Smithcourt Dr BS34 ...36 D6
Smithmead BS13 .....79 B5
Smoke La BS11 ......33 D6
Smyth Rd BS3 ....63 A3
Smyth Terr **3** BS3 ...63 C4
Smythe Croft BS14 ...80 A3
Smyths Cl BS11 ......33 B1
Snow Hill BA1 ....85 A1
Snow Hill Ho BA1 ....141 C4
Snowberry Cl Bristol BS32 36 E8
Weston-S-M BS22 .....89 A1
Snowberry Wlk BS5 ...50 E1
Snowdon Cl BS16 ....50 F4
Snowdon Rd BS16 ...50 F4
Snowdon Vale BS23 ..88 A1
Soapers La BS35 .....15 B8
Soaphouse Ind Est BS5 .64 E8
Sodbury Rd GL12 .....18 A4
Solent Way BS35 .....15 D7
Solon Ct BS13 ....78 F5
Solsbury Ct BA1 .....85 E3
Solsbury La BA1 .....85 F4
Solsbury View **18** BA1 .85 A1
Solsbury Way BA1 ....85 A2
Somer Ave BA3 ......132 F2
Somer Ct BA3 ....133 B1
Somer Ho **1** BA3 ...133 A1
Somer Lea BA3 ......138 D5
Somer Rd BA3 ....132 F2
Somerby Cl BS32 ....36 D7
Somerdale Ave
Bath BA2 ....101 D2
Bristol BS4 ....64 A1
Weston-S-M BS22 .....105 C8
Somerdale Cl BS22 ...105 C8
Somerdale Rd BS31 ...81 F7
Somerdale Rd N BS30,
BS31 ....81 F8
Somerdale View BA2 ..101 C2
Somerford Ct BS10 ...34 F1
Somermead BS3 .....63 C1
Somerset Ave
Weston-S-M BS22,BS24 .106 A8
Yate BS37 ....27 C4
Somerset Cl GL12 ....11 F4
Somerset Cres BS34 ..36 F5
Somerset Folly BA2 ...116 B2
Somerset Ho Bath BA2 .101 D4
12 Bristol BS2 ....143 C3
Somerset La BA1 .....84 E1
Somerset Mews BS23 .104 F6
Somerset Pl BA1 .....84 E1
Somerset Rd Bristol BS4 .64 B3
Clevedon BS21 ....57 E3
Portishead BS20 ......44 F5
Somerset Sq Bristol BS1 .143 B1
3 Nailsea BS48 ......59 E2
Somerset St Bath BA1 .141 C1
Bristol BS1 ....143 B1
Bristol,Kingsdown BS2 .143 A4
Somerset Terr BS3 ....63 D3
Somerset Way BS39 ..132 E6
Somerton BS24 ......105 A2
Somerton Cl BS15 ....65 E7
Somerton Rd Bristol BS7 .49 E6
Clevedon BS21 ....57 E1
Somervale Rd BA3 ...133 C2
Somervale Sch BA3 ..133 A1
Somerville Cl BS31 ...82 E2
Somerville Rd BS25 ..108 A4
Sommerville Rd BS7 ..49 E3
Sommerville Rd S **1** BS6 49 F2
Soper Gdns BS4 .....79 D7
Sophia Gdns BS22 ...89 B4
Sopworth Rd SN14 ...31 E5

Sorrel Cl BS35 ....8 D2
Soundwell Coll (Folly La Ctr)
BS2 ....64 A6
Soundwell Rd BS15,BS16 .51 D2
South Ave Bath BA2 ...101 D5
Portishead BS20 ......45 D6
Yate BS37 ....27 B1
South Bristol Bsns Pk
BS4 ....79 E7
South Bristol Ret Pk BS3 63 A3
South Bristol Trad Pk
BS3 ....62 F3
South Combe BS24 ...122 B6
South Croft Bristol BS9 .49 C7
Winscombe BS25 .....107 F2
South Ct BS32 ....24 D3
South Dene BS9 .....48 E6
South Gr Bristol BS6 ..49 C5
Pill BS20 ....47 C4
South Green St **9** BS8 .62 F6
South Hayes BS5 .....50 B4
South Hill BS25 ......107 F2
South Lawn BS24 ....105 F4
South Lawn Cl BS24 ..105 F4
South Lea Rd BA1 ....101 A8
South Liberty La
Bristol BS3 ....63 A1
2 Bristol BS3 ....63 B2
South Mdws BS40 ....92 E2
South Par Bristol BS1 .141 C2
Chew Magna BS40 ....96 B3
Weston-S-M BS23 .....104 D8
Yate BS37 ....27 E1
South Parade Cotts
BA2 ....102 C1
South Rd
Almondsbury BS32 ....24 E6
11 Bristol,Bedminster BS3 .63 C3
Bristol,Kingswood BS15 .65 D8
Bristol,Redland BS6 ..49 C2
Lympsham BS24 ......122 B1
Midsomer Norton BA3 .133 B1
Portishead BS20 ......45 D7
Timsbury BA2 ....116 B2
Weston-S-M BS23 .....87 C1
South Rock Ind Est BA3 138 D1
South Side BS49 .....91 E5
South St Bristol BS3 ..63 B3
Stratton-on-t-F BA3 ..138 F2
South Street Prim Sch
BS3 ....63 B3
South Terr **6** Bristol BS6 49 B2
Weston-S-M BS23 .....104 D8
South View Bath BA2 .102 C1
Bristol BS16 ....51 E5
Frampton Cotterell BS36 38 B7
Paulton BS39 ....132 E6
Portishead BS20 ......45 D7
Radstock BA3 ....133 D5
Timsbury BA2 ....116 B2
South View Bsns Pk
BS16 ....51 F5
South View Cres BS36 .38 D6
South View Pl BA3 ...133 B2
South View Rd BA2 ..101 D6
South View Rise BS36 .38 D6
South View Terr BS49 .74 B1
South Wlk BS37 ......27 E1
Southampton Gdns **2**
BS7 ....49 F5
Southampton Mews **1**
BS7 ....49 F5
Southbourne Gdns BA1 .85 B1
Southbourne Mans BA2 .142 B2
Southbow Ho **2** BS3 .63 A3
Southcot Pl BA2 .....141 C1
Southdown BS22 .....88 F4
Southdown Ave BA2 ..101 B3
Southdown Com Inf Sch
BA2 ....101 B3
Southdown Jun Sch
BA2 ....101 B3
Southdown Rd Bath BA2 101 B3
Bristol BS9 ....48 F8
Southend Ho GL12 ...18 A5
Southend Rd BS23 ...104 E4
Southern Ring Path **4**
BS21 ....57 B1
Southern Way BS21 ..57 C1
Southernhay
Bristol,Clifton Wood BS8 .142 B2
Bristol,Staple Hill BS16 .51 D4
Southernhay Ave BS8 .142 B2
Southernhay Cres BS8 .142 B2
Southey Ave BS15 ...51 E1
Southey Ct BS15 .....51 D1
Southey Rd BS21 ....57 D2
Southey St BS2 ......49 F2
Southfield
Norton St Philip BA2 ..136 F4
Radstock BA3 ....134 A2
Southfield Ave BS15 ..51 E1
Southfield Cl
Nailsea BS48 ....59 E3
Weston-S-M BS23 .....104 D2
Southfield Ct BS9 ....49 A7
Southfield Rd
Bristol,Cotham BS6 ..49 D1
Bristol,Eastfield BS9 ..49 A7
Nailsea BS19 ....59 F3
Southfield Rd Trad Est
BS48 ....59 F3
Southfield Way BS37 ..28 A4
Southgate BA1 ....141 C2
Southlands Bath BA1 ..84 B1
Bristol BS9 ....48 C8
Tytherington GL12 ....16 B4
Southlands Dr BA2 ...116 B2

Southlands Way BS49 .91 E5
Southleaze BS25 .....125 A6
Southleigh BS25 .....124 F8
Southleigh Mews BS8 .142 B4
Southleigh Rd BS8 ...142 B4
Southmead BS25 .....125 A8
Southmead Hospl BS10 .49 E8
Southmead Rd
Bristol BS10,BS34 ....35 E1
Weston-S-M BS22 .....105 B7
Southmead Way BS10 .49 E8
Southover Cl BS9 .....49 A8
Southover Rd BS9 ....115 D1
Southridge Hts BS24 .122 A8
Southsea Rd BS34 ....36 A8
Southside BS23 ......104 E8
Southside Cl BS9 .....48 B8
Southside Cres BS22 ..88 A4
Southstoke La BA2 ...118 F8
Southstoke Rd BA2 ...101 F1
Southview Cl BS24 ...105 D4
Southville Pl BS3 .....63 D4
Southville Prim Sch BS3 63 C4
Southville Rd Bristol BS3 63 C4
Weston-S-M BS23 .....104 E4
Southville Terr BA2 ...102 B4
Southway Ct BS21 ...57 D1
Southway Dr BS15 ...66 D5
Southwell St BS2 .....142 C4
Southwood Ave BS9 ..48 C8
Southwood Dr BS9 ...48 B8
Southwood Dr E BS9 ..48 C8
Sovereign Sh Ctr BS23 .104 E7
Spalding Cl BS7 ......50 A3
Spaniorum View BS35 .22 F2
Spar Rd Avonmouth BS11 33 D4
Yate BS37 ....27 D2
Spartley Dr BS13 .....78 F6
Spartley Wlk BS13 ...78 F6
Specklemead BS39 ...132 D5
Speedwell Ave **5** BS5 64 D7
Speedwell Cl BS35 ...8 D2
Speedwell Est **3** BS21 57 C2
Speedwell Rd BS5,BS15 51 A1
Speedwell Tech Coll
BS15 ....51 A1
Spencer Dr
Midsomer Norton BA3 .133 A2
Weston-S-M BS22 .....89 A4
Spencer Ho **6** BS1 ..143 B1
Spencer's Ct BS35 ...15 B5
Spencers Belle Vue
BA1 ....141 B4
Sperring Ct BA3 .....138 F8
Spey Cl BS35 ....15 C8
Spindleberry Gr BS48 .60 A2
Spinners End BS32 ...89 B4
Spinney Croft BS13 ...78 F5
Spinney Rd BS24 ....106 D4
Spinney The Bristol BS32 36 E7
Frampton Cotterell BS36 .38 B7
Portishead BS20 ......45 C4
Weston-S-M BS24 .....104 F1
Spires View **4** BS16 ..50 E5
Spout La GL9 ....41 D2
Spratts Bridge BS40 ..96 A3
Spring Cres BA2 .....141 C2
Spring Gardens Rd BA2 141 C2
Spring Gdns BS4 ....64 A1
Spring Ground Rd BS39 132 E5
Spring Hill
Bristol,Hopewell Hill BS15 51 E2
Bristol,Kingswood BS2 .143 A4
Weston-S-M BS22 .....88 B1
Spring Hill Dr BS22 ..88 E1
Spring Ho **2** BS35 ..15 C8
Spring La Bath BA1 ..85 B2
Dundry BS41 ....79 A1
Spring Leigh BS8 ....62 D6
Spring Rise BS20 ....45 C3
Spring St BS3 ....63 E4
Spring Street Pl BS3 ..63 E4
Spring Terr BS22 .....88 C2
Spring Vale BA1 .....85 B2
Spring Valley BA1 ...88 C2
Spring Wood Gdns
BS24 ....105 E3
Springfield
Norton St Philip BA2 ..136 E4
Peasedown St John BA2 .134 C7
1 Thornbury BS35 ....15 D8
Springfield Ave
Bristol,Ashley Down BS7 .49 F5
Bristol,Shirehampton BS11 .47 E6
Bristol,Vinney Green BS16 .52 A7
Weston-S-M BS22 .....88 D1
Springfield Bldgs
Midsomer Norton BS39 .132 D2
Radstock BA3 ....134 A3
Springfield Cl
Axbridge BS26 ....124 F2
Bath BA2 ....101 B5
Bristol BS16 ....52 A7
Springfield Cotts BS30 .83 A8
Springfield Cres BA3 .134 A3
Springfield Gdns BS29 .107 A3
Springfield Gr BS6 ..49 C5
Springfield Ho
Bristol BS6 ....142 C4
Portishead BS20 ......45 C4
Springfield Hts BA3 ..133 E4
Springfield Lawns BS11 47 D6
Springfield Pl BA3 ...133 E4
Springfield Rd
Bristol,Cotham BS6 ..49 D1

Springfield Rd continued
Bristol,Vinney Green BS16 ...**52** A7
Pill BS20 ....**47** C4
Portishead BS20 ....**45** B5
Springfields BS34 ......**36** A2
Springhill Cl BS39 ......**132** C6
Springleaze
Bristol,Knowle Park BS4 ...**64** A1
Bristol,Vinney Green BS16 ...**52** A7
Springwater Pk Trad Est
BS5 ....**64** E7
Springwood Dr BS10 ...**34** D3
Spruce Way Bath BA2 ...**118** E8
Bristol BS34 ....**35** F7
Weston-S-M BS22 ....**105** E8
Square The Alveston BS35 .**15** A4
Axbridge BS26 ....**125** C2
Banwell BS29 ....**107** B3
Bath BA2 ....**141** B1
Bristol BS1 ....**143** C2
Bristol,Knowle Park BS4 ...**64** A1
Bristol,Staple Hill BS16 ...**51** E4
Burrington BS40 ....**109** F3
Shipham BS25 ....**125** E7
Temple Cloud BS39 ....**114** E1
Timsbury BA2 ....**116** B2
Wellow BA2 ....**118** D1
Squire La BS40 ....**111** C1
Squires Ct BS30 ....**65** F4
Squires Leaze BS35 ....**8** D2
Stabbins Cl BS22 ....**89** B5
Stable Yd BA2 ....**101** C4
Stackpool Rd BS3 ....**63** C4
Staddlestones BA3 ....**138** F7
Stadium Rd BS6 ....**49** C5
Stafford Cres BS35 ....**8** B1
Stafford Pl BS23 ....**104** E8
Stafford Rd Bristol BS2 ...**50** A2
Portishead BS20 ....**45** E4
Weston-S-M BS23 ....**104** F7
Stafford St BS3 ....**63** D4
Staffords BS30 ....**66** A6
Stainer Cl BS4 ....**79** D7
Stalcombe La BA2 ....**99** B4
Stall St BA1 ....**141** C2
Stambrook Pk BA1 ....**86** A5
Stanbridge Cl BS16 ....**51** F6
Stanbridge Prim Sch
BS16 ....**51** F6
Stanbridge Rd BS16 ....**51** F6
Stanbury Ave BS16 ....**51** C5
Stanbury Rd BS3 ....**63** E3
Stancombe La BS48 ....**76** E7
Standfast Rd BS10 ....**34** F3
Standish Ave BS34 ....**24** C1
Standish Cl BS10 ....**34** F1
Standon Way BS10 ....**35** C2
Stane Way BS11 ....**47** C7
Stanfield Cl BS7 ....**50** C6
Stanford Cl BS36 ....**37** F8
Stanford Pl BS4 ....**79** D7
Stanhope Pl BA1 ....**141** A2
Stanhope Rd Bristol BS30 ..**65** F2
Weston-S-M BS23 ....**104** E3
Stanhope St BS2 ....**64** A5
Stanier Rd BA2 ....**141** A2
Stanley Ave
Bristol,Ashley Down BS7 ...**49** E3
Bristol,Newleaze BS34 ....**36** B2
Stanley Chase BS5 ....**50** E2
Stanley Cres BS34 ....**36** B2
Stanley Ct BA3 ....**133** B2
Stanley Gdns BS30 ....**66** B4
Stanley Hill BS4 ....**64** A4
Stanley Mead BS32 ....**24** E2
Stanley Park Rd BS16 .....**51** E3
Stanley Pk BS5 ....**50** C1
Stanley Rd
Bristol,Redland BS6 ....**49** C5
Bristol,Warmley BS15 .....**66** B8
Weston-S-M BS23 ....**104** F7
Stanley Rd W BA2 ....**101** D5
Stanley St
5 Bristol,Bedminster BS3 .**63** C3
Bristol,Upper Easton BS5 ...**64** A8
Stanley St N 12 BS3 ......**63** C3
Stanley St S BS3 ....**63** C2
Stanley Terr Bristol BS3 ...**63** C3
Radstock BA3 ....**134** A3
Stanley Villas 13 BA1 .....**85** A1
Stanshalls Cl BS40 ....**94** C8
Stanshalls Dr BS40 ....**94** C8
Stanshalls La BS40 ....**94** C8
Stanshaw Cl BS16 ....**51** A7
Stanshaw Rd BS16 ....**51** A7
Stanshawe Cres BS37 .....**27** C1
Stanshawes Court Dr
BS37 ....**39** E8
Stanshawes Dr BS37 ......**27** C1
Stanshaws Cl BS32 ....**24** C2
Stanton Cl BS15 ....**51** F1
Stanton Drew Prim Sch
BS39 ....**97** A2
Stanton Drew Stone Circles★
BS39 ....**97** A3
Stanton La BS39 ....**97** D4
Stanton Rd Bristol BS10 ...**35** E2
Chew Magna BS40 ....**96** B3
Stanton Wick La BS39 ....**97** B1
Stanway BS30 ....**66** C1
Stanway Cl BA2 ....**101** D1
Staple Gr BS31 ....**81** D5
Staple Grove Cres BS5 ....**65** B7

Staple Hill Prim Sch
BS16 ....**51** D4
Staple Hill Rd BS16 ......**51** B4
Staples Cl BS21 ....**57** E1
Staples Gn BS22 ....**89** B3
Staples Hill BA2 ....**120** C4
Staples Rd BS37 ....**27** C2
Stapleton Cl BS16 ....**50** D5
Stapleton Rd Bristol BS5 ..**50** B2
Bristol,Eastville BS5 ....**50** C3
Stapleton Road Junc
BS5 ....**50** B1
Star Ave BS34 ....**37** A4
Star Barn Rd BS36 ....**37** E7
Star La Bristol BS16 ......**50** F3
Pill BS20 ....**47** D4
Starcross Rd BS22 ....**89** A2
Starling Cl BS22 ....**105** E8
Starrs Cl BS26 ....**125** B2
Station App Bristol BS1 ...**143** C1
Pensford BS39 ....**97** D5
Weston-S-M BS23 ....**104** E7
Station Ave BS16 ....**51** A4
Station Ave S 3 BS16 .....**51** A4
Station Cl Backwell BS48 ..**75** F7
Bristol BS15 ....**66** C8
Chipping Sodbury BS37 ....**40** D8
Congresbury BS49 ....**91** C4
Station Ct BS5 ....**64** E8
Station La BS7 ....**50** A3
Station Lodge 8 BS23 ....**104** E7
Station Mead BA3 ....**138** D3
Station Rd
Acton Turville GL9 ....**42** F8
Axbridge BS26 ....**125** C2
Backwell BS48 ....**76** A6
Bath BA1 ....**101** C7
Blagdon BS40 ....**110** E3
Bristol,Ashley Down BS7 ...**49** F4
Bristol,Filton BS34 ....**36** A3
Bristol,Fishponds BS16 ....**51** A4
Bristol,Henbury BS10 .....**34** F4
Bristol,Lower Soundwell
BS15 ....**51** F3
Bristol,Montpelier BS6 ....**49** E2
Bristol,Newleaze BS34 ....**36** B2
Bristol,Patchway BS34 ....**36** C7
Bristol,Shirehampton BS11 ..**47** D5
Bristol,Shirehampton BS11 ..**47** D5
Bristol,Upper Knowle BS4 ..**64** D2
Bristol,Warmley BS30 .....**66** C7
Charfield GL12 ....**11** B5
Clevedon BS21 ....**57** D3
Clutton BS39 ....**114** E3
Coalpit Heath BS36 ....**38** C5
Congresbury BS49 ....**91** C4
Flax Bourton BS48 ....**77** A8
Freshford BA2 ....**120** C5
Iron Acton BS37 ....**26** D3
Keynsham BS31 ....**81** E6
Midsomer Norton BA3 .....**133** B2
Nailsea BS48 ....**59** F1
Pill BS20 ....**47** C4
Pilning BS35 ....**22** F4
Portbury BS20 ....**46** D3
Portishead BS20 ....**45** D6
Sandford BS25 ....**107** F4
Severn Beach BS35 ....**22** A6
Wellow BA2 ....**118** D1
Weston-S-M BS23 ....**104** E7
Weston-S-M,St Georges
BS22 ....**89** D2
Weston-S-M,Worle BS22 ...**88** F2
Wickwar GL12 ....**18** B7
Winterbourne BS36 ....**37** E4
Wrington BS40 ....**92** D2
Yate BS37 ....**27** C2
Yatton BS49 ....**74** B1
Station Rd Link BS15 .....**52** A2
Station Road Bsns Ctr
BS15 ....**52** A3
Station Road Workshops
BS15 ....**52** A3
Staunton Fields BS14 .....**80** C4
Staunton La BS14 ....**80** D3
Staunton Way BS14 ......**80** D4
Staveley Cres BS10 ....**35** C2
Staverton Cl BS32 ....**24** C1
Staverton Way BS15 .....**66** A7
Stavordale Gr BS14 ......**80** B6
Staynes Cres BS15 ....**65** E8
Steam Mills BA3 ....**138** F8
Stean Bridge Rd BS32 ....**36** E6
Steanbridge BS32 ....**36** D6
Steel Cl BS30 ....**65** F3
Steel Mills BS31 ....**81** F4
Steevens Ho (almshouses) 13
BS2 ....**143** C3
Stella Gr BS3 ....**63** A2
Stephen St BS5 ....**64** C8
Stephens Dr BS30 ....**65** F5
Stepney Rd BS5 ....**50** C1
Stepney Wlk BS5 ....**50** C1
Stepping Stones The
BS4 ....**64** E6
Sterncourt Rd BS16 .....**51** A7
Stevens Cres BS3 ....**63** F4
Stevens La BS24 ....**122** C3
Stevens Wlk BS32 ....**36** D8
Steway La BA1 ....**86** B6
Stibbs Ct BS30 ....**65** F4
Stibbs Hill BS5 ....**65** A7
Stickland BS21 ....**57** C1
Stidcot La GL12 ....**16** D5
Stidcote La GL12 ....**16** E5
Stile Acres BS11 ....**34** A1
Stilemead La BS40 ....**111** D1
Stileway Bsns Pk BS21 ....**73** B8

Stillhouse La BS3 ....**63** D4
Stillingfleet Rd BS13 .....**79** C5
Stillman St BS13 ....**78** A4
Stinchcombe BS37 ....**27** E1
Stirling Cl BS37 ....**27** D4
Stirling Rd BS4 ....**64** C3
Stirling Way BS31 ....**81** E4
Stirtingale Ave BA2 ......**101** C3
Stirtingale Rd BA2 ....**101** C3
Stitchings La BA2 ....**117** D7
Stitchings Shord La
BS39 ....**113** C4
Stock Hill BS35 ....**7** C1
Stock La BS40 ....**109** A7
Stock Way N BS48 ....**59** E2
Stock Way S BS48 ....**59** E2
Stockhill Cl BA3 ....**138** C3
Stockhill Rd BA3 ....**138** C2
Stockmead BS40 ....**109** B5
Stockwood Chambers
BS5 ....**64** C7
Stockwood Cres BS4 .....**63** F2
Stockwood Green Prim Sch
BS14 ....**80** E5
Stockwood Hill BS31 .....**81** C7
Stockwood La BS14 ......**80** E5
Stockwood Mews BS4 ...**64** F5
Stockwood Rd BS4 ......**64** F1
Stockwood Vale BS31 ....**81** C6
Stodelegh Cl BS22 ....**89** B3
Stoke Bishop CE Prim Sch
BS9 ....**48** D5
Stoke Bridge Ave BS34 ...**36** D6
Stoke Cotts BS9 ....**48** E4
Stoke Gifford Junc BS34 ..**36** E4
Stoke Gr BS9 ....**48** D5
Stoke Hamlet BS9 ....**48** F6
Stoke Hill Bristol BS9 .....**48** E3
Chew Stoke BS40 ....**112** D7
Stoke La
Bristol,Broomhill BS16 ....**50** E7
Bristol,Patchway BS34 ....**36** C8
Bristol,Westbury on Trym
BS9 ....**48** F6
Stoke Lodge Jun & Inf Sch
BS34 ....**36** C8
Stoke Mdws BS32 ....**24** D1
Stoke Mead BA2 ....**119** F7
Stoke Paddock Rd BS9 ...**48** D6
Stoke Park Rd BS9 ......**48** F4
Stoke Park Rd S BS9 .....**48** E4
Stoke Rd Bristol BS8,BS9 ..**49** A2
Portishead BS20 ....**45** D5
Stoke View BS34 ....**36** A3
Stoke View Pk 5 BS16 .....**50** F4
Stoke View Rd BS16 .....**50** F3
Stokefield Cl BS35 ....**8** B1
Stokeleigh Wlk BS9 ......**48** C5
Stokemead BS34 ....**36** C8
Stokes Croft BS1 ....**143** B4
Stokes Ct 1 BS30 ....**66** A4
Stone House Mews BS37 .**28** B1
Stone La BS36 ....**37** F3
Stone Monolith BS34 ....**35** E6
Stone with Woodford CE
Prim Sch GL13 ....**3** C4
Stoneable Rd BA3 ....**134** A3
Stoneage La BA2 ....**117** B2
Stoneberry Rd BS14 .....**80** B3
Stonebridge BS21 ....**57** D1
Stonebridge Pk BS5 .....**50** E2
Stonebridge Rd BS23 ....**104** F4
Stonechat Gdns BS16 ....**50** E6
Stonehenge La BS48 .....**59** E4
Stonehill BS15 ....**65** E4
Stonehill Ctr BS30 ....**65** E4
Stonehill Farm BS15 .....**65** E4
Stonehouse Cl BA2 ......**102** B4
Stonehouse La BA2 ......**102** B2
Stoneleigh BS40 ....**96** B3
Stoneleigh Cres BS4 .....**64** A2
Stoneleigh Ct BA1 ....**84** E3
Stoneleigh Dr BS30 ......**65** F5
Stoneleigh Rd BS4 ......**64** A2
Stoneleigh Wlk BS4 .....**64** A2
Stones Cross BA3 ....**133** B2
Stones Ct BS6 ....**49** B2
Stonewell Dr BS49 ....**91** D3
Stonewell Gr BS49 ......**91** D3
Stonewell La BS49 ......**91** D3
Stonewell Park Rd BS49 ..**91** D3
Stoney Littleton Long
Barrow★ BA2 ....**135** D7
Stoney Steep BS48 ......**60** A5
Stoney Stile Rd BS35 ....**15** A5
Stoneyard La BA3 ....**130** D2
Stoneyfield Cl BS20 .....**47** B5
Stoneyfields BS20 ....**47** B4
Stores Rd BS11 ....**33** C4
Stormont Cl BS23 ....**104** F3
Stothard Rd BS7 ....**50** B7
Stottbury Rd BS7 ....**50** A3
Stoulton Gr BS10 ....**35** A3
Stourden Cl BS16 ....**51** A7
Stourton Dr BS30 ....**65** F4
Stover Rd BS37 ....**27** B2
Stover Trad Est BS37 ......**27** B2
Stow Hill Rd GL12 ....**16** B6
Stowborough Cotts
BA2 ....**134** C7
Stowell Hill Rd GL12 .....**16** B6

Stowey Bottom BS39 ...**113** E5
Stowey Crossroads
BS39 ....**113** D5
Stowey Pk BS49 ....**91** D7
Stowey Rd BS49 ....**91** C8
Stowick Gdns BS11 ......**34** C3
Stradbrook Ave BS5 .....**65** B7
Stradling Ave BS23 ......**104** F5
Stradling Rd BS11 ....**34** C2
Straight St BS2 ....**143** C2
Straightmead BA3 ......**130** F1
Straits Par BS16 ....**51** B5
Stratford Cl BS14 ....**79** F3
Stratford Ct BS9 ....**48** F8
Stratford La BS40 ....**112** E1
Strathearn Dr BS10 .....**35** B2
Stratheden BS8 ....**142** A4
Strathmore Rd BS7 .....**49** F5
Stratton Cl BS34 ....**36** C7
Stratton Rd Saltford BS31 .**82** E3
Stratton-on-t-F BA3 ....**139** B1
Stratton St BS2 ....**143** B3
Strawberry Cl BS48 .....**59** D1
Strawberry Field BS26 ...**125** D2
Strawberry Gdns BS48 ...**75** D8
Strawberry Hill BS21 ....**57** F4
Strawberry La Bristol BS5 .**64** E7
Dundry BS13,BS41 ....**78** E3
Strawbridge Rd 10 BS5 ..**64** B7
Stream Cl BS10 ....**35** D3
Stream Side BS16 ....**51** F6
Stream The BS16 ....**37** B2
Streamcross BS49 ......**74** D1
Streamleaze
Chew Magna BS40 ....**96** B3
Thornbury BS35 ....**15** C8
Streamleaze Ct BS35 ....**15** B8
Streamside
Chew Magna BS40 ....**96** B3
1 Clevedon BS21 ....**57** F3
Streamside Rd BS37 .....**28** A1
Streamside Wlk BS4 .....**64** E3
Stredlings Yd BS2 ....**142** C4
Street End BS40 ....**110** D2
Street End La BS40 ......**110** D2
Street The
Acton Turville GL9 ....**42** F6
Alveston BS35 ....**15** B5
Bishop Sutton BS39 ....**113** D4
Bishop Sutton,Stowey
BS9 ....**113** F4
Burton SN14 ....**43** B4
Chew Stoke BS40 ....**112** D8
Chilcompton BA3 ....**138** D5
Compton Martin BS40 .....**129** B7
Farmborough BA2 ....**115** F6
Luckington SN14 ....**31** E4
North Nibley GL11 ....**5** D4
Olveston BS35 ....**14** A3
Radstock BA3 ....**133** F2
Ubley BS40 ....**111** D1
Winford BS40 ....**94** F1
Stretford Ave BS5 ....**64** D8
Stretford Rd BS5 ....**64** D8
Stride Cl BS35 ....**22** A6
Strode Comm BS35 ......**14** F5
Strode Gdns BS35 ......**14** F5
Strode Rd BS21 ....**57** C2
Strode Way BS21 ....**57** B1
Stroud Rd
Bristol,Patchway BS34 ....**35** F8
Bristol,Shirehampton BS11 ..**47** E5
Stroud Way BS24 ....**105** E7
Stuart Pl BA2 ....**101** D6
Stuart Rd BS23 ....**105** A5
Stuart St BS5 ....**64** C7
Studland Ct BS9 ....**49** B6
Stumpwell La GL12 ....**5** E2
Sturden La BS16 ....**37** C3
Sturdon Rd BS3 ....**63** A3
Sturmer Cl BS37 ....**27** E4
Sturmey Way BS20 ......**47** E3
Sturminster Cl BS14 .....**80** D6
Sturminster Rd BS14 ....**80** D7
Sulis Manor Rd BA2 .....**118** D8
Sullivan Cl BS4 ....**79** D6
Sumerlin Dr BS21 ....**57** F3
Summer Ct BS8 ....**142** B3
Summer Hill BS4 ....**64** A4
Summer House Way
BS30 ....**66** B7
Summer La
Banwell BS29 ....**106** E5
Burton SN14 ....**43** F3
Monkton Combe BA2 ......**119** D8
Weston-S-M,Locking BS29 .**106** D7
Weston-S-M,West Wick
BS22,BS24 ....**89** B1
Summer La N BS22 ......**89** A2
Summer Lane Parkhomes
BS29 ....**106** E4
Summer St 4 BS3 ....**63** C4
Summerfield BS22 ......**89** A3
Summerfield Rd BA1 .....**85** A1
Summerfield Sch BA1 .....**84** D1
Summerfield Terr BA1 ....**85** A1
Summerhayes BS30 .....**66** D5
Summerhill Jun & Inf Schs
BS5 ....**64** F8
Summerhill Rd Bath BA1 ..**84** D1
Bristol BS5 ....**64** F8
Summerhill Terr BS5 .....**64** F8
Summerhouse BS21 .....**59** D4
Summerlands BS48 ......**76** B5
Summerlands Rd BS23 ...**105** B8
Summerlays Ct BA2 .....**102** B6
Summerlea BA2 ....**117** A5

Summerleaze
Bristol BS16 ....**51** C3
Keynsham BS31 ....**81** E7
Summers Dr BS30 ....**54** A1
Summers Mead BS37 ....**27** E4
Summers Rd 4 BS2 .....**50** A1
Summers Terr 3 BS2 .....**50** A1
Sundays Hill BS32 ....**24** A4
Sundayshill La GL12 ......**9** D7
Sunderland Pl BS8 ......**142** B3
Sunderland St BA2 ......**141** C3
Sundridge Pk BS37 ......**39** E8
Sunfield Rd BS24 ....**105** E3
Sunningdale Bristol BS8 ..**142** B4
Yate BS37 ....**39** E8
Sunningdale Cl BS48 ....**60** A1
Sunningdale Dr BS30 ....**66** B6
Sunningdale Rd BS22 ....**88** F3
Sunny Bank Bristol BS15 ..**51** B1
Wick BS30 ....**67** B7
Sunny Bank Way BS24 ...**89** B1
Sunny Hill BS9 ....**48** C7
Sunny Wlk BS15 ....**51** B1
Sunnybank Bath BA2 ....**102** B4
Bristol BS16 ....**51** E6
Westerleigh BS37 ....**39** A3
Sunnybank Ct BS24 .....**89** B1
Sunnydene BS4 ....**64** D4
Sunnyhill Dr BS11 ....**47** E6
Sunnyhill Ho E BS11 .....**47** E6
Sunnyhill Ho W BS11 ....**47** E6
Sunnymead Bristol BS30 ..**66** D6
Keynsham BS31 ....**81** F3
Midsomer Norton BA3 ....**132** F2
Stratton-on-t-F BA3 ....**138** F2
Sunnymede Rd BS48 ....**59** D3
Sunnyside Bristol BS9 ....**48** E5
Clutton BS39 ....**115** B4
Farrington Gurney BS39 ...**132** B3
Frampton Cotterell BS36 ...**38** B8
Sunnyside Cres BS21 ....**57** D3
Sunnyside Farm Trad Est
BS20 ....**47** C2
Sunnyside La Bristol BS16 .**52** C1
Yate BS37 ....**27** C1
Sunnyside Rd
Clevedon BS21 ....**57** D3
Weston-S-M BS23 ....**104** E5
Sunnyside Rd N BS23 ....**104** E6
Sunnyside View BA2 .....**134** C7
Sunnyvale Clevedon BS21 .**57** B1
Peasedown St John BA2 ...**133** E8
Sunnyvale Dr BS30 ......**66** B3
Sunridge BS16 ....**51** D6
Sunridge Cl BA3 ....**138** F8
Sunridge Pk BA3 ....**138** F8
Sunrise Gr BS4 ....**64** D4
Sunset Cl BA2 ....**134** C7
Surrey Rd BS7 ....**49** E3
Surrey St BS2 ....**143** B4
Sussex Pl Bath BA2 ......**141** C1
Bristol BS2 ....**49** F1
Sussex St BS2 ....**64** A6
Sutherland Ave
Bristol BS16 ....**51** E7
Yate BS37 ....**27** D4
Sutherland Dr BS24 .....**105** D2
Sutherland Pl 9 BS8 .....**49** A2
Sutton Ave BS4 ....**64** D4
Sutton Cl BS22 ....**105** E8
Sutton Ct BS39 ....**113** F6
Sutton Hill Rd BS39 .....**113** D4
Sutton La BS40 ....**93** F1
Sutton Pk BS39 ....**113** D4
Sutton St BA2 ....**102** B7
Swainswick BS14 ....**79** F6
Swainswick Gdns BA1 ...**85** C2
Swainswick La BA1 ......**85** D4
Swainswick Prim Sch
BA1 ....**85** B5
Swaish Dr 2 BS30 ....**66** A4
Swallow Cl BA3 ....**139** B8
Swallow Ct BS14 ....**80** F6
Swallow Dr BS34 ....**35** E8
Swallow Gdns BS22 .....**105** E8
Swallow Pk BS35 ....**8** D3
Swallow St BA1 ....**141** C2
Swallows Ct BS34 ....**36** A4
Swallows The BS22 .....**105** D7
Swan Cl BS22 ....**105** E8
Swan Field BS37 ....**27** F2
Swan La BS36 ....**37** C8
Swancombe
Blagdon BS40 ....**110** E2
Clapton In Gordano BS20 ..**59** E8
Swane Rd BS14 ....**80** F6
Swanley La GL13 ....**4** B5
Swanmoor Cres BS10 ....**35** A4
Sweetgrass Rd 6 BS24 ..**106** A8
Sweets Cl BS15 ....**51** E2
Sweets Rd BS15 ....**51** E2
Swift Cl BS22 ....**88** F1
Swinhay La GL12 ....**11** B8
Swiss Dr BS3 ....**62** F2
Swiss Rd Bristol BS3 .....**62** F1
Weston-S-M BS23 ....**104** F7
Sycamore Cl
Bristol,Crofts End BS5 .....**50** E1
Bristol,Hanham Green BS15 .**65** B3
Nailsea BS48 ....**59** E2
Shipham BS25 ....**125** E8
Weston-S-M BS23 ....**105** A8
Sycamore Ct BS7 ....**49** E3
Sycamore Dr Bristol BS34 .**35** F7
Thornbury BS35 ....**8** C1
Sycamore Ho BS16 ......**51** C6
Sycamore Rd BA3 ....**134** B2
Sycamores BS23 ....**87** E1

Sydenham Bldgs BA2 . .141 A2
Sydenham Hill BS6 . . . . . .49 D1
Sydenham La BS1 . . . . . . .49 E1
Sydenham Rd Bath BA2 . .141 A2
Bristol,Cotham BS6 . . . . . .49 E1
Bristol,Totterdown BS4 . . . .64 A3
Sydenham Terr BA2 . . . . .102 C1
Sydenham Way BS15 . . . . .65 C3
Sydney Bldgs BA2 . . . . . .102 B6
Sydney Hill BS6 . . . . .102 B6
Sydney Ho BA2 . . . . .102 B7
Sydney Mews BA2 . . . . . .102 B7
Sydney Pl BA2 . . . . .102 B7
Sydney Rd BA2 . . . . .102 B7
Sydney Row BS1 . . . . . . .142 B1
Sydney Wharf BA2 . . . . . .102 B7
Sylvan Way BS9 . . . . .48 B7
Sylvia Ave BS3 . . . . .63 C2
Symes Ave BS13 . . . . .79 C4
Symes Pk BA1 . . . . .84 A2
Symington Rd BS16 . . . . . .51 B5
Syston Way BS15 . . . . .51 D1

T

Tabernacle Rd BS15 . . . . . .65 C6
Tackley Rd BS5 . . . . .50 B3
Tadwick La BA1 . . . . .85 A6
Tailor's Ct 5 BS1 . . . . . . .143 A3
Talbot Ave BS15 . . . . .51 C1
Talbot Rd BS4 . . . . .64 C2
Talgarth Rd BS7 . . . . .49 F4
Tallis Gr BS4 . . . . .79 D6
Tamar Cl BS35 . . . . .15 D7
Tamar Dr BS31 . . . . .82 A4
Tamar Rd Bristol BS2 . . . . .64 C6
Weston-S-M BS22 . . . . .89 A2
Tamblyn Cl BA3 . . . . .134 A3
Tamsin Ct BS31 . . . . .81 F5
Tamworth Rd BS31 . . . . . .81 E4
Tanhouse La BS37 . . . . . . .27 D7
Tankard's Cl BS8 . . . . . . .142 C3
Tanner Cl BS30 . . . . .65 F5
Tanner Ct BS30 . . . . .65 F5
Tanners Ct Bristol BS16 . . . .37 B1
Thornbury BS35 . . . . .15 B4
Tanners La SN14 . . . . .69 F8
Tanners Wlk Bath BA2 . .100 F5
Marshfield SN14 . . . . .69 F8
Tanorth Cl BS14 . . . . .80 A3
Tanorth Rd BS14 . . . . .79 F3
Tanyard The BS30 . . . . . . .66 B2
Tapsters BS30 . . . . .66 A4
Tara Cl BS36 . . . . .25 F1
Tarn Ho BS34 . . . . .36 A8
Tarnock Ave BS14 . . . . . . .80 A7
Tarnwell BS39 . . . . .97 A2
Tarragon Pl BS32 . . . . . . .36 F7
Taunton BS22 . . . . .89 B4
Taunton Wlk BS7 . . . . . . .50 A7
Taveners Wlk BS48 . . . . . .59 F3
Taverners Cl BS23 . . . . . .104 F4
Tavistock Rd Bristol BS4 . . .63 F1
Weston-S-M BS22 . . . . .89 A2
Tavistock Wlk BS4 . . . . . . .63 F1
Tawny Way BS22 . . . . . . .105 F3
Taylor Cl BS15 . . . . .65 F8
Taylor Ct BS22 . . . . .89 B4
Taylor Gdns BS13 . . . . . . .78 F4
Tayman Cl BS10 . . . . .49 E6
Tayman Ridge BS30 . . . . . .82 D8
Taynton Cl BS30 . . . . .66 C2
Teal Cl Bristol BS32 . . . . . .24 D2
Weston-S-M BS22 . . . . .88 F1
Teasel Mead BS32 . . . . . . .36 E7
Teasel Wlk BS22 . . . . . . .105 D7
Tech Coll BS15 . . . . .65 E8
Teddington Cl BA2 . . . . . .101 C4
Teesdale Cl BS22 . . . . . . .105 D8
Teewell Ave BS16 . . . . . . .51 E4
Teewell Cl BS16 . . . . .51 E4
Teewell Ct BS16 . . . . .51 E4
Teewell Hill BS16 . . . . . . .51 E4
Teignmouth Rd
Bristol BS4 . . . . .63 F1
Clevedon BS21 . . . . .57 E3
Telephone Ave BS1 . . . . .143 A2
Telford Ho Bath BA2 . . . .101 D3
Leigh Woods BS8 . . . . .62 E6
Telford Wlk BS5 . . . . .51 A1
Tellisford La BA2 . . . . . . .136 F4
Templar Rd BS37 . . . . .27 E3
Templars Way BS25 . . . . .125 E7
Temple Back BS1 . . . . . . .143 B2
Temple Beck E BS1 . . . . .143 C2
Temple Bridge Bsns Pk
BS39 . . . . .131 F7
Temple Circle Gyratory
BS1 . . . . .143 B1
Temple Ct BS31 . . . . .81 E5
Temple Gate BS1 . . . . . . .143 B1
Temple Gate District Ctr
BS3 . . . . .63 F4
Temple Inn La BS39 . . . . .114 E1
Temple Meads Sta BS1 . .143 C2
Temple Prim Sch BS31 . .81 F6
Temple Rose St BS1 . . . . .143 B1
Temple St Bristol BS1 . . . .143 B2
Bristol,Bedminster BS3 . . . .63 B2
Keynsham BS31 . . . . .81 F5
Temple Trad Est BS2 . . . . .64 C5
Temple Way BS1 . . . . . . .143 B2
Temple Way Underpass
BS2 . . . . .143 C3
Templand Rd BS13 . . . . . .78 F5
Tenby Rd BS31 . . . . .81 D4
Tenby St BS5 . . . . .64 B7

Tennessee Gr BS6 . . . . . . .49 C5
Tennis Court Ave BS39 . .132 D5
Tennis Court Rd BS39 . . .132 D5
Tennis Rd BS4 . . . . .64 A2
Tenniscourt Rd BS15 . . . . .52 A1
Tennyson Ave BS21 . . . . . .57 B2
Tennyson Cl BS31 . . . . . . .81 F6
Tennyson Rd Bath BA1 . .101 D7
Bristol BS7 . . . . .49 E5
Weston-S-M BS23 . . . . . .105 A3
Tenterk Cl BS24 . . . . .122 B6
Tenth Ave BS7 . . . . .36 B1
Tereslake Gn BS10 . . . . . .35 D4
Terrace The BS25 . . . . . . .125 E7
Terrace Wlk BA1 . . . . . . .141 C2
Terrell Gdns 13 BS5 . . . . .64 D7
Terrell St BS2 . . . . .143 A4
Terris Ct BS34 . . . . .36 E4
Terry Hill BA3 . . . . .140 D8
Terry Ho BS1 . . . . .142 C3
Tetbury Cl BS34 . . . . .36 C7
Tetbury Gdns BS48 . . . . . .60 A1
Tetbury Rd BS15 . . . . .65 B8
Teviot Rd BS31 . . . . .82 A4
Tewkesbury Rd 11 BS2 . . .50 A8
Teyfant Com Sch BS13 . . .79 E4
Teyfant Rd BS13 . . . . .79 E4
Teyfant Wlk BS13 . . . . . . .79 E4
Thackeray Ave BS21 . . . . .57 E4
Thackeray Ho BS23 . . . . .105 A5
Thackeray Rd BS21 . . . . . .57 E4
Thames Cl GL12 . . . . .11 A4
Thames Ho 9 BS35 . . . . . .15 C8
Thanet Rd BS3 . . . . .63 B2
Thatcher Cl BS20 . . . . .45 D4
Thatchers Cl BS5 . . . . .65 A8
Theatre Royal ★ BS1 . . . .143 A2
There-and-Back-Again La
BS1 . . . . .142 C2
Theresa Ave BS7 . . . . .49 E4
Theynes Croft BS41 . . . . . .62 B1
Thicket Ave BS16 . . . . .51 C3
Thicket Mead BA3 . . . . . .133 A2
Thicket Rd BS16 . . . . .51 C4
Thicket Wlk BS35 . . . . .8 C1
Thiery Rd BS4 . . . . .64 C2
Thingwall Pk BS16 . . . . . .50 E3
Third Ave Bath BA2 . . . . .101 D5
Bristol,Hengrove BS14 . . . . .80 B7
Bristol,Northville BS7 . . . . . .36 A1
Radstock BA3 . . . . .139 D7
Third Way BS11 . . . . .33 C2
Thirlmere Ct BS30 . . . . . . .66 D6
Thirlmere Rd Bristol BS34 . .36 A8
Weston-S-M BS23 . . . . . .105 A4
Thistle St 1 BS3 . . . . .63 B3
Thomas Ave BS16 . . . . . . .52 B8
Thomas Cl BS29 . . . . .107 A3
Thomas La BS1 . . . . .143 B2
Thomas Pring Wlk 1
BS5 . . . . .51 A1
Thomas St Bath BA1 . . . .141 C4
Bristol,Baptist Mills BS2 . . . .49 F1
Bristol,Kingsdown BS2 . . . .143 A4
7 Bristol,Russell Town BS5 . .64 B7
Thomas St N 12 BS2 . . . . .49 D1
Thomas Way BS16 . . . . . . .50 E7
Thompson Rd BS14 . . . . . .80 E6
Thomson Rd 7 BS5 . . . . . .64 B8
Thorn Cl Weston-S-M BS22 .89 B2
Yate BS37 . . . . .27 D1
Thornbank Pl BA2 . . . . . .141 A1
Thornbury Dr BS23 . . . . .104 D2
Thornbury Hospl BS35 . .8 C1
Thornbury Ind Pk BS35 . .15 B7
Thornbury Mus BS35 . .15 B8
Thornbury Rd
Alveston BS35 . . . . .15 A5
Weston-S-M BS23 . . . . . .104 C1
Thorndale BS8 . . . . .142 A4
Thorndale Cl BS22 . . . . . .105 D8
Thorndale Mews BS8 . . . .142 A4
Thornhayes Cl BS36 . . . . .38 A8
Thornhills The BS16 . . . . .51 B6
Thornleigh Rd BS7 . . . . . .49 E5
Thornmead Gr BS10 . . . . .35 A2
Thorns Farm BS37 . . . . . .27 E1
Thornycroft Cl BS7 . . . . . .50 B7
Thorpe Lodge 9 BS6 . . . .49 D1
Three Brooks La BS32 . . . .36 E8
Three Oaks Cl BS16 . . . . .51 C4
Three Queens' La BS1 . . .143 B2
Three Wells Rd BS13 . . . . .78 F4
Thrissell St BS5 . . . . .64 A8
Throgmorton Rd BS4 . . . . .79 F8
Thrush Cl BS22 . . . . .105 E8
Thurlestone BS14 . . . . . . .80 A6
Thurlow Rd BS5 . . . . .50 C2
Thurston's Barton BS5 . . . .50 E1
Tibberton BS15 . . . . .66 A8
Tibbott Rd BS14 . . . . .80 D5
Tibbott Wlk BS14 . . . . . . .80 D5
Tichborne Rd Bristol BS5 . .64 C7
Weston-S-M BS23 . . . . .87 E1
Tickenham CE Prim Sch
BS21 . . . . .58 F4
Tickenham Hill BS48 . . . . .59 E4
Tickenham Rd BS21 . . . . . .58 A4
Tide Gr BS11 . . . . .48 A8
Tidenham Way BS34 . . . . .23 F1
Tiffany Ct BS1 . . . . .143 B1
Tiledown BS39 . . . . .114 E1
Tiledown Cl BS39 . . . . . . .114 F1
Tilley Cl
Farmborough BA2 . . . . . . .116 A5
Keynsham BS31 . . . . .82 A2

Tilley La BA2 . . . . .116 A5
Tilling Rd BS10 . . . . .49 E7
Tilling Wlk BS10 . . . . .49 E7
Tilting Rd BS35 . . . . .8 E2
Timber Dene BS16 . . . . . . .50 D4
Timberscombe Wlk BS14 80 C5
Timbers The BA3 . . . . . . .139 B7
Timbury Rd Bristol BS3 . . . .63 E2
Farmborough BA2 . . . . . . .116 B5
High Littleton BS39 . . . . . .115 D1
Timsbury Village Workshops
BA2 . . . . .115 F3
Timsbury Wlk BS3 . . . . . . .63 E2
Tindell Ct 12 BS30 . . . . . .65 F4
Tinker's La
Compton Martin BS40 . . . .129 B7
Kilmersdon BA3 . . . . .140 B1
Tintagel Cl BS31 . . . . .81 D4
Tintern Ave BS5 . . . . .64 D8
Tintern Cl BS30 . . . . .65 F6
Tippetts Rd BS15 . . . . .65 D6
Tirley Ho BS34 . . . . .23 F1
Tirley Way BS22 . . . . .88 B2
Titan Barrow BA1 . . . . . . .86 C2
Tiverton Gdns BS22 . . . . . .89 A2
Tiverton Rd 2 BS21 . . . . . .57 E1
Tiverton Wlk BS16 . . . . . . .51 A2
Tivoli Ho BS23 . . . . .104 E8
Tivoli La BS23 . . . . .104 E8
Tockington Gn BS32 . . . . .14 B2
Tockington La BS32 . . . . . .24 A7
Tockington Manor Sch
BS32 . . . . .14 C2
Tockington Park La BS32 24 E8
Toddington Cl BS37 . . . . . .39 D8
Toghill La BS30 . . . . .68 A3
Toll Bridge Rd BA1 . . . . . .85 E3
Toll Down Way SN14 . . . . .43 A3
Toll House Ct 4 BS3 . . . . .63 A4
Toll Rd BS23 . . . . .121 F8
Tolland BS24 . . . . .105 A2
Tone Rd BS21 . . . . .57 D1
Top Rd BS25 . . . . .125 F7
Tor Cl BS22 . . . . .89 A2
Tormarton Cres BS10 . . . . .34 F4
Tormarton Intc BS37 . . . . .41 B1
Tormarton Rd
Acton Turville GL9 . . . . . . .42 E6
Marshfield SN14 . . . . .56 B3
Tormynton Rd BS22 . . . . . .88 E3
Toronto Rd BS7 . . . . .50 A8
Torpoint Rd BS3 . . . . .63 D2
Torrance Cl BS30 . . . . .66 D6
Torridge Rd BS31 . . . . . . .82 A4
Torrington Ave BS4 . . . . . .79 F8
Torrington Cres BS22 . . . . .89 A2
Tortworth Prim Sch
GL12 . . . . .10 C7
Tortworth Rd BS7 . . . . . . .49 E5
Torwood House Sch BS6 . .49 A3
Totnes Cl BS22 . . . . .89 A2
Totshill Dr BS13 . . . . .79 E4
Totshill Gr BS13 . . . . .79 E4
Tottenham Pl BS8 . . . . . .142 B3
Totterdown Bridge Ind Est
BS2 . . . . .64 A4
Totterdown La BS24 . . . . .105 A1
Totterdown Rd BS23 . . . .104 F4
Touching End La SN14 . . . .69 F8
Touchstone Ave BS34 . . . . .36 F5
Tovey Cl BS22 . . . . .88 E4
Tower Hill Bristol BS2 . . . .143 B3
Locking BS24 . . . . .106 D4
Tower House La BS48 . . . . .60 A4
Tower La Bristol BS1 . . . . .143 A3
Bristol,Warmley Tower
BS30 . . . . .66 B6
Tower Rd Bristol BS15 . . . .51 C1
Portishead BS20 . . . . .45 A4
Tower Rd N BS30 . . . . .66 B7
Tower Rd S BS30 . . . . .66 B5
Tower St BS1 . . . . .143 B2
Towerhead Rd BS29 . . . . .107 D3
Towerleaze BS9 . . . . .48 D3
Town Barton BA2 . . . . . . .136 F4
Town End BA2 . . . . .136 F4
Townsend
Almondsbury BS32 . . . . . . .23 F4
East Harptree BS40 . . . . . .130 A5
Townsend Cl BS14 . . . . . . .80 F5
Townsend La BS32 . . . . . . .24 A5
Townsend Rd BS14 . . . . . .80 F5
Townshend Rd BS22 . . . . .89 B5
Townwell GL12 . . . . .10 B2
Tozers Hill BS4 . . . . .64 C2
Tracy Cl BS14 . . . . .79 F7
Trafalgar Rd BA1 . . . . .84 B1
Trafalgar Terr 3 BS3 . . . . .63 B2
Tralee Wlk BS4 . . . . .63 D1
Tramway Rd BS4 . . . . .64 C3
Transom Rd BS1 . . . . . . .143 B2
Tranton La GL13 . . . . .2 C4
Tratman Wlk BS10 . . . . . . .34 F3
Travers Cl BS4 . . . . .79 D6
Travers Wlk BS34 . . . . . . .36 F5
Trawden Cl BS23 . . . . .88 A1
Tredegar Rd BS16 . . . . . . .51 B3
Tree Leaze BS37 . . . . .27 F2
Treefield Pl 5 BS2 . . . . . . .50 A2
Treefield Rd BS21 . . . . . . .57 D2
Treetops Cvn Site BS16 . .51 A8
Tregarth Rd BS3 . . . . .62 F1
Trelawn Cl BS22 . . . . .89 D2
Trelawney Ave BS5 . . . . . .64 D8
Trelawney Pk BS4 . . . . . . .64 D3

Trelawney Rd BS6 . . . . . . .49 C1
Trellick Wlk BS16 . . . . . . .50 E8
Tremes Cl SN14 . . . . .69 F8
Tremlett Mews 3 BS22 . . .89 B4
Trench La BS32 . . . . .24 C2
Trenchard Rd
Locking BS24 . . . . .106 D4
Saltford BS31 . . . . .82 D3
Trenchard St BS1 . . . . . . .142 C3
Trendlewood Pk BS16 . . . .50 E5
Trendlewood Way BS48 . . .60 A1
Trenleigh Dr BS22 . . . . . . .89 A2
Trentham Cl 7 BS2 . . . . . .50 A2
Tresham Cl BS32 . . . . .24 D2
Trevanna Rd BS3 . . . . .62 F1
Trevelyan Rd BS23 . . . . . .104 F7
Trevelyan Wlk
Bristol,Great Stoke BS34 . . .37 A5
Bristol,Henbury BS10 . . . . .34 F3
Treverdowe Wlk BS10 . . . .34 D3
Trevethin Cl BS15 . . . . . . .65 D7
Trevisa Gr BS10 . . . . .35 C4
Trewartha Cl BS23 . . . . . .104 F8
Trewartha Pk BS23 . . . . .104 F8
Trewint Gdns BS4 . . . . . . .79 F8
Triangle Ct BA2 . . . . .101 D5
Triangle E BA2 . . . . .101 D5
Triangle N BA2 . . . . .101 D5
Triangle S BS8 . . . . .142 B3
Triangle The
Clevedon BS21 . . . . .57 D3
Paulton BS39 . . . . .132 E6
Portishead BS20 . . . . .45 B5
Wrington BS40 . . . . .92 D2
Triangle Villas BA2 . . . . .101 D5
Triangle W Bath BA2 . . . .101 D5
Bristol BS8 . . . . .142 B3
Trident Cl BS16 . . . . .38 A1
Trim Bridge 3 BA1 . . . . . .141 B2
Trim St BA1 . . . . .141 B2
Trin Mills BS1 . . . . .143 A1
Trinder Rd BS20 . . . . .47 B4
Trinity CE Prim Sch GL9 . .43 A6
Trinity Coll BS9 . . . . .48 E4
Trinity Ct BS48 . . . . .59 C1
Trinity Mews 15 BS2 . . . .143 C3
Trinity Pl Bristol BS8 . . . .142 A2
Weston-S-M BS23 . . . . .87 C1
Trinity Rd Bath BA2 . . . . .102 B2
Bristol BS2 . . . . .64 A7
Nailsea BS48 . . . . .59 C1
Weston-S-M BS23 . . . . .87 C1
Trinity St Bath BA1 . . . . . .141 B2
Bristol BS2 . . . . .64 A7
Trinity Wlk Bristol BS2 . . .143 C4
Bristol,Newton BS2 . . . . . . .64 A7
Tripps Cnr BS49 . . . . .91 C7
Tripps Row BS41 . . . . .62 A1
Troon BS37 . . . . .39 E8
Troon Dr BS30 . . . . .66 B6
Troopers' Hill Rd BS5 . . . .65 A7
Tropicana Leisure Pool
BS23 . . . . .104 D6
Trossachs Dr BA2 . . . . . . .102 F3
Trowbridge Rd BS10 . . . . .35 C1
Trowbridge Wlk BS10 . . . .35 C1
Truro Rd Bristol BS3 . . . . .63 B3
Nailsea BS48 . . . . .60 A1
Trym Bank BS9 . . . . .48 D7
Trym Cross Rd BS9 . . . . . .48 C5
Trym Rd BS9 . . . . .49 A7
Trym Side BS9 . . . . .48 C5
Trymleaze BS9 . . . . .48 C5
Trymwood Cl BS10 . . . . . .34 F2
Trymwood Par BS9 . . . . . .48 D6
TT Trading Est BS37 . . . . .28 C1
Tucker St BS2 . . . . .143 C3
Tucker's La BS40 . . . . . . .128 E8
Tuckett La BS16 . . . . .51 C7
Tuckingmill La BS39 . . . . .98 C5
Tuckmill BS21 . . . . .57 B1
Tudor Cl BS30 . . . . .66 C3
Tudor Rd
Bristol,Baptist Mills BS2 . . . .49 F1
Bristol,Jefferies Hill BS15 . . .65 C5
Bristol,Lower Easton BS5 . . .50 C1
Portishead BS20 . . . . .45 A4
Weston-S-M BS22 . . . . .89 A4
Tuffley Rd BS10 . . . . .49 C8
Tufton Ave BS11 . . . . .48 A8
Tugela Rd BS13 . . . . .78 F7
Tuggy's La BA2 . . . . .119 E1
Tunbridge Cl BS40 . . . . . . .96 B2
Tunbridge Rd BS40 . . . . . .96 B2
Tunbridge Way BS16 . . . . .52 A8
Tunley Hill BA2 . . . . .116 E2
Tunley Rd BA2 . . . . .117 D2
Tunnel La BA3 . . . . .138 F5
Tunstall Cl BS9 . . . . .48 E4
Turley Rd BS5 . . . . .50 D1
Turnberry Bristol BS30 . . . .66 B6
Yate BS37 . . . . .39 E8
Turnberry Wlk 3 BS4 . . . .64 D1
Turnbridge Cl BS10 . . . . . .35 C3
Turnbridge Rd BS10 . . . . .35 C3
Turnbury Ave BS48 . . . . . .60 A1
Turnbury Cl BS22 . . . . . . .88 F3
Turner Cl BS31 . . . . .82 A5
Turner Ct BS22 . . . . .88 F3
Turner Dr BS37 . . . . .27 B1
Turner Gdns BS7 . . . . .50 B7
Turner Way BS21 . . . . .57 B1
Turner Wlk BS30 . . . . .66 D7
Turner's Terr BA3 . . . . . . .135 A1

Turners Ct 9 BS30 . . . . . .65 F4
Turnpike Cl BS37 . . . . .27 E2
Turnpike Gate GL12 . . . . .18 B6
Turnpike Rd
Axbridge BS26 . . . . .124 E1
Shipham BS25 . . . . .125 E8
Turtlegate Ave BS13 . . . . .78 E4
Turtlegate Wlk BS13 . . . . .78 E4
Turville Dr BS7 . . . . .50 A6
Tuscany Ho BS6 . . . . .49 A3
Tutton Way BS21 . . . . .57 D1
Tuttors Hill BS27 . . . . . . .126 C1
Tweed Cl BS35 . . . . .15 C8
Tweed Rd BS21 . . . . .57 C1
Tweed Rd Ind Est 2
BS21 . . . . .57 C1
Tweeny La BS30 . . . . .66 D6
Twenty Acres Rd BS10 . . .35 B2
Twerton Farm Cl BA2 . . .101 B6
Twerton Inf Sch BA2 . . . .101 A5
Twerton Park (Bath FC)
BA2 . . . . .101 B6
Twickenham Rd BS6 . . . . .49 C5
Twinhoe La BA2 . . . . .118 E2
Two Acres Cvn Pk BS21 . .44 B1
Two Acres Rd BS14 . . . . . .80 A7
Two Mile Ct BS15 . . . . . . .65 C8
Two Mile Hill Inf Sch
BS15 . . . . .65 C8
Two Mile Hill Jun Sch
BS15 . . . . .65 C8
Two Mile Hill Rd BS15 . . .65 B8
Two Stone La BS37 . . . . . .40 C8
Two Trees BS40 . . . . .127 E8
Twr The BS1 . . . . .143 B2
Twynings The BS15 . . . . . .51 E2
Tybalt Way BS34 . . . . .36 E5
Tydeman Rd BS20 . . . . . . .45 F5
Tyler Cl BS15 . . . . .65 E5
Tyler Gn 2 BS22 . . . . .89 B4
Tyler St BS2 . . . . .64 A6
Tyler's La BS16 . . . . .51 D5
Tylers Farm BS37 . . . . .27 F4
Tylers Way BS37 . . . . .27 F5
Tyndale Ave Bristol BS16 . .51 A5
Yate BS37 . . . . .27 D3
Tyndale Cl GL11 . . . . .5 E4
Tyndale Ct 7 BS6 . . . . . . .49 B1
Tyndale Mon The ★ GL11 . .5 E4
Tyndale View BS35 . . . . . .15 B8
Tyndall Ave BS8 . . . . .142 C4
Tyndall Ho 5 BS2 . . . . . . .143 C3
Tyndall Rd BS5 . . . . .64 B8
Tyndall's Park Rd BS8 . . .142 C4
Tyndalls Park Mews
BS2 . . . . .142 C4
Tyndalls Way BS10 . . . . . .49 E8
Tyne Ho 8 BS35 . . . . .15 C8
Tyne Rd BS7 . . . . .49 D3
Tyne St BS2 . . . . .50 A2
Tyning Cl Bristol BS14 . . . .80 A7
Yate BS37 . . . . .27 E2
Tyning End BA2 . . . . .102 B5
Tyning Hengrove Jun Sch
BS14 . . . . .80 A7
Tyning Hill BA3 . . . . .134 B3
Tyning La BA1 . . . . .85 B1
Tyning Pl BA2 . . . . .102 C2
Tyning Rd Bath BA2 . . . . .102 C2
Bathampton BA2 . . . . .85 F2
Bristol BS3 . . . . .63 F3
Peasedown St John BA2 . .134 D3
Saltford BS31 . . . . .82 E2
Winsley BA15 . . . . .120 E7
Tyning The Bath BA2 . . . .102 B5
Freshford BA2 . . . . .120 B4
Tynings BS39 . . . . .114 D3
Tynings Mews BS23 . . . . .104 E4
Tynings Sch The BS16 . . .51 E4
Tynings The
Clevedon BS21 . . . . .57 A1
Portishead BS20 . . . . .44 F1
Tynings Way
Clutton BS39 . . . . .114 E3
Westwood BA15 . . . . .120 F3
Tynning Terr 16 BA1 . . . . .85 A1
Tynte Ave BS13 . . . . .79 E3
Tyntesfield BS48 . . . . .60 F4
Tyntesfield Rd BS13 . . . . .79 A8
Tyrone Wlk BS4 . . . . .79 E8
Tyrrel Way BS34 . . . . .36 E5
Tythe Ct SN14 . . . . .70 A8
Tytherington Rd BS35,
GL12 . . . . .16 A6

U

Ubley CE Prim Sch
BS40 . . . . .111 D1
Ubley Dro BS40 . . . . .128 B7
Ullswater Cl Bristol BS30 . .66 D6
Weston-S-M BS23 . . . . . .105 A4
Yate BS37 . . . . .27 E3
Ullswater Dr BA1 . . . . .85 A2
Ullswater Rd BS10 . . . . . . .35 C1
Uncombe Cl BS48 . . . . . . .76 D7
Under Knoll BA2 . . . . . . .134 E8
Under La BS40 . . . . .93 D1
Underbanks BS20 . . . . . . .47 D4
Underdown Ho BS1 . . . . .143 A1
Underhill Ave BA3 . . . . . .132 F3
Underhill Dr BS23 . . . . . .104 D1
Underhill La BA3 . . . . . . .132 E2

Underhill Rd GL12 .....11 A5
Underleaf Way BA2 ....134 D7
Undertown BS40 ......129 A7
Undertown La BS40 ....129 A7
Underwood Ave BS22 ....88 B1
Underwood Cl BS35 .....15 A4
Underwood End BS25 ..108 A4
Underwood Rd BS20 ....45 C3
Unicorn Bsns Pk BS4 ....64 D5
Unicorn Pk BS4 ....64 D5
Union Pas BA1 ....141 C2
Union Pl BS23 ....104 D7
Union Rd 2 BS2 ....64 A6
Union St Bath BA1 ......141 C2
Bristol BS1 ....143 B3
Nailsea BS48 ....59 C1
Weston-S-M BS23 ....104 D7
Unity Ct BS31 ....82 A5
Unity Rd BS31 ....82 A6
Unity St Bristol BS2 .....143 C3
Bristol,Brandon Hill BS1 ..142 C2
Bristol,St George BS15 ....65 C8
Univ of Bath BA2 ......102 E5
Univ of Bristol BS8 ....142 C3
Univ of Bristol (Veterinary Science Dept) BS49 ...109 B6
Univ of Bristol Dept of Economics BS8 ....142 C3
Univ of Bristol Dept of Ed BS8 ....142 C3
Univ of Bristol Sch of Vetinary Science BS2 .142 C4
Univ of the West of England BS3 ....62 E4
Univ of the West of England Faculty of Health & Social Care BS16 ....50 E5
Univ of the West of England Frenchay Campus BS16 .36 E1
Univ of the West of England, St Matthias BS16 ......51 A5
University Cl BS9 ....48 F4
University Rd BS8 .....142 C3
University Wlk BS8 ....142 C3
Uphill Ct BS23 ....104 D2
Uphill Dr BA1 ....85 B2
Uphill Farm Cvn Pk BS23 ....104 E1
Uphill Prim Sch BS23 ..104 D2
Uphill Rd BS7 ....49 F5
Uphill Rd N BS23 ......104 D4
Uphill Rd S BS23 ......104 D2
Uphill Way BS23 ....104 D1
Upjohn Cres BS13 ....79 D3
Uplands Cl BA2 ....119 F7
Uplands Dr BS31 ....82 F2
Uplands Rd Bristol BS16 ..51 D3
Saltford BS31 ....82 F2
Uplands The BS48 ....75 C8
Upper Bath Rd BS35 ....15 B8
Upper Belgrave Rd BS8 .49 A2
Upper Belmont Rd BS7 ..49 E3
Upper Berkeley Pl BS8 .142 B3
Upper Bloomfield Rd BA2 ....101 D1
Upper Borough Walls BA1 ....141 C2
Upper Bristol Rd
Bath BA1 ....101 D7
Clutton BS39 ....114 D3
Weston-S-M BS22 ....88 B1
Upper Byron Pl BS8 ....142 B3
Upper Camden Pl BA1 .141 C4
Upper Chapel La BS36 ...38 C7
Upper Cheltenham Pl BS6 ....49 E1
Upper Church La
Bristol BS2 ....142 C3
Hutton BS24 ....105 D2
Upper Church Rd BS23 ..87 D1
Upper Church St BA1 ...141 B3
Upper Cranbrook Rd BS6 49 B4
Upper East Hayes BA1 ...85 B1
Upper Farm Cl BA2 ....136 F4
Upper Furlong BA2 ....116 B3
Upper Green La BS40 ...111 B7
Upper Hedgemead Rd BA1 ....141 B4
Upper Horfield Prim Sch BS7 ....50 A8
Upper Kewstoke Rd BS23 ....87 B1
Upper Lambridge St BA1 85 C2
Upper Lansdown Mews BA1 ....84 F1
Upper Maudlin St BS2 ..143 A3
Upper Merryfield BA3 ..139 E1
Upper Mount Pleasant BA2 ....120 A4
Upper Myrtle Hill BS20 ..47 C4
Upper New Rd BS27 ....125 F1
Upper Oldfield Pk BA2 .141 A1
Upper Perry Hill BS3 ....63 C4
Upper Pitching BA3 ....138 D5
Upper Rd BS39 ....130 E6
Upper Sandhurst Rd BS4 64 D4
Upper St Bristol BS4 .....64 A4
Dyrham SN14 ....54 D4
Upper Stanton BS39 .....97 A2
Upper Station Rd BS16 ..51 D4
Upper Stone Cl BS36 ...38 C7
Upper Strode BS40 .....111 F7
Upper Sydney St BS3 ....63 B3
Upper Terr BS11 ....34 B1
Upper Tockington Rd BS32 ....14 A2
Upper Town La BS40 ....94 C8
Upper Wells St BS1 ....142 C2
Upper York St BS2 .....143 B4
Upton BS24 ....105 A2
Upton La BS41 ....96 A8
Upton Rd BS3 ....63 B4
Urchinwood BS49 ....91 F4
Urchinwood La BS49 ....91 F4
Urfords Dr BS16 ....51 C6
Usk Ct 5 BS35 ....15 C8

V

Valda Rd BS22 ....88 C2
Vale Cres BS22 ....89 C2
Vale Ct BS8 ....142 A4
Vale End BS48 ....59 D1
Vale La BS3 ....79 C8
Vale Mill Way BS24 ....105 F8
Vale St BS4 ....64 A4
Vale The BS16 ....52 F6
Vale View BA3 ....134 A2
Vale View Pl BA1 ....85 B1
Vale View Terr BA1 .....85 F3
Valentine Cl BS14 ....80 B5
Valerian Cl BS11 ....47 F6
Valetta Cl BS23 ....104 F3
Valley Cl 6 BS48 ....59 E2
Valley Gdns Bristol BS16 ..51 F8
Nailsea BS48 ....59 E2
Valley Rd
Bristol,Bedminster Down BS13 ....79 A8
Bristol,Mangotsfield BS16 ..52 A5
Bristol,North Common BS30 66 D6
Clevedon BS21 ....57 F5
Leigh Woods BS8 ....62 C7
Portishead BS20 ....45 A2
Valley View
Chilcompton BA3 ....138 D3
Clutton BS39 ....114 E3
Valley View Cl BA1 ......85 B3
Valley View Rd Bath BA1 .85 C3
Paulton BS39 ....132 E6
Valley Way Rd BS48 .....59 E3
Valley Wlk BA3 ....133 B2
Valls The BS32 ....36 F6
Valma Rocks BS5 ....65 A6
Van Diemen's La BA1 ....84 F2
Vanbrush La BS16 ....50 E7
Vandyck Ave BS31 ....81 F6
Vane St BA2 ....102 B7
Varsity Way BS24 ......106 B6
Vassall Ct BS16 ....51 B5
Vassall Rd BS16 ....51 B5
Vattingstone La BS35 ....14 F5
Vaughan Cl BS10 ....34 F3
Vauxhall Terr 2 BS3 ....63 A4
Vayre Cl BS37 ....28 C1
Veale The BS24 ....122 C6
Vee La BS40 ....94 D8
Vellore La BA2 ....102 C7
Velvet Bottom Nature Res* BS40 ....127 F4
Venns Gate BS27 ......126 A1
Ventnor Ave 1 BS5 .....64 F8
Ventnor Rd
Bristol,Crofts End BS5 ....50 F1
Bristol,Filton BS34 ....36 B3
Venton Ct 5 BS15 ....65 B5
Venus La BS39 ....114 E3
Venus St BS49 ....91 E2
Vera Rd BS16 ....50 F2
Verbena Way BS22 ......89 A1
Vereland Rd BS24 ......105 E3
Verlands BS49 ....91 E5
Vernals La GL12 ....11 C8
Vernham Gr BA2 ....101 C1
Vernon Cl BS31 ....82 D3
Vernon La BS26 ....124 B3
Vernon Pk BA2 ....101 C6
Vernon St 5 BS2 ....63 F4
Vernon Terr BA2 ....101 C6
Vernslade BA1 ....84 A2
Verrier Rd BS5 ....64 C7
Verwood Dr BS30 ....66 C2
Vian End BS22 ....88 F4
Vicarage Cl BS22 ....89 A3
Vicarage Cotts 9 BS16 ..51 D5
Vicarage Ct 8 BS15 .....65 B5
Vicarage Gdns BA2 ....134 B7
Vicarage La
Barrow Gurney BS48 .....77 C6
Compton Bishop BS26 ...124 B3
Compton Dando BS39 .....98 D6
Hillesley GL12 ....19 D8
Norton St Philip BA2 .....136 E4
Olveston BS35 ....14 B3
Vicarage Rd
Bristol,Headley Park BS13 .79 A6
Bristol,Jefferies Hill BS15 ..65 B5
Bristol,Moorfields BS5 ....64 C8
Bristol,Southville BS3 ....63 B4
Coalpit Heath BS36 ......38 C6
Leigh Woods BS8 ....62 D6
Pilning BS35 ....22 C7
Vicars Cl BS16 ....51 B4
Victor Ho BS34 ....36 C3
Victor Rd BS3 ....63 C3
Victor St
8 Bristol,Russell Town BS5 64 B6
Bristol,St Philip's Marsh BS2 ....64 A4
Victoria Ave BS5 ....64 C7
Victoria Bldgs BA2 .....101 D6
Victoria Bridge Ct BA1 .141 A3
Victoria Bridge Rd BA1, BA2 ....141 A2
Victoria Cl Bath BA2 ....101 C5
Portishead BS20 ....45 D5
Thornbury BS35 ....8 B3
Victoria Cotts BA2 .....118 F7
Victoria Cres BS35 ......22 A6
Victoria Ct
6 Bristol,Cotham BS6 ....49 D1
Bristol,Westbury Park BS6 .49 A3
Portishead BS20 ....45 D5
Victoria Gdns
Batheaston BA1 ....85 F3
7 Bristol BS6 ....49 D1
Victoria Gr BS3 ....63 E4
Victoria Ho Bath BA1 ...101 D8
Keynsham BS31 ....81 F4
Victoria Jubilee Homes BS40 ....109 C6
Victoria Lodge BS22 .....88 E2
Victoria Par BS5 ....64 C8
Victoria Park Bsns Ctr BA1 ....101 D7
Victoria Park Com Jun & Inf Schs BS3 ....63 E3
Victoria Pk
Bristol,Fishponds BS16 ....51 A5
Bristol,Two Mile Hill BS15 ..51 D1
Weston-S-M BS23 ....87 D1
Victoria Pl
Bath,Combe Down BA2 ...102 C1
2 Bath,Lambridge BA1 ...85 C1
Bristol BS3 ....63 C3
Paulton BS39 ....132 D5
Weston-S-M BS23 ....104 D8
Victoria Quadrant BS23 104 E8
Victoria Rd
Avonmouth BS11 ....47 B7
Bath BA2 ....101 D6
Bristol,Jefferies Hill BS15 ..65 C5
Bristol,North Common BS30 66 D5
Bristol,St Philip's Marsh BS2 ....64 A5
Clevedon BS21 ....57 C3
Saltford BS31 ....82 D3
Victoria Sq Bristol BS8 ..142 A3
Portishead BS20 ....45 D5
Weston-S-M BS23 ....104 D7
Victoria St Bristol BS1 ..143 B1
Bristol,Staple Hill BS16 ...51 D5
Victoria Terr Bath BA2 ..101 D6
15 Bristol,Clifton BS8 .....62 F6
Bristol,St Philip's Marsh BS2 ....64 B5
Paulton BS39 ....132 E6
Victoria Wlk BS6 ....49 D1
Vigor Rd BS13 ....79 B5
Villa Rosa BS23 ....87 C1
Village Cl BS37 ....27 D1
Village The BS16 ....52 C7
Villice La BS40 ....129 A7
Villiers Rd BS5 ....50 B1
Vilner La BS35 ....15 B7
Vimpany Cl BS10 ....34 F3
Vimpennys La BS35 .....22 E1
Vincent Cl BS11 ....34 C2
Vine Gdns BS22 ....89 A2
Viner's La GL9 ....43 B5
Vinery The BS25 ....125 A7
Vineyard La GL12 ....11 F5
Vining Wlk 4 BS5 ....64 B8
Vinney La BS37 ....28 F8
Vinny Ave BS16 ....52 A7
Vintery Leys BS9 ....49 B7
Virginia Cl BS37 ....28 A1
Vivian St BS3 ....63 D3
Vivien Ave BA3 ....133 A2
Vowell Cl BS13 ....79 B4
Vowles Cl BS48 ....60 A3
Voyager Cl BS34 ....37 A4
Vulcan Ho BA2 ....141 C3
Vynes Cl BS48 ....60 A1
Vynes Ind Est BS48 ......60 A3
Vynes Way BS48 ....60 A1
Vyvyan Rd BS8 ....142 A3
Vyvyan Terr BS8 ....142 A3

W

Wade Rd BS37 ....27 A3
Wade St BS2 ....143 C3
Wadehurst Ind Pk BS2 ..64 A7
Wades Rd BS34 ....36 B3
Wadham Dr BS16 ....37 B1
Wadham Gr BS16 ....52 B5
Wadham St BS23 ....104 D8
Wagtail Gdns BS22 .....105 E8
Wainbridge Cres BS35 ...22 D7
Wainbrook Dr BS5 ......50 D2
Wains Cl 5 BS21 ....57 C2
Wainwright Cl 5 BS22 ...89 B4
Waits Cl BS29 ....106 F3
Wakedean Gdns BS49 ...74 A1
Wakeford Rd 1 BS16 ....52 A7
Walcot Bldgs BA1 .....141 C4
Walcot Ct BA1 ....141 C4
Walcot Gate BA1 ......141 C4
Walcot Ho BA1 ....141 C4
Walcot Inf Sch BA1 ....141 C4
Walcot Par BA1 ....141 C4
Walcot St BA1 ....141 C3
Walcot Terr BA1 ....141 C4
Waldegrave Rd BA1 .....84 E1
Waldegrave Terr BA3 ...134 A3
Walden Rd BS31 ....82 A4
Walford Ave BS22 ....89 C3
Walk Mill La GL12 ....11 F4
Walk The GL12 ....11 F5
Walker Cl
Bristol,Blackhorse BS16 ...52 A7
Bristol,Upper Easton BS5 ..64 B8
Walker Ct BS16 ....51 F5
Walker St BS2 ....142 C4
Walker Way BS35 ....15 B7
Walkers Dr BS24 ....105 F7
Wall Gn BS26 ....125 C1
Wallace La BS40 ....129 E3
Wallace Rd BA1 ....85 B1
Wallcroft Ho BS6 ....49 A3
Wallenge Cl BS39 ......132 F6
Wallenge Dr BS39 ......132 F6
Walley La BS40 ....113 B7
Wallingford Rd BS4 .....79 D7
Walliscote Ave BS9 .....49 C6
Walliscote Grove Rd 11 BS23 ....104 E7
Walliscote Prim Sch BS23 ....104 E7
Walliscote Rd Bristol BS9 .49 C6
Weston-S-M BS23 ....104 D6
Walliscote Rd S BS23 ...104 D4
Wallscourt Rd BS34 .....36 B2
Wallscourt Rd S BS34 ...36 B1
Wallsend La SN14 ....55 C5
Wally Court Rd BS40 ...112 E8
Walmsley Terr 4 BA1 ...85 B1
Walnut Ave BS37 ....28 A2
Walnut Bldgs BA3 .....134 A3
Walnut Cl Axbridge BS26 .125 B1
Bristol BS15 ....51 F1
Coalpit Heath BS36 ....38 C6
Easton-in-G BS20 ....47 A3
Keynsham BS31 ....81 C4
Nailsea BS48 ....75 E8
Thornbury BS35 ....8 D1
Weston-S-M BS24 ....105 B2
Walnut Cres BS15 ....65 F8
Walnut Dr Bath BA2 ....101 E4
Colerne SN14 ....70 F6
Walnut La BS15 ....66 A8
Walnut Tree Cl
Almondsbury BS32 ....24 A5
Ubley BS40 ....111 D1
Walnut Tree Ct BS49 ....91 D4
Walnut Wlk Bristol BS13 ..79 A6
Keynsham BS31 ....81 C4
Walsh Ave BS14 ....80 A7
Walsh Cl BS24 ....105 B2
Walshe Ave BS37 ....28 C1
Walsingham Rd BS6 .....49 E2
Walter St BS3 ....63 A4
Waltham End 2 BS24 ..106 A8
Waltining La BA2 ......100 E6
Walton BS24 ....105 A2
Walton Ave BS4 ....64 D5
Walton Bay House Park Homes BS21 ....44 B1
Walton Cl Bristol BS30 ...66 C1
Keynsham BS31 ....81 D4
Walton Cres BS40 ....94 F8
Walton Cross BS21 ......58 B7
Walton Heath BS37 .....27 F1
Walton Rd Bristol BS11 ...47 D6
Clevedon BS21 ....57 F4
Walton Rise BS9 ....49 A7
Walton St Bristol BS5 ....50 B1
Clevedon BS21 ....58 A7
Walwyn Cl BA2 ....101 A6
Walwyn Gdns BS13 ......79 C3
Wansbeck Rd BS31 .....82 A4
Wansbrough Rd BS22 ...89 B4
Wanscow Wlk BS9 ......49 B6
Wansdyke Bsns Ctr BA2 ....101 D4
Wansdyke Ct 9 BS14 ...80 B5
Wansdyke Prim Sch BS14 ....79 F4
Wansdyke Rd BA2 .....101 D1
Wansdyke Sch BA2 ....118 E8
Wansdyke Workshops BS31 ....82 A6
Wapley Hill BS37 ....39 E4
Wapley Rd BS37 ....40 B3
Wapping Rd BS1 ....143 A1
Warden Rd BS3 ....63 C4
Wardour Rd BS4 ....79 D8
Ware Ct BS36 ....37 D5
Wareham Cl BS48 ....59 D1
Warend Hill GL11 ....5 F6
Waring Ho BS1 ....143 A1
Warleigh Dr BA1 ....86 A3
Warleigh La BA1 ....103 C5
Warleys La BS24 ....89 C1
Warman Cl BS14 ....80 F6
Warman Rd BS14 ....80 F6
Warmington Rd BS14 ....80 C8
Warminster Rd
Bath BA2 ....103 B5
Bristol BS2 ....50 A2
Warmley Park Sch BS30 .66 B7
Warne Pk BS23 ....105 A6
Warne Rd BS23 ....105 A6
Warner Cl Bristol BS15 ...65 F6
Cleeve BS49 ....92 A7
Warns The BS30 ....66 A4
Warren Cl Bristol BS32 ...24 D3
Hutton BS24 ....105 D2
Warren Croft GL11 ....5 E4
Warren Gdns BS14 ......80 F5
Warren La BS41 ....77 E8
Warren Rd BS34 ....36 B3
Warren Way BS37 ....27 E3
Warren's Cl BS27 ......126 B1
Warrens Hill BS27 ......126 B1
Warrens Hill Rd BS27 ..126 D4
Warrilow Cl BS22 ....89 B5
Warrington Rd BS4 .....64 D2
Warry Cl BS48 ....60 B2
Warth La Pilning BS35 ....12 D3
Weston-S-M BS22 ....89 A8
Warwick Ave 7 BS5 .....50 B1
Warwick Cl Bristol BS30 ..66 B2
Thornbury BS35 ....8 A1
Weston-S-M BS22 ......105 C8
Warwick Gdns BS39 ....114 D3
Warwick Rd Bath BA1 ...101 B7
Bristol,Lower Easton BS5 ..50 B1
Bristol,Woolcott Park BS6 ..49 B1
Keynsham BS31 ....81 D4
Washing Pound La
Bristol BS14 ....80 B4
Nailsea BS48 ....59 B4
Washingpool Hill BS35 ..14 E1
Washingpool Hill Rd BS32 ....14 D2
Washingpool La BS11 ...33 F7
Washington Ave BS5 ....50 C1
Washpool La BA2 ......100 F2
Watch Elm Cl BS32 .....36 E6
Watchhouse Rd BS20 ...47 D4
Watchill Ave BS13 ......78 F6
Watchill Cl BS13 ....78 F6
Water La Bristol BS1 ....143 B2
Bristol,Hanham Green BS15 65 B2
Bristol,Upper Knowle BS4 ..64 D2
Bristol,Windmill Hill BS3 ..63 F3
Paulton BA3,BS39 ......133 A4
Pill BS20 ....47 C4
Water St BS40 ....129 F4
Water's La BS9 ....49 A7
Waterbridge Rd BS13 ....78 F4
Watercress Cl BS48 .....60 B2
Watercress Rd BS2 ......49 F3
Waterdale Cl BS9 ....49 C7
Waterdale Gdns BS9 ....49 C7
Waterford Cl BS35 ......15 D8
Waterford Pk BA3 ......133 E1
Waterford Rd BS9 ....49 B6
Waterhouse La BA2 ....119 F8
Waterloo Bldgs BA2 ....101 B6
Waterloo Ho BS20 ....47 D5
Waterloo Pl 19 BS2 ....143 C3
Waterloo Rd Bristol BS2 .143 C3
Radstock BA3 ....134 A2
Waterloo St Bristol BS2 .143 C3
9 Bristol,Clifton BS8 .....62 F7
Weston-S-M BS23 ....104 E8
Watermead Cl 9 BA1 ...141 B2
Watermill Cl GL12 ....9 E7
Watermore Cl BS36 .....38 C7
Waters Rd BS15 ....65 C8
Waterside Cres BA3 ...133 D1
Waterside Dr BS32 ......24 A1
Waterside La BA3 ......140 A6
Waterside Pk BS20 ......44 D4
Waterside Rd BA3 .....133 D1
Waterside Way BA3 ....139 D8
Watery La Bath BA2 ....101 A6
Doynton BS30 ....68 A8
Nailsea BS48 ....59 B2
Stratton-on-t-F BA3 .....139 A3
Winford BS40 ....95 B4
Wathen Rd BS6 ....49 F3
Watkins Yd BS9 ....49 A8
Watley's End Rd BS36 ...37 F7
Watling Way BS11 ....47 D7
Watson Ave BS4 ....64 D4
Watson's Rd BS30 ....65 F3
Watters Cl BS36 ....38 D6
Wavell Cl BS37 ....27 D3
Waveney Rd BS31 ....82 A3
Waverley Ct BS49 ....91 D3
Waverley Rd
Backwell BS48 ....76 A7
Bristol,Cotham BS6 ......49 C1
Bristol,Shirehampton BS11 .47 E6
Weston-S-M BS23 ....104 F4
Yate BS37 ....27 B2
Waverley St 8 BS5 ......50 A1
Wayacre Dro BS24 .....121 E6
Waycroft Prim Sch BS14 .80 E5
Wayfield Gdns BA1 ......85 F4
Wayford Cl BS31 ....82 A3
Wayland Ct BS16 ....51 A4
Wayland Rd BS22 ....88 E3
Wayleaze
Coalpit Heath BS36 ......38 D7
Westerleigh BS37 ....39 F3
Wayside BS22 ....88 D2
Wayside Cl BS36 ....38 B7
Wayside Dr BS21 ....57 E5
Weal Terr BA1 ....84 B2
Weal The BA1 ....84 C2
Weare Ct BS1 ....142 A1
Weatherley Dr BS20 .....44 F3
Weatherly Ave BA2 ....101 D2
Weavers Cl GL12 ....11 F4
Weavers Orch BA2 .....118 D1
Webb St BS5 ....64 A8
Webbington Rd BS26 ...124 C3
Webbs Heath BS30 ......66 E8
Webbs Mead BS40 .....112 D8
Webbs Wood BS32 ......36 F7
Webbs Wood Rd BS32 ...36 F7
Wedgewood Rd BS16 ....37 D1
Wedgwood Cl 4 BS14 ...80 B5
Wedgwood Rd BA2 .....101 A5
Wedlock Way BS3 ....62 F3
Wedmore Cl Bristol BS15 .65 F7
Weston-S-M BS23 ....104 F2
Wedmore Pk BA2 ......101 A3

Wedmore Rd
Clevedon BS21 .....57 B1
Nailsea BS48 .....75 E8
Saltford BS31 .....82 D4
Wedmore Vale BS3 .....63 E2
Weedon Cl 6 BS2 .....50 A2
Weekesley La BA2 .....116 D1
Weetwood Rd BS49 .....91 E5
Weight Rd 2 BS5 .....64 C7
Weind The BS22 .....88 D2
Weir La Abbots Leigh BS8 ..61 F5
Marshfield SN14 .....69 F8
Weir Rd BS49 .....91 E3
Well Cl Long Ashton BS41 ..62 B1
Weston-S-M BS24 .....105 B2
Winscombe BS25 .....125 A8
Well House Cl BS9 .....48 E3
Well La Badminton GL9 ....30 E5
Banwell BS29 .....106 E3
Yatton BS49 .....91 C8
Well Pk BS49 .....91 E4
Welland Rd BS31 .....81 F4
Wellard Cl 1 BS22 .....89 B4
Wellesley Prim Sch BS37 39 D6
Wellgarth Rd BS4 .....64 A2
Wellgarth Wlk BS4 .....64 A2
Wellington Ave BS6 .....49 E1
Wellington Bldgs BA1 .....84 B2
Wellington Cres BS7 .....49 E6
Wellington Ct BS21 .....57 C5
Wellington Dr Bristol BS9 49 D6
Yate BS37 .....27 B2
Wellington Hill BS7 .....49 E6
Wellington Hill W BS9 .....49 D7
Wellington La BS6 .....49 E1
Wellington Mews BS11 .....47 D5
Wellington Pk BS8 .....49 A2
Wellington Pl
Bristol,Frenchay BS16 .....37 B1
9 Bristol,Montpelier BS6 ..49 E1
Weston-S-M BS23 .....104 D7
Wellington Rd
Bristol BS2 .....143 C4
Bristol,Hopewell Hill BS15 .51 D2
Yate BS37 .....27 E3
Wellington Terr
20 Bristol BS8 .....62 F6
Clevedon BS21 .....57 D5
Wellington Wlk BS10 .....49 C7
Wellow Brook Mdw BA3 133 B2
Wellow La
Hinton Charterhouse BA2 .119 D1
Norton St Philip BA2 .....136 D5
Peasedown St John BA2 ..134 C6
Shoscombe BA2 .....134 E6
Wellow Mead BA2 .....134 B7
Wellow Rd BA2 .....135 B8
Wellow Tyning BA2 .....134 D7
Wells Cl Bristol BS14 .....80 C5
Nailsea BS48 .....60 B1
Wells Rd Bath BA2 .....141 B1
Bristol BS4 .....64 B2
Chilcompton BA3 .....138 F4
Clevedon BS21 .....57 D1
Corston BA2 .....100 A7
Dundry BS40,BS41 .....95 F7
Norton St Philip BA2,BA3 .136 C3
Paulton BS39 .....132 B7
Radstock BA3 .....133 E2
Wells Sq BA3 .....133 D1
Wells St BS3 .....63 A4
Wellsea Gr BS23 .....105 B7
Wellstead Ave BS37 .....27 D1
Wellsway Bath BA2 .....101 F3
Keynsham BS31 .....81 F3
Wellsway Pk BA2 .....118 D8
Wellsway Sec Sch BS31 .82 A5
Welsford Ave BS16 .....50 D4
Welsford Rd BS16 .....50 C4
Welsh Back BS1 .....143 A2
Welton Gr BA3 .....133 B3
Welton Prim Sch BA3 ..133 C2
Welton Rd BA3 .....133 E2
Welton Vale BA3 .....133 B2
Welton Wlk BS15 .....51 C2
Wemberham Cres BS49 ..74 A1
Wemberham La BS49 .....90 E8
Wenmore Cl BS16 .....37 D1
Wentforth Dr 2 BS15 .....51 C2
Wentwood Dr BS24 .....105 A1
Wentworth Bristol BS30 ..66 A6
Yate BS37 .....27 E1
Wentworth Cl BS22 .....89 A3
Wentworth Rd BS7 .....49 D3
Wescott Gr BS11 .....34 C2
Wesley Ave Bristol BS15 ..65 D5
Radstock BA3 .....133 C1
Wesley Cl
Bristol,Rose Green BS5 ....50 D1
7 Bristol,Upper Soundwell
BS16 .....51 D3
Wesley Coll BS10 .....34 F1
Wesley Ct BS23 .....104 F8
Wesley Dr BS22 .....89 A3
Wesley Hill BS15 .....51 D1
Wesley La BS30 .....66 B5
Wesley Pl BS8 .....49 A2
Wesley Rd Bristol BS7 ....49 E4
Radstock BA3 .....133 D1
Wesley St BS3 .....63 C3
Wessex Ave BS7 .....49 F7
Wessex Ct BS7 .....49 F7
Wessex Ho 10 BS2 .....143 C3
Wessex Rd BS24 .....105 B2
West Ave BA2 .....101 C5
West Broadway BS9 .....49 D6
West Cl BA2 .....101 A5
West Coombe BS9 .....48 D6
West Country Water Pk*
BS36 .....24 F2
West Croft Blagdon BS40 110 E2
Bristol BS9 .....49 C7
Clevedon BS21 .....57 B2
West Dene BS9 .....48 E6
West Dundry La BS41 ...78 E2
West End
Bristol,Kingsdown BS2 ..143 A4
Bristol,Southville BS3 ....142 C1
Thornbury BS35 .....7 C6
West End Farm Caravan Pk
BS24 .....105 E4
West End La BS48 .....75 A8
West End Trad Est BS48 ..59 B1
West Garston BS29 .....107 A3
West Gdns BS20 .....45 C5
West Gr BS6 .....49 F1
West Harptree Rd BS40 .129 F5
West Haven Cl BS48 .....76 A6
West Hay Rd BS40 .....92 C3
West Hill Nailsea BS48 ...60 A5
Portishead BS20 .....45 B5
West Hill Ct BS20 .....45 C6
West Hill Gdns
Radstock BA3 .....133 D1
Radstock BA3 .....133 E1
West Hill Rd BA3 .....133 D1
West La BS40 .....94 C8
West Lea Rd BA1 .....84 A1
West Leaze Pl BS32 .....36 E6
West Leigh Inf Sch BS48 .76 A6
West Links BS23 .....104 D2
West Links Cl BS22 .....88 B3
West Littleton Rd SN14 ...55 E2
West Mall BS8 .....62 F7
West Par BS9 .....48 C7
West Park Rd BS16 .....51 E5
West Pk BS8 .....142 B4
West Point Row BS32 .....24 C3
West Priory Cl BS9 .....49 A7
West Rd Lympsham BS24 .121 E1
Midsomer Norton BA3 ...133 A3
Yatton BS49 .....91 B7
West Ridge BS36 .....38 C7
West Rocke Ave BS9 .....48 D6
West Rolstone Rd BS24 ..90 A1
West Shrubbery 5 BS6 ...49 B2
West St Axbridge BS26 ...125 B2
Banwell BS29 .....107 A3
Banwell BS29 .....107 B3
Bristol BS2 .....143 C3
Bristol,Bedminster BS3 ....63 C3
1 Bristol,Kingswood BS15 .65 D8
Bristol,Oldland Common
BS30 .....66 C4
Tytherington GL12 .....16 B5
Weston-S-M BS23 .....104 D8
West Terr BA3 .....137 C1
West Town Ave BS4 .....64 D1
West Town Dr 2 BS4 .....64 D1
West Town Gr BS4 .....80 D8
West Town La BS4 .....64 D1
West Town Lane Jun & Inf
Schs BS4 .....64 C1
West Town Pk BS4 .....64 D1
West Town Rd
Backwell BS48 .....76 A5
Bristol BS11 .....47 C7
West Tyning BA2 .....99 B1
West View BS35 .....14 F4
West View Rd
Batheaston BA1 .....86 A3
Bristol BS3 .....63 B3
Keynsham BS31 .....81 E5
West Way
Bristol BS10,BS34 .....35 E4
Clevedon BS21 .....57 C3
West Wick BS24 .....89 C1
West Wick Rdbt BS24 ..106 B8
West Wlk BS37 .....27 E1
Westacre Cl BS10 .....35 A2
Westaway Cl BS49 .....91 C7
Westaway Pk BS49 .....91 D7
Westbourne Ave
Clevedon BS21 .....57 B2
Keynsham BS31 .....81 E5
Westbourne Cl 2 BS16 ..52 A7
Westbourne Cres BS21 ...57 B2
Westbourne Ct BS5 .....64 B8
Westbourne Gr 8 BS3 ...63 C3
Westbourne Pl BS8 .....142 B3
Westbourne Rd
Bristol,Downend BS16 .....51 F8
8 Bristol,Upper Easton
BS5 .....64 B8
Westbourne Terr BS16 ...51 B7
Westbrook Pk BA1 .....84 A2
Westbrook Rd Bristol BS4 80 D8
Weston-S-M BS22 .....88 D1
Westbrooke Ct BS1 .....142 A1
Westbury Court Rd BS9 .49 A7
Westbury Cres BS23 .....104 F2
Westbury Ct BS9 .....49 A7
Westbury Hill BS9 .....49 A7
Westbury La BS9 .....48 C7
Westbury Mews BS9 .....49 A7
Westbury Park Prim Sch
BS6 .....49 B3
Westbury Pk BS6 .....49 A4
Westbury Rd BS6 .....49 A4
Westbury Terr BA2 .....117 E5
Westbury View BA2 .....134 E8
Westbury-on-Trym CE Prim
Sch BS9 .....49 A8
Westcliff Coll F Ed BS23 .87 B1
Westcourt Dr BS30 .....66 B4
Westend La BS35 .....7 B6
Westend Rd GL12 .....17 E5
Westering Cl BS16 .....52 A5
Westerleigh Bsns Pk
Yate BS37 .....39 B8
Yate,Nibley BS37 .....27 A1
Westerleigh Cl BS16 .....51 F7
Westerleigh Rd
Bath BA2 .....102 B1
Bristol BS16 .....51 F6
Clevedon BS21 .....57 B2
Henfield BS16,BS36,BS37 ..38 D2
Pucklechurch BS16 .....53 C7
Westerleigh BS36,BS37 ...39 B5
Yate BS37 .....39 C8
Western Approach
Distribution Pk BS35 ..22 C4
Western Ave BS36 .....26 A1
Western Ct Bristol BS34 ..37 A4
Clevedon BS21 .....57 D3
Western Dr BS14 .....79 E6
Western Grange BS34 ...36 A3
Western La BS40 .....129 C3
Western Rd BS7 .....49 E6
Westex Ho BS23 .....105 B5
Westfield BS21 .....73 D8
Westfield Cl
Backwell BS48 .....76 A6
Bath BA2 .....101 E3
Bristol BS15 .....65 D5
Keynsham BS31 .....81 C5
Weston-S-M BS23 .....104 D2
Westfield Cres BS29 ...107 A3
Westfield Dr BS48 .....76 A6
Westfield Ho BA2 .....101 E3
Westfield Ind & Trad Est
BA3 .....139 C7
Westfield La BS34 .....36 E3
Westfield Pk Bath BA1 ..101 A7
Bristol BS6 .....49 B1
Westfield Pk S BA1 .....101 A7
Westfield Pl BS8 .....62 F7
Westfield Prim Sch
BA3 .....139 C8
Westfield Rd
Backwell BS48 .....76 A6
Banwell BS29 .....107 A3
Bristol BS9 .....49 A8
Weston-S-M BS23 .....104 D2
Westfield Terr BA3 .....133 D1
Westfield Way BS32 .....24 D2
Westgate BS1 .....142 B1
Westgate Bldgs BA1 ....141 B2
Westgate St BA1 .....141 B2
Westhall Rd BA1 .....101 D7
Westhaven Sch BS23 ...104 D2
Westland Ave BS30 .....66 C4
Westleigh Cl Bristol BS10 .35 D1
Yate BS37 .....27 C1
Westleigh Ct BS37 .....27 C1
Westleigh Pk BS14 .....80 B8
Westleigh Rd BS10 .....35 D1
Westmarch Way BS22 ...89 A4
Westmarsh BS35 .....7 B5
Westmarsh La BS35 .....7 B5
Westmead Gdns BA1 .....84 A2
Westmead Rd BS5 .....65 B7
Westminster Cl 1 BS9 ..49 A7
Westminster Rd BS5 .....64 D8
Westmoreland Dr BA2 .141 A2
Westmoreland Rd
Bath BA2 .....141 A1
Bristol BS6 .....49 B3
Westmoreland St BA2 ..141 A2
Westmoreland Station Rd
BA2 .....141 A1
Westmorland Ho BS6 ....49 A3
Westmorland Terr BS37 ..41 D7
Weston All Saints CE Prim
Sch BA1 .....84 A2
Weston Ave 4 BS5 .....64 D7
Weston Bsns Pk BS24 ..105 E5
Weston Cl BS9 .....48 C7
Weston Coll BS23 .....104 D8
Weston Cres BS7 .....49 E6
Weston Dro BS20 .....58 F8
Weston Euro Pk BS24 ..105 B4
Weston Express Bsns Pk
BS22 .....105 C6
Weston Farm La BA1 ....84 C2
Weston Gateway Tourist Pk
BS24 .....89 C1
Weston Ind Est BS24 ..105 B2
Weston La BA1 .....101 C8
Weston Lock Ret BA2 ..101 C6
Weston Lodge BS23 ....104 D8
Weston Milton Sta BS22 105 C7
Weston Miniature Rly*
BS23 .....104 D5
Weston Park Ct BA1 .....84 D1
Weston Park Prim Sch
BS11 .....47 F8
Weston Pk BA1 .....84 C1
Weston Pk E BA1 .....84 D1
Weston Pk W BA1 .....84 C1
Weston Rd
Bath BA1 .....101 D8
Brean TA8 .....121 A5
Congresbury BS49 .....91 B5
Failand BS8 .....61 C3
Long Ashton BS41,BS48 ...77 D8
Weston Ret Pk BS23 ...105 A6
Weston Sixth Form Coll
BS23 .....104 F2
Weston Way BS24 .....105 F2
Weston Wood Rd BS20 ...45 C3
Weston-Super-Mare Sea Life
Ctr* BS23 .....104 D6
Weston-super-Mare Sta
BS23 .....104 E7
Westonia BS22 .....88 E2
Westonian Ct BS9 .....48 C4
Westons Brake BS16 ....38 A1
Westons Hill Dr BS16 ....38 A1
Westons Way BS15 .....65 F7
Westover Cl BS9 .....34 F1
Westover Dr BS9 .....35 A1
Westover Gdns BS9 .....48 F8
Westover Rd BS9 .....35 A1
Westover Rise BS9 .....35 A1
Westpoint Trad Est BS15 .65 D7
Westview BS39 .....132 C5
Westview Orch BA2 ....120 B5
Westward BS41 .....62 B2
Westward Cl BS40 .....92 D2
Westward Dr BS20 .....47 C4
Westward Gdns BS41 ....62 B2
Westward Rd BS13 .....78 F7
Westway BS48 .....59 E2
Westwood Ave BS39 ...115 C2
Westwood Cl 2 BS22 ....88 F2
Westwood Cres BS4 .....64 D5
Westwood Rd Bristol BS4 .80 D8
Westwood BA15 .....120 F3
Westwood with Iford Prim
Sch BA15 .....120 F3
Westwoods BA1 .....86 B3
Wetherby Ct BS16 .....37 F1
Wetherby Gr BS16 .....37 F1
Wetherell Pl BS8 .....142 B3
Wetlands La BS20 .....45 C3
Wexford Rd BS4 .....79 D8
Weymouth Ct BA1 .....102 B8
Weymouth Rd BS3 .....63 D2
Weymouth St BA1 .....102 B8
Wharf La BS20 .....46 B5
Wharf Rd 6 BS16 .....50 F4
Wharfedale BS35 .....15 D8
Wharfside BS24 .....121 E3
Wharnecliffe Cl BS14 ....80 B5
Wharnecliffe Gdns BS14 .80 B5
Whartons 8 BS4 .....64 D1
Whatley Ct 9 BS8 .....49 B1
Whatley Rd BS8 .....49 B1
Wheatfield Dr
Bristol BS32 .....24 D1
Weston-S-M BS22 .....89 A5
Wheatfield Prim Sch
BS32 .....24 D1
Wheathill Cl BS31 .....81 D5
Wheelers Cl BA3 .....133 D2
Wheelers Dr BA3 .....133 C2
Wheelers Patch BS16 ....52 B5
Wheelers Rd BA3 .....133 D2
Whinchat Gdns BS16 ....50 F6
Whippington Ct BS1 ...143 B3
Whistley La BS40 .....129 F6
Whitby Rd BS4 .....64 C4
Whitchurch District Ctr
BS14 .....80 A5
Whitchurch La
Bristol BS13 .....79 B5
Bristol BS13 .....79 C5
Bristol,Witchurch BS14 ...79 E5
Dundry BS41 .....79 C1
Whitchurch Prim Sch
BS14 .....80 C4
Whitchurch Rd BS13 ....79 A6
White Cross Gate BS39 .131 F6
White Hill BA2 .....134 F6
White Horse Rd BA15 ..120 E7
White House La BS26 ..123 A3
White House Rd BS49 ...91 F8
White Lodge Pk BS20 ....45 D6
White Lodge Rd BS16 ....51 F4
White Ox Mead La BA2 .117 F1
White St BS5 .....143 C4
White Tree Rd BS9 .....49 B4
White Tree Rdbt BS6 ....49 A4
Whitebeam Ct BS5 .....64 E8
Whitebeam Ho BS16 .....51 C6
Whitebrook La BA2 ....134 A8
Whitecroft Way BS15 ....66 A7
Whitecross Ave BS14 ....80 C6
Whitecross La BS29 ...107 A4
Whitecross Rd
East Harptree BS40 .....129 F4
Weston-S-M BS23 .....104 E6
Whitefield Ave
Bristol,Jefferies Hill BS15 ..65 D5
Bristol,Whiteway BS5 .....51 A1
Whitefield Cl BA1 .....86 B4
Whitefield Rd BS5 .....51 A2
Whitefields BS37 .....28 C1
Whitegate Cl BS24 .....122 B6
Whitegates BS36 .....37 D6
Whitehall Ave BS5 .....50 E1
Whitehall Gdns BS5 .....50 D1
Whitehall Prim Sch BS5 .50 D1
Whitehall Rd BS5 .....64 C8
Whitehall Trad Est 4
BS5 .....64 C8
Whitehouse La
Bristol BS3 .....63 D4
Litton BA3 .....130 D3
Wraxall BS48 .....60 A6
Whitehouse Pl BS3 .....63 E4
Whitehouse Rd BS35 ....22 C7
Whitehouse St BS3 .....63 E4
Whiteladies Rd BS8 ....142 B4
Whitelands Hill BA3 ...134 B3
Whiteleaze BS10 .....49 C8
Whitemead Ho 3 BS3 ...63 A3
Whitemore Ct BA1 .....86 A4
Whiteoak Way BS48 .....75 D8
Whites Hill BS5 .....65 A6
Whitesfield Ct BS48 .....59 D2
Whitesfield Rd BS48 ....59 D1
Whiteshill BS16 .....37 D3
Whitewall La BS35 .....8 F1
Whiteway Ave BA2 .....101 A3
Whiteway Cl
Bristol St Anne's Park BS4 .64 E6
Bristol,Whiteway BS5 .....65 A8
Whiteway Ct 1 BS5 .....65 A8
Whiteway Mews BS5 .....65 A8
Whiteway Rd Bath BA2 .101 A3
Bristol BS5,BS15 .....51 A1
Whitewells Rd BA1 .....85 A2
Whitewood Rd BS5 .....50 F1
Whitfield Cl 8 BS16 .....51 D3
Whitfield Fishponds Com Sch
BS16 .....50 F4
Whitfield Ho 6 BS15 ....65 D8
Whitfield Rd BS35 .....8 C2
Whiting Rd BS13 .....79 A4
Whitland Ave BS13 .....79 B5
Whitland Rd BS13 .....79 B5
Whitley Cl BS37 .....27 C3
Whitley Mead BS34 .....36 E3
Whitling St BS40 .....95 A2
Whitmead Gdns BS13 ...79 C4
Whitmore Ave BS4 .....65 A3
Whitson Ho 1 BS2 .....143 C3
Whitson St BS1 .....143 A4
Whitting Rd BS23 .....104 E4
Whittington Dr BS22 ....88 D2
Whittington Rd BS16 .....51 C6
Whittock Rd BS14 .....80 D6
Whittock Sq BS14 .....80 D7
Whittucks Cl BS15 .....65 D4
Whittucks Rd BS15 .....65 C4
Whitwell Rd BS14 .....80 B8
Whytes Cl BS9 .....49 A8
Wick CE Prim Sch BS30 .67 B6
Wick Cres BS4 .....64 D3
Wick House Cl BS31 ....82 D3
Wick La Camerton BA2 ..116 F1
Lympsham BS24 .....121 E1
Pensford BS39 .....97 D3
Upton Cheyney BS30 .....67 A2
Wick Rd
Bishop Sutton BS39 .....113 C3
Bristol BS4 .....64 D4
Hewish BS24 .....89 F4
Lympsham BS24 .....121 D2
Pilning BS35 .....22 C7
Wick Wick Cl BS16 .....38 A1
Wickets The
Bristol,Northville BS7 .....35 F1
Bristol,Upper Soundwell
BS15 .....51 D2
Wicketts The BS7 .....35 F2
Wickfield BS21 .....57 C1
Wickham Cl BS37 .....40 D8
Wickham Ct Bristol BS16 .50 D5
Clevedon BS21 .....57 C3
Wickham Glen BS16 .....50 D5
Wickham Hill BS16 .....50 D5
Wickham View BS16 .....50 D4
Wicklow Rd BS4 .....79 E8
Wickwar Rd
Kingswood GL12 .....11 E4
Rangeworthy BS37 .....17 B1
Yate BS37 .....28 B5
Widcombe BS14 .....80 A6
Widcombe CE Jun Sch
BA2 .....102 B5
Widcombe Cl 3 BS5 .....65 A7
Widcombe Cres BA2 ...102 B5
Widcombe Hill BA2 ....102 C4
Widcombe Inf Sch BA2 .102 B5
Widcombe Par BA2 .....141 C1
Widcombe Rise BA2 ....102 B5
Widcombe Terr BA2 ....102 B5
Widmore Gr BS13 .....79 B5
Wigmore Gdns BS22 .....88 D2
Wigton Cres BS10 .....35 C2
Wilbye Gr BS4 .....79 D7
Wilcox Cl BS15 .....65 C6
Wildcountry La BS41,
BS48 .....77 E6
Wildcroft Ho BS9 .....49 B4
Wildcroft Rd BS9 .....49 B4
Wilder Ct BS2 .....143 B4
Wilder Ho BS2 .....143 B4
Wilder St BS2 .....143 B4
Willada Cl BS3 .....63 B2
William Daw Cl BS29 ...106 F3
William Herschel Mus*
BA1 .....141 B2
William Mason Cl 18 BS5 64 B7
William St Bath BA2 ....141 C3
Bristol,Hillfields BS16 .....51 B3
8 Bristol,Moorfields BS5 ..64 C8
Bristol,Newton BS2 .....64 A6
Bristol,St Pauls BS2 .....49 F1
Bristol,Windmill Hill BS3 ...63 E4
Williams Cl BS30 .....65 F3
Williamson Rd BS7 .....49 F3
Williamstowe BA2 .....102 C1
Willinton Rd BS4 .....79 F8
Willis Est BS2 .....49 F3
Willis Rd BS15 .....51 F2
Williton Cres BS23 ....104 F3
Willment Way BS11 .....33 D1
Willmott Cl BS14 .....79 F3
Willoughby Cl
Alveston BS35 .....15 A4
Bristol BS13 .....79 B7
Willoughby Rd BS7 .....49 E5

Willow Bank BS10 .....49 C7
Willow Bed Cl BS16 ..51 B6
Willow Cl Bath BA2 ..118 E8
Bristol,Cribbs Causeway
BS34 ....35 E7
Bristol,North Common BS30 66 D6
Charfield GL12 ....11 A4
Clevedon BS21 ....57 E3
Long Ashton BS41 .....61 F1
Portishead BS20 ....45 C4
Radstock BA3 ....133 E2
Weston-S-M,St Georges
BS22 ....89 D2
Weston-S-M,Uphill BS23 .104 E2
Wick BS30 ....67 B6
Willow Ct BS7 ....56 E4
Willow Dr Bleadon BS24 .122 C6
Hutton BS24 ....105 E2
Weston-S-M BS24 ....105 E5
Willow Gdns BS22 .....89 D2
Willow Gn BA2 ....101 E4
Willow Gr ◫ BS16 .....51 C2
Willow Ho BS13 ....79 D4
Willow Rd BS15 ....65 C3
Willow Sh Ctr The BS16 .51 E6
Willow The BA3 ....138 E2
Willow Way BS36 ......38 C6
Willow Wlk Bristol BS10 ..35 B3
Keynsham BS31 ....81 D4
Willowdown BS22 .....88 E4
Willowfalls The BA1 ...85 E3
Willows The
Bristol,Bradley Stoke BS32 .36 D8
Bristol,Frenchay BS16 ...37 B1
Nailsea BS48 ....59 F3
Yate BS37 ....27 D2
Wills Dr BS5 ....64 A8
Wills Way BS4,BS13 ...79 D6
Willsbridge Hill BS30 ...66 A2
Willsbridge Mill ★ BS30 .66 A2
Willway St BS3 ....63 D4
Wilmot Ct BS30 ....66 A6
Wilmots Way BS20 .....47 D4
Wilshire Ave BS15 ....65 D5
Wilson Pl BS2 ....143 C4
Wilson St BS2 ....143 C4
Wilton Cl BS10 ....35 C1
Wilton Gdns BS23 ....104 D7
Wiltons BS40 ....92 F2
Wiltshire Ave BS37 ....28 A3
Wiltshire Pl BS15 .....51 E3
Wiltshire Way BA1 .....85 A2
Wilverley Ind Est BS4 ..64 E1
Wimbledon Rd BS6 ....49 C5
Wimblestone Rd BS25 .107 F2
Wimborne Rd BS3 .....63 C1
Winash Cl BS14 ....80 D7
Wincanton Cl Bristol BS16 37 F1
Nailsea BS48 ....60 B1
Winchcombe Cl BS48 ..76 A8
Winchcombe Gr BS11 ..47 F5
Winchcombe Rd BS36 ..38 B8
Winchester Ave BS4 ...64 D3
Winchester Ct BS16 ...50 E6
Winchester Rd Bath BA2 101 D5
Bristol BS4 ....64 D3
Wincombe Trad Est BS2 .64 A4
Wincroft BS30 ....66 C4
Windcliff Cres BS11 ...47 E7
Windermere Ave BS23 .104 F4
Windermere Rd BS34 ..36 A8
Windermere Way BS30 ..66 D6
Windmill Cl BS3 ......63 E4
Windmill Farm Bsns Ctr
BS3 ....63 D4
Windmill Hill Bristol BS3 .63 D3
Hutton BS24 ....106 A2
Windmill La BS10 .....34 D3
Windmill Rd BS21 .....73 E8
Windrush Cl BA2 .....100 F4
Windrush Ct BS35 .....15 C8
Windrush Gn BS31 ....82 A4
Windrush Rd BS31 ....82 A4
Windscreens Ave BS2 ..64 A7
Windsor Ave Bristol BS5 ..65 B6
Keynsham BS31 ....81 E4
Windsor Bridge Rd BA1,
BA2 ....101 D7
Windsor Cl Bristol BS34 ..36 E4
Clevedon BS21 ....57 D2
Windsor Cres BS10 ....34 C4
Windsor Ct Bath BA1 ..101 C7
◫ Bristol,Clifton BS8 ..62 F6
Bristol,Downend BS16 ...51 E7
Wick BS30 ....67 C7
Windsor Dr Nailsea BS48 .59 E2
Yate BS37 ....27 D2
Windsor Gr ◫ BS5 ....64 B8
Windsor Pl Bath BA1 ..101 C7
Bristol,Clifton BS8 ....62 F6
Bristol,Mangotsfield BS16 .52 A5
Windsor Rd
Bristol,Longwell Green
BS30 ....65 F2
Bristol,Montpelier BS6 ..49 E2
Weston-S-M BS22 .....88 C2
Windsor Terr
Bristol,Clifton BS8 ....62 F6
Bristol,Windmill Hill BS3 .63 F4
Paulton BS39 ....132 E5
Windsor Villas BA1 ...101 C7
Windwhistle Circ BS23 .104 F4
Windwhistle La BS23 ..104 E1
Windwhistle Prim Sch
BS23 ....104 F3

Windwhistle Rd BS23 ..104 D3
Windy Ridge BA15 ....120 F3
Wine St Bath BA1 ....141 C2
Bristol BS1 ....143 A3
Wineberry Cl BS5 .....50 D1
Winfield Rd BS30 .....66 C7
Winford CE Prim Sch
BS40 ....94 F7
Winford Cl BS20 ......45 E4
Winford Gr BS13 ......79 A8
Winford La BS41 ......78 C1
Winford Rd BS40 .....95 F3
Winford Terr BS41 ....78 C5
Wingard Cl BS23 .....104 D2
Wingard Ct ◪ BS23 ..104 E5
Wingfield Rd BS3 .....63 E2
Winifred's La BA1 .....84 E1
Winkworth Pl ◪ BS2 ..49 F1
Winnowing End BS25 .108 A3
Winsbury View BA2 ....99 B1
Winsbury Way BS32 ...24 D1
Winscombe Cl BS31 ...81 D6
Winscombe Dro
Shipham BS25 ....125 D6
Winscombe BS25 .....125 A5
Winscombe Hill BS25 .124 F5
Winscombe Rd BS23 ..105 A7
Winscombe Woodborough
Prim Sch BS25 ......125 A6
Winsford St ◫ BS5 ....64 A8
Winsham Cl BS14 .....80 B5
Winsley CE Prim Sch
BA15 ....120 E7
Winsley Hill BA2 .....120 B6
Winsley Rd Bristol BS6 ..49 D1
Winsley BA15 ....120 F7
Winstanley Ho ◪ BS5 ..64 B6
Winstone Ct BS2 .....142 C3
Wint Hill BS29 ....107 B2
Winterbourne Hill BS36 .37 D5
Winterbourne Rd BS34 ..36 E6
Winterfield Pk BS39 ..132 E4
Winterfield Rd BS39 ..132 E5
Winters La BS40 ......93 D6
Winterstoke Cl ◫ BS3 ..63 B2
Winterstoke Commercial Ctr
BS23 ....105 A6
Winterstoke Ctr ◫ BS3 ..63 B2
Winterstoke Ho ◫ BS3 ..63 A3
Winterstoke Rd
Bristol BS3 ....63 A2
Weston-S-M BS23,BS24 .105 B4
Winterstoke Underpass
BS3 ....62 F4
Winton St BS2 ....63 F4
Wistaria Ave BS37 ....28 A1
Wisteria Ave BS24 ...105 D2
Witch Hazel Rd BS13 ..79 E3
Witchell Rd BS5 ......64 C7
Witcombe BS37 ....39 C7
Witcombe Cl BS15 ....51 F1
Witham Rd BS31 .....82 A3
Witherlies Rd BS16 ...50 F6
Withey Cl W BS9 .....48 F5
Witheys The BS14 ....80 C4
Withies La BA3 ......139 A4
Withies Pk BA3 .....138 F8
Withington Cl BS30 ...66 C2
Withleigh Rd BS4 .....64 B2
Withy Cl BS48 ....59 F3
Withy Cl E BS9 ....48 F6
Withyditch La BA2 ...117 C4
Withymead Rd SN14 ...70 A8
Withypool Gdns ◪ BS14 .80 B5
Withys The BS20 ......47 D4
Withywood Com Sch
BS13 ....79 A5
Withywood Gdns BS13 ..78 F4
Withywood Rd BS13 ..78 F4
Witney Cl BS31 ....82 D3
Woburn Cl BS30 ......65 F5
Woburn Rd BS5 ......50 B3
Wolferton Rd BS7 ....49 F2
Wolfridge Gdns BS10 ..35 A4
Wolfridge La BS35 ....14 F4
Wolfridge Ride BS35 ..14 F4
Wolseley Rd BS7 .....49 D3
Wolvers Hill Rd BS29 .106 E6
Wolvershill Ind Units
BS29 ....106 C6
Wolvershill Pk BS29 ..107 A3
Wood End Wlk BS9 ...48 C6
Wood Hill BS49 ......91 E6
Wood Hill Pk BS20 ....45 D7
Wood Kilns The BS49 ..74 A1
Wood La Axbridge BS26 .125 D2
Clapton In Gordano BS20 .59 E8
Horton BS37 ....19 A1
Weston-S-M BS23 .....87 F1
Wood Rd BS15 ....65 D8
Wood St Bath BA1 ...141 B2
Bath,Beechen Cliff BA2 .141 B1
Bristol BS5 ....50 B2
Woodacre BS20 ......45 E7
Woodbine Rd BS5 ....64 D8
Woodborough Cres
BS25 ....125 A7
Woodborough Ct BS25 .125 A6
Woodborough Dr BS25 .125 A6
Woodborough La BA3 .134 A4
Woodborough Rd
Radstock BA3 ....134 A3
Winscombe BS25 ....124 F8
Woodborough St BS5 ..50 B1
Woodbridge Rd BS4 ..64 A2
Woodbury La BS8 ....49 A2
Woodchester Bristol BS15 51 E3
Yate BS37 ....39 E7

Woodchester Rd BS10 ..49 C7
Woodcliff Ave BS22 ...88 C1
Woodcliff Rd BS22 ....88 C1
Woodcote BS15 ......65 D6
Woodcote Wlk BS16 ..51 B2
Woodcroft BS39 .....113 C3
Woodcroft Ave BS5 ...50 D1
Woodcroft Cl BS4 ....64 E4
Woodcroft Rd BS4 ....64 E4
Wooddene BS25 .....125 A8
Woodend BS15 ....65 D6
Woodend La BS35,GL13 ..2 E1
Woodend Rd BS36 ....38 C7
Woodfield Rd BS6 ....49 B2
Woodford Cl BS48 ....60 A1
Woodford Ct ◪ BS23 .104 E5
Woodgrove Rd BS10 ..34 D2
Woodhall Cl BS16 .....51 F6
Woodhill Ave BS20 ....45 D6
Woodhill Ct BS20 .....45 D6
Woodhill Rd BS20 ....45 D6
Woodhill Views BS48 ..59 F3
Woodhouse Ave BS24 .24 D7
Woodhouse Cl BS32 ..24 D6
Woodhouse Gr BS7 ...49 E6
Woodhouse Rd BA2 ..101 A6
Woodhurst BS21 .....105 A7
Woodington Ct ◫ BS30 .65 F4
Woodington Rd BS21 ..57 C1
Woodland Ave BS15 ...51 D2
Woodland Cl Bristol BS15 .51 C2
Failand BS8 ....61 B4
Woodland Ct BS9 .....48 C3
Woodland Glade BS21 .57 E5
Woodland Gr
Bath,Claverton Down BA2 .102 E5
Bath,Weston Park BA1 ..84 C1
Bristol BS9 ....48 D6
Woodland Pl BA2 ....102 D5
Woodland Rd
Bristol BS8 ....142 C4
Cromhall GL12 ....10 B4
Nailsea BS48 ....59 E3
Weston-S-M BS23 ...104 D4
Woodland Terr
Bristol,Kingswood BS15 ..65 E7
Bristol,Woolcott Park BS6 .49 B2
Woodland Way
Bristol BS15 ....51 C2
Failand BS8 ....61 B4
Woodlands
Axbridge BS26 ......125 D2
Bristol,Mangotsfield BS16 .51 E6
Bristol,Patchway BS34 ..24 D3
Tytherington GL12 ....16 B6
Weston-S-M BS23 ....87 D1
Woodlands Ct
Bristol BS32 ....24 B3
◫ Bristol BS32 ......24 C2
Woodlands La
Almondsbury BS32 ...24 E5
Bristol BS32 ....24 D5
Woodlands Pk Bath BA1 .85 C2
Bristol BS32 ....24 C3
Woodlands Rd
Charfield GL12 ....11 A4
Clevedon BS21 ....57 C4
Portishead BS20 .....45 D8
Tytherington GL12 ....16 B6
Woodlands Rise BS16 ..51 D6
Woodlands The BA2 ..116 F3
Woodleaze BS9 ......48 B6
Woodleigh BS35 ....8 C1
Woodleigh Gdns BS14 ..80 C6
Woodmancote BS37 ..39 D8
Woodmancote Rd ◪ BS6 49 E1
Woodmans Cl BS37 ...40 B8
Woodmans Rd BS37 ..40 C8
Woodmans Vale BS37 ..40 C8
Woodmarsh BS14 ....80 A4
Woodmead Gdns BS13 .79 C4
Woodmead La BS30 ..54 A1
Woodmill BS49 ....74 A1
Woodpecker Ave BA3 .139 B8
Woodpecker Cres BS16 .53 C4
Woodpecker Dr BS22 .105 E8
Woods Hill BA2 ......120 A6
Woodside Bristol BS9 ..48 D3
Midsomer Norton BA3 .132 E1
Woodside Ave BS24 ..105 B2
Woodside Ct BS23 ...105 A8
Woodside Gdns BS20 ..44 E5
Woodside Gr BS10 ....34 D3
Woodside Rd
Bristol,Downend BS16 ...51 C7
Bristol,Kingswood BS15 ..65 C7
Bristol,St Anne's Park BS4 .64 E6
Clevedon BS21 ....57 C5
Coalpit Heath BS36 ...38 E6
Woodspring Ave BS22 .88 B3
Woodspring Cres BS22 .88 A3
Woodspring Mus ★
BS23 ....104 E8
Woodspring Priory ★
BS22 ....71 C1
Woodstock Ave BS6 ...49 C1
Woodstock Cl BS15 ...65 F8
Woodstock Rd
Bristol,Redland BS6 ...49 C2
Bristol,Woodstock BS15 ..65 F7
Weston-S-M BS22 ...105 B8
Woodstock Sch BS10 ..34 C8
Woodview
Chilcompton BA3 ....138 E5
◪ Clevedon BS21 ....57 F3
Paulton BS39 ....132 C5
Woodview Cl BS11 ....47 E7

Woodview Dr BS49 ....92 B8
Woodview Terr
Nailsea BS48 ....59 F2
Weston-S-M BS23 ...105 A6
Woodward Ave BS37 ..27 B1
Woodward Dr BS30 ...65 F4
Woodwell Rd BS11 ...47 E5
Woodyleaze Dr BS15 ..65 D6
Wookey Cl BS48 ......75 F8
Woolcot St BS6 ......49 B2
Wooler Rd BS23 .....104 E8
Woollard La BS14,BS39 ..98 A4
Woolley La BA1 ......85 A4
Woolley Rd BS14 .....80 E5
Woolvers Way BS24 ..106 B6
Wootton Cres BS4 ....64 E6
Wootton Pk BS4,BS4 ..64 B1
Wootton Rd BS4 .....64 F6
Worcester Bldgs BA1 ..85 B1
Worcester Cl Bristol BS16 .51 B2
Peasedown St John BA2 ..134 D7
Worcester Cres BS8 .142 A4
Worcester Ct BS8 ...142 A4
Worcester Gdns BS48 ..75 C8
Worcester Pk BA1 ....85 B2
Worcester Pl BA1 ....85 B2
Worcester Rd
Bristol,Clifton BS8 ...142 A4
Bristol,Hopewell Hill BS15 .51 D1
Worcester Terr Bath BA1 .85 B1
Bristol BS8 ....142 A4
Wordsworth Ho BS34 ..36 A8
Wordsworth Rd
Bristol BS7 ....50 B7
Clevedon BS21 ....57 C2
Weston-S-M BS23 ...105 A3
Workshop Rd BS11 ....33 C4
World's End La BS31 ..82 C5
Worldsend La GL13 ....2 E7
Worle Ct BS22 ....88 F3
Worle Inf Sch BS22 ...88 E2
Worle Moor Rd BS24 .105 F8
Worle Parkway BS22 ..89 B1
Worle Sch BS22 ....88 E2
Worle Sta BS22 ....89 B2
Worlebury CE Fst Sch
BS22 ....88 B2
Worlebury Cl BS22 ....88 B3
Worlebury Hill Rd BS22,
BS23 ....88 B2
Worlebury Park Rd BS22 .88 A2
Worlebury St Pauls CE Fst
Sch BS22 ....88 B3
Wormcliff La SN13 ....86 F3
Worrall Mews ⑩ BS8 ..49 A2
Worrall Pl ⑪ BS8 ....49 A2
Worrall Rd BS8 ......49 A2
Worrel's La BS16,BS36 ..37 D3
Worsley St BS5 ....64 D7
Worthing Rd BS34 ....35 F8
Worthings The BS24 ..122 B1
Worthy Cl BS15 ......65 F6
Worthy Cres BS24 ...122 B1
Worthy La ◪ BS23 ...104 E8
Worthy Pl ◪ BS23 ...104 E8
Worthy Rd BS11 .....33 D7
Worthys The BS32 ....37 A6
Wotton Rd Charfield GL12 .11 B5
Iron Acton BS37 .....26 F5
Kingswood GL12 .....11 F5
Wrangle Farm Gn BS21 .57 E2
Wrangle The BS24 ...105 F7
Wraxall CE Prim Sch
BS48 ....60 B4
Wraxall Gr BS13 .....79 A8
Wraxall Hill BS48 .....60 C5
Wraxall Rd BS30 .....66 A6
Wren Cl Bristol BS16 ..50 E7
Weston-S-M BS22 ...105 D8
Wren Dr BS16 ....51 A6
Wrenbert Rd BS16 ....51 D5
Wright Way BS16 .....50 E8
Wrington CE Prim Sch
BS40 ....92 E2
Wrington Cl BS34 ....36 C7
Wrington Cres BS13 ..79 A7
Wrington Hill BS40 ...92 F5
Wrington La BS49 ....91 E5
Wrington Mead BS49 ..91 E5
Wrington Rd BS49 ....91 F4
Writhlington Ct BA3 ..134 C2
Writhlington Sch BA3 .134 C1
Wroughton Dr BS13 ..79 D4
Wroughton Gdns BS13 .79 D4
Wroxham Dr BS34 ....36 C8
Wyatt Ave BS13 ......78 F5
Wyatt Cl BS13 ....78 F5
Wyatt's Cl BS48 ......59 D2
Wyatts View BS4 .....64 E6
Wychwood BS15 .....65 E6
Wyck Beck Rd BS10 ..35 A3
Wycliffe Rd BS9 ......49 B7
Wycliffe Row ◪ BS3 ..63 F4
Wycombe Gr BS4 ....64 D2
Wye Croft Cl BS10 ....35 D3
Wye Ct BS35 ....15 C8
Wyedale Ave BS9 ....48 C7
Wykis Ct BS15 ....65 E5
Wyllie Ct BS22 ....89 A5
Wymbush Cres BS13 ..79 C5
Wymbush Gdns BS13 ..79 C5
Wyndam Ct BS2 ....143 B4
Wyndham Cres
Bristol BS4 ....65 A3
Easton-in-G BS20 ....47 B4
Wyndham Way BS20 ..45 E5
Wynstones The BS15 ..65 C7
Wynter Cl BS22 ......89 A3

Wyvern Cl BS23 .....104 F7
Wyvern Com Sch BS23 .104 F5
Wyvern Mews BS23 ..104 F7
Wyvern Villas BS9 ....49 A8

Y

Yadley Cl BS25 ......125 A7
Yadley La BS25 .....125 A6
Yadley Way BS25 ....125 A7
Yanel La BS25 ......108 B5
Yanleigh Cl BS13 .....78 D6
Yanley La BS41,BS13 ..78 C7
Yarbury Way BS24 ....89 B1
Yarrow Ct BS22 ......89 A5
Yate Rd BS37 ....26 F3
Yate Rocks BS37 .....27 F7
Yate Sta BS37 ....27 D4
Yatton BS13 ....78 F8
Yatton Inf & CE Jun Schs
BS49 ....91 C8
Yatton Sta BS49 ......74 A1
Yeamen's Ho BS1 ...143 B1
Yeatman Cl BS39 ....113 C4
Yelverton Rd BS4 ....64 E1
Yeo Bank La BS21 ....72 F1
Yeo Cl BS23 ....105 A5
Yeo Ct Clevedon BS21 ..57 C5
Congresbury BS49 ....91 D4
Yeo La BS41 ....61 F1
Yeo Moor BS21 ......57 E2
Yeo Moor Jun & Inf Schs
BS21 ....57 E2
Yeo Valley Way BS48 ..60 B2
Yeo Way BS21 ....57 B2
Yeolands Dr BS21 ....57 B1
Yeomans Cl BS9 ......48 D5
Yeomans Orch BS40 ..92 E3
Yeomanside BS14 ....80 C5
Yeomead BS48 ....59 F3
Yeomeads BS41 ......61 F1
Yeoward Rd BS21 ....57 E1
Yew Tree Cl
Bishop Sutton BS39 ..113 D4
Langford BS40 ......109 E6
Nailsea BS48 ....59 C1
Yew Tree Cotts BS40 .110 E3
Yew Tree Ct BS14 ....80 B5
Yew Tree Dr Bristol BS15 .51 F3
Weston-S-M BS24 ...106 B8
Yew Tree Gdns
Easton-in-G BS20 ....47 C4
Nailsea BS48 ....59 C1
Sandford BS25 .....108 A4
Yew Tree La
Compton Martin BS40 .129 A7
Kingston Seymour BS21 ..73 B1
Yew Tree Pk BS49 ....91 D3
Yewcroft Cl BS14 .....80 A4
Yewtree Batch BS40 ..94 A1
Yomede Pk BA1 .....101 A7
York Ave BS7 ....49 F4
York Bldgs BS3 ......63 E4
York Cl
Bristol,Bromley Heath BS16 37 F1
Bristol,Stoke Gifford BS34 .36 D4
Weston-S-M BS22 ...89 A4
Yate BS37 ....27 E4
York Ct BS2 ....143 B4
York Gdns Bristol BS8 ..62 F6
Winterbourne BS36 ...37 F8
York Pl
Bristol,Brandon Hill BS1 ..142 C2
Bristol,Victoria Park BS8 .142 B3
York Rd
Bristol,Lower Easton BS5 ..50 C1
Bristol,Montpelier BS6 ..49 E1
Bristol,Staple Hill BS16 ..51 E4
Bristol,Windmill Hill BS3 ..63 E4
York St Bath BA1 ....141 C2
◪ Bristol,Baptist Mills BS2 .50 A2
◫ Bristol,Redfield BS5 ..64 C7
Bristol,St Pauls BS2 .143 B4
◪ Bristol,Westbury Park
BS8 ....49 A2
Weston-S-M BS23 ...104 D7
Youngs Ct BS16 ......52 B8
Youngwood La BS48 ..75 D7

Z

Zetland Rd BS6 ......49 D2
Zig Zag BS21 ....57 D4
Zinc Rd BS11 ....33 C3
Zion Hill BA3 ....138 B7